PAINTBRUSH

File

Save	Ctrl-S

Edit

Undo	Ctrl-Z
Cut	Ctrl-X
Copy	Ctrl-C
Paste	Ctrl-V

View

Zoom In	Ctrl-N
Zoom Out	Ctrl-O
View Picture	Ctrl-P

Text

Bold	Ctrl-B
Italic	Ctrl-I
Underline	Ctrl-U

TERMINAL

Edit

Copy	Ctrl-C
Paste	Ctrl-V
Send	Ctrl-Shift-Ins

CARDFILE

Edit

Undo	Ctrl-Z
Cut	Ctrl-X
Copy	Ctrl-C
Paste	Ctrl-V
Index	F6

Card

Add	F7
Autodial	F5

Search

Go To	F4
Find Next	F3

CALENDAR

Edit

Cut	Ctrl-X
Copy	Ctrl-C
Paste	Ctrl-V

View

Day	F8
Month	F9

Show

Previous	Ctrl-PgUp
Next	Ctrl-PgDn

Alarm

Set	F5

Options

Mark	F6
Special Time	F7

CALCULATOR

Edit

Copy	Ctrl-C
Paste	Ctrl-V

RECORDER

Stop Recording	Ctrl-Break

MASTERING WINDOWS™ 3.1

SPECIAL EDITION

ROBERT COWART

San Francisco • Paris • Düsseldorf • Soest

ACQUISITIONS EDITOR: *Dianne King*
DEVELOPMENTAL EDITOR: *Christian T.S. Crumlish*
EDITORS: *Stefan Grünwedel, Carol Henry, and Brenda Kienan*
PROJECT EDITOR: *Abby Azrael*
TECHNICAL EDITORS: *Sheldon M. Dunn, Sheila Dienes, and Dan Tauber*
WORD PROCESSORS: *Ann Dunn and Chris Meredith*
SERIES DESIGNER: *Based on a design by Amparo del Rio*
PRODUCTION ARTISTS: *Lucie Zivny, Suzanne Albertson, and Helen Bruno*
LINE ART: *Delia Brown and Cuong Le*
SCREEN GRAPHICS: *Cuong Le*
PAGE LAYOUT AND TYPESETTING: *Len Gilbert, Claudia Smelser, Deborah Maizels, and Dina F Quan*
PROOFREADERS: *Rhonda M. Holmes and Elisabeth Dahl*
INDEXER: *Nancy Guenther*
COVER DESIGNER: *Archer Design*
PHOTO ART DIRECTION: *Ingalls + Associates*
COVER PHOTOGRAPHER: *David Bishop*

Library of Congress Card Number: 91-68096
ISBN: 0-89588-842-4

Manufactured in the United States of America
10 9 8

To my mother, who doesn't do windows

Acknowledgments

I am indebted to the talented people at SYBEX for their invaluable assistance. Special thanks go to Dr. R.S. Langer and Dianne King for their support in acquisitional, developmental, financial, and contractual matters; Managing Editor Barbara Gordon for coordinating everything; Production Manager Bret Rohmer for his support; my developmental editor, Christian Crumlish; my editor, Stefan Grünwedel, for his patience; Mac Dunn for his technical editing; Dan Tauber for technical help; page proofer Rhonda Holmes; Screen Queen Delia Brown; Amparo del Rio for her book design; Lucie Zivny, production artist; Deborah Maizels, typesetter; and everybody else who worked behind the scenes all the way to shipping the book out the door.

For their work on this Special Edition, I'd like to thank my editors, Carol Henry and Brenda Kienan; my project editor, Abby Azrael; my technical editor, Sheila Dienes; proofreader Elisabeth Dahl; production artists Suzanne Albertson and Helen Bruno; and typesetters Len Gilbert, Deborah Maizels, Claudia Smelser, and Dina Quan.

Not to be overlooked are the people responsible for the distribution and sales of SYBEX books, including the one you're holding. SYBEX has its own independent sales and marketing force working to get these books onto shelves around the world—from small independent bookstores to the national chains. Thanks to Alan Oakes, Executive Vice President; Roger Gershon, Vice President Marketing; John McCarthy, Vice President Sales; and Marsha Copeland, academic coordinator. Thanks to you and the rest of the crew in Alameda and around the country, I can pay my rent!

Finally, many heartfelt thanks go out to the multitalented, "can-do" Beverly Hill (yes, that's her name, not her address) for her generous aid in writing, reviewing, scheduling, and formatting, and for overall friendship and support! Thanks also to Kevin Bachus for additional font material and tips & tricks. And special thanks to another multitalent—my dear friend and writing colleague Dr. Steve Cummings—whose writing and research assistance made the chapters on DDE & OLE, supercharging Windows, and using fonts, come together.

CONTENTS AT A GLANCE

TABLE OF CONTENTS

Chapter 6

Chapter 7

Chapter 8

PART TWO

THE SUPPLIED PROGRAMS

Chapter 9

Chapter 10

Chapter 11

PART THREE

ADVANCED TOPICS

Chapter 17

Chapter 18

PART FOUR

TROUBLESHOOTING AND TIPS & TRICKS

Chapter 20

Chapter 21

APPENDICES

Appendix A

Appendix B

Appendix C

Introduction

This book is designed to help you get the most out of Windows 3.1 with the least amount of effort. I've written this book with both the novice and the experienced PC user in mind. The intention was to produce a volume that would prove both accessible and highly instructive to all Windows users.

From the outset, this book does not require that you have a working knowledge of Windows—only a modicum of familiarity with DOS. So if you are **new to Windows**, a bit PC-literate, and ready to learn, this book is a good choice. I think you'll find it easy to read and not over your head. There are lots of everyday examples to explain the concepts, and there's even a little humor thrown in to cut the usual computer-book boredom.

If you're a **power user**, familiar with earlier versions of Windows and the intricacies of DOS, the explanations and procedures, along with the Fast Tracks included in many chapters, will quickly bring you up to speed with Windows 3.1. In addition, Part III, "Advanced Topics," and Part IV, "Troubleshooting and Tips & Tricks," will be useful on a number of counts. In Part III, the chapter on PIFs explains how to get the most from your DOS applications in Windows by taking advantage of Windows' memory-management and multitasking features. The DDE and OLE chapter explains the ins and outs of data exchange and object linking and embedding and the multimedia chapter explores the possibilities for adding audio, video, and MIDI elements to your Windows setup. If you want to supercharge your Windows setup for high performance, there's a chapter on that, too, covering hardware and software modifications, hard disk management, video accelerator cards, and so forth. The networking chapter covers procedures for running Windows on popular networks. In Part IV, the troubleshooting chapter is a definite must for all Windows users. I've collected many useful tips (over 200!) to save you time and make Windows computing much more efficient. The last chapter reviews products you can use with Windows.

If you haven't installed Windows yet, consult Appendix A. And for those days when you don't have a mouse (such as when you're using a laptop computer), Appendix B's compilation of shortcut key commands should be a welcome boon. Appendix C introduces the networking capabilities of Windows for Workgroups, which Microsoft made available in 1992. And, of course, for all Windows users, the inside front and back covers of the book provide information that you'll want to refer to regularly.

All in all, I've tried to address the major topics that most Windows users are likely to need, then carefully chosen notable and savory value-added information, and supplied it all in one place.

WHY THIS BOOK?

Although there are manuals supplied with Windows, they have to include every detail about Windows—probably more than you care to know about or want to wade through. The explanations in the manuals are also sometimes vague. So I've done the legwork for you in advance: I've boiled down the manuals, experimented for many months on various machines from laptops to supercharged 486s, and then written a book explaining Windows in normal, everyday English.

In researching this book, I've tried to focus on not just the "how to's" but also on the whys and wherefores. Too many computer books tell you only how to perform a sample task without explaining how to apply it to your own work. In this book, step-by-step sections explain how to perform specific procedures and descriptive sections explain general considerations about what you've learned. As you read along and follow the examples, you should not only become adept at using Windows, but you should also learn the most efficient ways to accomplish your own work.

WHAT'S NEW WITH WINDOWS 3.1?

Windows 3.1's improvements over 3.0 include the following:

- Easier installation
- Improved online tutorial
- More stable operation; programs crash less often
- Faster, more flexible Program Manager allows more groups; window and icon size and placements are remembered between sessions
- StartUp group allows easy assignment of programs to run automatically when you bring up Windows
- Large assortment of icons for assigning to applications in your Program Manager groups
- A "drag and drop" feature for some applications; for example, dragging a file into a Print Manager window or icon will immediately print it
- Screen and printer fonts are more accurate and easy to manage, with new TrueType fonts
- Print Manager is faster and its performance improved
- Multimedia capabilities for audio, video, and MIDI allow support of multimedia applications as they become available
- A few multimedia utility programs are included: Sound Recorder, MIDI Mapper, and Media Player
- Object linking and embedding (OLE) for seamless integration of documents created with multiple applications
- Improved network support
- Real mode has been eliminated to improve performance on 286, 386, and 486 machines
- More supplied PIFs for common non-Windows applications
- Improved virtual-memory management allows more non-Windows

applications to run at once

- Adjustable font size and full mouse support for non-Windows applications running in a window
- Automatic reconnection to network printers and drives after a workstation crashes or when booting
- Character Map application lets you easily insert nonkeyboard characters, such as math and Greek symbols, into documents
- Complete indexed Help system for Windows and context-sensitive help for many Windows dialog boxes
- More color settings, including some for LCD screens
- Screen-saver utility built into the Control Panel
- Easier-to-use standard File dialog boxes for opening and saving files
- Improved SMARTDrive performance with delayed write-through speeds up disk reads and writes

Subsequent to the release of Windows 3.1, Windows 3.11 was released. This is an upgrade to Windows 3.1 which is very moderate in nature. Actually, it is nowhere near as dramatic as the upgrade from Windows 3.0 to Windows 3.1. In fact, many people didn't even notice that it happened. Most of the improvements were internal to Windows, such as improved memory and disk caching, and more efficient disk access through the use of 32-bit virtual device drivers. The upshot is that, from the user's point of view, very little has changed other than Windows becoming a bit faster and more reliable. Cosmetically, the only change was that a toolbar was added to the File Manager. This is discussed in Chapter 4. Since the differences between Windows 3.1 and Windows 3.11 are so minimal, this book uses the more popular moniker Windows 3.1 throughout.

Perhaps you have heard about Windows 95, the next generation of Windows. As with the jump to Windows 3.1 from 3.0, Windows 95 will be the natural upgrade path for most Windows users. Within several years most Windows users will have upgraded to Windows 95. However, just as with earlier versions of DOS, there will be many who are perfectly content with Windows 3.1 and who don't wish to take the time out to learn a whole new operating system, or whose PC doesn't have enough speed or RAM to run it. Windows 95, though superior in many ways to Windows 3.x, works quite a bit differently. Despite the fact that Windows 95 looms large on the PC horizon, I believe that the time you spend learning to use Windows won't be wasted, nor the benefits short-lived since Windows 3.1 (or something very similar) is likely to be around for a good long time.

WHAT YOU NEED IN ORDER TO USE THIS BOOK

There are a few things about your level of knowledge and your computer setup that this book assumes.

What You Should Know

If you are new to computers, you should at least have some understanding of DOS, the PC's disk operating system. Though Windows takes much of the effort out of using DOS, it's still a good idea for you to understand how DOS works so that you'll know what Windows is doing for you. Though I'll be covering techniques for performing typical DOS tasks in Windows—such as copying files, formatting disks, and moving between directories—I'm assuming that you already understand why you'd want to do these things in the first place. Of particular importance is an understanding of disk files, disk directories, and the differences between data files and program files. You may want to take some time out to bone up on these topics if your knowledge is shaky.

What You Should Have

In order for this book to make sense, and for Windows to work, it is assumed that you have the following:

- An IBM PC-AT, 80386, 80486, or compatible computer with at least one megabyte of RAM.
- A hard disk with a minimum of five to eight megabytes of free space on it.
- A monitor that is supported by Windows. When run, the Setup program (explained in Appendix A) shows you a list of the supported monitors.

- A printer, obviously, if you want to use Windows to print out your work on paper. Some of the exercises in this book will cover printing. Though not necessary for most of the book, it will be to your advantage if you have a printer.
- A mouse. Though you can operate Windows without a mouse (from the keyboard), it's quite a bit more cumbersome to do so. The mouse makes almost all Windows operations so much easier that you really should get ahold of one. In order to leave more room in the book for useful information about Windows, most instructions will assume you have a mouse.

HOW THIS BOOK IS ORGANIZED

There are four parts to this book:

Part I This consists of eight chapters, introducing Windows and then covering all the essentials of Windows usage. After reading and following along on your computer, you'll know how to control the Windows graphical environment, run programs, copy data between programs, and manage your files. You should definitely read these chapters if you've never used Windows before.

Part II This covers the supplied programs—the Windows accessories. There you'll learn all the ins and outs of Write, Terminal, Paintbrush, Notepad, Cardfile, Recorder, Calendar, Calculator, and Character Map. Though not the most sophisticated programs in their respective classes, these programs are well thought out, handy, and thrown in for free with Windows.

Part III This gets into the finer aspects of Windows operations. Here you'll learn how to fine-tune your non-Windows applications to run best within Windows, how to supercharge your Windows system, how to use OLE and DDE, the multimedia options, networking commands, and fonts effectively.

Part IV This is a special section chock full of troubleshooting advice for solving sticky problems, hundreds of tips to help you get the most out of Windows, and a round-up of products you might find useful with Windows.

Appendices Appendix A tells you how to install Windows on your computer and Appendix B lists shortcut keys. Appendix C introduces Windows for Workgroups.

CONVENTIONS USED IN THIS BOOK

There are a few conventions used throughout this book that you should know about before beginning. First, there are commands that you enter from the keyboard and messages you receive from Windows that appear on your screen. When you have to type something in, the instruction may be shown on a line by itself, like this:

WIN /S

or it might be included right in a line like this: "Now type **WIN /S**." More often than not, responses from Windows will be shown in figures so that you can see just what the screens look like. Sometimes, though, I'll skip the picture and just display it in a different font like this:

Cannot read from drive A

Second, you'll see two pages before each chapter and sections within the chapters that look like this:

To do the following,

1. **Do this...**
2. **Do this...**
3. **Do this...**

These are called Fast Tracks. The ones at the front of the chapter give you information quickly and show you where to go for more explanation. The style of Fast Track shown above always follows a major heading. Because such a Fast Track is an abridged version of the text that follows it, it's easy to review the steps to accomplish a certain task. This is handy if you've already read the book but forget the exact steps involved. However, if you're reading the book or learning about a procedure for the first time (and you're not in a big rush), just skip the Fast Track and read the more detailed instructions that follow it.

Finally, there are also many margin notes in this book. They are positioned in the left margin, next to the material to which they refer. There are four kinds of margin notes: Note, Tip, Speedtip, and Caution:

Notes give you information that is pertinent to the procedure or topic being discussed next to it.

Tips indicate practical hints that might make your work easier.

Speedtips are like tips, but they always contain information that will help speed up your work.

Cautions alert you to something very important. Generally, they inform you about the potential problems you might encounter if you were to follow a procedure incorrectly or without careful forethought.

BEFORE YOU BEGIN...

Before you begin working with Windows, make sure you have installed the program on your computer's hard disk. A large portion of what appears to be a software problem is often the result of incorrect installation. If your copy of Windows is already installed and operating correctly, you have no need to worry about this and can move ahead to Chapter 1. However, if you haven't installed Windows, you should do so by turning to Appendix A, which covers the Windows Setup program.

PART ONE

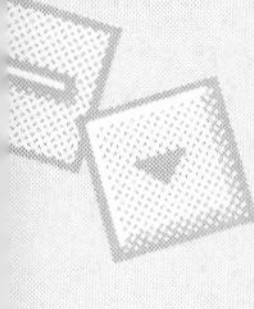

The Essentials

P

Part I consists of eight chapters, in which you will learn the rudiments of Windows 3.1. This is an essential section to read, even if you've used earlier versions of Windows, since numerous aspects of Windows 3.1 are new. The first chapter explains what Windows is and generally how it works. Chapters 2 and 3 explain how you run and manage your programs with the Program Manager. Chapter 4 shows you how to work with and manage disk files with the File Manager. Chapter 5 explains how to customize various aspects of Windows with the Control Panel. Chapters 6 and 7 discuss installing and using your printer. Finally, Chapter 8 covers techniques for copying information between programs with the Clipboard.

FAST TRACK

CHAPTER 1

FAST TRACK

To start Windows, ... 8

make sure you've installed Windows properly (see Appendix A). Boot up your computer as usual. Type **WIN** ↵.

About windows: 10

A window is used to contain each group, program, or document you're working with. You can have multiple windows on the screen at once. You can easily switch between them. A window can use the whole screen (called *maximized* size) or be sized down to fill just a portion of the screen (called *restored* size). Windows can overlap ("cascade"), or be adjusted in a "tiled" fashion so you can see them all at once.

To minimize a window, ... 16

first activate the window. Then, position the mouse pointer on the Minimize Box (the down arrow in the upper-left corner of the window) and click. The window reduces to an icon, and the window's name is shown below the icon. (This is also called iconizing the window.)

To restore a Window from an icon, ... 16

double-click on the icon. If you prefer, you can click once, and when the Control menu appears above the icon, press ↵, type **R**, or click on the word *Restore*. The window returns to its previous size.

To maximize a Window, ... 16

activate the window, and then click on the Maximize box (the up arrow in the upper-right corner of the window). The window expands to fill the entire screen or the entire program window if it's a document. The Maximize box changes to a Restore box with both up and down arrows. Click on this box to once again restore the window to its previous size.

To adjust a window's size manually, ... 16

position the cursor on any edge or corner of the window that you want to resize. The cursor shape will change to a two-headed pointer. Keeping the mouse button depressed, drag the window edge or corner to the desired position, and then release the mouse button.

To get help, ... 31

open the Help menu and select Contents or How to Use Help.

To exit Windows, ... 42

activate the Program Manager window and double-click the Control box. You will be asked to confirm exiting and possibly to close any open applications.

CHAPTER 1

FEATURING

An Overview of the Windows Interface

Types of Windows, Menus, and Dialog Boxes

The Help System

What Is Windows?

icrosoft Windows (or simply Windows) is a software program that makes your IBM PC (or compatible) easy to use. It does this by simplifying the computer's *user interface*—a buzzword that refers to the way you give your computer commands, the way you interact with it.

Usually the interface between you and the computer consists of the screen and the keyboard: you interact with the computer by responding to what's on the screen, typing in cryptic commands at the DOS command line to do your work. (DOS stands for Disk Operating System; it is the software that makes your IBM computer run.) DOS often isn't very intelligent at interpreting your commands and most people consider it awkward or intimidating as a user interface. These commands can be confusing and difficult to remember. Who wants to learn lots of computer gobbledygook just to see what's on your disk, copy a file, or format a disk? Thus, many people try to get by with just a rudimentary knowledge of DOS—or opt for the Apple Macintosh instead. I know people in both clubs. A good friend of mine who recently bought an expensive PC explained to me that she wasn't going to buy DOS because she heard it was just a pain to use. She didn't understand that DOS is a necessary evil—a bit like the gasoline in your car.

Windows changes much of this. What's been missing from the PC is a program that makes the computer easy to use. Windows is just such a program. With Windows, you can run programs, enter and move data around, and perform DOS-related tasks simply by using the *mouse* to point at objects on the screen. (A mouse is a small electronic gadget that you move around on the table next to your computer.) Of course, you also use the keyboard to type in letters and numbers.

With Windows, instead of typing in commands such as

```
copy c:\*.* a:
```

to copy all files from drive C to drive A, you just use the mouse to point at the names of the files you want to copy and click on a few command names. Windows interprets your actions and tells DOS and your computer what to do.

In addition to making DOS housekeeping tasks such as creating directories, copying files, deleting files, formatting disks, and so forth, easier, Windows makes running your favorite *applications* easier, too. (An application is a software package that you use for a specific task, such as word processing. WordPerfect is an example of an application. In this book, I'll use the words *program* and *application* interchangeably.)

Windows owes its name to the fact that it runs each program or document in its own separate *window.* (A window is a box or frame on the screen.) You can have numerous windows on the screen at a time, each containing its own program and/or document. You can then easily switch between programs without having to close one down and open the next.

Another feature is that Windows has a facility—called the Clipboard—that lets you copy material between dissimilar document types, making it easy to *cut* and *paste* information from, say, a spreadsheet into a company report or put a scanned photograph of a house into a real estate brochure. In essence, Windows provides the means for seamlessly joining the capabilities of very different application programs. Not only can you paste portions of one document into another, but by utilizing more advanced document-linking features—called Dynamic Data Exchange (DDE) and Object Linking and Embedding (OLE)—those pasted elements remain "live." That is, if the source document (such as some spreadsheet data) changes, the results will also be reflected in the secondary document containing the pasted data.

As more and more application programs are written to run with Windows, it'll be easier for anyone to learn how to use new programs. This is because all application programs that run in Windows use similar commands and procedures.

Windows comes supplied with a few of its own handy programs, and we will discuss them in this book. There's a word-processing program called Write, a drawing program called Paintbrush, a communications program called Terminal for connecting to outside information services over phone lines, small utility programs that are helpful for keeping track of appointments and notes, a couple of games to help you escape from your work, and a few others.

THE ORIGINS OF WINDOWS

Years of research went into developing the prototype of today's popular graphical user interfaces. It was shown in the early 1980s that the graphical user interface, in conjunction with a hand-held pointing device (now called the mouse), was much easier to operate and understand than the older-style keyboard-command approach to controlling a computer. A little-known fact is that this research was conducted by the Xerox Corporation and first resulted in the Xerox Star computer before IBM PCs or Macintoshes existed. It wasn't until later that the technology was adapted by Apple Computer for its Macintosh prototype, the Lisa.

For several years now there have been graphical user interfaces for IBM PCs. Windows (from Microsoft) and GEM (from Digital Research) have been the two primary contenders. Another similar interface, DESQView, is fairly popular, but its appearance on the screen is not as sophisticated as Windows, since it doesn't take advantage of higher-resolution graphics. Recently Windows took the lead, particularly since IBM officially endorsed it in 1989, and since so many software companies have written programs designed for it.

So now, with this new version of Windows (version 3.1), we have the latest incarnation of a type of computer interface that has, in effect, been in the making for close to a decade and promises to become a well-ensconced standard. I believe that the time you spend learning to use Windows won't be wasted, nor the benefits short-lived, since Windows (or something very similar) is likely to be around for some time.

Before going on in this book, make sure you've read the introduction to this book and installed Windows correctly on your computer. You use the Setup program for installation, as explained in the appendix.

In this chapter you'll learn the basics of how Windows works. If you've never used Windows before, you should read this chapter thoroughly while experimenting with Windows on your computer. This is because it covers all the basic concepts and skills you'll need to understand and use Windows. You should feel free to experiment, if with some caution. Even if you're already familiar with Windows, you might still want to skim this chapter, particularly if you've only used Windows version 2, to pick up the material that relates to versions 3.0 and 3.1 (hereafter referred to as "3.X").

If at any time while reading this chapter you have to quit Windows to do other work or to turn off your computer, just jump to the end of the chapter and read the section called "Exiting Windows." Also, if at any time you don't understand how to use a Windows command or perform some procedure, read the section near the end of this chapter that covers Windows' built-in Help facility.

If you truly get stuck and don't know how to escape from some procedure you're in the middle of, the last resort is to reboot your computer and start up Windows again. Though this isn't a great idea, and you may lose part of any documents you're working on, it won't hurt Windows or your computer. You reboot your computer by pressing the Ctrl, Alt, and Del keys simultaneously; by pressing the reset switch on your computer; or by turning your computer off, waiting about ten seconds, and then turning it on again.

STARTING WINDOWS

To start Windows, follow these steps:

1. Boot up your computer in the usual way. The DOS prompt appears (usually the C prompt, though your computer may show a different drive name such as D:).
2. At the DOS prompt, type **WIN** and press Enter.

The Windows sign-on screen appears for a few moments and then disappears. After a few more moments, during which parts of the program are being retrieved from the hard disk, the Windows starting screen appears, looking approximately like that in Figure 1.1. Your screen may look a bit different.

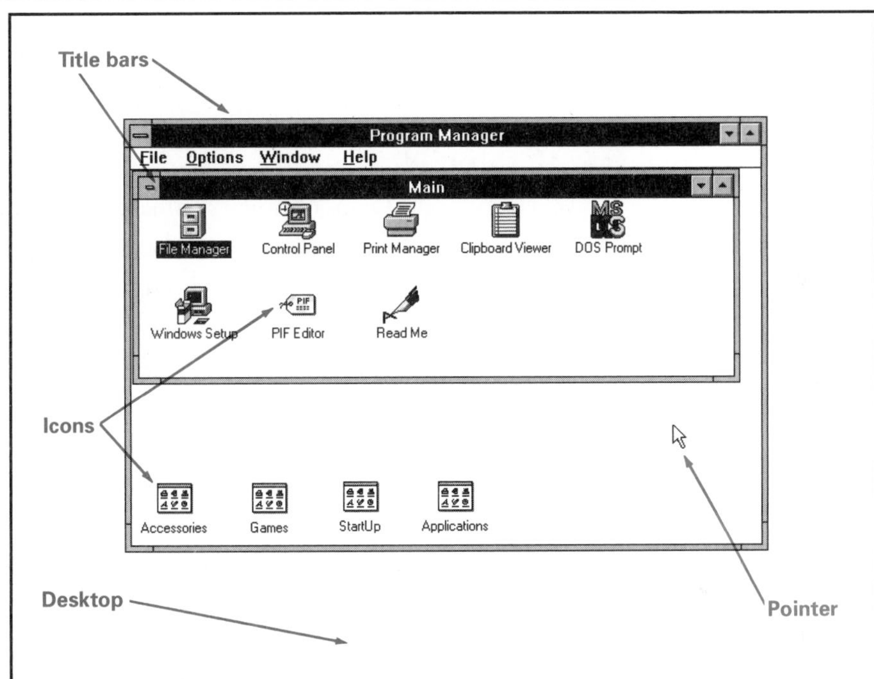

FIGURE 1.1: *The initial Windows screen. This "starting screen" belongs to the Windows application Program Manager, the part of Windows that organizes your program for you.*

PARTS OF THE WINDOWS SCREEN

Now let's take a quick look at the three basic parts of the Windows startup screen: the Desktop, windows, and icons. Once you understand these three essential building blocks, we'll look closer at them, examining the finer details of each.

THE DESKTOP

The *Desktop* is your overall work area while in Windows. It's called the Desktop because Windows uses your whole screen in a way that's analogous to the way you'd use the surface of a desk. As you work in Windows, you move items around on the Desktop, retrieve and put away items (as if in a drawer), and perform your other day-to-day tasks. You do all of this using graphical representations of your work projects. The analogy of the Desktop falls a bit short sometimes, but it's useful for understanding how the program helps you to organize your activities. Because of this graphical representation, working with your programs is often faster and easier than it would be with DOS.

THE WINDOWS

When you want to do some work, you open up a program or document with the mouse or keyboard, and a *window* opens on the Desktop. This is similar to pulling a file folder or notebook off the shelf, placing it on the desk, and opening it up. In Windows, you do this for each task you want to work on.

Windows usually starts up by displaying the Program Manager window. As explained more in Chapter 2, the Program Manager is the part of Windows that organizes and runs programs that you do your work with. It is actually a program itself, and thus appears in a program window.

Just as with a real desktop, you can have a number of projects scattered about, all of which can be in progress. You can then easily switch between your projects, be they letters, address lists, spreadsheets, games, or whatever. This is unlike normal PC computing under DOS where you have to "put away" one project before opening the next.

Of course, if you happen to be a neatnik, you can opt to have only one document or program open at a time, and keep the Desktop clutter-free, so to speak. But there are advantages to the messy-desk approach. For example, you can view two documents (such as a spreadsheet and a report you are writing about) simultaneously by placing each document side by side in separate frames that you size to fit on the screen, as you see in Figure 1.2. This approach also allows you to copy material from one document to another a bit more easily.

Another feature designed into Windows is that it can be instructed to remember certain aspects of your work setup each time you quit. For example, if you use a certain group of programs regularly, you can set up Windows to come up with those programs already running—or ready to run

FIGURE 1.2:
Windows lets you see several documents simultaneously.

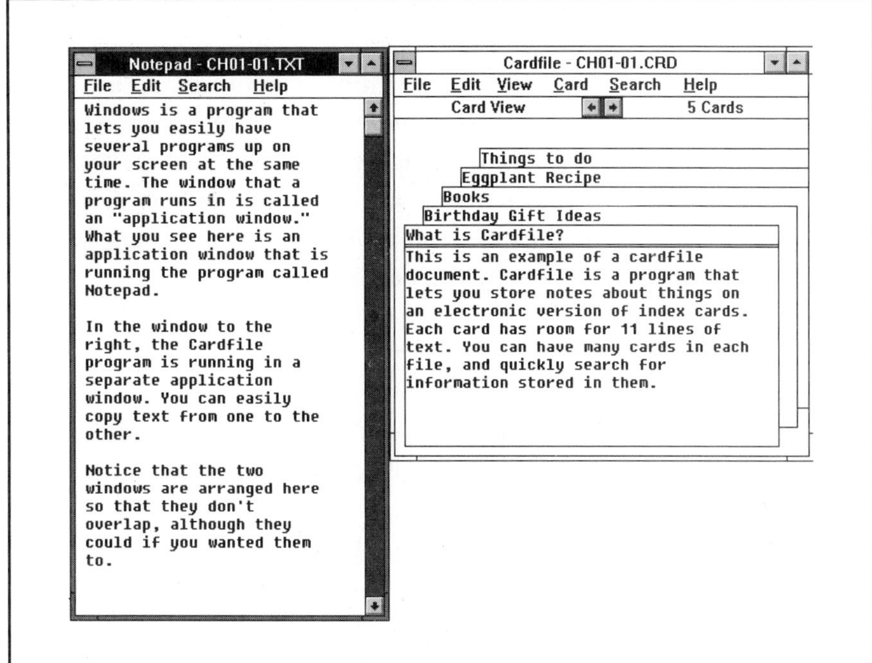

with just a click of the mouse. Programs you use less frequently will be stored away, within easy reach, but not cluttering your Desktop.

Icons

Icons are the third basic element of the Windows screen. At the bottom of the Program Manager window in Figure 1.1 you see several small symbols with names under them. These are called *icons.* Windows uses icons to represent documents and programs when they are not currently opened up in a window. They may be sitting on the Desktop waiting to be worked with, or they may be programs that are actually running but have temporarily been shrunk down to get them out of the way for the moment. When a program or document is *minimized* (also called *iconized*) in this way, it's as if the program is in suspended animation: the program or document is still available, but you can't use it.

A special class of icon, called a *group icon,* is used to represent a collection of programs that you decide to group together for convenience. As you will see in Chapter 2, the Program Manager uses group icons to help you organize your programs.

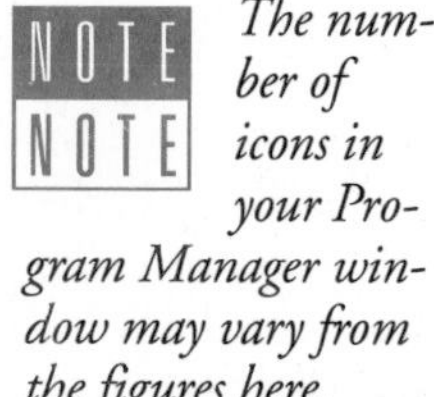

The number of icons in your Program Manager window may vary from the figures here.

You will have at least five group icons—Main, Accessories, Startup, Main, and Games—within your Program Manager window. (You may only see four icons at the present time, since the Main icon has been opened into a window that you are quite likely looking at.) If you chose to have the Windows Setup program install your existing applications, you will see an icon called Applications as well.

TYPES OF WINDOWS

Now let's look a little more closely at the various parts of the Desktop. There are two possible types of windows that you'll encounter: *application windows* and *document windows.*

Application Windows

Application windows are those that contain a program that you are running and working with, such as Microsoft Word, Excel, PC Paintbrush, WordPerfect, and so on. Most of the work that you do will be in application windows. Figure 1.3 shows a typical application window, sometimes called a *parent window.*

Document Windows

Some programs designed for Windows applications will let you work on more than one document at a time. For example, Microsoft Word for Windows allows you to have multiple documents open at once, in separate document windows. Instead of running Word several times in separate application windows, you just run it once in an application window and open several document windows within the application window. Figure 1.4 shows Microsoft Word with two document windows open inside it. Document windows are sometimes called *child windows.*

FIGURE 1.3:

An application window

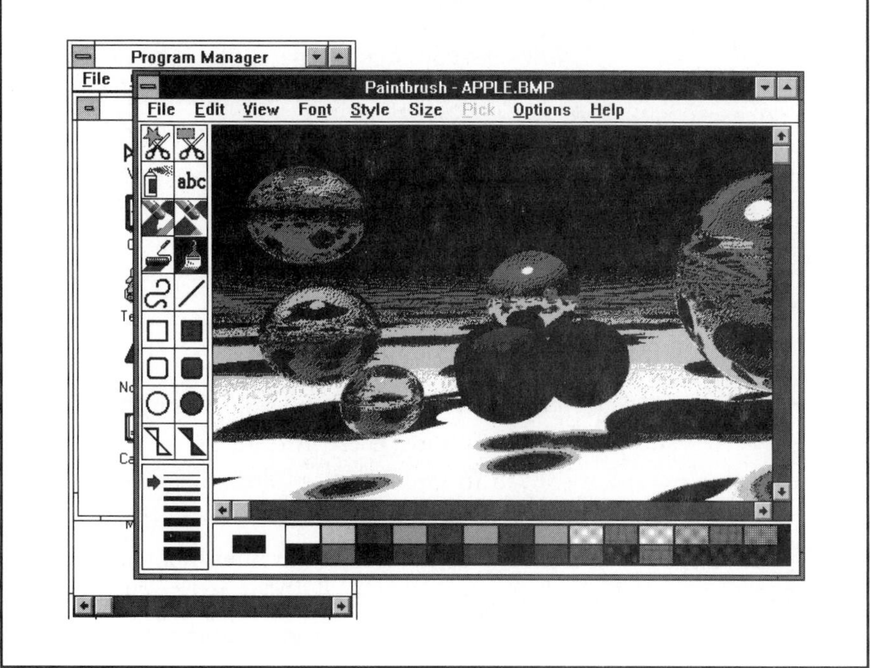

FIGURE 1.4:

Two document (child) windows within an application (parent) window

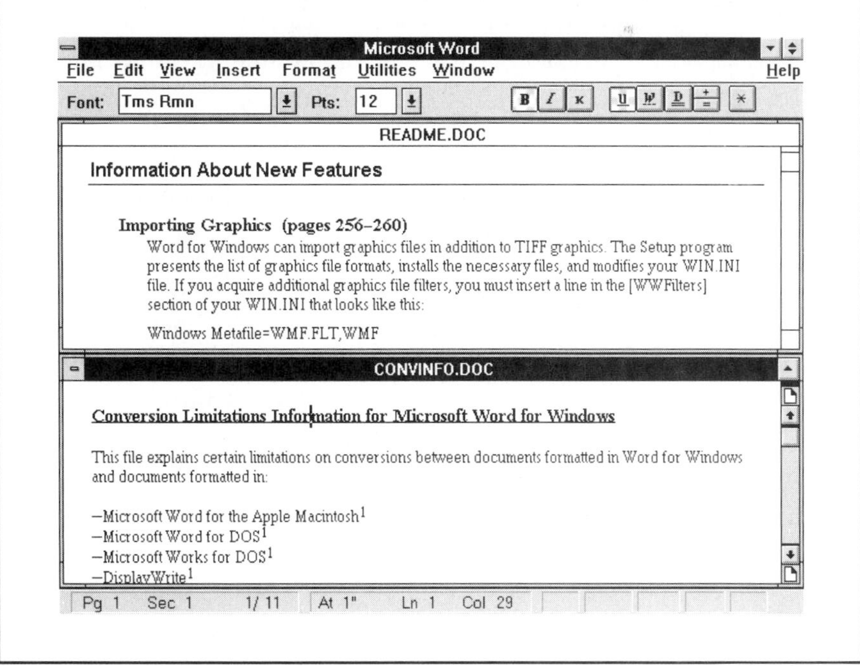

ANATOMY OF A WINDOW

Now let's consider the parts of a typical window. The first time you start Windows, the Desktop comes up in the arrangement shown in Figure 1.1 (please refer to it or look at your screen). Notice that there are two windows open already—the Program Manager window and the Main window.

THE TITLE BAR

The name of each program or document appears at the top of its respective window, in what's called the *title bar.* In this case, the title bars read Program Manager and Main. But if you were running another application, its name would be shown there instead.

In an application window, the name of the application is often followed by the name of the file being worked on. For example, in Figure 1.5, the Notepad application is running in a window. The title reads Notepad, followed by the file being edited, NETWORKS.TXT.

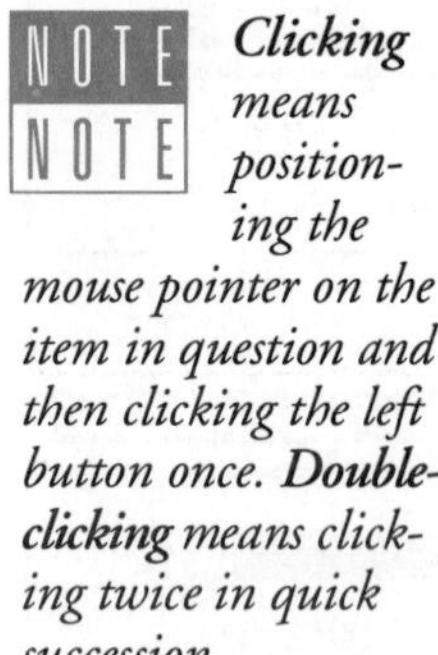

***Clicking** means positioning the mouse pointer on the item in question and then clicking the left button once. **Double-clicking** means clicking twice in quick succession.*

The title bar also serves another function: it indicates which window is *active.* Though you can have lots of windows on the screen at once, there can be only one active window at any given time. The active window is the one you're currently working in. When a window is made active, it jumps to the front of other windows that might be obscuring it, and its title bar changes color. (On monochrome monitors, the intensity of the title bar changes.) You make a window active by clicking anywhere within its border.

MINIMIZE AND MAXIMIZE BUTTONS

There are two small buttons at the right end of the title bar with small arrows (triangles) in them. The button with the arrow facing up is called the *Maximize button.* The other one is called the *Minimize button.* After a window has been maximized, the Maximize button changes to the *Restore button.* Restore buttons have both up and down arrows. These are little control buttons with which you quickly change the size of a window.

FIGURE 1.5:

Parts of a typical window

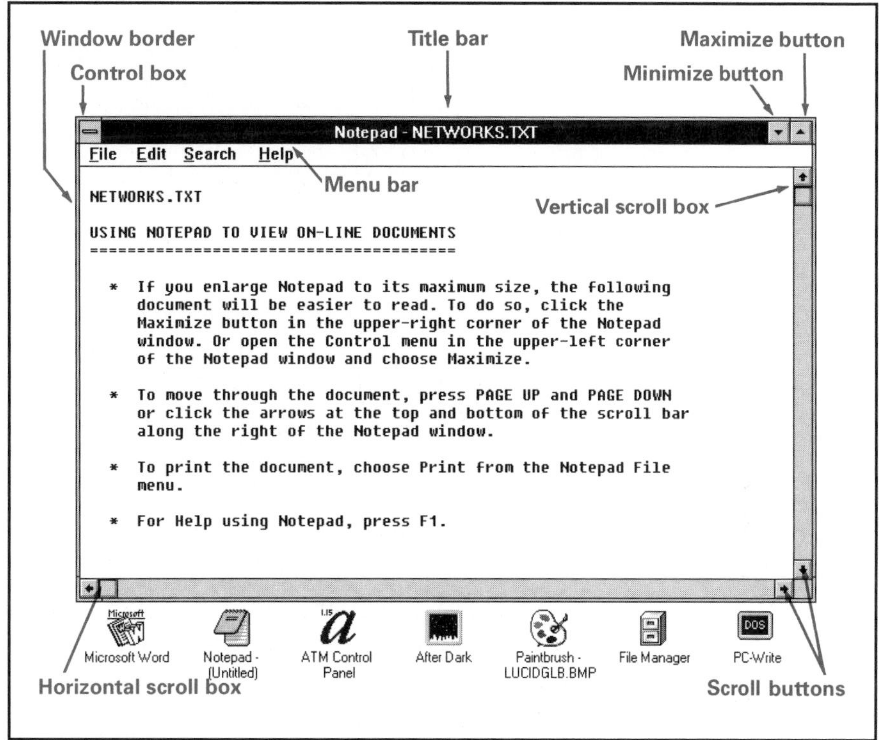

There are essentially three sizes that a window can have:

- Minimized: the window becomes an icon at the bottom of the Desktop, where it's ready to be easily opened again, but takes up a minimum of screen space.
- Normal: the window is open and takes up a portion of the Desktop, the amount of which is determined by how you manually size the window, as explained in the next section. This is also called the *restored* size.
- Maximized: the window takes up the whole Desktop. When you maximize a document window, it expands to take up the entire application window. This may or may not be the entire screen, depending on whether the applicaton has been maximized.

Here are the basic mouse techniques to quickly change the size of a window. Try these techniques on the Main window (or any other window that might be on your screen) to get the idea of it:

To Minimize a Window

1. You have to activate the window, so click anywhere within its perimeter.
2. Position the mouse pointer (the arrow that moves around on the screen when you move the mouse) on the Minimize button (the down arrow) in the upper-right corner of the window and click. The window reduces to the size of an icon. The window's name is shown below the icon so you know where it is.

To Restore a Window from an Icon

- Double-click on the icon.

To Maximize a Window

1. Activate the window by clicking within its perimeter.
2. Click on the Maximize button.

The window expands to fill the entire screen, or the entire program window if a document is being maximized. (Child windows are limited to the size of their parent window.)

The Restore button replaces the Maximize button. Clicking on this button will once again restore the window to its previous size.

To Manually Adjust the Size of a Window

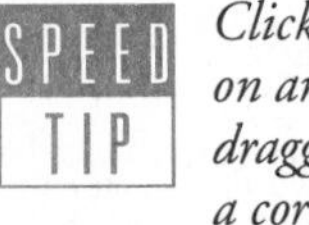

Clicking on and dragging a corner allows you to change both the width and height of the window.

Carefully position the cursor on any edge or corner of the window that you want to resize. When you are in the right position, the cursor shape changes to a two-headed arrow, as you can see in Figure 1.6. Press the mouse button and hold it down. A "ghost" of the window's outline moves with the arrow to indicate that you are resizing the window. Drag the window edge or corner to the desired position and then release the mouse button. (*Dragging* simply means keeping the mouse button depressed while moving the mouse.)

FIGURE 1.6:

Changing a window's size by dragging its corner

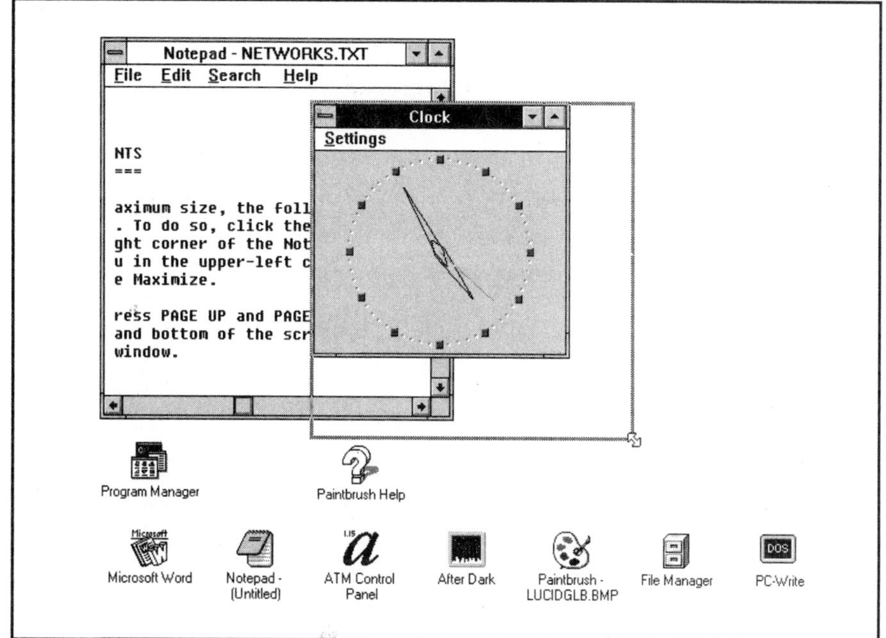

The Control Box

The box at the left end of the title bar is called the Control box. (It's supposed to look like a little file cabinet drawer with a handle on it, because it has to do with controlling files.) It has two functions. First, it opens a menu, called the Control menu. Figure 1.7 shows a Control box with its Control menu open. This is the same menu you get when you single-click on an iconized window. It only comes up when you single-click. Most of the commands here let you control the size of the window. (Menus are covered in detail later in this chapter.)

NOTE *Pressing Alt-Hyphen opens the Control box of the active child window; Alt-Spacebar opens the Control box of the active parent window.*

Second, the Control box for a program or document will close the window (terminate the program or close the document) when you double-click on it. If you double-click on the Control box of a group window (such as the Main window), it iconizes the window.

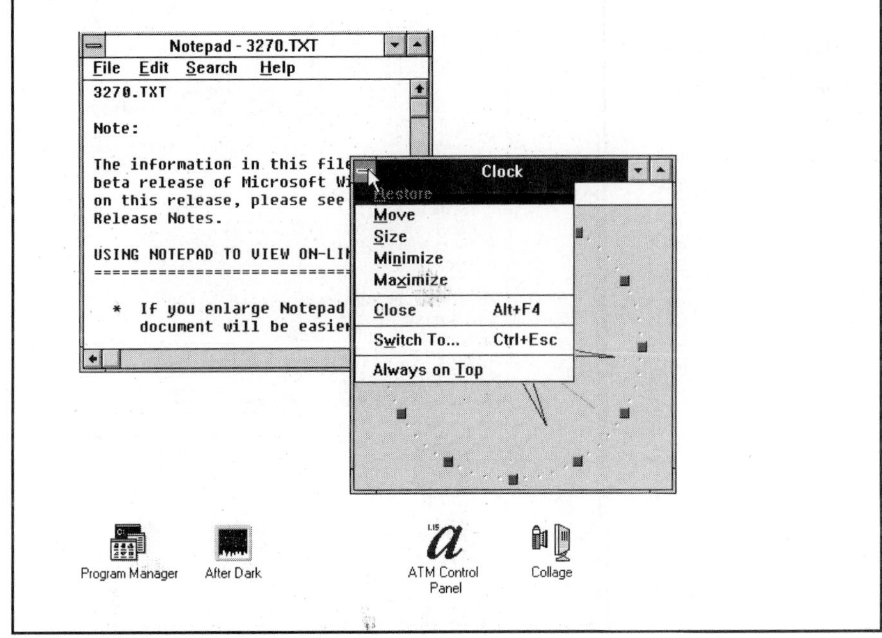

FIGURE 1.7: *Single-clicking on the Control box brings up the Control menu. Double-clicking quits the program or document, eliminating the window.*

Scroll Bars, Scroll Buttons, and Scroll Boxes

On the bottom and right edges of many windows, you'll find *scroll bars, scroll buttons,* and *scroll boxes.* These are used to "pan across" the information in a window: up, down, left, and right. This is necessary when there is too much information (text or graphics) to fit into the window at one time. For example, you might be writing a letter that is two pages long. Using the scroll bars lets you move around, or scroll, within your document to see the section you're interested in, since two full pages of text won't be displayed in a window at one time. Scrolling lets you look at a large amount of data through what amounts to a small window—your screen. Figure 1.8 illustrates this concept. Many Windows operations, such as listing files on your disks, reading Help screens, or displaying lots of icons within a window require the use of scroll bars and boxes.

Scroll bars have a little box in them called the *scroll box* or *elevator.* Just as an elevator can take you from one floor of a building to the next, the scroll bar takes you from one section of a window or document to the next. The

FIGURE 1.8:

Scrolling lets you work with more information than will fit on your screen at one time.

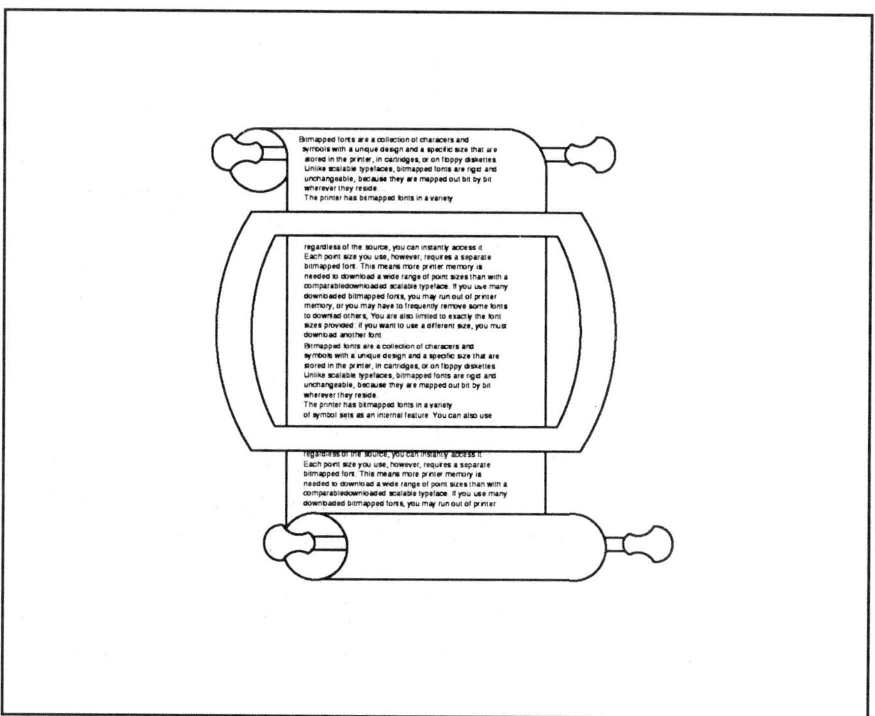

elevator moves within the scroll bar to indicate which portion of the window you are viewing at any given time. By moving the elevator with your mouse, you cause the document to scroll.

Try these exercises to see how scroll bars and boxes work:

1. With the Main window open (in normal, not maximized size), size the window so that it shows only three icons, such as File Manager, Control Panel, and Print Manager (see Figure 1.9). A vertical scroll bar appears on the right edge of the window. This indicates that there are more icons in the window than are visible, since the window is now so small. What has happened is that one icon is now out of view.
2. Drag the elevator up and down by positioning the pointer on the elevator, holding the mouse button down, and moving the mouse. Notice that as you do this, the elevator moves along with the pointer and the window's contents are repositioned.

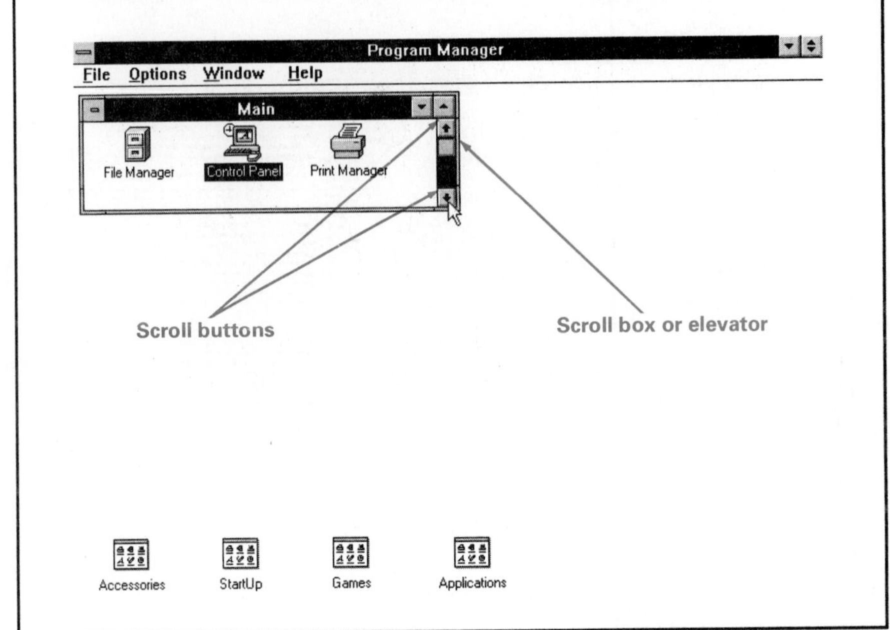

FIGURE 1.9:
A scroll bar appears to indicate that there is more in the Main window than is currently visible.

3. Now try another approach to scrolling. Click on the scroll buttons (the little arrows at the top and bottom of the scroll bar). With each click, the elevator moves a bit in the direction of the button you're clicking on. If you click and hold, the elevator continues to move.
4. One more approach is to click within the scroll bar above or below the elevator. Each click scrolls the window up or down a bit.

This example used only a short window with relatively little information in it. In this case, maximizing the window or resizing it just a bit would eliminate the need for scrolling, and is probably a better solution. However, with large documents or windows containing many icons, scrolling becomes a necessity, as you'll see when you learn how to use Windows' built-in Help System.

ALL ABOUT MENUS

The *menu bar* is a row of words that appears just below the title bar. (It appears only on application windows. Document windows do not have menu bars.) If you click on one of the words in the menu bar (called menu *names*), a menu opens up, displaying a series of options that you can choose from. It is through menus that you tell all Windows applications what actions you want carried out.

SPEED TIP *You could also have pressed Alt-F to open the File menu. If there is an underlined letter in any menu's name, holding down the Alt key and pressing that letter opens the menu.*

Try this as an example:

1. With the Program Manager window open and active, click on the word *File* in the menu bar. A menu opens, as you see in Figure 1.10, listing eight options. You can see why it's called a menu; it's a bit like a restaurant menu listing things you can order.
2. Click on the other names in the menu bar (Options, Window, or Help) or press the key to see the other menus and their choices.

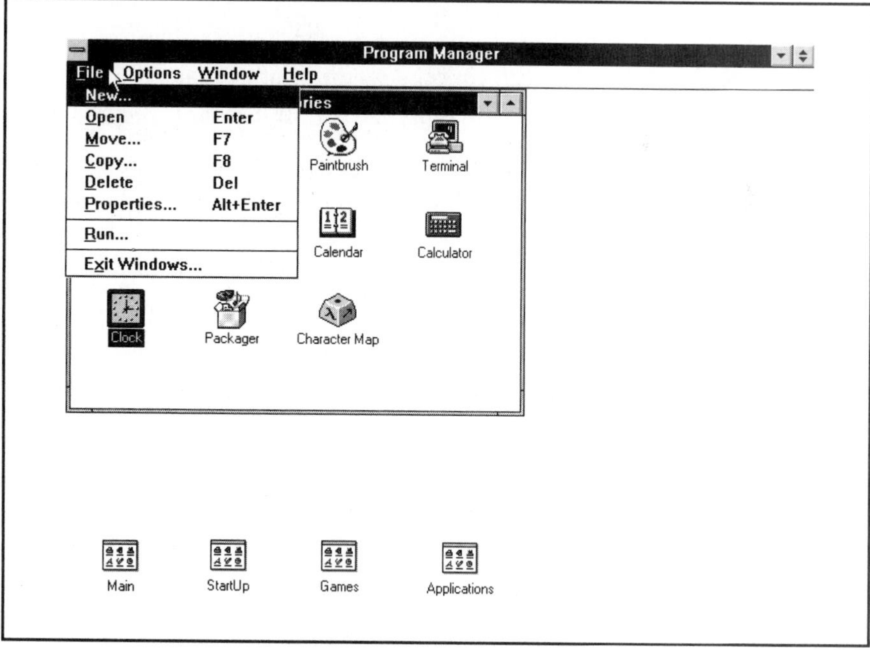

FIGURE 1.10: *Opening a menu by clicking on its name in the menu bar*

At this point, don't select any of the commands just yet. We'll begin using the commands in a bit.

Each menu name, when clicked on, will open up its own menu, with choices somewhat relevant to the menu's name. The names on the menu vary from application to application, but there are always several that are the same, such as File, Edit, and Help. It may take a while for you to become familiar with the commands and which menus they're located on, but it will become more automatic with time. In any case, it's easy enough to look around through the menus to find the one you want.

Selecting Menu Commands

Once a menu is open, you can select any of the commands in the menu that aren't dimmed. (The dimmed command names are ones that are not available at the time.) You can select a menu command in several ways:

- by typing the underlined letter in the command name
- by clicking on the command name
- by highlighting the command name using the arrow keys and then pressing Enter

You can cancel a menu (that is, make the menu disappear without selecting any commands) by simply pressing the Esc key, or by clicking anywhere outside of the menu.

Special Indicators in Menus

Windows and Windows applications menus often have special symbols that tell you more about the menu commands. For example, examine the menus in Figure 1.11. Notice that many of these commands have additional words or symbols next to the command name. For example, the New command (for creating a new file) has ellipses (three dots) after it. Other commands may have check marks, triangles, or key combinations listed beside them. Here are the meanings of these words or symbols:

A Grayed (Dimmed) Command Name

When a command is shown as *grayed,* or *dimmed,* it means that this choice is not currently available to you. A command can be dimmed for a number of reasons. For example, a command for changing the typestyle of text will

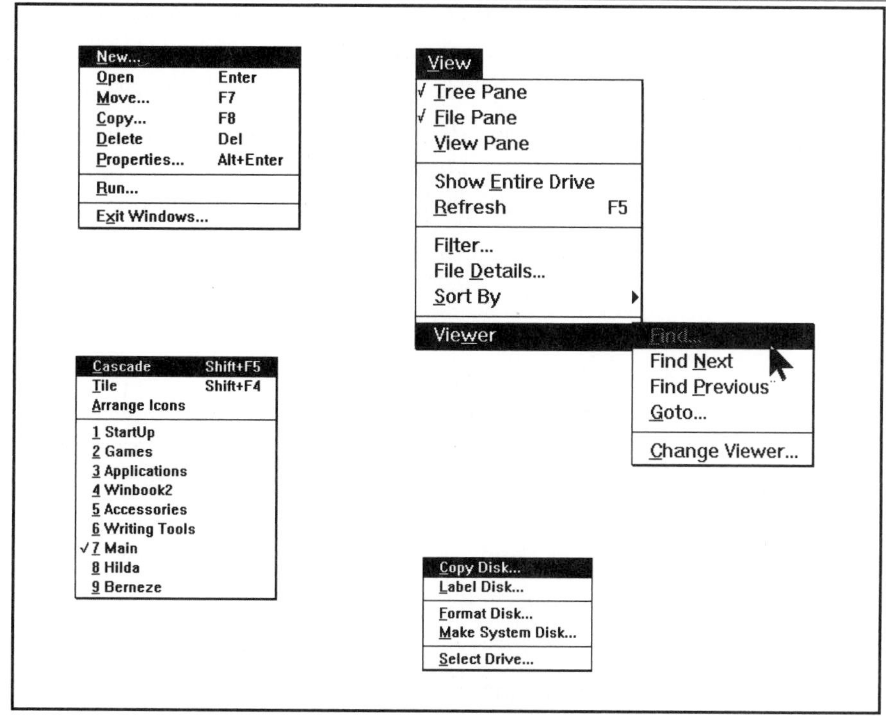

FIGURE 1.11: *Typical menus*

be grayed if no text has been selected. Other times, commands will be grayed because you are in the wrong program mode. For example, if a window is already maximized, the Maximize command on the Control menu will be dimmed, since this choice doesn't make sense.

Ellipses (...)

Ellipses next to a command mean that you will be asked for additional information before Windows or the Windows application executes the command. When you select the command, a dialog box will appear on the screen, asking you to fill in the needed information. (We will discuss dialog boxes in the next section of this chapter.)

A Check Mark (✓)

A check mark preceding a command means the command is a toggle that is activated (turned on). A *toggle* is a command that is alternately turned off and on each time you select it. It's like a toggle switch or those old car high-beam switches on the floor that you step on to change between high beams and low beams. Each time you select one of these commands, it switches from *active* to *inactive.* If there is no check mark, then the command or setting is inactive. This is typically used to indicate things like whether selected text is underlined, which font is selected, what mode you are in within a program, and so on.

A Triangle (▶)

A triangle to the right of a menu command means that the command has additional subchoices for you to make. Choosing such a command brings up a *cascading menu* (because the next menu starts to the right of the previous one and runs down from there, a bit like a waterfall of menus). You make selections from a cascaded menu the same way you would from normal menus. The upper-right example in Figure 1.11 shows a cascaded menu.

A Key Combination

Some menu commands list keystrokes that can be used instead of opening the menu and choosing that command. For example, in the Program Manager's File menu (shown in Figure 1.10), you'll notice that the Open command could be executed by pressing the Enter key, and the Delete command could be executed by pressing the Del key. These alternative time-saving keystrokes are called *shortcut keys.*

ALL ABOUT DIALOG BOXES

A dialog box will always appear when you select a command with ellipses (...) after it. Dialog boxes pop up on your screen when Windows or the Windows application program you're using needs more information before continuing. Some dialog boxes ask you to enter information (such as file names), while others simply require you to check off options or make choices from a list. The list may be in the form of additional sub-dialog boxes or submenus. In any case, after you enter the requested information, you click OK and then Windows or the application program continues on its merry way, executing the command.

Though most dialog boxes ask you for information, other boxes are only informative, alerting you to a problem with your system or an error you've made. Such a box might also request confirmation on a command that could have dire consequences or explain why the command you've chosen can't be executed. These alert boxes often have a big letter *i* (for "information") in them, or an exclamation mark (!) if the warning is more important. Generally, these boxes only ask you to read them and then click OK (or cancel them, if you decide not to proceed). Some boxes only have an OK button. Let's look at some typical dialog boxes and how they work.

Moving between Sections of a Dialog Box

As you can see in Figure 1.12, dialog boxes often have several sections to them. You can move between the sections in three ways:

- The easiest way is by clicking on the section you want to alter.
- If you are using the keyboard, you can press the Tab key to move between sections and press the spacebar to select them.
- You can also use the Alt key with the underlined letter of the section name you want to jump to or activate. Even when you are using a mouse, the Alt-key combinations are sometimes the fastest way to jump between sections or choose an option within a box.

Entering Information in a Dialog Box

Now let's consider how you enter information into dialog boxes. There are six basic types of sections in dialog boxes: text boxes, check boxes, option buttons, command buttons, list boxes, drop-down list boxes, and file dialog boxes. Figure 1.12 illustrates these areas.

Once you've jumped to the correct section, you'll need to know how to make choices from it. Here is a list explaining how to use the sections:

Text Boxes

In this sort of section, you are asked to type in text from the keyboard. Sometimes there will be text already typed in for you. If you want to keep it as is, just leave it alone. To alter the text, simply type in new text. If the existing

FIGURE 1.12:

Typical dialog boxes, showing text boxes, option buttons, drop-down list boxes, and command buttons

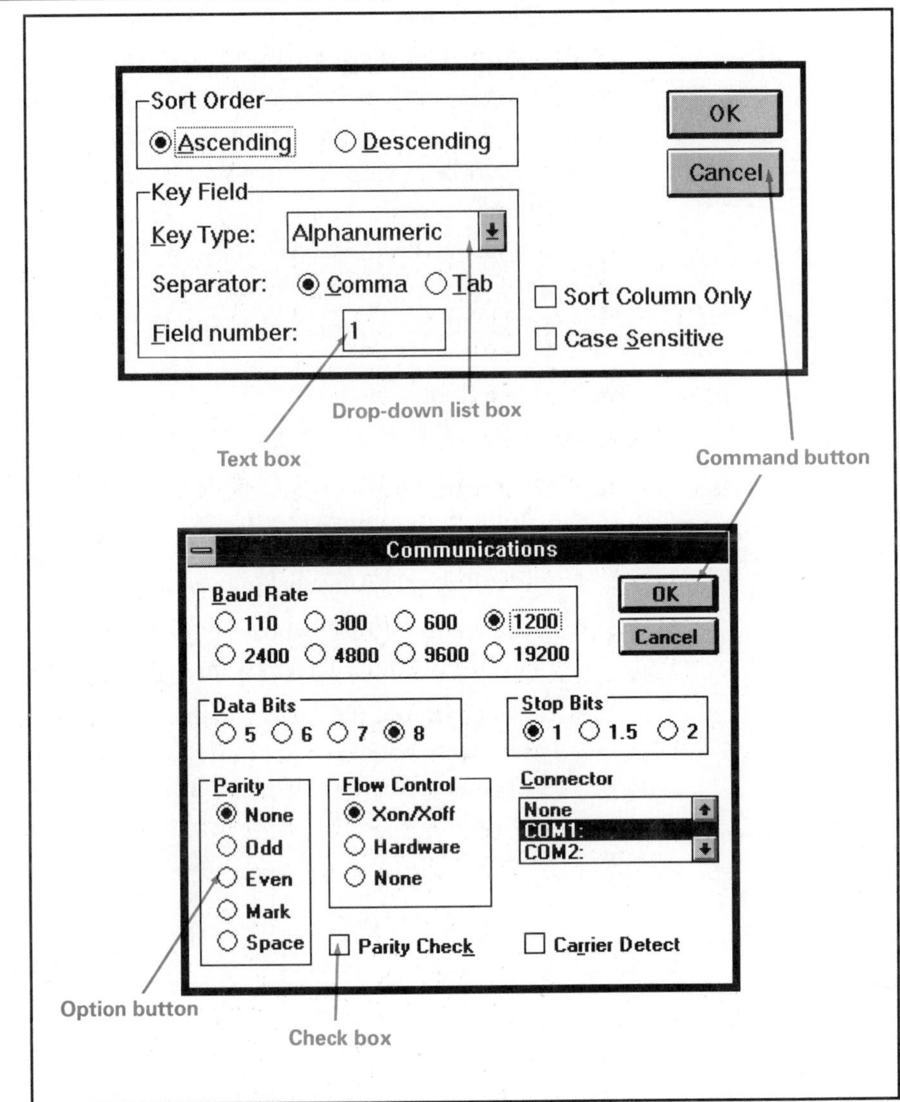

text is already highlighted, then the first key you press will delete the existing entry. If it is not highlighted, you can backspace over it to erase it. You can also edit existing text. Clicking once on highlighted text will *deselect* it and cause the *text cursor* (a vertical blinking bar) to appear when you put the pointer inside the text area. You can then move the text cursor around using the arrow keys or the mouse and insert text (by typing) or delete text (by pressing the Del key). Text is inserted at the position of the text cursor. Text boxes are most often used for specifying file names when you are saving or loading documents and applications, or specifying text to search for in a word-processing document.

Check Boxes

Check boxes are the small square boxes. They are used to indicate nonexclusive options. For example, you might want some text to appear as bold *and* underlined. Or, as another example, consider the Communications dialog box in Figure 1.12. In this box, you can have both the Parity Check and the Carrier Detect set on or off. These are toggle settings (as explained previously) that you activate or deactivate by clicking on the box. When the box is empty, the option is off; when you see an ×, the option is on.

Option Buttons

Unlike check boxes, which are nonexclusive, option buttons are exclusive settings. They are also round rather than square, and only one can be set on at a time. For example, using the same Communications dialog box referred to above, you may select 5, 6, 7, or 8 data bits in the Data Bits section of the dialog box. Clicking on the desired button turns it on (the circle will be filled) and turns any previous selection off. From the keyboard, you first jump to the section, then use the arrow keys to select the option.

Command Buttons

Command buttons are like option buttons except that they are used to execute a command immediately. They are also rectangular rather than boxes or circles. The most common command buttons are the OK and Cancel buttons found on almost every dialog box. Once you've filled in a dialog box to your liking, you click on the OK button and Windows or the application executes the settings you've selected. If you change your mind and don't want the new commands on the dialog box executed, click on the Cancel button. There is always a command button that has a thicker border; this is the button that will be executed if you press Enter. Likewise, pressing the Esc key always has the same effect as clicking on the Cancel button (that's why there's no underlined letter on the Cancel button). Some command buttons are followed by ellipses (...). These commands will open additional dialog boxes for adjusting more settings. Other command buttons include two >> symbols in them. Choosing this type of button causes the particular section of the dialog box to expand so that you can make more selections.

List Boxes

> **SPEED TIP** *You can quickly jump to an option in a list box by typing the first letter of its name. If there are two choices with the same first letter and you want the second one, press the letter again, or press the down arrow key.*

List boxes are like menus. They show you a list of options or items from which you can choose. For example, when choosing fonts to display or print text in, Windows Write shows you a list box. You make a selection from a list box the same way you do from a menu: by just clicking on it. From the keyboard, highlight the desired option with the arrow keys and then press Enter to choose it. Some list boxes are too small to show all the possible selections at once. In this case, there will be a scroll bar on the right side of the box. Use the scroll bar to see all the selections. Some list boxes let you make more than one selection, but most only allow one. To make more than one selection, press the spacebar to select or deselect any item, or hold the shift key down and click on additional list items with the mouse.

Drop-Down List Boxes

Drop-down list boxes are indicated by a small underlined arrow in a box to the right of the option. The current setting is displayed to the left of the little arrow. Clicking on the arrow opens a list that works just like a normal list box, and has scroll bars if there are a lot of options. Drop-down list boxes are used when a dialog box is too crowded to accommodate regular list boxes.

File Dialog Boxes

A dialog box like one of the two shown in Figure 1.13 often appears when using Windows and Windows applications. This type of box, called a file dialog box, is used to select files from your hard disk or floppy disks. Though used in a variety of situations, you're most likely to run into file dialog boxes when retrieving or saving a file from within an application program.

File dialog boxes vary somewhat from program to program, but they roughly work in identical fashion. Typically the box is divided into two main sections, listing files on the left, and directories on the right. In some applications, directories are represented by a folder as you see in the upper example

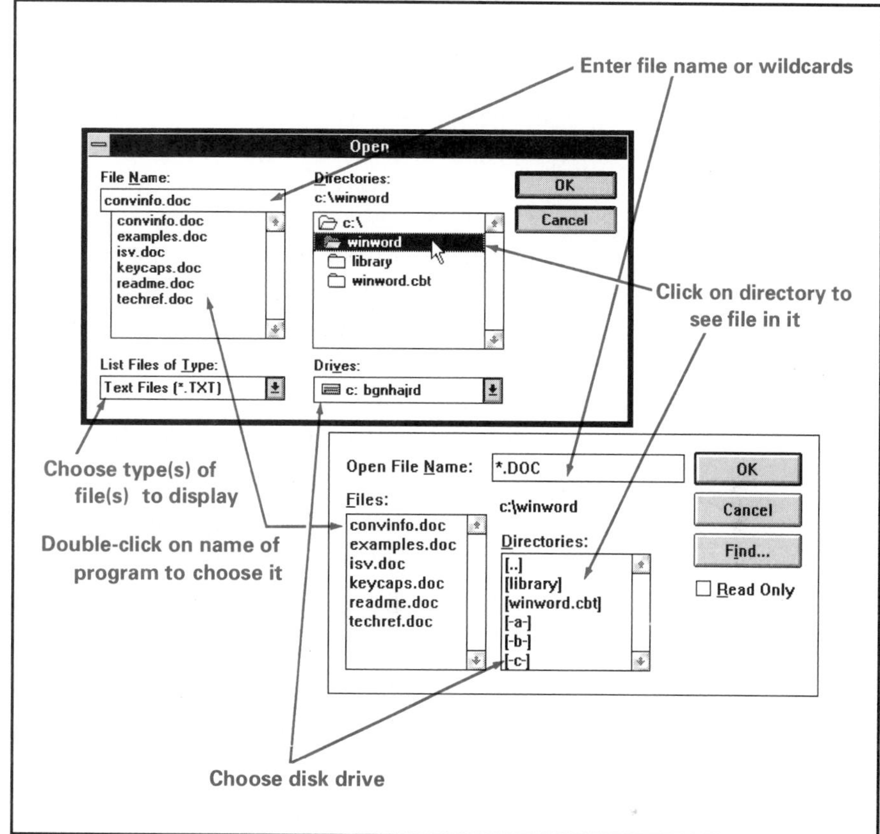

FIGURE 1.13:
A file dialog box lets you scan through directories to load or save a document. Here you see two typical file dialog box types. The upper one is the newer Windows 3.1 style.

in the figure. In others, notably older programs not specifically designed for Windows 3.1, you only see the directory's name enclosed in brackets, as shown in the lower example.

Here's how you move through directories to find or name a file:

1. Make sure the correct disk drive is chosen down in the lower-right side of the box. Open the drop-down list box and select another drive if necessary. If using an older file box, you don't have a drop-down list for the drive. To change drives, you scroll to the bottom of the directory list and double-click on the name of the drive (e.g., [–a–], [–b–], [–c–]) to change drives.

2. Select a directory on the right side by double-clicking on its folder or name. The directory's files appear in the list to the left. If you don't see the directory you're aiming for, you may have to "move down" or "back up" the directory tree a level or two, particularly if the disk you're looking at has multiple levels of subdirectory levels on it. (See Chapter 4 for a review of DOS directory theory.) In newer style boxes, you'd double click on the folder just above the one that's currently open to back up a level, or on the folder below the current one to move down a level. In older-style boxes, you'll have to double-click on the two dots (..) at the top of the directory list to back up one directory level. Each double click backs up one directory level. To move down a level, click on any directory name enclosed in brackets.
3. If you want to see only certain types of files, open the List Files of Type box (if there is one) to select the type of files you want to see (such as programs, or all files). If the options offered don't suit your needs, or if you're using the older-style box, you can type in DOS-like wildcards in the File Name area, then press Enter to modify the file list accordingly. For example, to show only Lotus 1-2-3 worksheet files, you'd enter *.WK? in the File Name area and press Enter.
4. Once the file you want is visible in the file box at the left, double-click on it, or highlight it, and click on OK.

When saving a file for the first time, the file won't exist on the drive yet, so it won't show up in the file list box; you'll be giving it a name. To do this, select the drive and directory as outlined above, then move the cursor to the File Name area and type in the file name and extension. Make sure to delete any existing letters in the text area first, using the Backspace and/or delete keys. (For more information about selecting, editing, and replacing text, see Chapter 8, under "Techniques for Selecting Text.")

GETTING HELP WHEN YOU NEED IT

TO GET HELP,

open the Help menu and select Contents or How to Use Help.

So far, you've gotten a fairly detailed overview of the Windows interface. However, we haven't used any programs other than the Program Manager yet, so some of this information is still academic, unless you have experimented on your own with dialog boxes and windows. Perhaps you have tried running some other programs such as Notepad or Cardfile, which would provide additional opportunities for experimentation. (Running programs is covered in the next chapter.) In any case, there will be times when you don't remember or understand how to use an operation or command. Luckily, you don't always have to drag out a book or manual to get some quick help. The people at Microsoft have done a very good job of developing a built-in Help facility for this version of Windows. Once you learn how to use it, it'll answer many of your questions. Windows applications from other software companies should have a help system that works the same way as described below.

To Get Help

To get help on what you're doing, open the Help menu (it's always the menu farthest to the right). The menu lists several choices, the number of which depends on the program you're using. You're probably using the Program Manager at this point, so there will be four choices, plus a choice called About Program Manager.

Each of the options at this stage is a general category that allows you to choose just what kind of help you need. Windows Tutorial takes the novice through a step-by-step guided tour of Windows. If you know how to use Windows but aren't sure where to begin seeking help about a specific feature, choose How to Use Help. Choosing Contents brings up a list of topics about the application you're using. (Pressing F1 instead of opening the Help menu opens the Help Contents directly.) Search for Help On opens up a dialog box where you can type in a word or select a topic for Help to give you more information about.

How to Use Help is the only Help command that brings up the same information for all applications (see Figure 1.14). The window is called "How to Use Help," and it contains help about how to get help. There are features in this window that are common to all Help windows, so I will discuss these features first:

- The first sentence reads, "If you are new to Help, choose Help Basics." To experiment some, position the pointer on the underlined words Help Basics. Notice that the cursor changes to the shape of a pointing finger, as shown in Figure 1.14. Microsoft calls this pointing finger the hand icon. Any word or phrase in a list that appears lighter (or green, if you have a color monitor) and is underlined with such a solid line is a topic. Clicking on a topic causes Help to jump to the section in the online manual (the documentation that is on your hard disk) that is relevant to the word or procedure you're interested in. You will see a new Help window with information about the topic you selected. (Click on the Back button to get back to the screen you started from.)

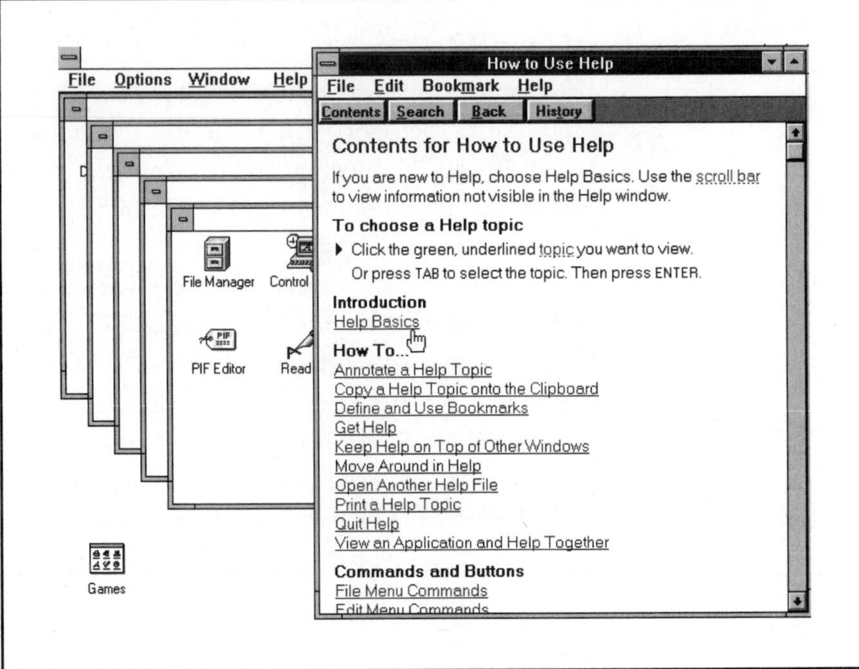

FIGURE 1.14: *A typical Help screen, in this case showing information on using Windows Help*

- Within the text of Help windows some words appear lighter (or green) and are underlined with a dotted line. These are called *hotspots* and are terms for which there is a definition that you can see. To see the definition, position the pointer on the term (once again, the cursor changes to the hand icon) and click. The definition pops up in a window like that shown in Figure 1.15. To close the box, just click again or press any key on the keyboard.
- Occasionally you'll encounter hotspots that are graphics instead of words. They don't look any different from other graphics in the Help windows, but the pointer turns into the hand icon when it's positioned over them. View information about hotspot graphics as you do other hotspots. There are a few key combinations that highlight the hotspots in a Help window, making it easy to locate and select them. Tab advances to the next hotspot, Shift-Tab moves to the previous hotspot, and Ctrl-Tab highlights all the hotspots as long as you hold both keys down.

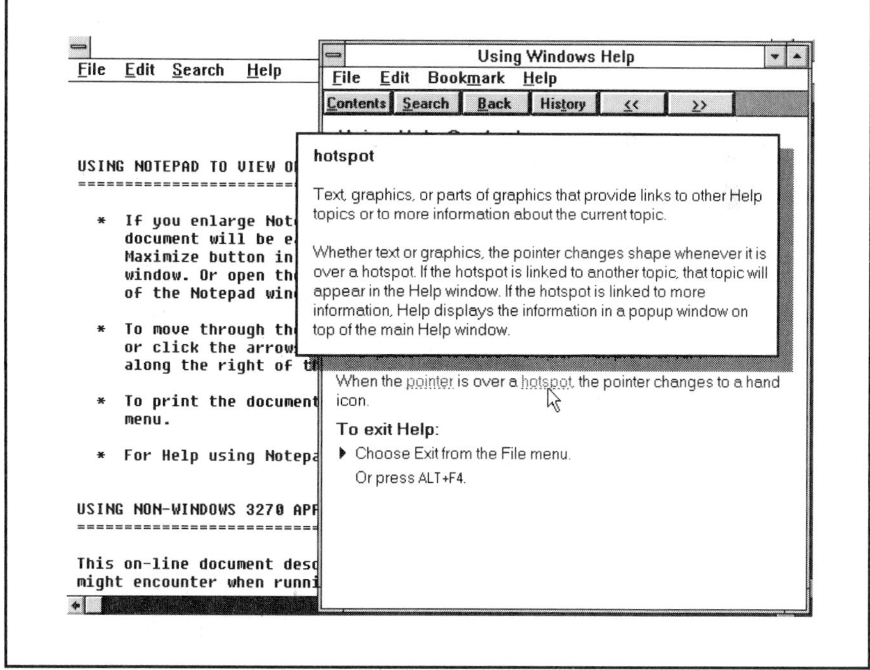

FIGURE 1.15:

Dotted-underlined words are hotspots. Click on a dotted-underlined word to see its definition.

- Another feature you may see is a list of topics with a boxed plus sign (+) preceding them, as in Figure 1.16. These are hotspots that will reveal helpful hints about certain options. Just position the pointer over the square and click. To close the pop-up box, click again.

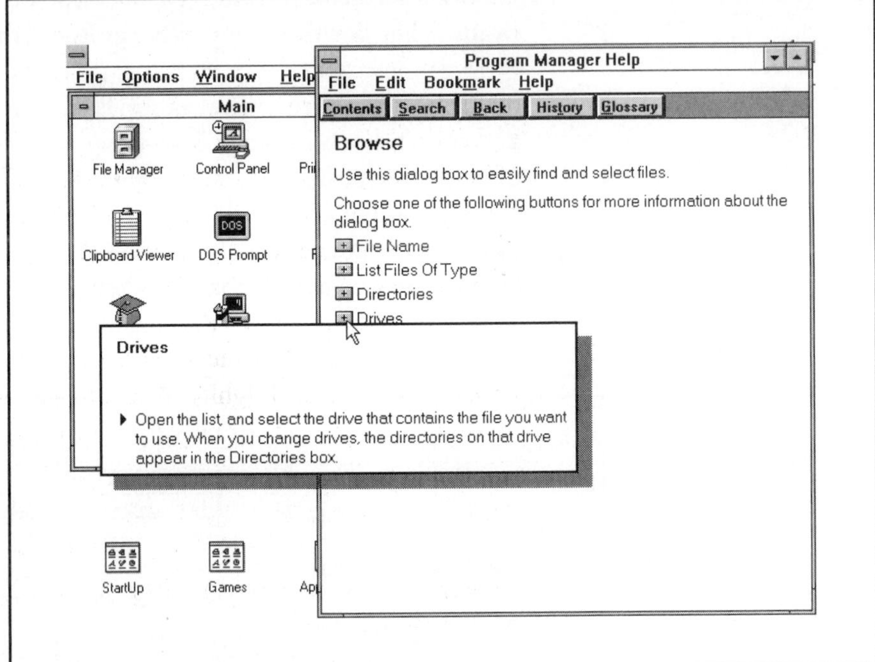

FIGURE 1.16: *Plus-sign hotspots explain an option*

THE HELP BUTTONS

Beneath the title bar, most Help screens have both a menu bar and a row of five to seven command buttons. I'll discuss the more noteworthy menu choices later in this section. Here's what the command buttons do when you click on them:

Contents: This jumps you directly to the list of Help contents for the application you are using. The Contents list is a good starting point for getting help and a good place to return to after reading Help on one item if you want to see more on another, unrelated item. Pressing F1 from an application takes you to this list without opening the Help menu.

Search: This button lets you look for a specific word or topic. There is a list of key words for each topic in the Help system. This command shows you those words in a list box. (You see the same box by choosing Search for Help On from the main Help menu.) You can select the subject you want to read about, or you can type in a word you want Help to look up. As you begin typing, the list will scroll to the word you've entered, assuming that there's a match. If the word you type isn't found there, Help jumps to the key word spelled most similarly. When the topic you want help on is highlighted, click on Show Topics or press Enter. Another list of topics related to the one you just indicated appears in the lower box of the Search screen. Sometimes it's just the general topic itself; other times there will be several new choices. Highlight the one you want to read and click on the Go To button (or press Enter). If you don't find the topic you want, click on the Cancel button (or press Escape).

Back: This lets you back up through the Help topics you have already viewed in the reverse order that you viewed them (meaning, the most recent first). When you have backed up as far as you can go, the Back button is grayed.

History: This brings up a little box within the current Help screen that lists the Help screens you've consulted in the reverse order that you viewed them. The most recent is at the top of the list. By using the History box, instead of backing up to a previous topic by clicking on Back until the screen you want reappears, you can just double-click on the topic in the History box. If you click on Back while the History box is open, you'll see the topics you already looked at in the order that they appear in the list. Each topic is added to the top of the list as you view it again.

<<: This is the Browse Backward button. If the Browse buttons appear on a Help screen, it means that some topics related to the current one can be viewed one after another by pressing one of the Browse buttons. Each click on the button returns you to the previous topic in the series. When you reach the first topic, the button becomes grayed.

>>: This is the Browse Forward button. It advances you to the next screen in the series of related topics. When you reach the end of the series, the button is grayed. Not all Help screens have this button.

Glossary: This button opens up the Windows Help Glossary, where you can get definitions of all the hotspot terms you'll encounter in Windows. To view a definition from the Glossary, position the hand icon on the term you want defined, and click. After reading the definition, click again or press any key on the keyboard to close the pop-up box. When you're finished using the Glossary, click on the Close Glossary button.

Keeping a Specific Help Screen Handy

There are several ways to keep a specific help screen easily available. First, you can shrink the Help window down to a size where you can still read it, but it doesn't take up the whole screen. Make it a small wide band at the bottom or side of the screen, for example, and resize your other windows to accommodate it, as in Figure 1.17.

Another solution is to minimize it, leaving more of your screen available for the application you're working with. Leave just enough space to see the icon on the Desktop. When you need to read the Help topic again, just double-click on the icon. This is particularly helpful for quickly recalling lists of key commands or other information that is difficult to remember.

A third technique is to open the Help screen's Help menu and choose Always on Top. Now it won't disappear when you switch back to the application. You can resize the Window, too.

You can only have one Help screen open at a time, however; so if you want to refer to a few topics' Help screens while you're working on a project, another feature, Bookmark, is a good tool for you to become familiar with. Bookmark allows you to create a list of the topics you most often refer to. Once you find a topic the first time and add it to the Bookmark list, you can

FIGURE 1.17:

Keep Help windows handy while working in Windows

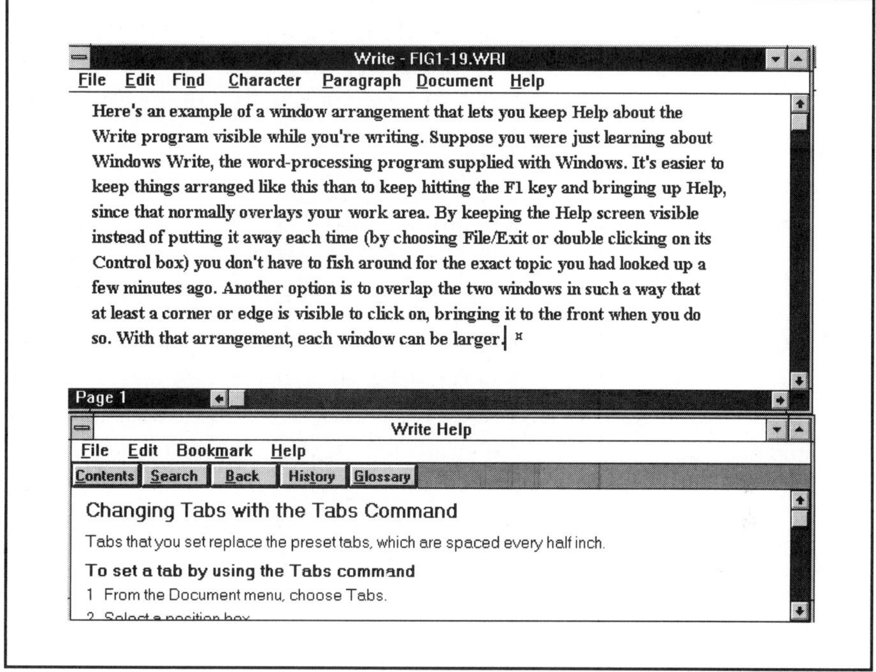

jump to that Help screen quickly the next time simply by choosing the topic from your personal list.

To define your bookmarks:

1. Open the Help screen and locate the topic you want to create a bookmark for.
2. When the desired topic Help screen is open, choose Bookmark ➤ Define.
3. In the Bookmark Define dialog box (see Figure 1.18) you have the option of giving the bookmark a name or leaving it with the topic name. Type in a new name if you want to. Choose OK. The dialog box closes and you return to the topic Help screen. If you open the Bookmark menu again, you will see the topic listed.

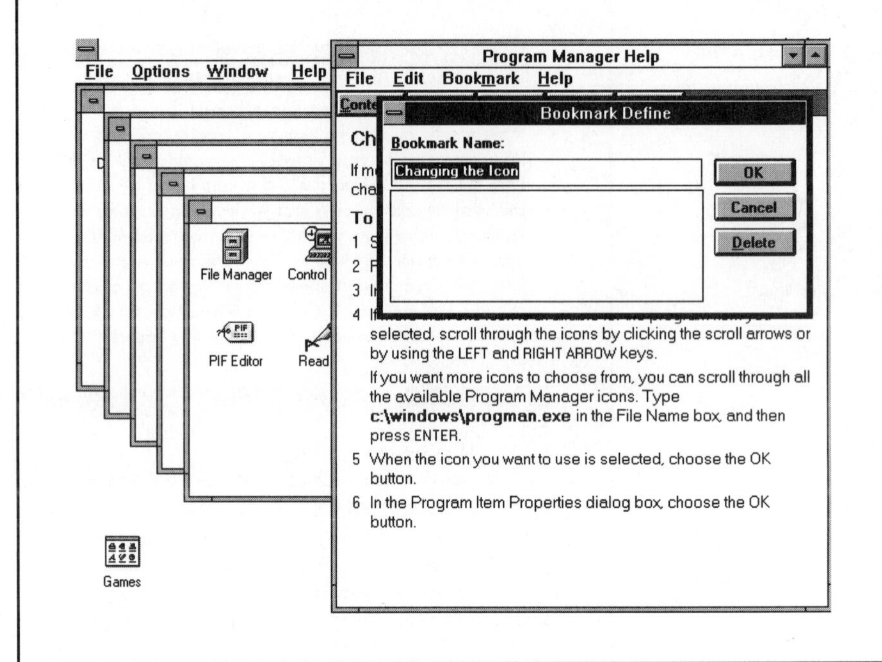

FIGURE 1.18:

Find help quickly by bookmarking Help topics.

To view one of your bookmarked topics later on, choose Help ➤ Contents ➤ Bookmark, then choose the topic by clicking on it. If more than nine topics are bookmarked, choose More from the Bookmark list, then click on the topic in the Go To dialog box.

To remove a bookmark from the list, follow the same steps that you did to define it, but in the Bookmark Define dialog box, choose Delete.

Remember that How to Use Help is a system-wide Help screen, so its list of bookmarks will be separate from those that you create while getting help within a particular application. For this reason, you should define bookmarks for a specific project from the Contents or Search options of Help. To bookmark general Windows topics, define them from the How to Use Help screen. Experiment with defining bookmarks from each of the Help menu options to see which list they end up in.

When Help Doesn't Help

In some cases, Help just won't tell you what you're interested in the first time around. Try spending some time wandering through the help screens. There is a lot of information in the Help files supplied with Windows and the Windows accessories. Sometimes the Search command won't find what you need to know, but the information is in the Help system in another context.

Modifying the Help Screens

You can add your own notes to a Help topic. This is useful for reminding yourself of things you've figured out about an application program or where to find information on some topic that eluded you last time you looked. Each topic can have only one annotation, but it can be quite long. An annotation is like a note that you "paper clip" to the topic. To make an annotation:

1. Get to the Help screen where you want to attach the note.
2. Open the Edit menu of the Help window and choose Annotate.
3. Type your notes into the dialog box that appears (Figure 1.19). You can edit the text using the Backspace key, the delete key, and the arrow keys.
4. When you are finished, click on Save. A paper clip now shows up before the topic title on the Help screen you're reading.

You can read the annotation on any Help topic (if there is a paper clip there) by either clicking on the paper clip or choosing Edit ➤ Annotate. You can delete an annotation by opening the Annotation dialog box again and clicking on Delete.

Copying the Help Screens

There may be occasions when you would find it useful to copy information from Help topics into a document or another application. For example, if you are preparing a training manual for employees in your company who are learning WordPerfect for Windows, you may find useful guidelines within WordPerfect's Help utility that you want to incorporate rather than retyping

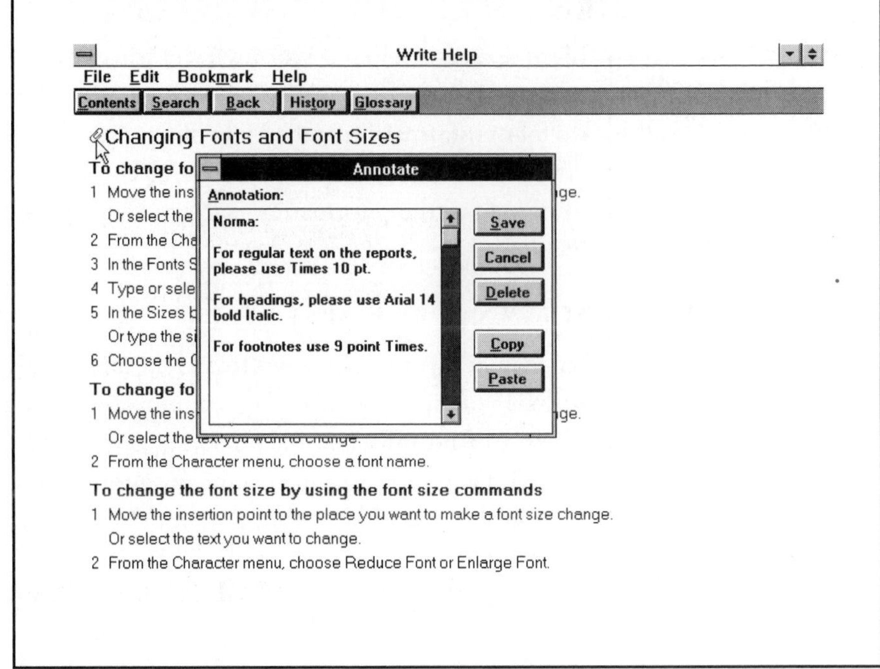

FIGURE 1.19: *Adding your own notes to a Help topic with Annotation*

it all. This feature can also save you time using Help if you annotate one topic with related information from another topic.

Copying is done by way of Windows' Clipboard. The entire Help topic may be copied, or only selected portions of it. (Graphics from a Help topic cannot be copied to the Clipboard, however.) For a complete discussion of Clipboard and text selection techniques, see Chapter 8. I'll briefly outline the steps here for copying to the Clipboard from Help:

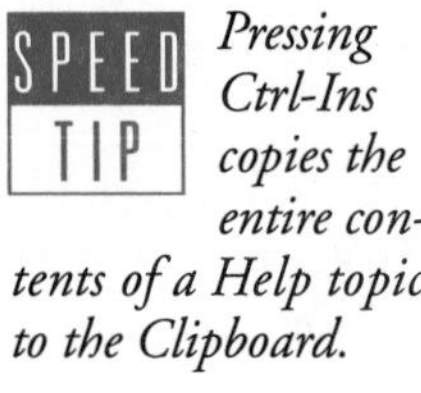

Pressing Ctrl-Ins copies the entire contents of a Help topic to the Clipboard.

1. Within the active Help topic window, open the Edit menu and choose Copy.
2. A duplicate of the Help topic appears in the text space of the dialog box, as shown in Figure 1.20. To copy all of it, just click on the Copy button. If you want to copy only a portion of it, select the desired text, then click on Copy. Note that the text may extend past the edge of the small window, but you can scroll over to see

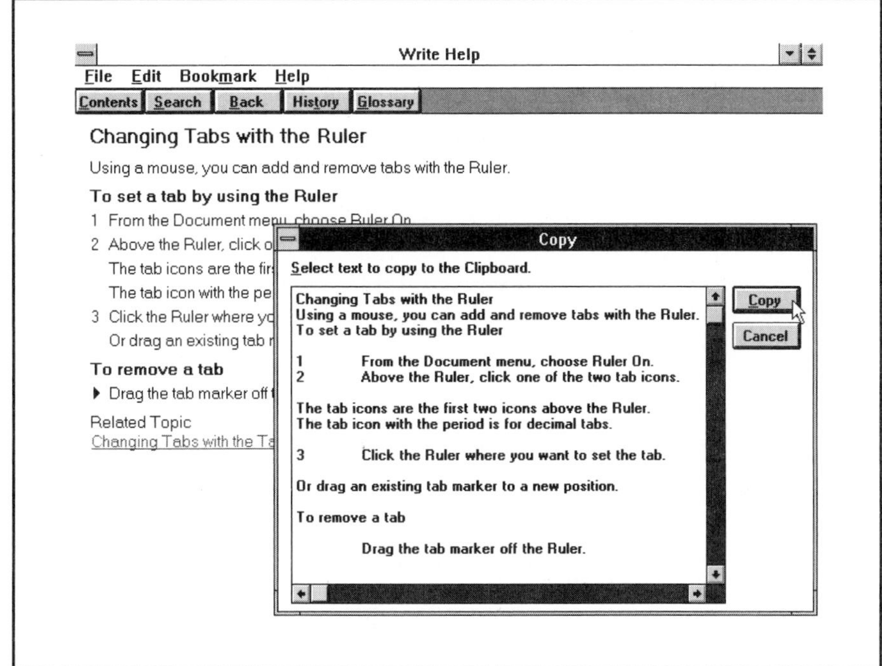

FIGURE 1.20: *Copying text from a Help topic*

it using the horizontal scroll bar. Or, if you resize the Help topic window to make it as narrow as the Copy box, the text will wrap so you can see it all.

To annotate another Help topic with the information you just copied, follow the steps above. But when the annotation dialog box appears, instead of typing in your notes, click on the Paste button, or press Shift-Ins. The text box fills up with the information you just copied from the other topic. In some cases there may not be enough space for the entire annotation to fit in the text box. You will see a message if that is the case. You can then decide how to edit the annotation.

Printing Help Topics

It is also possible to print a Help topic on paper. This is done from the topic window's File menu. Choose File ➤ Print. If you want to change the settings of the printed copy, see the section on printing options in Chapter 6.

EXITING WINDOWS

TO EXIT WINDOWS,

activate the Program Manager window and double-click the Control box. You will be asked to confirm exiting and possibly to close any open applications.

When you're finished with a Windows session, you should get back to the DOS prompt before turning off your computer. This ensures that Windows saves your work on disk correctly, and that no data are lost. Even if you are running an application in Windows and you close that application, you'll want to exit Windows, too, *before* turning off your computer. When Windows is running another application, that application is running "on top of" the Program Manager. Thus, to exit Windows, you're actually exiting the Program Manager. Here are the steps for correctly exiting Windows:

1. Close any applications that you have running in Windows. (This is almost always done with the application's File ➤ Exit command.) If you forget to do this, the Program Manager will remind you, upon exiting, that there are some open files that need saving, and will close others for you without asking. If you have DOS applications running, you'll have to close them manually before Windows will let you exit. Windows alerts you to this by highlighting the DOS icon. Open its window, quit the DOS application, and enter **EXIT** at the DOS prompt, if necessary.
2. Open the Program Manager window.
3. If you want the Program Manager to remember which group windows were open and how they were arranged at the time of exit, choose Options ➤ Save Settings on Exit.
4. Choose Exit Windows from the File menu of the Program Manager window, or simply double-click on the Control box.
5. Click on OK in the following dialog box and you'll be returned to the DOS prompt.

FAST TRACK

CHAPTER

2

FAST TRACK

What is the Program Manager? **47**

The Program Manager is one of the supplied Windows applications. However, it's always running while you are in Windows. Its function is to organize and run your programs efficiently. It creates the icons for your programs, and controls program windows.

Two modes of Windows operation: **50**

- Windows can be run in two modes, Standard and 386-Enhanced. Which mode you run in depends on your needs and your hardware.
- Standard mode requires a 286, 386, or 486 and has all the advantages of 386-Enhanced mode except multitasking and the ability to run DOS programs in a window.
- 386-Enhanced mode requires a 386 or 486 machine. Windows automatically runs in the highest possible mode.

To control the mode you run Windows in, ... **50**

include an argument after WIN (S for Standard, /386 for 386-Enhanced) when starting the program.

To run a program from an icon, ... **53**

find the icon and double-click it.

To run a program using the Run command, ... **57**

select File ➤ Run and enter the program name.

To run a program from the File Manager, ... 59

double-click on the program's file name.

To switch to another running application, ... 63

- activate that application's icon or window.
- press Ctrl-Esc to bring up the Task List.
- press Alt-Esc or Alt-Tab to cycle through running applications.

To switch between applications using the Task List, ... 64

click on any application window's Control box (all programs running in a window have a control box) or click on an iconized application. Choose Switch To from the menu. The Task List appears. Double-click the application you want to jump to, or highlight it and click on Switch To. (You can also open the Task List by double-clicking the desktop or pressing Ctrl-Esc.)

To quickly organize your screen, ... 66

use the Task List's other commands. End Task closes the highlighted application. Cascade and Tile neatly organize the open windows in two different fashions. Arrange Icons lines up the icons on the screen.

CHAPTER 2

FEATURING

- Six Ways to Run Your Programs
- Running Multiple Sessions of a Program
- Switching between Applications

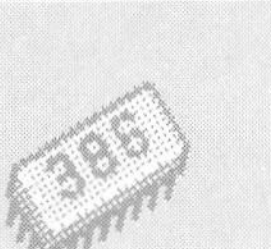

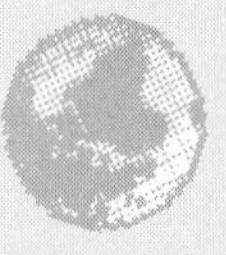
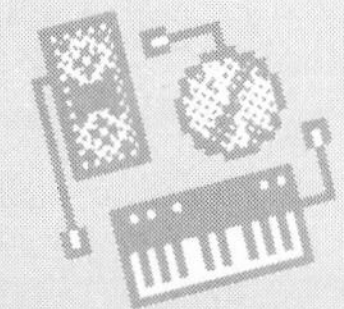
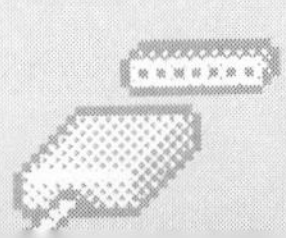

Using the Program Manager

efore continuing in this chapter, make sure you are familiar with the use of dialog boxes, menus, and the various elements of typical windows. See Chapter 1 if you are in doubt about any of these. If you need some more practice identifying these elements, or if your facility with the mouse is wanting, run the tutorial program.

This chapter explains the essentials of using the Windows Program Manager. It covers the basics of how to run your programs from within Windows.

WHAT IS THE PROGRAM MANAGER?

The Program Manager is the heart of Windows. It's the part of Windows that is always running, either as a window, or as an icon, while you are using Windows. With the Program Manager's commands, you run your own programs, switch between them, and copy material between windows.

The Program Manager is, in effect, a conductor that directs the flow of data and keeps track of where you are and what you're doing while using Windows (see Figure 2.1). It lets you run programs, remembers which window contains which program, remembers which window is active, and, along with Windows, works to control the computer's hardware (such as the printer, screen, hard disk, and RAM) to let you switch easily between your tasks.

In addition, the Program Manager helps you organize your programs. A feature in the Program Manager lets you assign icons to your programs. You can then use these icons to select which programs you want to run. Instead of typing in the name of the program you want to run at the DOS command line, you just click on the program's icon.

Once you've got your icons created, the Program Manager also lets you organize your program icons into groups, each with its own window, for easier access. For example, you might want to have all your accounting programs in one group and all your writing programs (word processor, spell-checker, etc.) in another group.

You already have at least five program groups in your Windows setup: Main, Accessories, Applications, StartUp, and Games. Each group is represented by an icon, or, if the group is open, its contents are displayed in a window.

Each group contains a number of programs. If you open a group by double-clicking on its icon, a window will open, displaying the programs in that group. In Figure 2.2, I've opened the Accessories group icon. All the icons in the resulting window represent the accessory programs supplied with Windows.

If you told Windows to install your existing Windows programs and your non-Windows applications, you'll have two other group icons—Applications and Non-Windows Applications—that you can open and examine.

Later, in Chapter 3, we'll cover the techniques for creating new program icons and new groups to contain those icons. But first, we'll cover techniques for running programs that already have icons.

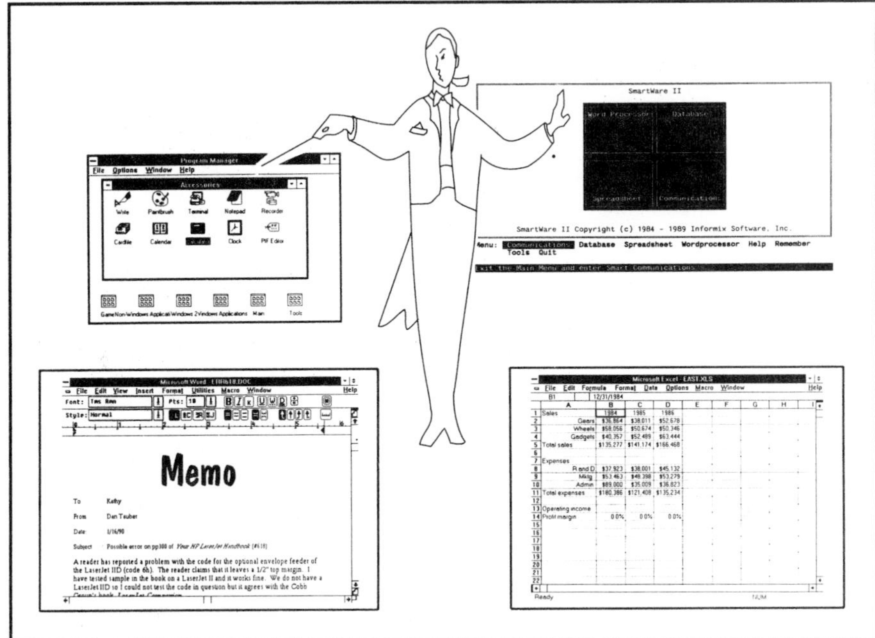

FIGURE 2.1:
The Program Manager manages your system resources and applications whenever you are in Windows

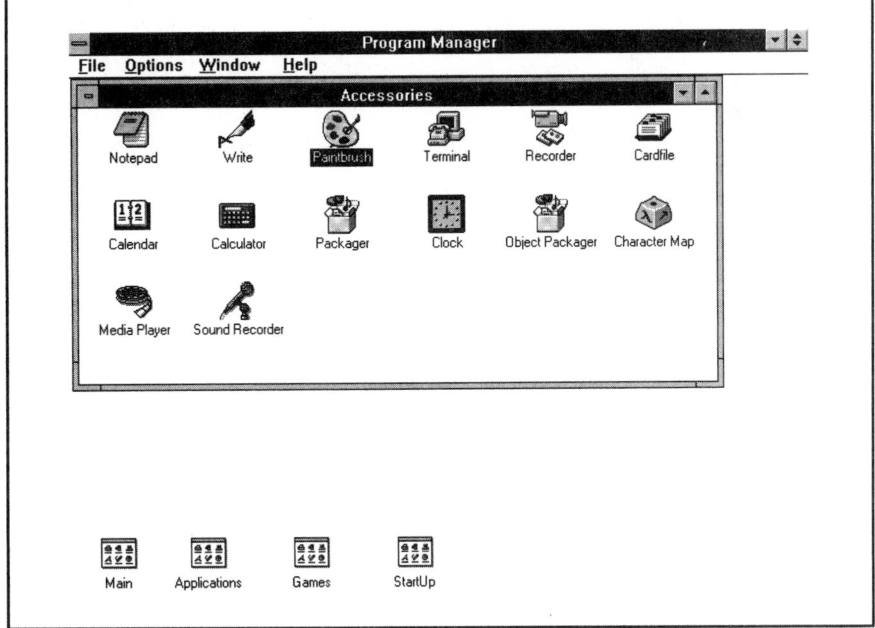

FIGURE 2.2:
The Accessories group window, showing the programs it contains. Each icon is a program.

CONSIDERATIONS FOR RUNNING PROGRAMS IN WINDOWS

Though the purpose of the Program Manager is to let you forget about many of the details of what's happening in your computer, it's in your interest to understand the basic concepts of the Program Manager so that you can control it. Without this knowledge, you can get lost trying to do simple things that you may already know how to do perfectly well in DOS.

The most obvious of these things is the simple task of running programs. As you know, one of the primary advantages of Windows over DOS is that it lets you run more than one program at a time. In addition, this often allows you to copy material from one program to another more easily. However, not all programs will utilize the Windows graphical interface to the same degree. Some programs (those not designed for Windows) will only run in what's called *full-screen mode,* wherein they take over the whole screen. In this case, the Windows Desktop disappears while the program is running and the program appears as it would if you were running it from DOS. Windows applications, however, will appear in a normal window, complete with menus and so forth.

There are several important points to know concerning your system and how Windows will run applications for you. One consideration is that the number of programs that will run simultaneously depends on the amount of memory in your computer (that's RAM, not hard-disk space). Since programs and documents vary in size, it's not possible to calculate an exact number of programs that can run in a given amount of RAM. Generally, the more memory you have the better. Windows will warn you if you are running out of memory.

Second, whether a non-Windows program can run in a window or has to run full-screen depends on your computer's innards and the mode in which you are running Windows. As you may know, there are four different types of CPU (Central Processing Unit) chips that are used as the heart of IBM-type personal computers. Listed in decreasing order of their speed and power, these chips, sometimes called *microprocessors,* are the 80486, 80386, 80286, and 8088 or 8086. Rather than referring to particular brands and models of computers, PC's are often classed by their CPU. Thus, in popular computer lingo, there are the 486, 386, 286, and PC or XT machines.

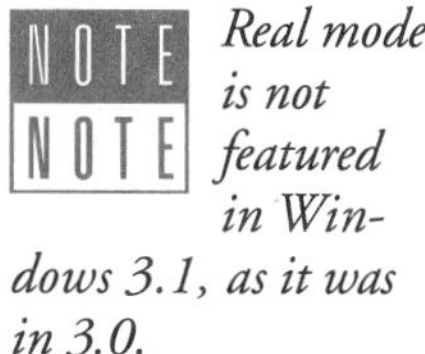

Real mode is not featured in Windows 3.1, as it was in 3.0.

There are also two *modes* that Windows can run in: Standard and 386-Enhanced. Most non-Windows (DOS) applications will run in a window if you have a 486 or 386 computer and are running Windows in 386-Enhanced mode. (The modes are explained below.) If you have a 286 computer, non-Windows applications must run full-screen. If you have an 8086 or 8088 computer you cannot run Windows 3.1—but you *can* run Windows 3.0.

With any of the types of machines and modes, Windows can actually handle your Windows programs with *multitasking*—that is, in such a way that they *appear* to be running simultaneously, thanks to a little computer chicanery. In reality, each program runs for a short period of time in turn, one after the other. So, the processing is not actually simultaneous. But the switching between programs happens so quickly that it appears to be simultaneous. As a result, your computer could be sorting a database and calculating a spreadsheet while you are writing a letter or working on some other task.

In Standard mode, multitasking takes place with Windows programs only. When a non-Windows program is active, other programs are temporarily suspended from operation. In 386-Enhanced mode, however, multitasking includes non-Windows applications.

If you are in doubt about which mode you're running Windows in, select the About Program Manager command from the Program Manager's Help menu. A dialog box will display the mode and the amount of RAM still available for use. Windows installs itself appropriately for your system when you run the Setup program. However, you can change the mode by adding a parameter to the WIN command when you start Windows, as follows:

COMMAND	EFFECT
WIN /S	Starts Windows in *Standard* mode, which is the normal operating mode for Windows. It requires an 80286 or 80386 machine and at least 1MB of memory. More memory will speed things up and allow more programs to run simultaneously.

COMMAND	EFFECT
WIN /386	Starts Windows in *386-Enhanced* mode, which requires an 80386 or 80486 machine with 2MB or more of memory. It lets you run non-Windows applications within a window, rather than full-screen. It also supports multitasking.
WIN	Starts Windows in the default mode, on the basis of Windows' assessment of the type of computer and amount of memory you have.

SIX WAYS TO RUN YOUR PROGRAMS

There are several ways to run programs from Windows, some easier than others. Here are the six basic techniques:

- Double-click on a program icon. (As an alternative, you can highlight the icon and press Enter.)
- Double-click on the DOS Prompt icon in the Program Manager's Main window. Then run a DOS program from the DOS prompt (e.g., from the C> prompt).
- Add program icons to the StartUp group. They will run automatically when you run Windows.
- Choose the Run command from the File menu of the Program Manager or File Manager and enter the name of the program. (The File Manager is explained in the next chapter.) If you enter the command **COMMAND.COM**, the DOS prompt will appear.
- In File Manager, double-click on a program file (.EXE, .COM, .PIF., or .BAT) or a file whose extension has an "association" with a particular application program from a directory window in the File Manager.
- Press the "shortcut key" you've assigned to a program. The program runs immediately. (Shortcut keys are described in Chapter 3.)

Regardless of the technique you use to run application programs, the following will be true:

- If the program is a Windows application, it will appear in a window.
- If it's a DOS application, it will run full-screen. If you're running in 386-Enhanced mode, you can then display it in a window by pressing Alt-Enter.
- You can switch between DOS and Windows applications easily, without having to quit either one. Techniques for doing so are explained later in this chapter, in the section "Switching between Applications."

Now let's look closer at the procedures for running programs and switching between them.

Running Programs from Icons

TO RUN A PROGRAM FROM AN ICON,

find the icon and double-click it.

The technique you choose for running a program depends on how frequently you use it. For programs you use a lot, I suggest you put them in groups, make up icons for them, and run them by double-clicking on them. For programs you use less frequently, use the other procedures listed in the next several sections.

Here's an example of running a program from an icon and working with it:

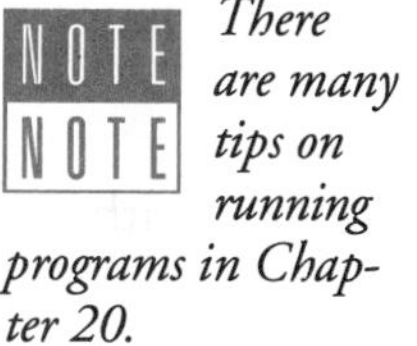

There are many tips on running programs in Chapter 20.

1. Open the Program Manager or activate its window (if it isn't active already).
2. Expand the Accessories group icon to a window by double-clicking on it. There are 17 programs in the Accessories group.

3. Double-click on the Calculator icon. This tells Windows to run the program. The Calculator accessory will appear on the screen in its own window, as you see in Figure 2.3. (If the Minimize on Use option has been checked in the Options menu, the Program Manager will be reduced to an icon after it loads the Calculator.)

4. While the Calculator is open, try experimenting with it. Try changing the calculator to a scientific format by choosing the Scientific command from the View menu. You can move the calculator around the screen by dragging its title bar. Notice that if you click within the Program Manager window, a portion of the calculator will be covered by it. Clicking on the Calculator window again causes the calculator to "come to the front" of the stack of windows.

5. Click on the Minimize button to reduce the Calculator to an icon on the Desktop.

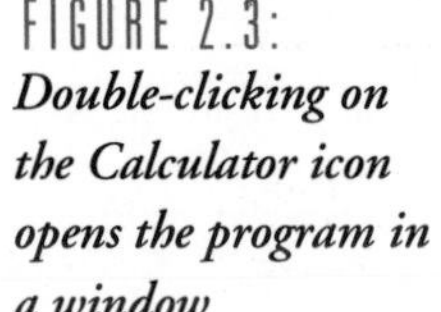

FIGURE 2.3: *Double-clicking on the Calculator icon opens the program in a window*

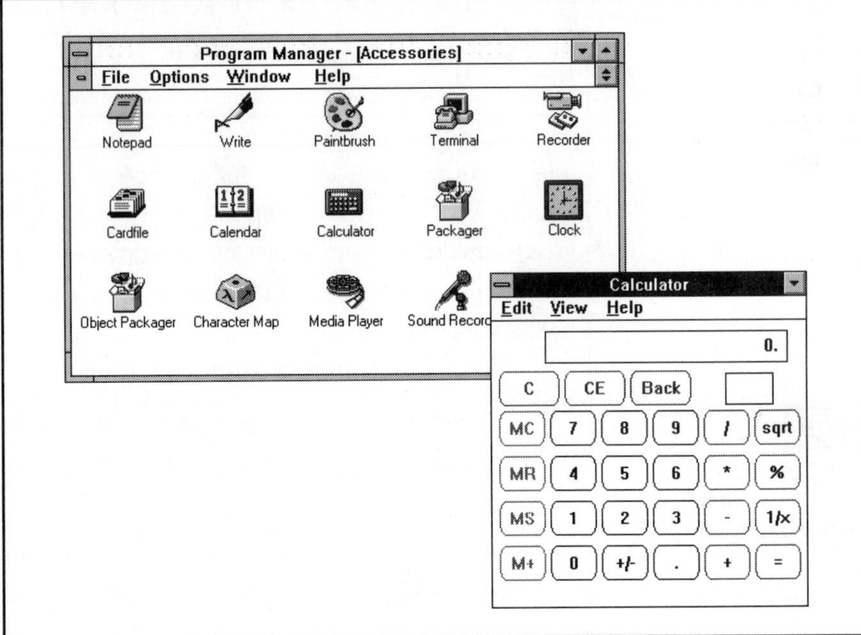

6. If you don't see the icon on the Desktop, it is because the Program Manager's window is covering it. If the window is maximized, click on the Program Manager's Restore button, then resize the window so you can see the bottom portion of the Desktop. Your screen should look something like that in Figure 2.4. Since the calculator is now on the Desktop, it is in effect running. It is more quickly available for your use than if you were to run the program again. This is because Windows keeps the program in RAM rather than having to load it from your hard disk again.
7. Double-click on the Calculator icon at the bottom of the screen; it appears more quickly than it did the first time.
8. Now we'll exit, or *close,* the Calculator program. Double-click on the Control box.

You've just run the Calculator program, reduced it to an icon, restored it to a window, and then closed it. While it was an icon, it was technically still

FIGURE 2.4:
The Calculator reduced to an icon on the Desktop

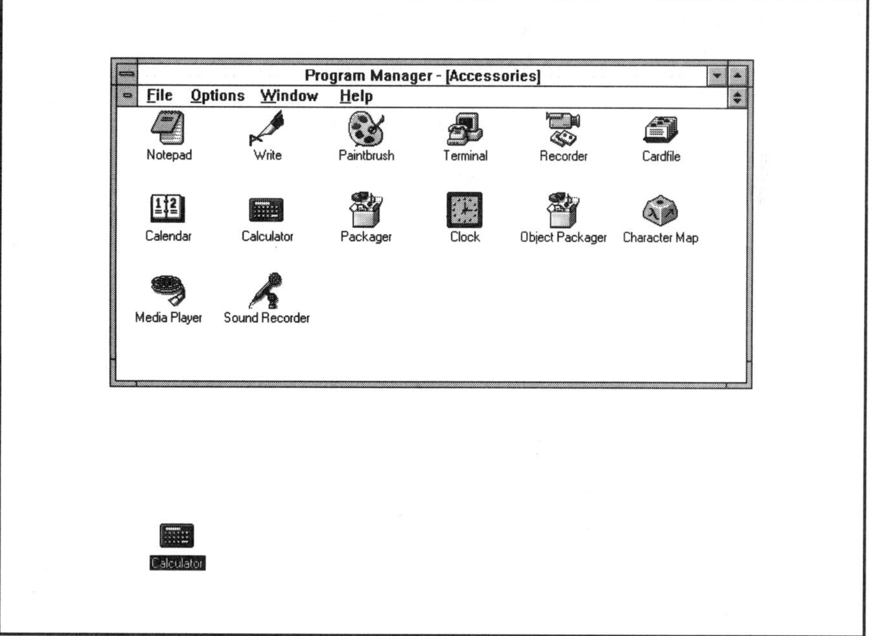

running, though you couldn't see it or work with it. The advantage of iconizing the program was that it was made easily available to you, even if the Program Manager had been iconized and other windows were open on the screen.

Try running the other accessory programs supplied with Windows. The clock is a particularly easy one, since all it does is display a sizeable clock on your screen. Notepad, Calendar, Write, and Cardfile are also fairly easy to figure out. (These are covered in more detail in Chapter 12.) Try opening several windows, one for each program, and then switching between them by clicking on their respective windows. Switching between programs is discussed later in this chapter.

If you know you have a program running but can't seem to find its window or icon, it's probably covered up by another window. Look on the Desktop by moving windows around or iconizing them. Don't click on the program's icon in the Program Manager window or other group window a second time. That will run the program again, and you'll have *two* sessions of the same program running, instead of just switching to the one you wanted. An easy way to find a program is by pressing Ctrl-Esc and selecting it from the Task List (see "Switching between Applications" later in this chapter).

Running Programs from the Startup Group

Perhaps you use the same application programs and documents every day, or at least every time you run Windows. So why should you have to boot up Windows and then click on each program you want to run every time? There is an easier way. You can instruct Windows to run specific programs or open documents of your choice when you start Windows. Anything that can be given an icon in Program Manager can be started up automatically upon running Windows.

For example, take a look at my StartUp group below. I have Windows automatically running a Microsoft Word document I'm working on, a DOS session, Daybook (for managing my appointments), File Manager, After Dark (a screen-saver program), my Notepad "to do" list, Collage (a screen-capture program), Big Cursor (enlarges the pointer on my screen), Clock, and ATM (Adobe's font manager program). (Notice that I also have a Program Manager icon in my StartUp group. The reason for and advantage of placing Program Manager in the StartUp group is explained under "Running and Selecting Applications" in Chapter 20.) All these programs and files load when I start Windows.

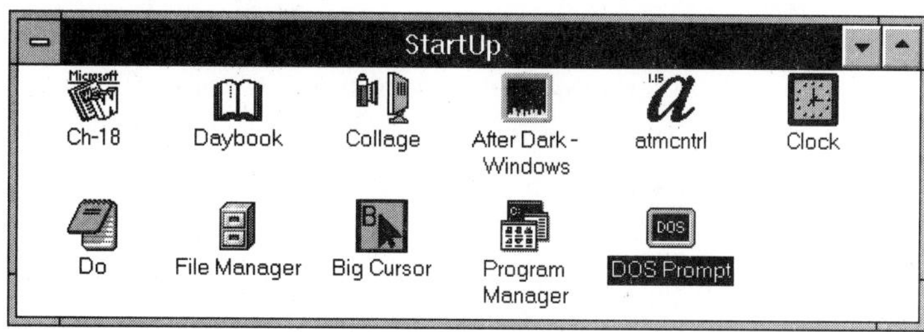

In Windows 3.0, this convenience was only made possible by altering your WIN.INI file's LOAD and RUN statements, which was a hassle. The StartUp group added with version 3.1 simplifies the process considerably. You just move or copy the desired icons into the StartUp group and the rest is done by Windows. The next time you start up Windows, the programs will all run. Of course, this will slow down the initial loading of Windows, since it takes time to run the programs and open any documents you've included in the group. You'll probably decide to change your StartUp group once in a while, just as people alter their AUTOEXEC.BAT files in DOS. When you no longer want to have a particular program or document loaded at startup time, just drag its icon into another group, or delete it altogether (see Chapter 3). Take care when deleting icons, though. You may want to use them again sometime. Rather than deleting, consider moving an icon into another group, possibly a group with a name such as "Old StartUp," unless you want to recreate the icon next time you need it. (I show you how to create icons in Chapter 3.)

Running Programs with the Run Command

TO USE THE RUN COMMAND,

select File ➤ Run and enter the program name.

Both the Program Manager and the File Manager (the File Manager is covered in Chapter 4) have a Run command in their File menus. This command lets you run a program by typing its name just as you would from the DOS prompt. The only difference is that you type it into a dialog box instead of at the DOS command line. You may also specify parameters that you normally give to your program when you call it up from DOS. A parameter is a word or letter you enter before or after the name of the program. For example, the line

```
WS.COM C:\FILES\MYLETTER
```

would run WordStar and open the file MYLETTER in the FILES directory on the C drive.

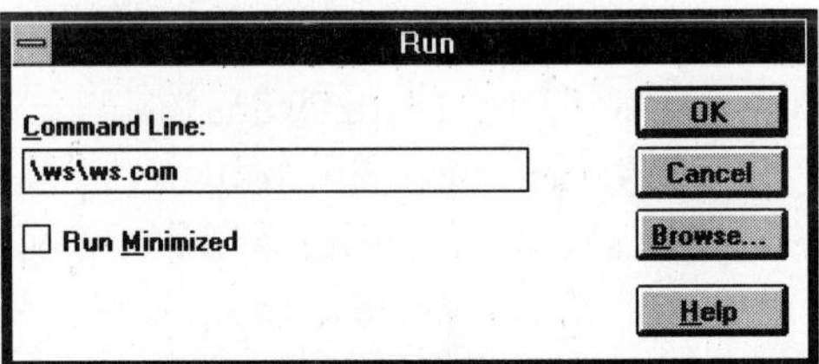

Here's an example of running a DOS program using the Run command. Suppose you wanted to run a non-Windows program such as WordStar from Windows and you didn't want to go about making up an icon for it:

1. Open the File menu on the Program Manager's window.
2. Choose Run. A dialog box appears, prompting you to enter a DOS command:

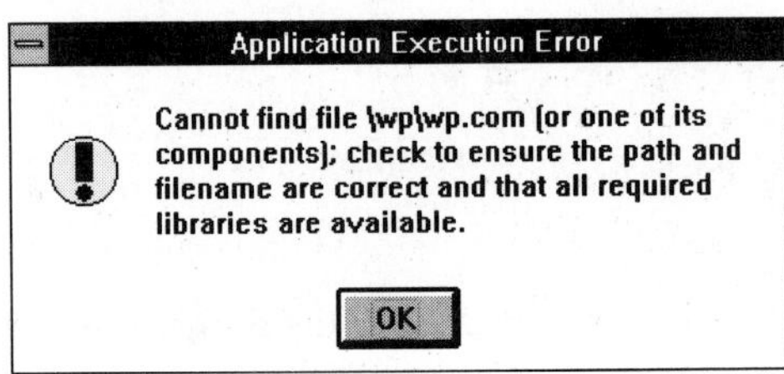

3. Type in **WS.COM** (or another program name) and press Enter. Precede the program name with the drive and directory if they are not in your computer's normal search path. Type the exact name, including extension, if there is one. If you want the program to be minimized to an icon immediately, click on the Run Minimized check box before clicking on OK.

If you don't specify the program's directory in the command, the program you want to run has to be in the current directory (typically the C:\WINDOWS directory) or a directory on the search path specified in your AUTOEXEC.BAT file. Otherwise, Windows will not find the program, and will display a dialog box like the one shown below. It doesn't mean the program isn't on your disk, only that Windows can't find it. Either change your path command or enter the path name before the program name.

Running Programs from the File Manager

TO RUN A PROGRAM FROM THE FILE MANAGER,

double-click on the program's file name.

You can also run programs from the File Manager, which is covered thoroughly in Chapter 4. The File Manager lets you see a directory of files, just as the DIR command in DOS does. However, one of the differences is that you can just double-click on a file's name to run it. Running programs from the File Manager in this way is useful when you're not sure exactly how to spell the name of the program but would recognize it if you saw it. It's also useful when you don't know the location of the program. A search command in the File Manager can find it for you. Once it's located, you can just double-click on it. All these details are covered in Chapter 4. But as a short introduction to running programs this way, here are the basic steps:

1. Run the File Manager and open the directory containing the desired program.

2. Double-click on the program's file name, as shown in Figure 2.5. It must be a file with a .COM, .EXE, .PIF, or .BAT extension, or a document that has a program associated with it (associations are covered in Chapter 4). For example, a .TXT (text) file will run since there is an association between .TXT files and the Notepad program. Clicking on a .TXT file runs the Notepad application and opens the text document in a window. It's an easy way to read or edit text files as long as they have that extension.

3. When you are through running the program, exit it as usual. If you were running full-screen, you will be returned to Windows. If you were running in a window, the window will be closed.

Running Programs from the DOS Prompt

If you like, you can run DOS programs from the DOS prompt. This is handy for running programs you very rarely use, or if you want to be able to type in a series of commands at the DOS prompt without having to type each one into the Run dialog box. The Program Manager has a DOS Prompt

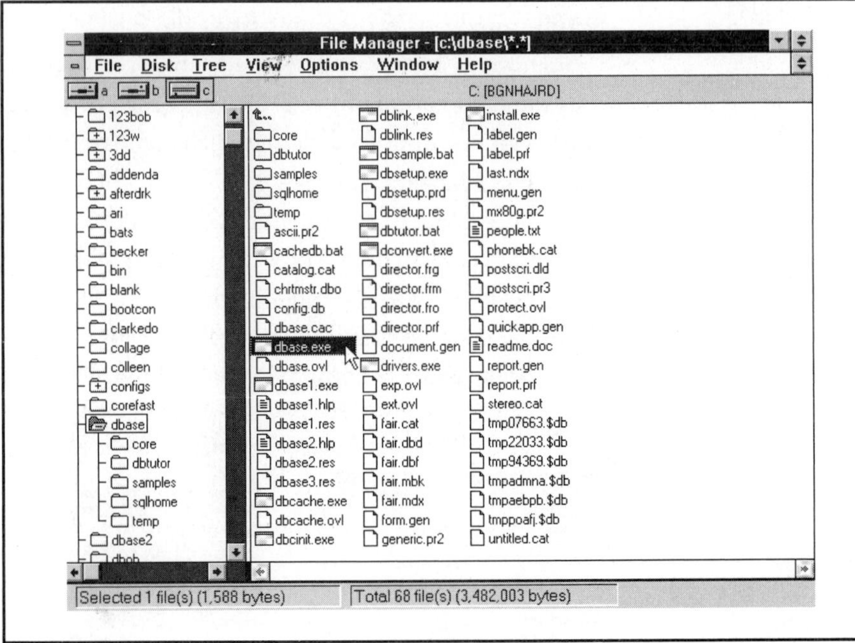

FIGURE 2.5: *Running dBASE by double-clicking on it within the File Manager*

icon in the Main group window for this purpose, so you don't have to leave Windows to do this:

1. Double-click on the MS-DOS Prompt icon in the Program Manager's Main group to bring up the command line.
2. Type in DOS commands as you normally would, just as if Windows weren't running.
3. When you are finished using the DOS prompt, type **EXIT** and you will be returned to Windows. It is also possible to leave DOS active and switch between open applications, as discussed in the section "Switching between Applications."

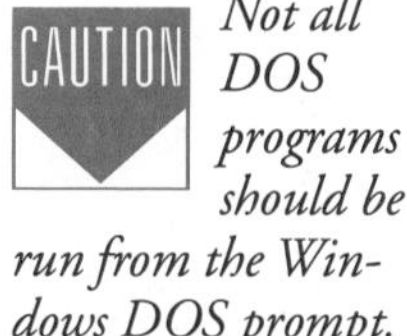

Not all DOS programs should be run from the Windows DOS prompt.

Certain DOS programs should *not* be run from the Windows DOS prompt. Technically speaking, any program that modifies the file allocation table (FAT) should be run from outside of Windows. That is, you should quit Windows and return to DOS to use them. If you don't, you could end up losing your work and causing your files to become jumbled. Most notably, this applies to the CHKDSK command when used with the /F option to recover lost fragments of files. (CHKDSK by itself can be used without trouble.) Also, programs that undelete erased files or those that defragment or optimize the hard disk, such as the Norton Utilities, should be run outside of Windows.

RUNNING ADDITIONAL SESSIONS OF THE SAME WINDOWS PROGRAM

As you know, Windows is designed to let you run several programs at one time and switch between them. However, there's no reason why the programs you run have to be different ones. One could have several copies of the same Windows program running simultaneously.

For example, if your word-processing program doesn't let you edit more than one document at a time, you could run it twice and use Windows to switch between them. Then you could use the Windows Clipboard to cut and copy text between programs (the Clipboard is covered in Chapter 8).

Each running copy of the program is called a *session*. You can have as many sessions of a Windows program as you want, limited only by your computer's memory. As an example of running multiple sessions, try this experiment:

1. Open the Accessories group in the Program Manager.
2. Double-click on the Calculator icon. This runs the Calculator program.
3. Position the Calculator window so that the Calculator icon is visible.
4. Double-click on the Calculator icon again. This runs it again. (The first calculator may disappear, but that's because it's on the Desktop, behind the Program Manager's window.) Double-click several more times, so that you have six calculators running.
5. Minimize the Program Manager window so that you can see the Desktop. You should have about six calculators sitting there in a jumble. Arrange them by dragging them by their title bars, and set them up to look interesting, perhaps like the way I did it in Figure 2.6.

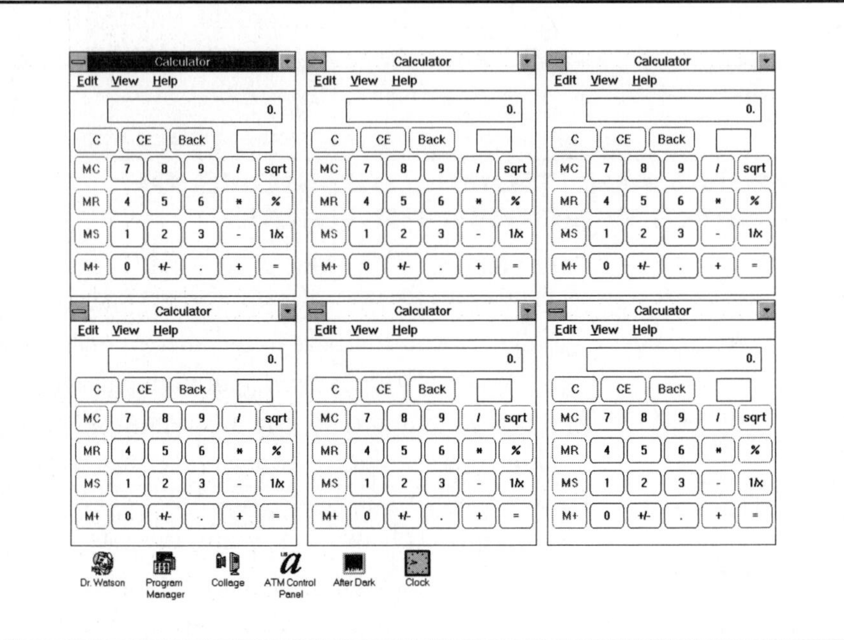

FIGURE 2.6: *Six sessions of the Calculator program running simultaneously*

6. Now close all except one of the Calculator windows. (Remember, you do this by double-clicking on the Control box of each window.)

SWITCHING BETWEEN APPLICATIONS

TO SWITCH TO ANOTHER RUNNING APPLICATION,

- **click on that application's icon or window.**
- **press Ctrl-Esc to bring up the Task List.**
- **press Alt-Esc or Alt-Tab to cycle through running applications.**

Often you'll have a number of applications open at one time. They'll either be in windows or reduced to icons on the Desktop—or they won't be visible, because when you are running a full-screen application, Windows temporarily disappears, along with any windows or icons. At other times you may have a lot of windows stacked on top of each other, making some of the applications difficult to see, especially if they're all maximized. Things can get pretty confusing with so much going on, and you may begin to lose track of your tasks.

Remember that you can only really be working on one window at a time—the active window. (The active window is identified by its title bar being a unique color or intensity.) To jump back to a given task you'll have to reactivate its window. There are a number of tricks for doing this. I'll explain each briefly, then discuss them in more detail in separate sections below:

TIP *Click the Cascade or Tile command buttons in the Task List dialog box to neatly rearrange all the open windows and bring them into view. Then click on the one you want to activate.*

- When you can see the window of the application you want to switch to, the easiest thing is just to click on it.
- Bring up the Task List dialog box by clicking on the Control box of any application window or the icon of any currently running program. Then choose the Switch To command. (Faster ways to open the Task List are to double-click anywhere on the Desktop background or press Ctrl-Esc.) Once the Task List is open, select

the application you want to switch to by double-clicking it or by highlighting it and clicking on Switch To.

- From any application, press Alt-Esc or Alt-Tab. Each press will move you to another of the open applications.

Below are the details for each of these approaches.

Choosing the Application Window You Want

If you can easily see the application window you want to activate, simply click anywhere within its perimeter. This will make the window jump to the front of whatever was lying on top of it. The active window's menu bar will change in color or intensity to indicate its newly activated status. (The colors that Windows uses can be altered with the Control Panel, covered in Chapter 5.)

If you like using this approach, adjust your application windows so that just a little edge of each one is visible at all times. All you need is to leave a corner or edge. Then you just click on the small exposed section. Figure 2.7 shows an example of several application windows arranged such that their title bars are easily visible.

Another solution to Desktop clutter is to keep all of your running programs iconized along the bottom of the Desktop. Then when you want to open an application, double-click on its icon. When you want to switch to another application, iconize the current one first, then double-click on the one you want to open up next. This will leave the Desktop uncluttered and allow you to see all your icons easily.

Using the Task List

The Task List makes switching between applications very easy, because Windows will show you a list of the current applications. Here's how to use the Task List:

1. Open the Task List in one of the ways already described. The Task List appears on your screen. It'll look something like the one below. The active application will appear first in the list,

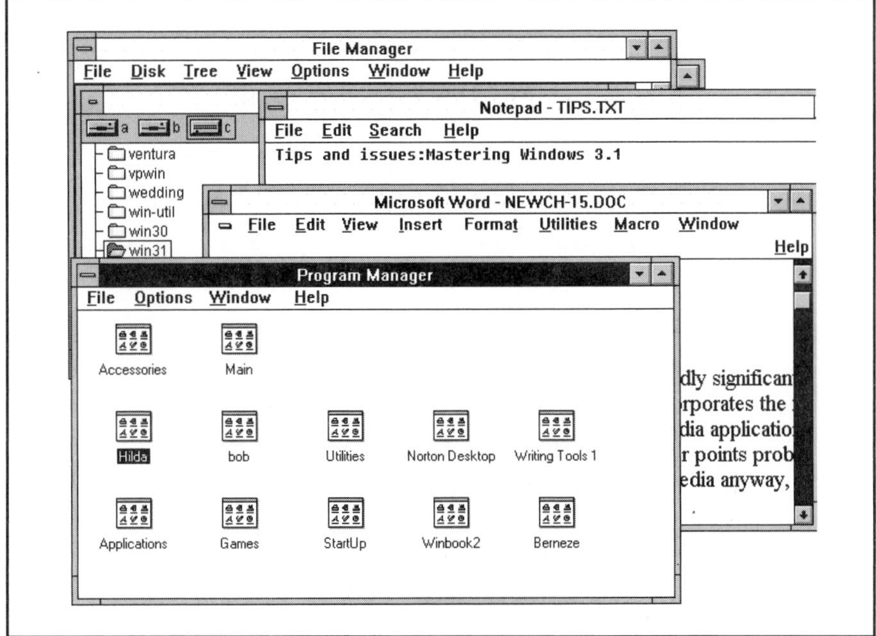

FIGURE 2.7:
You can arrange your application windows so that you can easily click on their title bars

with its name highlighted. The application you were using prior to that will be second in the list, and so on.

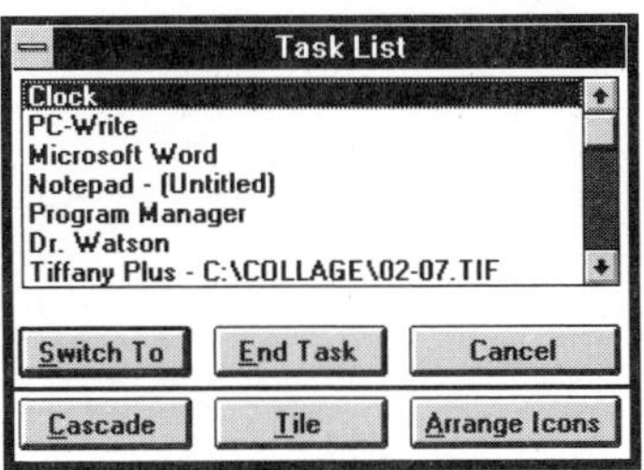

2. Select the name of the program you want to switch to in one of the following ways:

- Type its first letter to jump to it. If more than one application starts with the same letter, type the letter again.
- Press the ↓ key until it is highlighted.
- If there is a scroll bar, use it to scroll to the desired program.

3. Switch to the desired application by

   - pressing Enter
   - double-clicking it
   - clicking the Switch To button

The task (application window) you selected will be activated. If the application is a full-screen one, Windows will disappear and the program's screen will reappear. If the application can run in a window and is currently running as an icon, it will be restored to its former size.

Notice that the Task List has four other command buttons besides Switch To and Cancel: End Task, Cascade, Tile, and Arrange Icons. These are all useful to helping you switch between and organize your various application windows. Here's what each does:

End Task closes the application you highlight, unless it is a DOS application. (You have to close DOS applications manually before Task List will allow you to end the task.)

Cascade causes all the open Windows to be sized and staggered in such a way that the title bar and edge or corner of every window are visible, as in Figure 2.8. DOS sessions or full-screen applications will be shown as icons at the bottom of the screen.

Tile causes all the open windows to be sized and lined up like tiles on a bathroom wall (see Figure 2.9). DOS sessions or full-screen applications will be shown as icons at the bottom of the screen.

Arrange Icons lines up all the icons on your Desktop. You could drag them around with the mouse, but this command does it faster.

Using Alt-Key Shortcuts

Finally, you can use Alt-Esc and Alt-Tab to switch between applications. Both key combinations work in a similar fashion, but with some subtle distinctions. Each time you press either of them, Windows will jump to the next application. This works even while in full-screen applications. Here are the differences between the two:

Alt-Esc cycles through the applications that are running in the order that they appear in the Task List. If the application is in a window,

FIGURE 2.8:

Choosing Cascade from the Task List lines up the open application windows like this for your convenience

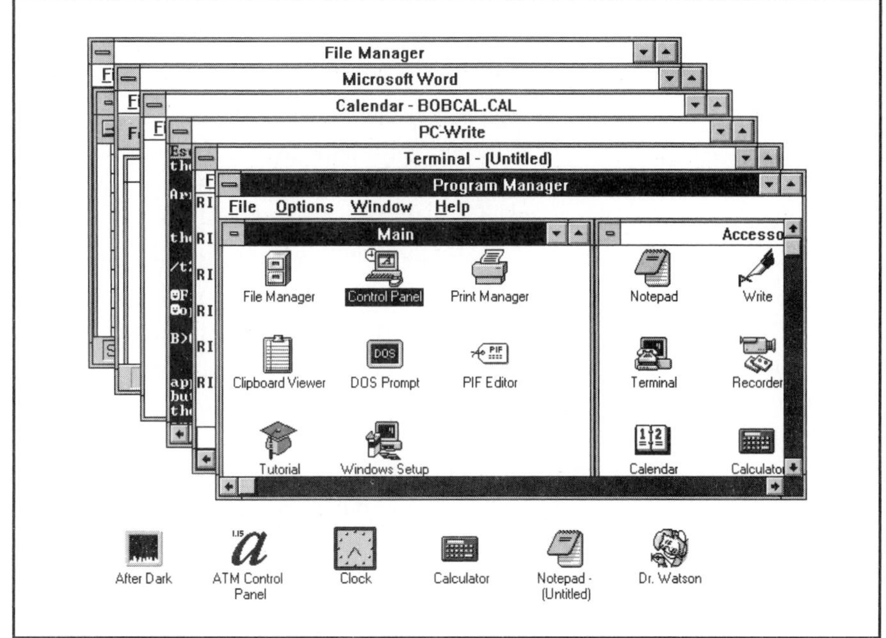

FIGURE 2.9:

Choosing Tile from the Task List lines up the open application windows like this

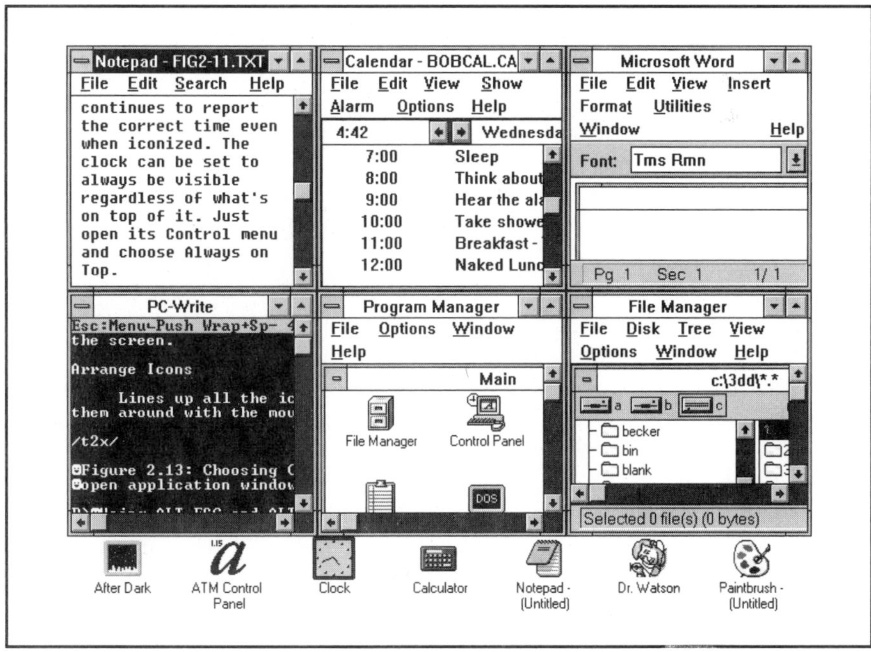

pressing Alt-Esc activates the window; if the application is a non-Windows application or is iconized, Alt-Esc highlights the icon. To activate the iconized application, press Enter or double-click the icon.

When running in 386-Enhanced mode, you can toggle a non-Windows application between full-screen and windowed display by pressing Alt-Enter.

Alt-Tab cycles through the applications that are running in a slightly different way than Alt-Esc. If you press and release both keys, you toggle between the last two active applications. If you want to cycle through all the running applications to activate another one, hold the Alt key down; each subsequent press of the Tab key will show the name of the next application on-screen. When the name of the application you want to activate appears, release the Alt key. This cycling method is probably preferable to the Alt-Esc method described above.

Although using these keyboard shortcuts is the fastest way to switch between applications if you have several running and want to shuttle back and forth between them quickly, the Task List may be the most reliable source for seeing just which applications you have running. Sometimes icons hide behind windows or other icons, and you may not notice that you have multiple sessions of an application running as you cycle through them.

FAST TRACK

CHAPTER

3

FAST TRACK

1. Run Windows Setup from the Main window.
2. Select Options ➤ Set Up Applications.
3. Choose either to search for applications or specify an application.

1. Select File ➤ New from the Program Manager window.
2. Choose Program Group and click on OK.
3. Enter the name of the new group in the Description text box and click on OK.

open the Main group and run the Setup program. On the dialog box that appears, open the Options menu and choose Set Up Applications. Indicate the drives that the programs are on and click OK (you might want to change the extension). Click on the name of each program you want to add and click OK. Then exit the Setup program via the Options menu.

1. Select File ➤ New from the destination window for the new icon.

2. Choose Program Item and click on OK.
3. Enter the name of the new icon in the Description text box.
4. In the Command Line text box, enter the command that you would type at the DOS prompt to run the program (including path if necessary).
5. Fill in the Working Directory text box with the name of the directory you want the program to default to, if different from that specified in the AUTOEXEC.BAT path.
6. Click on the Change Icon button to select the icon.

To make a copy of an icon, ... 88

hold down the Ctrl key and drag the icon either to a different place in the same window or to another window or group icon.

To create an icon for a file, ... 92

1. Click on the icon of the file's application.
2. Choose File ➤ Properties.
3. Put the file name in the Description line.
4. Add a space and the file name to the end of the Command Line entry.

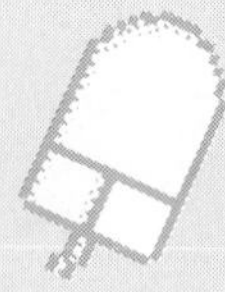

CHAPTER 3

FEATURING

Creating Program Icons and Groups

Using Setup to Create Icons

Copying and Moving Icons

Changing an Icon's Properties

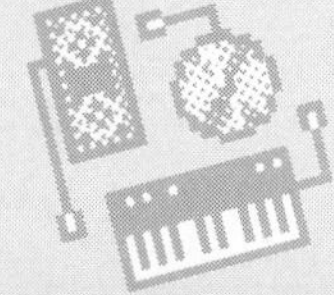

Creating and Using Groups

hapter 2 introduced you to the Program Manager and explained the essentials of running programs within Windows. This chapter tells you how you use the Program Manager to set up your own icons for Windows and non-Windows programs and how to create new groups to hold those icons.

Recall that the Program Manager arranges applications (such as the ones supplied with Windows) into groups. Though you can run applications directly from the Program Manager or File Manager with the Run command, it's more convenient to open the group they're stored in and double-click on the icon of the application you want to run.

There are two types of icons, *group icons* and *program icons:*

- Group icons all look the same (they have six miniature icons on them) and they only show up within the Program Manager's window. You can't drag them outside the window. When you double-click a group icon, a *group window* opens, displaying program icons assigned to that group.

- Program icons simply represent your programs. Double-click on one to run the program it represents.

So the relevant questions are how do you create an icon for each of your applications and how do you then assign them to groups?

SIZING CONSTRAINTS OF GROUP WINDOWS

As you'll recall from the discussion of Windows anatomy in Chapter 1, there are both parent and child windows. The Program Manager is an application, and group windows are child windows within the Program Manager. Therefore, as with other types of windows, group windows can be resized and moved and even iconized, but they can never be larger than the Program Manager's window. So if you can't see all the icons in your group window and want to make it bigger, you'll have to maximize the Program Manager window before you can make the group window fill the screen.

When you resize a group window, some of the icons may not show up. This is because they may be beyond the perimeter of the window. If you choose the Arrange Icons command from the Window menu, they will reappear. If you want Windows to rearrange your icons automatically whenever you resize a particular group window, choose Auto Arrange from the Options menu.

INSTALLING AND RUNNING WINDOWS APPLICATIONS

Windows applications come in two basic flavors—those designed for Windows 3.X, and those designed for previous versions of Windows. When you use either the Windows Setup program or the New command to install an application, Windows checks to see whether it's a Windows application or not. If so, it uses an icon built into the application and adds it to the destination group. If you're adding the program via Windows Setup, Windows will put the new program icon into the Applications group, unless you specify otherwise. It's then your choice either to leave it there or move it to another group. If you're installing the program with the New command, it goes into the active group window.

Windows applications can only be run from Windows. If you try to run a Windows application from DOS, you will see this message:

This program requires Microsoft Windows.

This message varies somewhat from application to application. Some Windows applications (for example Microsoft Excel and Word for Windows) are smart enough to start Windows automatically in order to run. So you can start Excel by typing **EXCEL** at the DOS prompt and pressing Enter. This brings up Windows and then runs Excel.

When you run a Windows application from within Windows, the application is first checked for its status. If the program was not designed for Windows 3.X, you will see the message shown in Figure 3.1. Microsoft recommends that you choose Cancel and then get an updated version of the program, one designed for Windows 3.X.

When running older programs, you may have some odd problems with

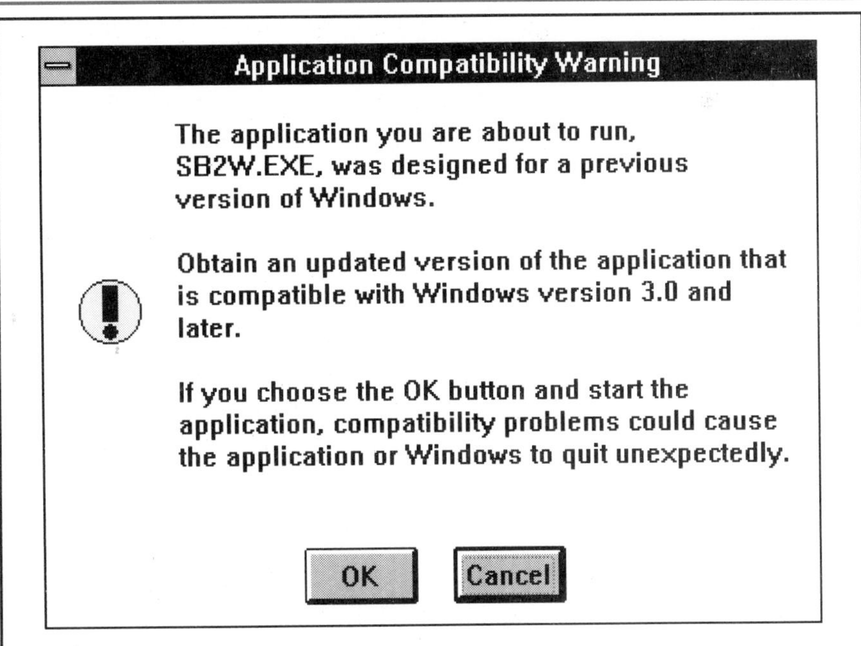

FIGURE 3.1: *This application compatibility warning message appears when you attempt to run a program that is not designed for Windows 3.X*

fonts, bitmap pictures, or colors not being displayed correctly. In addition, your program might become what the Windows manual calls "unstable," which means it's likely to bomb. As the warning suggests, it's best to get an updated version of your program.

CREATING PROGRAM ICONS

TO CREATE PROGRAM ICON(S),

1. **Run Windows Setup from the Main window.**
2. **Select Options ➤ Set Up Applications.**
3. **Choose either to search for applications or specify an application.**

When you installed Windows on your computer, its setup program may have already created a group for your applications, called—not surprisingly—"Applications." Both Windows and non-Windows applications icons landed in this group.

Generally speaking, the installation program is only successful at recognizing most popular non-Windows programs. So you may have many programs that didn't show up as icons, leaving you wondering what happened to them. For these non-Windows programs, you'll have to make icons for them, as described later in this chapter.

Here's how you can create icons for a program you've added to your hard disk since installing Windows, or for programs that Windows overlooked during installation:

1. Open the Main group.
2. Run the Windows Setup program by double-clicking on it. A dialog box will appear, showing the current parameters of your Windows setup.
3. Open the Options menu and choose Set Up Applications.

In the Setup Applications dialog box, Windows will ask if you want to search for applications or specify one. You will probably want to choose the second option when you only have one application to set up. The first option allows you to set up several applications at once. Depending on which option you choose, there will be two different ways to accomplish the application's setup.

Specifying an Application

I'll outline the shorter approach first—setting up a single application:

1. Choose the setup option that specifies an application.
2. Click OK.
3. In the Setup Applications dialog box, first enter the application's path and file name. Type in the search path. If you're not sure what it is, click on Browse and select the appropriate one from the list in the File dialog box.
4. Click OK. The program path and file name now appear in the first line of the dialog box.
5. The default program group is Applications. If you want to specify a different group, open the drop-down list by clicking on the Program Group area, then click on the new group name. (If the group does not exist, you will have to leave Windows Setup to create it.)
6. When the setup specifications are correct, click OK. Windows will add the program to the group.
7. Exit Windows Setup from either the Options menu or the Control box.

Now you can open the group window where you added the application and see the new icon. You can even run it now if you want to.

Searching for Applications to Set Up

When you want to set up more than one application in group windows, you can compile a list of them with the Setup option to search for applications. Even if all the applications won't ultimately be in the same group, you can set them up at the same time, then move them around later. (To find out how to do this, see "Moving a Program Icon into a New Window" later in this chapter.)

1. Choose the setup option that searched for applications and click on OK.
2. Windows will ask which drives to search for applications. Path allows you to search the current path specified in the AUTOEXEC.BAT file. The list then shows other disks that are available (whether they are network driven or in your computer will be indicated). Choose any or all appropriate drives. To save time and limit the search, you might want to select Path only, or a specific hard disk if you have more than one.
3. Click OK and the setup program will do its best to find applications to set up for you. A gauge indicates the status of the search. When Windows Setup is finished looking for programs, they'll be displayed in a dialog box like the one in Figure 3.2.
4. If you want to add them all, just click on Add All. Otherwise, click on the name of each program you want added. To deselect an application, click it again. (Notice as you highlight each one that its complete path and file name appear in the lower left-hand corner of the dialog box. If you are unsure of what a highlighted program is, this information may help you identify it.) When you've highlighted all the programs you want to set up, click on Add. The list of names will show up in the box on the right.
5. Click on OK and Windows will add the programs to the Applications group.

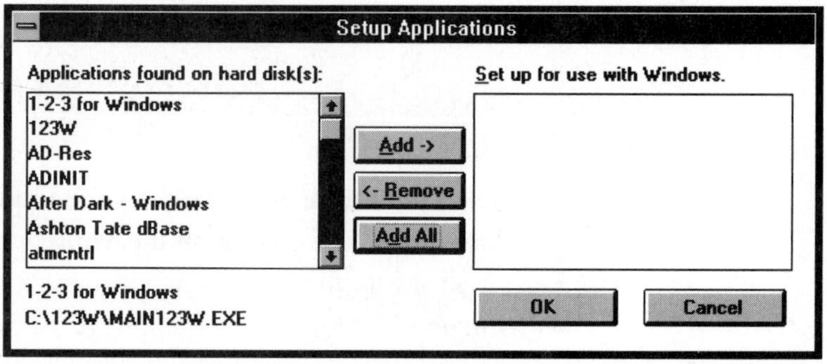

FIGURE 3.2:

Letting the Windows Setup program create the icons for your applications. Here you see which applications were found on the hard disk.

6. Exit the setup program from either the Options menu or the Control box. To see the new programs in the Applications group, open the window (if it isn't already open) and find the icons.

CREATING YOUR OWN GROUP

TO CREATE A GROUP,

1. **Select File ➤ New from the Program Manager window.**
2. **Choose Program Group and click on OK.**
3. **Enter the name of the new group in the Description text box and click on OK.**

Creating a new group is simple. As an example, here are the steps to make up a group called "Writing Tools." This is actually a group I have on my computer. It contains the programs I use most frequently for writing projects:

1. Open the Program Manager window.
2. Open the File menu and select New.
3. From the dialog box that appears, choose Program Group, as shown below, and click on OK.

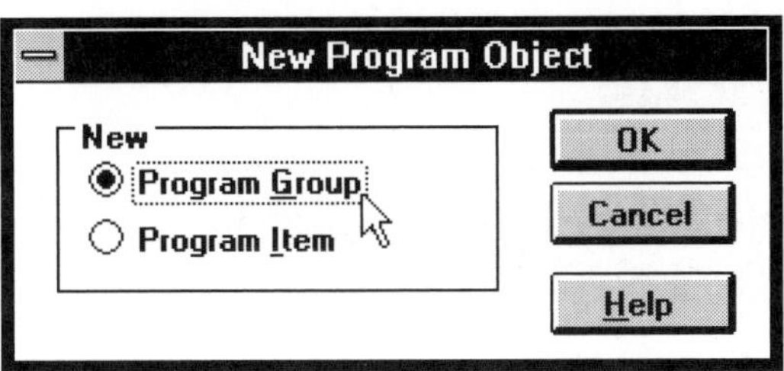

4. Another dialog box will appear. This is the Program Group Properties dialog box. It has two text sections, Description and Group File:

Description is the name that will appear under the group's icon and in the title bar of the group's window.

Group File is the name of the file that Windows puts on your hard disk to hold information about the group. This file is invisible to you. Windows creates the name for you, so you're not required to fill this line in. If you do, the name you supply will be used. Don't leave an extension, since .GRP (for "group") is automatically added by the Program Manager.

Enter **Writing Tools** in the Description text box.

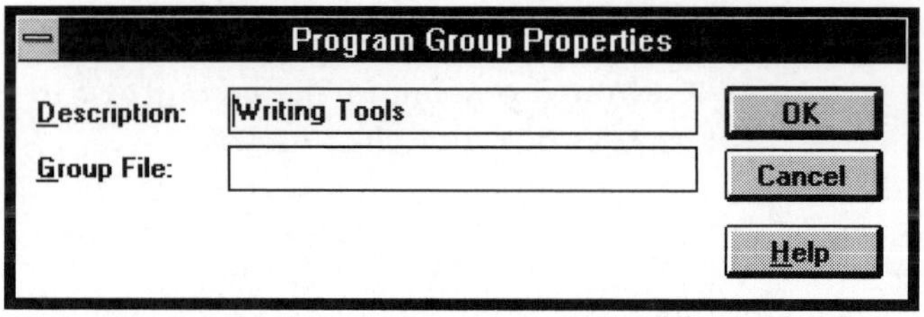

Program Group Properties
Description: Writing Tools
Group File:
OK
Cancel
Help

5. Click on OK and a new, empty group window appears. Notice that its title bar reads Writing Tools.

If you decide later that you want to change the name of the group, select the Properties command from the Program Manager's File menu and type the new name into the Description line. Don't change the Group File name, however.

ADDING APPLICATIONS TO A GROUP

> NOTE *Windows groups should contain no more than 40 application icons.*

Once you have a group created, the next step is to add programs (and/or documents) to it. This can be done in a variety of ways:

- Program icons can be *moved* into the new group from an existing group by dragging the icons from one group window to another. (One other approach is to drag a file from a File Manager window. This will be covered in Chapter 4.)

- Program icons can be *created* while the new group window is active. Windows will then automatically add the new program icon to the group.
- Program icons can be *copied* into the new group from existing groups. This creates a duplicate icon in the new group.

These techniques can also be used with existing groups, incidentally. So if you already have a group set up, it's easy to modify its contents to accommodate changes in your work patterns, or to update it when you buy a new program or want to delete an old one. Note, however, that it's a good idea to leave the supplied groups (Main and Accessories) as they are, since Windows expects to find its supplied programs in a particular arrangement. Add your own groups for other programs.

Moving a Program Icon into a New Window

This example takes you through the two ways to move the Solitaire icon (in the Games group) into the Writing Tools group you created above.

Dragging a Program Icon

The easiest way to move an icon from one group to another is to drag it with the mouse. This is how it's done:

1. Open the Games window.
2. Drag the Solitaire icon from the Games window to the Writing Tools window or icon (see Figure 3.3). (Make sure not to double-click on the icon or the program will run.)
3. Writing Tools now contains the Solitaire program icon. This will remain the case even if you close and then reopen the two groups.
4. Now move the Solitaire program back to its original position.

Moving a Program Icon Using the Move Command

You can also move applications or documents from group to group using the Move command from the Program Manager File menu. Here are the steps

FIGURE 3.3:

Moving a program icon from one group to another by dragging with the mouse

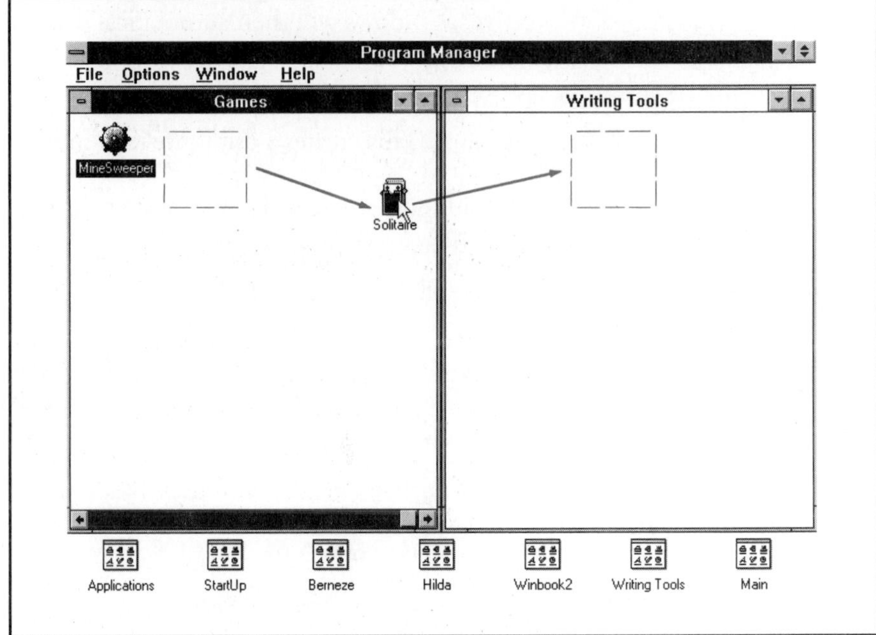

to perform the same move as above—putting Solitaire in the Writing Tools group instead of the Games group:

1. Open the Games window (the group window that contains the application you want to move).
2. Highlight Solitaire (the application you will move).
3. Open the Program Manager File menu and choose Move. The Move Program Item dialog box opens. Solitaire is identified as the program item, Games as the group to move it from, and Accessories as the default destination (To) group.
4. Scroll through the list of other group windows in the drop-down list box until you find Writing Tools. Highlight it.
5. Click on OK. The dialog box closes and the Games window returns to the screen, but it no longer has the Solitaire icon in it.
6. Double-click on the Writing Tools icon (if its window is not already open) to see that Solitaire now appears there.

Creating Your Own Program Icon

TO CREATE A PROGRAM ICON,

1. **Select File ➤ New from the destination window for the new icon.**
2. **Choose Program Item and click on OK.**
3. **Enter the name of the new icon in the Description text box.**
4. **Enter the line in the Command Line text box that you would type at the DOS prompt to run the program (including path if necessary).**
5. **Fill in the Working Directory text box with the name of the directory you want the program to default to, if different from that specified in the AUTOEXEC.BAT path.**
6. **Click on the Change Icon button to select the icon.**

The example in this section will show you how to create an icon for the WordStar word-processing program (which is a non-Windows application). You can apply this technique to Windows programs just as easily. You tell Windows the name of the icon and the name of the program it is to represent. Windows then creates the new icon and places it in the active window. Follow all the steps in this section to successfully create a new icon:

Getting Started

To open the Program Item Properties box directly, press and hold the Alt key while double-clicking the program icon.

1. Activate the Writing Tools window.
2. Select New from the Program Manager's File menu. A dialog box appears.

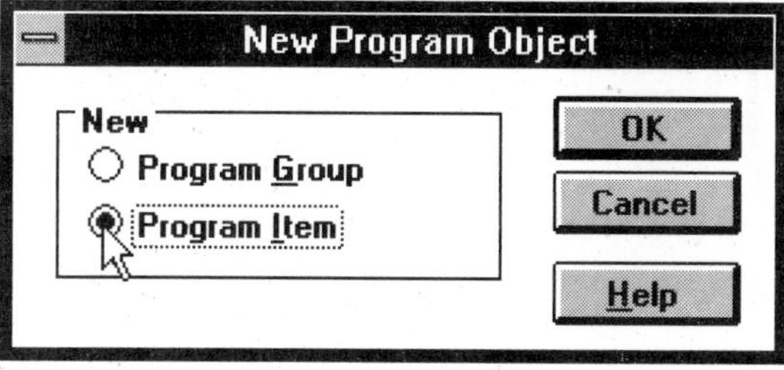

3. Choose Program Item and click OK. The Program Item Properties dialog box appears. There are four lines that you have to fill in—Description, Command Line, Working Directory, and Shortcut Key.

The following sections discuss each area of the Program Item Properties dialog box (see Figure 3.4).

Describing Your Icon

Description is the name you want under the icon and in the title bar when the program is running. If you don't type anything into this area, Windows will assign the program name specified in the Command Line entry without the file name extension. But it makes more sense to give the icon a name that will help you remember what it's for.

Specifying the Command Line

Command Line is the command that the icon gives to DOS when you double-click it. This information is essential:

1. Type the name of the program you want the icon to run (see Figure 3.4). Be sure to include the extension of the program's file name. You should also include the file's path name if the drive

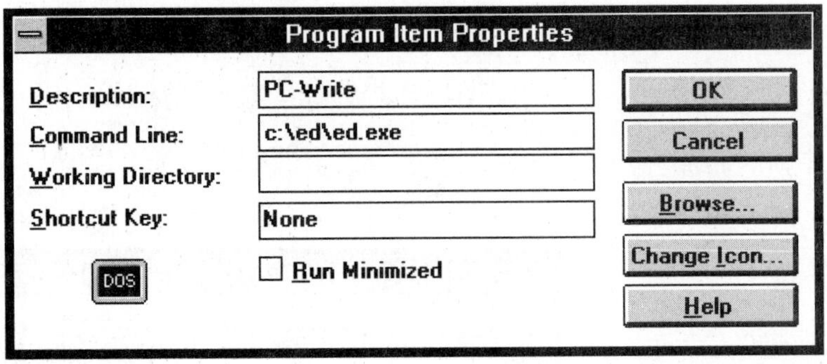

Program Item Properties
Description: PC-Write
Command Line: c:\ed\ed.exe
Working Directory:
Shortcut Key: None
DOS
Run Minimized
OK
Cancel
Browse...
Change Icon...
Help

FIGURE 3.4: *Setting up the properties for a new icon (note that you include the entire path name and extension of the file on the command line)*

and directory that it is stored in is not included in your computer's search path as stipulated in your AUTOEXEC.BAT file. For example, if the program is WP.EXE and that file is stored in \WP, then the command line \WP\WP.EXE should be used unless \WP is included in your path.

2. Since typos and syntax errors can make entering path information troublesome, Windows provides a Browse button which allows you to select the correct Command Line entry from a list of files available on your various disks. This is very helpful if you don't know the exact specifications for a file. Click on Browse, then look through the directories in the Files dialog box. (See the section Files Dialog Boxes in Chapter 1 if you need to review how this is done.) Remember that unless you change the file type, Browse will only search for files with extensions of .EXE, .PIF, .COM, and .BAT.
3. Select the program from the list and click on OK. Windows fills in the Command Line text box for you.

You can also add a file name to the Command Line text box that will cause a particular document to be opened when you click on this icon. See the section "Creating Icons for Individual Documents" later in this chapter to find out how this is done.

Assigning a Working Directory

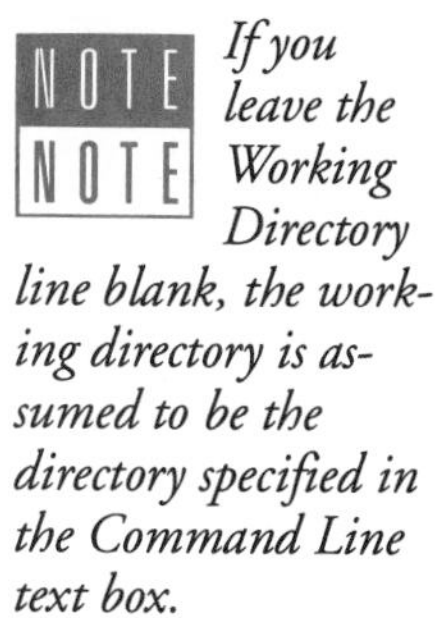

If you leave the Working Directory line blank, the working directory is assumed to be the directory specified in the Command Line text box.

Working Directory is the directory where the program or document files for the application are located and where new files will be placed when you save your work (unless you specify otherwise when saving and retrieving). The directory you specify here becomes the "current" DOS directory while the application is running.

Typically this will be the directory where the files your application needs to run are located. Complicated application programs with lots of support files containing such things as fonts, dictionaries, thesauruses, and so forth are cases in point.

Some simpler programs don't need access to additional files, or don't mind looking around for them in other directories via the search path set up by your AUTOEXEC.BAT file. With such programs, you can specify a working directory that is different from the Command Line directory, and all will be well. The result will be a different default directory when you go to save or retrieve files—just a convenience of not having to keep typing in a new path when performing such a process.

For example, say you wanted to start PC-Write (which is in the \ED directory), but you want it to come up with \LETTERS as the current directory. Make sure the path for the program itself

```
C:\ED\ED.EXE
```

is in the Command Line text box. Then, enter the desired default directory

```
C:\LETTERS
```

on the Working Directory line. Windows will switch to the \ED directory to run the program, and then to C:\LETTERS directory where your document files are located.

The startup directory can also be set by the program's PIF file. This is explained in Chapter 13.

Saving Time with Shortcut Keys

Shortcut Keys allows you to define a key combination that will open this application directly rather than having to go through the regular procedures of clicking on icons or switching between applications. For example, you could define a shortcut key that would allow you to run your WordPerfect program or document simply by pressing Ctrl-Alt-W. For more information about using shortcut keys, see Chapters 13 and 20.

Assigning an Icon to a Program

Once the Properties information is filled in, the final step is to decide which icon you want to use to identify the program. This is purely a subjective matter and doesn't influence the workings of your program:

1. Click on the Change Icon button in the Program Item Properties dialog box. You'll see the Change Icon dialog box.

2. In the Current Icon area you will see one or more icons associated with the file name displayed. The MS-DOS icon is appropriate for most DOS programs. Windows applications usually have their own icons that will automatically be chosen when you add the program, but you can look through other program's icons for some variety. To do this, select Browse.

3. In the Browse dialog box, choose one of the file names. PROGMAN.EXE is a good one, since it contains lots of icons. MORICONS.DLL contains about 100 icons.

4. Once you've selected the file whose icons you want to see, click OK.

5. You're back at the Change Icon dialog box and the file name has changed to the one you just selected. The new icons appear, as shown in Figure 3.5. To scroll through them, use the scroll bar or the arrow keys.

6. When the one you want to use is highlighted, click OK or press Enter.

FIGURE 3.5:

Windows chooses an icon for each application you add, but you can choose your own. After selecting a file whose icons you want to view, click OK to see the available icons.

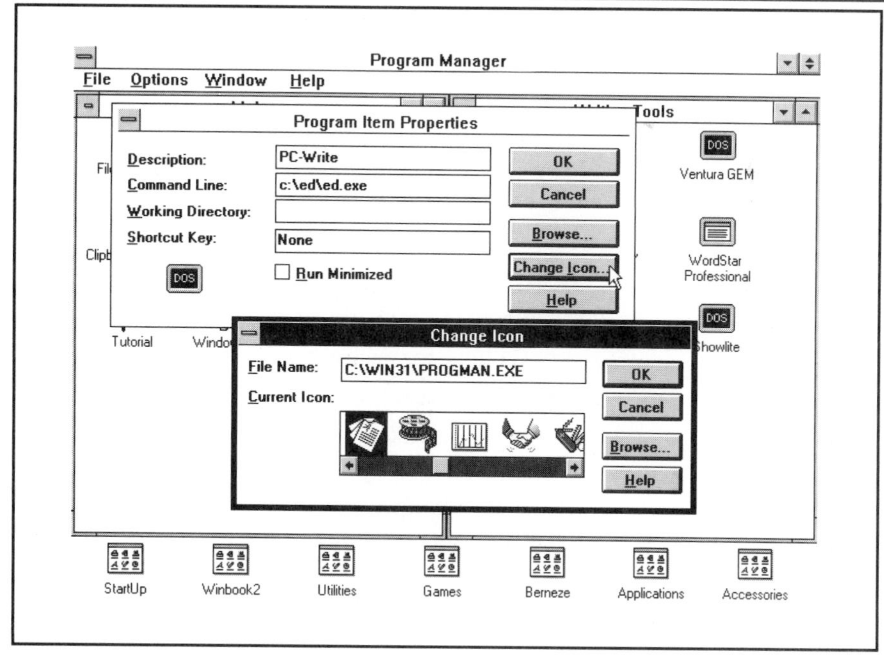

Setting the Run Minimized Option

NOTE *Working Directory, Shortcut Key, and Run Minimized are new properties in Windows 3.1.*

When you run the program you've just set up, it's possible to have it start up as an icon. This is useful if you want to have a program available to switch to while using other applications, but don't want its window to be open as a matter of course. This is often done with programs in the StartUp group. All you have to do is set the Run Minimized check box on by clicking on the empty box in the Program Item Properties dialog box. The program will start up as an icon on your Desktop, which you can restore as you would any iconized program.

When you're all finished creating your icon, click OK in the Program Item Properties box to close it and return to the Program Manager. When you look in the group window where your program resides, you'll see the new icon.

COPYING AN ICON FROM ANOTHER WINDOW

TO MAKE A COPY OF AN ICON,

hold down the Ctrl key and drag the icon either to a different place in the same window or to another window or group icon.

NOTE *Icons don't take up much RAM or hard disk space. However, **running** too many additional copies of a particular application may lead to low memory messages from Windows.*

Suppose you want the same program to be included in more than one group. This would be useful in a number of different situations. For instance, perhaps several people use the same computer and some of the same programs. An easy way to organize each person's programs is to set up a group for each. You can name each group after the person's name: Bob, Hilda, Berneze, and so on. Then, for each icon you want duplicated, you just create it once and copy it into the respective group windows. There are two ways to do this. I'll discuss the easiest way first.

Copying an icon from one group to another in the Program Manager does not copy the program itself, as does the DOS COPY command. In the above example there is still only one copy of WS.EXE on the hard disk, not four. The copy command just changes the group (.GRP) file for each group to include the new icon. Thus, you can make many copies of an icon without worrying about cluttering up your hard disk or using up lots of hard disk space.

Copying an Icon by Dragging

The easiest way to copy an icon from one group to another is to drag it there:

1. If necessary, create the groups to which you want to copy the icon.
2. Open the group window containing the icon you want to copy and select the icon by clicking on it once.
3. Press and hold down the Ctrl key, then drag the icon to the destination window. As with moving an icon, it isn't necessary for the destination window to be open. You can drag the program icon to the destination group icon, too.

You can Ctrl-drag the program icon into as many groups as you want.

Copying an Icon Using the Copy Command

You can also copy a program icon into another group using the Program Manager Copy command. The dragging method is so much easier, though, that you would probably only use this if you don't have your mouse hooked up:

1. Create the groups into which you want to copy the icon.
2. Open the group window containing the icon you want to copy, and select the icon by clicking on it once.
3. Open the File menu and choose Copy. The Copy Program Item dialog box appears. It has a drop-down list from which you choose the destination group for the icon. Open the list by clicking on the down arrow. Groups are listed in alphabetical order. Your screen should look something like Figure 3.6. (Notice that I've tiled the two group windows.)
4. Choose the desired destination group from the list and click on OK. A copy of the icon is then added to the new group.
5. Repeat the process to copy the icon to other groups. I've copied the WordStar Professional icon to each of my coworkers' groups, as you can see in Figure 3.7.

FIGURE 3.6:

When copying program icons to another group using the Copy command, you choose the destination group from this dialog box.

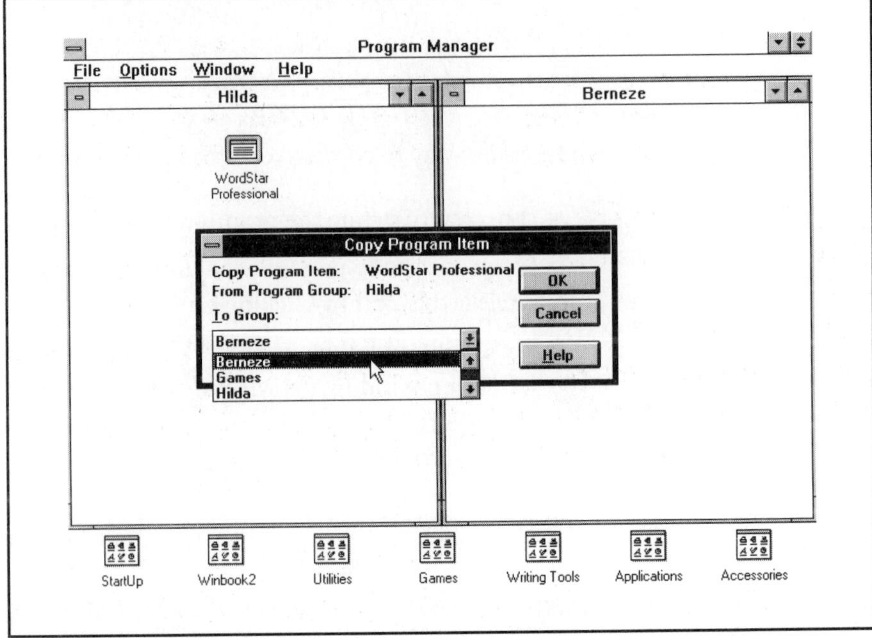

FIGURE 3.7:

The result of copying a program icon to several program groups

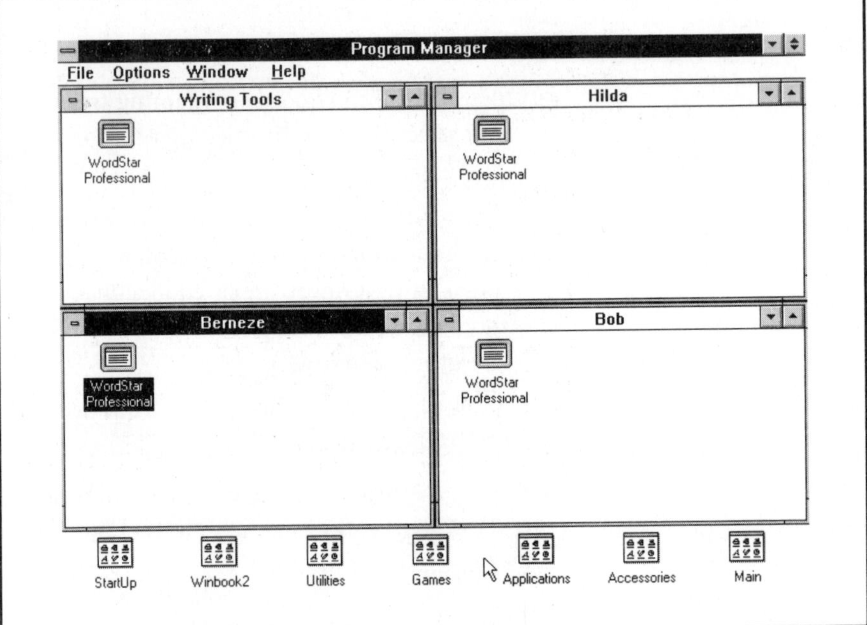

MODIFYING THE PROPERTIES OF DUPLICATE ICONS

Once an icon is copied, you can alter it to suit specific needs, should you want to. This applies regardless of whether you've copied the icon to a different group or within the original group. Copying to the same group lets you make up slightly different versions of the icon for different purposes.

For example, each of your coworkers may want to start up WordStar with a different default directory or have it automatically open a particular document when run.

These types of alterations are done by tailoring the properties of the icon via the Properties command on the Program Manager's File menu, as follows:

1. Select the icon to be altered.
2. Open the File menu and select the Properties command. The Program Item Properties dialog box appears. (This is the same box you use to create a new program icon, so you may recognize it.)
3. Alter the icon's Description, Command Line, and/or Working Directory entries to your needs, and click on OK. The dialog box below shows the command line altered to start WordStar with the current directory set to \HILDA\LETTERS. Note that for this to work, WS.EXE would have to be in a directory listed in the AUTOEXEC.BAT search path. Note also that the name of the icon has been changed to read Hilda's WordStar Professional.

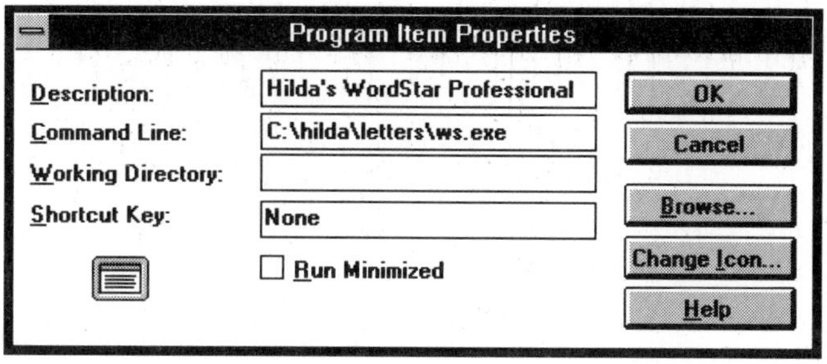

CREATING ICONS FOR INDIVIDUAL DOCUMENTS

TO CREATE AN ICON FOR A FILE,

1. **Click on the icon of the file's application.**
2. **Choose File ➤ Properties.**
3. **Put the file name in the Description line.**
4. **Append the file name to the Command Line entry, leaving a space in between.**

You can also open a document file directly from the File Manager. This is covered in Chapter 4.

You can create icons for individual documents. Clicking on such an icon then opens a specific document in an application program. For example, an icon could be set up to run WordStar and open the file called PROPOSAL. This would be just like entering

```
WS PROPOSAL
```

at the DOS prompt.

To do this, click on the WordStar icon and select Properties from the File menu. Modify the Command Line entry in the Program Item Properties dialog box so that it reads

```
WS.EXE PROPOSAL.WS
```

If the document is in another directory, add the path name, such as

```
C:\WS\WS.EXE \BUSINESS\PROPOSAL.WS
```

You should also change the icon's name to "Proposal" to remind you which document opens when you click on it.

If there are a number of documents you use regularly, just use the Copy command to create as many icons for the same program as you need. Then modify them accordingly, with each one set to open a different document. Figure 3.8 shows such a group of icons. They all run Microsoft Excel, but each one opens a different spreadsheet.

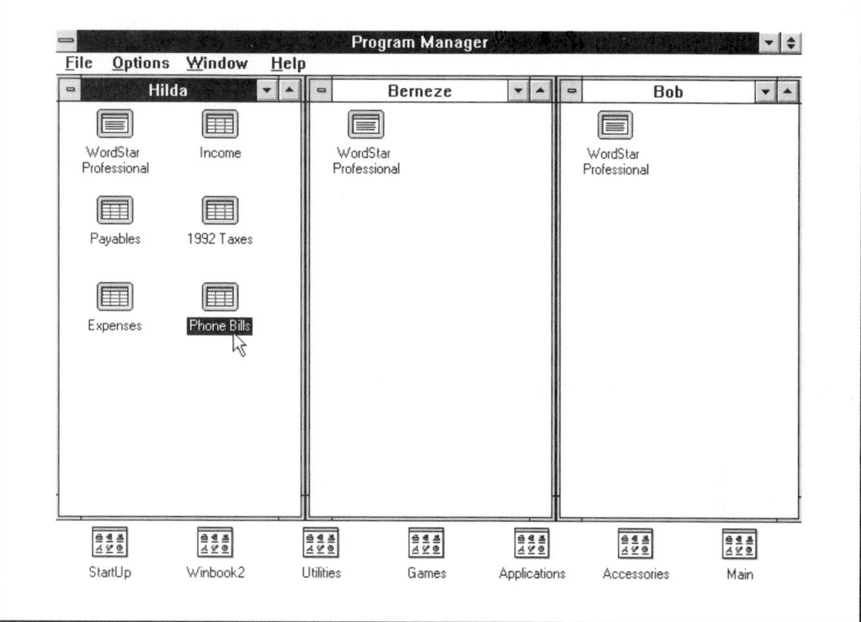

FIGURE 3.8: *You can make up icons that run the same program but open different documents. These are all Excel documents set to open various spreadsheets. The Command Line entry for each icon opens a different document.*

RUNNING PROGRAMS FROM A FLOPPY DISK

You can create icons that are set up to run programs from a floppy disk rather than from the hard disk. This isn't something you're likely to do regularly, but it can be done. Here's how.

1. Specify the drive name in the Command Line entry of the Program Item Properties dialog box, such as:

   A:\XTREE.EXE

2. Insert the proper disk in drive A when setting up the properties of the icon or Windows will give you a warning message, saying that the path is invalid. (If this happens, just click on OK, and the icon will be created anyway.)
3. Windows will present the Removable Path Specified dialog box, alerting you to the fact that the file you're making an icon for might not be available at a later time. Click on Yes.

4. Run the program as usual. If you have the wrong disk in the floppy disk drive, Windows will alert you to this fact with the relatively obscure message seen below. Replace the disk, OK the dialog box, then run the program again.

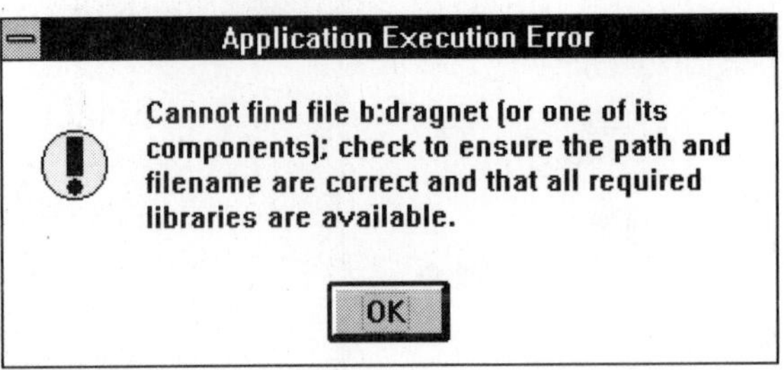

DELETING PROGRAM ICONS

Deleting a program icon doesn't delete the program itself from your hard disk. Chapter 4 shows you how to do that.

Occasionally you'll need to delete programs from your groups. Perhaps you'll stop using a program often enough to warrant having an icon for it, and would be willing to run it via the Run command. Or perhaps you'll switch to a new spreadsheet program and want to delete the old one and its icon from your system and replace it with a new one. Whatever the reason, deleting a program icon is occassionally necessary. Here are the steps for doing so:

1. Open the group window containing the icon you want to eliminate.
2. Highlight the icon.
3. Select Delete from the File menu (or press Del). The dialog box below asks you if you're sure you want to delete the icon. Click on Yes and the icon will be deleted from the group window.

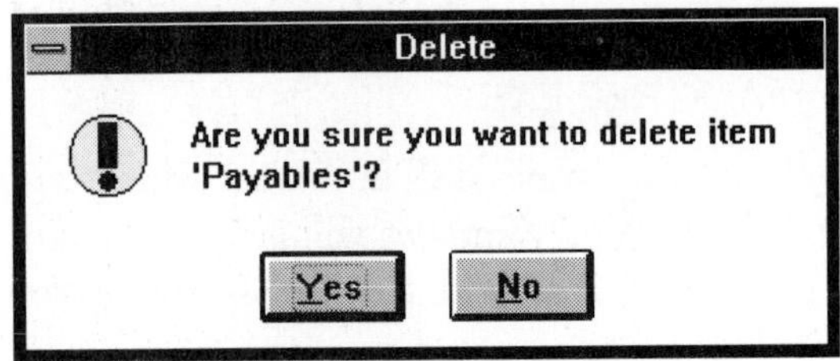

DELETING GROUPS

Just as you may need to delete program icons, you can delete group icons and windows. When you delete a group, all the program items in the group are erased, too. This doesn't delete the programs or documents, however; it only erases the group's .GRP file:

1. Select the group icon (it must be iconized, not open as a window). If the Control menu opens, click again to close it (or press Esc). The icon's name must be highlighted, but the Control menu closed.
2. Press Del, or select Delete from the File menu. You'll see the dialog box shown below. Click Yes to delete the group.

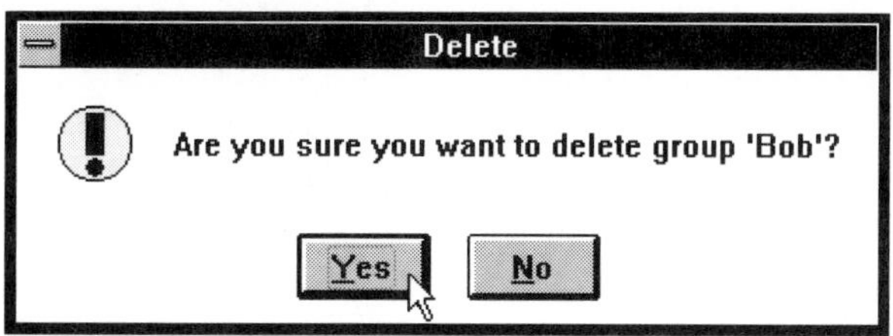

CUSTOMIZING OTHER PROGRAM ICON PARAMETERS

There are numerous parameters that will affect how a non-Windows program runs from Windows, beyond those discussed in this chapter. For example, you may want to stipulate how the program should use the screen and keyboard, how much RAM it requires, how much of the computer's processing power is used on each program (386 and 486 machines only), and so forth.

Normally, Windows sets these parameters according to built-in defaults designed to work with most programs. In most cases, then, all that is required in the program icon creation process is to fill in the description and command line entries in the Program Item Properties dialog box, as you've already learned how to do in this chapter. Occasionally you will want to exercise more control over the way Windows runs a program. To do this, you have to create what's called a *PIF file* (for Program Information File) or use a PIF file supplied with the program. Chapter 13 covers PIF files and the use of the PIF Editor. If you've installed a program from the Program Manager and it doesn't run properly, you can probably cure the malady by creating a PIF file for it.

FAST TRACK

CHAPTER

4

FAST TRACK

To create a directory, ... **109**

select the parent directory and choose File ➤ Create Directory.

To delete a directory, ... **110**

select the directory and press Del.

To move the separator bar in the drive window, ... **111**

- Position the pointer over the split bar until the pointer becomes a double arrow, then drag the bar to the left or right to adjust the size of the tree and file windows.
- Choose View ➤ Split and move the bar with the right or left arrow key. Press Enter when the window is split to your liking.

To sort a directory listing, ... **115**

open the View menu and choose which way you want to sort (by name, type, size, or modification date).

To show specific files, ... **116**

choose View ➤ By File Type. Turn on the check boxes for file types to include, and/or type in a filter criterion in the Name text box.

To refresh the screen, ... **120**

press F5.

To create an association, ... 126

1. Select a file that has the extension in question.
2. Choose File ➤ Associate.
3. Enter the name (and path) of the program to associate with the extension.

To move a file to a different directory, ... 132
drag its icon to the directory in the tree window.

To move a file/directory to another drive, ... 137

1. Select the file/directory.
2. Hold down the Alt key.
3. Drag the selection to the drive icon.

To copy a file, ... 138

1. Select the item.
2. Hold down the Ctrl key.
3. Drag the selection to the destination.

To format a disk, ... 143
place the disk in the drive and choose Disk ➤ Format Disk.

CHAPTER 4

FEATURING

A Review of the DOS Directory Structure

Copying, Moving, and Deleting Files & Directories

Searching for Files

Setting Up Associations

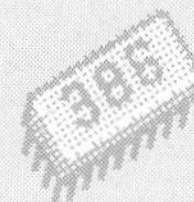

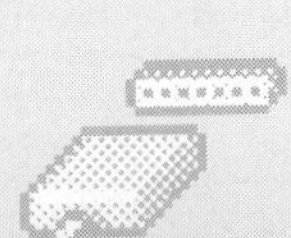
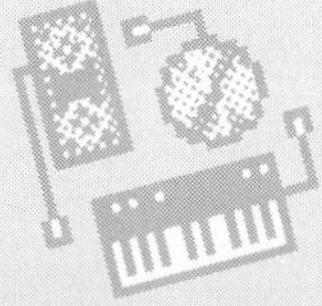

Using the File Manager

One of the most confusing aspects of DOS (or any computer operating system for that matter) is the job of managing your files. Most application programs nowadays consist of numerous files. Add to this the plethora of files you are likely to collect and create, and your hard-disk directory can easily become impossibly cluttered. With the advent of affordable high-capacity hard disks (80, 110, or even 200 megabyte disks are not uncommon these days), hard-disk housekeeping becomes even more of a necessity.

If you've used DOS to any degree, you know it can be quite a hassle to keep your files organized and up-to-date, not to mention perform the often overlooked chore of making backup copies of important documents and programs. File-management tasks via the DOS interface require exacting attention to syntax and spelling, both of which are sometimes difficult or tedious to remember. One of the more grueling jobs in DOS—copying files between directories—is enough to challenge even the multilingual or the highly computer-literate.

Even if you remember the proper syntax for a complex DOS file-management command, make one misspelling and your carefully constructed command bombs, with DOS issuing a dispassionate and hieroglyphic reply such as

```
Bad command or file name
```

or

```
Not ready error reading drive A
Abort, Retry, Fail?
```

Who but those of us with the lowest self-esteem would choose anything other than Retry? It's enough to intimidate even seasoned computerites.

Then there's the job of purging your disks of unnecessary or obsolete files. Typing in the name of each file name you want to eliminate is simply a pain, and one false move with the ERASE or DEL commands can wreak havoc on your files. For example

```
ERASE *.WK?
```

would erase all the 1-2-3 worksheets in the current directory in about the same amount of time it takes to realize you've locked your keys in the car. And just like your car, DOS doesn't bother to ask, "Yo! Do you really want to do this?"

True, the advent of DOS 5 and its shell program has made file management much easier than before. However, the Windows 3.1 File Manager is superior to the DOS shell in its features and ease of use. Your hard disk's directories can be displayed in separate windows, from which you employ the "point and shoot" approach to copy, move, or delete any file(s) you choose. You just select the desired files and drag them to their new directories or drives. You can even run programs or open document files by double-clicking on their names. You can elect to see only certain files, sort them in various orders, search the entire disk for a certain file, even format floppy disks. You can also create and delete directories.

A REVIEW OF DOS DIRECTORIES

This book assumes you understand the basics of the DOS directory structure and have used DOS commands to perform directory-related file housekeeping. However, if you're a little rusty on the topic, the File Manager won't make much sense to you. So here's a thumbnail sketch of directory workings.

DOS stores all files in directories on your disk. A *directory* is simply a collection of files. Directories let you keep files together that are somehow related. Typically you'll keep related work files, such as letters, in one directory, spreadsheets in another, and so forth. With occasional limitations imposed by specific programs, you can organize your files any way the spirit strikes you.

Directories are organized in a system analagous to a "tree," as illustrated in Figure 4.1. In fact, the organization of directories is called the *directory tree.* The directories are organized in a hierarchical manner, from the *root* (the most basic level) to various branches off the root (directories), and branches off those branches (subdirectories).

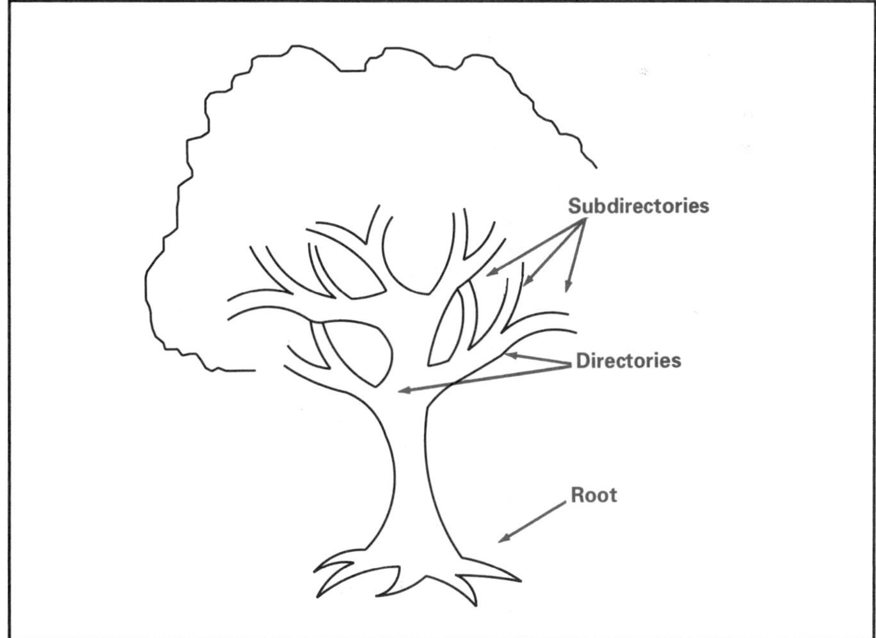

FIGURE 4.1:

The DOS directory-tree structure. Directories are organized from the root outward.

It is possible that you've never used directories before, since, theoretically, you can put all your files in the default directory (the root), though there is a limit to the number of files you can store in the root directory. If you've never created a new directory, it's possible (though not likely) that all your files are stored in the root directory. However, it's wise to divide things up according to the way you work, by creating appropriate directories and assigning your files to them according to some sensible scheme.

The root directory is always indicated by a single backslash (\). All other directories have names that you assign. For example, the Windows Setup program created a directory branch called WINDOWS. Subordinate to WINDOWS, it created another branch called SYSTEM. The official name of the system directory is C:\WINDOWS\SYSTEM. This is called the directory's *path name.* The name describes the path you'd take to get to the directory, just as if you were climbing the tree—from the root up to the particular branch. Notice that the \ (indicating the root) precedes the directory name and that branches in the path name are also separated by a backslash.

In working with directories, the main thing to keep in mind is the "you can't get there from here" rule. To switch between distant branches there are times when you have to remember their relationship to the root. For example, if you were working in the \WINDOWS\SYSTEM directory and wanted to save a file in the \LETTERS\PERSONAL directory, you'd typically have to back up to the root level first, then select the LETTERS directory, and finally select the PERSONAL directory. When working with most applications and some dialog boxes in Windows (especially the File Open, File Save, and Browse dialog boxes), you'll need to remember this.

STARTING THE FILE MANAGER

To run the File Manager, open the Main group and double-click on the File Manager icon. This will bring up the File Manager's initial screen, as shown in Figure 4.2. If you have used the File Manager before, the window's size may be different, since the File Manager has an option that saves its setup, just as the Program Manager does, when you exit Windows.

FIGURE 4.2:

The File Manager screen, showing the directory structure (on the left) and the directories and files (on the right) of the root directory

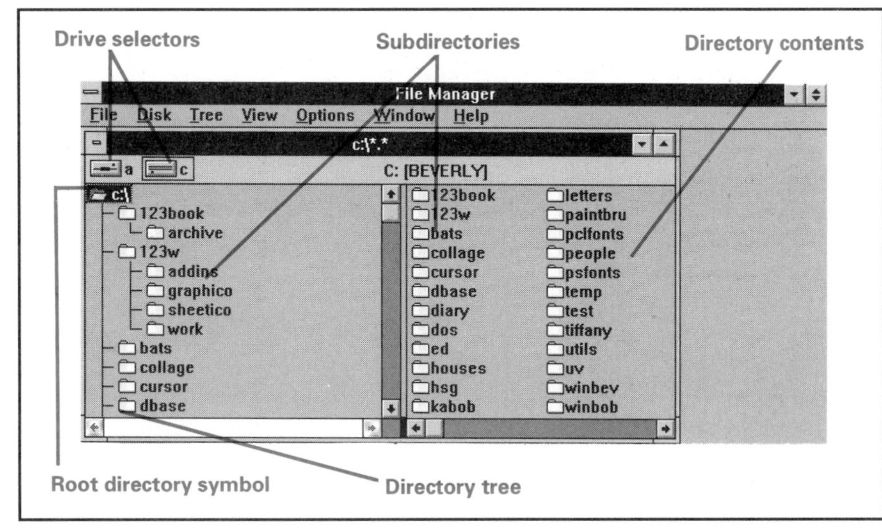

Change directories and file names from lowercase to uppercase letters (and vice versa) by selecting Options ➤ Font.

What you see is the main File Manager window and a child window within it showing the directories on your hard disk. Whenever you request to view a directory or disk drive's contents, they'll be displayed in a child window. You can open as many child windows as you want, each showing different (or identical) directories and/or drives. Then you can copy and move files between them, delete files, or run programs. This section outlines how to carry out each procedure.

You may see this toolbar in your File Manager window. You can turn the toolbar on or off by choosing View/Toolbar. The illustrations in this chapter show the toolbar turned off.

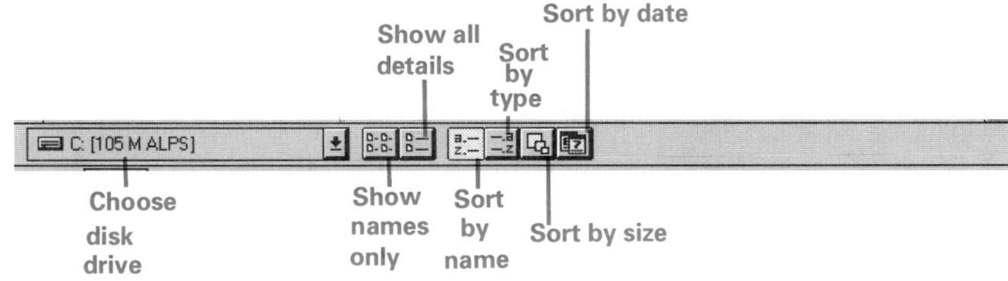

Displaying Directory and File Views

When you run the File Manager, the directory window for the current drive is the first thing you see. It lists all the directories on the current drive and their contents. The window is split into two *panes*: the left side for the directory tree and the right side for the directory contents.

If your window isn't split, open the View menu. You have three choices of view:

Tree and Directory displays both panes.

Tree Only displays only the tree pane.

Directory Only displays only the directory (or file) pane.

NOTE *If you are running Windows for Workgroups, your toolbar will include icons for sharing your dirves and connectiong to network drives that others have shared. The procedures for sharing and connecting to network drives are covered in Chapter 17.*

For purposes of discussion, choose Tree and Directory. You now see the tree on the left, and on the right the contents of whatever directory is currently selected (highlighted) in the tree.

Notice the line that displays the letter (and volume name if there is one) of the selected disk drive. On the left end you see icons representing the disk drives on your system. The one that is outlined is the currently selected drive. If you have a hard drive and a floppy drive, you'll see icons labeled A and C, or B and C. If you have two floppy drives, you'll have all three, A, B, and C. Any additional drives, including a RAM drive or network drives, will have distinct icons, too. To the right of the drive icons you'll see the disk drive and volume name.

If the child window is not maximized within the File Manager window, it will have a title bar. The title bar shows the disk drive and the currently selected directory and file path. When the child window is maximized, the File Manager title bar carries this information. Moving the directory highlight up and down in the tree causes the title bar to change to reflect the path of the highlighted directory. (Use the up and down arrow keys, or single-click with the mouse.)

The Tree Pane

The tree is a graphical representation of your disk layout. Each file folder icon symbolizes one directory, and the straight lines connecting them indicate how they're related. The name of each directory appears after the icon. If you have more directories than can be seen at one time, the window will have a scroll bar which you can use to scroll the tree up and down.

To see as many directories as possible at one time, maximize both the File Manager and the child windows. It makes working with a directory tree much simpler. (Remember that the maximum size of a child window is determined by the size of the parent window. If you want the directory window to take up the whole screen, you have to maximize the File Manager window, too.)

The Status Line

You may or may not see a status line at the bottom of the window, displaying the amount of available room your drive has and the number and size of the files listed. You can turn this on or off. Turning it off frees up a little more space for displaying directories and files. Choose Options ➤ Status Bar to change the setting.

Switching Drives

SPEED TIP *You can also change drives by pressing Ctrl and the drive letter. Thus, Ctrl-A switches to drive A, Ctrl-B to drive B, etc.*

To switch drives, you simply click on the appropriate drive icon. If you choose a floppy drive icon (ones with a single line in the middle, instead of two lines), you'll have to insert a floppy disk in the selected drive or you'll get an error message.

Once you change drives, the File Manager examines the new drive and displays its directories in the tree pane. Usually your floppies will have only one directory (the root) so you'll see only one file folder. A hard disk typically has many directories. The next section explains how to see the different levels of directories and how to see which directories contain additional subdirectories.

WORKING WITH DIRECTORIES

Once you have the correct drive selected, you can work with the various directories and files it contains. Before getting into working with files, let's first consider how the File Manager displays and manipulates your drive's directories. Activate the tree pane again by clicking on it.

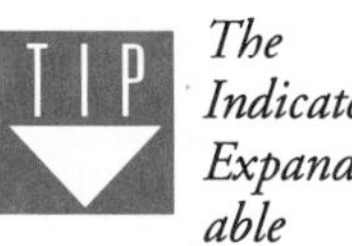

The Indicate Expandable Branches option slows the File Manager down when it is set on. Once you have your directories where you need to be in the File Manager, turn this option off.

Expanding and Collapsing Directory Levels

There's an option on the Tree menu that shows you which directories contain additional subdirectories. You set this option on by choosing Tree ➤ Indicate Expandable Branches. Once it is on, some file folders in the Directory Tree window have a plus sign (+) in them. Others have a minus sign (–). The plus indicates that there are additional subdirectories attached to the directory, and that these are not currently showing. A minus indicates that all the immediate subdirectories are currently visible.

The first step when using any directory is to select it. Only one directory can be selected at a time. You select a directory by clicking on it, typing its first letter, or moving the highlight to it with the arrow keys. When selected, the directory icon and name become highlighted:

You can jump quickly to a directory name by typing its first letter on the keyboard. If there is more than one directory with the same first letter, each press of the key will advance to the next choice.

- Double-click on any directory that has either a plus or minus sign in its file folder. The directory will alternately expand or collapse one level with each double-click.
- Select the directory you want. Then open the Tree menu and select Expand One Level. This shows the next directory level. Or choose Expand Branch to see all the directories subordinate to the selected one (if there are more levels).
- The fastest way to see the entire subdirectory structure of your disk is to select Tree ➤ Expand All. This displays all the branches. Figure 4.3 illustrates the effect.
- The fastest way to collapse all the branches is to double-click on the topmost folder (the root). To reopen just the first level, double-click once again on the root icon or select Tree ➤ Expand One Level.

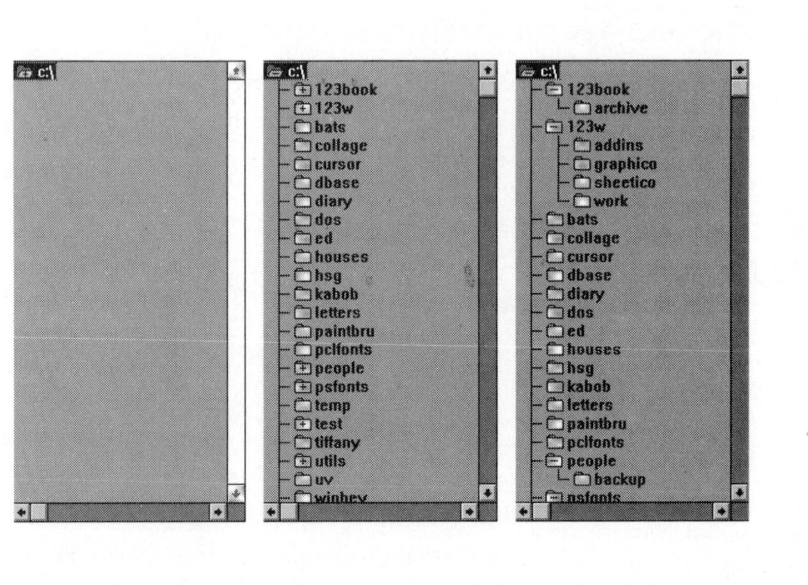

FIGURE 4.3:

The effect of the Tree menu's Expand commands (from left to right): Collapse Branch, Expand One Level, and Expand All

Notice that every time you select a directory, its contents are displayed in the directory-contents side of the window. The contents include subordinate directories (listed first and looking like little folders just as they do in the left window), followed by the list of files.

If you want to change the order in which files are sorted, (by name, extension, etc.) you can do so. See the section "Sorting the Directory Listing" later in this chapter.

Creating a Directory

TO CREATE A DIRECTORY,

select the parent directory and choose File ➤ Create Directory.

Creating a directory is easy, and because of the graphical nature of the directory tree, it's much easier to visualize what you're doing than when creating directories from the DOS command line. Once you've created a new directory, you can employ the file commands or mouse procedures explained in the next section to copy or move files into it:

1. From the tree pane, select the directory under which you want to create a subdirectory. If you select the root, then the directory will be created directly off of it.
2. Choose File ➤ Create Directory. A dialog box will appear.
3. Type in the name of the new directory and click on OK.

Below you can see the effect of selecting the Winbook directory and adding a subdirectory called Chap-4.

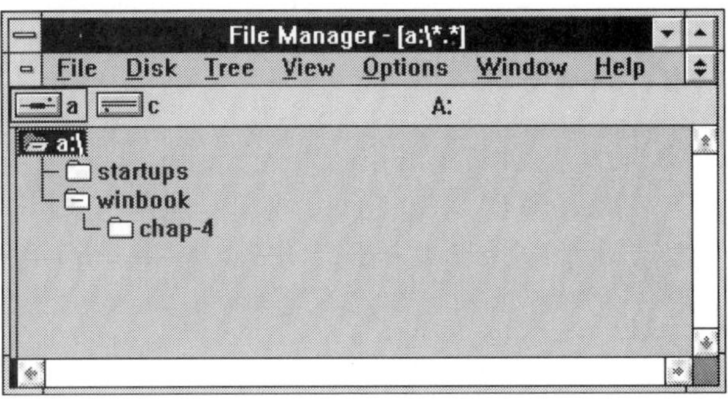

Deleting a Directory

TO DELETE A DIRECTORY,

select the directory and press Del.

Deleting a directory in DOS is a pain. You have to remove all the files first, then delete the directory. In the File Manager it's much simpler. You can do it in one step. But since it's so easy, you have to be careful. One false move and you've wiped out a directory and all its files!

Luckily, the default settings for File Manager require you to confirm the operation before the files and directory are all erased. Obviously you should be very careful when using this command. Make sure you really want to trash *all* the files in the directory first. Once deleted, files can be easily recovered only immediately thereafter with a file-recovery program such as Norton Utilities or the UNDELETE program supplied with DOS 5.

1. In the tree window select the directory you want to delete.
2. Select File ➤ Delete or press Del. A dialog box will appear with the name of the directory in it. You can name a different directory if you want, but normally you'd just leave it as is.
3. Click on OK and the following confirmation box appears:

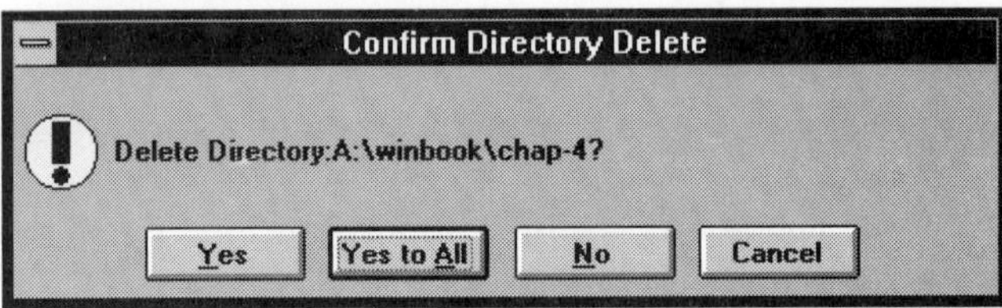

SPEED TIP *To quickly erase an entire floppy disk, select the drive and then select the root. Turn off the confirmations and press Del. (Make sure to set the confirmations back on to prevent accidental erasures on other drives.)*

4. Do you really want to delete the directory and all its files? If so, click on Yes to All.

If you click on Yes in the above dialog box with the confirmation messages set on, you will keep clicking on Yes for each file before it is deleted. If you click Yes to All, all files will be deleted with no further ado.

You can tell File Manager not to bug you about each deletion if you want to, via the Confirmation dialog box (the procedure and consequent effects are detailed in the "Working with Files" section below.) However, be cautious when cancelling confirmation settings, since they are designed to prevent accidental file erasure. On the other hand, if you really want to erase a whole branch—or the entire disk for that matter—in short order, turning them off lets you do just that. Simply set all the confirmations off, select the directory to delete (even as high as the root) and press Del. All the files in the directory as well as all subordinate directories and their files will be deleted.

WORKING WITH FILES

TO MOVE THE SEPARATOR BAR IN THE DRIVE WINDOW,

- **Position the pointer over the split bar until it becomes a double arrow, then drag the bar to the left or right to adjust the size of the tree and file windows.**
- **Choose View ➤ Split and move the bar with the right and left arrow keys. Press Enter when the window is split to your liking.**

Once you've selected the correct drive and directory, you can copy, move, delete, run, open, or print any files you wish. You do all your work with files by selecting them in the file window and dragging file icons around or choosing commands from the File menu:

1. As an example, try opening any directory. (Make sure you're on the right drive first—probably C.) Notice that when the directory is open, its file folder icon opens up, as shown in Figure 4.4.
2. The contents of the directory are shown in the right side of the window. Notice the complete path name of the directory in the window's title bar. Enlarge the window (if it isn't already enlarged) to see more of the files. Notice that each file has an icon. File Manager chooses these icons on the basis of each file's extension.

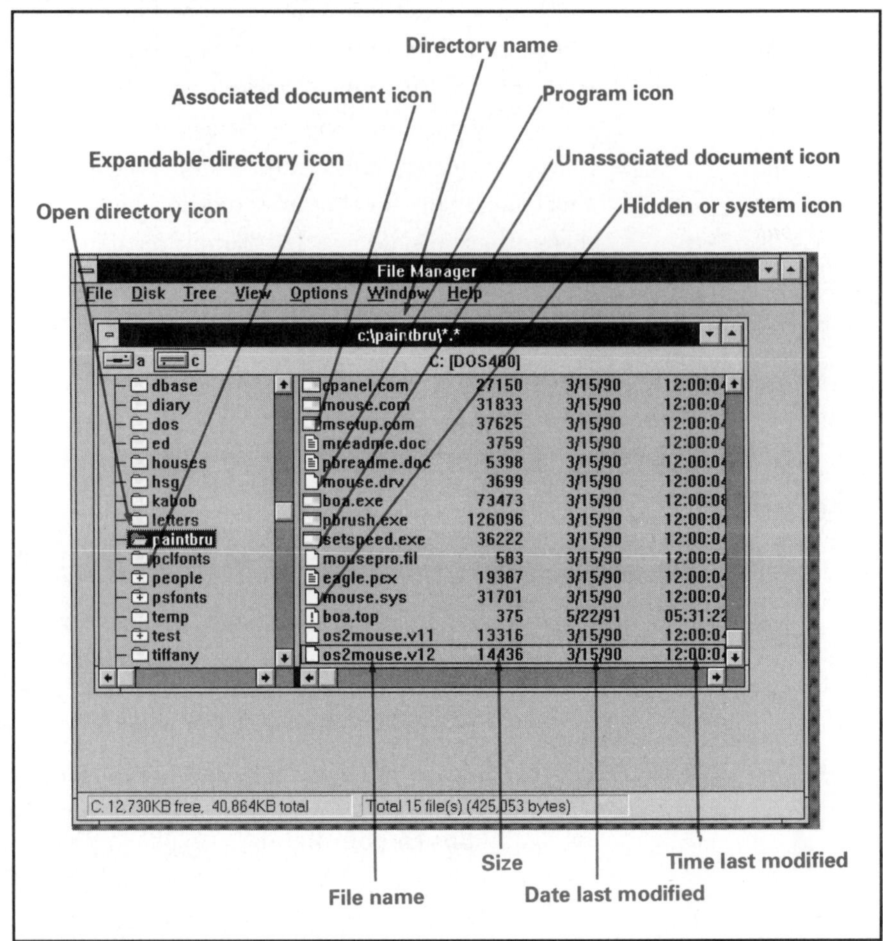

FIGURE 4.4:

A typical File Manager display, with a directory folder icon open and all file details visible

Here are the icon types and what each represents:

Icon	File Type
	Directory files. These will open a Directory Window when clicked on.
	Program and batch files. These will run when clicked on.

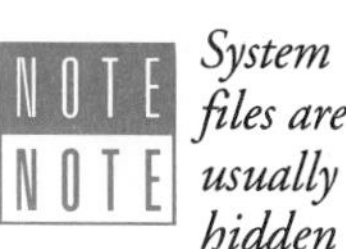

System files are usually hidden and constitute the operating system for your computer. Deleting or moving them can render your system inoperable. Hidden files that aren't system files are often created by other programs for their own use. Only delete them if you have deleted the application that uses them.

Icon	File Type
	Document files that have an association. These will open and run the program that created them at the same time.
	System or hidden files. Unless you turn on the option to show system or hidden files, these will not be listed in your contents window.
	All other files. Double-clicking on these will do nothing except get you an error message.

Modifying a Directory Listing to Show Specific Information

Normally the file pane shows all the files in the directory with as little information about each as possible. You just see the file name and an icon. If you want to see more detailed information about the files, including files' names, sizes, attributes, and last modification date or some other combination of these, you can opt to do so. The View menu has three commands to help out:

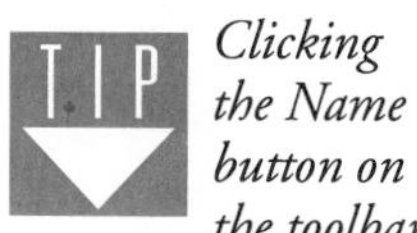

Clicking the Name button on the toolbar is a shortcut for displaying only file names. Clicking the All Details button shows all the details.

Name lists only the name and icon of each file. Use this setting to see the greatest number of files in the window. As you can see in Figure 4.5, Windows packs in three times as many files this way than when all the information is displayed. This is the default setting.

All File Details lists all the data (name, size, date and time of last modification, and attributes).

Partial Details lets you set various options from the dialog box shown in Figure 4.6. The choices are self-explanatory. File attributes are Read Only, System, Hidden, and Archive. (These are covered below, in "Changing File Attributes.") Once you have the settings you need, clicking on OK will save the setup, and the File Manager will use it to display directories until you change it.

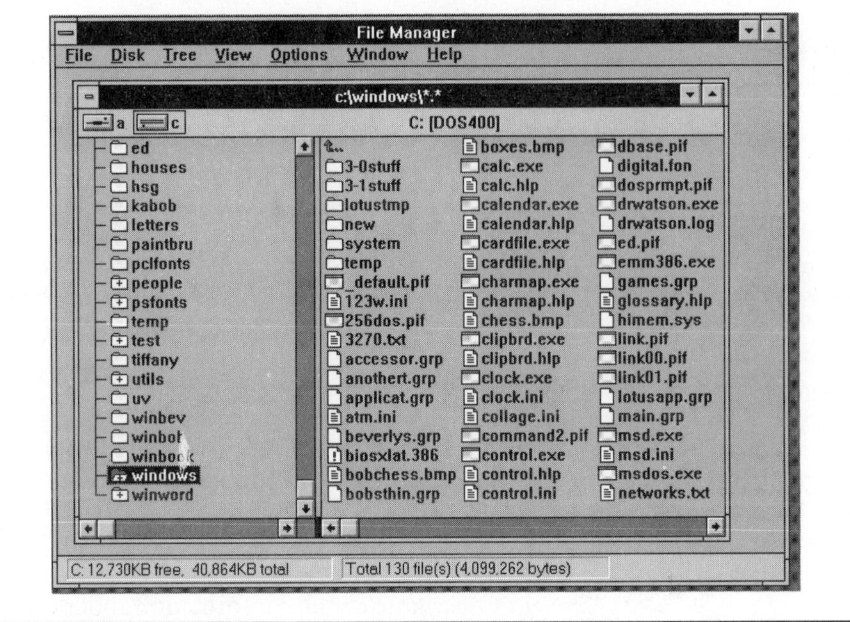

FIGURE 4.5:

Choosing View ➤ Name packs the maximum number of files on the screen.

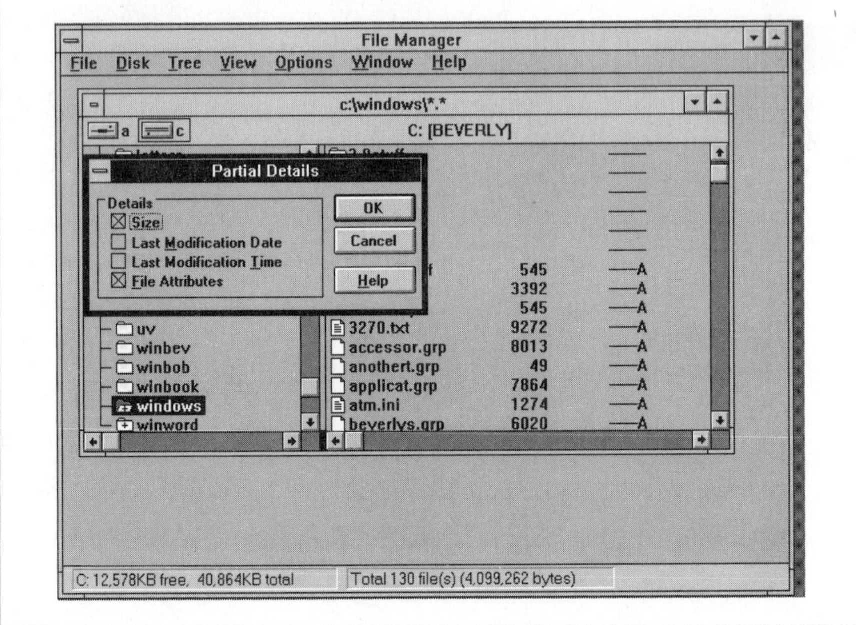

FIGURE 4.6:

Show file size and attributes for the Windows directory by choosing View ➤ Partial Details and setting them on.

Sorting the Directory Listing

TO SORT A DIRECTORY LISTING,

open the View menu and choose which way you want to sort (by name, type, size, or modification date).

Normally the directory contents are alphabetically sorted according to their names, with directories listed first and files following them. Using the View menu, you can elect to sort on the basis of other information. For example, Figure 4.7 shows the files in the Zip directory sorted by type, meaning by file extension (the last three letters after the period in the file's name).

Notice that when sorting by type, the file names are alphabetized within each extension, and extensions that start with numbers appear before letter extensions.

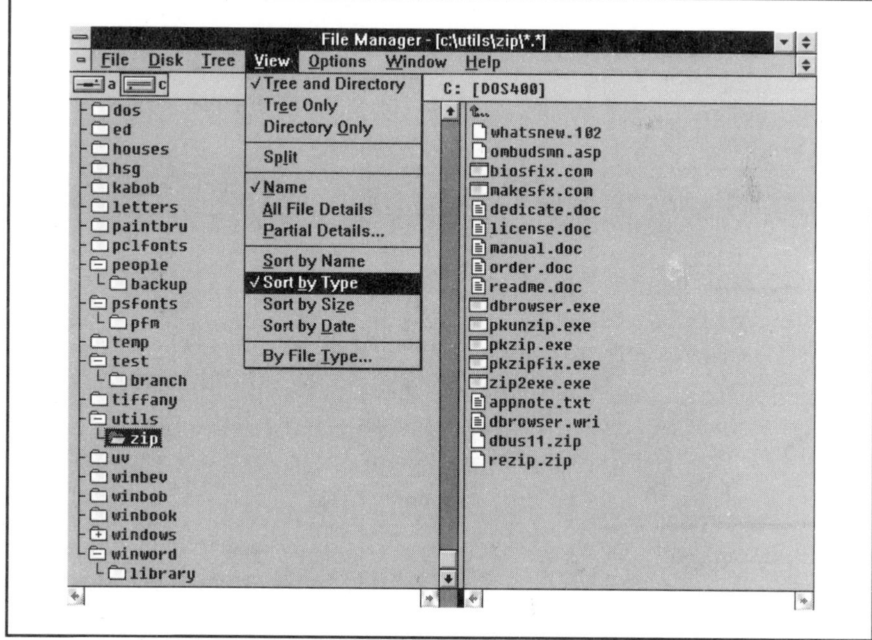

FIGURE 4.7: *See all the files in a directory by extension by choosing View ➤ Sort by Type. Other Sort options organize directory contents accordingly.*

Whichever setting you choose will now apply to all directories you view until you change it, even in future sessions with the File Manager if you elect to save the settings when you exit (Options ➤ Save Settings on Exit).

SHOWING ONLY SPECIFIC FILES

TO SHOW SPECIFIC FILES,

choose View ➤ By File Type. Turn on the check boxes for file types to include, and/or type in a filter criterion in the Name text box.

You can choose to see only specific files in a directory window, temporarily hiding the rest. This is similar to specifying wildcards for a file name when using the DOS DIR command. For example, at the DOS prompt you might type the following command to see all the executable program files:

```
DIR *.EXE
```

Or, as another example, you might type

```
DIR 198?.WK3
```

to see all files with 198 as the first three of four characters and .wk3 as the extension. Or you might type

```
DIR ACCOUNTS.WK3
```

to look for a file with this exact name. (If the asterisk and question mark in the above examples leave you in the dark, read "Using Wildcards to Limit File Listings" below to learn more about them.)

With Windows, these same DOS rules for listing files apply. The only difference is that you use a dialog box instead of entering the command at the DOS prompt. Also, as a convenience, the dialog box has the most common options included as check boxes. This means you won't have to enter the most common extensions. To limit a directory listing, follow these steps:

1. Choose View ➤ By File Type. The dialog box shown below appears.

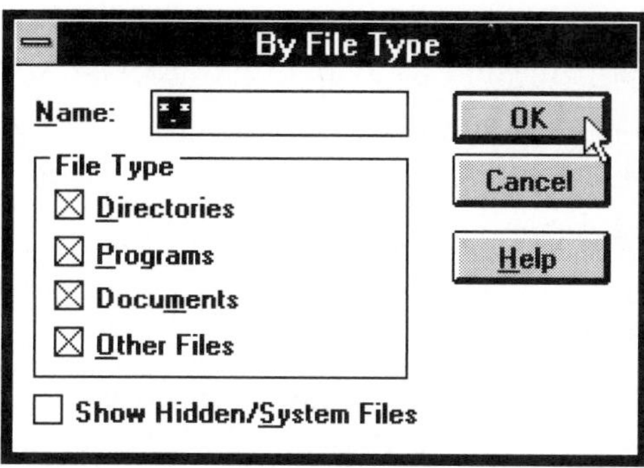

2. Normally all four File Type boxes are checked, meaning that all files (except hidden and system files) are shown. Leave an × next to only the types of files you want to see, and click on OK.

Using Wildcards to Limit File Listings

In displaying or searching for files, the * and ? wildcards can be quite useful in limiting the files you want the computer to show you. When you specify particular parameters for file names, you are in essence putting a filter on the file names to help the computer identify what you don't want it to find or show. (The computer filters out any files that don't satisfy the parameters you've specified with your wildcards.)

These wildcards follow standard DOS conventions. File names are divided in two: the name on the left side of the period that identifies its contents and the extension on the right side that identifies what type of file it is. An * represents all characters to the right of it and a ? replaces a single character. Be aware that you can only have an * *and* a ? on the same side of the file name if the ? is to the left of the *.

In the above examples, ***.EXE** means that you want to see all the .EXE type files, regardless of what program they are for. If you were to specify **ACCOUNTS.***, you would see a list of all the files about ACCOUNTS on your disk, whether text, graphics, Lotus 1-2-3 worksheets, or otherwise. The file specification **198?.WK3** will bring up all Lotus 1-2-3 worksheet files for the years 1980 through 1989, or any variation that you may have used when naming the files. You can use as many question marks as you need to define your needs accurately, but you can only use one * on each side of the file name.

Here are a few more examples. To see all the files with three letters in their first name and ws as an extension, you would type **???.WS**. Type *. to see all files with no extension. Like the ?, the * can also be used in combination with other letters or numbers. To see all correspondence to people whose names begin with *P*, type **P*.LTR**. Finally, *.* equates to all files.

Entering Your Own Criteria

NOTE *These settings will now apply to all directories you select. To select different files in another directory, change the By File Type settings again.*

Sometimes you'll want to limit a directory listing to a very specific subset of files. It's likely that the choices in the dialog box are too general for this. So, you just type in the DOS filter as you would if you were using the DIR command from the DOS prompt. The file manager will only display files with names that meet the filter criteria:

1. Type the file name or wildcard filter into the Name portion of the dialog box.
2. Set the four File Type check boxes on, unless you want to eliminate some groups of files from the listing. If you want hidden or system files to show as well, set that box on.
3. Click on OK. The listing will be updated, and the window's title bar will reflect the current file filter. (If the contents listing doesn't seem to change to reflect your settings, choose Window ➤ Refresh or press F5.)

Figure 4.8 shows the file pane listing just the help files (files with the extension .HLP). This was obtained by entering ***.HLP** into the Name area of the By File Type dialog box.

If when viewing a directory listing you ever notice that a multitude of files have suddenly disappeared, don't panic. You probably limited the listing via View ➤ By File Type command. Look at the drive window's title bar. It should read *.*. If it doesn't, select the command again, make sure the Name line reads *.*, and check the four check boxes (or five if you want to include hidden/system file types). All files should be displayed again.

FIGURE 4.8:

This directory window shows only Windows files with the extension .HLP because *.HLP *was typed into the Name section of the View* ➤ *By File Type dialog box, as shown.*

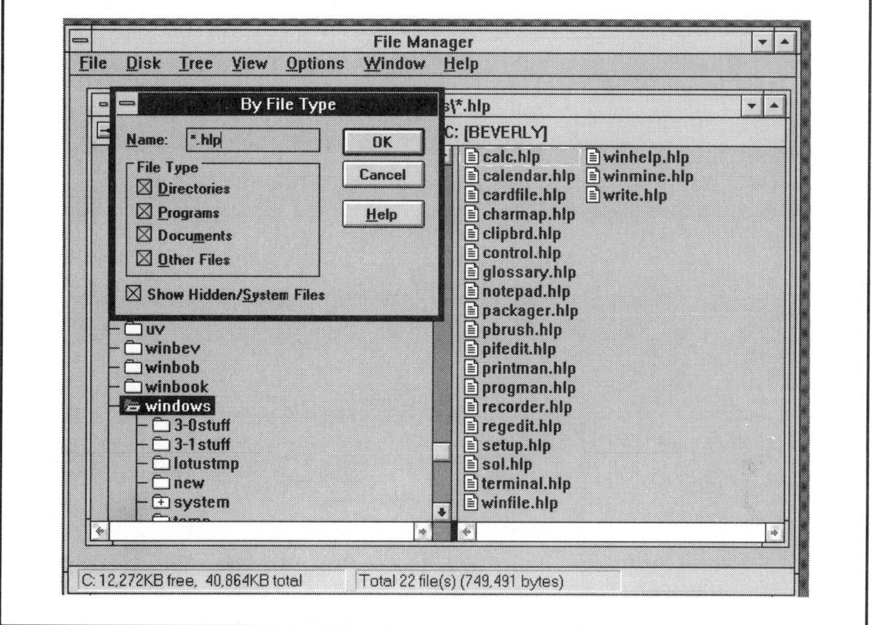

VIEWING MORE THAN ONE DIRECTORY AT A TIME

There are two ways to select a drive to display its directory contents. Each way yields a different result. The first leaves only one window open and replaces its contents with the new information when you select a new drive or directory. The other opens additional windows for each drive. There are advantages to each.

The first method eliminates clutter by keeping unnecessary windows from filling up your screen. But having more than one window open at a time lets you copy and move files between directories and drives with less effort.

To open additional drive windows, either double-click on the drive icon of your choice or choose Window ➤ New Window. New Window brings up a second window identical to the first one. You can then change the drive or directory by the usual means.

Open as many windows as you wish. The title bar of each displays the selected drive, directory, and whether a file-selection filter is in use (i.e., the file type). If multiple windows have the same directory selected, the title bar information will be followed by a number.

Choose Window ➤ Tile (Shift-F4) or Window ➤ Cascade (Shift-F5) to tile or stack your windows (see Figure 4.9).

If you expect to need quick access to each drive window later, adjust the windows to a usable size, then iconize them. The next time you double-click them, they'll pop up in the size and location in which you left them.

FIGURE 4.9: *You can have multiple directory listings on the screen at once. After opening the windows, choose Window ➤ Tile to arrange them neatly.*

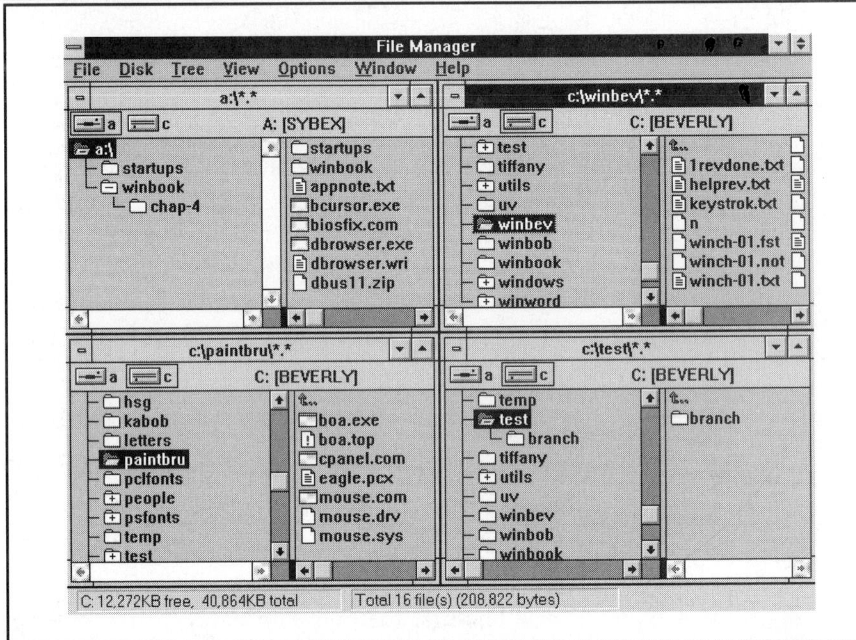

Refreshing the Directory

TO REFRESH THE SCREEN,

press F5.

Sometimes other programs will affect the contents of a drive window that's open. For example, you might switch to a program window and edit a file that's also displayed in the current drive window, changing its size (in bytes). Normally Windows will take care of this type of situation, updating the information in the current drive window after it senses that another program has altered one of its files. However, there are times when this doesn't happen reliably. Particularly when you are connected to a network, Windows may have trouble detecting that a directory's contents have changed. This will also be an issue if you change floppy disks and want to see the directory of the new disk. If you suspect that a directory may have been changed in some way that isn't reflected in the directory pane, just press F5 or choose the Window ➤ Refresh command.

Searching for a Specific File

As hard disk storage capacities have skyrocketed in recent years, looking for a specific file when you can't remember where you put it can be a real headache. If you have a lot of directories, opening each one and examining the files can take a ridiculous amount of time. Even in DOS, the DIR command is no help, since you have to keep switching directories and retyping the command. Some utility programs such as Norton's FileFind are real time savers if you're using DOS. But what about within Windows? Well, the Microsoft people were thoughtful enough to build such a utility into the File Manager—only it's superior to FileFind because the files it finds are plopped into a window that you can keep on the screen or iconize for later access. Here's how to use it:

SPEED TIP *To search the entire drive, click in the tree pane and press Home before you choose File ➤ Search. (Home always returns you to the top of the active drive window.)*

1. Select File ➤ Search. The dialog box shown in Figure 4.10 appears.
2. Type in the name of the file you're looking for. Use wildcards if you want. (To review wildcards, see "Using Wildcards to Limit File Listings" earlier in this section.)
3. Fill in the Start From line. As a default, the search starts from the current (highlighted) directory. This is like switching to a directory in DOS with the CD command before issuing a DIR command.
4. If you want to search down all the subordinate branches from the current directory to the end of the branch, click the Search All Subdirectories check box.

5. If you want to search the whole disk, check the Search All Subdirectories box and enter \ into the Start From line.
6. Click on OK. Windows will conduct the search on the current disk (floppy or hard) and display its search results in a new window called Search Results (see Figure 4.10). If the File Manager status bar is on, it will tell you how many files were found. If no files were found, a message to that effect will appear on the screen. To cancel a search in progress press Esc.

Windows helps you fill in the Search dialog box with whatever is selected in your active File Manager window. The selected directory will be in the Start Search From text box and the extension of any selected file will be in the Search For text box.

Your Search Results window is like any other window (you can tile it, iconize it, move it around, resize it, and so on). You can also think of it as any file pane—you can move, copy, delete, and rename files, and you can perform these and other actions the same way you do from the drive windows. However, if you exit File Manager, the Search Results window will not

FIGURE 4.10:

You can search for a file using the File ➤ Search command. The results of the search are displayed in a Search Results window.

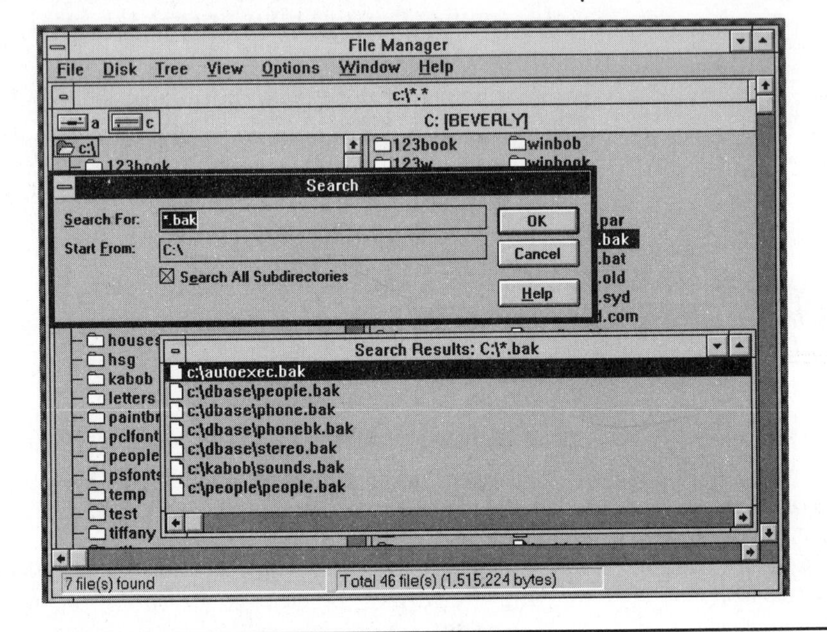

be saved. Therefore, if you want to return to it later, instead of closing File Manager, just iconize it, and your search results will not be lost.

The next time you conduct a search, the Search Results window's contents will be erased and then replaced with the new search results.

Selecting Files in a Directory Pane

Now let's return to the regular directory pane. Before you can work with the files in a directory, you have to select one or more of them. As with other objects in Windows, you select files by highlighting them. Here are various methods of selecting (and deselecting) files:

To Select One File

Click once on the file. Notice that the status line (the last line in the File Manager window) indicates that one file is selected.

To Select More Than One File

1. Click on the first file to select.
2. Press the Ctrl key and hold it down.
3. Click on each additional file you want to select.

To Select a Group of Consecutive Files

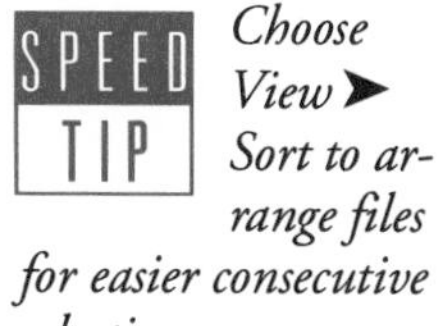

Choose View ➤ Sort to arrange files for easier consecutive selecting.

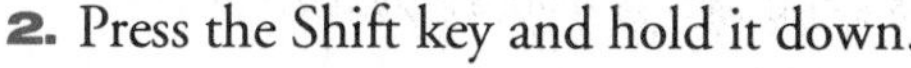

1. Click on the first file in the series.
2. Press the Shift key and hold it down.
3. Move to the bottom of the group you want to select and click again. All the files between the first and last click will be selected.

To Select Several Groups of Consecutive Files

1. Select the first group as described above.
2. To select the second group, hold down the Ctrl key and click on the first file in the second group.
3. Press the Shift and Ctrl keys simultaneously and click on the last file in the second group. Repeat Steps 2 and 3 for each additional group.

Figure 4.11 shows three groups of files selected in this way.

To Select All the Files in a Directory

1. Choose File ➤ Select Files.
2. From the Select Files dialog box, choose Select with the File(s) space set to *.*.

SPEED TIP *If all the files you want to select have similar names, use the Search command to find them. Then select them in the Search Results window.*

To Select Particular Files

The File ➤ Select Files command provides a way to select specific files in a directory. Just as in the Search dialog box, you can use wildcards, extensions, or file names to filter your selections:

1. Choose File ➤ Select Files.
2. Enter appropriate file information in the File(s) text box.
3. Choose Select.

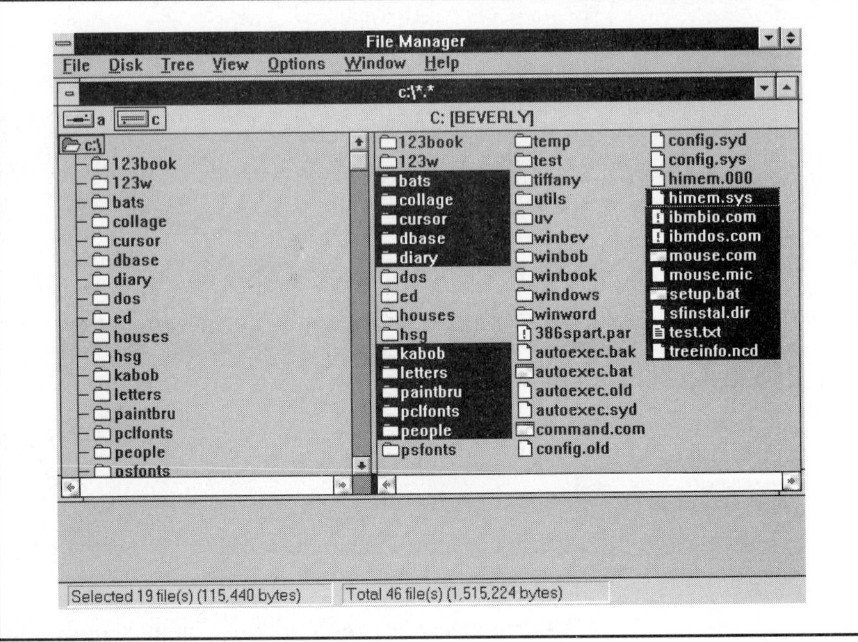

FIGURE 4.11: *You can select several nonconsecutive groups of files*

To Deselect File(s)

- To deselect all the files currently selected, either click on a single file (release the Shift key first) or choose File ➤ Select Files ➤ Deselect with *.* in the File(s) space.
- To deselect a single file from a group of selected files, hold down the Ctrl key and click on the file again.
- To deselect files with a common element, choose File ➤ Select Files ➤ Deselect with the appropriate file information entered in the File(s) space.

Once highlighted, a file or group of files can be operated on via the mouse or the commands in the File menu. Open the File menu and you will see the commands shown in Figure 4.12. Here's what each one does (a few are not explained here because they are discussed elsewhere):

> **Open** opens a document file, such as a letter, report, or worksheet, by running the program associated with it, and then opening the document itself. You can also open a document by double-clicking

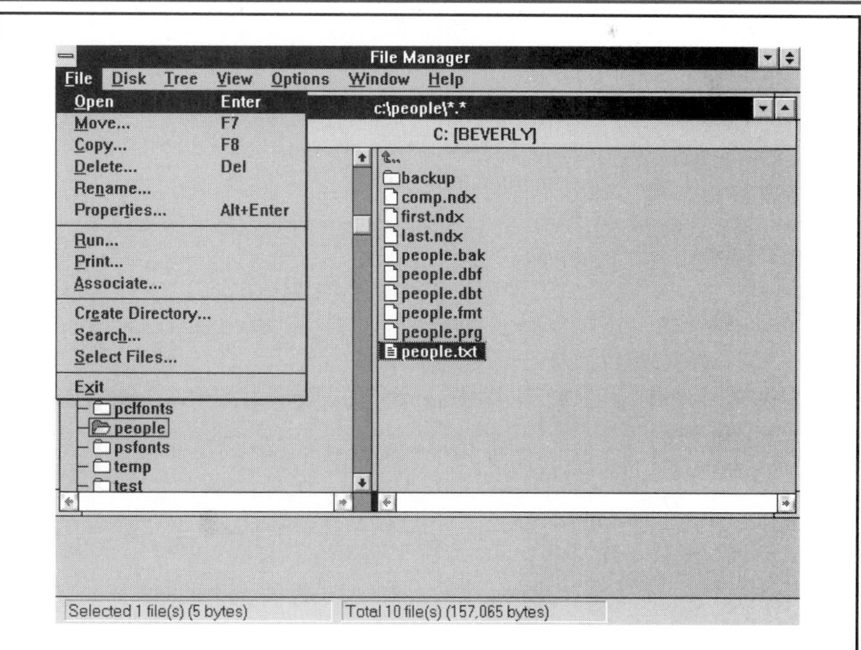

FIGURE 4.12: *To work with a file, select it by clicking on it, then open the File menu. Notice the status line, which indicates the number of files selected and total size of the selected file(s).*

it. Except for the supplied Windows programs, this requires setting up an association first (discussed later in this chapter). If the file is a program, this runs the program. The file must be a program file (with a .BAT, .EXE, .COM, or .PIF extension).

Move moves file(s) to another directory or drive.

Copy copies file(s) to another directory or drive.

Delete deletes selected file(s).

Rename renames selected file(s).

Properties sets the DOS file flags for selected file(s). Flags are explained below in the section titled "Changing File Attributes."

Run presents a dialog box into which you can type a program name (with a .BAT, .EXE, .COM, or .PIF extension). This is like typing a program name from the DOS prompt.

Print prints text files. Use it only with ASCII files, such as those created by Notepad.

Associate tells Windows what application a document was created with. The program will then be run when you open the document. (This command is discussed next.)

Create Directory creates a subdirectory under the selected root or directory.

Search searches a drive and/or directory for files that you specify by name or using wildcards.

Select Files selects directory files by name or per wildcard specifications.

About Associations

TO CREATE AN ASSOCIATION,

1. **Select a file that has the extension in question.**
2. **Choose File ➤ Associate.**
3. **Enter the name (and path) of the program to associate with the extension.**

An *association* is simply a way of telling Windows what program to run for each type of file extension. For example, if you click on a file that has a .CRD extension, Windows will run the Cardfile program (CARDFILE.EXE) and open the file you clicked on. There is already an association made up for .CRD files and stored in the Windows program, which is why it works. But you can make up your own associations. For example, say you use lots of Lotus 1-2-3 files. Many 1-2-3 files have the extension .WK3. You can set up an association that tells Windows "when I click on a .WK3 file, run Lotus 1-2-3 and open the file I clicked on."

Obviously the trick to using associations is to have a consistent system for your files' extensions. Not all programs require specific extensions, so you may have to impose your own rules. For example, I never use extensions on my word-processing files—I just keep them in separate directories, one for each program. To use an association, I'd have to start adding some unique extension to my file names. I could use .WS for my WordStar files, .PCW for my PC-Write files, and so on.

Default Associations

These are the most important associations that are already set up:

FILE EXTENSION	ASSOCIATED PROGRAM
.CRD	Cardfile
.CAL	Calendar
.CLP	Clipboard
.HLP	Help
.TRM	Terminal
.TXT	Notepad
.INI	Notepad (these files are used by Windows)
.WRI	Write
.REC	Recorder
.BMP	Paint

All associated files are assigned a special icon (called a *document icon*) in the directory windows so that you can see which documents can be opened just by double-clicking them. The icon is a lined page with a bent corner.

Creating an Association

To actually set up an association you just perform the following steps once. It will then affect all documents, data files, etc., with the same extension:

1. Open a directory that contains a file for which you want to make an association.
2. Single-click on any file that has the extension in question. (If you double-click, you'll get an error message saying that there isn't an association for that type of file.)
3. Choose File ➤ Associate. A dialog box will appear (see Figure 4.13). Enter the exact name and path of the program that you want to run when you double-click this type of file. (If your PATH command in your AUTOEXEC.BAT file contains the directory the program is in, you can omit the directory.)

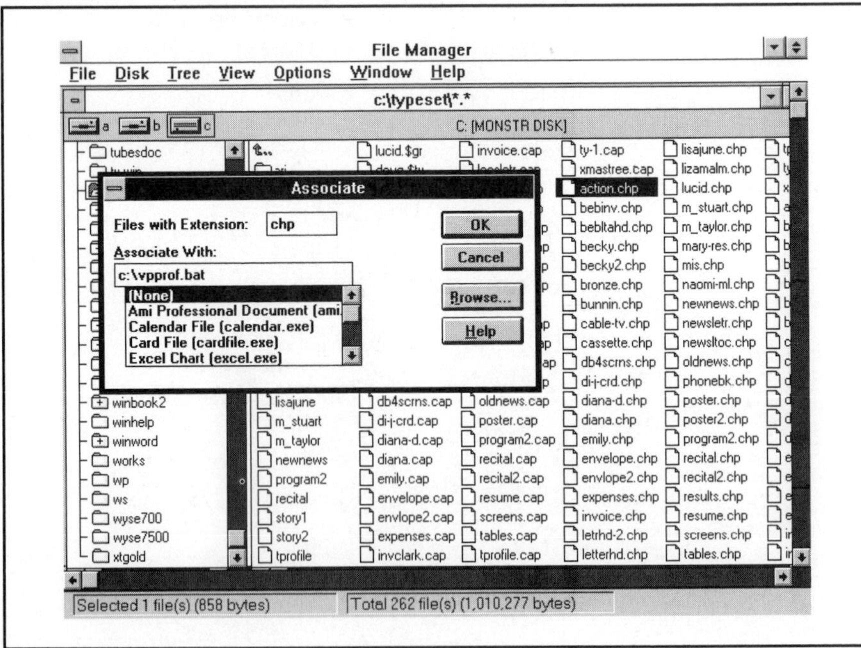

FIGURE 4.13: *Creating an association. This setup links all .CHP files with Ventura Publisher. After this, when any .CHP file is double-clicked, Windows will run VPPROF.BAT, which tells Ventura to open the selected document.*

In Figure 4.13, I've created an association between .CHP files and Ventura Publisher Professional. Since Ventura uses a batch file in the root directory to start up, I've used the name of the batch file as the file with which to associate my .CHP files.

OPENING DOCUMENTS FROM THE FILE MANAGER

Once documents are associated with applications, you can open them easily from the File Manager. Simply double-click the file name or icon in a directory pane. Windows will run the application and open the document in a window. If the program can't run in a window and requires full-screen mode, the File Manager will disappear until you exit the program.

If a document doesn't have an association, you can still tell Windows to open it. However it's a little tricky. Here are the steps:

1. Open the directory containing the document.
2. Open the directory containing the application program (if they're not both in the same directory).
3. If you have two windows open, adjust them so that both their contents can be seen.
4. Drag the document's icon to the application's icon, as shown in Figure 4.14, and release the mouse.

A dialog box will ask you to confirm the action (see Figure 4.16). In this instance I dragged the document WINCH-01.FST into ED.EXE (PC-Write):

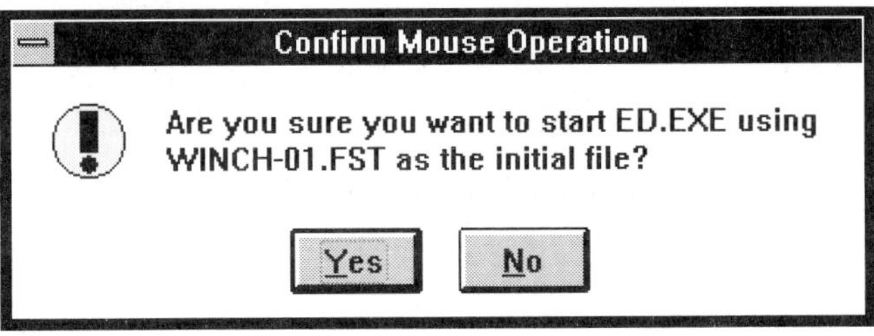

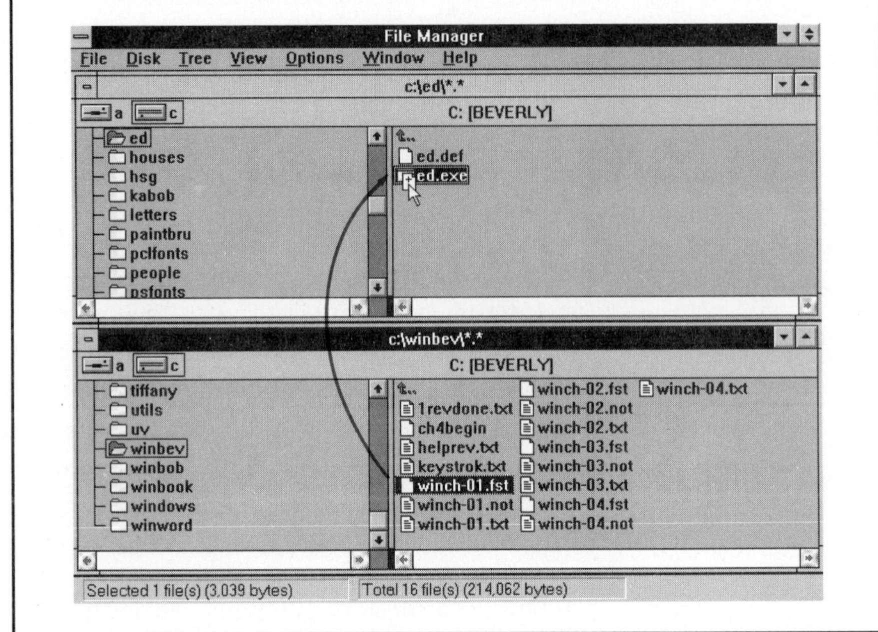

FIGURE 4.14: *To run a program and open a document at the same time, drag the document icon into the application icon.*

File Manager now has a feature that allows you to view files by dragging an icon into an open application window. See Chapter 16 for more about how this works.

Running Programs from the File Manager

As mentioned earlier, you can run programs directly from the File Manager. You do not have to return to the Program Manager to bring up a DOS prompt or create a program icon. This is most useful for occasionally running a program that you don't use often. Here are two ways to run programs:

- Double-click on the program name. It should be an .EXE, .COM, .PIF, or .BAT extension.
- Choose File ➤ Run. Type the name of the program into the dialog box. Include the path name if it's not part of your system's PATH command. (But always include the extension.)

PRINTING FROM THE FILE MANAGER

You can print many types of files from the File Manager. When you print this way, the File ➤ Print command runs the application, loads the selected file, and executes the application's Print command, sending the selected file to the Window's Print Manager, which handles the printing.

There are a few advantages to this approach. It makes printing very easy—you just drag the file(s) into the Print Manager icon or window and printing commences. But the file must have an association, or this technique won't work. (Even then, not all applications support this technique for printing.)

You may also find that you have more control over your hard copy if you print using the source application's File menu, since some applications let you set print options (such as headers and footers, landscape or portrait page orientation, etc.) before you print. Printing from File Manager gives you no options other than convenience.

To print from the File Manager:

1. Select the file you want to print.
2. Choose File ➤ Print. A dialog box appears with the file's name typed in, as you can see in Figure 4.15. Change it if you want to, and then click on OK.

The file(s) will be sent to the Print Manager, from where it is spooled—a process wherein printing is done behind the scenes, letting you get back to work. (The Print Manager and spooler are covered in detail in Chapters 6 and 7.)

There is a shortcut method of printing files from the File Manager: you can drop a file's icon onto the Print Manager icon or window. Here's how it's done:

1. Run the Print Manager by double-clicking its icon from the Main group.
2. Size the File Manager and Print Manager windows so they are both visible on the Desktop.
3. Drag the file(s) you want to print into the Print Manager window. (When the file leaves the File Manager window it will turn into the international "no can do" symbol—a circle with a diagonal line through it—but when it makes it to the Print Manager, it returns to a normal document icon.) When the document icon is

FIGURE 4.15: *Printing a file from the File Manager*

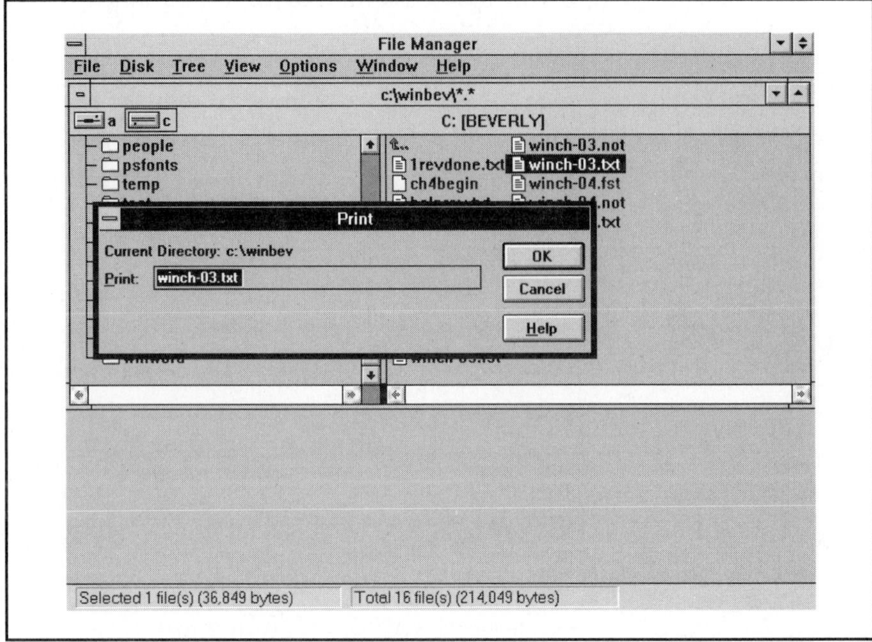

positioned over the Print Manager, it has a plus sign in it. This indicates that the document is being copied into the Print Manager, rather than being moved.

4. Release the mouse button. The application that is associated with the document will open with the document loaded in a window (e.g., if the file is a .DOC file, Microsoft Word will run and open the .DOC file). Then the application's print dialog box will pop up momentarily and a small window will report that the file is printing.

Moving Files

TO MOVE A FILE TO A DIFFERENT DIRECTORY,

drag its icon to the directory in the tree window.

Sometimes you'll want to move a file or group of files from one directory to another. Once again, this process is normally a real pain if you are using the DOS prompt, which requires you to copy the files to the new directory and then erase the old ones.

The File Manager makes this potentially tedious task a breeze. You select the files to be moved and then drag them as a group to the new destination. (Keep in mind that *moving* is not *copying*. After the operation, there is still only one copy of the files you've moved—they're just in a new location.)

The new destination can be an open window, an iconized window, a folder in the tree pane, a disk-drive icon in the drive window, or a group icon or window in the Program Manager. You've got a lot of choices. The rule of thumb is this: If you want to move it, try selecting it and dragging it to the new location. If Windows can't do it, you'll be told, but the chances are good that you can drag a file or a directory to almost any icon or window.

Here are the general steps for moving files around:

1. Open the directory containing the file you want to move.
2. Adjust your display so that an icon, folder, or window of the destination is visible. Maximizing and/or tiling the windows can make this easier.
3. Select the file you want to move.
4. Drag it to the destination icon, folder, or window. As you do so, the icon will disappear from the original location and the mouse pointer will change to a document icon. (If you're moving more than one file, the icon will look like a stack of three little pages.)
5. Release the mouse button. You'll see a dialog box asking you to confirm that you want to move the files, as shown below.
6. Click Yes to complete the move.

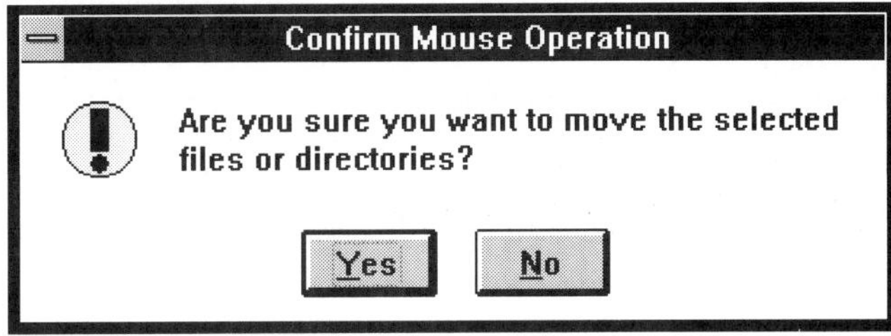

If you attempt to move files between drives without holding down the Alt key, Windows will assume that you only want to *copy* them. In that case, a plus sign will appear in the file icon when it's dragged beyond its window and into the new drive window.

Moving Directories

The File Manager lets you move complete directories or directory branches. When you move a directory, all the files in the directory are automatically moved.

You can select the directory to be moved either from the tree pane or from the directory (file) pane. Just drag the directory's folder from either pane to the new destination:

- When you move a directory to another directory, Windows adds it below the destination directory.
- When you move a directory from one drive into another drive's icon, it gets added below the current directory in the destination drive.

More often than not, people want to move directories around on the same drive, a bit like rearranging their living-room furniture. This is extremely easy with the File Manager. After using this feature, you'll wonder how you ever did without it:

1. Select the directory you want to move (in either pane) and drag it to its new location. As you slide the mouse over its possible targets, a line forms around the target, indicating where the directory will land if you release the mouse button.
2. When you release the mouse button, the directory will be added as a subdirectory one level below the destination directory (and any subdirectories will be arrayed below it as before).

Moving Multiple Directories Simultaneously

You can move the contents of more than one directory at a time, but unless they are connected by a descending branch you have to do this from a directory (file) pane, not from the tree pane. For example, suppose you wanted directories One, Two, and Three to be subdirectories under a directory called Four. You could do this by dragging one directory at a time as explained above. But it's faster to do it in one fell swoop. Select directories One, Two, and Three in the directory pane. Drag them as a group to Four in the tree pane. Figure 4.16 shows one way of doing this and the resulting dialog box. Figure 4.17 shows the change to the directory tree. Notice that directories One, Two, and Three were added under Four as subdirectories. Unless you change the confirmation settings, File Manager asks you to confirm your actions before actually moving the directories.

Entering the Destination from the Keyboard

Sometimes just typing in the name of the destination is easier than dragging the files and directory icons around, especially if you're fast at the keyboard. With this technique, the destination does not have to be visible. Just select the source files or directories and choose File ➤ Move. Type the name of the destination drive and directory into the dialog box that appears. Figure 4.18 shows an example of this. Notice that if multiple files are selected, the From box lists them all, end to end, with a space separating the names. You can

FIGURE 4.16:

Dragging multiple directories into a destination directory. The source directories will become subdirectories of the destination directory.

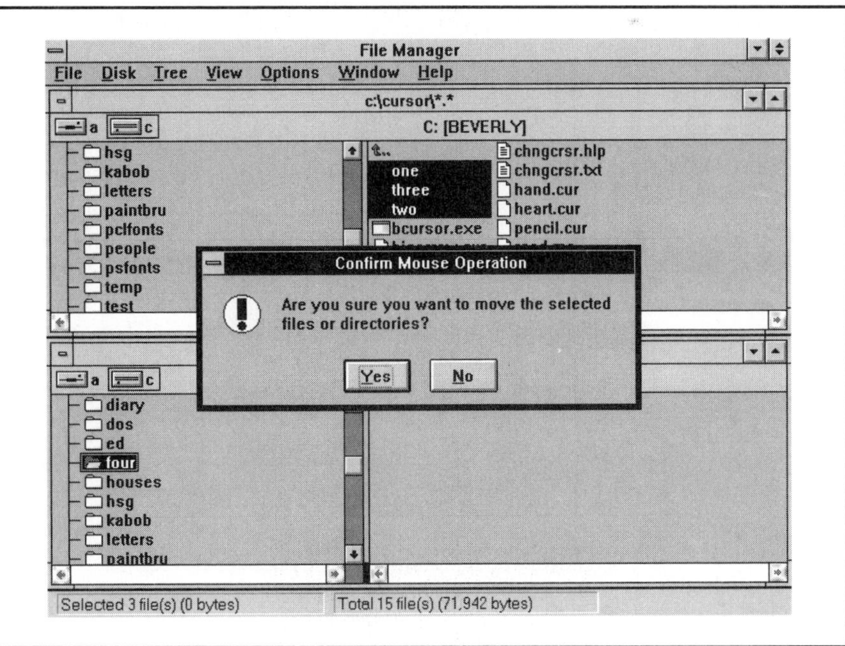

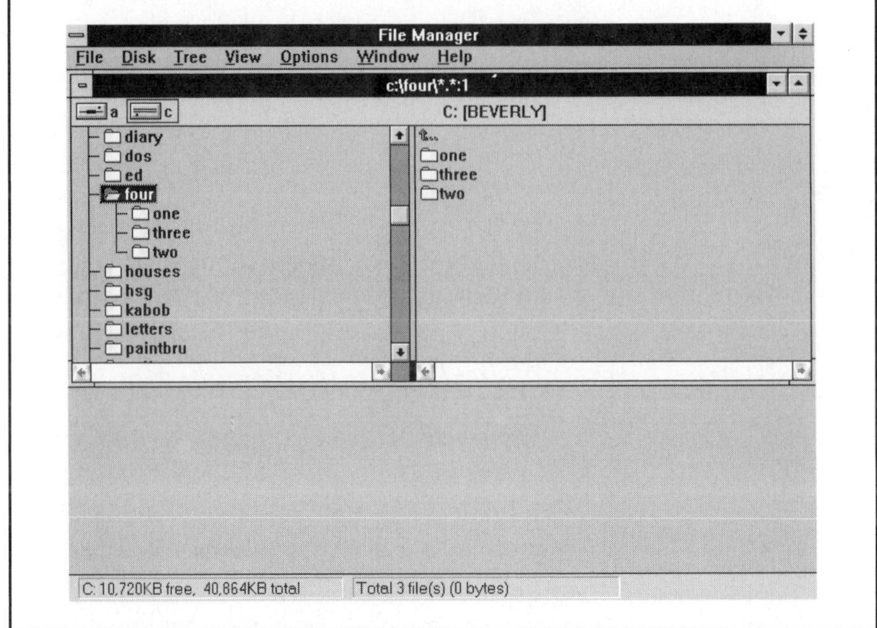

FIGURE 4.17:

The result of moving directories One, Two, and Three into directory Four. Notice the altered directory tree.

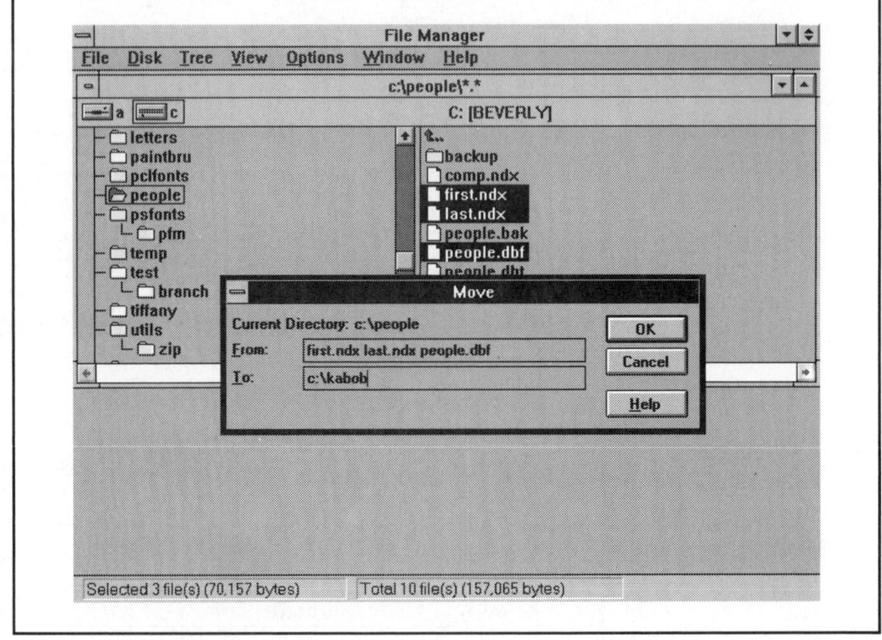

FIGURE 4.18:

You can use the Move command to move files. This is sometimes easier than setting up the screen to accommodate the dragging technique of file moving. Simply select the files, choose File ➤ Move, and type in the destination directory.

type in more names this way, or leave the From line alone. When moving a directory, remember that it will be added below the destination directory.

Moving Files and Directories to another Disk Drive

TO MOVE A FILE/DIRECTORY TO ANOTHER DRIVE,

1. **Select the file/directory.**
2. **Hold down the Alt key.**
3. **Drag the selection to the drive icon.**

Moving files and directories to another disk drive can be done several ways:

- Open windows for the source and destination drives, then drag the directories or files from one to the other.
- Select the source files or directory(s), choose File ➤ Move and type in the destination drive and directory.
- Select the source files or directory(s) and drag them into the destination drive icon as described below.

You can drag selected files or directories to another drive using the drive icons at the top of the drive window. The File Manager will use the current directory of the target drive as the final destination. To do this:

1. Select the files or directories.
2. Hold down the Alt key, since you're moving them to another drive.
3. Drag them into the destination drive icon. If you're moving the directories or files to a floppy drive, make sure you have a formatted disk in the drive, or you will get an error messsage.
4. A dialog box will ask if you want to move the items. Click Yes. (If the dialog box asks about copying (not moving), you forgot to hold down the Alt key. Click on No and try again.)
5. After you move a directory, the File Manager asks if you want to delete the original. When moving files, you are not asked this (they are just deleted).

When you are moving files about, particularly to a floppy, there may not be enough room on the floppy for all the source files. File Manager shows you how many bytes you've got selected in the status bar of its window. When you click on the drive window for the floppy, the status bar tells you how much room is left on it. So, if you open one window for the floppy and one for the hard disk directory you're copying from, you can switch back and forth between the two to make sure you aren't going to run out of space during the moving process. Figure 4.19 shows one possible setup.

Copying Files

TO COPY A FILE,

1. **Select the item.**
2. **Hold down the Ctrl key.**
3. **Drag the selection to the destination.**

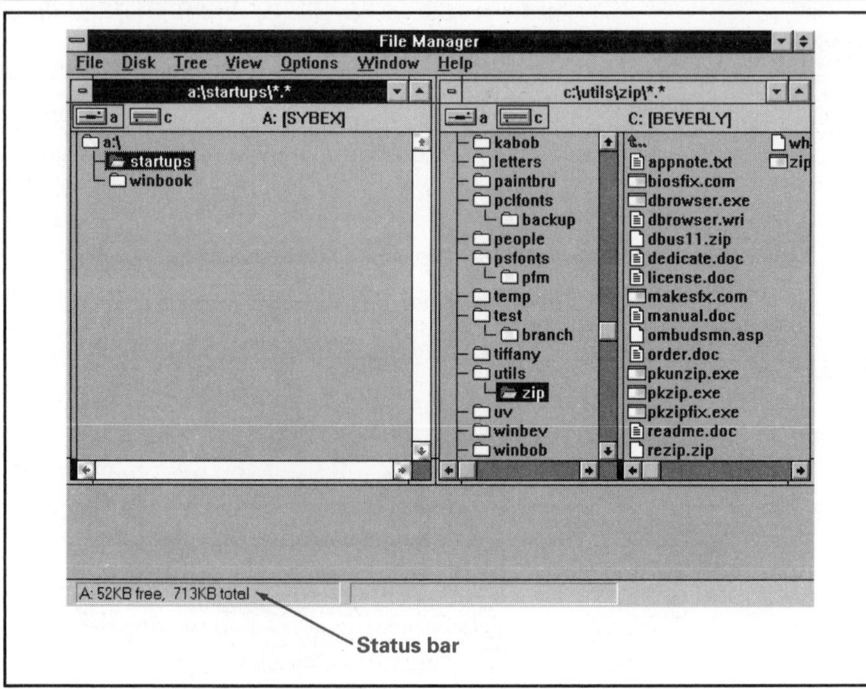

FIGURE 4.19: *Before moving (or copying) files to a floppy, make sure you have enough room. Check the status bar for the available space on the floppy and the total size of the files selected.*

Copying differs from moving in that it duplicates the items you're working with. Copying is often used for transferring files between computers, for installing software into your computer, or as a safety backup procedure. Making a copy of a file or directory ensures you have a backup in case of some catastrophe like spilling your morning cappuccino on the floppy containing your tax return spreadsheet (and it's April 15th) or on the Ph.D. dissertation you just spent five years researching. The other thing it protects you against is the ominous "hard-disk crash." That's when your hard disk inexplicably croaks, taking everything with it.

Though there are programs specifically designed to back up your entire hard disk in an efficient manner, the Copy command is useful enough for making backups of individual files.

Making the Copy

You can drag files into a Program Manager group to easily add a program or document icon to the group. The file must be a program or associated document. Arrange your screen so the destination icon or group window in the Program Manager is showing. Then drag the selected directory or files from File Manager into it.

Just as with moving, you can stipulate the source and destinations of items by selecting the Copy command. If you select the source items using the mouse, they'll be inserted into the From line. Then you just type in the To information.

You copy files and directories virtually the same way you move them (see the previous section), with a couple of exceptions:

1. Arrange the screen so that source and destination windows, icons, files, or drives are visible.
2. Select the item(s) to be copied.
3. Press the Ctrl key.
4. Drag the items to their destination drive, icon, window, or directory, and release.
5. Answer dialog boxes appropriately. Check the dialog box to make sure it says Copy, not Move. Make sure you see the correct destinations, too. If not, type in the changes or try again.

Copying a File to the Clipboard

You can copy a file from File Manager directly to the Clipboard so that it can be linked or embedded in another document. This procedure uses the Copy command. Here's how it's done:

1. Select the file you want to copy.
2. Choose File ➤ Copy or press F8.
3. In the Copy dialog box, click on Copy to Clipboard.
4. Click on OK.

Once you've followed the above steps, you can open the Clipboard Viewer to see the document (or see a note saying it can't be displayed). You can find Clipboard Viewer in the Main group of the Program Manager (unless you moved it). From the Edit menu of an appropriate application (one that can accept the file you just put on the Clipboard) you can then paste the file's contents into a document. (The Clipboard is covered in detail in Chapter 8, and Object Linking and Embedding is covered in Chapter 14.)

After any form of copying, the originals are left intact, so you don't have to worry about losing anything if you make a mistake. The only thing to worry about is copying a file on top of a file with the same name. File Manager will ask you if you want to overwrite the old file with the new one, unless you have turned off this confirmation message (see the next section).

Changing the Confirmation Settings

The File Manager has some safeguards against accidental erasure of files and directories. Usually it's a good idea to leave these settings as they are. Once you have more experience with the ways of the File Manager, though, you might want to change them so they don't nag you every time you want to overwrite an old file or delete a directory that has a bunch of subdirectories under it that you also want deleted:

1. Choose Options ➤ Confirmation.
2. The dialog box shown below appears. The Confirm On… settings have the following meanings:

   File Delete asks for okay to delete files.

Directory Delete asks for okay to delete directories.

File Replace asks for okay to overwrite an existing file.

Mouse Action asks for okay any time you attempt to copy, delete, or move files or directories with the mouse.

Disk Commands asks for okay to format or copy a disk.

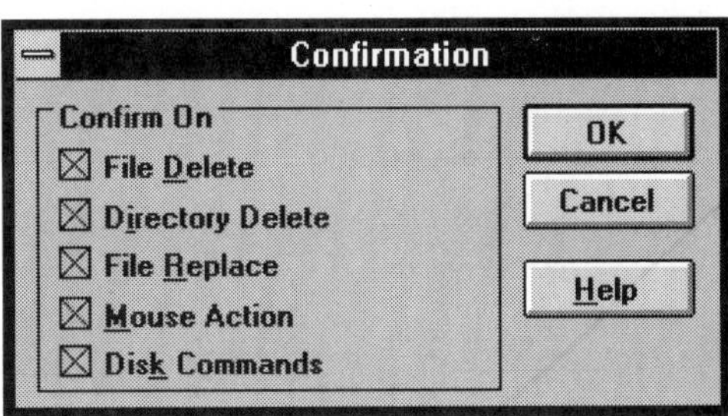

Deleting Files

Deleting files means erasing them! It's difficult to recover them after they're deleted. Delete a file by following these steps:

1. Select the file(s).
2. Press Del or choose File ➤ Delete. A dialog box appears.
3. Check the information in the box. If it's correct, click OK. If not, cancel it or change the information by typing in another file name. You can add a drive letter and path, just as with the DEL command in DOS.

Renaming Files and Directories

Renaming files is done in a manner similar to deleting. It simply changes the name of the file or directory selected. This command can also be used with directories:

1. Select the item to be renamed.
2. Choose File ➤ Rename. A dialog box appears.
3. Type in the new name and click on Rename.

CHANGING FILE ATTRIBUTES

Changing file attributes is easier with Windows than with DOS, by far. You simply select the files, open a dialog box and set the check boxes appropriately. The most common setting change for files is to set them to Read Only. Once this is set, nobody can accidentally erase or overwrite them.

Here's how to set the various attributes:

1. Select the file(s) whose attributes you want to alter.
2. Choose File ➤ Properties.

The following dialog box appears:

Check the boxes appropriately. Here are the meanings of the choices:

Read Only won't allow users to make changes to the file.

Archive indicates the file has been modified since the last backup. This is used by backup programs such as the DOS BACKUP command.

Hidden will hide the file from directory listings in DOS and directory windows in File Manager (unless you choose View ➤ By File Type ➤ Show Hidden).

System tells Windows and DOS that this is an operating system file. It will normally be hidden (unless you choose View ➤ By File Type ➤ Show System).

WORKING WITH DISKS

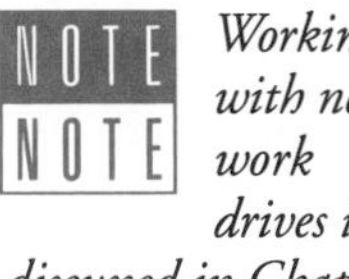

Working with network drives is discussed in Chapter 17.

The File Manager has a few features that apply specifically to managing your disks, particularly floppy disks. These commands make the process of formatting disks and copying disks a bit simpler. There's also a command for changing the volume label of a disk, the optional name that each floppy or hard disk can be assigned, typically for archival purposes.

FORMATTING DISKS AND MAKING SYSTEM DISKS

TO FORMAT A DISK,

place the disk in the drive and choose Disk ➤ Format Disk.

CAUTION *Formatting erases all data from the disk! Reversing the process is difficult if not impossible.*

What with the myriad disk capacities and sizes around these days, formatting a floppy disk can turn out to be quite an exercise in futility. The DOS manual is usually not much help either. There are enough options to the format command to choke a rhino. You might become a real fan of Windows just for its formatting command. Here's how to format a disk now:

1. Put the disk to be formatted in the floppy drive.
2. Choose Disk ➤ Format Disk.
3. The dialog box you see below appears. Use the drop-down lists to set the drive and disk capacity of the floppy.

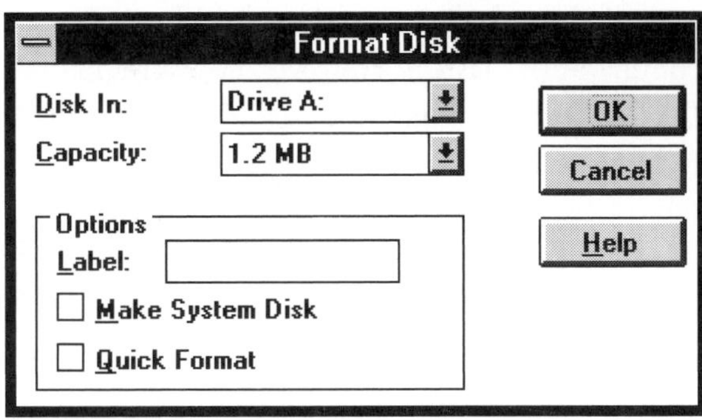

4. In the Options section of the box, you may give the disk a name by typing in a label. Then check on Make System Disk and/or Quick Format if appropriate. Select Make System Disk if you want the disk you're formatting to be able to boot up a computer from the A drive. The necessary hidden system files and COMMAND.COM will be copied to it during the formatting process. Quick Format deletes the file allocation table and root directory of the disk, but the disk is not scanned for bad sector areas. Use this option only for disks that have been formatted before.
5. Click OK. The confirmation message you see below appears:

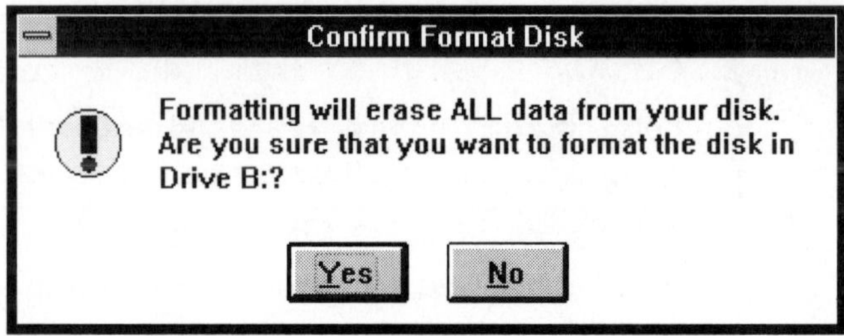

6. If you want to go ahead and format the disk, click Yes. You will be informed of the progress.

Copying Disks

You can make copies of disks two ways. If the disks have the same capacities, you can use the Copy Disk command. If they do not, you can't; you have to use the Copy command as explained earlier. Just select all the files with wildcards (*.*) in the From section of the Copy dialog box and perform the copy.

If the two diskettes have the same capacities, use the Copy Diskette command (it's faster). However, be aware that this command, like the DOS DISKCOPY command, erases everything on the destination disk before creating an exact copy of the source disk:

1. Put the source disk in one drive and the destination disk in the other. If you only have one drive, insert the source disk in it.
2. Click on the drive icon for the source disk.
3. Choose Disk ➤ Copy Diskette.

4. If you have two drives, you'll have to choose the destination drive from the dialog box.
5. Follow the instructions on the screen. If you only have one drive, you'll have to swap the disks a few times.

Changing a Disk's Label

All floppy and hard disks can have a volume label. This is not the paper label on the outside, but a name encoded into the directory on the disk. It shows up when you type DIR at the DOS prompt and on the top line of the drive window when you switch to that drive in the File Manager. The label really serves no functional purpose other than to identify the disk for archiving purposes. When you format a disk in DOS or with the File Manager, you are given the chance to assign a volume label. File Manager lets you change a disk's label after the fact, should you need or want to. Here's how:

1. Insert the disk in the drive.
2. Choose Disk ➤ Label Disk.
3. Type the label into the dialog box (up to 11 characters) and click on OK.

FAST TRACK

CHAPTER

5

FAST TRACK

double-click on Colors in the Control Panel. Choose an existing color scheme from the list or assign particular colors by clicking on Color Palette. Choose the screen element whose color you want to change and click on a color square.

use the font installer that came with the font. If there isn't one, then use the Control Panel's. Put the font on the hard disk. Then choose Fonts from the Control Panel. To add to the font, click on Add, choose the font file from the file box, and click OK. To remove a font, select it from the Fonts box and click on Remove. (Printer fonts are installed from the Printer Setup dialog box.)

choose Ports from the Control Panel. Click on the port, select the settings from the dialog box, and click OK.

choose Mouse from the Control Panel. Drag the slider to alter tracking and double-click speed. Reverse the buttons if you want to. Mouse Trails creates a shadow of the mouse path.

To fine-tune the Desktop, ... 167

choose Desktop from the Control Panel. Choose a wallpaper or pattern for the Desktop background. Set icon spacing, granularity (a grid for sizing windows), cursor blink rate, and border width for all windows. Set the screen saver options if you want one to activate when your computer is idle.

To set network options, ... 175

choose Network from the Control Panel (available only with networks). Options vary depending on the network.

To alter international settings, ... 175

choose International from the Control Panel. Adjust the country, language, keyboard layout, measurement, list separator, date, time, currency, and number format defaults.

To set the time and date, ... 178

choose the Date/Time icon. Click on the arrows to alter or set the current date and time.

CHAPTER 5

FEATURING

Customizing Your Desktop

Changing Screen Colors

Adding and Removing Fonts

Making Other System Settings

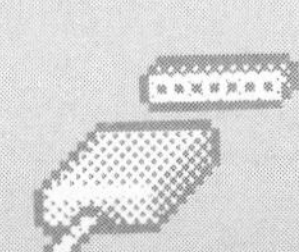
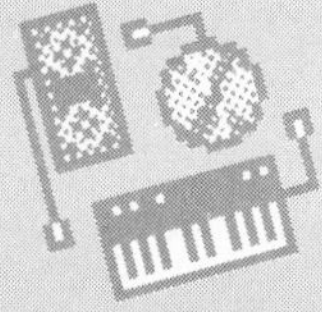

Customizing Windows with the Control Panel

Though you may, up to this time, have been using Windows pretty much as it comes out of the box, there are numerous alterations you can make to customize Windows to your liking—adjustments to screen colors, mouse speed, key repeat rate, fonts, and networking options to name a few. Most of these adjustments are not necessities as much as they are niceties that make using Windows just a little easier. Some are more imperative, such as setting up Windows to work with your brand and model of printer. In any case, these adjustments are made via the Control Panel. Once set, the changes are stored in the Windows initialization file (WIN.INI) and loaded when you run Windows again.

OPENING THE CONTROL PANEL

NOTE *Printers, Drivers, MIDI Mapper, Network, and Sound are not covered in this chapter. Refer to Chapter 6 for information about setting up printers and Chapter 15 for details regarding installation and removal of video, audio, MIDI, and CD-ROM device drivers, and assigning system sounds.*

You open the Control Panel by switching to the Program Manager, opening the Main group, and double-clicking on the Control Panel icon. The Control Panel window then opens, as shown in Figure 5.1.

There will be between 11 and 14 items to choose from, depending on whether or not you are running Windows in 386-Enhanced mode, are using a network, and/or have a MIDI board installed. You will see the 386 Enhanced icon only if you are running in that mode and the network icon only if you are currently hooked up to and running on a network. The icons are as follows:

Color: sets the colors (or gray levels) of various parts of Windows' screens, title bars, scroll bars, and so forth.

Fonts: adds and deletes typefaces for your screen display and printer output.

Ports: sets up the serial ports on your computer for use with various communications programs and serial printers.

Mouse: sets the speed of the mouse pointer's motion relative to your hand motion and how fast a double click has to be to have an effect. You can also reverse the functions of the right and left buttons.

Desktop: sets the background pattern or picture for the Desktop (it doesn't have to be just a plain color). Also sets the blinking rate of the cursor and allows you to choose the screen saver, icon spacing, sizing grid, and Alt-Tab task-switching mode.

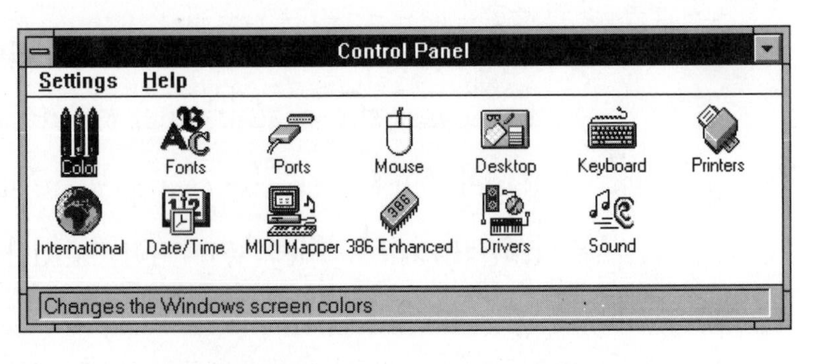

FIGURE 5.1: ***The Control Panel window. Each item opens a window from which you can make adjustments.***

Keyboard: sets the rate at which keys repeat when you hold them down.

Printers: selects which printer to print to, which port to use, and which paper orientation and size will be used when you print. Also used to install *printer drivers.* (Printers and printer drivers are covered in Chapter 6.)

International: sets how Windows displays times, dates, numbers, and currency.

Date/Time: sets the current date and time.

MIDI Mapper: allows reassignments of MIDI patch numbers, channel numbers, and key numbers so that nonstandard synthesizers can play MIDI sound files properly.

Network: varies with the network type. Possibly lets you log on and off the network, change your user ID and password, log onto network drives, use network printers, and send electronic mail to other network users.

386 Enhanced: sets specifics about time and resource contention between programs running simultaneously in 386 mode.

Sound: turns off and on the computer's beep, or adds sounds to various system events if you have a sound board.

Drivers: installs or removes sound, CD-ROM, video, MIDI, and other device drivers.

SETTING THE SCREEN COLORS

TO RESET THE SCREEN COLORS,

double-click on Colors in the Control Panel. Choose an existing color scheme from the list or assign particular colors by clicking on Color Palette. Choose the screen element whose color you want to change and click on a color square.

The Color icon lets you change the way Windows assigns color to various parts of the screen. If you're using a monochrome monitor (no color), altering the colors may still have some effect (the amount will depend on how you installed Windows), so it's not just for systems with color screens.

Windows sets itself up using a default color scheme that's fine for most screens—and if you're happy with your colors as they are, you might not even want to futz around with them.

However, the color settings options for Windows are very flexible and easy to modify. You can modify the color setting of just about any part of a Windows screen. For those of you who are very particular about color choices, this can be done manually, choosing colors from a palette or even mixing your own with the Custom Colors feature. Once created, custom colors and color setups can be saved on disk for later use or automatically loaded with each Windows session. For more expedient color reassignments, there's a number of supplied "canned" color schemes to choose from.

In some cases the screen driver that you chose (or that was automatically chosen) when installing Windows has some effect on the display of colors, too. You may want to experiment with these by running Windows Setup again (it's in the Main group), choosing Options ➤ Change System Settings, and choosing a variation on your display type from the Display drop-down list. Specifically, if you're using a monochrome VGA display that can render colors as shades of gray, select VGA (which is color) instead of VGA with Monochrome Display. Then experiment with the Color Panel color schemes to create a more pleasing display. Your setup will have more of a 3-D look since colors will be displayed as differing shades of gray. In fact, the figures for this book were taken from just such a setup, with some fine tuning for the scroll and title bars.

Upon opening the Color icon, you see the dialog box shown in Figure 5.2. The various parts of the Windows graphical environment that you can alter are shown (and named) in the bottom portion of the dialog box. As you select color schemes, these samples change so that you can see what the effect will be without having to go back into Windows proper.

Loading an Existing Color Scheme

Before playing with the custom color palette, first try loading the supplied ones; you may find one you like:

1. Click open the drop-down Color Schemes list box.
2. Choose a selection whose name suits your fancy. The colors in the dialog box will change, showing the scheme. Try them out.

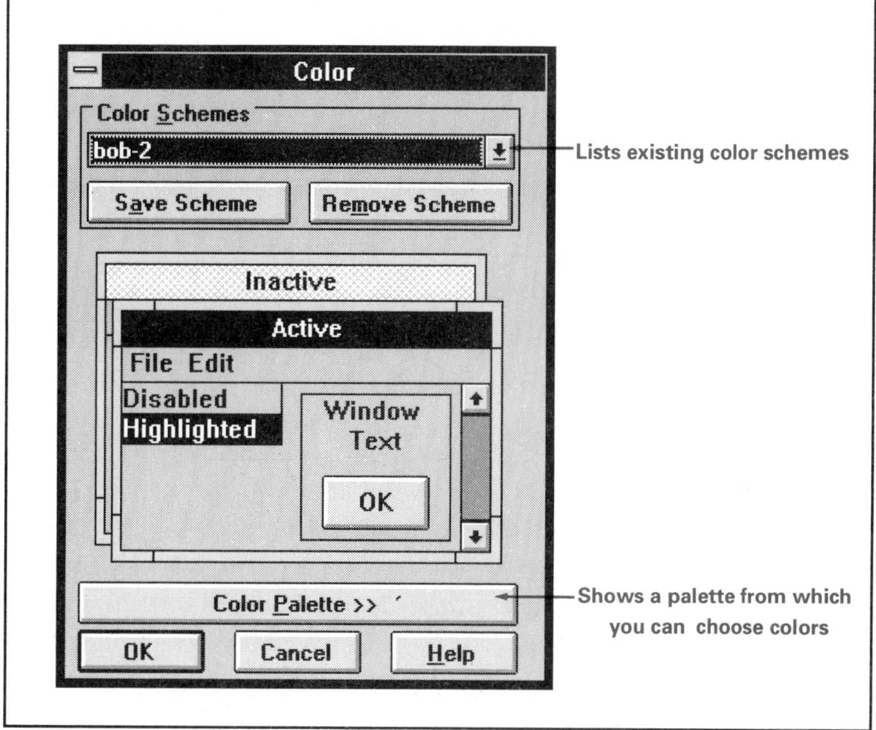

FIGURE 5.2:

The dialog box for setting the colors. Choose existing color schemes or click on Color Palette to set up your own. As you can see, I've defined one called "Bob-2."

TIP *You can toggle a drop-down list box open and closed by pressing Alt-↓ or Alt-↑.*

Some are garish, others more subtle. Adjusting your monitor may make a difference, too. (You can cycle through the different supplied color schemes without selecting them from the drop-down list: with the Color Schemes space highlighted, just press the ↑ and ↓ keys. The sample screen elements will change to reflect each color scheme as its name appears in the Color Schemes box.)

3. Click on OK to apply the settings to all Windows activities.

Microsoft has incorporated a few color schemes that may enhance the operation of your computer:

- Colors come in solid and dotted shades. Solid colors may speed up the time it takes Windows to update your screen as you move from application to application. Several supplied color schemes, including Windows Default, use only solid colors. Also, choosing the same color for your active and inactive window borders will save time.

- On most LCD screens, Windows appears in reverse video (like a photo negative) unless you flip a switch or use a built-in utility program to reverse the screen from white to black. If you don't have such a switch, try one of the supplied LCD color schemes to rectify the problem.
- Those of you with a Plasma screen may want to use the Plasma Power Saver color scheme. It uses darker colors, which use less power than lighter colors.

Choosing Your Own Colors

If you don't like the color schemes supplied, you can make up your own. It's most efficient to start with one that's close to what you want, and then modify it. Once you like the scheme, you may save it under a new name for later use. Keep in mind that you have to use solid colors for the following elements: Window Frame, Window Text, Window Background, Menu Bar, Menu Text, Active and Inactive Title Bar Text, Button Face, Button Text, Disabled Text, Highlight, and Highlighted Text. If you use a nonsolid color (one with a dot pattern), Windows adjusts it to become a similarly tinted solid color. Here are the steps:

1. Select the color scheme you want to modify.
2. Click on the Color Palette button. This expands the dialog box, as shown in Figure 5.3. You now have 48 colors to choose from and another drop-down list to select the screen element you want to change.
3. From the Screen Element drop-down list box, choose the element of the screen that you want to alter. Note that clicking on the different areas of the sample screen at left changes the element title shown in the Screen Element box. Experiment with clicking on them to see what comes up. Some (like the OK button) cycle through two or three elements as you click repeatedly. This is often an easier way to select the element you want to modify than selecting a title from the drop-down list box.

FIGURE 5.3:

The expanded Color dialog box. Choose an element and then assign a color by clicking on it.

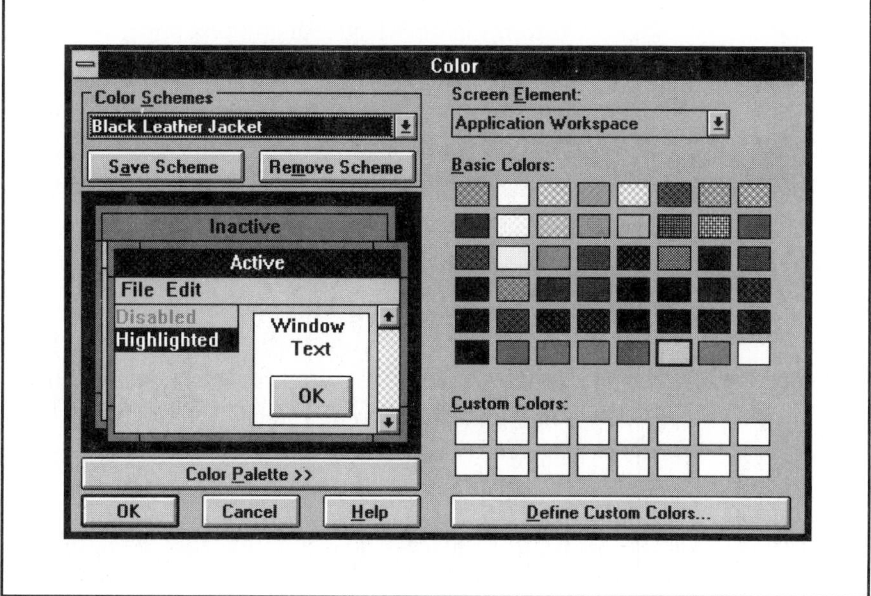

4. Click on one of the 48 colors (or patterns and intensity levels, if you have a monochrome monitor) to assign it to the chosen element.
5. Once the color scheme suits your fancy, you can save it. (It will stay in force for future Windows sessions even if you don't save it, but you'll lose the settings next time you change colors or select another scheme.) Click on Save Scheme.
6. Type in a name for the color scheme and click on OK.

If you want to remove a scheme (such as one you never use), select it from the drop-down list and click on the Remove Scheme button.

Making Up Your Own Colors

If you don't like the colors that are available, you can create your own. There are 16 slots at the bottom of the color palette for storing colors you set using another fancy dialog box called the color refiner.

Click on Define Custom Colors in the expanded Color dialog box. The Custom Color Selector dialog box appears (see Figure 5.4). There are two cursors that you work with here. One is the *luminosity bar* and the other is the *color refiner cursor.* To make a long story short, you simply drag these around one at a time until the color in the box at the lower left is the shade you want. As you do, the numbers in the boxes below the color refiner will change. *Luminosity* is the amount of brightness in the color. *Hue* is the actual shade or color. All colors are composed of red, green, and blue. *Saturation* is the degree of purity of the color; it is decreased by adding gray to the color and increased by subtracting it. You can also type in the numbers or click on the arrows next to the numbers if you want, but it's easier to use the cursors. When you like the color, click on Add Color to add the new color to the palette.

You can switch between a solid color and a color made up of various dots of several colors. Solid colors look less grainy on your screen but give you fewer choices. The Color|Solid box shows the difference between the

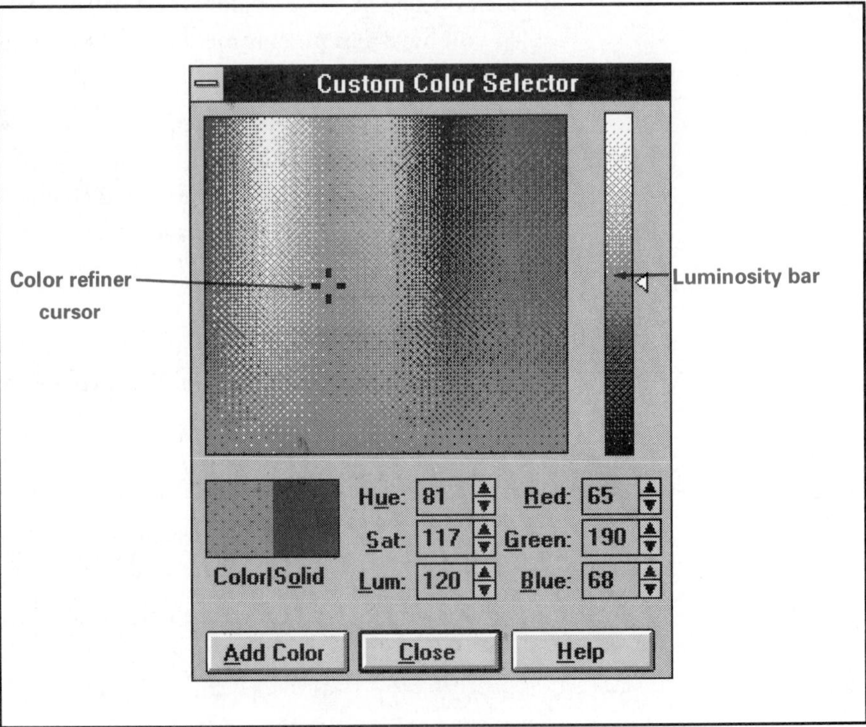

FIGURE 5.4: *The custom color selector lets you create new colors*

two. If you click on this box before adding the color to the palette, the solid color closest to the actual color you chose will be added instead of the grainier composite color.

Once a color is added to the palette, you can modify it. Just click on it, move the cursors around, and then click Add Color again. Click on Close to close the dialog box. Then continue to assign colors with the palette. When you are content with the color assignments, click on OK. If you decide after toying around that you don't want to implement the color changes, just click Cancel.

ADDING AND REMOVING FONTS

Fonts are the various type styles that you can use when composing a document, viewing it on the screen, or printing it on paper. Fonts add visual impact to your documents to help you express your words or numbers in a style that suits your audience. They can also increase readability.

As an example of some fonts, Figure 5.5 shows three of the most popular type styles in today's printing: Courier, Times, and Helvetica (called Arial in Windows). Fonts are specified by size as well as by name. The size

FIGURE 5.5:
Various fonts and point sizes

This is Times New Roman
This is Courier
This is Arial
18 point Arial
18 point Times New Roman
20 point Script
70 pt

of a font is measured in *points.* A point is $1/72$ of an inch. In addition, fonts styles include **bold**, *italic,* and underlining.

Windows comes supplied with a reasonable stock of fonts, some of which are installed on your hard disk and integrated into your Windows program during the setup procedure. The number and types of fonts installed depend on the type of screen and printer you have. When you told the setup program what type of printer you had, a printer driver was installed. The printer driver includes a set of basic fonts for your printer.

Some application programs, such as word processors, may have additional fonts supplied with them—fonts not included with Windows—that you may want to use. Fonts can also be purchased separately from companies who specialize in typeface design, such as Bitstream, Inc. and Adobe Systems, Inc.

Font packages usually come with their own setup programs, which will automatically install the fonts into your Windows system for you. When this is the case, you should just follow the instruction manual supplied with the font package. If there is no such installation program, you use the Control Panel's Fonts program to install the font(s). This program also lets you remove fonts from your Windows setup and lets you set options for TrueType fonts, which are discussed below.

There are several classes of fonts used with Windows:

- *Vector fonts* use straight line segments and formulas to draw letters. They can be easily scaled to different sizes. These are primarily used on printing devices that only draw lines, such as plotters.
- *TrueType fonts* are generated either as *bitmaps* or as soft fonts, depending on your printer. The advantage of TrueType fonts is that they will print exactly as seen on the screen. (TrueType fonts were added to Windows 3.1 to solve many of the earlier problems associated with differences between how fonts appear on screen and how they print.)
- *Printer fonts* are fonts stored in your printer (in its ROM), stored on plug-in cartridges, or downloaded to your printer by Windows when you print. Downloaded fonts are called *soft fonts.*
- *Screen fonts* control how text looks on your screen. They come in predefined sizes, such as 10 point, 12 point, etc.

Prior to Windows 3.1, both printer and screen fonts often had to be added for each typestyle you wanted to add to your setup. Now, TrueType fonts simplify matters, since adding a TrueType font installs both printer and screen fonts simultaneously. In addition, TrueType fonts will look identical (though perhaps with differences in smoothness or resolution) regardless of the printer with which you print them.

When you print a document, Windows checks your printer driver file to see if it includes the fonts you put in the document. If the printer or printer driver does not supply the font, Windows attempts to find a happy solution. In most cases, Windows will handle day-to-day printing jobs just fine. If your printer has a soft font already in it (from plug-in font cartridges or in its ROM) and Windows doesn't have a screen font of that type, Windows will usually substitute another, similar screen font with the correct size for displaying your work on the screen. Even though it might not look exactly like the final printout, the line length and page breaks on your screen will be accurate.

Adding Fonts

If no installation program came with your fonts, or if you want to add some TrueType fonts to your system, follow these steps:

1. Open the Fonts window by double-clicking on its icon in the Control Panel window. The dialog box is shown in Figure 5.6. All the installed fonts are displayed in the Installed Fonts section.
2. Click on any font name and you'll see an example of it in a variety of sizes displayed in the lower portion of the box. A description of the font will appear below the box. If the font is a vector or TrueType font, no sizes are listed after the name, since they can be printed or displayed in any size. If the font is a bitmapped font, the sizes available are listed after the font's name. The size of the font file is shown in the bottom portion of the box as well. A typical TrueType font uses approximately 70K.
3. Click on Add. A dialog box appears, as shown in Figure 5.7. Choose the correct drive and directory where the fonts are stored.
4. Choose the fonts you want to add. If you want to select more than one, extend the selection by Shift-clicking (to select a range) or Ctrl-clicking (to select individual noncontiguous fonts).

FIGURE 5.6:

You open this dialog box to see what the installed fonts are.

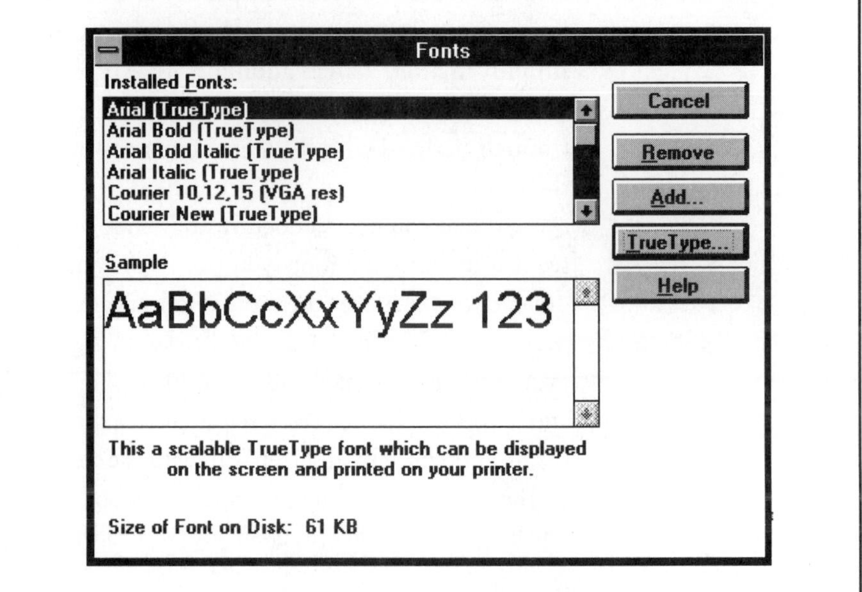

FIGURE 5.7:

This is the dialog box from which you need to choose a font file to add.

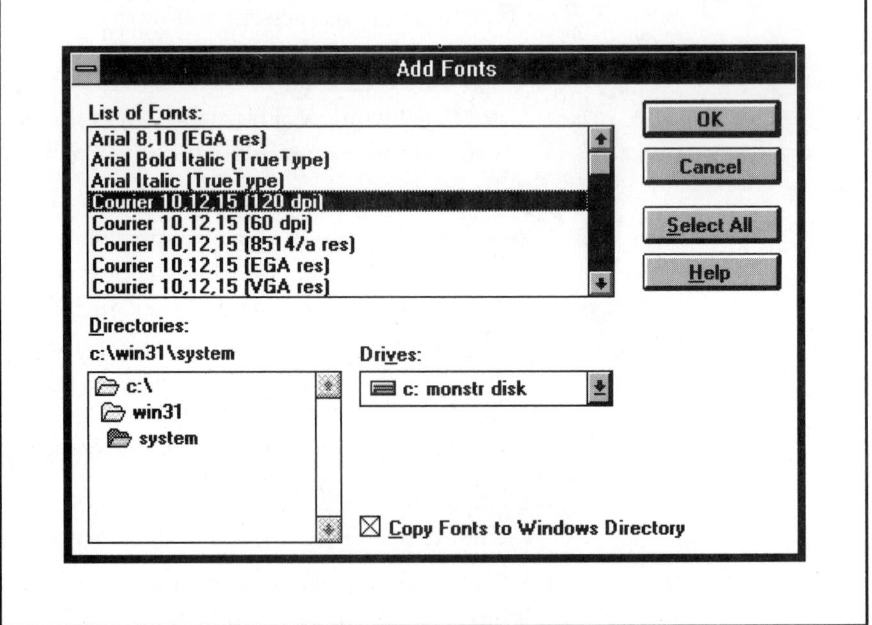

5. When fonts are installed, the installation program normally copies them to the \WINDOWS\SYSTEM directory. However, font files are pretty large. So, if your hard disk is low on space, you might want to tell Windows to use the fonts where they are, such as in another directory or on another drive (such as a network drive, a floppy, or other DOS partition). Turn off the Copy Fonts to Windows Directory check box to do this.
6. Click on OK. The font(s) will be added to your font list.
7. The Fonts dialog box reappears. Close it and you're done. The new font(s) should be available for your Windows applications.

If you try to install a font that's already in your system, the installer won't let you, so don't worry about accidentally loading one you already have.

TrueType Options

As mentioned above, TrueType fonts take up a fair amount of disk space. They also take up valuable memory (RAM) when they are activated (which is the default when you run Windows). Windows is already memory-hungry without any help from TrueType fonts. So, if your system is underendowed in the RAM department (i.e., you've gotten messages from Windows before that say you are low on memory), you have a couple of font options that might reclaim some needed memory.

Choose TrueType from the Fonts dialog box. The TrueType options box comes up with two choices:

Enable TrueType Fonts

Show Only TrueType Fonts in Applications

If you disable TrueType fonts, you'll increase the amount of memory for Windows to run applications and open documents. By the same token, if you choose to show only TrueType fonts, that will turn off vector and bit-mapped fonts, which will also save memory. So the moral is this: If you're having a memory shortage, either:

- turn both check marks **on**, enabling TrueType fonts and disabling other types of fonts.
- turn both check marks **off**, which enables all fonts except TrueType.

Click on OK to finalize the choice. A dialog box advises you to restart Windows and offers a Restart button. The changes you made don't take effect until you do so. Click on the Restart button.

Fonts are not removed from your disk when they are disabled. You can reactivate them again from the same dialog box. The Fonts list in the Fonts dialog box will be adjusted to show what's currently active in your Windows setup—and thus the fonts that will be available to you from your Windows applications.

Removing Fonts

Removing fonts is similar to adding fonts, except you use the Remove button. Deleting individual fonts or font sets increases the available memory in your computer, letting you run more programs simultaneously. If you are having memory limitation problems, you could gain some room by eliminating fonts you never use. However, don't remove the MS Sans Serif font set, since it's used in all the Windows dialog boxes.

To remove a font, follow these steps:

1. Open the Fonts dialog box by clicking on its icon in the Control Panel window. The dialog box shown in Figure 5.6 comes up. All the installed fonts are displayed in the Installed Fonts section.
2. Select the name of the font or fonts you want to remove.
3. Click on Remove.
4. A dialog box asks you to confirm the removal. If you want to remove the font from your disk as well as from your Windows setup, check the Delete Font File from Disk check box.
5. Choose the Yes button.

Unless you are sure that you don't use a particular font, I suggest you do *not* remove it from your disk. Try deleting it from the system to determine whether you miss the font in any applications. Then delete it from your disk later if you really want to. (To do *that* you'll have to add it first, then delete it again with the Delete Font File from Disk check box set on.)

SETTING THE SERIAL PORTS

TO CONFIGURE A SERIAL PORT,

choose Ports from the Control Panel. Click on the port, make the settings from the dialog box, and click OK.

If you've ever used the DOS MODE command to set up the communications parameters of your computer's serial COM ports, you know that it's a hassle to remember the exact syntax and *arguments* (the numbers and letters you type after the command) required for a specific setup. Since most programs that use the serial ports (such as communications programs, mouse drivers, or slow-speed networks) take care of setting the COM ports, it's rare that you need to deal with these directly anyway. As a case in point, the Terminal program supplied with Windows has its own dialog box for making the appropriate settings for baud rate, parity, stop and start bits, etc. But there is the occasional exception, such as when you're using a serial printer connected to a COM port, and you need to initialize the port's settings.

In any case, should the need arise, the Control Panel lets you easily set the COM port parameters—and it sure beats using the MODE command to do it, since you just choose the settings from a dialog box. Here's how:

1. Double-click the Ports icon in the Control Panel window. A dialog box appears.

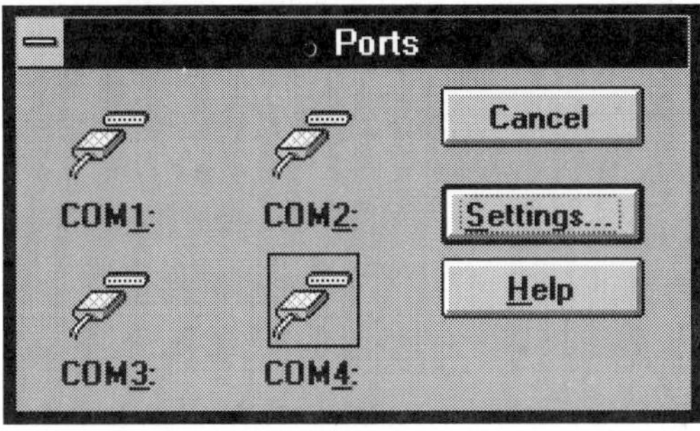

2. You can set up the parameters of any of the four possible COM ports. (LPT ports cannot be altered because they are not serial ports and do not have settings.) Click on the icon corresponding to the port you want to alter.

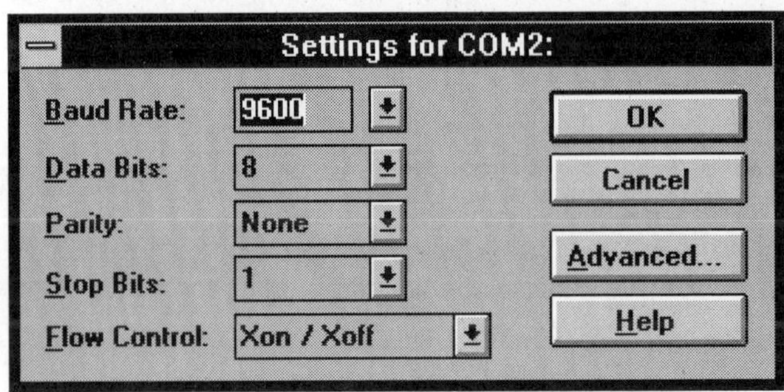

3. Now make the settings applicable to the job you're doing. Each space has a drop-down list where you can make your choices. The settings should match the settings of the equipment you are connecting to the port. If you're in doubt about them, consult the manual supplied with the external equipment. You may also want to refer to a book specializing in the use of asynchronous serial communications interfaces, such as *The RS-232 Solution (2nd Edition),* by Joe Campbell (SYBEX).
4. If you want to alter the port address of the COM port or change the IRQ request line (hardware interrupt), click on Advanced and set them from the resulting dialog box. (These settings require an understanding of the interrupt and port assignments of your hardware and possible conflicts with other ports or cards such as network interface cards in the system, so make sure you do your homework first. Otherwise, leave them alone.)
5. Click on OK. You return to the Ports dialog box.
6. Change other ports if necessary, then click Close when you're finished.

ADJUSTING THE MOUSE

TO ADJUST THE MOUSE,

choose Mouse from the Control Panel. Drag the slider to alter tracking and double-click speed. Reverse the buttons if you want to. Mouse Trails creates a shadow of the mouse path.

You can adjust four aspects of your mouse's operation:

- Tracking speed
- Double-click speed
- Left-right button reversal
- Mouse trails

Tracking speed is the speed at which the mouse pointer moves relative to the movement of the mouse. Believe it or not, mouse motion is actually measured in *Mickeys!* (Somebody out there has a sense of humor.) A Mickey equals 1⁄100 of an inch of mouse movement. The tracking-speed setting lets you adjust the relationship of Mickeys to *pixels.* (Pixels are the dots on your screen.) If you want to be very exact in your cursor movement, you'll want to slow the tracking speed, requiring more Mickeys per pixel. However, this requires more hand motion for the corresponding cursor motion. If your desk is crammed and your coordination is very good, then you can increase the speed (fewer Mickeys per pixel). If you use the mouse with non-Windows programs (such as Ventura Publisher or AutoCAD), you might want to adjust the Windows mouse speed to match that of your other programs so you won't need to mentally adjust when you use such programs.

Incidentally, if you think the mouse runs too slowly in your non-Windows applications, there is a fix. MouseWare is a memory-resident program that lets you adjust the tracking speed for non-Windows programs. It's available from Metroplex Digital Corporation, P.O. Box 815729, Dallas, TX 75381-5729. Phone (214) 231-8944. Also, if you're using a Logitech mouse, a program called Click that is supplied with the Logitech mouse lets you easily control its tracking. See the Logitech manual for details.

Double-click speed determines how fast you have to double-click to make a double-click operation work (that is, to run a program from its icon, to close a window by double-clicking its Control box, or to select a word by double-clicking on it while in Write). If the double-click speed is too fast, it's difficult to make things happen. If it's too slow, you end up running programs or opening and closing windows unexpectedly. However, I find the slowest speed to work well for me.

Left-right button reversal simply switches the function of your mouse's buttons. For lefties, being able to switch the mouse buttons may be a boon. If you use other programs outside of Windows that don't allow this, however, it might just add to the confusion. If you only use the mouse in Windows programs and you're left-handed, then it may be worth a try.

Mouse trails creates a shadow of the mouse's path whenever you move it. Some people find it annoying, but for those of you who have trouble finding the pointer on the screen, it's a blessing. Mouse trails are particularly helpful when using Windows on laptop computers, where the pointer often "submarines"—disappears when you move it. (This option won't appear if the display driver you're using doesn't support Mouse Trails.)

Here are the steps for changing Mouse options:

1. Double-click on the Mouse icon in the Control Panel window. The dialog box shown below appears.

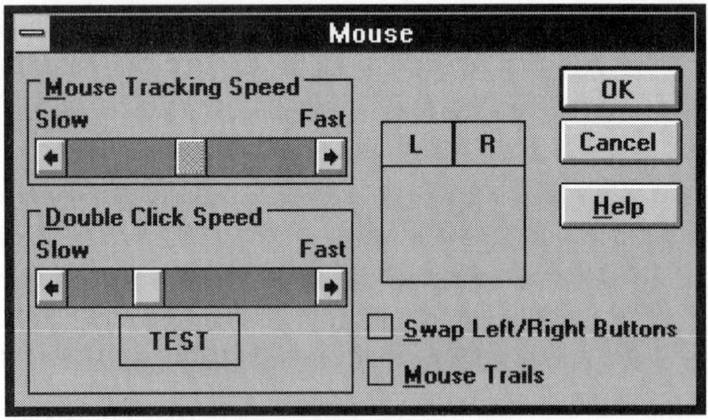

2. Drag the sliders within their scroll bars to adjust the mouse speed parameters.

3. Notice that the tracking speed changes instantly. Move the cursor around to test the new speed. Double-click on the Test button to try out the new double-click speed. The color in the box will change if the double click registered.
4. Click on the Swap Left/Right Buttons check box if you want to switch them. (This change takes effect immediately, so once you set this check box on, start clicking with the right button.)
5. Click on the Mouse Trails button if you want to be followed everywhere you go.
6. Click OK when you're happy with all your settings.

FINE-TUNING THE DESKTOP

TO FINE-TUNE THE DESKTOP,

choose Desktop from the Control Panel. Choose a wallpaper or pattern for the Desktop background. Set icon spacing, granularity (a grid for sizing windows), cursor blink rate, and border width for all windows. Set the screen saver options if you want one to activate when your computer is idle.

There are several alterations that you can make to the Windows Desktop. You can change the following:

- Background patterns
- Background wallpaper
- Sizing grid
- Border width of all windows
- Icon spacing
- Cursor blink rate
- Screen saver
- Alt-Tab switching style

The *patterns* and *wallpaper settings* simply let you decorate the Desktop with something a little more festive than the default screen. Patterns are repetitious designs, such as the woven look of fabric. Wallpaper uses larger pictures that were created by artists with a drawing program. You can create your own patterns and wallpaper or use the ones supplied. Wallpapering can be done with a single copy of the picture placed in the center of the screen or by tiling, which gives you multiple identical pictures covering the whole screen. Some of the supplied wallpaper images cannot be used if you are low on memory. This is because the larger bit-mapped images take up too much RAM. If an image can't be used, the Control Panel will inform you when you try to select it.

The *sizing grid* is an invisible grid that causes the borders of windows to "snap" into place. It makes aligning windows easier. It also affects the alignment of icons. The grid's setting is called *granularity.* If the setting is zero, the grid is off. The range is 0 to 49. Each increment of 1 corresponds to 8 pixels on the screen. I find a setting of 1 or 2 to be sufficient.

The *border width setting* lets you make the borders of windows wider for visibility purposes, I suppose. When windows are tiled, thicker borders may help you to distinguish between them visually; and when resizing windows, thicker borders are easier to grab. The borders of windows in this book have been set to 4. The range is 0 to 49.

Icon spacing determines the distance between icons, both on the Desktop and in group windows. Increasing the spacing prevents icon names from overlapping each other, but sometimes makes icons harder to find since they will be spaced out across more of the Desktop and are thus more likely to be obscured by a window. I use a spacing of 106.

Cursor blink rate determines how fast the vertical bar (called the insertion point or text cursor) blinks. On some screens, it's easier to see if the speed is altered. The text cursor appears whenever you are editing text (in the text portion of a dialog box, in a Cardfile document, in a Notepad document, etc.).

Screen Saver, when set on, will blank your screen or display a moving image or pattern if you don't use the mouse or keyboard for a predetermined amount of time.

In the Applications section of the dialog box there's only one option: "Fast Alt+Tab" Switching. Normally this is enabled and causes Windows to display a thin box in the middle of your screen when you press Alt-Tab (and keep Alt pressed down) to switch between applications:

Notice that the icon and the name of the application and document (if one are active) are displayed in the box. As explained at the end of Chapter 2, each press of the Tab key (while Alt is depressed) cycles through the list of running applications. If you disable this feature, you will not see the box in the middle of the screen. Instead, with each Tab press you'll see the application's window perimeter or icon wherever it's currently located on the screen. The bummer with this setup is that you have to look all over the screen to see which application is going to become active when you release the Tab key. I recommend leaving this option enabled.

Follow these general procedures to adjust any of the Desktop features (some are covered in greater detail later):

1. Double-click on the Desktop icon in the Control Panel window. The dialog box shown in Figure 5.8 appears.
2. Select the pattern or wallpaper you want. You'll have to try each one to see the effect because they don't go into effect until you leave the dialog box. You can only have either at one time, not both. You can, however, see a sample and a close-up of a pattern (called a cell) by choosing Edit Pattern. From there you can edit the pattern by turning pixels on and off with a click of the mouse.
3. If you choose Wallpaper, click on Tile or Center.
4. Set the cursor blink rate by sliding the box in the scroll bar or clicking on the arrows at either end of it. You can see the effect as soon as you move the mouse cursor off the slider button.
5. Adjust the border width and grid spacing (granularity) by clicking on the ↑ and ↓ buttons or by clicking on their assigned values and typing in the desired new value.

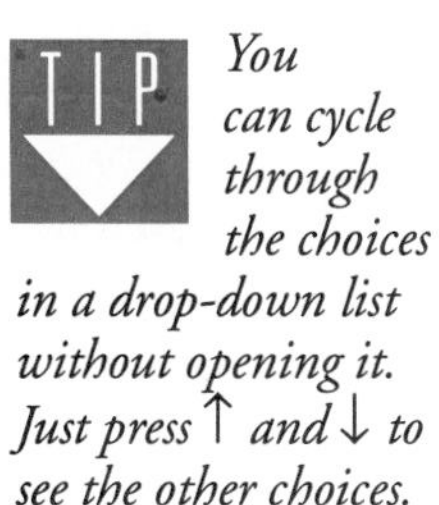

You can cycle through the choices in a drop-down list without opening it. Just press ↑ and ↓ to see the other choices.

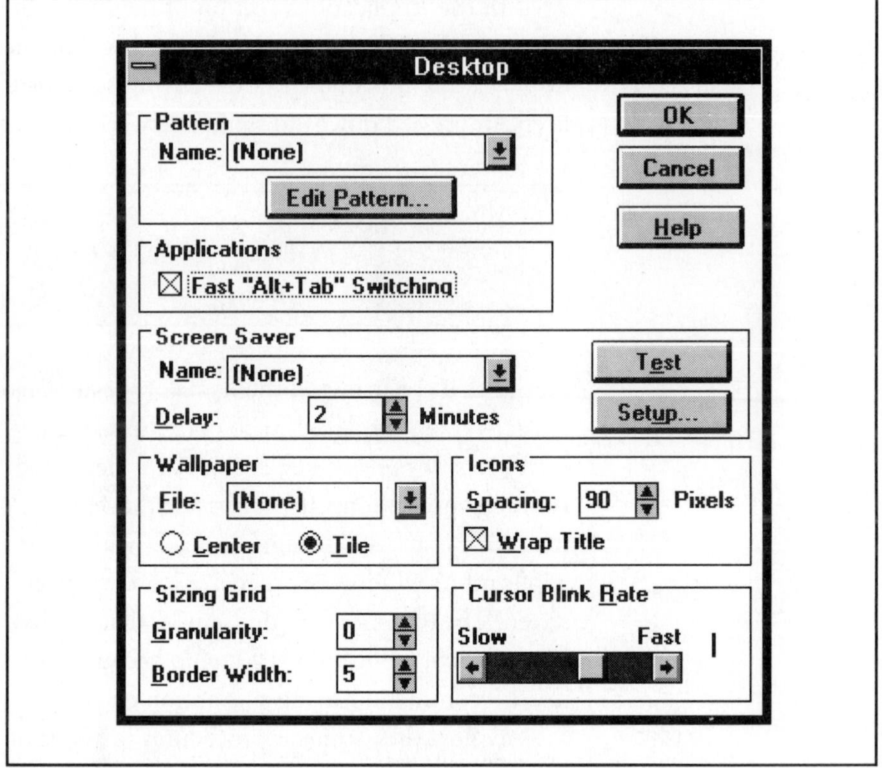

FIGURE 5.8: *Setting the many Desktop options*

6. Select a screen saver if you want one and adjust the settings to suit yourself.
7. Click on OK.

Unfortunately, this is one of those boxes that you'll have to open, reset, and OK a million times to see all the patterns and wallpaper choices, and to see the effect of changing the border size and granularity. Anyway, with some experimentation, you'll find the settings you like.

Figure 5.9 shows some of the patterns and wallpaper selections supplied with Windows.

Changing a Pattern

If the supplied patterns don't thrill you, make up your own with the built-in bit-map editor. You can either change an existing one or design your own. If

FIGURE 5.9:

Some of the supplied patterns and wallpapers

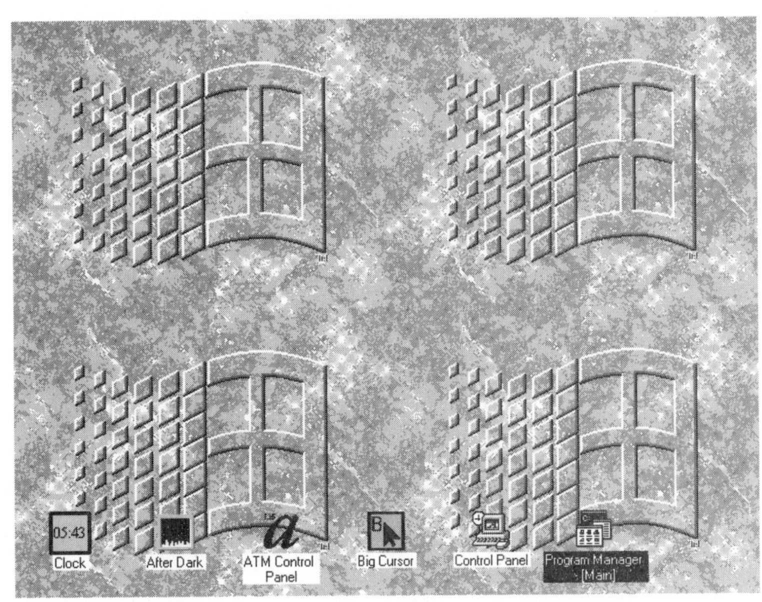

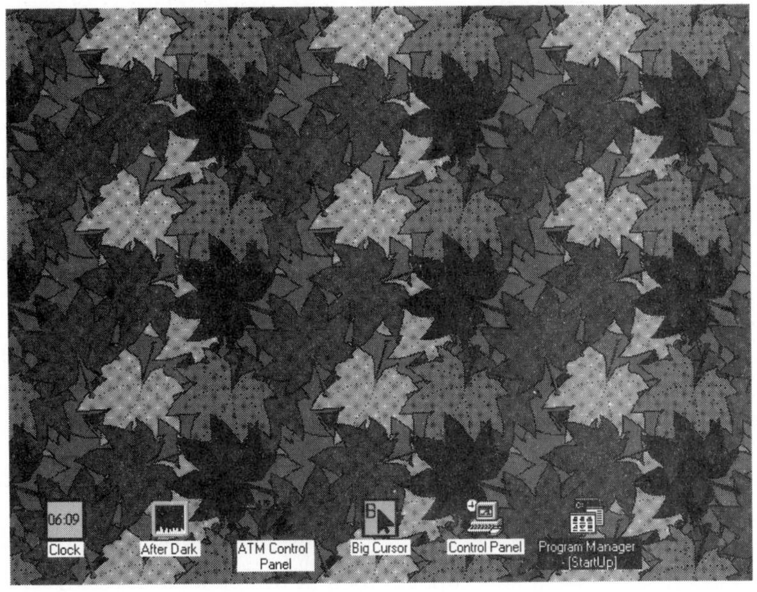

you want to design your own, choose None from the Name drop-down list before you begin. Otherwise, choose a pattern you want to play with:

1. Click on Edit Pattern in the Desktop dialog box. A new dialog box appears.

2. In the Name text box, type in a name for the new pattern.
3. Create the pattern by clicking in the large box (this is the cell). What you are doing is defining the smallest element of the repeated pattern. It is blown up in scale to make editing it easier. Each click reverses the color of one pixel. The effect when the pattern is applied across a larger area and in normal size is shown in the Sample section to the left.
4. When you like the pattern, click on Add and the pattern is added to the list. You can then select it later from the Desktop dialog box.

If you later want to remove a pattern, select the pattern while in the editor and click on Remove.

Loading a New Slice of Wallpaper

The images used in wallpaper are actually .BMP files. These are bit-mapped files created by programs such as Paintbrush. Other programs create bit-mapped .BMP files too, though, so the sky's the limit as far as what you can use as wallpaper. For example, you could use a scanned color photograph of your favorite movie star, a pastoral setting, some computer art, a scanned Matisse painting, or a photo of your pet lemur. Figure 5.10 shows an example of a custom piece of wallpaper.

You can also edit the supplied .BMP files with Paintbrush if you want. And since Paintbrush will read .PCX files and convert them to .BMP files, you can also use virtually any .PCX file as wallpaper. Just load it into Paintbrush by selecting File ➤ Open. In the Open dialog box, open the List Files of Type drop-down list box and choose PCX file (*.PCX) to display available .PCX files. Then choose the desired file and click on OK.

Here's how to load a new .BMP file and display it as wallpaper:

1. Create the image with whatever program you want, so long as it saves it as a .BMP bit-mapped file.
2. Copy the file into the Windows directory. Only then will it appear in the list of wallpaper options.
3. Choose it from the Desktop dialog box. (If you leave Desktop open while creating your .BMP file in Paintbrush, the Wallpaper File list won't show the new file until you close Desktop and reopen it.)

FIGURE 5.10:

A custom piece of wallpaper created with Micrografx Designer

Loading a Screen Saver

Screen savers reduce the wear on your monitor by blanking it out after a certain period of inactivity. The screen saver options allow you to choose or create an entertaining video ditty that will greet you when you return to work. You also set how much time you have after your last keystroke or mouse skitter before the show begins. Here's how it's done:

1. In the Screen Saver section of the Desktop dialog box, choose a name from the drop-down list. (The default screen saver is basic black.)
2. To see what it looks like, click on Test. Your screen will go black and then begin its antics. The show continues until you hit any key or move your mouse.
3. If you want to change anything about it, choose Setup.
4. Depending on which screen saver you chose, you'll have a few possible adjustments, such as speed, placement, and details pertinent to the graphic. Play with the settings until you're happy with the results.
5. The last choice in the Setup dialog box is Password Options. If you set password protection on, every time your screen saver is activated you will have to type your password into a box to return to work. This is good if you don't want anyone else tampering with your files or seeing what you're doing. It can be a pain, though, if there's no particular need for privacy at your computer. Don't forget your password, either, or you'll have to reboot to get back to work. Click the Password Protected check box if you want protection.
6. Choose Set Password to define or change your password.
7. In the dialog box that appears, type in your new password. You won't see the letters, just an asterisk for each letter (to preserve confidentiality).
8. For confirmation that you typed it correctly, type it again in the Retype New Password text box. If there is a discrepancy between the two, you'll get an error message. Reenter the password. (If you're changing a password, the steps will be approximately the same. Enter your old password first, then the new one and its confirmation.) When it is correct, click on OK.

9. Back at the Desktop dialog box, set the number of minutes you want your computer to be idle before the screen saver springs into action. In the Delay space, either type in a number or use the up and down arrows to change the time incrementally.
10. When all the settings are correct, click on OK.

NETWORK OPTIONS

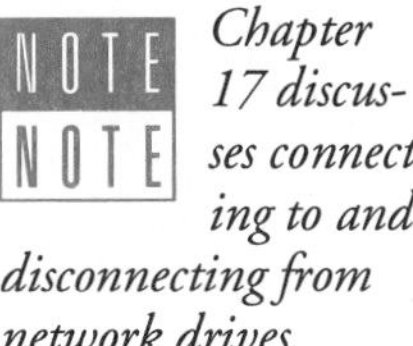

Chapter 17 discusses connecting to and disconnecting from network drives.

If you see a network icon in the Control Panel dialog box, this means you are connected to a network and the network software is running. Beyond that, it is difficult for me to predict here just what you will see when you click the icon. The dialog box that you see (if any) when you click this icon will depend on the type and brand of network attached. It's likely that you will have some choices such as logging on and off the network, selecting printers, passwords, and exchanging electronic mail (E-mail) with other network users.

INTERNATIONAL SETTINGS

TO ALTER INTERNATIONAL SETTINGS,

choose International from the Control Panel. Adjust the country, language, keyboard layout, measurement, list separator, date, time, currency, and number format defaults.

The International settings customize your Windows for use in other countries. If you're using Windows in English in the United States, don't bother making any changes unless you want to rearrange the keyboard to act like a Dvorak keyboard. (The Dvorak keyboard layout rearranges the keys for faster typing than the familiar—but old-fashioned—QWERTY layout, but you have to relearn the key locations.) The settings made from this box pertain exclusively to Windows and Windows applications. Other programs won't take advantage of them. Even some Windows applications won't. You should do some experimenting with the settings to see if they make any difference, or read the application's manual for information about how to set the formats for it.

Choosing International from the Control Panel displays the dialog box you see in Figure 5.11. The international settings and their explanations are shown below:

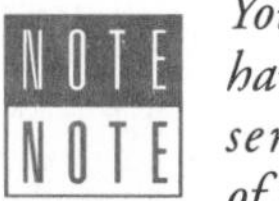

You may have to insert one of the Windows floppy disks when making changes if Windows needs some files.

Country selects which country you're in. All other settings change in accordance with the accepted practices in that country. Only bother changing the other options if necessary.

Language selects the language Windows will use as a default. Some applications use this information when processing your data or text.

Keyboard Layout sets the type of keyboard layout, with variations for each country and language.

Measurement displays Metric or English units.

List Separator: In the sentence "Well, it's one, two, three, what are we fighting for…" the list separator is a comma. In other languages, items listed in a sentence are separated by other punctuation marks.

Date Format sets dates from a myriad of formats such as 3/6/53; 03/06/53; 3/6/1953; 06–03–1953; March 6, 1953; and others. This is useful for programs that pop the date into text at the touch of a key, or that translate dates from one format to another.

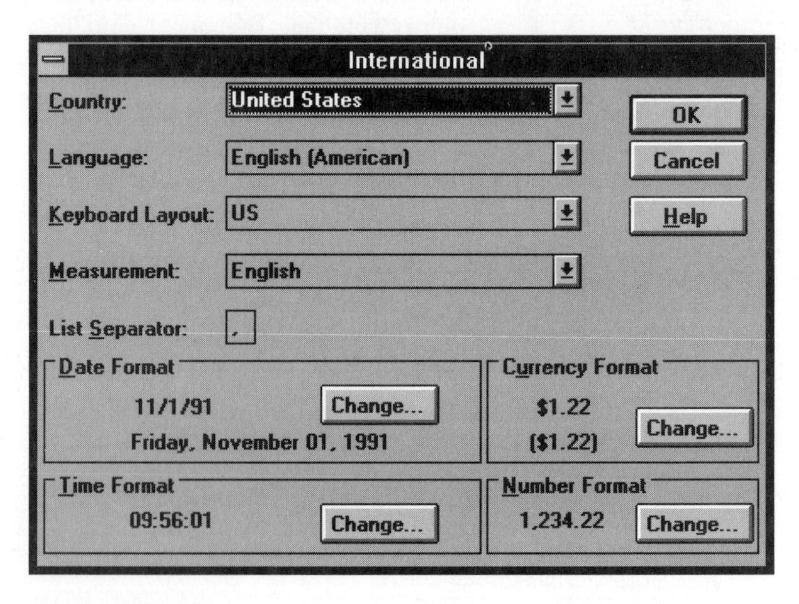

FIGURE 5.11: *The International dialog box. Changes you make here affect only the applications that use the internal Windows settings for such functions.*

Time Format allows for 12- or 24-hour time indication, AM or PM indicators, choice of separators, and leading zeros.

Currency Format sets the currency indicator and location and number of decimal digits.

Number Format displays numbers with or without decimals, commas, or leading zeroes, and with different decimal separators.

To change the settings:

1. Click on the International icon in the Control Panel dialog box.
2. Choose Country, Language, Keyboard Layout, and Measurement from the drop-down lists.
3. Set date, time, currency, and number formats via additional dialog boxes that appear when you click on the Change button in their respective sections. Examples of the current settings are shown in each section, so you don't need to change them unless they look wrong.

CHANGING THE KEY-REPEAT RATE

There's only one thing to change via the Keyboard icon—the key-repeat rate. Most keys repeat when you hold them down. This setting lets you change the speed:

1. Double-click on the Keyboard icon in the Control Panel dialog box. The box below appears:

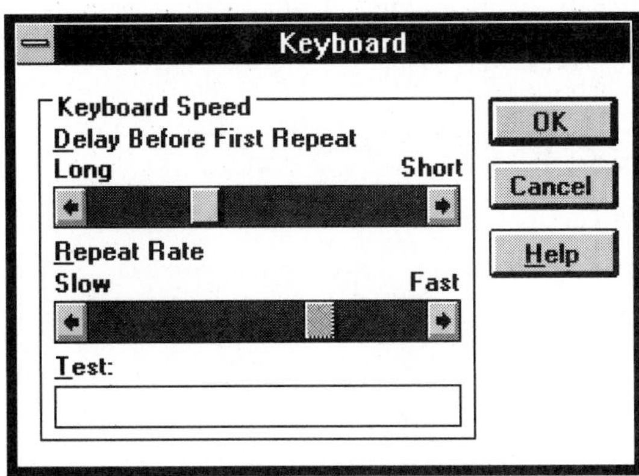

2. Drag the slider to change the key-repeat speed.
3. Test the key-repeat speed by clicking in the Test text box and holding down a letter key. If it's too slow or fast, adjust and try again.

SETTING THE DATE AND TIME

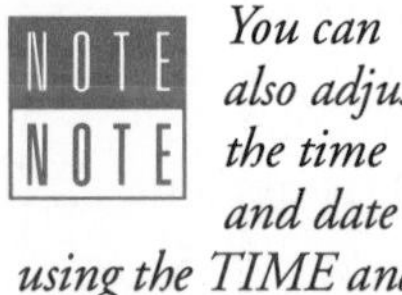

You can also adjust the time and date using the TIME and DATE commands from DOS.

The Date/Time icon lets you adjust the system's date and time. These are used for date- and time-stamping the files you create and modify. All programs use these settings, regardless of whether they are Windows or non-Windows programs. (This icon doesn't change the format of the date and time—just the actual date and time. To change their *format,* choose the International icon from the Control Panel.)

1. Double-click on the Date/Time icon. The dialog box below appears.

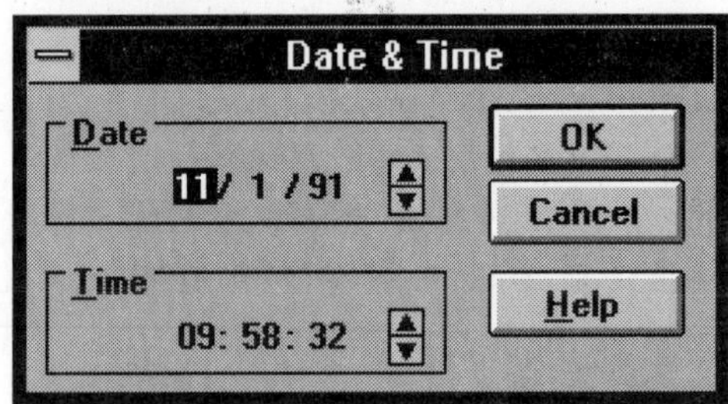

2. Adjust the time and date by typing in the corrections or clicking on the arrows.

MAKING 386-ENHANCED SETTINGS

If you are running in 386-Enhanced mode, you'll have an additional icon in your control panel. This icon is labeled "386-Enhanced" and looks like a computer chip. When clicked on, it brings up the dialog box shown in Figure 5.12.

FIGURE 5.12:

The 386-Enhanced dialog box, reachable from the Control Panel

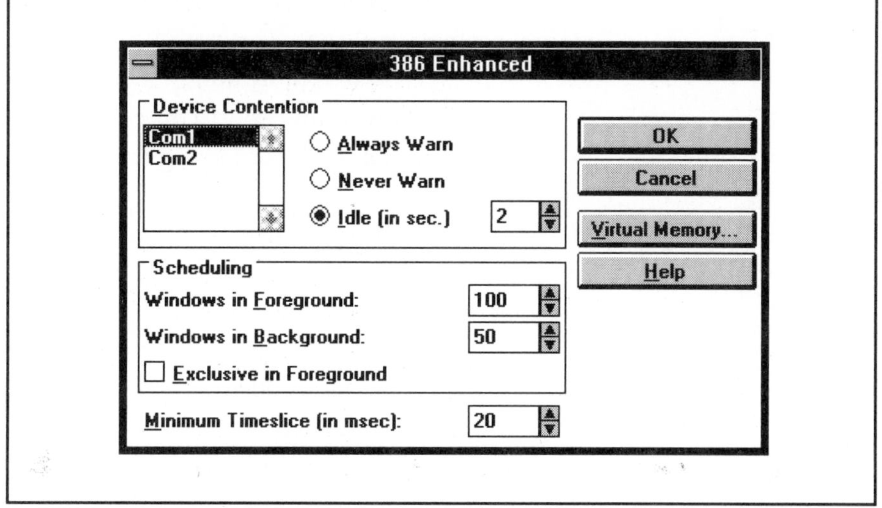

Unlike PIF settings or those you make from a running application, the settings you make from this dialog box affect *all* running programs. This includes both Windows and non-Windows programs. The settings will stay in effect until you change them.

The Device Contention Settings

The first section of the dialog box, Device Contention, controls the way Windows handles situations in which simultaneously running applications try to gain access to the same port.

For example, suppose you printed a spreadsheet from a Windows program such as Microsoft Excel and then switched to a non-Windows program and tried to print from that, too. If both programs expected to print to the same port, there would be a data collision, resulting in a garbled mess in your printout. When two applications expect unimpeded access to the same port, you have what's called a "hardware contention problem."

If you're only running Windows programs, you can forget about this section, since Windows arbitrates such problems automatically. As I explain in Chapter 7, the Print Manager handles all Windows application printing chores, preventing contention by virtue of print queueing. Hardware contention problems only occur between Windows and non-Windows applications, or between two or more non-Windows programs.

You can avoid printer-port contention quite easily. Just remember not to print from a non-Windows program when another application is printing to the same printer on the same port. That's the easiest rule of thumb. If you have several printers (such as network printers) connected to different ports, you can print one job to each port without trouble. Just be diligent in remembering what you've sent where and wait until the print job for a port is over before sending it another.

To help prevent data collisions on a port, Windows provides the dialog box settings. To use the settings, select the port in question and click on one of the three options. Here's what each one does:

Always Warn: If one program is already using the port and another one tries to, Windows will warn you in a dialog box. You will then have the option of selecting which program should have access to the port. In most cases, you should use this setting.

Never Warn: You will not be warned about device contention problems. Multiple programs will be allowed access to the same port. Results may be undesirable, however, with the typical example being garbage printouts or printouts containing information from two or more documents—a sort of unintentional merging of documents. If you know that no two programs will ever try to gain access to the port at the same time, or you want to ensure that Windows won't tie up your operations by displaying a warning dialog box, use this setting.

Idle: The time you enter here determines how much time should pass between applications' use of the device in question to prevent Windows from displaying the warning message. The range is 0 to 999 milliseconds.

As explained above, if the Always Warn option is set on, Windows will alert you if two programs try to access the same port at *exactly* the same time. However, programs don't always use a port continuously, and this could cause a problem. If there is a temporary lull in activity on a port or device, Windows could mistakenly allow another program to use it when the first program wasn't really through with it. For example, you might be using the COM1 port with a communications program. If you were distracted momentarily, perhaps to go answer the door, it's likely that no data would be flowing across the COM1 port. Windows could then assume you were finished using the port. Another program might then seize the port, ruining your communications session even if the Always Warn option were set on. To prevent this, you'd want to increase the idle time.

Foreground and Background CPU Scheduling

The second section determines how CPU time is split between Windows and non-Windows programs during multitasking. To comprehend the settings, it's important to understand that Windows applications are always multitasked, even in Standard mode. You cannot control the timeslicing or CPU allocation for those applications. Windows shares the CPU time equally among them. What we're dealing with here are settings that determine the amount of CPU time that Windows programs will *give up* to non-Windows programs running in 386-Enhanced mode. In Standard mode, this is not an issue, since a non-Windows program, when active, takes over all the CPU time. In 386-Enhanced mode, however, CPU time can be shared between non-Windows and Windows programs. All the Windows programs are treated as one program, all receiving the same amount of time. Here are the descriptions of each setting (you may want to refer to the section on advanced PIF settings in Chapter 13 for more detailed descriptions of these settings):

Windows in Foreground: This determines the relative amount of CPU time allotted to all Windows applications when one Windows application is running in the foreground (active). As long as one Windows application is active, they will all get CPU time determined by this setting. The important issue is the ratio between this setting and the sum of the Foreground settings for all other non-Windows programs that are running. (Their *background priority* PIF settings, described earlier in this chapter, determine this ratio). If your Windows applications slow down considerably when non-Windows programs are running in the background, you might try increasing this number. (You could also try decreasing the non-Windows applications' background priority, or setting their back ground- execution options off.)

Windows in Background: This determines the relative amount of CPU time that all Windows programs collectively receive when running in the background—that is, when a non-Windows program is the active window.

Exclusive in Foreground: When set on, this option prevents all non-Windows applications from running whenever *any* Windows application is in the foreground.

Minimum Timeslice Setting

The Minimum Timeslice check box determines the minimum amount of time allotted to any application before Windows redirects the CPU to the next application. Normally this is set to 20 milliseconds. Thus, up to fifty applications could be serviced every second. (Keep in mind, however, that all running Windows applications taken together are treated as a single application.) Increasing this number will improve the overall efficiency of your programs. This is because the switching process in and of itself requires CPU time. So, reducing the number of times the CPU switches among applications per second leaves more CPU time for your applications. However, Windows appears to run more smoothly when the switching rate is faster (timeslice is smaller). If you want to increase the smoothness of Windows, decrease this number. If you want to increase the efficiency of your programs marginally, increase the number. If you don't know what to do, leave it alone, since the default of 20 is a reasonable compromise arrived at through experimentation by the engineers at Microsoft.

Virtual Memory Settings

Clicking the Virtual Memory button brings up a dialog box that allows you to set the size and type of your "swap file." Windows uses this free space on your hard disk to simulate additional system RAM, increasing the number of programs you can run simultaneously. Formerly managed in Windows 3.0 using SWAPFILE.EXE, it's now much easier to check your current swap file settings and alter them. The use of this button is explained in Chapter 16.

FAST TRACK

CHAPTER

6

FAST TRACK

To begin installation of a new printer driver, ... 189

open the Control Panel and select Printers. Click on Add. Select your printer's name and model from the list box. Follow the instructions on the screen regarding inserting any necessary disk(s) in the floppy drive. Repeat for each printer you want to install.

To make connections to your printer, ... 193

open the Control Panel and select Printers. Highlight the printer to have a port assigned to it. Click on Connect. From the Connect dialog box, select the port, timeout, and fast printing options.

To choose various printer options, ... 198

open the Control Panel and select Printers. Choose the printer and click on Setup. Set the paper size, trays, and print orientation. See additional options by clicking on Options.

To set the default printer, ... 200

from the Printers dialog box, double-click the printer name. The default printer is used by programs that don't give the option of changing printers at print time.

To choose a network printer, ... 201

log onto the network. From the Printers dialog box, choose Connect. Click on Network. Set the printer path and password (if necessary). Click on Connect.

To remove a printer and driver from your setup, ... 202

from the Printers dialog box, highlight the name of the printer you want to remove. Click on Remove.

If your printer isn't listed in the driver list, ... 203

check the compatibility list for a driver that will work with your printer. If there isn't one, contact Microsoft to see if there is a new driver available. If there isn't, contact the printer manufacturer for a Windows 3.1 driver.

CHAPTER 6

FEATURING

Installing, Connecting, and Removing a Printer

Choosing Print Options

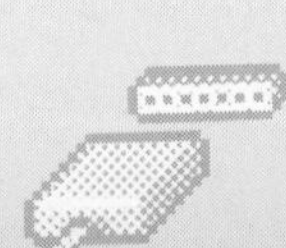

Installing a Printer

hen you installed Windows, you may have elected to install a printer. If you did, Windows ran the Control Panel and executed the printer installation program that is triggered when you click on the Printers icon in that window. Thus, you may be somewhat familiar with the procedure. If your printer is already installed and seems to be working fine, then you can probably skip over this chapter. However, if you need to install a new printer, want to modify or customize your current installation, or add an additional printer(s) to your setup, then read on. This chapter will cover how to:

- install a new printer
- install a printer if it's not listed
- select the printer port
- configure your printer setup

- set the default printer
- select a printer when more than one is installed
- set specific printing options
- print over a network
- remove a printer from your setup

ABOUT PRINTER INSTALLATION

The first thing to know when installing printers is that there's a file in your Windows directory that contains sundry data pertaining to printers. It's called PRINTERS.WRI. You should read this file because it's full of helpful hints not included in the manuals. It's the latest scoop about printing with Windows, and it's so recent that I can't even include it reliably in this book—it changes too often, particularly as Microsoft adds new printers to their list. You may have already read it if you elected to read the online documentation during the Windows setup, though it may have made no sense at that time.

In any case, the easiest way to read it is to get into the File Manager, open the Windows directory, and double-click on PRINTERS.WRI. Since it's a .WRI file, and such files are associated with the Write application, it will load into a Write window. There are instructions at the beginning of the file explaining how to use it. There's lots of technical gobbledygook in the file, too, which you can forget about if you don't understand it or if it doesn't apply to your particular printer or printing jobs.

One point to remember: The way you configure your printer while in Windows only affects printing from Windows applications. Non-Windows (DOS) applications don't use these settings or the drivers, even if you run the program from within Windows. See Chapter 7 for more details about printing with Windows and DOS applications.

The overall game plan for installing a printer is to:

- install the printer driver file onto your hard disk from a floppy disk, either supplied with Windows or with your printer
- select the printer's port and relevant port settings

Once these steps are complete, your printer should work, and you probably won't need to do anything more. However, there are several more customizations you can make to your setup along the way. You may want to:

- select printer settings relevant to page orientation, scaling, type of paper feed, halftone imaging, and when file header information (such as a PostScript "preamble") is sent to the printer
- specify the amount of time you want Windows to keep trying to print a document before alerting you to a printer problem
- select the default printer if you have more than one printer installed
- choose whether your printer should substitute its own fonts for certain TrueType fonts

If you only want to modify one of the settings for your currently installed printer, look for the section that explains that topic and skip to it. You may, however, have to work your way up to the dialog box that contains the pertinent setting. Figure 6.1 shows all the dialog boxes associated with setting up a PostScript printer, and the paths taken to arrive there. Figure 6.2 shows a similar path for an HP LaserJet printer. (The dialog boxes for your printer may look a bit different.)

INSTALLING THE PRINTER DRIVER

TO BEGIN INSTALLATION OF A NEW PRINTER DRIVER,

open the Control Panel and select Printers. Click on Add. Select your printer's name and model from the list box. Follow the instructions on the screen regarding inserting any necessary disk(s) in the floppy drive. Repeat for each printer you want to install.

A printer driver is a file whose job is to translate the data you want to print so that your printer knows how to print them. Windows needs special printer drivers to work with your printer, and many such drivers are included

FIGURE 6.1:

The complete road map of printer setup dialog boxes for a PostScript printer

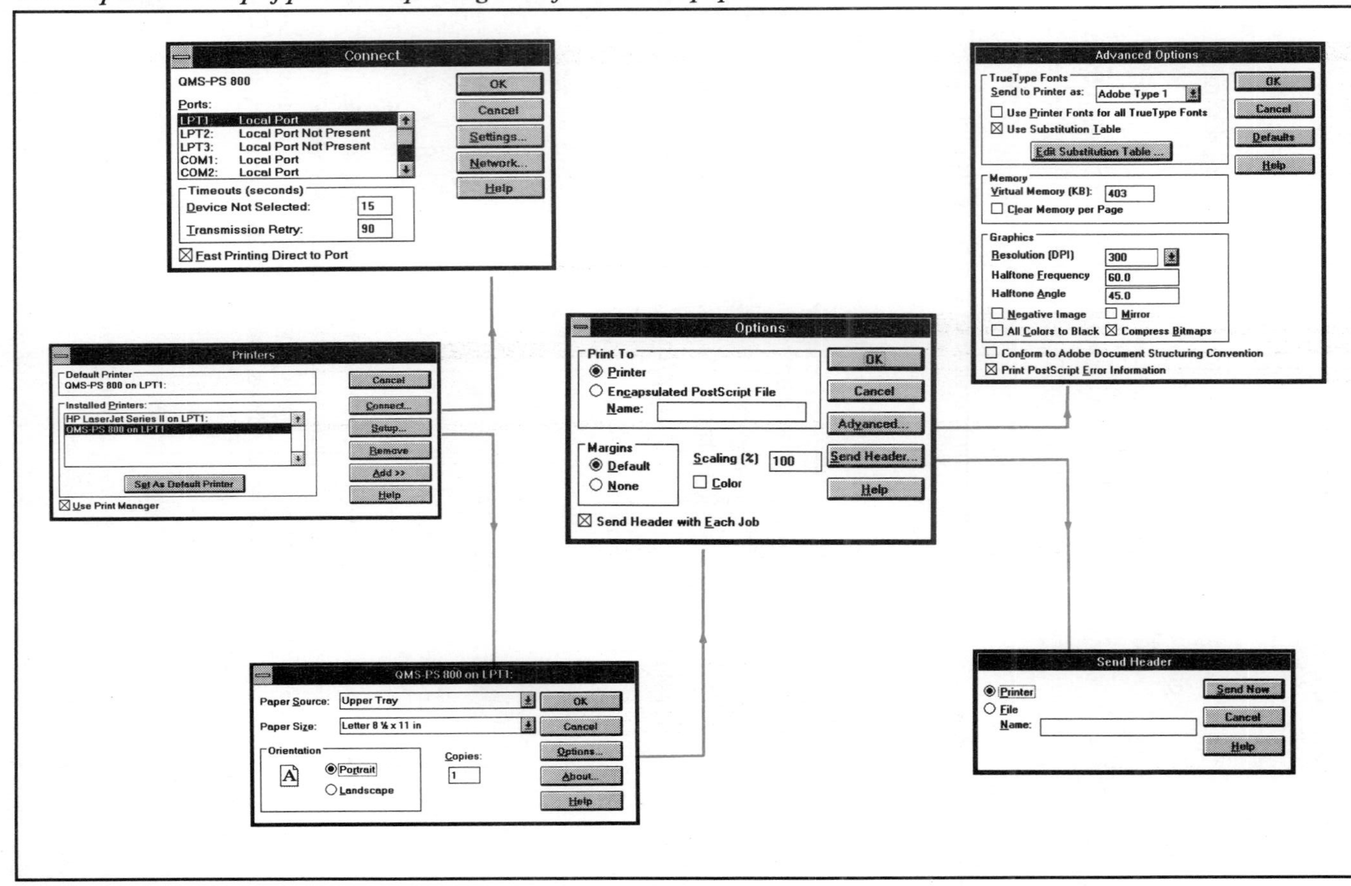

FIGURE 6.2:

The complete road map of printer setup dialog boxes for an HP LaserJet printer

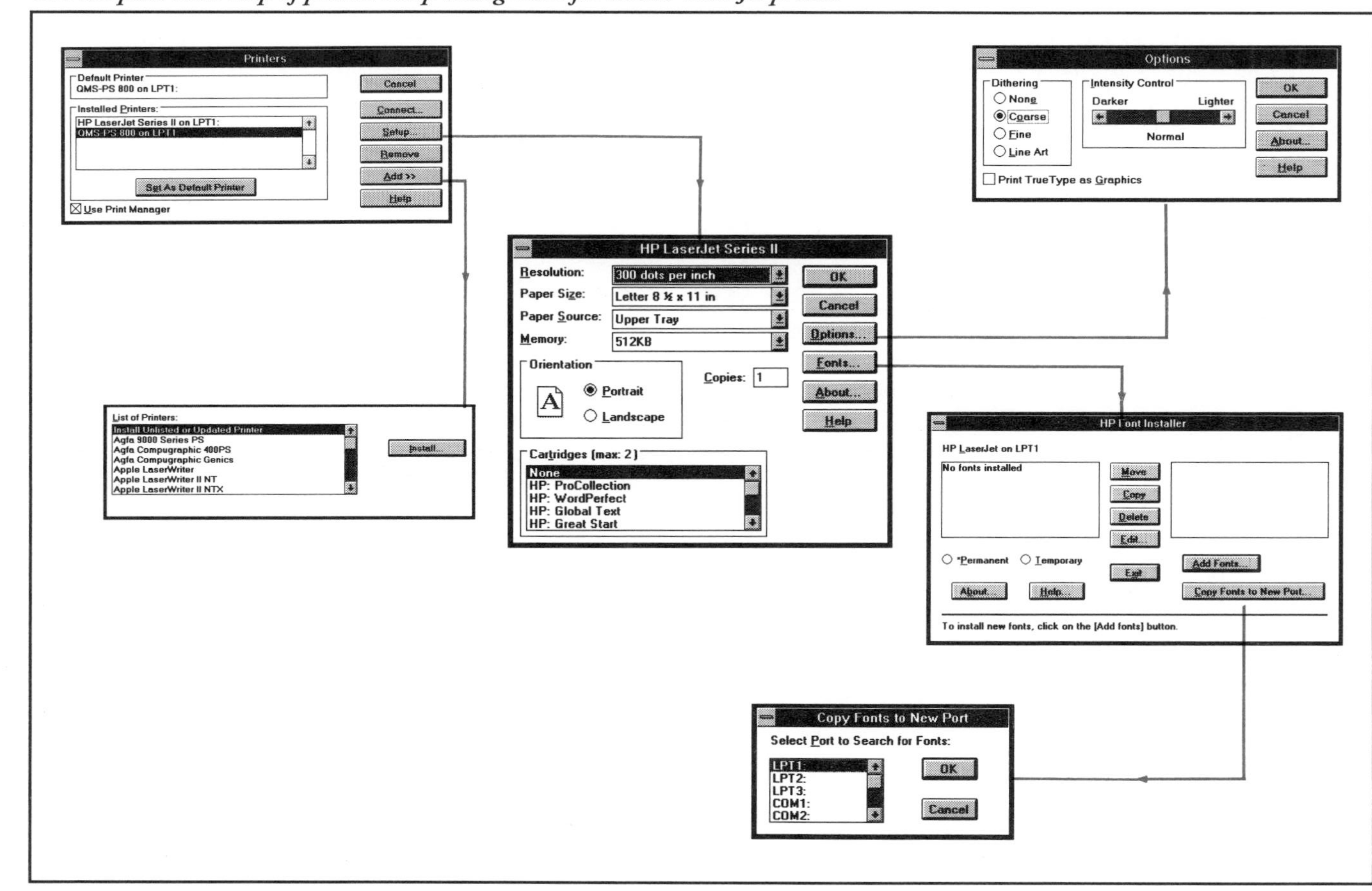

with Windows. In cases where a driver for your printer isn't included with Windows, the printer's manufacturer may be able to supply one. The procedure for installing manufacturer-supplied drivers is covered at the end of this chapter.

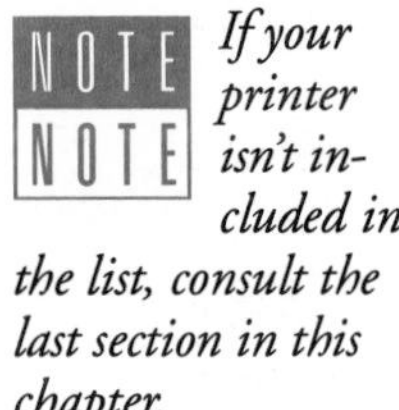

If your printer isn't included in the list, consult the last section in this chapter.

A good printer driver will take advantage of all your printer's capabilities, such as its built-in fonts and graphics features. A poor printer driver may succeed in printing only draft-quality text, even from a sophisticated printer.

Install the printer driver by following these steps:

1. Open the Control Panel and double-click on Printers.
2. From the resulting dialog box, click on Add. The dialog box expands to look like that shown in Figure 6.3. (If no printers were previously installed, you don't have to click on Add; the box expands automatically.)

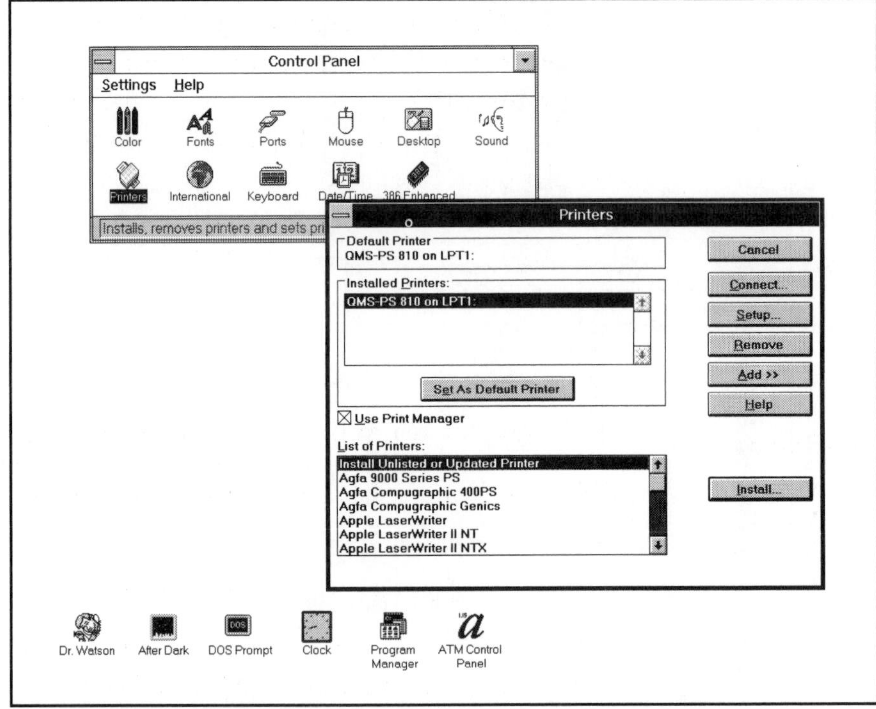

FIGURE 6.3:

The main printer dialog box. From here you can install or remove a printer, or modify any printer setup.

3. Select your printer from the list. Make sure to select the exact printer model, not just the correct brand name. Consult your printer's manual if you're in doubt about the model.
4. Click on Install. You will likely be instructed to insert one of your Windows disks into a floppy drive so that Windows can copy the appropriate printer driver from it onto your hard disk. If necessary, insert the disk, make sure the path name of the drive is correct, and click on OK (e.g., if using drive B, just change the A:\ to B:\). If the printer driver with the correct name is already on the hard disk, then you won't be instructed to insert a disk; the existing driver will be used.
5. You'll be alerted to insert additional disks if they are needed for the font files. Just follow the instructions on screen. The printer name is added to the Installed Printers box. The first printer in the list is the "default" printer in the Default Printer text box.

If you want to install additional printers, you can do so at this point or later. Just repeat the above steps. The first printer you install will automatically be set to the active state and assigned to the LPT1 printer port, as indicated in the Installed Printers list. Additional printers will be set to the inactive state, and will not be assigned a port. In either case, you must at least assign the port before trying to print with them, or it's likely that the additional printers won't work.

CONNECTING THE PRINTER

TO MAKE CONNECTIONS TO YOUR PRINTER,

open the Control Panel and select Printers. Highlight the printer to have a port assigned to it. Click on Connect. From the Connect dialog box, select the port, timeout, and fast printing options.

Once you've finished the above steps by installing the driver for your printer, the next steps involve assigning a port and setting the timeouts. This is called making a connection.

Assigning the Port

Here you tell Windows where your printer is physically hooked up to your computer. As a default, Windows assigns a printer to LPT1 (also called a *parallel port*), but you can alter this assignment via these steps:

1. The Printers dialog box should still be on your screen. If it isn't, select Printers from the Control Panel again.
2. Select the printer whose port you are setting.
3. Click on the Connect button. This brings up the Connect dialog box, as shown in Figure 6.4.
4. Click on the port you want to use:

   LPT1:, LPT2:, LPT3: The most common setting is LPT1, since most PC-type printers hook up to the LPT1 parallel port.

FIGURE 6.4:

You set the printer port assignments from this box

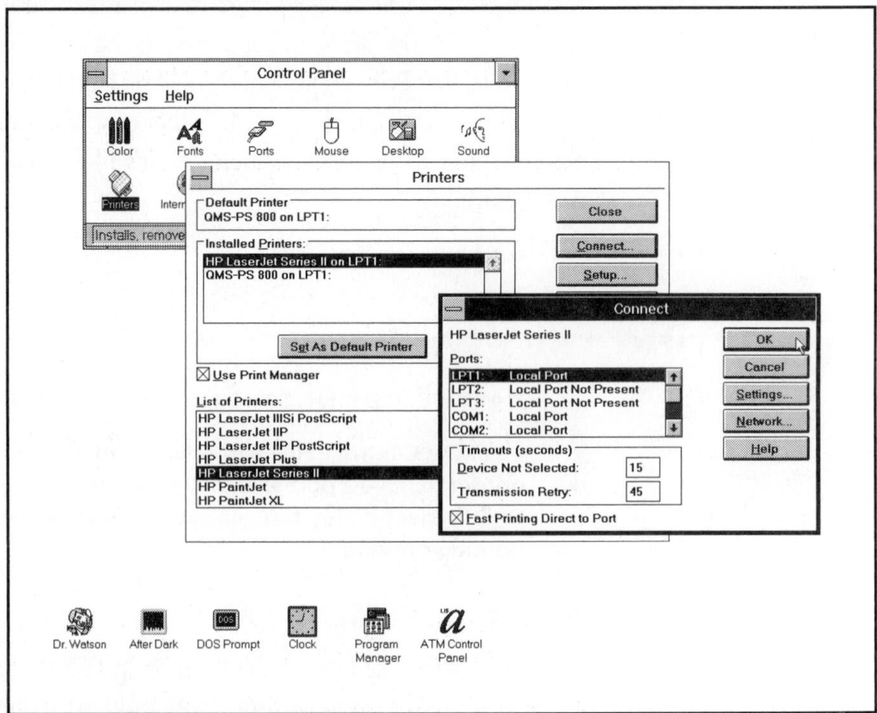

COM1:, COM2:, COM3:, COM4: If you know your printer to be of the *serial* variety, then chances are it's connected to the COM1 port. If COM1 is tied up for use with some other device, such as a modem, then use COM2. (Make sure your printer is actually connected to a serial port assigned to COM2. Refer to your computer's manuals or ask someone who knows.) If you choose a COM port, the Settings button becomes active. You should click on it to check the communications settings in the resulting dialog box. Set the baud rate, data bits, parity, stop bits, and flow control to match those of the printer being attached. Refer to the printer's manual to determine what the settings should be.

EPT: If you're using an IBM Personal Pageprinter or other printer that required installation of a specially supplied printer circuit card in your computer, use this setting.

FILE: This is for printing to a disk file instead of to the printer. Later the file can be sent directly to the printer, or sent to someone on floppy disk or over a modem. Printing to files is covered in more detail in Chapter 7.

LPT1.DOS, LPT2.DOS These choices are similar to the LPT1: and LPT2: options. The difference here is that a connection using these ports prints from Windows applications through DOS and your computer's BIOS, instead of directly to the ports using Windows' drivers. You only have to use this setting if you have special memory-resident printing software that loads before Windows, such as an AppleTalk printer driver or a program that switches your printer between HP LaserJet and PostScript emulation. If you aren't having success printing through the normal LPT1: and LPT2: connections, try these. (In Windows 3.0 these ports were called LPT1.OS2 and LPT2.OS2—and if you upgraded from 3.0 you may still see these names for the ports.)

Setting the Timeouts

There are several other options in the Connections box to consider. The first is the *timeouts.* When there's a problem with your printer, such as running out of paper, applications (and DOS) often aren't very nice about it.

The result can be a printing job that gets unceremoniously terminated, or the appearance of a not very lucid description of the problem on your screen, such as

DOS error writing device PRN
Abort, Retry, Fail?

Other times you're left sitting and waiting while your laser printer's data light happily flashes, particularly when printing graphics, which can seem to take an eternity. Quite reasonably, you assume that everything's fine. That is, until you realize that you've downed two cups of coffee waiting for your one-page report to print.

The culprit precipitating some of these printing migraines is called a timeout. Printers, programs, and operating systems like DOS don't always agree on how long to wait in the case of an error before throwing in the towel. So, while you're busily adding paper to the tray or changing a ribbon with the printer top open, or before you've remembered to put the printer *online* to begin with, something just decides to give up.

The timeout settings determine how long Windows should wait before issuing an error message, should it appear that there is some malady with your printer. Of course, the error message dialog box, just like the DOS Retry message, lets you retry the transmission from the point where it stopped, so long as you're around to monitor the printing process—it's no big deal if your setting isn't perfect.

You can alter the default timeout settings as follows. From the Printer dialog box, click on Connect (if the box isn't already open as a result of setting the port assignment). In the Connect dialog box, there are two timeout settings:

Device Not Selected: If your printer is *offline,* how long should Windows wait before sending a message to that effect? Offline is a state wherein the printer is temporarily disconnected from the computer and cannot receive data. Many printers automatically go offline when you remove the paper tray or they run out of paper. Some printers also have a panel switch that takes them offline. Make sure the printer is online before you start to print. This setting is normally 15 seconds, but you may want to increase it if, for example, the printer is quite a ways from the computer and changing paper takes a while. Increasing this timeout would let you correct the problem and continue printing without having to tell Windows to retry the print job.

Transmission Retry: Printers and computers communicate with each other about the progress of their data transmission. When the printer receives some data, it acknowledges this to the computer. The computer then sends the next portion of data. If for some reason, other than being offline, the Windows Print Manager doesn't receive an acknowledgment from the printer (the reasons vary from printer to printer), the Transmission Retry setting comes into play. The default setting is 45 seconds, which is long enough for most purposes. If printing from your application regularly results in an error message about transmission problems, and retrying seems to work, increase the setting.

Allowing Fast Printing from DOS Applications

The last option in the Connect dialog box is a check box option, Fast Printing Direct to Port. The default setting for the box is on. You would normally leave this setting as is.

Here's the technical explanation for this option. Some DOS (non-Windows) applications send data to your printer by way of *DOS interrupts* rather than print directly to the port. Using DOS interrupts prevents two or more programs from printing simultaneously through the same port. Software engineers sometimes use this method to ensure proper behavior of their programs. Unfortunately, this technique has the side effect of slowing down the printing process. Since most programmers know this, a bulk of DOS programs print directly to the port instead of through DOS.

Determining whether an application program uses DOS interrupts or prints directly to the printer isn't easy. If you are installing a printer that you know is going to be used by applications that use DOS interrupts, you should turn off the option box.

Once your port, timeout, and fast printing options are set, click on OK. The port is assigned. The name of the port now appears to the right of the printer's name.

CHOOSING PRINT OPTIONS

TO CHOOSE VARIOUS PRINTER OPTIONS,

open the Control Panel and select Printers. Choose the printer and click on Setup. Set the paper size, trays, and print orientation. See additional options by clicking on Options.

Next you can make choices that will affect what your printouts look like, such as paper orientation, black intensity, font selections, scaling, and dithering pattern for printing complex images such as scanned photographs. You can make changes to some of these settings from the File menu of most Windows programs later on, when you're ready to print from that program. But making the settings now determines the default settings that will be assumed until such a time. The more advanced settings such as font substitution and dithering can only be reached from these dialog boxes.

From the main Printers dialog box select the printer whose options you want to configure and click on Setup. A dialog box like that shown in Figure 6.5 will appear.

The options and settings in your dialog box may be different from the ones shown here.

The options that you have will depend on the type of printer device you installed. Some options may be unavailable for your printer. In any case, here are all the possible options, with an explanation of each:

Resolution: Some printers can render graphics in more than one resolution. The higher the resolution, the longer the printing takes, so you can save on time with your drafts by choosing a lower resolution. For finished, high-quality work, choose the highest resolution.

Paper Size: Normally, it's assumed you're using 8½-by-11-inch paper. Change this if you are using a different paper size. There are eight available sizes.

Paper Source: Some printers have more than one tray (for paper of different lengths). You can choose which tray or bin to use, whether the paper will be fed manually or by a tractor. Tractor-feed paper has holes along the edges for sprockets to feed it into the printer.

FIGURE 6.5:

You configure options for a specific printer in this dialog box

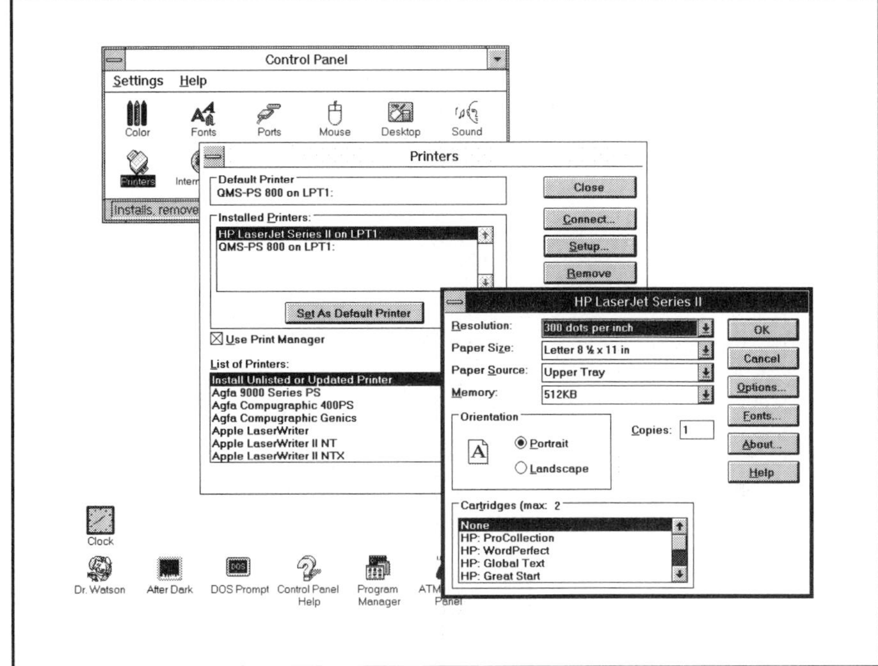

Memory: How much memory (RAM) your printer has. This setting applies primarily to laser printers. If you don't know the amount, just leave this setting as is, or consult the printer's manual.

Orientation: Page orientation. Normal orientation is Portrait, which, like the portrait of the Mona Lisa, is taller than it is wide. Landscape, like a landscape painting, is the opposite.

Cartridges: This section lists the possible font cartridges available for your printer (at least the ones known about at the time the driver was made). It also shows you how many cartridges can be physically plugged into your printer at one time. If two cartridges can be plugged in, select two names by holding down the Shift key while clicking on the names. This information is then used in the font dialog boxes in various Windows programs so that you can change the font of selected text.

Copies: Controls the number of copies of each page you print. Normally you want just one. But if you always print more than one, change the setting.

Fonts: This button lets you choose additional font cartridges or downloadable font files (sometimes called *soft fonts*) for your printer. Don't confuse these with fonts supplied with Windows. This button refers to fonts and cartridges that you purchase from other manufacturers (such as Bitstream, Hewlett-Packard, Adobe, and others) or your computer dealer.

Options: Some printers will have additional options available, as determined by the brand and model of printer. To change these options, click on Options. Then make the adjustments from the resulting dialog boxes. For information about each of the settings, click on the Help button in the dialog box. (The Help screens have hot spots that explain each of the settings.)

Make the changes you want and click on OK. This will return you to the Printers dialog box to make the settings described in the next section.

SELECTING THE DEFAULT PRINTER

If you've installed more than one printer (regardless of port), Windows needs to know which one is the default printer. The default printer will be used by programs that don't give you a choice of printers. It will also be the one that Windows always assumes you want to use unless you choose another printer with the Control Panel or with an application's printer setup dialog box.

To select the default printer:

1. From the Printers dialog box, double-click the name of the printer to be set as the default printer, or highlight it and click on Set As Default Printer.
2. Check to see that the dialog box section labeled Default Printer reflects the new default printer.

CHOOSING A NETWORK PRINTER

TO CHOOSE A NETWORK PRINTER,

log on to the network. From the Printers dialog box, choose Connect. Click on Network. Set the printer path and password (if necessary). Click on Connect.

Assuming your Windows system is successfully hooked up to a local area network (LAN) that has a network printer on it, you should be able to print from that printer. However, you'll have to select the printer from a different dialog box, called Network-Printer Connections.

First, make sure you've installed Windows correctly for use on the network. Please refer to the Windows manual and your network manual for more information.

You should also have run the network software upon booting up and logged on in such a way that there is a network printer currently assigned and available to your system. Only then are you able to choose a specific network printer:

1. From the main Printers dialog box, choose Connect.
2. From the Connect dialog box, click on Network. A new dialog box appears. The contents of this box will depend on the type of network you are using.
3. Choose the port you want to use. (Check your network operations manual if you don't know which port your printer is connected to.)
4. Enter the name of the network printer. Your network may allow you to see a list of the available network printers and choose one. Click on Browse to try this.
5. If you have previously connected to printers on the network (during the current or previous Windows sessions), clicking on Previous may display a list of those connections, making it easier to reconnect.
6. Type in the password if necessary.

7. Click on Connect. The printer is connected to Windows and the printer name appears in the Current Printer Connections list. If there was already a printer connected to that port, you'll be alerted to the conflict, which you will have to correct before the connection is made.
8. Click on Close.

When you want to disconnect a network printer from Windows, highlight the printer and click on the Disconnect button. (See Chapter 7 for more information about printing over a network.)

REMOVING A PRINTER

TO REMOVE A PRINTER AND DRIVER FROM YOUR SETUP,

from the Printers dialog box, highlight the name of the printer you want to remove. Click on Remove.

If you get a new printer and decommission the current one, you should remove the old printer from the list of available drivers and printers. This process also removes the associated printer driver file unless another printer relies on it. This frees up disk space and reduces hard disk clutter. However, it doesn't remove all the fonts that might be associated with the driver. This could be a problem if disk space is tight, since fonts can take up considerable room. To remove fonts, use the Fonts command from the Control Panel, as described in Chapter 5.

To remove a printer from the installed printers list:

1. Open the Printers dialog box by clicking on Printers in the Control Panel.
2. In the Installed Printers box, highlight the name of the printer you want to remove.
3. Click on Remove. You are asked to confirm the removal.
4. Click on OK. You will be returned to the main Printers dialog box. Click Close to leave that box.

WHAT TO DO IF YOUR PRINTER ISN'T ON THE INSTALLATION LIST

If your printer isn't listed in the rather huge list of printers supplied with Windows, there is still hope. Many off-brand printers are designed to be compatible with one of the popular printer types, such as the Epson MX series, Hewlett-Packard LaserJet, or Apple LaserWriter.

The Windows manual comes with a hardware compatibility listing which you should check just to see if your printer is listed. If it is, then you can use the driver designed for the printer that yours is compatible with.

If your printer is not listed there, it may still be compatible. Check the manual supplied with the printer and look for any indication of compatibility. It's usually listed up front, along with the description of the printer, or in the back if there is a technical description of operating modes. Setting the printer in a compatibility mode may require the adjustment of switches in the printer. Again, check the printer's manual for these.

Finally, if it looks like there's no mention of compatibility anywhere, you may have a printer manufactured by a company that simply wanted to build a better mouse trap. And they might have. (There's always room for improvements when it comes to printers!) It's possible that the manufacturer has a printer driver for Windows 3.1 that they will send you upon request. It's also possible that Microsoft has a new driver for your printer that wasn't available when your copy of the program was shipped. Contact Microsoft Corp. at (206) 882-8080 and ask for the Windows Driver Library Disk which will contain all the latest drivers. (They may ask for the serial number of your program or some other identification.)

Assuming you *do* obtain a printer driver, follow these instructions to install it:

1. Follow the instructions described early in the chapter under "Installing the Printer Driver." However, instead of selecting the name of the printer (which isn't in the list), scroll to the top of the list and pick Install Unlisted or Updated Printer.
2. Click on Install.

3. Windows will ask you to insert the proper disk(s) and press Enter.
4. You may have to copy other files associated with the driver. They should be copied into the \WINDOWS\SYSTEM directory unless otherwise directed by instructions supplied with the printer driver.
5. Follow the instructions described in "Assigning the Port" to continue the installation.

FAST TRACK

CHAPTER

7

FAST TRACK

To print from a Windows application, ... 211

check that the printer and page settings are correct. Select the Print command on the application's File menu, fill in whatever information is asked of you, and click OK.

To view the print queue, ... 213

open the Print Manager window, either from its icon at the bottom of the screen (if something is printing or the Print Manager is active), or by double-clicking on the Print Manager icon in the Main group.

To pause the printing process, ... 217

from the queue window, click on the large Pause button in the upper-left corner. The Print Manager will stop sending data to the printer, and the current print job (the one with the printer icon to the left of its information line) will be temporarily suspended. (The printing may not stop immediately because your printer may have a buffer that holds data in preparation for printing. The printing will stop when the buffer is empty.)

To resume the printing process, ... 217

from the queue window, click on the large Resume button in the upper-left corner. The Print Manager will continue sending data to the printer, starting where it left off.

To set the printing priority (and so affect the speed), ... **218**

open the Print Manager's Options menu and choose Low, Medium, or High Priority.

To print on a network, ... **220**

1. Select Options ➤ Network Connections in the Print Manager window and choose the relevant button to check the connection.
2. Select Options ➤ Printer Setup, then click on Setup to verify that the correct printer is selected in the application's Setup dialog box.
3. Print the file.

To print from non-Windows applications, ... **227**

because you cannot use the Print Manager, you print using the same procedures as from DOS.

To print to a disk file, ... **228**

1. Make sure the correct printer driver is installed.
2. Run Print Manager.
3. Choose Options ➤ Printer Setup.
4. Click on Connect. From the Ports box, choose File.
5. Exit the boxes, return to your application, and print.
6. Type in the File name when prompted.

CHAPTER 7

FEATURING

Print Manager Basics

Managing the Print Queue

Printing on a Network

Printing from Non-Windows Applications

Printing to and from a Disk File

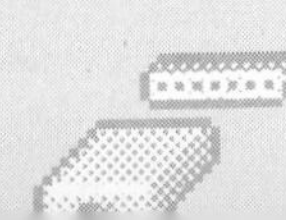
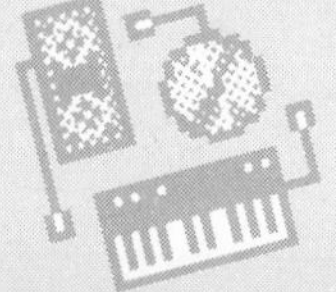

Using the Print Manager

nce you have your printers set up, as described in Chapter 6, Windows uses the Print Manager to print your documents. Just as the Program Manager and File Manager help you organize programs and files, the Print Manager helps organize printing tasks within Windows. Thus, whenever you print from a Windows application, the Print Manager automatically takes control of the printing job, using the selected printer driver and setup options.

Unfortunately, the Print Manager does not work with non-Windows applications. A program has to be designed a certain way to function with the Print Manager. However, this doesn't mean you can't print from non-Windows applications while running Windows. You can, but unless you are running in 386-Enhanced mode, your computer will be tied up during the printing process, just as if you were printing with DOS outside of Windows. That process is discussed later in the section "Printing from Non-Windows Applications."

PRINT MANAGER BASICS

When you print from non-Windows programs in DOS, your computer and printer take over the show. You're reduced to taking a coffee-break, going for a jog around the block (probably not a bad idea), or pulling out a pencil and paper to continue your work. This is because most programs won't let you print a document and work on another one at the same time.

There are many programs available (called *spoolers*) that let you do this, however, and you may have tried one. They'll let you print from DOS applications and go immediately back to work, while the program prints your files in the *background.*

A spooler program (PRINT.COM or PRINT.EXE, depending on your version of DOS) is supplied with your copy of DOS. It lets you specify a list of files to be printed (such a list is called the print *queue*), and then prints them while you return to your work. However, using it is awkward at best.

Though there are better spoolers available for use with DOS, these accessory programs are still only as elegant as their user interface. And they do not guarantee equal success with all programs. Some programs print just fine, and others not so well.

Because of the consistency in the design of programs created for Windows, a task such as printing can be controlled in a more sophisticated manner than normally allowed under DOS. The Print Manager is the program that provides that control. It handles all printing tasks within Windows. It's a well-designed spooler with the graphical interface and convenience typical of Windows applications. When printing with the Print Manager you can:

- immediately go back to work, even with another application.
- start other programs and print from them, too. Print Manager just adds subsequent documents to the queue.
- automatically utilize all the capabilities of the printer driver and setup you installed. Your settings for such options as number of copies, paper tray, page orientation, and so forth, are automatically used during the print job so you don't have to set them each time, though you can change the defaults if you like.
- easily see which jobs are currently being printed or are in the queue waiting to be printed. A window displays this information along with an indication of the current print job's progress.

- add jobs to the print queue the same way you print them individually. The Print Manager handles the details.
- easily rearrange the order of the print queue or delete jobs from it.
- adjust how much of your computer's computing time goes to printing instead of to your work.
- temporarily pause or resume printing without causing printer problems.
- print to a local printer, or to a network printer if you are connected to a network.

You can also bypass the Print Manager and print directly to the printer port to speed up printing on a network.

PRINTING FROM WINDOWS APPLICATIONS

TO PRINT FROM A WINDOWS APPLICATION,

check that the printer and page settings are correct. Select the Print command on the application's File menu, fill in whatever information is asked of you, and click OK.

As explained above, Windows applications automatically take advantage of Print Manager. If you print from Notepad, for example, it will automatically run the Print Manager, which then handles the print job. All of the printer settings you make from the Control Panel's printer dialog boxes then go into effect, since the Print Manager uses the printer driver and printer setup you have already established. (There is one exception to this. When configuring a printer from the Control Panel, there is an option in the Printers dialog box that lets you turn off the Print Manager. When that check box is turned off, all print jobs will bypass the Print Manager and go directly to the printer. No spooling will occur, and your computer will be tied up until the print job is concluded. This can speed up printing on some networks.)

The exact appearance of your printed documents may vary from program to program, though, depending on the degree to which your Windows application can take advantage of the printer-driver setup. Some programs, such as Write, let you change fonts, for example, while others, such as Notepad, don't. Consult the program's manual to figure out what options are supported by your applications. You might have to experiment a bit by actually printing several times before you're satisfied with the results.

In general, the way Print Manager works is this: When you print from a Windows program, it actually prints to a disk file instead of directly to the printer. Print Manager then spools the file to the assigned printer(s), coordinating the flow of data and keeping you informed of the progress.

To print from any Windows application with the Print Manager, follow these steps:

1. Check to see that the printer and page settings are correct. Some applications provide a Printer Setup or other option on their File menu for this.
2. Select the Print command on the application's File menu and fill in whatever information is asked of you.
3. Click on OK. The application writes the printer file to the hard disk and tells Windows to start up the Print Manager (if it isn't already running). The Print Manager icon appears at the bottom of the Desktop and, depending on the application, you may see a little message box informing you that a document is being printed.
4. Click the Cancel button on this box (or follow other instructions depending on the program) if you want to abort the printing before it is added to the Print Manager queue. If you don't get to the Cancel button fast enough, don't worry. You can still stop the printing from the Print Manager window (see "Deleting a File from the Queue" later on).
5. Wait for the document to print, or go back to work. If there is an error, the Print Manager will alert you. When the document is finished printing, the Print Manager icon will disappear from the Desktop (assuming the queue is empty), as Windows closes Print Manager to free up memory.

PRINTING FROM THE FILE MANAGER

You can quickly print Windows applications document files by dragging them from a File Manager window into the running Print Manager. This is an easy way to add files to the print queue. Just run File Manager, then run Print Manager. Then drag your document files either into the Print Manager icon or window. Printing will commence. The documents must have associations or the printing won't work.

VIEWING THE PRINT QUEUE

TO VIEW THE PRINT QUEUE,

open the Print Manager window, either from its icon at the bottom of the screen (if something is printing or the Print Manager is active), or by double-clicking on the Print Manager icon in the Main group.

Once you have a number of documents printing in the queue, there's more you might want to know about the status of your print jobs. Probably the thing you'll want to do most often from the Print Manager's window is check the status of the queue—which job is currently printing, which printer it's printing to, and what percentage of the job is finished printing. You also may want to see the names and sizes of other print jobs in the queue.

To experiment with viewing the queue, try printing something handy. An easy thing to open and print is a topic from the Help system. Follow these steps if you want to experiment:

1. Run the Print Manager by double-clicking its icon. (It's in the Program Manager's Main group.) The opening screen comes up and looks like the one you see in Figure 7.1. Maximize the window.
2. Choose Help ➤ Contents, then move the hand cursor to the topic "Print Your Documents" in the Print Manager Help window and click on it to open the Help screen. Adjust it so that the top third of the Print Manager window is still showing.
3. Set up your printer with paper and make sure it's online.

FIGURE 7.1: *The initial Print Manager screen with no print jobs pending*

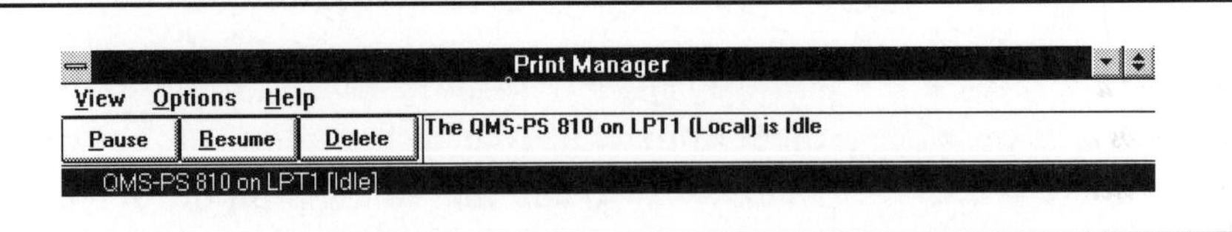

4. Choose File ➤ Print Setup from the Help window, make sure the correct printer is selected, and close Print Setup.
5. Choose File ➤ Print Topic. The Help topic "Printing Your Documents" is printed to a disk file, and then the disk file is added to the print queue as shown in Figure 7.2 (although the list shows the file name as "Untitled"). Printing should commence immediately.
6. Click on the Pause button in the Print Manager window. This will stop the printing and you can then add some more items to the queue before the first one finishes and vanishes from it. Notice that the message line indicates that the printer is paused.
7. In the Help window, use the Browse button to view other topics, such as the commands. Print each of them. They'll be added to the queue and there should then be three files waiting to print. Since the printer is paused, nothing will be printing. Your screen will look something like Figure 7.3.

NOTE *You can hide the file size and the date and time information of queued files if you want to. Open the View menu and set the Print File Size and Date/Time Sent toggles to the off position.*

You may notice the following pieces of information in the print queue screen:

- The message box reports the name, port, and status of the printer. If you click on a file in the queue, the message box changes to indicate which printer and port the file is being sent to.
- The first line of the queue indicates the name of the printer, its status, and which port it's connected to. This is called the *queue information line.*
- Below that, each print job queued up for that printer occupies one line. These lines are called *file information lines.* The currently

FIGURE 7.2:

Printing a file from any Windows application automatically adds the file to the print queue.

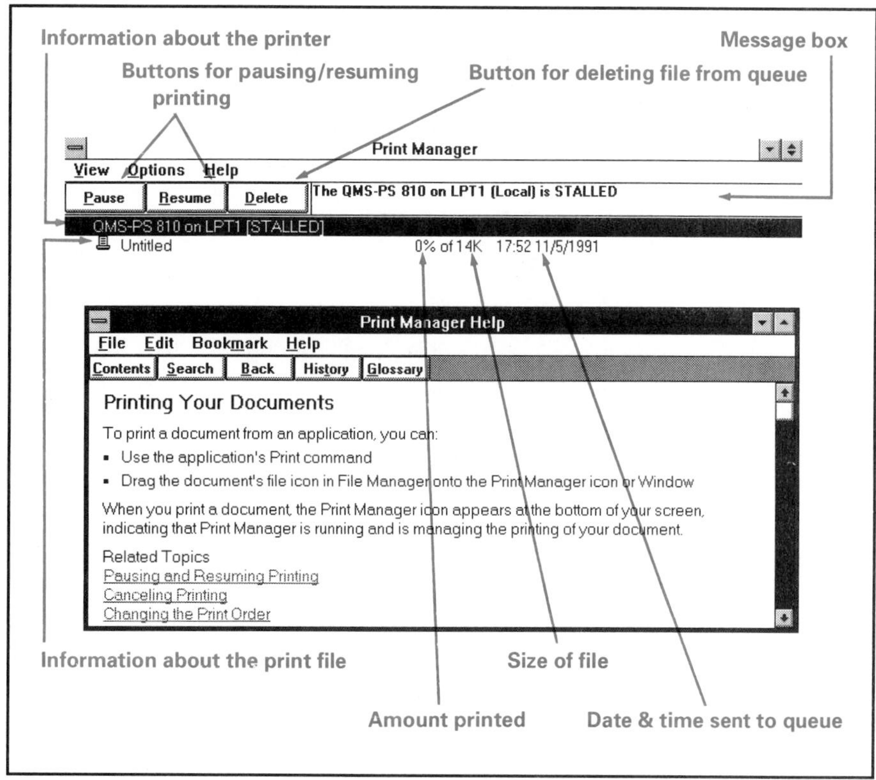

printing file shows a printer icon to its left. Subsequent jobs have numbers to their left, indicating their position in the queue. To the right of the numbers are the name of the originating application, the document being printed, the size of the file, and the time and date the file was put on the queue. If a file is printing, the percentage of the file that has been printed appears on its information line just to the left of the file size (e.g., 35% of 15K).

- If files have been queued to other printers (including network printers), there will be additional printer information lines and file information lines.

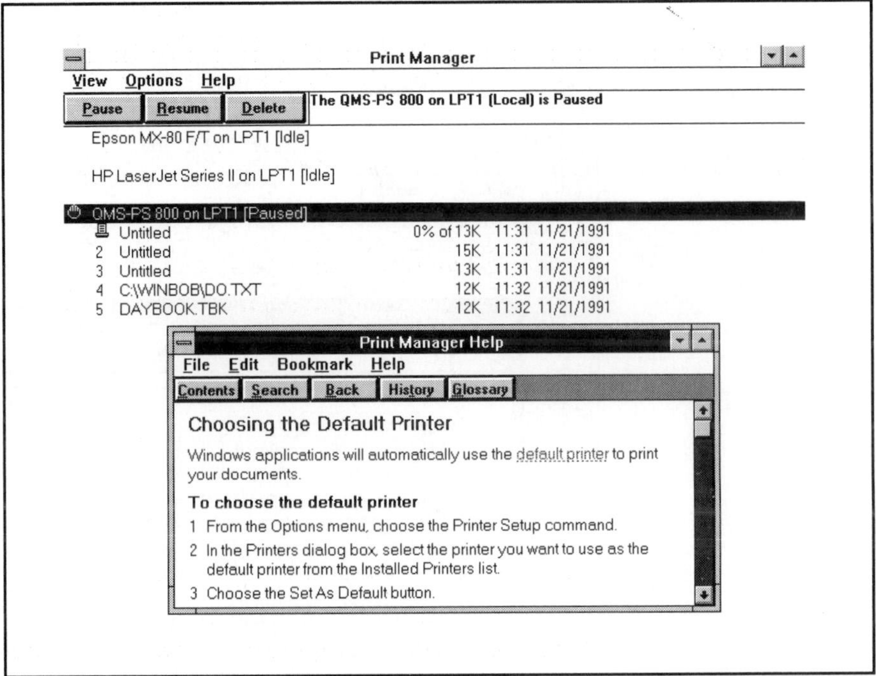

FIGURE 7.3: *Printing additional documents adds them to the queue.*

DELETING A FILE FROM THE QUEUE

After sending a file to the queue, suppose you reconsider printing it. Perhaps you want to edit the file and print it later. If so, you can simply remove the file from the queue:

1. Select the file by clicking on it in the queue.
2. Click the Delete button in the Print Manager window.
3. A dialog box appears, asking for confirmation. Click on OK.

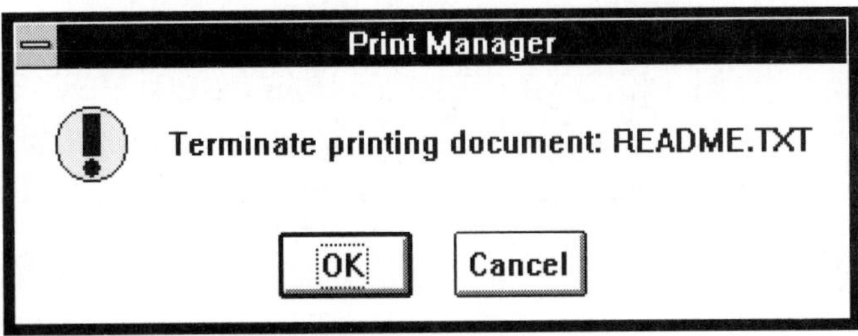

Sometimes (especially with laser-type printers) deleting a file while it's printing in graphics mode necessitates resetting the printer to clear its buffer. To reset, either turn the printer off then on again, or use the Reset option, if available.

If you want to cancel *all* print jobs:

1. Choose View ➤ Exit.
2. In the confirmation box, click on OK. If you don't click OK, Print Manager continues to operate and the files will continue to print, even though you may think you exited Print Manager and cancelled all printing.

PAUSING THE PRINTING PROCESS

You can temporarily halt the printing process for Windows applications at any time. This may be useful in cases where you want to adjust the printer for some reason, or to quiet the printer (if it's a dot-matrix or impact type) so you can take a phone call, have a conversation, etc.

To pause the printing process, click on the Pause button in the queue window. The Print Manager stops sending data to the printer, and the current print job (the one with the little printer to the left of its information line) is temporarily suspended. (The printing may not stop immediately because your printer may have a buffer that holds data in preparation for printing. The printing will stop when the buffer is empty.)

To resume the printing process, click on the Resume button. The Print Manager will continue sending data to the printer, starting where it left off.

REARRANGING THE QUEUE ORDER

Once you have several items on the queue, you may want to rearrange the order in which they're slated for printing. Perhaps a print job's priority has increased because it's suddenly needed for an urgent meeting, or you have to get a letter in the mail. Whatever the reason, it's easy to rearrange the print queue:

1. Click on the file you want to move and hold the mouse button down. The mouse pointer changes to a large arrow.
2. Drag the file to its new location. A dotted rectangle surrounds each file as you pass over it, indicating the position your file would jump to were you to release the mouse button.
3. Release the mouse button when you have the dotted rectangle in the correct spot. Your file is inserted in the queue, above the currently outlined file.

SETTING THE PRINTING SPEED

TO SET THE PRINTING PRIORITY,

open the Print Manager's Options menu and choose Low, Medium, or High Priority.

Your computer can actually do only one thing at a time. It's only through computer sleight-of-hand that your machine appears to be working at two jobs simultaneously. This is achieved by splitting its *CPU time* between tasks, focusing on each one in a round-robin fashion. The CPU, or Central Processing Unit, is the chip that does the actual "computing" in your computer. CPU time is the amount of time the CPU spends on a given task, and splitting time between two or more tasks is called time slicing. In time slicing, CPU time is doled out by using a formula that prioritizes the tasks. Normally each task gets the same priority, and thus the same amount of CPU attention (a bit like dealing out cards in a poker game—the old "one for me, one for you" routine).

Obviously, there is only a finite amount of CPU time available. In a given period of time the CPU can only do so much computing. Luckily, many programs do not come close to taxing the capabilities of the lightning-fast CPU. For example, with most word processors, the CPU is usually left twiddling its thumbs between the letters you type at the keyboard.

Running the Print Manager requires some CPU time, just like other programs, and it'll slow down whatever program you're working with. Whether the slowing is perceptible or not depends on what else you're doing in Windows. If you are doing work that requires considerable CPU attention (such as spreadsheet calculations, database sorting, or desktop publishing), printing can slow down the response time of your computer—sometimes to the point of aggravation.

NOTE *You can adjust the prioritizing of CPU time for other applications, too. This is discussed in Chapter 13.*

For this reason, the Print Manager lets you adjust the amount of CPU time it gets. It does this by letting you adjust the time-slicing formula. For example, you might double the amount of time you get for your applications, thus decreasing the amount the Print Manager gets ("one for you, two for me"). This translates to increasing the priority of your application and decreasing the priority of the Print Manager. The result will be increased speed for your application and decreased speed for printing. It is also possible to increase the priority of printing.

Three commands on the Print Manager's Options menu adjust the priority. If you notice that your other applications run too slowly while printing is going on, open the Options menu and choose one of the speed settings described below. The settings remain in effect until you change them again. They only affect printing through the Print Manager:

Low Priority: This reduces the CPU time spent on printing.

Medium Priority: This is the default setting. Printing gets CPU priority equal to that of other applications.

High Priority: If you want to speed up the printing, you can try this command. If your other applications slow down too much, then go back to Medium.

PRINT MANAGER MESSAGES

Sometimes the Print Manager wants to alert you to a condition that may require your intervention in some way. Perhaps the printer runs out of paper, goes offline, or has paper jammed in it. Three commands on the Options menu let you determine how Print Manager's messages will be displayed in such instances:

Alert Always: If there is a problem, your computer will beep and the Print Manager will pop up a dialog box regardless of what other programs or windows you are using.

Flash if Inactive: If the Print Manager is iconized or its window is open but not active, then the icon or the title bar in the window will flash and you'll hear a beep. When you restore or activate the window, the error message will then appear.

Ignore if Inactive: If the Print Manager is iconized or its window is open but not active, nothing will happen. Printing will just stop.

PRINTING WITH NETWORK PRINTERS

TO PRINT ON A NETWORK,

1. **Select Options ➤ Network Connections in the Print Manager window and choose the relevant button to check the connection.**
2. **Select Options ➤ Printer Setup, then click on Setup to verify that the correct printer is selected in the application's Setup dialog box.**
3. **Print the file.**

If you're connected to a network that is supported by Windows, you may have some additional options when printing and using the Print Manager. The options you have depend on the type of network you're connected to. With the most comprehensive network setup, you can:

- print to a network printer instead of to the printer connected directly to your computer (the local printer)
- view the print queue of only the files you sent to the network printer
- view the *entire* print queue for the network printer you are connected to

- view the print queue for network printers that you're not connected to
- print directly to the network printer, without using the Print Manager—possibly increasing printing efficiency
- tell Print Manager not to *poll* (repeatedly request) the network's printer server for queue information, thus decreasing the demand on the network and increasing network efficiency

PRINTING TO A NETWORK PRINTER

To print to a network printer, you must be logged on to the network and have selected the network printer for your output. Connecting to a network printer can be achieved

- through the Printers option on the Control Panel as discussed in Chapter 6.
- from the Print Manager—a simpler alternative.

Here's how:

1. Choose Options ➤ Network Connections. The Network-Printer Connections dialog box appears.
2. Choose the relevant button to review the current connection, reinstate a previous one, or make a new one:

   New Connection connects to a new printer. You'll have to enter the path and (possibly) password.

   Connect connects to the printer shown in the network path box.

   Browse browses the network for printers that are available.

   Current Printer Connections shows a list of network printers to which you're currently connected.

   Previous shows a list of network printers and paths you've been connected to before.

   Disconnect terminates the connection to the printer whose name is in the Printer Connections box.

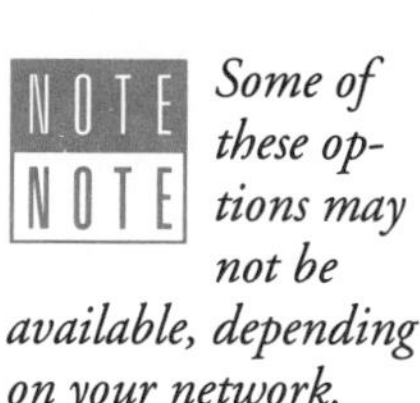
Some of these options may not be available, depending on your network.

Once you're connected to the network printer and you want to print from an application:

1. Activate the application's windows and open its Printer Setup dialog box (if it has one) to make sure the correct printer (network

rather than local) is selected. If it isn't, choose the network printer you wanted.

2. Go ahead and print from your application. The Print Manager will automatically start up and handle the print job as described in "Printing from Windows Applications" at the beginning of this chapter.

Some applications print to the default printer and don't allow you to choose a printer at print time. If your job seems to be going to the wrong printer, choose Options ➤ Printer Setup in the Print Manager and make your network printer the default printer. Then try printing again.

Viewing the Queue for Network Printers

Just as with a local printer, you'll probably want to check the network queue occasionally to see when your print jobs are coming up. This is particularly important on a busy network where there may be many people waiting for print jobs to be completed. You may not be able to speed things up, but at least you'll know whether you should go out for lunch or not!

There are two basic categories of network printers—those you're connected to (via the Control Panel's Printer settings) and those you aren't. Print Manager lets you look at the queue for each type.

Viewing Your Queue Only for a Network Printer You're Connected To

When you print to a network printer, the queue for your print files shows up just as it does when you print to a local printer. That is, the files are added to the queue in the order you sent them to the printer, and are displayed in that order. You may rearrange or delete them if you wish. However, you should be aware that the queue you see doesn't reflect all the print jobs slated for the printer. Other network users may have sent jobs to the printer, too. If you don't care about that, just go back to work. If you want to see the entire queue for your printer or another network printer, read the two sections below.

Viewing the Entire Queue for a Network Printer You're Connected To

If you want to see the entire queue—that is, your files and other users' files destined for printing on a particular printer—do the following:

1. Click on the network printer's information line in the Print Manager window. This should highlight it, as shown in Figure 7.4. (If the network printer doesn't appear in the window, then you are not logged on to the network or not connected to the network printer. Check with your network manager or your network manuals.)
2. Choose View ➤ Selected Net Queue. The queue for the network printer appears as a window. It will have scroll bars if there are more jobs in the queue than can be displayed at one time. An example is shown in Figure 7.5.
3. When you are finished examining the information, close the window.

FIGURE 7.4:

To see the queue for a network printer, first highlight it by clicking on it, as shown here.

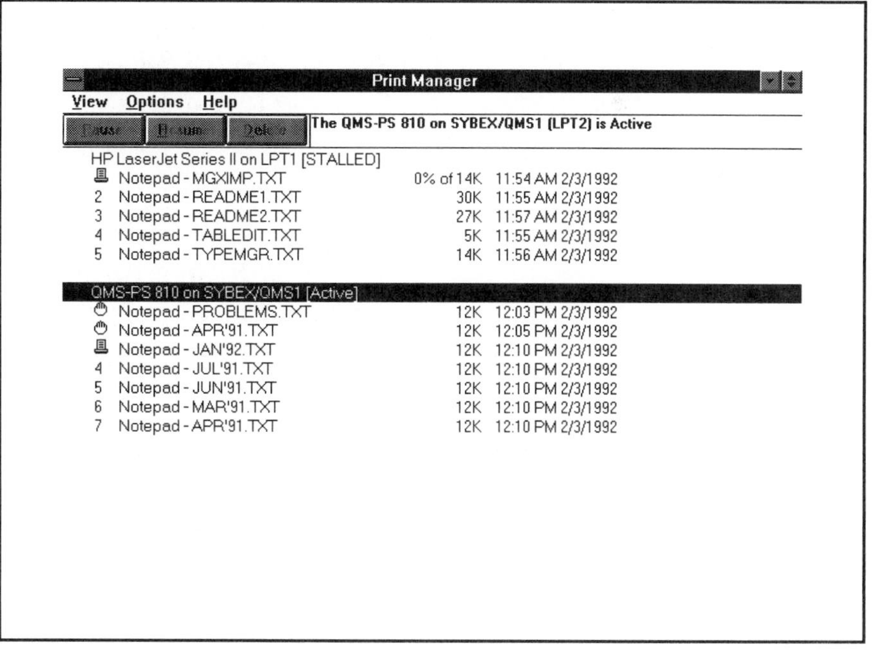

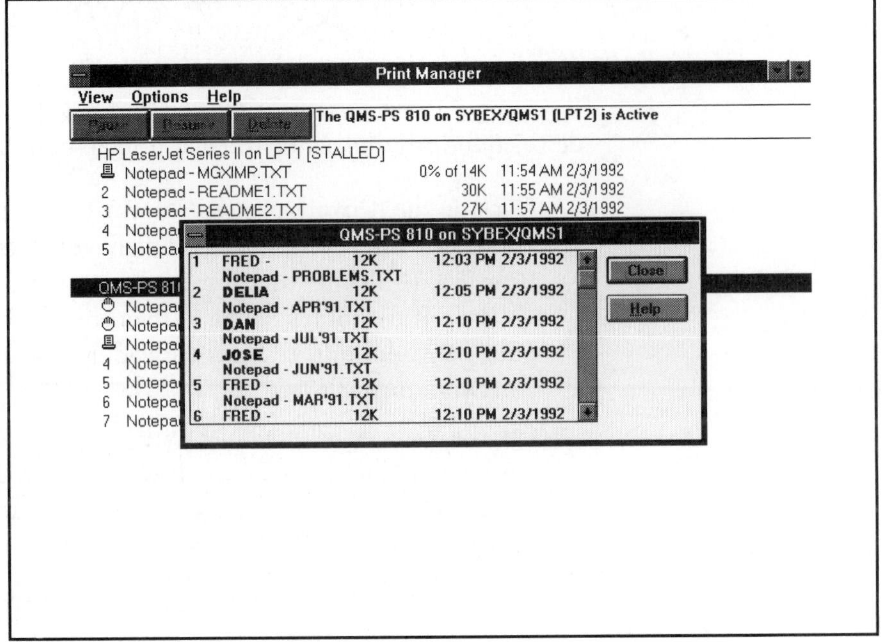

FIGURE 7.5:

A display of the selected network printer's queue appears when you choose the Selected Net Queue command.

Viewing the Network Queue for a Printer You're Not Connected To

Sometimes you may want to see the queue for a network printer that isn't the one you're currently connected to. This can help you determine whether there is a printer on the network that has a shorter queue. You could conceivably switch to that printer before sending your print job down the line and save yourself some waiting. (You would first have to connect yourself to the new printer via the Print Manager's Options menu or Control Panel's Printer dialog boxes before printing.)

1. Choose View ➤ Other Net Queue. A small text box appears at the bottom of the Print Manager window, asking you for the path name of the network printer's queue.
2. Type in the queue's name. This might be a rather complex name, similar to a DOS path name. You might need to refer to your network manager or the manuals supplied with your network to determine the exact path and printer name.

3. Click on View. The queue for the printer appears. An example of such a queue is shown in Figure 7.6.
4. You can view other queues by typing in another name and clicking on View again, if you want. Otherwise, close the window when you are finished.

Updating the Queue Information

If the Print Manager window is left open, the queue will periodically be updated to reflect changes on the network, such as new print jobs added to the queue or completed print jobs leaving the queue. If you minimize the window, the queue will not be updated, but this doesn't matter, since you can't see it anyway. However, it *does* cut down on network data flow. Whenever you restore the Print Manager window, the queue information will be updated.

If you leave the window open and don't want to wait for the periodic update, but want an update immediately, you can choose View ➤ Refresh. This will update the queue information immediately.

FIGURE 7.6:

Use the Other Net Queue command to see the queue for a network printer to which you're not currently connected.

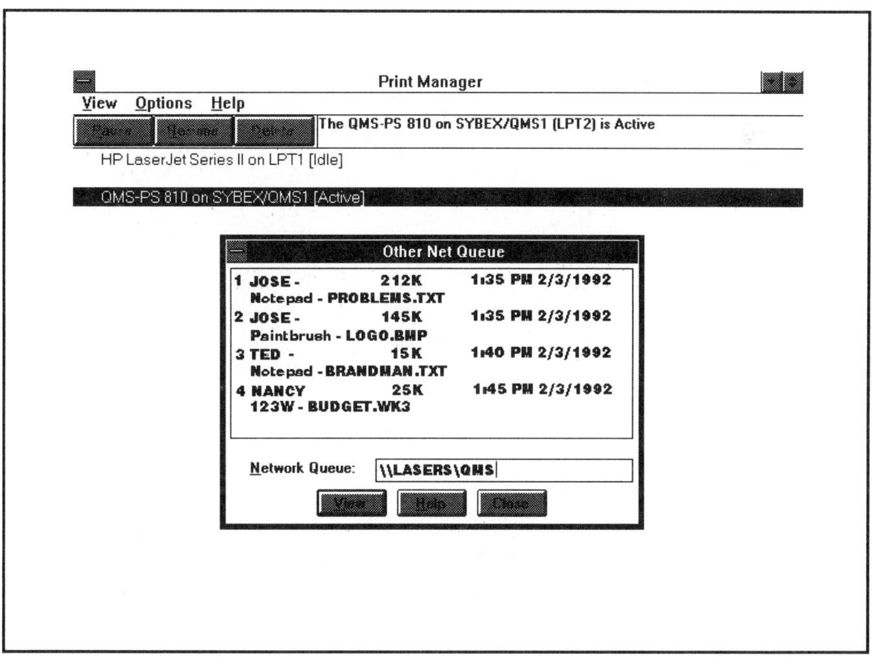

If you want to leave the window open and you don't want to add to the network's traffic by having Print Manager request a periodic update, you can do this:

1. Choose Options ➤ Network Settings. The Network Options dialog box appears.
2. Turn off the Update Network Display check box.
3. Click on OK.

From this point on, only updates pertaining to *your* print job(s) will be reflected in the queue. No other network queue information will be updated until you reset this box.

Printing through the Print Manager for Network Printing

When you are connected to a network, Windows normally prints directly to the network printer, not through the Print Manager. This speeds up your printing by eliminating an additional *software layer* (set of instructions for the CPU to process) in the print procedure. There are times when you might not want to bypass the Print Manager, however. For instance, you may want to use the Print Manager's error checking features. Also, in some odd cases, printing directly to the network may be slower than using the Print Manager. This depends on your network and the application you're printing from. You may want to experiment with a setting on the Network Options dialog box that lets you determine whether the Print Manager is engaged or not during the process of printing. Regardless of this setting, you'll still be able to view the queue.

To print through the File Manager:

1. Choose Options ➤ Network Settings. The Network Options dialog box appears.
2. Set the Print Net Jobs Direct check box on or off, as desired. When it's off (unchecked), printing passes through the Print Manager.
3. Click on OK.

PRINTING FROM NON-WINDOWS APPLICATIONS

You cannot take advantage of the Print Manager when you are printing from non-Windows applications. This is because non-Windows applications are not designed to cooperate with the Print Manager, and haven't the slightest idea what's going on vis-à-vis Windows. Though you can run non-Windows applications from Windows, they are subject to certain limitations, one of which is not being able to use the Print Manager or the printer driver(s) you've installed. Consider these points:

- Make sure you have properly installed the DOS application so that it works with your printer. Read the application's manual(s) to determine what printer drivers and/or procedures you need to follow in order to print correctly.
- Do not rely on Windows to handle any aspect of the printing process.
- Do not try to print from multiple non-Windows programs or from a mix of Windows and non-Windows programs at the same time on the same port. Unless you are running in 386-Enhanced mode, this will cause the output of the files to be mixed together like a computer cocktail! In 386 mode, you will be warned of the impending blending, but in Standard mode, you won't. As rules of thumb, remember the following: Unless you're running in 386 mode, print a bunch of files only when they're all from Windows applications. When you want to print from a non-Windows program, do it when nothing else is in the Print Manager's queue, or, if necessary, when the queue is paused.

If you *really* want to print a non-Windows application document with the Print Manager, it may be possible to have a compatible Windows application handle the printing. For example, Notepad will read ASCII files. Write will read ASCII and Microsoft Word for DOS files. Microsoft Word for Windows, WordPerfect for Windows, and Ami Pro will read numerous DOS word processing and graphics file formats, too. Microsoft Excel will read Lotus 1-2-3 and dBASE files, and so on. Do a little research on file-format compatibilities, and then use the appropriate Windows application to open and print the file from within Windows. This may also give you the ability to format the files with fonts and other refinements to look more pleasing, particularly in the case of programs such as dBASE that have little in the way of printer support. The Print Manager will then kick in and handle the details of queuing.

PRINTING TO A DISK FILE

TO PRINT TO A DISK FILE,

1. **Make sure the correct printer driver is installed.**
2. **Run Print Manager.**
3. **Choose Options ➤ Printer Setup.**
4. **Click on Connect. From the Ports box, choose File.**
5. **Exit the boxes, return to your application, and print.**
6. **Type in the File name when prompted.**

Sometimes you may want to print to a disk file rather than to the printer. When you print to a disk file, the output from the application program that normally would go out the printer port on the back of your computer and over a cable to the printer goes instead into a file on a floppy or hard disk. You might think the file would then be just a copy of the file you were printing. Usually it isn't. This is because it contains all the special formatting codes that control your printer—codes that change fonts, margins, page breaks, and attributes such as underlines, bolding, and so on. Print files destined for PostScript printers include their PostScript preamble, too (unless you defeat the PostScript header downloading process via the Control Panel by selecting Printers ➤ Setup ➤ Options ➤ Header and check Already Downloaded). A *preamble* is a series of codes sent to the printer at the start of each print job.

In any case, printing to a file gives you several options not available when printing direct to the printer:

- You can send the file to another person either on floppy disk or over the phone lines with a modem and a communications program such as the Terminal program supplied with Windows (see Chapter 10). That person can then print the file directly to a printer (if it is compatible) with Windows or the DOS COPY command. They don't need the application program that created the file and they don't have to worry about any of the printing details such as formatting, setting up margins, etc. It's all in the file.

- You can print the file later. Maybe your printer isn't hooked up, or you only have a dot-matrix printer and you want to print on a laser printer somewhere else, or there's so much stuff on the queue that you don't want to wait, or you don't want to slow down your computer or the network by printing now. Later you can copy the file to the printer with the File Manager's Print command or the DOS command COPY. The Print command uses the Print Manager, so you can queue up as many files as you want, prepare the printer, and then print them without having to be around.
- Sometimes print files are used by applications for specific purposes. For example, you may want to print part of a database to a file that will later be pulled into a company report. Or you might want to print an encapsulated PostScript graphics file to be imported into a desktop publishing document.

In some applications this choice is available in the Print dialog box. If not, the general game plan is this: You modify your printer driver to print to a file rather than to a port. Then, whenever you use that printer, it'll use all the usual settings for the driver, but will send the data to a file of your choice instead of to the printer port:

1. In Print Manager, choose Options ➤ Printer Setup. The Printers dialog box appears.
2. In the Installed Printers box, select the printer that will eventually be used to print the file. If you want to print the file as ASCII text only, with no special control codes, you should install the Generic/Text Only printer driver. Then select that as the destination printer. If you want to print to an encapsulated PostScript (EPS) file, install a PostScript driver, such as the Apple LaserWriter. Choose Setup, then Options. From the Options dialog box, choose Encapsulated PostScript File and type in the name of the file.

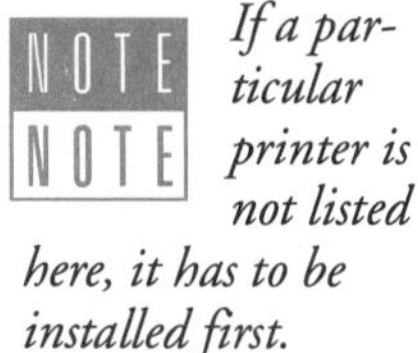

If a particular printer is not listed here, it has to be installed first.

3. Click on Connect. The Connect dialog box appears.
4. Select FILE: from the Ports list box.
5. Click on OK to return to the Printers dialog box.
6. Make sure the Setup settings are correct by clicking on Setup and checking them.
7. Return to the Control Panel by clicking on Close.
8. Print from the application. You'll be asked to specify a file name for the output. To be safe, type in the complete path name for the file, including its drive letter (e.g., C:\LETTERS\WILMA.PRT).

Be aware that until you reset your printer's configuration to its previous port assignment, you'll be printing to a file whenever you use this printer from any application. To reset the printer to its normal port, use the steps above but choose the proper port instead of FILE: from the Connect dialog box's Port list box.

PRINTING FROM A DISK FILE

To print the file later, follow either of these steps:

- From DOS, get to the DOS prompt and enter the command

  COPY *filename port*

  where *filename* is the file you want to print and *port* is the port your printer is connected to. For example, if the file were named BUDGET.TXT and the printer were connected to LPT1:, the following command would print it from DOS:

  ```
  COPY BUDGET.TXT LPT1:
  ```

- From Windows, run or switch to the File Manager and drag the file into a running Print Manager window or icon.

The printing process is a troublesome procedure that is fraught with maladies and pitfalls. Indeed, you may have already encountered difficulties on your own while attempting to print a document. If you find yourself frustrated by all the confusing connections that you can (and have to) make both in Windows and on the printer itself, I advise you to refer to the "Printer Problem Solving" section in Chapter 19. There I give you a troubleshooting checklist that should cover many situations you might encounter, as well as give you a couple of printing tips.

FAST TRACK

CHAPTER

8

FAST TRACK

To cut to the Clipboard, ... **241**
highlight the text/graphic(s) and select Edit ➤ Cut.

To copy from a non-Windows application, ... **243**

1. Press Alt-Enter to run a full-screen application in a window.
2. Open the Control box and select Edit ➤ Mark.
3. Use the mouse to select the text/graphic(s).
4. Open the Control box and select Edit ➤ Copy.

To copy an image of an active window, ... **245**
size the window and press Alt-PrtScr.

To paste into a Windows application, ... **247**
position the insertion point and select Edit ➤ Paste in the application.

To paste Clipboard material into a non-Windows application, ... **250**
if the application is in full-screen mode, position the cursor where you want the Clipboard material pasted. Press Alt-Esc to get back to Windows. Get to the desktop, click once on the destination application's icon to open the Control menu, and choose Paste.

The application will reappear with the new material pasted in (you may have to move the cursor before the pasting occurs).

If the application is in a window (386 mode only), activate the window and position the cursor where you want the Clipboard material pasted. Open the Control box and choose Edit. Then choose Paste from the cascading menu.

To view the Clipboard's contents, ... **253**
run Clipboard from the Main group.

To save the Clipboard to a file, ... **255**
choose File ➤ Save As from the Clipboard Viewer.

To empty the Clipboard, ... **256**
press Del or choose Edit ➤ Delete while in the Clipboard Viewer.

CHAPTER 8

FEATURING

Selecting Text and Graphics

Cutting, Copying, and Pasting

Working with the Clipboard's Contents

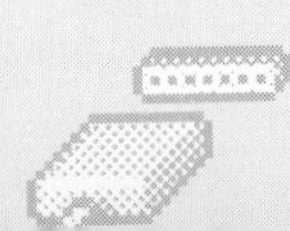
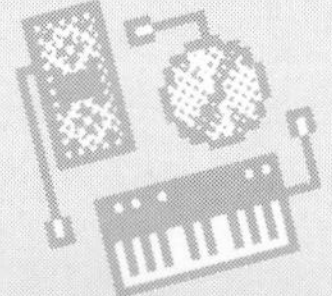

Copying Material with the Clipboard

One of the characteristics of a perfect operating system environment would be an almost seamless meshing of simultaneously running programs. Though this has never been realized completely by any computer system thus far, Windows bridges a few significant gaps, as you've seen. The ability to run several programs at once and switch among them at will—even while printing in the background—is a strong move in this direction.

Consider another issue—that of copying data between the programs. Ideally, all computer programs should be able to read each other's documents or cut and paste information between them. Unfortunately, this is rarely the case. Many programs use proprietary file and data formats designed to work optimally with the particular program. These are often promoted by marketing departments of software companies in the hopes that they will eventually become the established standard. As a result, sharing data between programs is seldom easy, and often creates more headaches than it's worth. If you've ever tried to print a dBASE data file in, say, Ventura Publisher or copy a portion of a Lotus 1-2-3 file into a WordStar file, you know what I mean.

These days, however, more and more conversion programs and utilities to help in the process are becoming available or are supplied with programs. For example, Microsoft Word for Windows can read and write numerous text and graphics file formats. The database management program Paradox and desktop publishing program Ventura Publisher both offer a plethora of conversion options. Standards are now emerging to expedite the process of data transfer between programs, and with time more elegant and effortless solutions are becoming available.

The emergence of Windows is facilitating the development of seamless data sharing on PCs. The Windows vehicles for data exchange are threefold: the Windows Clipboard, Dynamic Data Exchange (DDE), and Object Linking and Embedding (OLE). This chapter explores the simplest and most often used of these, the Clipboard. (DDE and OLE are covered in Chapter 14.)

The Clipboard is a built-in utility program that aids the process of copying information between applications. Though not capable of making significant conversions between file formats or performing any radical sleight-of-hand to miraculously render all programs compatible, the Clipboard is extremely handy for many everyday tasks.

Using the Clipboard, you can mark a portion of text or graphics in one application window and drop it into the destination window of another. The Clipboard works with both text and graphics and on both Windows and non-Windows programs, within certain limitations that mostly pertain to non-Windows applications.

Functionally, the Clipboard acts a bit like a real clipboard. It's a temporary storage area onto which you can "clip" a small amount of data that you can keep easily at hand. You copy or cut the information out of an active window or from the File Manager's Copy dialog box. Then when you want to use the information, a simple command pops it into a new location, either in the same window or in another one.

The Clipboard uses system resources (RAM and disk files) to hold the information temporarily. This information waits on the Clipboard until you want to copy or move it to a new location, typically a document that is open in a window. The information stays on the Clipboard until you delete it, replace it, or exit Windows. This means that you can use the information in it more than once, dropping it into several documents if you want to, or into several places in the same document. You can also store and retrieve Clipboard information to and from a disk for later use.

You use the cut, copy, and paste approach with the Clipboard. If you've worked with a Mac program such as MacWrite or are familiar with PC or Windows programs such as Microsoft Word or Works, you're already familiar with these techniques. *Cutting* means removing the information from its source location and putting it onto the Clipboard. When you cut information, it is deleted from its source window. *Copying* information, as the name implies, leaves the original intact, simply placing a duplicate of it on the Clipboard. *Pasting* is the process of inserting whatever is on the Clipboard into the destination document.

TECHNIQUES FOR SELECTING TEXT

Cutting and copying text requires a procedure called *selecting*—and though it is easy to learn, it is a bit less simple to explain. (If you already do know how to select text, skip to the next section.)

The exact way you select material in Windows programs may vary slightly from program to program, but the same techniques generally apply, particularly to text. There may be some shortcuts in specific programs, so you should read the manual or help screens supplied with the program. Graphics programs allow a wider variety of selection techniques, and some of those are discussed below in the section "Techniques for Selecting Graphics."

Write is covered at length in Chapter 9.

To illustrate how you select, cut, copy, and paste text, the following exercises work with a Write file (PRINTERS.WRI) supplied with Windows. Since these procedures are used in many other Windows programs, you'll be able to apply what you learn here to more than just the Clipboard.

SELECTING BY DRAGGING

Before you can select anything, you have to open the document it's in. In this case, open the file called PRINTERS.WRI, which was copied onto your

If you want to select more text than fits in a window, keep dragging the mouse pointer all the way to the edge of the window. The text will scroll and be selected until you release the mouse button.

hard disk during installation. This is one of the last-minute information files supplied with your copy of Windows. Depending on when you bought Windows, you may or may not have this exact file. If not, use another .WRI file. Recall that you can open the file by starting Write (found in the Accessories group) and choosing File ➤ Open, or you can open the File Manager, display the directory the file is in, and double-click the file. Since there's an association set up between .WRI files and Write, Write will start with the document file opened. Then maximize the window so you can work with it more easily.

Now select some text. Assume you want to copy the second paragraph of text into another document. You'll have to select that paragraph.

1. Position the insertion point just before the first letter of the second paragraph.
2. Click and hold the left mouse button down.
3. Drag the mouse toward you (moving the pointer toward the bottom of the screen) while holding the button down. As you do so, the text is highlighted.

You can move the mouse left, right, up, and down to refine the selection, for as long as you keep the button depressed. You might notice that if you move the cursor toward the top of the screen, above the initial point of your selection, the selection sort of reverses. That is, the starting point now appears to be the end point. This is because the first place you click when making a selection acts as an *anchor point;* it stays stationary. As long as the mouse button is depressed, all text between the anchor point and the cursor will be selected. Release the mouse when the text you wanted to select is highlighted. Figure 8.1 shows some selected text in a Write document.

Selecting by Shift-Clicking

There's another way to select text (some graphics programs work this way, too). It's called *shift-clicking.* Try these steps:

1. "Deselect" any text you've selected by clicking anywhere on the text. It doesn't matter where. This will collapse the highlighted selection.

2. Move the cursor to the beginning point of the section to be selected and click.

3. Move the mouse to the end of the section you want to select. (Note that you can use the arrow keys and the scroll bars to move to a position in the text that is not visible.)

4. Press and hold down the Shift key and then click the mouse (this is shift-clicking). The text between your two clicks is now selected.

5. Close the Write file for the time being. If asked whether you want to save any changes to the file you were experimenting with, say No.

Some applications let you select text by clicking in the far-left margin. One click selects the current line, and selection is extended by dragging the mouse down. Some programs also have a Select All command that selects everything in the file.

In most text-based Windows applications, selected text will automatically be replaced by the first symbol (letter, number, symbol, or punctuation mark) you press on the keyboard. This makes the process of deleting unwanted text and inserting new text fast, but it also means you should be careful when

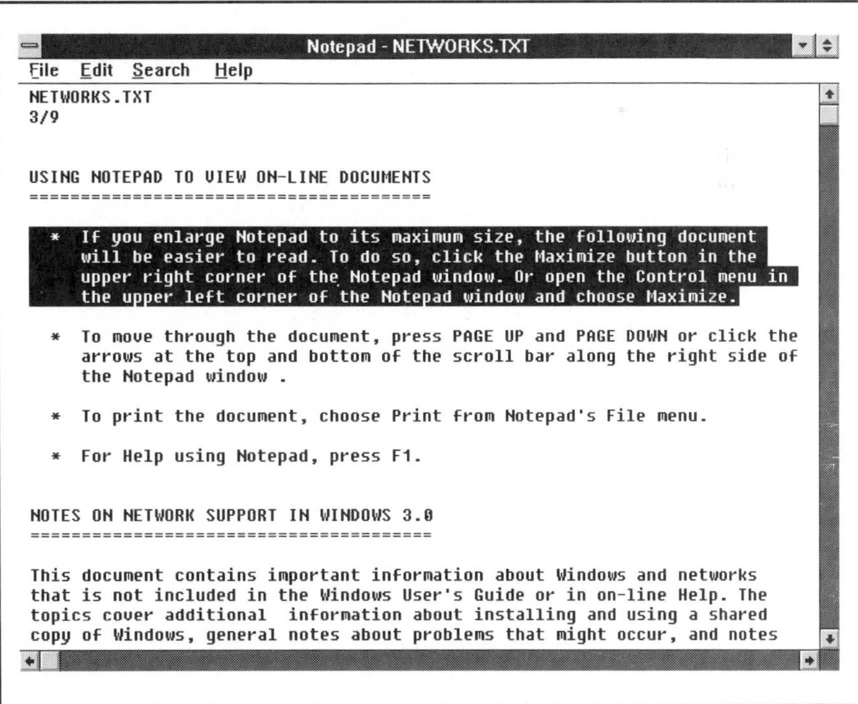

FIGURE 8.1:

You can select text in most Windows applications by dragging the mouse over the text to be selected. Depress the mouse button in the upper-left corner of the text, then move the mouse down and to the right. When you release the mouse button, the selection is made.

selecting text. If you type a letter, the text may disappear and be replaced by the single letter. If this happens, some applications will let you recover the lost text by selecting Edit ➤ Undo.

TECHNIQUES FOR SELECTING GRAPHICS

Paintbrush is covered at length in Chapter 11.

You select graphics approximately the same way as you do text. As an example, let's run the Paintbrush program supplied with Windows, then load a picture and select a portion of it:

1. Start the Paintbrush program by double-clicking its icon.
2. When Paintbrush comes up, maximize the window.
3. Choose File ➤ Open. Double-click on WINLOGO.BMP in the Open dialog box. The Windows logo appears. (Incidentally, this is one of the Desktop backgrounds you might recall from Chapter 5. It's really a .BMP file that you can edit in Paintbrush if you want.)
4. Once the picture loads, click on the right of the two scissor boxes in the upper-left side of the screen. These scissor boxes are the tools that Paintbrush uses for selecting portions of a picture. It is typical of graphics programs to have several types of *tools* for selecting items or areas.
5. Position the cross-hair cursor near the lower-right corner of the logo. Click and hold.
6. Drag the mouse down and to the right to draw a box around a portion of the logo and release the mouse button. A dotted line appears; this is the selected section of the picture. You can now cut it, copy it, or move it—among other things. Figure 8.2 shows the effect of clicking in its middle and dragging it slightly.
7. Try the other selection tool—the scissor with the star. This one works more like a lasso: you can capture any arbitrarily shaped area.
8. Close the Paintbrush application and document. Don't save the changes. If you do, you will mess up your Windows logo.

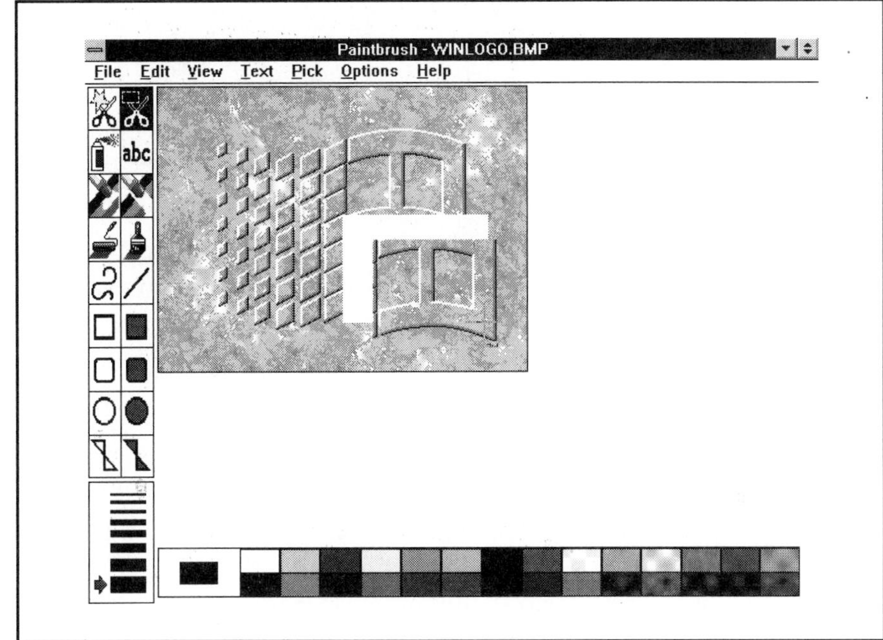

FIGURE 8.2:

Selecting graphics is a bit different from selecting text. The techniques vary more between applications. Here, a section of a Paintbrush picture has been selected and then dragged a bit.

CUTTING TO THE CLIPBOARD

TO CUT TO THE CLIPBOARD,

highlight the text/graphic(s) and select Edit ➤ Cut.

You can cut to the Clipboard only from Windows applications. You can't cut from non-Windows applications, though you can copy from them (as explained later).

When cutting from a Windows application, you first select the information you want to cut and then use the application's Edit menu to cut the material. The information automatically goes into the Clipboard. Here are the typical steps:

1. Open the document you want to cut material from, if it isn't already open and on the screen.
2. Select the information to be cut. Exactly how you do this depends on the application. It's possible to cut a combination of

text and graphics, as well as one or the other. Refer to the application's manual for specifics about its particular selection capabilities and quirks.

3. Choose Cut from the application's Edit menu. The selected section of text or graphics will most likely vanish. Actually it's still alive, only it's captured and living in Clipboard Land.
4. Follow the steps in "Pasting Information from the Clipboard" to paste the stuff you've just cut into a new location.

COPYING TO THE CLIPBOARD

As explained earlier, the distinction between cutting and copying is that copying leaves the original information intact. Copying is not limited to Windows applications, unlike cutting. Copying also gives you a wider variety of options as far as what you can copy:

- selected text or graphics from Windows applications
- selected text from non-Windows applications (386-Enhanced mode only)
- a bitmap image of the active window (386-Enhanced mode only)
- an image of the entire screen
- an entire file to the Clipboard from File Manager (for use with OLE)

The technique you use depends on the type of application and whether the program is running full-screen or in a window. Each variation is described below.

COPYING SELECTED TEXT OR GRAPHICS FROM WINDOWS APPLICATIONS

The method for copying a selected area of text or graphics is similar to that used for cutting. Specifically:

1. Open the document you want to copy material from if it isn't already open and on the screen.

2. Select the information to be copied. Exactly how you do this depends on the application. It's possible to copy a combination of text and graphics, as well as just one or the other. Refer to the application's manual for specifics.
3. Choose Copy from the application's Edit menu. The selected section of text or graphics does not appear to change. However, a copy of it is now placed on the Clipboard.
4. Follow the steps in this chapter's section "Pasting Information from the Clipboard" to paste the copied information elsewhere.

Copying Selected Text or Graphics from Non-Windows Applications

TO COPY FROM A NON-WINDOWS APPLICATION,

1. **Press Alt-Enter to run a full-screen application in a window.**
2. **Open the Control box and select Edit ➤ Mark.**
3. **Use the mouse to select the text/graphic(s).**
4. **Open the Control box and select Edit ➤ Copy.**

You can copy a selected area of graphics or text from non-Windows programs. However, you can only do this when you're running in 386-Enhanced mode and the non-Windows program is running in a window (not full-screen). If the program won't run in a window, you're out of luck. (You can't copy from some graphics programs for this reason.)

You can pull any text from a non-Windows application, including text that isn't actually in a document, such as program menus and instructions. Whatever you copy is dumped on the Clipboard as text or bit-mapped graphics, and can then be pasted into any Windows program that will accept text or graphics from the Clipboard (e.g., Notepad, Write, Cardfile, Paintbrush, Terminal, Microsoft Word, etc.).

Note that some non-Windows programs may appear to be in text mode (because they are displaying text) but are not. In this case, copying text may not work as expected. Microsoft Word, for example, can run in graphics mode in an attempt to better represent the final printed page. If you copy text from Word in this mode, however, you will be surprised to find that what's been copied to the Clipboard is a graphic—not text—and thus can't be successfully pasted into another text file and edited as text. Switch Word back to text mode before copying, though, and you will succeed:

1. Make sure you're running in 386-Enhanced mode. If you're in doubt about your mode, open or activate the Program Manager window and choose Help ➤ About Program Manager. The dialog box will report the current operating mode.
2. Open the non-Windows application from which you want to copy text. It must be running in a window, not full-screen. If it's currently in full-screen mode, press Alt-Enter to move it into a window. (Some applications can't run in a window. Chapter 13 talks more about such quirks and considerations.)
3. In your application, open the document to be copied from, and scroll it so you can see the text to be copied. (You can only copy text that's actually on the screen.)
4. Open the window's Control box and choose Edit ➤ Mark.
5. With the mouse, select the text or graphics area to be copied. Start in the upper-left corner of the desired text, and move the mouse down to the lower-right corner. The selected area will be highlighted. An example is shown in Figure 8.3, where I've selected some text from a WordStar document. Notice that the moment you first click in the window, its menu bar changes. The word *Select* precedes the window name, indicating that you're in *select mode*. You can't use your application again until you finish the selection process or press Esc.
6. Open the window's Control box again and choose Edit ➤ Copy. This places the selection on the Clipboard. (You can just press Enter as a shortcut for this step.)
7. Follow the steps under "Pasting Information from the Clipboard" to paste the copied information elsewhere.

FIGURE 8.3:

To select text or graphics from a non-Windows application in 386-Enhanced mode, first window the document and choose Edit ➤ Mark from the Control box. Then select the desired text or graphic. Finally, press Enter to copy to the Clipboard.

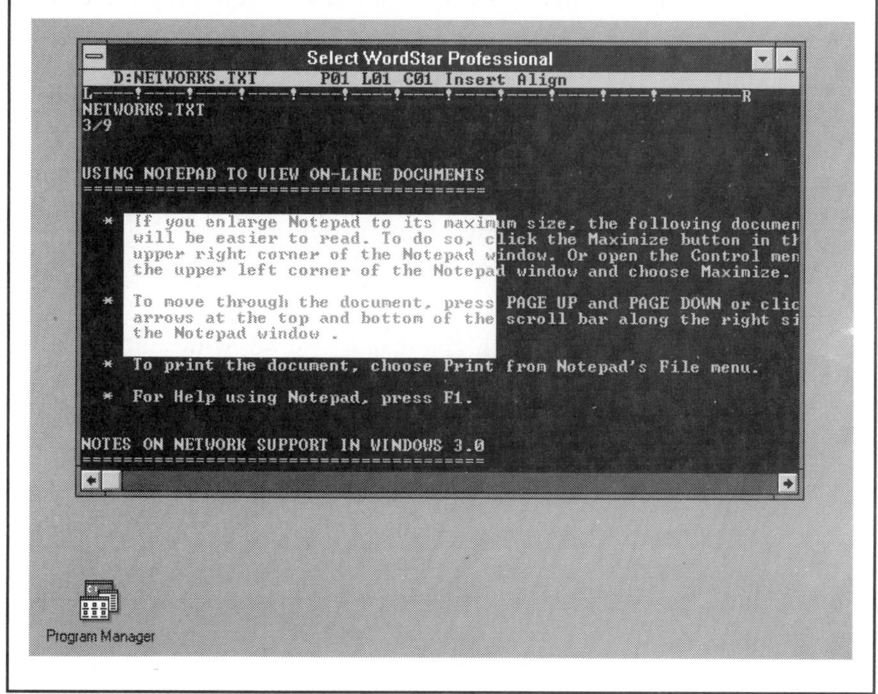

Copying a Bit-Mapped Image of the Active Window

TO COPY AN IMAGE OF A WINDOW,

size the window and press Alt-PrtScr.

If you are running in 386-Enhanced mode, you can copy the complete contents of the active window to the Clipboard. The window may contain either a Windows or non-Windows application. The Clipboard translates the window's image into a .BMP (bit-mapped) file format that some graphics programs, such as Windows Paintbrush, can read and print. It's like taking a photograph of the window.

Copying a window in this way can be useful if you're writing instruction manuals for Windows programs. You can pull the file into a program such as Paint, modify it if necessary, and then save it on disk as a file. Then,

If you don't want to work with the window's image yet, save it to a disk file for later use. See the section "Saving the Clipboard's Contents to a File" later in this chapter.

when creating your manual, pull this picture into the word-processing program or desktop publishing program in which the manual is being laid out. You may have to convert the .BMP file to another file format first if your layout program can't use .BMP files. Paintbrush will convert to PCX format, which is readable by many programs such as Ventura and PageMaker. Note that windows are graphic images, so even the text captured as part of a window is really graphics, not text.

Incidentally, the active window isn't always the window running the application you're using. The active window is sometimes an auxiliary window, such as a dialog box. So, you can capture individual dialog boxes for your instruction manuals, too. The color or shade of the title bar tells you which window is the active window.

Another point to consider if you are creating images for instruction manuals is this: There are several programs available for capturing screens and windows that are more capable than the Windows Clipboard. The ones used for this book are called Collage Plus (Inner Media, Inc.) and Tiffany Plus (Anderson Consulting and Software), and are very flexible in their capture modes and file formats, including gray-scaling capabilities. Other programs to consider are Pixelpop (MHS Partners), Hotshot Graphics (Symsoft Corp.), and HiJaak (Inset Systems, Inc.).

Here are the steps for copying the active window's image onto the Clipboard:

If Alt-Prt-Scr doesn't seem to succeed in copying the image, try Shift-PrtScr. Some older keyboards use this key combination instead.

1. Open the desired application in a window.
2. Adjust and size the window as needed.
3. Press Alt-PrintScreen. (Some keyboards label this key PrtScr or something similar.) The image will be copied to the Clipboard.
4. Follow the steps under "Pasting Information from the Clipboard" to paste the copied information elsewhere.

Copying a Bit-Mapped Image of the Entire Screen

Suppose you want to capture an image of the entire screen, as opposed to a particular window. You don't even have to be running in 386-Enhanced mode to do this; Standard mode will suffice:

1. Set up the screen you want the image of, adjusting and sizing windows as needed.
2. Press PrtScr.
3. The image will be copied to the Clipboard.
4. Follow the steps under "Pasting Information from the Clipboard" to paste the copied information elsewhere.

If pressing PrtScr doesn't seem to succeed in copying the image, try Shift-PrtScr or Alt-PrtScr instead.

Note that when copying the screen image in Standard mode, only text screens can be copied. Any non-Windows program running in graphics mode (such as Microsoft Word) will not be copied. In 386-Enhanced mode, DOS applications running in graphics mode *can* be copied.

PASTING INFORMATION FROM THE CLIPBOARD

Once you've got something on the Clipboard, you have two choices. You can paste it into a document you're working with (or that you open subsequently) or you can save it to a file. Saving to a file is described later in the section "Working with the Clipboard's Contents." Here we'll consider the possibilities for pasting. Specifically, you have two major pasting choices:

- pasting information into Windows applications
- pasting into non-Windows applications

Here's the scoop on each option.

Pasting Information into Windows Applications

TO PASTE INTO A WINDOWS APPLICATION,

position the insertion point and select Edit ➤ Paste in the application.

NOTE *You don't have to be just copying between different applications. These techniques can move text or graphics around within the same application, or between two document windows running in the same application.*

Pasting into Windows applications is a simple procedure. Most Windows applications have a Paste command on their Edit menus. This is designed to work with the Clipboard for the express purpose of transferring information between documents or from place to place within a single document. The documents can even have been created by different applications.

To paste information successfully, all you have to do is set up the right conditions, and then issue the command:

1. Activate the window that will receive the information.
2. If you're pasting text, move the text cursor to the position where you want the copied or cut text to be inserted and click. If you're using other types of programs, figure out if the program has an "insertion point" tool or icon. Such a tool is used to tell the Clipboard where pasted material should begin. (Check the application's manual if you don't know how its insertion point works. Some programs don't use one.)
3. Choose Edit ➤ Paste. The Clipboard's contents will appear in the destination window.

If the material is text, it will flow into the text stream at the point of the cursor. If it is graphics, the technique for pinpointing the destination within a document depends on the application. In Paintbrush, a selected section appears in the upper-left corner of the screen. Other programs may require you to preselect the box, cell, or other starting location for the insertion. In most cases, the pasted material will automatically be selected after it is dropped in, so that you can manipulate it by moving, changing font, color, size, etc. If you decide the destination was wrong, make sure it's all still selected and choose Edit ➤ Cut, press Delete, or choose Edit ➤ Undo (if the application has it). Then reposition and paste again.

Figures 8.4 and 8.5 show, respectively, examples of text and graphics being pasted into documents. Figure 8.4 shows a section of text cut from Cardfile into a Microsoft Word for Windows document. Figure 8.5 shows a section of one graphic file pasted into another.

Keep in mind that until you cut or copy again, or clear the Clipboard's contents (explained at the end of this chapter), the information is still on it. You can paste as many times as you want. Figure 8.6 shows the effect of repeatedly pasting and moving slightly the same portion of a graphics file

FIGURE 8.4:

To paste text on the Clipboard into a Windows application, position the insertion point and click. Then choose Edit ➤ Paste. The text will appear at the insertion point.

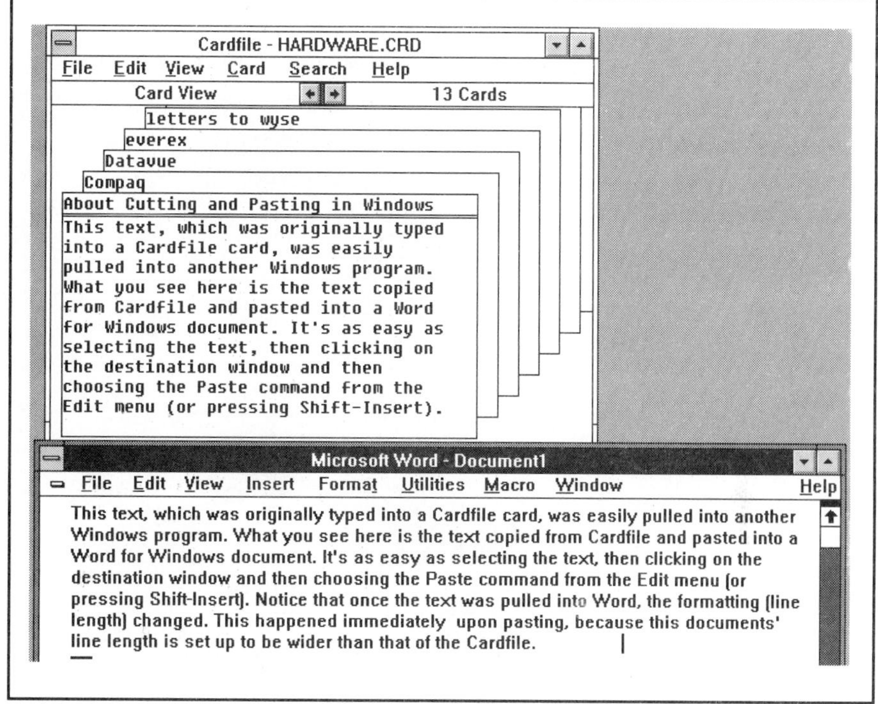

FIGURE 8.5:

To paste an image or graphic from the Clipboard, position the insertion point and click (if possible). Then choose Edit ➤ Paste. The graphic appears at the insertion point, or is placed in the window at some predetermined location.

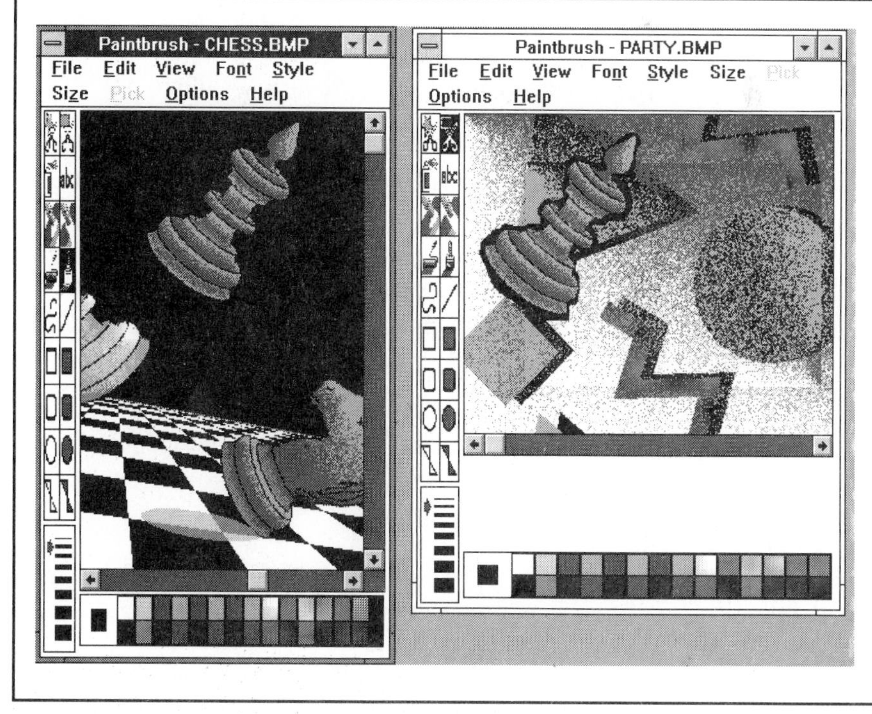

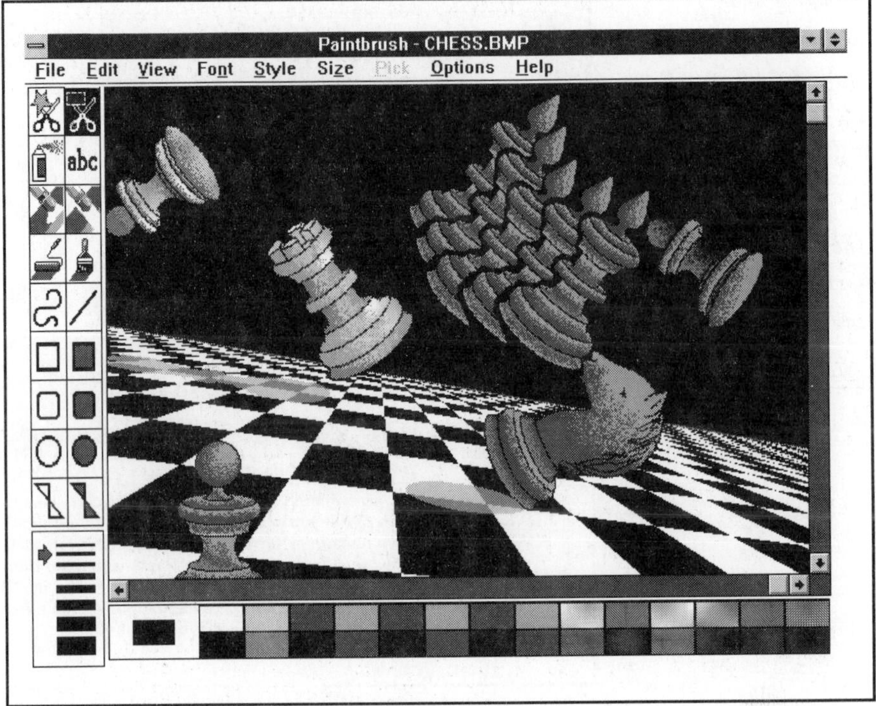

FIGURE 8.6:

Since material stays on the Clipboard after a Paste command, you can paste again. Here you see several pastings of the same graphic—in this case, a bishop.

within the Paintbrush program. This was done using a graphic called CHESS.BMP, supplied with Windows 3.0.

Pasting Text into Non-Windows Applications

NOTE *To transfer graphics, you'll have to cut or copy the graphic into a program such as Paintbrush, PC Paintbrush, or CorelDRAW and then save the file in a format that's transferable.*

Finally, let's consider pasting information into non-Windows applications. This is a bit trickier and the results are not highly guaranteed, since non-Windows applications are not always that well-behaved. They also do not operate by the same principles in terms of how they accept data. Also keep in mind that any formatting contained in text will be lost in the transfer.

There are two main permutations of pasting text when using non-Windows applications:

- pasting into full-screen, non-Windows applications
- pasting into windowed, non-Windows applications (386 mode only)

Here's the scoop on each:

Pasting into Full-Screen, Non-Windows Applications

The following steps assume that you have some text on the Clipboard:

1. Start up the destination application in full-screen mode.
2. Using whatever method applies to the application, position the cursor at the location where you want to insert the Clipboard's material.
3. Switch back to Windows by pressing Alt-Esc. Adjust your windows so you can see the icon for the non-Windows application at the bottom of the Desktop.
4. Click once on the program's icon. This opens the Control menu.
5. Choose Edit ➤ Paste from the Control menu. (If you're running in 386-Enhanced mode, choose Edit and then Paste from the cascading menu.) The text will be copied into your document. If the Clipboard's contents were not deemed appropriate for pasting, Windows will say No appropriate data in Clipboard.

What happens is this: The Clipboard's contents are transferred to the computer's keyboard buffer. The text is then inserted at the insertion point as though you were typing the text on the keyboard. For this procedure to work correctly, the program you are using must conform to certain DOS standards for accepting keyboard input and displaying it on the screen. Be aware that your application may not accept information in this way. There's no harm in trying, though, so give it a whirl. If things look really screwy when you try pasting, then quit your application without saving the changes. Your file will still be okay.

Pasting into Windowed, Non-Windows Applications

Pasting into a non-Windows application that is running in a window is similar to the above procedure. You have to be running in 386-Enhanced mode, of course, since that's the only mode that allows running non-Windows applications in a window. Here are the steps:

1. Open the destination application in a window. (Press Alt-Enter if you need to switch it.)
2. Make sure you're not in Select mode. (The title bar will tell you; press Esc if you are.)
3. Move the application's cursor to the insertion point, using whatever means are normal for the application (arrow keys, mouse, etc.).
4. Open the application's Control box and choose Edit ➤ Paste. The text will be inserted.

The caveats described above for pasting into full-screen, non-Windows applications apply less to this approach, since Windows is orchestrating the display and keyboard operations for your program when it is running the application in a window. Figure 8.7 shows an example where I inserted Clipboard text from a Help screen into a WordStar file running in a window.

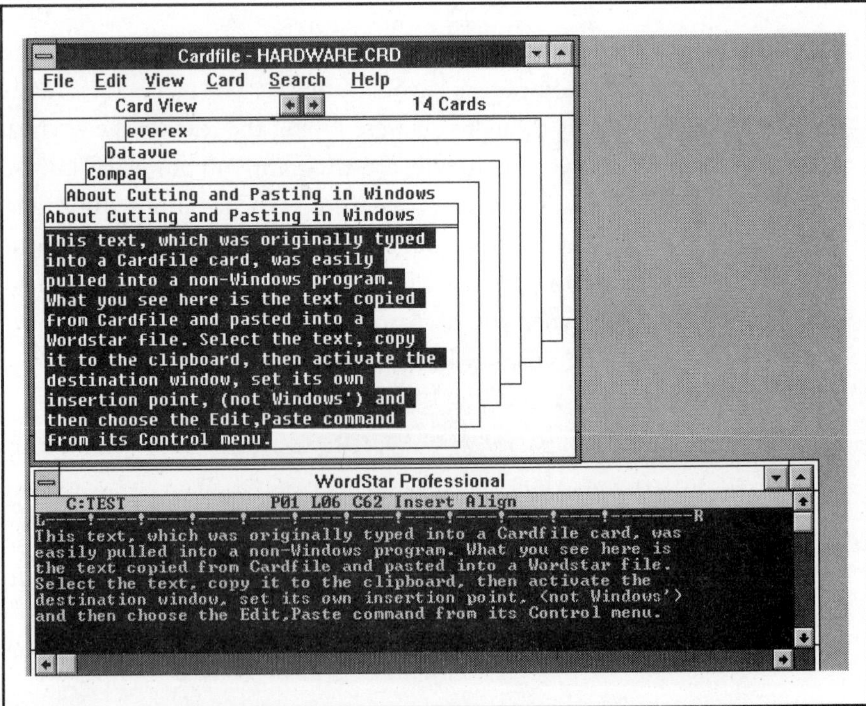

FIGURE 8.7:

To paste text into a non-Windows application running in a window, position the cursor and select Edit ➤ Paste from the Control box.

WORKING WITH THE CLIPBOARD'S CONTENTS

To print the Clipboard's contents, paste them into an appropriate document and print from there.

Sometimes you'll want to do more than simply cut, copy, and paste information between applications. The Clipboard program has some other, free-standing capabilities of its own that allow you to do the following:

- view the Clipboard's contents
- save the Clipboard's contents to a file
- retrieve the contents of a Clipboard file
- clear the Clipboard's contents

The purpose and particulars of each of these is described below.

VIEWING THE CLIPBOARD'S CONTENTS

Sometimes you'll forget what's on the Clipboard. Since every time you cut or copy in any application the contents are replaced with the new material, it's easy to forget what's in the Clipboard's memory. Here's how to view the contents:

1. Run the Clipboard Viewer program by double-clicking on its icon in the Program Manager's Main group.
2. The Clipboard Viewer window comes up, displaying its current contents. Figure 8.8 shows an example of this.

The contents may be displayed slightly differently from the way they looked when you copied them. For example, line breaks in text may be in new positions. Don't worry about that. The material should still be intact and will be okay when you paste it.

As you may know, graphics and text both have a considerable amount of potential formatting material associated with them, such as font size and type, and graphics settings for color, resolution, gray-scaling, and so forth. When you cut or copy material, the Clipboard does its best to capture all the relevant information. Then when you paste, the destination program has to

FIGURE 8.8:

Opening the Clipboard Viewer program displays the Clipboard's contents—in this case, LEAVES.BMP.

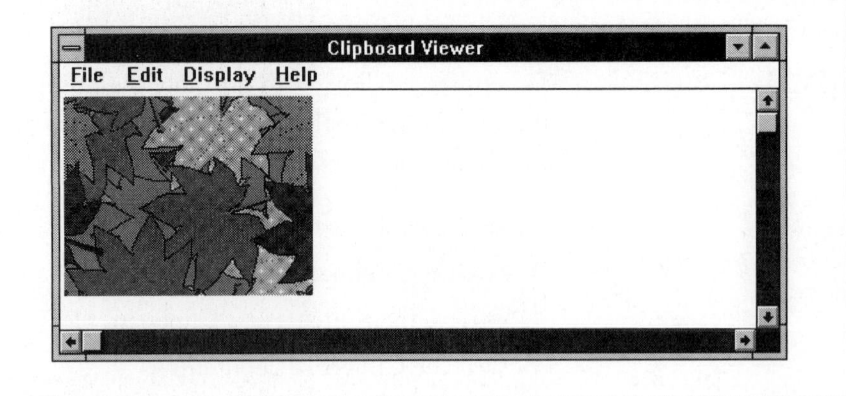

figure out what information it can use and what it can ignore. The whole process is pretty iffy, considering all the possible variables. That is why viewing the contents of the Clipboard doesn't always reveal all of what's actually there in detail. However, the application you cut to or copy from supposedly tells the Clipboard which formats the data can be viewed and accepted in. If there's more than one choice, you'll be allowed to change the view via the Display menu. By changing the display format, you may get a more accurate representation of the Clipboard's contents. The Auto setting returns the view to the original display format with which the material was shown.

When you paste into another Windows program, incidentally, the destination program does its best to determine the optimal format for accepting the information. This isn't determined by the Display menu's setting or current Clipboard window display.

For purposes of experimentation, you can leave the Clipboard's window on the screen somewhere. Then open a few other programs, such as Notepad and Paintbrush, and open a document for each. Size the windows so you can see all of them, including the Clipboard. Now go back and forth between Notepad and Paintbrush, copying selected sections of text and pictures with the Edit menus. Notice how the contents of the Clipboard change each time you use the Copy command.

Saving the Clipboard's Contents to a File

TO SAVE THE CLIPBOARD TO A FILE,

choose File ➤ Save As from the Clipboard Viewer.

Normally when you exit Windows, or cut or copy anything new onto the Clipboard, you'll lose the contents. Occasionally you may want to save the Clipboard contents to a file. This way you can resurrect it later (as explained in the next section) and paste it again. However, the Clipboard uses a proprietary file format that isn't readable by other popular programs. No doubt utility programs from other companies to convert Clipboard files to usable formats will eventually become available. Until that time, you'll have to use Clipboard as a middleman to drop text and graphics into your documents, rather than saving them as files and then reading them directly:

1. Open or switch to the Clipboard.
2. Choose File ➤ Save as. The Save As dialog box will appear.
3. Type in a name for the saved file. As usual, you can change the path name and extension. However, you're best off leaving the extension as .CLP, since Clipboard uses this as a default when you want to reload the file.
4. Click on OK. The file will be saved, and can be loaded again as described below.

Retrieving the Clipboard's Contents

To reload the contents of a .CLP file onto the Clipboard (and necessarily obliterate the current contents of the Clipboard), do the following:

1. Open or activate the Clipboard window.
2. Choose File ➤ Open. The Open dialog box will appear.

3. Select the file you want to pull onto the Clipboard. (Only .CLP files can be opened.) Click on OK.
4. If there's something already on the Clipboard, you'll be asked if you want to erase it. Click on OK if you do.
5. Change the display format via the Display menu if you want (assuming there are options available on the menu).

Clearing the Clipboard

TO EMPTY THE CLIPBOARD,

press Del or choose Edit ➤ Delete while in the Clipboard Viewer.

Keeping information on the Clipboard decreases the amount of memory available for other applications in Windows. If you're running Windows on a machine with limited memory, or if you need to have a sizable number of applications open at once, you should keep the Clipboard free of items that consume a significant amount of memory. Even if the item you clipped to it isn't large in appearance, the memory space required by Clipboard for the information may be considerable, especially since some items are stored in multiple formats. This means several copies of the information may coexist in RAM. If you're getting warning messages from Windows indicating that running another application isn't possible because of a RAM shortage, try clearing the Clipboard, as follows:

1. Open the Clipboard.
2. Choose Delete from the Edit menu, or press Del.
3. Choose OK from the dialog box. The Clipboard's contents will be deleted.

To get an idea of how much RAM an item on the Clipboard is using, select the item, and then check the free memory amount from the Program Manager (Help ➤ About Program Manager). Then clear the Clipboard and check again. The amount of RAM required to hold the item will equal the difference between the two numbers, assuming you didn't load or close any other programs or documents between these steps.

PART TWO

The Supplied Programs

Part II consists of four chapters, which discuss the basic applications programs that are supplied with Windows—the Accessories. Chapter 9 delves into the Write word-processing program quite thoroughly. Chapter 10 discusses the use of Terminal—the telecommunications program—for connecting to information services, bulletin board systems, and other computers. Chapter 11 details the use of Paintbrush, the drawing program supplied with Windows. In Chapter 12, I cover most of the remaining programs—Notepad, Calculator, Calendar, Recorder, Cardfile, Character Map, and Clock. The more advanced programs are discussed in Part III.

FAST TRACK

CHAPTER 9

FAST TRACK

To turn on the ruler, ... **275**

choose Document ➤ Ruler. Triangles indicate the left and right indents for the paragraph currently containing the insertion point. The small dot on the left side of the ruler indicates the position of the first-line indent.

To format the whole document, ... **284**

select the entire document by holding down Ctrl and clicking in the left margin. Then make the paragraph settings. This applies to character settings as well.

To format text, ... **285**

select the text to be affected, if it's already been typed. Open the Character menu and choose the desired format. To change the font, choose the Font command and select the font from the dialog box.

To set tabs, ... **288**

- Choose Document ➤ Tabs. In the dialog box, type the desired tab locations.
- Click on a tab icon in the ruler. In the area just below the ruler, click where you want the tab to be. You can drag the tab marker left or right to reposition it, if necessary.

To search for a word, ... **293**

choose Find ➤ Find. Type in the text you want to locate. Press Enter or click on Find Next. If you want to find complete words only or want to match upper- or lowercase, check those options in the dialog box.

To replace a word, ... **293**
choose Find ➤ Replace. Type in the text to be found and the replacement text. Select check boxes as necessary.

To copy between two Write documents, ... **297**
you have to run Write twice and load one document in each window, then arrange them on-screen and copy and paste.

To create a page break, ... **301**
place the cursor where you want to break a page and press Ctrl-Enter.

To create a header or footer, ... **302**
select Document ➤ Header or Document ➤ Footer, enter the text, and make other adjustments. Click on Return to Document.

To add a graphic to a document, ... **304**

- ◆ Select Edit ➤ Paste to insert a graphic from the Clipboard.
- ◆ Select Edit ➤ Move Picture, move the pointer, and click the mouse to move the graphic sideways.
- ◆ Select Edit ➤ Size Picture, move the pointer, and click the mouse to resize the graphic.

To save a file, ... **310**
choose File ➤ Save, enter the file name, determine the directory, and click OK.

CHAPTER 9

FEATURING

Entering and Editing Text

Formatting Characters and Paragraphs

Creating Headers and Footers

Setting Up Columns

Searching and Replacing Words

Importing Graphics

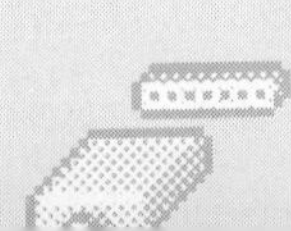

Using Write for Simple Word Processing

This chapter begins with a tutorial that gives you the opportunity to learn how to create and edit a word-processing document. Along the way, you can experiment with the major procedures involved in a simple Windows-based word processor. Many of the techniques discussed in this chapter are applicable to other Windows programs as well. So you'll benefit from following the specific exercises—particularly if you're new to Windows.

One of the freebie applications supplied with Windows is called Windows Write, or just Write. This is a simple but useful word processor. It boasts few significant frills compared to hefty programs like Microsoft Word for Windows, WordPerfect, or Ami Pro, but will suffice for you to write letters, reports, or anything that doesn't require sophisticated formatting. Besides, the price is right, so you can't complain.

Though not a heavyweight at formatting text, Write accepts, displays, and prints graphics pasted to it from the Clipboard; it also supports OLE. (See Chapter 14 for more about OLE.) Write lets you create word-processing documents of virtually any length, limited only by the capacity of your disk drive, and it has a fair number of features that make it useful as an everyday workhorse.

After entering and editing your document, we'll extend your skills by discussing the various formatting features you can easily apply to your documents. Included in the discussion is information on how to:

- format individual characters with font, style, and size alterations
- format paragraphs by changing line spacing, indents, and margins
- set the tab stops to aid you in making tables
- quickly search for and replace specific text
- include headers and footers
- paginate your document correctly
- incorporate and edit graphics
- copy text between two Write documents
- save and print files

CREATING YOUR FIRST DOCUMENT

Every document you create in Windows, or any other program for that matter, is stored by your computer in a file. The first step in creating your document will be to tell Windows that you want to begin a new file.

To open a new Write document, open the Accessories group and double-click on the Write icon. Write will come up and open a new document window for you. Your screen should now look like that shown in Figure 9.1.

There are several things to notice on your screen. As usual, up at the top you see the menu and title bars. The menu bar offers options for writing, editing, and formatting text. Try pulling down each menu now, just to take a look at the various selections you have at your fingertips. You may even want to choose some of the menu choices that have dialog boxes associated with them (indicated by the ellipsis after the name). You can always press Esc (or click on Cancel) to back out of a dialog box.

Referring to your screen or to Figure 9.1, notice that the title bar shows Untitled as the file name, since you haven't named the document yet. Notice, too, that the cursor sits blinking in the upper-left corner of your screen with another symbol to its right. This little boxy symbol indicates the end (bottom) of the document. Since you haven't typed in anything yet, the only thing between the top and bottom of the document is the insertion point.

FIGURE 9.1:

The initial Write screen with no text in the document

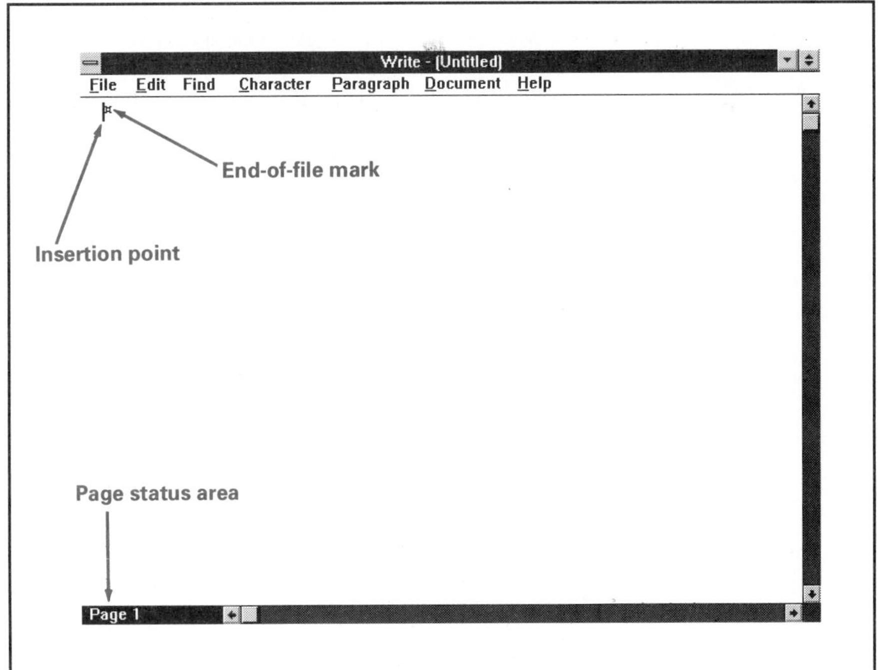

ENTERING TEXT

Now begin creating a document. You may type in anything you want. However, to establish a consistent text for me to refer to later on in this chapter, try entering the following text, a hypothetical news story. (For purposes later on, keep the two misspelled words, *Pizza* and *sight,* as they are.) If you are at all unfamiliar with word processors, first read the steps that follow this text:

NEWS FLASH

Society for Anachronistic Sciences
1000 Edsel Lane
Piltdown, PA 19042

The Society for Anachronistic Sciences announced its controversial findings today at a press conference held in the city of Pisa, Italy. Pizza was chosen as the sight for the conference because of its celebrated position in the annals of Western scientific history. The Society has made public its annual press conferences for well over 300 years and, as usual, nothing new was revealed. According to its members, this is a comforting fact and a social service in an age when everything else seems to change.

Begin entering the text into your new file, following the steps outlined here. If you make mistakes while you are typing, use the Backspace key to back up and fix them. If you don't see an error until you are long past it you'll learn how to fix such errors later:

1. Type **NEWS FLASH** on the first line.
2. Next, press Enter twice to move down a couple of lines to prepare for typing the address. Notice that pressing Enter is necessary for adding new blank lines in a word-processing document. Pressing the ↓ key will not move the cursor down a line at this point or create new lines; you will only hear an error beep from your computer if you try this.
3. Enter the first line of the address; then press Enter to move down to the next line. Repeat this process for the last two lines of the address. So far this should remind you of using a typewriter.
4. Press Enter twice to put in another blank line.
5. Begin entering the body of the story. Don't forget to leave in the spelling mistakes so that we can fix them later on. You shouldn't press Enter at the end of each line because Write will automatically wrap to the next line for you. This is called *word wrapping.* All you have to do is keep typing—and leave only one space between sentences, not two.

EDITING YOUR TEXT

Editing is simply the process of making changes, either major or minor, to your document. Everyone who uses a word processor inevitably develops his or her own style of editing. Some people like to print out a document and edit on paper, fix the errors, and then print again. Others find editing on the screen more efficient. You will no doubt decide for yourself later.

The first step in editing is learning how to move around in the text. While actually entering the text above, you probably seldom found it necessary to move the cursor around to any great extent. For the most part, you left if alone and it moved along by itself as you typed. But now for editing purposes you'll want to move up and down quite a bit in order to fix misspelled words and change other things.

SCROLLING IN THE DOCUMENT

As with other Windows programs, you typically scroll using the scroll bars. You can also use the PgUp and PgDn keys to scroll your text a screen at a time. The sample press release you've typed in is not long enough to warrant any scrolling, so add some creative sentences and paragraphs of your own to the text so that the whole story extends beyond one screen.

Scrolling with the Keyboard

Practice scrolling by following these instructions:

1. Press the PgUp key. (If you don't have an extended keyboard, make sure NumLock is toggled off; otherwise pressing that key will type the number 9 instead of scrolling the text.) Pressing PgUp moves you up one screen toward the beginning of your document.
2. Press PgDn. This has the opposite effect.

Scrolling with the Mouse

When you work with large documents, the scroll bar can be a guide to the relative position of the cursor within the document:

1. Put the pointer somewhere in the scroll bar itself, either above or below the elevator, and click to move a screenful at a time.

Clicking above the elevator moves you towards the top; clicking below moves you towards the bottom of the text.

2. Drag the elevator and pull it to any particular point on the scroll bar.

Consider the scroll bars to be a sort of measuring stick for your document, with the top of the bar representing the beginning of your document and the bottom of the bar the end. By dragging the elevator to the approximate relative position you want to scroll to, you can get close to your desired spot quickly. The horizontal scroll bar works the same way as the vertical bar, but is only useful if your document is more than a page wide.

Moving the Cursor

The *cursor* marks the position where letters appear when you type. As you may recall from the previous chapter's discussion about pasting text from the Clipboard, this is also called the *insertion point.* Editing your text involves moving the insertion point to the correct location and then inserting text, removing words, fixing misspellings, or marking blocks of text for moving, copying, or deletion. Obviously the easiest way to do this is just to point and click. The insertion point will jump from wherever it is to the position where you clicked.

You can also use the arrow keys, though, which may be easier at times. Here are some exercises to try:

NOTE *After positioning the cursor, don't forget to click. Otherwise, you'll end up making changes in the wrong place—wherever the cursor happens to be.*

1. Move to the second line of the story and click just before the *t* in the word *sight.* This will position the insertion point just before that letter.
2. Press → again and hold it down for a few seconds. Notice that once the key begins to repeat, the cursor moves faster. When it gets to the end of the first line, it wraps around to the second and third lines. Now press ← and hold it down. When the cursor gets to the beginning of the document, your computer starts to beep because the cursor can't go any farther.
3. Press ↓. Hold it down for a while and notice what happens when the cursor reaches the bottom of the screen. The text scrolls up. The reverse happens when the cursor is at the top of the screen and you press the ↑ key.

4. Press Ctrl-→. Each press of the arrow key moves ahead one word. Ctrl-← moves a word at a time in the other direction.

Since writing relies heavily on the keyboard, Write provides many keyboard combinations that can be used to move the insertion point. These are listed in Table 9.1. Note that the 5 key is used in combination with some arrow keys. This means the 5 key on the numeric keypad. (Make sure NumLock is turned off or you'll just get a *5* when you press the 5 key.) If you don't have a numeric keypad, you can't use these commands.

Making Selections in Write

Much of editing with a word processor centers around manipulating blocks of text. A *block* is a portion of your text, letters, words, or paragraphs. Many of the commands in Windows programs use this idea of manipulating blocks

TABLE 9.1: *Keyboard Combinations in Write*

PRESS	TO JUMP TO THE
Ctrl-→	Next word
Ctrl-←	Previous word
5 →	Next sentence
5 ←	Previous sentence
Home	Beginning of the current line
End	End of the current line
5 ↓	Next paragraph
5 ↑	Previous paragraph
Ctrl-PgDn	Bottom of the window
Ctrl-PgUp	Top of the window
PgDn	Next Page
PgUp	Previous page
Ctrl-Home	Beginning of the document
Ctrl-End	End of the document

of information, sometimes text or other data, such as numbers.

You must select a block before you can work with it. As long as an area of a document is selected, it will become the center of attention to Write and will usually be treated differently than the rest of the document. Some menu commands will affect the selection and nothing else. This remains the case until the block is "deselected" when you click elsewhere or select another block.

Be careful not to press any keys other than the cursor-movement keys after you've made a selection. If you type **A**, for example, the whole selection will be replaced by the letter *A*. If this happens accidentally, choose Edit ➤ Undo from the menu bar *before doing anything else* and your text will be returned to its previous state.

Once you've selected a section of text, you can manipulate it in any number of ways: you can cut or copy it, change its font size, alter the paragraph formatting, and so forth. Try these exercises to get the hang of selecting.

Selecting an Arbitrary Text Area with the Mouse

Selection is particularly intuitive and simple with the mouse. Mouse selection was also explained in Chapter 8 for copying and cutting to the Clipboard. Try this:

1. Deselect any possible selections you may have made already by clicking somewhere in the text. It doesn't matter where.
2. Move the pointer to the beginning of a word somewhere (you may have to scroll the window).
3. Hold the left mouse button down and move the pointer down several lines. As you move the mouse, the selection extends. When you let up on the button, the selection is completed.
4. Click anywhere again to deselect the selection.

The *anchor point* is the point you first clicked. Dragging downward extends the selection downward from the anchor point. If you were to keep the mouse button down and drag *above* the anchor point, the selection would extend from the anchor point upward.

Selecting an Arbitrary Text Area with the Shift Key

You can also use the Shift key in combination with the arrow keys or the mouse to select an arbitrary amount of text:

1. Deselect anything you already have selected.
2. Move the cursor to the beginning of any word in the first paragraph. Now press Shift-→. The selection advances one letter with each press (unless you hold the key down too long, in which case it moves by itself and selects several letters).
3. Press Shift-↑ five times. Notice that as you move up past the anchor point, the selection reverses, moving upward in the text.
4. Press Shift-Ctrl-→. The selection advances a word with each press.
5. Release the keys and click somewhere to deselect.
6. Click on the first word in the second paragraph.
7. Hold down the Shift key.
8. Click on a word in the middle of the paragraph. This changes the selection: it's now from the new anchor point to the point where you clicked.

Selecting a Word at a Time

Often you'll want to select a word quickly, either to delete it or to change some aspect of it, such as its font size. You can do this easily by double-clicking. Let's say you want to change *Western* in the first paragraph to *Eastern:*

1. Double-click on the word *Western* to select it.
2. Press Del to delete it. (Using Del doesn't put it on the Clipboard, incidentally. It just deletes it.)
3. Type **Eastern**.

Selecting a Line or Series of Lines

There's a shortcut for selecting an entire line or quickly selecting a series of entire lines:

1. Move the mouse pointer into the left margin. It changes into an arrow. This margin is called the *selection area.*
2. Position the pointer to the left of the first line of the first paragraph and click the mouse to select the entire line.
3. Starting from the same place, hold down the mouse button and drag the pointer down the left margin, selecting each line the pointer passes.

Selecting an Entire Sentence

If you don't like a particular sentence and want to cut or move the whole thing, you can do so easily:

1. Hold down the Ctrl key.
2. Click anywhere on the first sentence in the first paragraph. The whole sentence will be highlighted.

Selecting an Entire Paragraph

Here's a shortcut for selecting an entire paragraph:

1. Move the cursor into the selection area (left margin) next to the first paragraph.
2. Double-click. The entire paragraph will be highlighted.

Dragging the pointer in the margin while still holding the mouse button down will select additional paragraphs.

Selecting an Entire Document

Sometimes you'll want to select the whole document. This can be useful for changing the font size or type of all the text, or changing other attributes, as discussed below. There's no menu choice for this, but it can be done with a key combination:

1. Move the cursor into the selection area.

2. Hold down Ctrl and click the mouse. The entire document will become selected.

Making Some Changes to the Text

Now that you know how to get around and select portions of text, you can begin to correct some of the typos in your letter.

Deleting Letters

Let's start with the second sentence of the first paragraph, where the word *site* is misspelled as *sight:*

1. Position the cursor between the *i* and *g* in *sight.*
2. Press Del. This removes the misplaced *g.* Notice also that the space closed up where the *g* was when you deleted the letter, pulling the letters to the right to close the gap.
3. Repeat this to remove the *h.*
4. Move the cursor one character to the right and add the *e.*

Notice that the line opened up to let the *e* in. Unlike on a typewritten page, lines on a computer screen are flexible, letting you insert the letter—in fact, so flexible that you may have noticed that Write rewraps all the lines of the paragraph almost instantly as you insert text.

Many simple errors can be fixed using the Del or Backspace key. But suppose you wanted to delete an entire word, sentence, or paragraph. You could do this by moving to the beginning or end of the section you wanted to erase and then holding down Del or Backspace, respectively, until the key erased all the words, letter by letter. But this is an unpredictable method. If you're not careful, you'll often erase more than you intended to. This is where selecting a text block comes in.

Deleting Words

For our second change, select the word *Pizza* in order to delete it and then replace it with *Pisa:*

1. Select the word *Pizza* at the beginning of the second sentence in the first paragraph.

2. Open the Edit menu and choose Cut, since we want to delete the currently selected word.

The word disappears and now you can type in **Pisa**. (You may have to add a space after the word, depending on how you selected *Pizza.*) All of this may seem like a lot of work just to change a few letters, but for larger selections you will find it's worth the effort.

Let's try another approach. Here's a shortcut for replacing a word or selection with some other text:

1. Double-click on *annual* in the third sentence.
2. With *annual* highlighted, type in **yearly**. Notice that *annual* is deleted. This saves the extra step of choosing Cut from the Edit menu.

Inserting Letters

You can insert any number of letters, words, or paragraphs wherever you want within a document. This is called *inserting.* You may know that some word processors allow you to deactivate insertion in favor of *overwriting,* where newly typed letters overwrite the old ones instead of pushing them to the right. Write does not let you do this. The advantage is that you will never accidentally type over some text you want to keep. The disadvantage is that you will have to take action to delete unwanted text.

MOVING SELECTED BLOCKS

The editing process often involves moving large portions of text, such as sentences and paragraphs, within a document. Rather than inserting a block of text by retyping it, you can pick it up and move it from one place to another with the Cut, Copy, and Paste commands covered in the last chapter.

Here's an example of the Paste command that will reverse the order of the first two paragraphs in our letter:

1. Move to the top of the document.
2. Select the "News Flash" line (actually a paragraph) with whatever technique you prefer—and carefully select the blank line immediately below the paragraph, too, since you want a blank line between the paragraphs after the move. Just drag the mouse a little

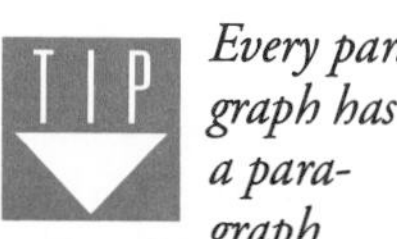

Every paragraph has a paragraph mark. Paragraph attributes such as alignment, tab settings, and margins are contained in it. Copying this mark is an easy way of copying attributes from one place to another.

further down. If you double-clicked in the margin to select the paragraph, press Shift to retain the paragraph selection and then double-click to the left of the blank line. You'll know the blank line is selected when a thin strip at the left margin becomes highlighted. (This is the normally invisible *paragraph mark* associated with the blank line.)

3. Open the Edit menu and choose Cut (or just press Ctrl-X without opening the menu).
4. Move the insertion point to the place where you want to insert the paragraph, which happens to be just before the *T* of the word *The* in the first main paragraph.
5. Choose Edit ➤ Paste or press Ctrl-V.
6. Give yourself a little more practice by returning the moved paragraph to its original position.

Sometimes after moving paragraphs around, you may have to do a little adjusting, such as inserting or deleting a line or some spaces. You can always insert a line with Enter. If, after a move, you have extra blank lines, you can delete them by putting the insertion point on the first space of a blank line (the far left margin) and pressing the Backspace key. This moves the cursor up and "pulls" up all the text to the right of (and below) the cursor by one line.

FORMATTING PARAGRAPHS

TO TURN ON THE RULER,

choose Document ➤ Ruler On. Triangles indicate the left and right indents for the paragraph that the insertion point is currently in. The small dot on the left side of the ruler indicates the position of the first-line indent.

Paragraphs are the most essential division of your text when it comes to formatting or controlling its looks. A paragraph is defined by Write as any text terminated by a *carriage return* (that is, the Enter key). So even a single letter, line, or word will be treated as a paragraph if you press Enter after it. Write handles each paragraph as a separate entity, each with its own formatting information. The press release you created early in the chapter uses a standard block paragraph format typical of many business letters. In that format, a paragraph's first line is not indented, so you separate paragraphs with a blank line. Also notice that the right margin is ragged, rather than straight (or *justified*).

These and other qualities affecting the looks of your paragraphs can be altered while you are entering text, or at any time thereafter. As you change the format settings, you immediately see the effects. Bold letters will look bold, centered lines centered, italic letters look slanted, and so forth.

For most documents, you may find that you are happy with Write's default format. Write applies the standard default format for you, carrying it from one paragraph to the next as you type. If you decide you'd rather use a different format for a new document, you just alter some settings and begin typing away. Then everything you type into the new document will be formatted accordingly until you change the settings.

The *ruler* helps you keep track of where you are typing on the page, much like the guide on a typewriter. It also lets you alter the format of paragraphs by clicking on icons and symbols displayed within its boundaries. These alterations can be made from the Paragraph menu as well, but the ruler makes it easier. Figure 9.2 shows the ruler and its sections. Normally the ruler is off (*hidden*), but you can turn it on if you wish to:

- Choose Document ➤ Ruler On to show it.
- Choose Document ➤ Ruler Off to hide it.

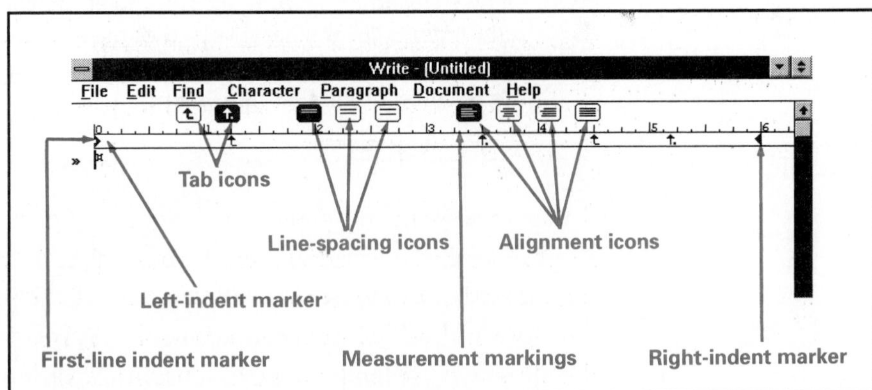

FIGURE 9.2: *The ruler helps you align text, change line spacing, and set tabs.*

Hiding the ruler lets you see extra lines of your text in the document window, but, as you'll see later, the ruler is useful to have around. (Figures in this chapter will be shown with the ruler on.) The ruler has markings on it to help you gauge where your text will fall across the printed page, and to help you set up tab stops. Each inch is marked with a number and each eighth of an inch is marked by a small line. (You can change the ruler to show centimeters via the Document Page Layout dialog box, though.)

Notice the ▶ and ◀ marks. These indicate the left and right indents (sometimes called *margin settings*), respectively. There is also a small square dot within the ▶ mark on the left side of the ruler, though it's not easily visible. This controls and indicates the setting of the first-line indent for each paragraph. The ruler can also show tab settings. The use of those settings will be explained later.

VIEWING AND ALTERING PARAGRAPH SETTINGS

Paragraph formatting falls into three categories with Write: *alignment, spacing,* and *indents.* The following sections explain and illustrate these categories. Unless otherwise noted, the examples here use inches as the basic unit of measure. If you wish to indicate another unit, such as centimeters, you can use the Document ➤ Page Layout command to do so.

ALIGNMENT

TO CHANGE THE ALIGNMENT OF A PARAGRAPH,

place the insertion point in the paragraph or select a range of paragraphs. Open the Paragraph menu and choose the type of alignment you want, or click on the appropriate alignment icon in the ruler.

Alignment refers to where the text in a paragraph sits within the margins. *Left* is the default, causing text to be flush with the left margin (and ragged right). *Center* centers every line of the paragraph. *Right* causes text to be flush with the right margin (and ragged left). *Justified* causes both sides of the text to be flush with the right and left margins. (This adds spaces between words and letters to fill out shorter lines.)

Many printers can do what's called *microspaced justification,* a technique for spreading out the words and letters so that justified text looks more evenly spaced. Yours may be able to, but you should probably try printing out a justified document before deciding whether to use this format.

Figure 9.3 shows four paragraphs, each one with a different type of alignment. To display or modify the settings for a given paragraph, you click the cursor anywhere on it and then view or change the setting either from the ruler or from the Paragraph menu. Anytime you position the insertion point in a paragraph, the rulers and menu will reflect that paragraph's current settings.

Viewing Paragraph Alignment

1. Move the insertion point to the paragraph in question and click.
2. If the ruler is on, look at it. The icons will indicate the alignment settings, as shown in Figure 9.4. The current setting is highlighted.

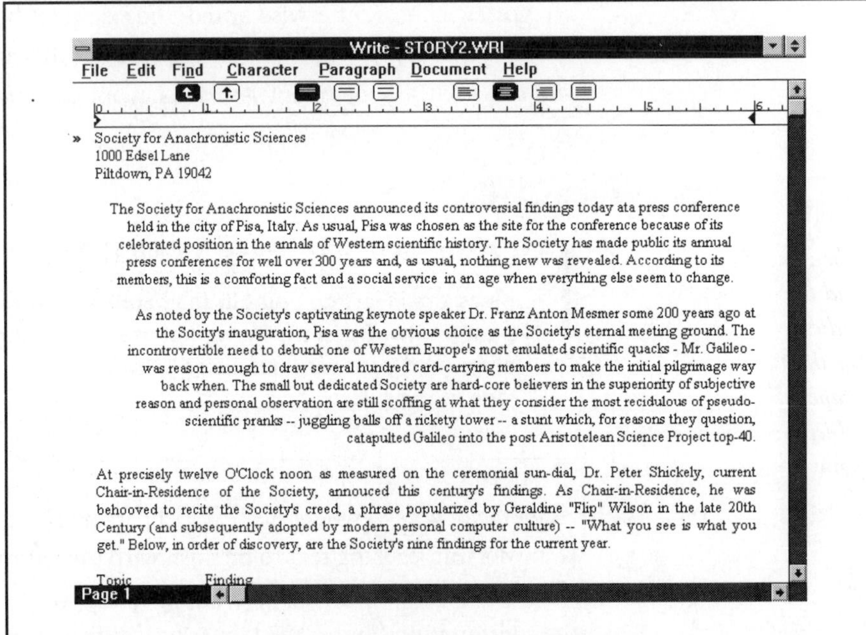

FIGURE 9.3: *Four types of alignment (from top to bottom): left, centered, right, and justified*

3. Open the Paragraph menu. There will be a check mark next to the current paragraph's alignment setting. Figure 9.5 shows an example of a centered paragraph's menu.

FIGURE 9.4:

These icons in the ruler indicate and allow you to alter the alignment settings for a paragraph or selected paragraphs.

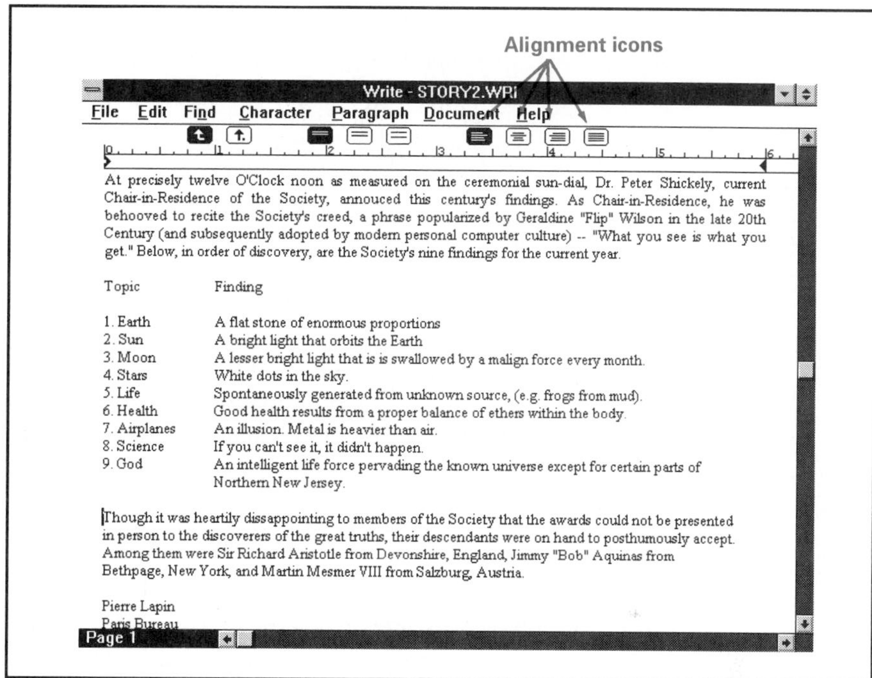

FIGURE 9.5:

The Paragraph menu and the ruler always indicate the settings for the current paragraph (the one in which the insertion point is positioned).

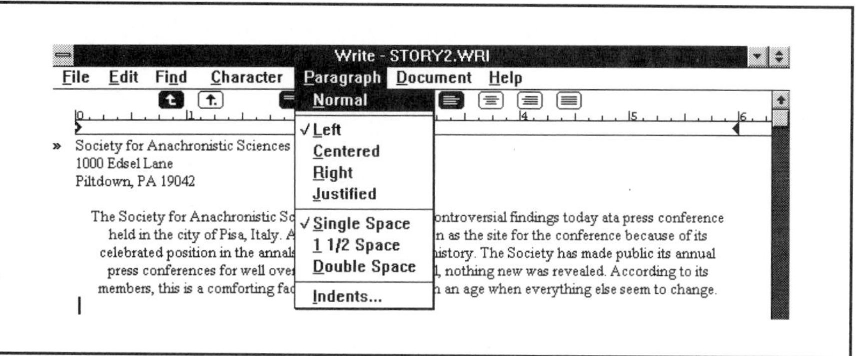

Altering the Paragraph Alignment

You can change the settings for a paragraph almost as easily as you can display them:

1. Move the insertion point to the paragraph or select several paragraphs (even a portion of each paragraph will suffice).
2. Open the Paragraph menu and choose the alignment you want.
3. As an alternative, if the ruler is showing, click on one of its four alignment icons (this is faster).

LINE SPACING

TO CHANGE THE LINE SPACING OF A PARAGRAPH,

place the insertion point in the paragraph or select a range of paragraphs. Click on the ruler icon that represents the line spacing you want, or choose a line spacing from the Paragraph menu.

Line spacing determines the amount of space between lines within the paragraph. Normally you'll want to use single or double spacing. However, you can also have 1½-spaced lines. (Text in font sizes of 24 points or over is not affected by line spacing.) To change the line spacing of a paragraph or paragraphs:

1. Move the insertion point to the paragraph in question (or select several paragraphs). There need not be text on the line yet. (On a new line you must do this before you begin typing.)
2. If the ruler is on, look at it. The icons will indicate the line-spacing settings, as shown in Figure 9.6. Click on the icon representing the line spacing you want.
3. As an alternative, open the Paragraph menu. There will be a check mark next to the current line-spacing setting. Change the setting by simply choosing another one.

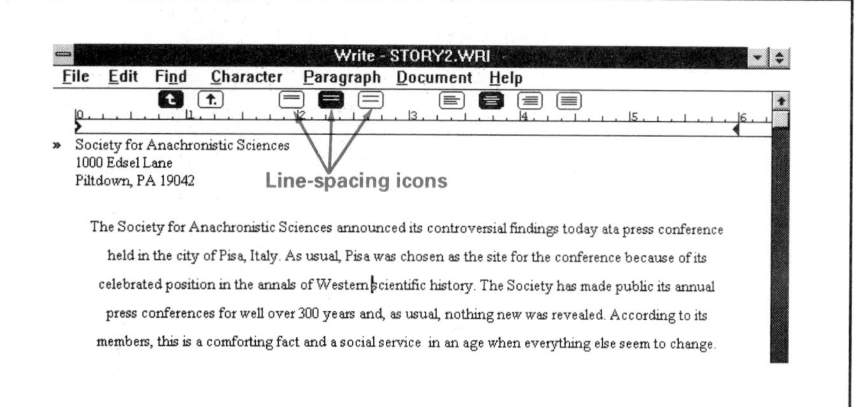

FIGURE 9.6: *These icons in the ruler indicate and allow you to change the line-spacing settings for the current paragraph or selected paragraphs.*

INDENTS

TO CHANGE THE INDENTATION OF A PARAGRAPH,

place the insertion point in the paragraph or select a range of paragraphs. Choose Paragraph ➤ Indents and enter the desired indents. If the ruler is on, you can drag the indent markers instead.

Indents fall into three categories: *right indent, left indent,* and *first-line indent.* Every paragraph has settings for each, and each paragraph's settings can be different. As with the other paragraph settings, these are carried from one paragraph to the next as you type, or you can change them after the fact. You set indents via the Paragraph menu's Indents command or by dragging the indent symbols on the ruler (see Figure 9.7).

The settings determine how far in from the left and right margins your text will appear. (They do not determine how far from the edge of the page the text will appear, however. That's established by the *margins.*) The first-line indent determines the starting position of the first line of each paragraph.

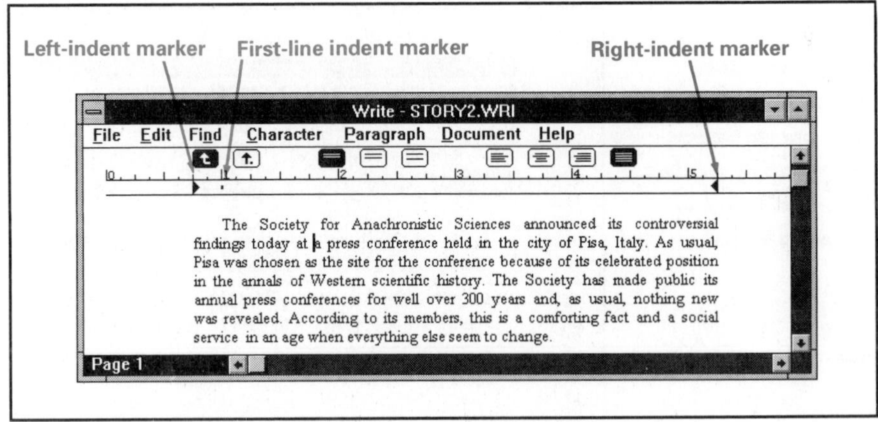

FIGURE 9.7: *Dragging these symbols with the mouse changes the right, left, and first-line indents*

Setting the Left or Right Indent

You can change the left or right indent by either selecting the command from the menu or using the ruler. Here's the first method:

1. Place the insertion point in a paragraph or select several paragraphs whose settings you want to change.
2. Choose Paragraph ➤ Indents. The Indents dialog box (shown below) will appear. Type in the desired indent and click on OK. If you type in just a number, it's assumed to be in inches. You can type **cm** after the number to indicate centimeters.

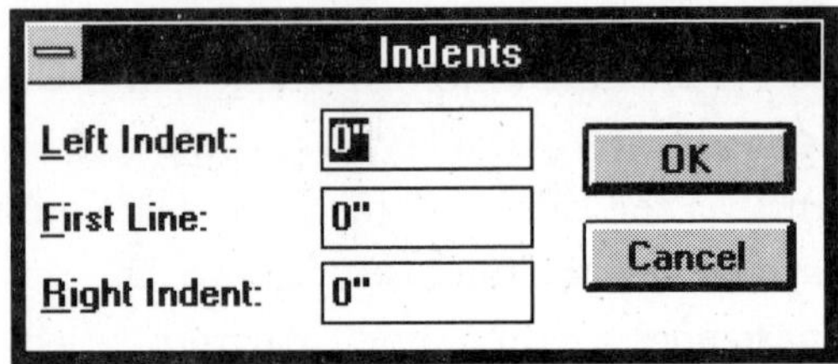

If the number you enter isn't acceptable, Write will tell you. This usually happens when you accidentally enter a value that is too large for the paper your printer driver is set up for.

You can also use the ruler to change the left or right indent:

1. Place the insertion point in the paragraph or select several paragraphs whose settings you want to change.

2. Turn on the ruler, if it's off, by choosing Document ➤ Ruler On.
3. Drag the left-indent marker in the ruler (▶) to a new position. To get to the marker, you may first have to move the square dot sitting on top of it (that's the *first-line indent* symbol, which I'll explain next). Move the dot a bit, grab the triangle, drag it to the new position, and then move the dot back.

Setting the First-Line Indent

If you want to indent the first line on a typewriter, you have to hit the Tab key or press the spacebar several times. It's easier to let Write do it for you with its first-line indent setting. This also lets you modify the look of a letter after the fact, since you can adjust the first line indents. You might write a letter in block form, then decide to change it to half-inch indents.

The first-line indent setting establishes the relative indent for the first line of each new paragraph. Note that the setting is *in addition to* the left indent. So if the left indent is 1" and the first line indent is 0.5", the first line will start 1.5" from the left margin. Incidentally, setting the first-line indent to a negative number, such as –0.5, will cause it to hang out that amount from the left indent. This is sometimes called a *hanging indent,* or an "outdent." To change the first-line indent:

1. Place the insertion point in the paragraph or select several paragraphs whose settings you want to change.
2. Choose Paragraph ➤ Indents. The Indents dialog box will appear. Type in the first-line indent amount and click on OK.
3. As an alternative, drag the first-line indent marker (the square dot) in the ruler to the new indent position.

In either case, Write will immediately reformat the paragraph in accordance with the new settings. Figure 9.8 shows examples of three different indent setups.

Reverting to the Normal Settings

One of the most popular formats for paragraphs is what's already set up as the *default* (normal) *paragraph:* single-spaced, left-aligned, and indents of

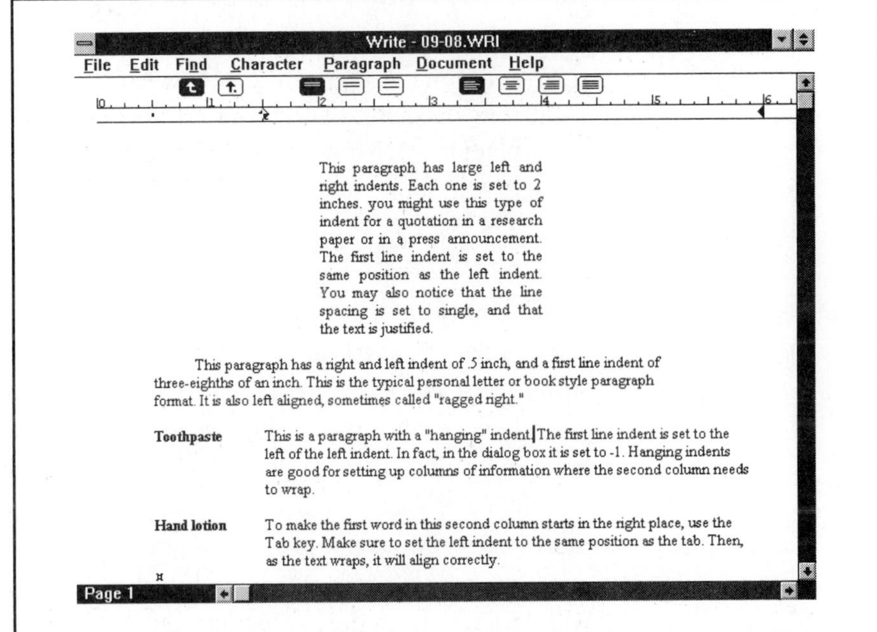

FIGURE 9.8: *Three different indent setups. (The last two paragraphs use the same settings.)*

zero. Simply open the Paragraph menu and choose Normal for the current or selected paragraphs to revert to this setup.

Reformatting the Whole Document

TO FORMAT THE WHOLE DOCUMENT,

select the entire document by holding down Ctrl and clicking in the left margin. Then make the paragraph settings. This applies to character settings as well.

You'll often want to reformat an entire document. That is, you'll print out the document, look at it, and quickly realize it should have been 1½ spaced, or should have smaller (or larger) first-line indents, etc. Since each paragraph has its own settings, it can be a pain to alter each paragraph one at a time. But remember, settings are applied to *all* selected paragraphs, so just select the whole document first, and then change the settings.

FORMATTING CHARACTERS

TO FORMAT TEXT,

select the text to be affected, if it's already been typed. Open the Character menu and choose the desired format. To change the font, choose the Font command and select the font from the dialog box.

Write includes commands for altering the look of the individual letters on the printed page. This is called *character formatting*. Commands for character formatting are on the Character menu. You can use character formatting to emphasize a section of text by making it bold, underlined, or italicized. Or you may want to change the size or even the type style (*font*) of the characters. On many printers, you can combine various character formats.

Just as with paragraph formatting, Write starts you off with a *regular* font, style, and line position (not super- or subscripted). (The Regular font means the standard font for the default printer.)

The Fonts dialog box will show you what sizes and font names are available for your particular printer. As with most Windows programs, Write measures character sizes in *points*. Typical point sizes are 9 to 14 for Regular text. (This book is printed in 10 point Garamond Light.) Typical newspaper headlines may appear in anything up to 60 points or so. Figure 9.9 shows some examples of actual point sizes in Times Roman (Tms Rmn).

Character formatting can be achieved in three ways:

- from the Character menu
- from the Fonts dialog box
- with shortcut Ctrl-key combinations

You can change the formatting of individual characters, selected blocks of text, or the whole document. Character formatting does not apply to paragraphs as a whole, unless they're actually selected.

FIGURE 9.9:

Comparative type sizes

12 point

15 point

24 point

60 point

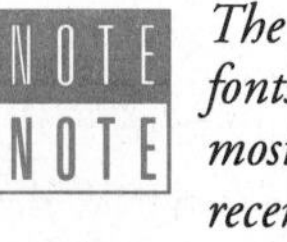

The three fonts you most recently used appear on the Character menu, so you can easily switch among them. The type size for each is the font's default size, usually 10 or 12 points.

The icon next to the font name tells you whether it is a TrueType or Printer font. The explanation below the Sample box tells you how your printed document will compare to what you see on the screen.

To change the formatting of characters you've already typed, follow these steps:

1. Select the text character(s) to be altered. You can select a single letter, a sentence, a paragraph, the whole document, etc.
2. Choose the new character format from the Character menu, or use any of the Ctrl-key combinations listed on the menu as shortcuts.

Note that some of these can be combined. For example, text can be bold, underlined, *and* italicized all at once. To clear any settings, choose Regular or simply press F5. Choosing Regular does not reset the typeface or size, it only resets the five attributes listed in the Character menu: bold, italic, underline, superscript, and subscript.

If the font name you want isn't listed on the menu, select Fonts. A dialog box will appear, from which you can choose the font name and type size you want, as you see in Figure 9.10.

Select the name of the font you want from the list. Then choose the size by clicking on it. You may have more options than are immediately visible, so scroll through the list if you don't see what you're looking for. You can type in the point size rather than choosing it from the list if you like. If your printer can scale fonts to any integer size (as PostScript printers can), use this technique to select type sizes that don't appear on the list.

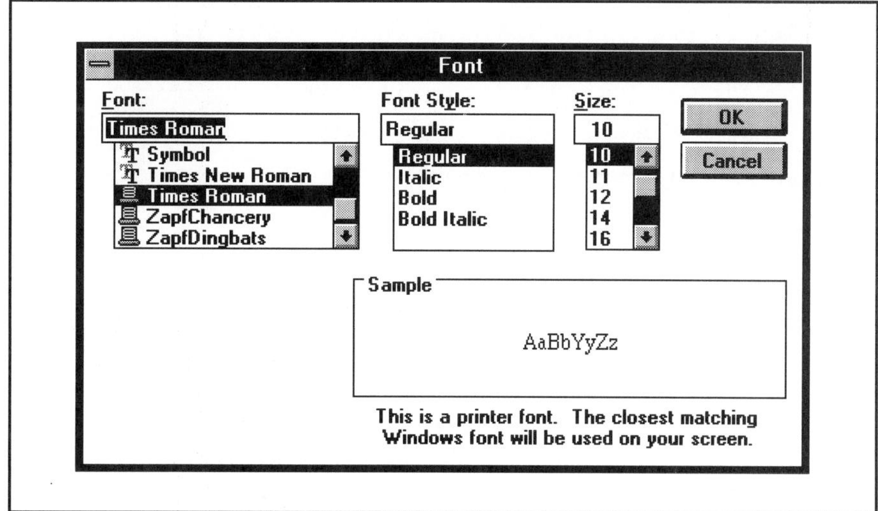

FIGURE 9.10:

To change the font, select some text, choose Character ➤ Fonts, and then choose the font name, style, and size from this dialog box.

There is a shortcut for changing font size quickly. Choose Character ➤ Enlarge Font or Reduce Font. Each time you select one of these commands, the font size is bumped up or down by one setting. This achieves the same effect as opening the font box and clicking on the next smaller or larger font size. When you reach the upper or lower size limit, nothing further happens.

Formatting Characters as You Type

You can also change formats as you type. Subsequent characters will be entered with the new settings—and remain in force until changed. This is particularly handy for italicizing or boldfacing words as you type:

1. Type in your text as usual.
2. When you get to the point where you want to change the style, open the Character menu and choose the new format you want, or press the Ctrl-key combination.
3. Press F5 to continue typing regular text.

Note that the menu choices and Ctrl-key combinations are toggles. So you could also press Ctrl-B once to start typing bold characters and press it again to revert to unbolded text. (This would be especially useful if you were typing a passage in italics, for instance, and wanted to bold a word, then go back to unbolded italics.)

WORKING WITH TABS

TO SET TABS,

- **Choose Document ➤ Tabs. In the dialog box type in the desired tab locations.**
- **Click on a tab icon in the ruler and then click in the area just below the ruler where you want the tab to be. You can drag the tab marker left and right to reposition it if you have to.**

As with a typewriter, you can vary the tab settings to suit your needs. For complex multicolumn tables, you'll probably want to set up your own custom tab stops. Default tabs are already set up across the page in half-inch increments. These tabs don't show up in the ruler. You can, however, have as many as 12 of your own tabs that will show up in the ruler, and they will apply to the entire document.

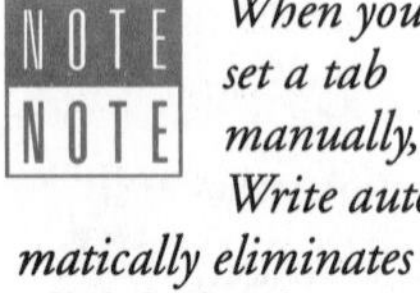

When you set a tab manually, Write automatically eliminates all default tab stops to the left of that one.

In addition to "normal" tabs, which are left-aligned, you can also set decimal-aligned tabs. Left-aligned tabs line up on the left, beginning at the tab. Decimal tabs align text at the decimal point. This is useful for aligning columns of numbers with decimal points in them, such as monetary figures.

Write does not include an option for right-aligned tabs, but you can simulate them by setting a decimal tab, as long as you don't use more than one period with text at that tab stop. Text you enter will right-align until a period is entered, at which point it begins aligning around the period. Figure 9.11 shows a table created with both normal and decimal tabs. There are two ways to set and alter tabs:

- from the Tabs dialog box
- from the ruler

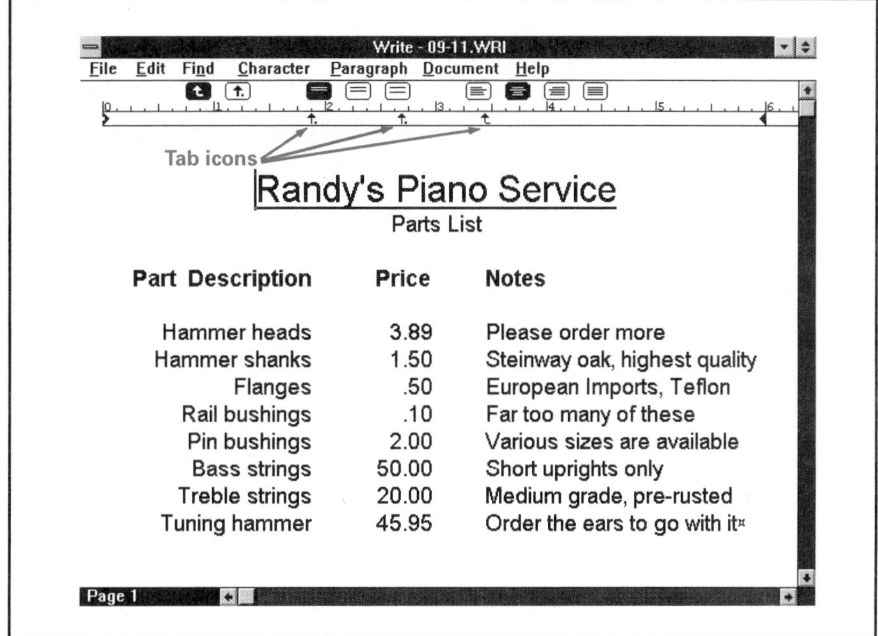

FIGURE 9.11:

A three-column table showing left-, right-, and decimal-aligned tabs. Notice that the right-aligned tab column uses a decimal-tab setting.

Setting Tab Stops from a Dialog Box

To set tabs from a dialog box, you choose Document ➤ Tabs. A dialog box appears, as shown in Figure 9.12. There are 12 rectangular sections, one for each possible tab. You type in the position of each tab (e.g., 2.5 or 5.75) in a box. You don't have to fill all the boxes, only ones you want. They can be entered in any order (for example, you could type 7.5 in the first box and 2.5 in the second). The next time you open the Tabs dialog box, they will be arranged correctly, from left to right in ascending order.

You then decide whether you want the tab stops to be left-aligned or decimal. For a decimal stop, click on the Decimal check box below the tab location. For left alignment, leave it off.

After you click on OK, the tabs will be set. The ruler will have new tab markers (little upward pointing arrows) in it to indicate the new tab positions, and the text will be adjusted immediately.

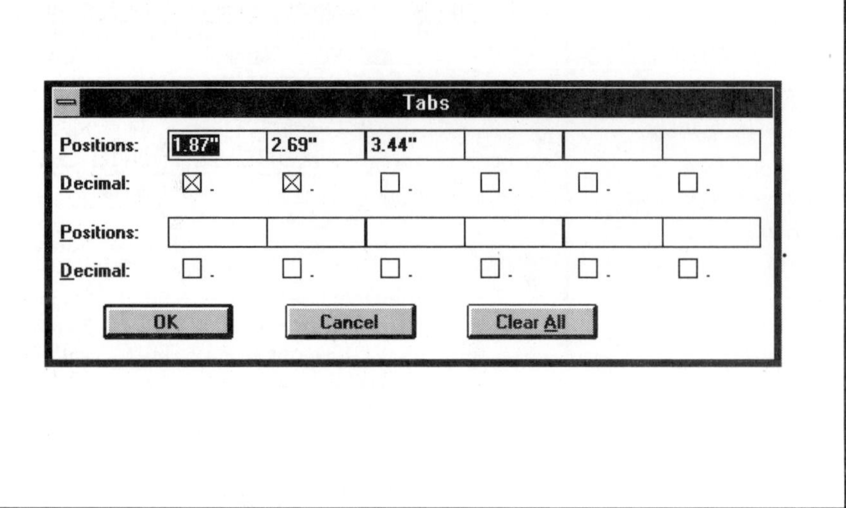

FIGURE 9.12: *You can set the 12 possible tabs from this box. Type the position in inches (or centimeters if your ruler has been set to centimeters from the Page Layout dialog box). There are three tabs set here: one at 1.87 inches, one at 2.69 inches, and one at 3.44 inches. The first two are decimal-aligned tabs.*

Setting Tab Stops from the Ruler

If you're good with the mouse, setting tabs is much easier and faster with the ruler. Here's how to do it:

1. Get the ruler on-screen. Notice the two leftmost icons in the ruler. One has a bent stem. This is the left-aligned tab icon. The other one is for decimal tabs. (See Figure 9.11)
2. Select the kind of tab you want by clicking on the tab icon in the ruler.
3. To position a tab, click on the correct spot just below the measurement indicator (in the narrow band where the indent markers reside). The tab marker will be added at the spot where you clicked. You can drag the tab marker left and right to fine-tune it any time. The text affected will be adjusted immediately.

Repositioning Existing Tab Stops

You can easily change existing tabs for a table or list to play with the look and size of your layout without ever having to retype columns or add or delete spaces between them. Just bring up the Tabs dialog box and make the changes. Or, from the ruler, just click on the tab markers you want to change and drag them one way or the other.

Clearing Tab Stops You Have Set

You can clear any of your custom tab stops at any time, either from the ruler or from the dialog box. To clear a tab from the ruler:

1. Click the tab marker you want to delete and hold down the left mouse button.
2. Drag the marker down into the document as though you were pulling it off the ruler. It will disappear.

Any text formerly aligned at that tab will move right to the next one. If you remove the last tab stop from the ruler, the text will move left, aligning on the default tab stops.

To clear tabs from the dialog box:

1. Choose Document ➤ Tabs.
2. Double-click in any box that has a tab setting you want to axe. Then press Del. If you want to clear all the tabs, just click on Clear All.
3. Click on OK. Any text aligned at deleted tabs will move right to the next one.

USING UNDO TO REVERSE MISTAKES

The Undo command on Write's Edit menu helps accommodate our propensity for 20/20 hindsight. You may spend five minutes thinking about an editing or formatting change, make it, and then decide after all that you wish you hadn't.

Undo is, quite understandably, the first selection on the Edit menu. You'll most heartily appreciate it when you use it to salvage portions of text that you accidentally deleted. Undo can reverse the following:

- Block deletions made with the Delete command from the Edit menu or the Del key on the keyboard. Choosing Undo jumps back to the place in your text where the deletion occurred and replaces the deleted text.
- Individual or multiple letters that you erased using the Del or Backspace keys. Undo remembers the last place you deleted letters, jumps back to that location, and retypes the letters in their original places. Unfortunately, it will return only the last letter or series of letters erased. That is, once you move the cursor to another location using any of the cursor-movement keys and delete again, the previous deletion is lost.
- Selected blocks directly deleted and replaced by typing new text on the keyboard. As mentioned earlier in the chapter, a simple way of replacing a selected block of words with new words or letters is to type in the new text after selecting the part you want to replace. Undo will reverse this type of deletion.
- New text that you typed in. This can be undone (erased) back to the last time you issued a command.
- Character and paragraph formatting changes (if you select the Undo command immediately after making the change).

When you realize you've done something that you regret, select Edit ➤ Undo. Unlike in real life, it usually works in Write. Remember, though, that the Undo command can only recall the last action. If you decide you have made a mistake, either while entering or deleting, you must undo the damage before using any other editing or formatting commands.

Another salient point: Not all commands can be undone. For example, Undo will not return a section of text to its original location once it has been moved. After you've moved a block of text, you'd have to reverse the procedure step by step if you decide it was better off where it was. That's just one example. There are too many others to list. If you'd like to undo an action and you're not sure if you can, just select Edit ➤ Undo. If it does the wrong thing, such as undoing something you did an hour ago, then you know that your last action couldn't be undone. Select Undo again and you'll be returned to the state you were in just before the Undo. Then fix the problem manually.

SEARCHING FOR AND REPLACING TEXT

TO SEARCH FOR A WORD,

choose Find ➤ Find. Type in the text you want to search for. Press Enter or click on Find Next. If you want to find complete words only or match upper- or lowercase, check those options in the dialog box.

TO REPLACE A WORD,

choose Find ➤ Replace. Type in the text to be found and the replacement text. Set the check boxes on as necessary.

Write offers Find and Replace commands to look for specific letters, words, or series of words in your text. Once the word processor finds the text, you can have it automatically replace that text with other text if you wish. Though Write calls these searching commands Find and Replace, this type of operation is more typically referred to as *search and replace.*

You can also use searching to get to a particular place in your document quickly. If you put unique markers (for example, ##1, *aaa*) in your text, you can search for them to move from one part of a document to another specific point. (Another way to do this is to use the Find ➤ Go To Page command if you know the page you want to get to. It doesn't take you to a specific location on a given page, however, only to the top of the page—and it requires that you update the pagination first, as explained later in this chapter.)

Using Find and Replace together, you can replace abbreviated words with the full word after you're done typing. For example, in preparing the manuscript for this book, I replaced *W* with *Windows* and *wp* with *word processor.* This eliminated lots of repetitive typing.

Finding a Specific Word or Text String

Here's how to use Find to locate a specific word or group of words:

1. Choose Find ➤ Find. The dialog box you see in Figure 9.13 will appear.
2. Type the text you're searching for and press Enter or click on Find Next. The cursor moves to the next instance of that text.
3. To find out if there are any other occurrences of the text, click Find Next again or just press Enter. Write will try to find the text again. Write always remembers the last word you searched for, so you can repeat the action more easily. It also scrolls the document for you, so you can see the text if and when it's found.

When there are no occurrences of the text you're searching for and the entire document has been searched, a dialog box will appear, saying:

Find complete.

Just press Enter or click on OK. If no occurrences of the word are found at all, a dialog box will appear, saying:

Text not found.

Just press Enter or click on OK.

FIGURE 9.13:

The Find dialog box. Type the word you want to find and set the options. As set, this will search for the word "golf."

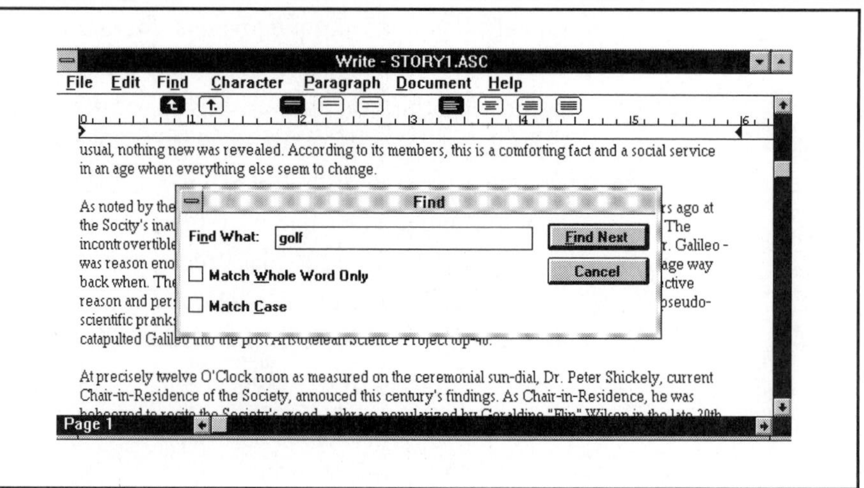

There are two other options when searching: whole-word matching and case matching. Sometimes you'll want to search for a word that could also be embedded in other words. For example, the word *pot* would be found in the word *potato.* If you don't want the search to stop at *potato,* set the Match Whole Word check box on before doing the search.

If you set the Match Case check box on, the search will find only text that exactly matches the case of the text you type in the Find What area. For example, if you had typed in the word *Golf,* it would not find *golf.*

The Find command always starts at the current cursor location and searches to the end of the document. Then it wraps around to the beginning and continues until it again reaches the cursor.

Keep in mind that the dialog box is actually a window and can be moved around the screen. You may want to adjust the size and position of your document window so that the Find window doesn't overlap it. Better yet, move the Find window. Otherwise, if you are doing lots of searching, it will occasionally hide the found word and you won't be able to see it. The Find window stays on the screen, ready for searching until you close it.

Another handy command is Find ➤ Repeat Last Find. Using it, you can repeat a search without having the Find dialog box on the screen. After closing the box, either choose Find ➤ Repeat Last Find, or simply press F3. This makes it easier to proceed with your search without interference from the Find window.

Replacing Specific Words

To replace a text string with another text string you use the Replace dialog box:

1. Choose Find ➤ Replace. A slightly larger dialog box appears. There is an additional text area in the dialog box called Replace With. This is where you type in the text that you want the found text to be changed to.
2. Set the Match Whole Word Only or Match Case check boxes on if you need them to aid in the search.
3. Now click on Find Next, Replace, Replace All, or Replace Selection. Here's what each does:

   Find Next: finds the next occurrence of the word, but doesn't change anything.

Replace: changes the next or currently highlighted occurrence of the word and then moves on to find and highlight the next occurrence. This happens very quickly.

Replace All: automatically finds and changes all occurrences of the word. You don't get to see what's happening.

Replace Selection: causes an automatic search and replace within the selected text area. (This option is only available if you have an area of text selected.)

4. Depending on which option you chose, you may want to continue the process by clicking again on a button.
5. Close the window when you're through by clicking on Close.

Tips for Using Search and Replace

The search and replace commands have a number of other options that you may want to use from time to time. When searching, you can use a wildcard character to broaden the range of possible matching words that Write will find. Say you wanted to find all words that started with *t,* had four letters, and ended with *l.* For the search word, then, you would type in **t??l.** The question marks are wildcards that will match with any letter. Thus, both *tool* and *teal* would be found. Or you could search for all five-letter words, say, by using **?????** as the search criterion.

Here are some other special characters that Write recognizes with the search and replace commands:

TYPE THIS	TO FIND OR REPLACE
^w	White space. White space is any combination of spaces, tabs, nonbreaking spaces, new lines, paragraph marks, and hard page breaks. This cannot be used as a Replace item.
^d	A page break (described later in this chapter)
^p	A paragraph mark (the invisible mark used to separate paragraphs)
^t	A tab
^?	A question mark

TYPE THIS	TO FIND OR REPLACE
^	A caret
?	Any character

To enter one of the special characters in the search or replace string, press Shift-6 to get the caret (^).

COPYING BETWEEN TWO DOCUMENTS

TO COPY BETWEEN TWO WRITE DOCUMENTS,

you have to run Write twice and load one document in each window, then arrange them on-screen and copy and paste.

You may often need to copy portions of text between two documents. Many professionals use word processors because they enable them to use "boilerplate text" to piece together new documents from existing ones. This is particularly useful for constructing legal documents or contracts that regularly include standard clauses or paragraphs. A more domestic example is creating a series of somewhat similar letters to a number of friends.

Since Windows lets you have multiple programs running at once, you have a fair amount of flexibility here. Though Write doesn't let you open more than one *document* at a time, Windows *will* let you run more than one *session* of Write. So you can run Write for each document you want to open. (The number of simultaneous sessions of Write you can have open at one time depends on the mode you're running in, the amount of RAM you have, and the size of the documents. Each copy of Write itself takes up 33K of RAM.)

Once your documents are open, you can select text from one, copy or cut it, and then open another window, position the cursor, and paste it in. Adjust the windows so that you can see enough of each document to easily select and insert text. Figure 9.14 shows an example of two Write documents open simultaneously.

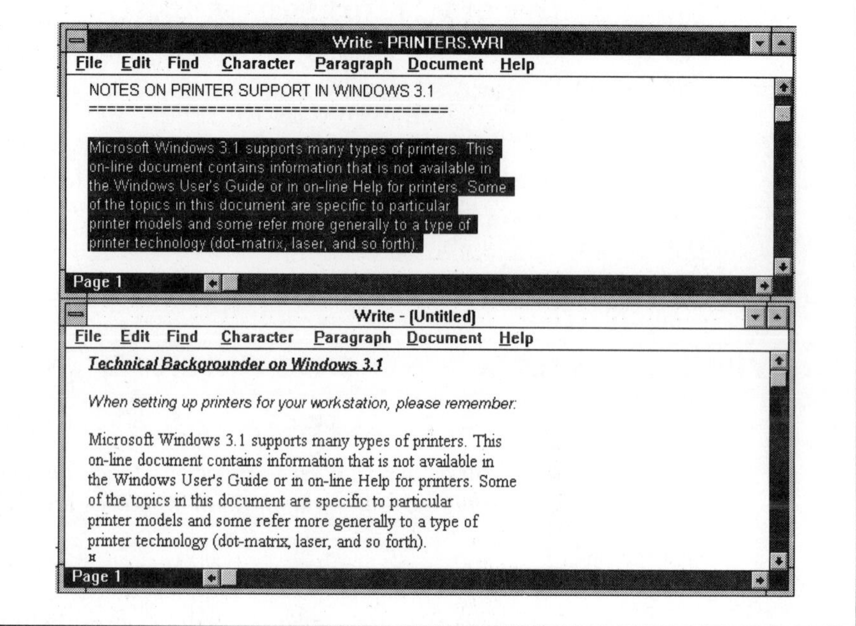

FIGURE 9.14: *You can run multiple copies of Write and load a different document into each window. This lets you transfer material easily between them or switch between writing tasks.*

Of course you can use the multiple Write windows for simply writing or viewing more than one document at a time, too. For example, you may be working on several news stories, several letters, or several chapters of a book. Just iconize the documents you're not actively working on but want to have close at hand.

Here are the general steps for opening two Write documents and transferring material between them:

1. Run Write and open the first document (or just leave the window as is if you're creating a new document).
2. Adjust the window so it takes up the top half of the screen.
3. Switch to the Program Manager and run Write again.
4. Open the file from which you're going to be cutting or copying.
5. Adjust the position of this window to fit the lower half of the screen.

6. Minimize the Program Manager and any other active programs to get them out of the way. Close programs you're not using to free up more memory. This should leave nothing but two Write documents on the screen.

7. Cut, copy, and paste to your heart's content, switching between the windows. The Clipboard will temporarily store whatever you copy or cut so you can switch between the documents, exchanging the information.

USING OPTIONAL HYPHENS

TO HYPHENATE A WORD,

place the insertion point at the optimal hyphenation point and press Ctrl-Shift-hyphen.

NOTE *Write always breaks a word at a real hyphen, such as in "helter-skelter." Use an optional hyphen to tell Write where to break a regular word. The optional hyphen remains invisible until the word is broken.*

Write does not handle hyphenation automatically. As a result, the words on some lines in a justified paragraph will have large spaces between them. This is because Write is doing its best to keep the left and right margins flush. Sometimes it has to push a large word to the next line and add spaces among the remaining words on the line. As a reasonable cure for such problems, you can insert what are called *optional hyphens* into your text. These are invisible codes that tell Write where to break a given word, and usually suffice to fix the most obviously "loose" lines. Figure 9.15 shows two examples of a justified paragraph, the second one with rebroken optional hyphens.

Here are the steps for entering optional hyphens into a word that you want Write to hyphenate:

1. When you see a loose line, try hyphenating the first word on the next line. Position the insertion point at the optimal hyphenation point.

2. Press Ctrl-Shift-hyphen (the hyphen key is above the *P* on most keyboards).

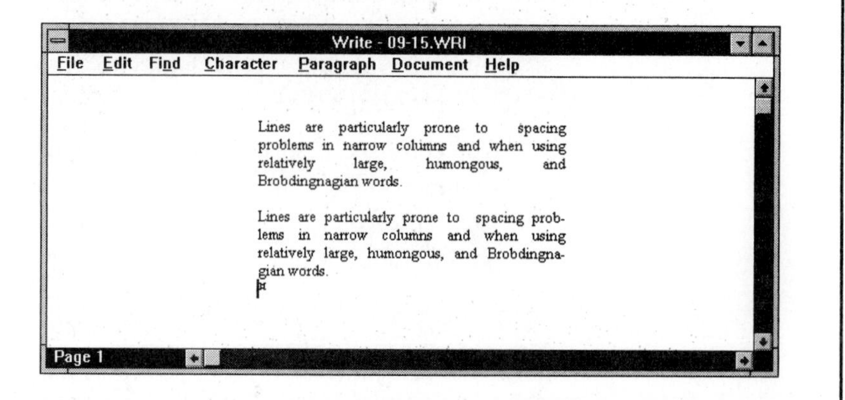

FIGURE 9.15: *Inserting optional hyphens will show Write where to break a long word so it can better justify a line. Here you see the same line before and after hyphenating the words "Brobdingnagian" and "problems."*

The word should split, with the first section being pulled up to the previous line. If nothing happens, the first part of the word would not fit on the previous line. Try inserting another optional hyphen earlier in the word, if possible.

PERFORMING PAGINATION AND INSERTING PAGE BREAKS

The word *pagination* refers to the numbering of pages. If we were still printing on continuous, long rolls of paper as the Egyptians did with their papyrus scrolls, pagination could be dispensed with. Because current tradition requires breaking text into separate pages, Write lets you preview the pages on your document as best it can. This way you can see just where the page breaks occur, and thus where your text will be divided into pages when printed.

As you scroll through a long document, Write shows page breaks as a double arrow (>>) in the left margin of the screen. Also, the status line indicates what page the cursor is on.

Like any good word processor, Write automatically minds the page breaks for you. Write even prevents against *widow* and *orphan lines*: short, single lines that might otherwise be left hanging alone at the beginning or end of a page.

Automatic Pagination

As you edit your text, Write doesn't bother to repaginate for you. Repagination only occurs when you select File ➤ Repaginate. You'll have to do this before printing, or the page numbers may be wrong. To repaginate the document:

1. Choose File ➤ Repaginate. The dialog box shown below will appear:

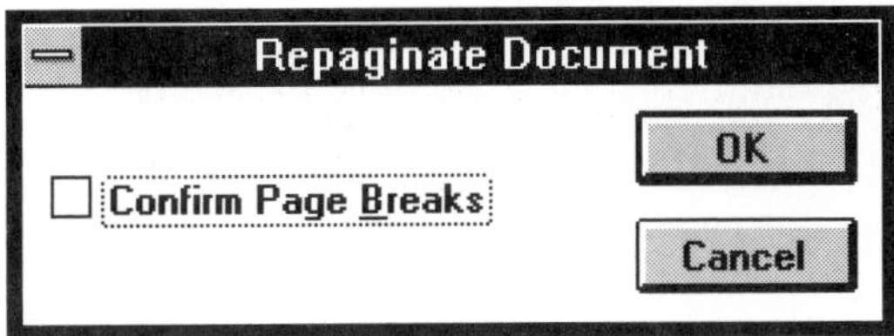

2. Click on OK, or if you want to confirm each page break and possibly make adjustments up or down, click on the Confirm Page Breaks box and then click on OK.

The document will be correctly paginated, and the page-break markers will be repositioned within the document. If you chose to confirm the page breaks, you'll see the dialog box shown in Figure 9.16, with a highlight on the line that is the first line of the next page. You can always move the break up, which would shorten the page. You can't always move it down, though, because the printed page is only so long and Write knows this. Clicking on Down will result in a beep if there's no more room left on the page. You'll then have to move the break up or leave it as it was.

Manual Page Breaks

TO CREATE A PAGE BREAK,

place the cursor where you want to break a page and press Ctrl-Enter.

You can break a page and start a new page at any point. For example, you might want to create a title page with just a few words on it, or break before a table that would otherwise get cut in half. You could enter lots of blank

FIGURE 9.16:

When you've chosen to confirm the page breaks, you'll see this dialog box. Use the buttons to move or confirm the break.

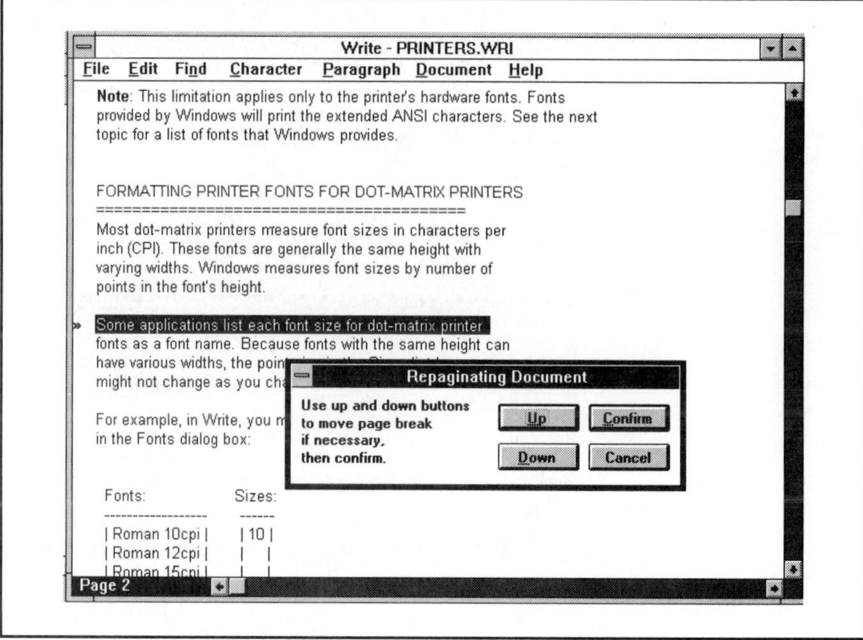

paragraphs to move down to the second page, but that's a hassle, and it will be unreliable if you ever edit the text above the paragraph marks again, because you might change the number of lines and misalign the break point. Instead, you can insert manual page breaks at specific locations in the text.

When you get to the position where you want to break to the next page, press Ctrl-Enter. A dotted line will appear across the screen, as shown in Figure 9.17.

WRITING HEADERS AND FOOTERS

TO CREATE A HEADER OR FOOTER,

select Document ➤ Header or Document ➤ Footer, enter the text, and make other adjustments. Click on Return to Document.

Once you've successfully entered and edited a document, you may want to fine-tune it prior to printing. One of the changes you'll probably want to

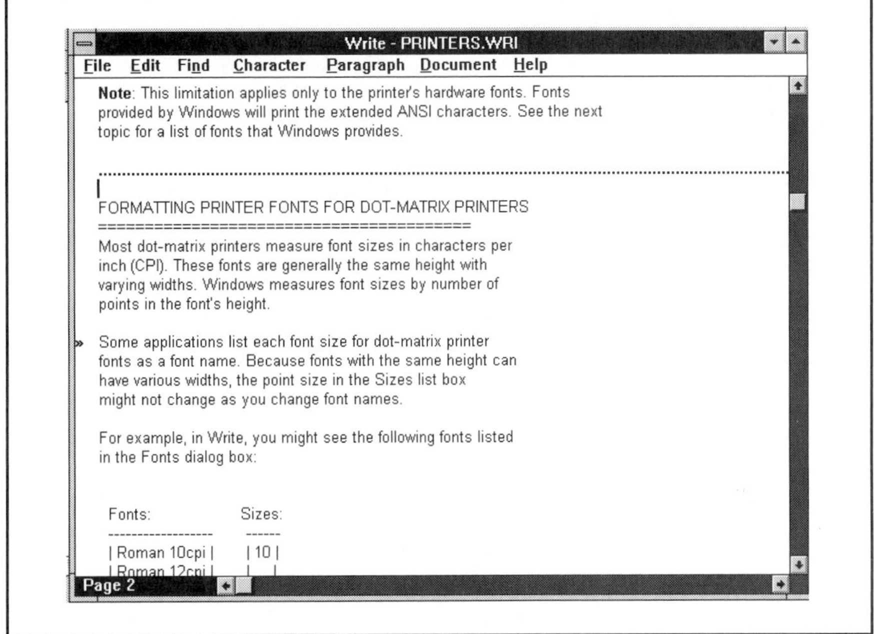

FIGURE 9.17:
Enter a manual page break by typing Ctrl-Enter. The dotted line appears to indicate the break. Delete it as you would any character in Write.

make is the addition of headers and footers that will print on each page.

A *header* is a line of text that appears at the top of every printed page, such as a page number or chapter title. *Footers,* which print at the bottom of the page, typically contain similar text. Write lets you include headers, footers, or both in each document.

Headers and footers can include text that you enter in the Header and Footer windows and/or the page number for each page. You can also opt to start the header or footer on the second page rather than the first, in case you want a title page for the document.

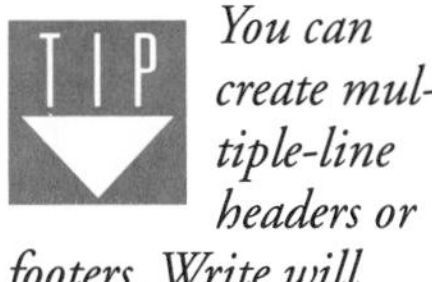

You can create multiple-line headers or footers. Write will compensate for the multiple lines by decreasing the amount of text it prints on each page of the document.

To add a header or footer, choose Header or Footer from the Document menu. A new window appears. (It looks like a new document but it isn't.) The footer screen is shown in Figure 9.18. Type in the header or footer as you want it to print. If you want the page number to appear as part of the text, click on Insert Page # in the dialog box. The word *(page)* will be inserted in the text. This is the code that Write uses to print the page number.

Don't forget that since headers and footers can include anything that normal text can, you can change the alignment, font, and size, too. For page numbers, you will typically use center or right alignment. If you want some

FIGURE 9.18:

The footer window with a sample footer. Type in any text you want in the footer and format it to meet your needs. Then set the options from the dialog box shown.

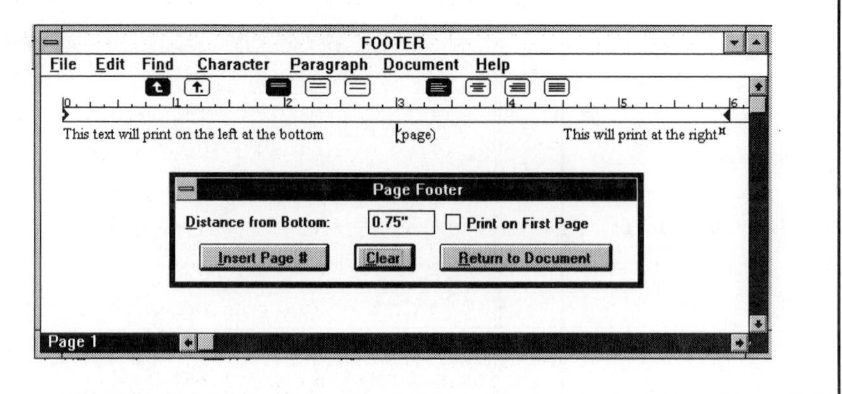

text on the left margin, some in the middle, and some on the right, use tabs and spaces to position text across the screen. Clicking on Clear erases everything, letting you start from scratch.

If you want the header or footer to print on the first page, set that check box on. In many cases, one or both are left off the first page.

Click on Return to Document when you are satisfied with the header or footer. It will not appear on your screen. Headers and footers only appear when printed, so you might want to test out your settings by printing a few pages.

ADDING GRAPHICS TO YOUR WRITE DOCUMENT

TO ADD A GRAPHIC TO A DOCUMENT,

- **Select Edit ➤ Paste to insert a graphic from the Clipboard.**
- **Select Edit ➤ Move Picture, move the pointer, and click the mouse to move the graphic sideways.**
- **Select Edit ➤ Size Picture, move the pointer, and click the mouse to resize the graphic.**

Although it's sort of a bare-bones word processor, Write *does* allow you to insert graphics into your documents. You can get the picture or graphic from other Windows applications such as Paintbrush. Once you've inserted them in the document, you can then cut, copy, or paste them. You can also change a graphic's size or move it around. With this feature you can add your company logo to every letter you print, put your picture on your letterhead, or put a map on a party announcement. Figure 9.19 shows examples of graphics inserted into Write documents.

Of course, you'll have to create the graphics in another program since Write doesn't let you create graphics. For a photo, have the photograph digitized with a scanner and then loaded into a Windows program that reads files created by the digitizer. Then copy the picture onto the Clipboard and paste it into Write. In Write, graphics created with color drawing programs are converted to black-and-white, and all graphics are displayed in a screen resolution comparable to what your printer is capable of. Sometimes the image may seem a bit distorted on-screen because of your monitor's *aspect ratio* (ratio of height to width display), but it should print out okay.

In addition to copying graphics into documents, Windows also allows what it calls *object linking* and *embedding*. Embedding is similar to copying, but with an important difference: you can edit embedded graphics within Write, rather than having to return to the application where the graphic was created to make changes and then recopying it to Write. Linking connects two files so that when you update information in one file, the graphic that is linked to it automatically changes to reflect the update. Chapter 14 covers object linking and embedding in detail. The discussion below explains how to perform the basic commands for graphics manipulation within Write.

Importing a Graphic from the Clipboard

To import a graphic into your document, follow these steps:

1. Get the picture on the Clipboard by copying it from the source application, such as Paintbrush. As long as it can be cut or copied, you can paste it into Write.
2. Open the Write document or activate its window.
3. Position the insertion point on the line where you want the picture to start and select Edit ➤ Paste.

FIGURE 9.19:

Examples of graphics in Write documents. Graphics are imported from the Clipboard and then can be moved and sized.

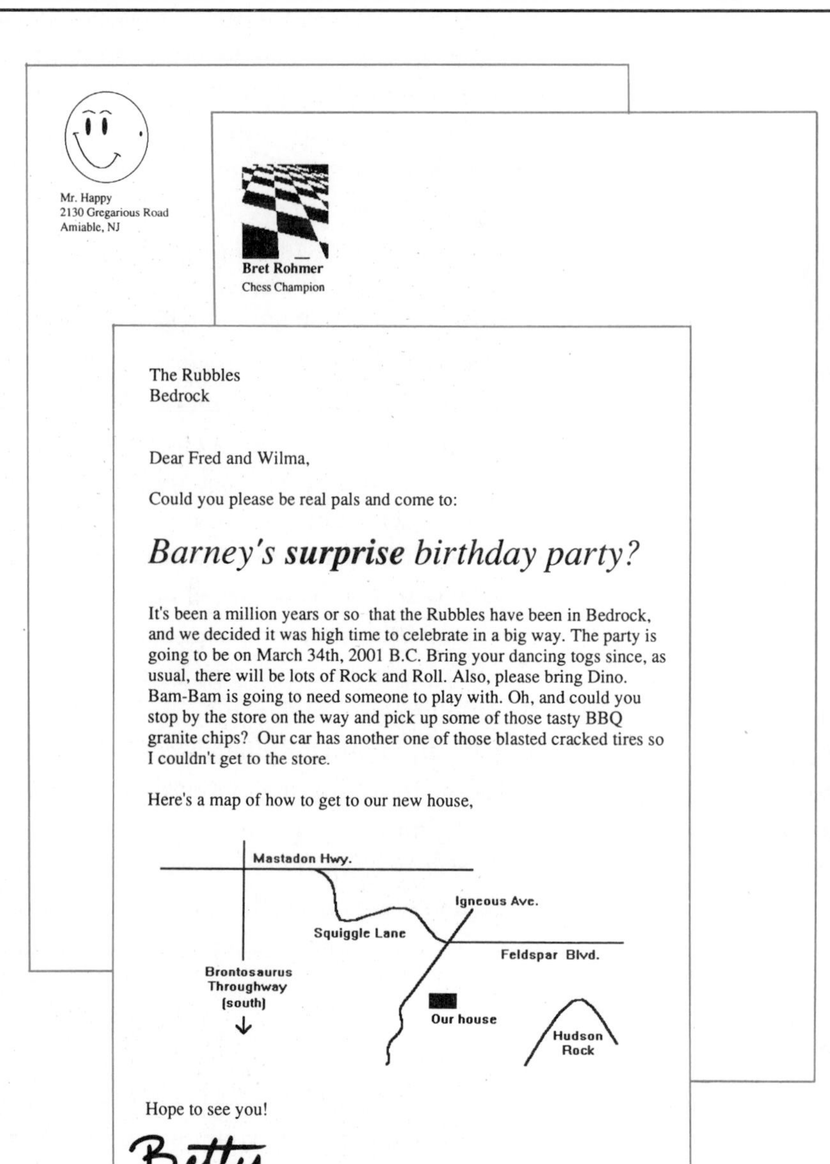

The graphic will be dropped into the document at the left margin. Figure 9.20 shows an example. Now you can move it horizontally or resize it with the commands explained next.

POSITIONING THE GRAPHIC

NOTE *To move a graphic up or down, you have to cut it, reposition the insertion point, and paste again on a new line.*

Once the graphic is pasted in, you can move it around:

1. Place the insertion point on the graphic. It will become highlighted.
2. Choose Edit ➤ Move Picture.
3. Use the arrow keys or mouse to move it to a new location (but don't click the mouse button—just move it). The cursor changes shape (to a square) and a dotted box indicates the graphic's potential new position as you move the cursor around. You can only move left or right, not up and down. (To cancel the move, press Esc.)

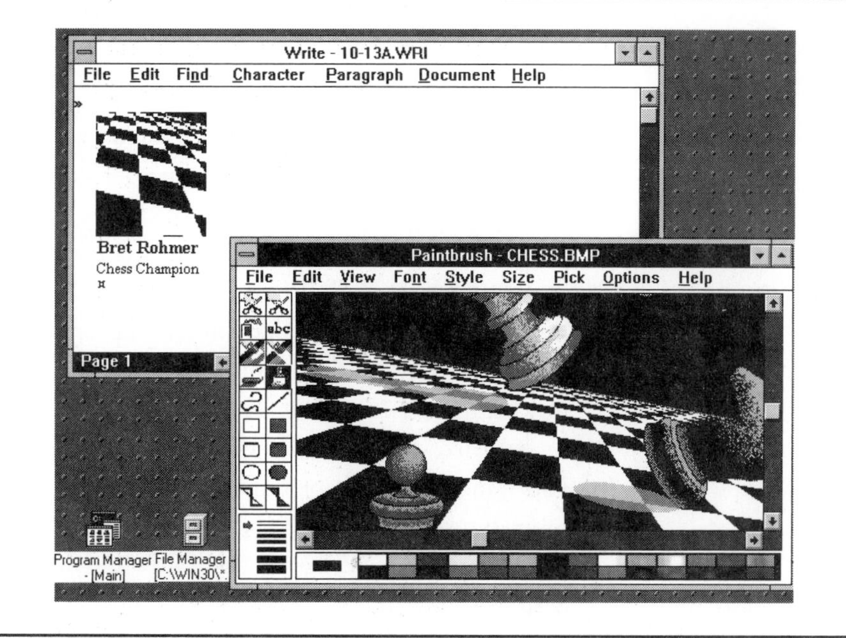

FIGURE 9.20: *The Windows 3.0 flying chess board picture CHESS.BMP copied from Paintbrush into a Write document*

4. Click or press Enter when the position is correct. The hourglass "please wait" cursor will appear for a second while Write thinks about things, and then the graphic will move.

SIZING THE GRAPHIC

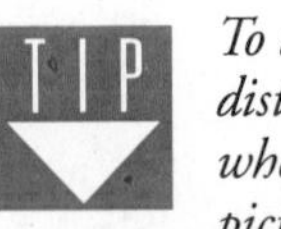

To avoid distortion when the picture is printed, keep the x and y values (in the status line) the same, and keep them in whole numbers rather than fractions.

You can resize a graphic, too. Here's how:

1. Select the graphic by clicking on it or placing the insertion point on it.
2. Select Edit ➤ Size Picture. The cursor changes shape. Stretch or shrink the frame of the picture just as you would a window. Notice that you can distort the picture if you want to, by making it long and skinny or short and fat. Pressing Esc will return the picture to its previous size.
3. Click the mouse or press Enter. Undo will return it to its previous state after it's been resized.

OPENING DOCUMENTS STORED IN OTHER FORMATS

As you may have noticed when opening and saving Write files, there are some options that pertain to file formats, conversion, and so on. Normally you'll just open and save Write .WRI files using the defaults in the dialog boxes. The defaults open only files with the .WRI extension and, upon saving, store them in the proprietary format that Write expects. However, since not all text files are alike (different programs use different codes to store formatting information), this gives rise to the need for dealing with other text file formats.

When you open a file that doesn't have a .WRI extension, Write asks if you want the file to be converted. You should have no problem opening many types of files created by Windows programs without converting. This is because many Windows programs use ANSI standard text files, which Write also needs.

However, there are times when you'll want to convert the file, or at least try to. For example, when you load a Microsoft Word file, you'll have to convert it. You should have no trouble here. If you load another type of file, and it doesn't look right on the screen, try opening it again and doing a conversion the second time. If it still doesn't look right, chances are you can't use it in Write without modifying it.

Typical conversion problems have to do with the line endings and the loss of paragraph and character formatting. You'll almost certainly lose the formatting when you load a file from a major word-processing program not made by Microsoft. That's just the way the cookie crumbles in the business world. Microsoft wants to lock you in. If you want to load a file from another program, the best idea is to convert the file to Word format through some utility. You can also try copying to the Clipboard and then into the Write document. This may work at least for the text. The formatting will be lost, though.

Opening straight ASCII files (such as the kind made by PC-Write) doesn't work correctly because Write will treat each line as a separate paragraph. This is because ASCII files have a "carriage return/line feed" pair at the end of each line, by definition. Your text will look okay at first, but you'll only be able to make format changes one line at a time. There is a way around the problem, though, using the Change command. It's a three-step conversion process:

1. Execute a search and replace. Search for all real paragraph separations by looking for ^P^P (this assumes there is a blank line between paragraphs and thus two paragraph-end marks in a row) and replace these with some unique character string such as %%. (Note that to find a paragraph mark you have to set Match Lower/Uppercase to off.)
2. Search for all the paragraph marks (^P) and replace them with nothing. (Don't type anything in the Replace With box.) This kills all the paragraph marks that are screwing up the formatting.
3. Search for the unique markers (%% in this example) and replace them with a paragraph mark (^P). This puts a paragraph mark at the end of each paragraph, where they belong as far as Write is concerned.

I've tried this with PC-Write files and it works fine. The other thing to know about foreign file formats is that Write works with files in RAM. Thus, the size of the files you can work with is limited by the amount of free RAM in your system. If you're having space-limitation problems, close some applications, get more memory, or use another program to edit the file.

SAVING YOUR WORK

TO SAVE A FILE,

choose File ➤ Save, enter the file name, determine the directory, and click OK.

Write stores parts of your document in RAM while you work on it. However, RAM is not a permanent storage area; thus your work will be lost when you turn off your computer unless you first save it to disk.

You save your documents with two commands: File ➤ Save and File ➤ Save As. The first time you save a document, Windows applications such as Write will ask you for a name to give your document. After the initial save, Write assumes you want to use the current name, unless you indicate otherwise by using the Save As command.

In general, it's a good idea to save your work any time you can't afford to risk losing it, such as when you have done so much editing that having to revert to the last version of your document would be bothersome. I try to save about every 15 minutes.

Save your file as follows:

1. Choose File ➤ Save. The Save As dialog box appears, since this is the first time you've saved this file and Write needs to ask you for the name. Your screen should look like the one shown in Figure 9.21.
2. Ensure that the correct drive and directory are selected.
3. Type in a file name and press Enter. Write will add the .WRI extension to the end of the file name automatically. Names must comply with DOS standards—i.e., be no longer than eight characters long before the period and not contain the characters *, ?, >, or a space.

FIGURE 9.21:

The Save As dialog box. After making sure the drive and directory are right, type in the file name.

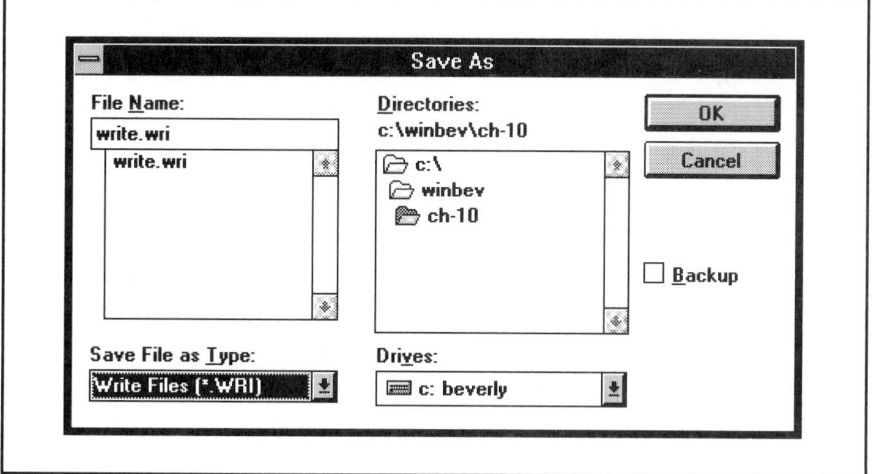

If you're not sure how to use this dialog box, please refer to the discussion of file dialog boxes in Chapter 1 and the discussion of drives and directories in Chapter 4.

The Save File as Type drop-down list box is normally set to store the file in .WRI format. The various formats in which you can save a file are discussed below. You don't alter these settings unless you want to create a file that other word processors or other types of programs can read:

Word for DOS: This stores the file in a format readable by Microsoft Word. However, graphics in your Write file will be lost.

Word for DOS/Txt Only: This saves the file as an "unformatted Microsoft Word" file. This can be read by Word, but will have no formatting information in it.

Text Files: This option causes the file to be saved without the character and paragraph formatting. It is stored as a Windows ANSI text file. This file could be opened by a text editor such as PC-Write, WordStar, or Sidekick as a plain text file.

All Files: This option doesn't affect the format in which the file is saved. It displays all files in the selected directory, rather than only those with a specific extension such as .WRI or .DOC.

The check box for making a backup copy will be set off. If you turn this on, Write makes a backup copy of the file each time you save it. This backup file is given the extension .BKP. If you save the file in Word format, the backup file is given the extension .BAK. The first part of the file name is left unaltered.

PRINTING YOUR DOCUMENT

When you are about ready to print, don't forget to save your file first, just in case the computer or the printer goes berserk in the process and you lose your file. To print, just choose File ➤ Print. You'll be presented with a dialog box asking you about the following options:

Copies: The number of copies of each page to be printed.

Print Range: If you want to print all the pages, click on All. If you want to print specific pages only, click on Pages and type in the page numbers you want to print. Make sure to repaginate first, so you know the correct page numbers! If you want to print only text that you selected, click on Selection.

Print Quality: Depending on the capabilities of your printer, this may offer several resolutions to print in. Lower resolution (sometimes called "draft") will speed up printing at the cost of a coarser appearance. This prints a bare-bones copy of the document with nothing but the text. Pictures are printed as empty boxes, and there is no text formatting. If the option is dimmed, your printer doesn't support it.

Print to File: If you want to save the file to another file that contains DOS printer commands, set this check box on. When you click on OK to close the Print dialog box, you will enter the output file name in the Print to File dialog box that comes up.

Collate copies: If you are printing more than one copy, this option orders the pages into collated groupings (e.g., 1–3, 1–3, rather than 1, 1, 2, 2, 3, 3).

Setup: This button appears on many Windows applications' Print dialog boxes. It allows you to choose the printer you want to print to, the paper orientation (portrait or landscape), paper size and feed, and other options (determined by your printer).

Turn on the printer, make sure it has paper and is online, and press Enter or click on OK.

FAST TRACK

CHAPTER

10

FAST TRACK

1. Run Terminal and enter the phone number you want to dial.
2. Set the communications parameters, the terminal emulation, the terminal preferences, and the modem commands from the Settings menu.
3. Make sure baud rate, data bits, stop bits, and flow control are the same for both computers.

1. Choose Transfers ➤ Receive Text File.
2. Type in the file name, choose options from the dialog box, and click OK.
3. Click the Pause button to skip unwanted text; click on Resume to continue capturing.
4. Click Stop to save and close the file.

1. Choose Settings ➤ Text Transfers and set the desired options.
2. Choose Transfers ➤ Send Text File and enter the file name.
3. Choose any line-feed options and click on OK.

To send a binary file, ... 342

1. Choose Settings ➤ Binary Transfers and set the desired error-checking protocol.
2. Tell the other computer to receive a file.
3. Choose Transfers ➤ Send Binary File and enter the file name.
4. Click on OK.

To receive a binary file, ... 342

1. Choose Settings ➤ Binary Transfers and set the desired error-checking protocol.
2. Tell the other computer to send the file.
3. Choose Transfers ➤ Receive Binary File and enter the file name.
4. Click on OK.

To exit your communications session, ... 351

1. Log off the service or other computer.
2. Choose Phone ➤ Hangup.
3. Close Terminal by double-clicking its Control box.

CHAPTER 10

FEATURING

Setting Up Your Hardware and Software

Making the Connection

Interacting Online

Uploading and Downloading Files

Using the Function Keys

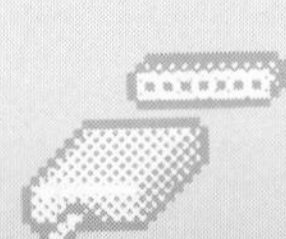

Using Terminal for Telecommunications

The Terminal program supplied with Windows lets you and your PC make contact with other computers to exchange or retrieve information. With Terminal and the right hookups, you can share data with other computers, whether they are in your own house, around the block, or on the other side of the world. Information shared this way typically consists of electronic mail, instant stock quotes, or complete files (such as word-processing or spreadsheet documents). Many people use communications programs to connect to their company's computer so that they can work from home—sometimes called *telecommuting.*

There are many types of information available for use with PCs and communications programs. Nowadays, many clubs and organizations have their own dial-up Bulletin Board Systems (BBSs) where members can leave messages and read notices of interest. Numerous BBSs also provide a wide variety of public-domain software and shareware that anyone with a computer, a modem, and a communications program can have just for the taking. With your PC, a modem, and Terminal, you can start to take advantage of the conveniences of computer communications.

The information in this chapter is necessarily somewhat general. Since a communications program such as Terminal can be used to connect to an almost endless variety of information services and computers, it's impossible to cover all the specific situations. What's more, each service typically has its own way of logging on, transmitting and receiving files, and so on, which adds another complication. So instead of demonstrating exact procedures, I'll discuss all the aspects of the Terminal program and explain the general steps you'll have to understand in order to use it effectively.

SETTING UP YOUR COMMUNICATIONS SYSTEM

In most cases, you'll be using Terminal to communicate with outside dial-up services such as CompuServe, Dow Jones News/Retrieval, the Source, or MCI Mail, or to call up a friend's or colleague's computer to exchange files. The other computer can even be of a different type, such as a Macintosh. This type of communication from a distance (as opposed to communication between computers in the same room) uses telephone lines and modems, which must be connected to the computers. The word *modem* stands for "modulator/demodulator." It provides the electronic connection between your computer and the phone line by converting digital information from your computer into an analog signal. On the other end of the line, the receiving modem does just the reverse (see Figure 10.1).

Though you can run Terminal to experiment with it, you can't use it over the phone without having a modem. To connect a modem, you'll need an unused COM port and external modem/cable combination, or an unused COM

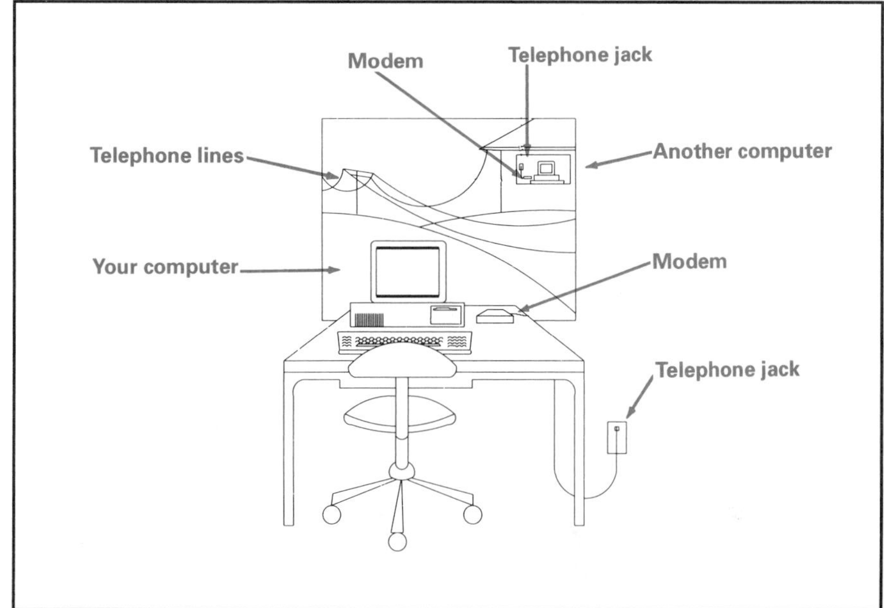

FIGURE 10.1: *A telecommunications setup, which consists of two computers, two modems, and interconnecting wires*

port, along with a modem card installed inside your computer. (If you don't have a free COM port, Terminal will warn you when you start it up, though it will still run.)

In either case, the general installation procedures are similar. You install the modem, plug your telephone line into it, and run a communications program (in this case, Terminal).

The main distinguishing factor among modems is the speed at which they can transfer data over the phone lines. As of this writing, the most popular modems transmit data at 1200 or 2400 baud. The word *baud* refers to the number of bits of data transferred in one second. The larger the number, the faster the transmission.

Since we can't cover all the ins and outs of modem purchasing here, we'll leave the purchase and installation details to you. However, my advice is to purchase a modem that uses Hayes-compatible commands. *Hayes compatibility* lets you take advantage of some useful features of Terminal (and most other communications programs) such as the ability to dial the phone for you automatically, redial busy numbers, and so on. If you don't have a Hayes-compatible modem, you can still use Terminal, since two other popular modem types—the MultiTech and TrailBlazer—are also supported. If you don't have any of these, there's a dialog box into which you can enter the particular commands used by your modem. You'll just have to do a little research first unless you know the commands already.

Make sure you have installed your modem properly, following instructions in the modem's manual, before continuing. Incorrect modem installation (most often caused by improper switch settings) is a frequent cause of communications problems.

BEGINNING A COMMUNICATIONS SESSION

TO PREPARE FOR A COMMUNICATIONS SESSION,

1. **Run Terminal and enter the phone number you want to dial.**
2. **Set the communications parameters, the terminal emulation, the terminal preferences, and the modem commands from the Settings menu.**
3. **Make sure baud rate, data bits, stop bits, and flow control are the same for both computers.**

Begin a session by double-clicking on the Terminal icon in the Accessories group. A Terminal window appears. The status line at the bottom of the screen is blank because you aren't currently connected to another computer for communications.

Next you have to set up various parameters before you can begin communicating with the other computer. Actually, Terminal has built-in defaults for these settings, which may, by chance, suffice for your session. However, success is not guaranteed since there are so many variables. Usually you'll need to set some parameters and modify others at least a little. You should go through the following five sections carefully to establish that the settings are correct for your communications session. While doing so, keep in mind that the settings on both ends of the communications link must be identical. Once you have the settings correct, you can save them to a .TRM file so that next time you can just load the file and be guaranteed success without having to resort to your memory.

Incidentally, the Terminal program supplied with Windows 3.1 can use the setup (.TRM) files you may have created with versions 2 or 3.0 of Windows Terminal. If you have created files containing setup information for your most frequently used communications sessions, you'll be able to load them in the new Terminal program with the Open command on the File menu.

The five groups of parameters you need to check and possibly alter are as follows:

Phone Number, for setting the telephone number you want to dial.

Terminal Emulation, for choosing among three types of terminals that the Terminal program can cause your screen and keyboard to simulate. Both the remote computer and your software must be set to the same terminal type to communicate correctly.

Terminal Preferences, for determining how data will be displayed on your screen and how Carriage Returns and Line Feeds will be processed. The screen for text display, cursor shape, number of text columns per screen, and several other parameters may need adjusting here, too.

Communications, for setting the speed and format for data sent between the two connected computers.

Modem Commands, for telling Terminal what kind of modem you have. If your modem is not listed, you can enter the commands that Terminal should use to control your modem.

MAKING THE PHONE NUMBER SETTINGS

If you have a Hayes-type modem, Terminal can dial the phone number of the remote computer for you. But to have your modem do this, you have to fill in the Phone Number settings as follows:

1. Choose Settings ➤ Phone Number and you'll see the Phone Number dialog box.

2. Type in the phone number you want your modem to dial. You can type in the number in any of the following forms:

   1-(510)-555-1111

   1-510-555-1111

   15105551111

   555-1111 (if you are calling a local number)

   The dashes and parentheses won't affect the dialing.

If you're using an alternative long distance service such as Sprint, MCI, or others, and you don't have direct access to the carrier by simply dialing, you can enter all the digits necessary into the box (up to a maximum of 100 digits). You can also insert commas into the phone number to tell your modem to pause before moving ahead to the next digit. On Hayes-compatible modems, each comma results in a two-second pause. At least one comma is usually necessary for alternative services, since it can take several seconds for the second dial tone to come on after the initial connection to the service. Here's an example showing the number you'd use to dial long distance via an alternative service to MCI Mail in Oakland, California, from a company phone requiring a 9 to get an outside line. Assume the relevant numbers are as follows:

To get an outside line: 9

Your long distance access number: 555-1311

Your private access code: 8273645

The number you're calling: 510-555-1111

Then the number you'd type into the Phone Number field would be

```
9,555–1311,,8273645,510–555–1111
```

Notice the placement and number of commas. You may have to change the number of commas (particularly of the double set) on the basis of how many rings it takes for your long distance service to answer and then come on with the second dial tone. Hayes-type modems do not acknowledge when the phone on the other end of the line has been answered, so you compensate for this with the commas.

There are three other sections in the Phone Number dialog box. You should set them according to your needs. Here are the meanings of each; chances are good that the default settings will work fine:

Timeout If Not Connected In 30 Seconds: *Timeout* means "give up" here. This setting tells Terminal how long you want it to wait after dialing the phone number of the other computer before hanging up. Normally Terminal tries to connect to the other modem for 30 seconds, after which it hangs up. You may have to increase the time setting if you find that Terminal is hanging up too soon. If you're using a long distance service that takes a few seconds to click in, or the modem on the other end takes several rings to answer, add ten seconds to the timeout value and try again.

Redial After Timing Out: Do you want Terminal to try dialing again after "timing out" and hanging up? Turn this check box on if you do. Since *timing out* can result from the the other computer's phone line being busy, setting this on gives you a better chance of getting through. It's like having the computer act like a telephone's automatic redial button.

Signal When Connected: When this is set on, your computer will beep if a connection is made. This is particularly useful when you might not be paying attention to the computer while waiting for a connection, or if you've iconized the Terminal application and can't see its window.

SETTING THE TERMINAL EMULATION

Before PCs were invented, people used computer *terminals* to communicate with one another and with mainframe computers. Terminals are essentially nothing but a screen and keyboard with which data can be entered and displayed. They have no internal computing power or disk storage, as does your PC. Since more than one manufacturer made such terminals, certain standards had to be established regarding how data were displayed on the terminal screens and how keyboards worked.

These standards continue today and apply to communications setups using PCs as well as to terminals. As the name implies, Terminal, among other things, makes your PC act like an old-style terminal, but with the added brains and storage capabilities of a computer. Some of these added brains allow your PC to be a chameleon—*emulating* more than one type of terminal with a change of options in a dialog box.

In telecommunication, there first has to be an agreement between the two computer systems about what kind of terminal is at each end. So before beginning a communications session, you have to figure out what the other computer expects, and then try to meet the requirements. This is called setting your *terminal emulation.* To set or check the terminal emulation, choose Settings ➤ Terminal Emulation. The small dialog box you see below appears:

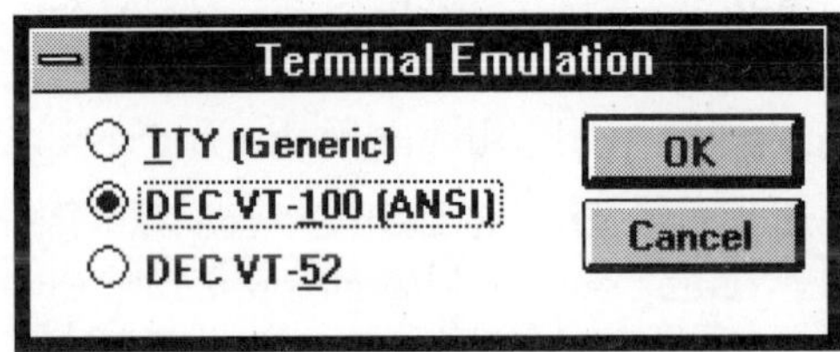

The DEC VT-100 ANSI (default) setting should work for most purposes. If you find your screen acting unpredictably or displaying bizarre letters, try the TTY (Generic) setting. The settings are described below:

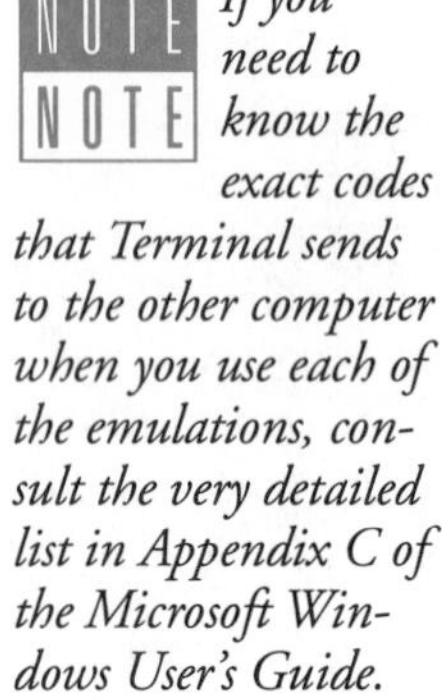

If you need to know the exact codes that Terminal sends to the other computer when you use each of the emulations, consult the very detailed list in Appendix C of the Microsoft Windows User's Guide.

TTY (Generic) has the highest level of compatibility of the three. However, it is the least sophisticated. If you do not know which terminal emulation to use, try this. It makes your PC emulate what's known as a "dumb" terminal, meaning that the only formatting codes it uses in communicating to the remote computer are carriage return, backspace, and tab characters.

DEC VT-100 (ANSI) emulates a standard ANSI terminal. Use this for communicating with mainframes as though using a DEC VT-100, VT-220, or VT-240 terminal or compatible. Many IBM PC-based bulletin board services use ANSI, too.

DEC VT-52 emulates the DEC VT-52 terminal. Use this for information services such as CompuServe and The Source, BBSs, electronic mail services, and so on.

Setting the Terminal Preferences

You should at least check the next group of settings before making a connection to another computer. Normally, you won't have to change the terminal settings, but occasionally you will. To see or alter the terminal settings, choose Settings ➤ Terminal Preferences. The Terminal Preferences dialog box appears, as shown in Figure 10.2.

There are nine settings to look at in this box:

Terminal Modes

This group has three check boxes that affect how information will appear on your screen:

Line Wrap causes incoming text that is longer than the width of your screen to wrap to the next line. Normally, line wrap is set on.

Local Echo "echoes" what you type on your keyboard to your screen, so you can see what you're typing. It may sound strange, but in some communications sessions you may find you can't see what you're typing, because the remote computer may not be programmed to echo your transmission back to your screen. Normally this will not be a problem, but if you find you are typing "in the dark," simply set Local Echo on. With two PCs running Terminal,

FIGURE 10.2:

From this dialog box you make fine adjustments to the terminal emulation. Most of these are cosmetic refinements for your convenience.

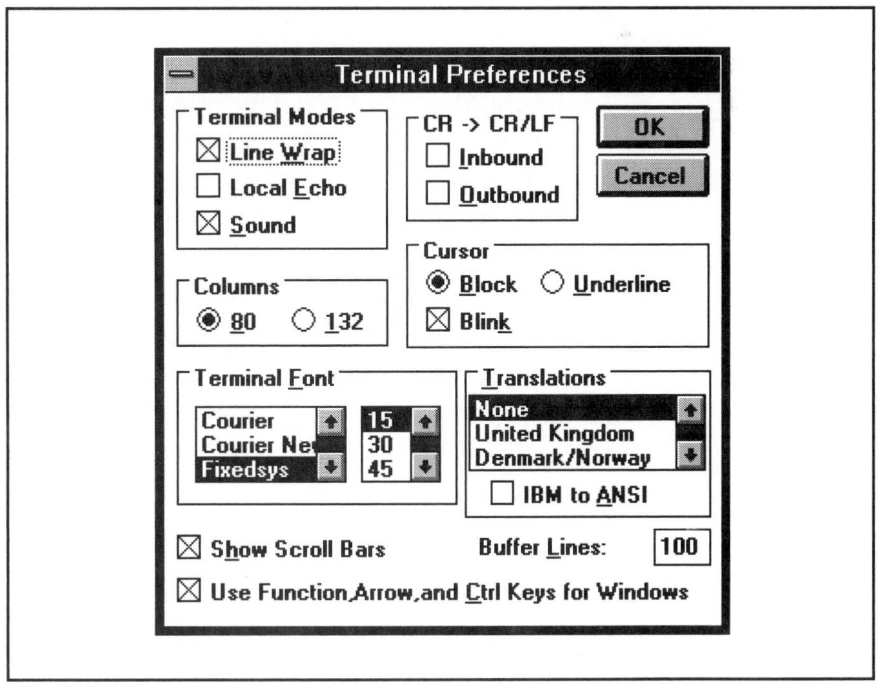

both should have Local Echo on. On the other hand, if you see double characters on the screen (such as HHEELLLLOO!!), turn Local Echo off.

Sound toggles the beep off and on. Sometimes the remote computer will send your computer the code that causes a beep sound. You may want to disable this if you find it annoying.

CR → CR/LF

The section CR → CR/LF is included to deal with some remote (sometimes called *host*) computers' habit of not moving the cursor down a line and moving back to the left side of the screen after sending the previous line of text. If all the incoming data appear on a single line that gets continually rewritten, or the cursor moves to the right margin and seems to get stuck, try setting the Inbound option on. For most sessions, however, leaving both boxes off will work fine. The options are as follows:

Inbound adds a *linefeed* (moves down a line) to the end of incoming lines.

Outbound adds a linefeed to the end of outgoing lines.

Columns

This setting can change the number of characters accepted before Terminal wraps the data to the next line. Instead of showing only 80 columns of characters across the screen (including spaces), the 132 setting results in the appearance of scroll bars on the Terminal window. You'll have to scroll to the right to see columns in excess of 80.

If the sending computer doesn't know you can receive 132 columns per line, however, it may continue to send carriage returns and linefeeds after 80 columns. In this case, you wouldn't see any change by selecting this option. However, many BBSs and information services have online commands for telling their system how many columns your screen can handle.

Cursor

Nothing more than a cosmetic alteration, the cursor setting modifies the look of the text cursor on the screen:

Block: The cursor appears as a large block, the height of a capital letter.

Underline: The cursor takes the shape of the familiar underline you see in DOS and in most DOS applications.

Blink: This is normally on, but turning it off stops the blinking (a welcome relief!).

Terminal Font

Another cosmetic option, this one determines which font and type size Terminal will use to display both incoming and outgoing characters. This is actually a thoughtful feature. Enlarging the font gives tired eyes a break when you're doing lots of telecommunications. If you increase the font size beyond a size that will allow a complete line of text to fit in the window, scroll bars will allow you to scroll horizontally to see it. However, it's rather a nuisance to do this, and it's better to stick with a smaller size, such as 12 to 14 point.

Translations

When you send a text file to or type interactively with a computer in another country, codes are interpreted somewhat differently from how they are in the U.S. To eliminate this problem, Terminal has a translation capability that converts the codes according to the International Standards Organization (ISO) 7-bit codes. If you're communicating with a computer in another country, select that country from the list. (Your country should already be set from the Control Panel's International icon.) The option box for IBM to ANSI converts the IBM extended character set used on many PCs to the ANSI character set used by Windows. This applies only to "extended characters," not normal letters, numbers, and punctuation marks. This will not likely need changing, so you can leave this box set off.

Show Scroll Bars

This is normally on, but you can turn it off. Having the scroll bars on lets you scroll to see information that is off the screen—a very useful feature. With many communications programs, information that scrolls off the top of the screen is "lost"; that is, you can't view it again. In Terminal, however, text you type or receive while in interactive communications sessions is stored in a *buffer,* which is discussed further below.

Buffer Lines

Normally this setting is 100 lines, but it can range from 25 to 400. With a setting of 100, Terminal will store the last 100 lines that scrolled off the top of the window in the temporary buffer—and if the scroll bars are on, you can scroll back up to see them. Note that you will have to scroll back down before you can see what you're typing.

Use Function, Arrow, and Ctrl Keys for Windows

This setting is normally selected. When set on, all function keys, arrow keys, and the Ctrl key are used by Windows and not passed on to the other computer. This way you can still use commands like Ctrl-Esc to open the Task List. If you want these keys to send their respective codes to the remote computer instead, turn this check box off.

SETTING THE COMMUNICATIONS PARAMETERS

If you plan to use the defaults, you can skip this section. Chances are good that a communications session will be successful using the defaults, since they were designed to work with most services.

Once you've made the phone, emulation, and preference settings, you should check the communications parameters. Choosing Settings ➤ Communications brings up the dialog box shown in Figure 10.3. All of these options, except Connector and Carrier Detect, have to be identical on each end (in each computer) before successful communications can begin. If you are in doubt about how to set one of them, there's a simple solution. Just find out what the settings are for the computer at the other end of the line and set yours accordingly. If you can't find out what those settings are, try the default settings that show up when you open a new document. If those don't work, then start systematically altering the settings one at a time.

Let's look at the eight groups of options one by one:

Baud Rate

As discussed before, baud rate determines the speed at which data are transferred between your PC and the computer at the other end of the line. You'll need to set the baud rate to match that of your modem and that of the remote computer's modem. In other words, all parts of the communications link must be set for the same speed.

Some modems can sense the baud rate automatically and adjust themselves accordingly. Others cannot do this and must be set with switches. You should consult your modem's instruction manual regarding this. If baud rates are mismatched, you will fail to get a connection, or you may see weird characters or punctuation marks on your screen instead of normal text.

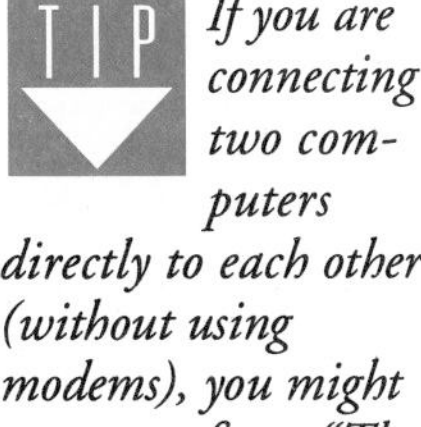

If you are connecting two computers directly to each other (without using modems), you might want to refer to "The RS-232 Solution (Second Edition)" by Joe Campbell (SYBEX).

Most communication via modem (as opposed to direct connection to another local computer, as explained later in this chapter) takes place at 300, 1200, or 2400 baud. It usually makes sense to use as fast a speed as possible to minimize the connect time over the phone. However, poor phone connections—not infrequent with long distance calls—can require dropping your speed down a notch (from, say, 2400 to 1200) to avoid loss of data. Also, most information services, such as CompuServe, charge twice as much for 2400 baud connect time as for 1200 baud.

Data Bits

The Data Bits setting refers to the number of *bits* (the smallest division of computer information) you want to send out in each packet of data. For example, each letter is typically stored in your computer as eight bits. (Eight bits is called a *byte.*) Suffice it to say that this setting is almost always going

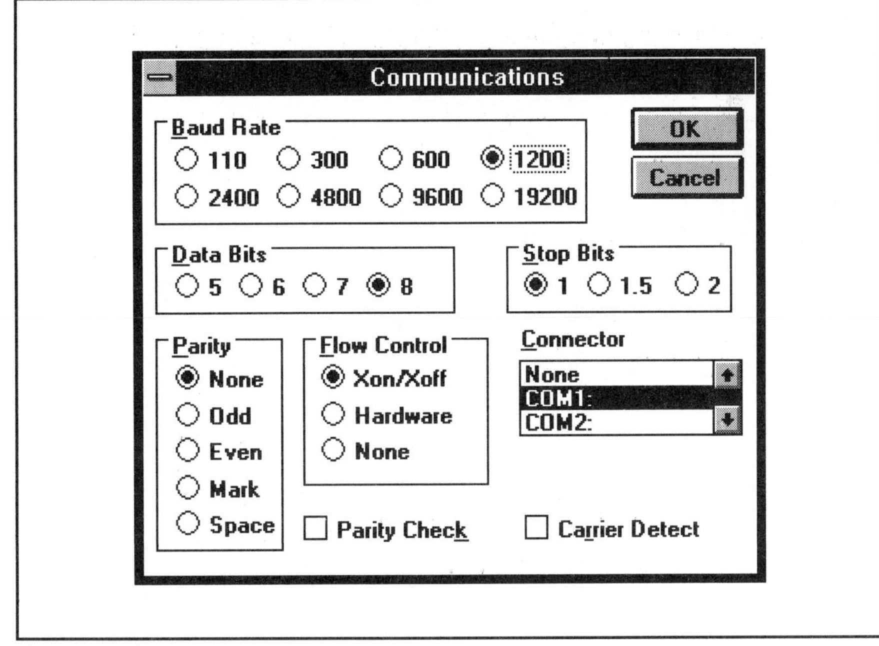

FIGURE 10.3: *The Communications dialog box. From here, you set the parameters that directly affect how the computers on each end of the communications link transfer data. All settings except for the COM port and Carrier Detect must be identical for both computers.*

to be 8, and must be 8 if you are intending to transfer binary files between computers. Binary files include all programs and any documents that consist of more than plain ASCII characters. Thus, formatted word-processing documents, spreadsheets, and graphics documents are binary files. The other popular standard is 7 bits. The 5- and 6-bit options are rarely used. Change this setting only if you are specifically told that the other system uses a setting other than 8 bits.

Stop Bits

Stop bits are used by the computers on both ends to indicate the end of one character and the beginning of the next. You can probably leave this setting as is (1). Change this setting if you are specifically told that the other system uses 2 or 1.5 stop bits.

Parity

Parity is a means by which the communications software can check if an error has occurred in the transmission of each byte of data. Parity can only be used if you have set the Data Bits parameter to 7. Otherwise parity should be left at None. If you are specifically told that the other system uses parity checking, find out what kind and change this setting.

Flow Control

In the process of receiving and sending data, the computers on each end of the line often have to attend to other tasks as well, such as storing information on disk. Sometimes these tasks can distract the receiving computer from handling its incoming data. As mentioned in Chapter 6 (in the discussion of printer connections), *handshaking* is used to prevent data from falling through the cracks during these processes. Handshaking provides a way for the two computers to agree when to stop and start the sending process so that other contingencies can be handled.

Most often, at least when using modems, the Xon/Xoff convention (or *protocol*) will be employed. When the receiving computer wants the sending computer to pause, it transmits an Xoff (a Ctrl-S) signal. When ready to receive data again, it sends an Xon (Ctrl-Q) signal. This is the default setting, and will work for most dial-up information services.

When connecting computers to each other directly via a cable (without a modem), you may want to use the Hardware setting. To use this option, you must make sure you have a special kind of cable. If you know that the other computer uses no handshaking, select None from the dialog box. Regardless of which handshaking setup you are using, remember that both computers must use the same type.

Connector

The last section of the Communications dialog box lets you tell Terminal which *port* your modem is connected to. Most PCs have two serial communications ports, called COM1 and COM2, though more fully expanded systems may have COM3 and COM4 as well. The default is for Terminal to use COM1 as the port. Your COM1 port may be tied up for use with a printer or other device, though, in which case your modem should be connected or set up for another port.

Parity Check

When this is set on, you will see every byte, even if a parity error was detected. In other words, you might see the wrong character, as in the following:

```
Welcome to Do-Dad Enterprises Online Database:
Please enter your $qssword
```

If Parity Check is set off (the default), you'll see a question mark in place of any byte (character) in which an error was detected. Seeing the question mark is more useful than seeing the byte for most purposes, as it will clue you in to the fact that the character was lost and that you will have to fill in the gaps. For example, if you see this when working interactively with another computer:

```
Welcome to Do-Dad Enterprises Online Database:
Please enter your ??ssword
```

you can assume some information was lost, and that the correct word is *password.* This setting has no effect if the parity is set to None.

Incidentally, when sending files rather than communicating interactively, errors such as these can be automatically detected and usually corrected if you use an error-checking scheme. This is explained in the section "Sending Binary Files" later in this chapter.

Carrier Detect

Normally the modem determines whether the modem on the other line is actually connected and ready to send and receive data. It knows this by detecting the presence of a carrier, which is a high-pitched tone. If the carrier is detected, the modem relays this to your computer and Terminal alerts you to this fact. Only then can you begin your communications session. If for some reason the modem isn't detecting the carrier (and Terminal isn't acting as if you're online), try setting this check box on. Then Terminal will use its own method of detecting the carrier.

SETTING THE MODEM PARAMETERS

The final step before beginning your session is to set the modem parameters:

1. Choose Settings ➤ Modem Commands. The box you see in Figure 10.4 will appear.
2. You probably won't have to modify anything in this box except the type of modem you have. Select the type of modem you have or one that's compatible with it. Check your modem's manual for compatibility information.

If you don't have a modem that's listed in the Modem Defaults group (or one that's compatible), choose None. If the modem accepts software commands,

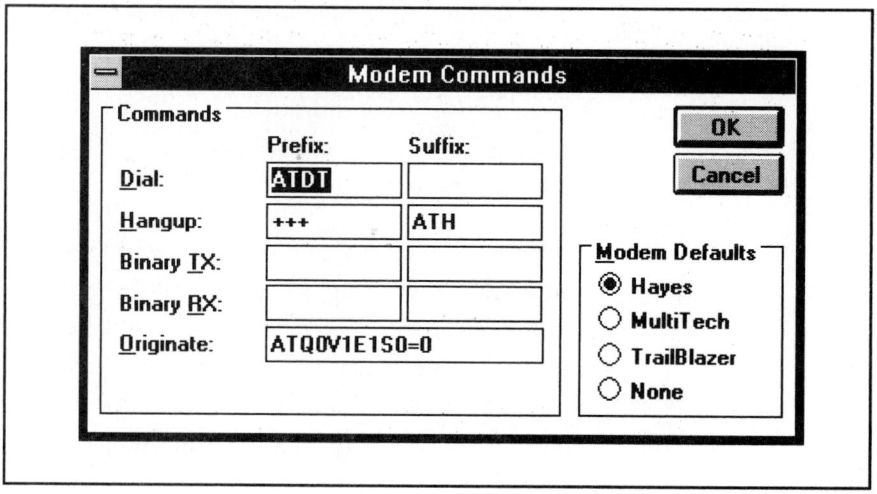

FIGURE 10.4:

The Modem Commands dialog box. From here you select your modem type or fill in the commands your modem expects. Check the modem's manual for campatibility with one of the default types; then you won't have to bother with the boxes.

If you don't have a modem that's listed in the Modem Defaults group (or one that's compatible), choose None. If the modem accepts software commands, you should type in the commands in the appropriate boxes in the Commands section of the dialog box. Some commands have two parts—a prefix and suffix. The *prefix* generally tells the modem the class of command it is going to receive, or requests attention from the modem. The *suffix* then supplies the specifics of the command. Check your modem's manual for the commands it uses.

The Prefix section of the Dial row in the dialog box sends a command to your modem before dialing a phone number. Terminal will send whatever command you enter here prior to dialing the number. For example, you may want to tell your modem how many rings to allow before giving up trying to connect with the remote computer. Or if you don't have a touchtone service, you can tell the modem to use pulse dialing instead. Or you can set up the modem to answer an incoming call. As an example, to dial with pulses from a Hayes modem, change the ATDT prefix to ATDP.

If you don't type in the commands, you can still use the modem. You'll just have to control the modem manually (if it has switches for that purpose) or type in the commands at the keyboard while connected to the modem.

Making a Connection

Once your settings are correct, make the connection to the remote computer. To initiate the connection, choose Phone ➤ Dial. A dialog box will appear, telling you that the number is being dialed, and counting down the seconds from the Timeout value you set earlier.

The phone number being dialed (along with the commands telling the modem how to dial it) shows up in the work area of the screen, like this:

```
ATDT5401114
```

If your modem has a speaker in it, you may also hear the number as it is being dialed. When the phone on the other end is picked up, you may hear some high-pitched tones indicating that the modems are "talking" to each other.

If the connection is successful, you may see the word

```
CONNECT
```

on the screen. From then on, everything you type on the keyboard will be sent to the other computer. If you have the function-key indicators showing (choose Settings ➤ Show Function Keys), the time indicator will change to show the elapsed time, informing you of the amount of time your computer has been connected to the remote machine.

If the connection is not successful, after about 15 seconds you will probably see the words

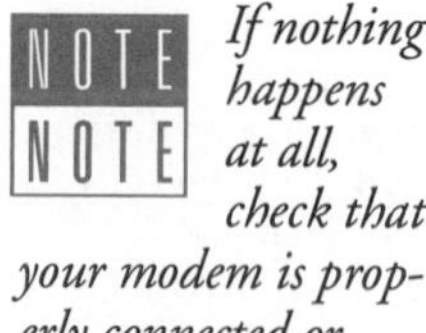

If nothing happens at all, check that your modem is properly connected or turned on.

NO CARRIER

just under the phone number. This means the modem gave up trying to make a connection. Typical reasons for failure at this point are the following:

- The other phone was busy.
- The other phone/modem didn't answer.
- The modems are set at different baud rates so they didn't recognize each other.

If the phone number you dialed is busy, your modem may report the word BUSY to the screen and you may hear the busy signal on the modem's speaker. Usually the modem will hang up and wait for a message from the computer to try again. To dial again, choose Phone ➤ Dial again.

If you want to stop a dialing that is in progress, click on Cancel in the Dialing box.

Saving Your Settings

With some practice you'll see that only a few of the settings need alteration for each new type of communications session. What's more, once you have the details of a particular hookup ironed out, you can save your settings on disk for future use. Your settings are saved as a file with a .TRM extension. To save your settings:

1. Choose File ➤ Save. The familiar Save As dialog box will appear.
2. Give your file a name, preferably one that will help you remember which information service or computer the settings are for.

SENDING AND RECEIVING DATA

Assuming the connection proceeds without difficulty, you can begin to transfer data between computers. What you do now depends entirely on what the other computer expects from you. If you are calling an information service, BBS, or a mainframe computer, you will typically have to sign on to the remote system by typing your name and possibly a password. If you are calling a friend's computer or connecting locally, you can probably just begin typing as I will describe here. In any case, once the initial connection is made, there are several ways that you can begin to transfer data between the two computers. The next several sections describe these techniques and how to use them.

TRANSMITTING DATA IN INTERACTIVE MODE

TO CAPTURE TEXT AS IT COMES IN,

1. **Choose Transfers ➤ Receive Text File.**
2. **Type in the file name, choose options from the dialog box, and click OK.**
3. **Click the Pause button to skip unwanted text; click on Resume to continue capturing.**
4. **Click Stop to save and close the file.**

TO SEND OUT TEXT,

1. **Choose Settings ➤ Text Transfers and set the desired options.**
2. **Choose Transfers ➤ Send Text File and enter the file name.**
3. **Choose any line-feed options and click on OK.**

The simplest way to transfer data is directly from your keyboard. As mentioned earlier, once you're connected to the other computer, everything you type is automatically sent to it. Conversely, characters typed at the other computer will be sent to your computer, showing up on your screen. Sending and receiving data this way is called working in *interactive* or *terminal* mode. Communication sessions often begin in terminal mode, with each person typing to the other's screen.

Terminal mode is often used, too, when connecting to many of the information services and electronic mail services that are interactive in nature. With these, you type certain commands to the host computer and it responds by sending you some data. As information comes over the line to your computer, it will appear on the screen, as shown in Figure 10.5. As you type, your text will appear on the screen as well.

As each new line of text is received or typed in by you, it will scroll upward in the Terminal window. Once it reaches the top of the window, it disappears from view, though the information is retained in the buffer. To recall the information, use the vertical scroll bar. Then scroll back down to continue interacting with the other computer.

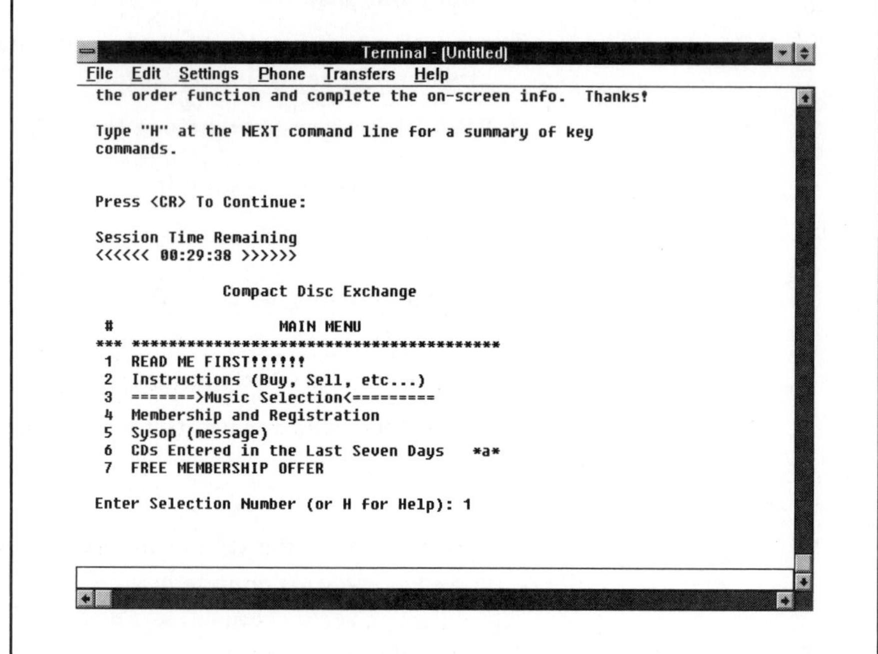

FIGURE 10.5:

A typical interactive session. Notice that the user entered the number 1 at the bottom of the screen in response to the prompt from the sender.

Capturing Text

There will be times when you'll somehow want to save incoming data while you're in Terminal mode so you can work with it later. You can *capture* incoming text at any time during a communications session with the Receive Text File command on the Transfer menu and save it in a disk file for later reading, printing, or editing. Here is the basic procedure for capturing text:

1. Choose Transfers ➤ Receive Text File.
2. A standard file dialog box appears, asking you to name the file in which you want the captured text stored. Select the directory and type in the name, but don't press Enter yet.
3. There are several options you might want to choose from before saving the file:

   Append File adds the incoming text to the end of the preexisting file you choose from the file box. This is useful for archiving a series of electronic mail conversations with a particular person, for example, or compiling information about a particular topic. Using this method, you can keep capturing data, even from session to session, into the same file.

   Save Controls saves control characters (formatting codes above ASCII 128) that might be in the file.

   Table Format converts two or more consecutive spaces into tabs. This is a great convenience if you're receiving lists of information that you later want to format and print. With spaces converted to tabs, you can adjust the tab alignment and spacing later in your word processor. You can also use proportionally spaced fonts and still have the columns line up.
4. Click on OK. The file will be opened and the status line at the bottom of the window will appear, showing the number of bytes (characters—including spaces, carriage returns, and linefeeds) that have been "captured," and the file they are being saved in (see Figure 10.6).
5. Continue with your session. Whatever you type will be captured too, along with the incoming text. When you want to stop capturing text, click on Stop in the status line. The status line message will disappear and the text will be stored on the disk.

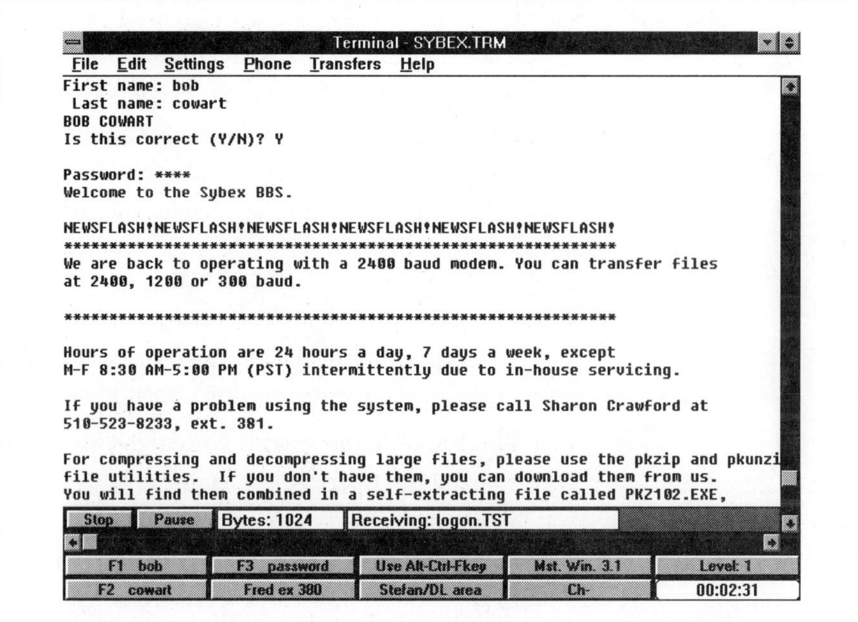

FIGURE 10.6:

You capture text to a file with the Transfers ➤ Receive Text File command. The status line changes to the file name and the number of bytes received. Stop or pause the capturing with the buttons at the bottom-left corner of the window.

Capturing Selected Portions of Text

During text capturing there may be sections of text you don't want to save interspersed with portions you do. A case in point would be reading menu choices or sign-on messages from BBSs, MCI Mail, or CompuServe. You can turn text capture on and off at will to accommodate this situation. Here's how to do it (assuming you've already chosen Transfers ➤ Receive Text File, there will be a Pause button in the status line and text capturing will be active):

1. Click on Pause in the status line when it looks as though a section of unwanted text is coming across the screen. This pauses the capturing, even though your session continues on-screen as though nothing happened. The button changes to read Resume instead of Pause.
2. When you want to start capturing again, click on Resume. All subsequent text will be added to the file.

Sending Text

Obviously just sending text to another computer by typing it in from your keyboard isn't very efficient. Terminal gives you an alternative to this approach by letting you send documents already prepared by a word processor or other program. This is a much more efficient method of data transfer.

There are two ways to do it. One method uses error correction to ensure that the other computer receives your file without any loss of data. This is discussed in the next section. The other technique does not use error correction, but it is compatible with a wider variety of host computers.

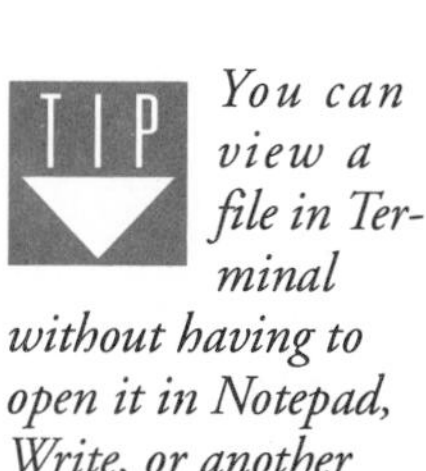

You can view a file in Terminal without having to open it in Notepad, Write, or another program. Choose Transfers ➤ View Text File and enter the file name. Use the Pause button to control the scrolling.

The Send Text File command on the Transfers menu is the method without error correction. Use this command to send letters via electronic mail services, BBSs, and information services. By composing your messages first with a word processor or text editor, you can minimize the connection time (and resultant cost).

Note, however, that you can use the Send Text File command only with ASCII files (i.e., plain text files without control codes in them), so make sure the file you want to send was created, or at least saved, as an ASCII file from whatever program you created it in. You cannot send programs (files with the extensions .EXE or .COM) with this command. Captured text files are ASCII files, as are all Notepad files and Write files saved in Text Only format. Typically, electronic mail services such as MCI Mail receive files in this format.

Before sending a text file you might want to check the settings in the Text Transfers dialog box. To do so,

1. Choose Settings ➤ Text Transfers. A dialog box will appear. It has three settings of importance. You can have Terminal send information a line at a time, a character at a time, or using the standard flow control. Standard Flow Control is the control setting you made in the Communications dialog box (see Figure 10.3). It's probably the way you want to send text files, and it's probably Xon/Xoff, which is the most popular standard. You should choose Line if the system you're sending to wants to receive text a line at a time, send back an acknowledgment, and then request the next line. Sending text a character at a time is very rarely used, and is extremely slow besides.

2. If you created the text in a word processor, the lines of text in the file may have a length that suits your needs but not those of the person receiving the file. You can predetermine the line length for the receiving party if you like. Turn on the Word Wrap check box and set the line length (number of characters) you desire.

Now to actually send a text file, follow these steps:

1. Make a connection to the other computer.
2. Choose Transfers ➤ Send Text File.
3. A dialog box will appear (see Figure 10.7). Enter the file name or select it from the Files list box.
4. Consider the two option boxes. If you want to add a linefeed to the end of each line of text you send, check the Append LF option. If you want to strip out the line feeds from the end of each line you send, check Strip LF. (See "Setting the Terminal Preferences" earlier in this chapter for a discussion of linefeeds.) Then click OK. You might have to talk with the person running the other computer to determine whether he or she wants line feeds added or excluded. Or you could try sending a few small files and vary the selection to see which one works best.

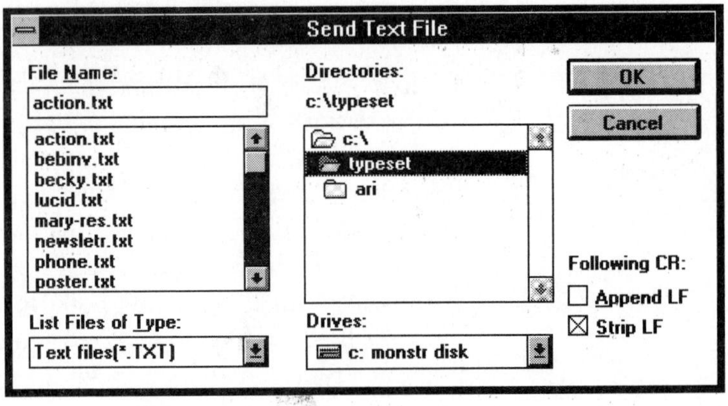

FIGURE 10.7:

To send a text file, choose Transfers ➤ Send Text File. Select or enter the file name, set the check boxes, and click on OK.

5. The status line will come on at the bottom of the window, and the text will scroll up the screen as the file is sent so that you can monitor the progress of the transfer. The status line also has a document bar in it that graphically displays the amount of the file that has been sent and the amount remaining, as shown in Figure 10.8.

6. You can pause, resume, and stop the transmission by clicking on the buttons in the status line or choosing the identical commands in the Transfers menu. When Terminal reaches the end of the file, the status line disappears.

If you notice that letters are missing at the beginning of each new line of text on your screen, you will have to stop the transfer and change the Flow Control setting in the Text Transfers dialog box. Choose Line at a Time and enter a value greater than the default of 1/10 of a second as the Delay Between Lines setting. For example, enter a 2 in place of the 1, for a 1/10-second delay. The Delay Between Lines setting controls how long Terminal will pause at the end of each line before beginning the transmission of the next line.

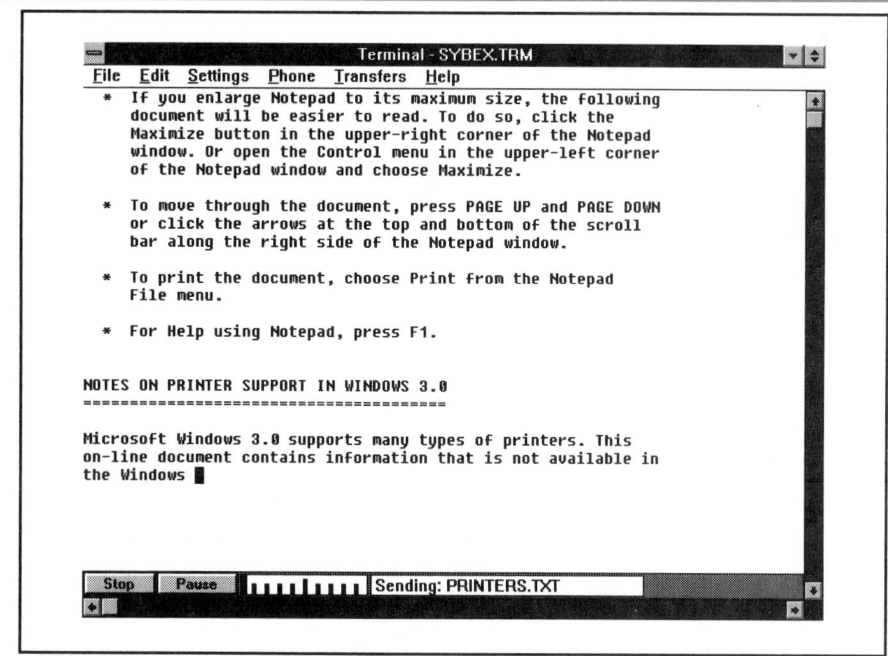

FIGURE 10.8:

When you send a file, the status line will appear, reporting the file being sent and the progress of the transmission. It also lets you stop, pause, or resume the transmission.

Sending and Receiving Files

TO SEND A BINARY FILE,

1. **Choose Settings ➤ Binary Transfers and set the desired error-checking protocol.**
2. **Tell the other computer to receive a file.**
3. **Choose Transfers ➤ Send Binary File and enter the file name.**
4. **Click on OK.**

TO RECEIVE A BINARY FILE,

1. **Choose Settings ➤ Binary Transfers and set the desired error-checking protocol.**
2. **Tell the other computer to send the file.**
3. **Choose Transfers ➤ Receive Binary File and enter the file name.**
4. **Click on OK.**

It's not uncommon for data to be lost or corrupted during the transmission process over telephone lines, particularly when long distances are involved. As we all know, long distance lines often suffer from noise, static, or even other people's conversations accidentally being crossed with ours. Usually we just put up with the noise, asking the other party to repeat their last sentence, or we redial the call.

Computers are less tolerant of such maladies. Noise on the line between two computers can cause a plethora of erratic data alterations during a file transfer. In response to this, computer scientists have devised numerous error-detection and error-correction schemes to determine whether errors have occurred in transmission, and have found various methods to correct them. Terminal uses two of these schemes with its Receive Binary File and Send Binary File commands from the Transfers menu.

The first one, the XModem protocol, is an error-detection and correction scheme devised by Ward Christensen and given to the public in 1977 for use on microcomputers, which were just then becoming available. X-Modem is now widely used and supported by many communications programs as well as some information services, such as CompuServe. The other one, Kermit, is functionally similar.

NOTE *In addition to catching errors in transmission, these protocols allow you to transmit all types of files, including programs, spreadsheets, and graphics. It doesn't matter what's in the file.*

Error-detection and correction schemes divide a file into a series of small sections, called *blocks.* The blocks are then sent sequentially, and each one is accompanied by a mathematically calculated code based on the contents of the block. After getting the block, the receiving computer sees whether its contents match this calculated code. If they do, the sending computer is advised to send the next block. If there is a discrepancy, the receiving computer asks the sending computer to retransmit the block until it's received properly. This process continues until the entire file is transmitted error-free.

The XModem protocol has two modes—CRC (Cyclical Redundancy Check) and checksum. Some receiving systems may have one but not the other. Terminal, when set to transfer binary files with the XModem CRC setting, tries CRC first, and then switches to checksum mode if the other system isn't responding.

Obviously, the system on the other end has to be using the same error-detection scheme or the computers won't be able to communicate about the success or failure of the transmission. In fact, the transfer will not even begin. Nothing will happen. Between Kermit and XModem, you should be able to send binary files to most other systems, since most communications programs support one or the other, or both.

Sending Binary Files

NOTE *You can't pause a binary transfer, but you can stop it in midstream by clicking on Stop or choosing Stop from the Transfers menu.*

To send a binary file, follow these steps:

1. Make sure you're online (connected).
2. Choose Settings ➤ Binary Transfers.
3. From the dialog box, choose the error-detection protocol you want to use (the one the receiving system uses).

4. Make sure the receiving computer is ready to receive an XModem or Kermit file. How you do this depends on the computer system, BBS, or information service to which you are connected. If you are sending a file to another PC, you may want to type a message in Terminal mode telling the operator to do what is necessary to prepare for receiving the file.
5. Choose Transfers ➤ Send Binary. A file dialog box will ask for the name and type of the file. Type in the path and file name or use the file and directory list boxes to locate the file, and then click on OK. This will begin the file transfer.

The progress of the transfer will be reported in a status line. You won't see the file on the screen (if it's not all text it would look like garbage anyway). If errors are detected, they will be reported in the status bar next to Retries. If more than ten consecutive errors are detected during transmission, Terminal will abort the sending process.

As a recap of sending binary files, consider the following: a binary file will arrive just as you sent it, with no modifications (for example, no adding or stripping of linefeeds). All types of files, including program files, can be sent and received as binary files. Formatted text as well as program files must be transmitted as binary files, or information will be lost. If you want to send such files to another person through an electronic mail service that doesn't accept binary files, such as MCI Mail, you will have to use a utility program that converts binary files into a special type of encoded 7-bit file before sending it. The receiving party will then have to reconvert the file on his or her end with the same utility program.

Receiving Binary Files

You'll want to use the Receive Binary File command to receive files from other PCs, BBSs, or information services that support the XModem or Kermit protocol. This will ensure that they are received without error. Receiving a binary file is essentially the reverse of sending one:

1. Choose Settings ➤ Binary Transfers and select XModem or Kermit, depending on the protocol that the other computer uses to send binary files.

2. In interactive mode, tell the sending computer to send the file. How you do this depends on the computer and program(s) involved. With some systems, you control the sending from your computer. In other cases, a person at the other end issues the command. BBSs typically will say something like:

   Ready to receive Y/N?

   or

   Press Enter to start download

3. Choose Transfers ➤ Receive Binary File. The file dialog box appears because you are telling Terminal to save the incoming data as a file. Enter the file name (and path if not the current path) or choose it from the directory and file boxes. Do this quickly, since the other computer is already trying to send the file. It will wait, but usually not too long.

4. Click on OK or press Enter, and the transmission should begin. A dialog box will appear, indicating the number of bytes received, the name of the file being transmitted, and a Stop button in case you want to bail out. You won't see the file on the screen.

If errors are detected during the transmission, they'll be reported next to the word Retries. If more than ten consecutive errors are detected during transmission, Terminal will abort the receiving process.

Since Terminal doesn't know the size of the file being sent to it, there isn't a little gauge indicating how long the whole transmission is going to take. Occasionally, you may run out of disk space while receiving a file. This is a real hassle, particularly if you've spent half an hour receiving most of a large file only to get an error message from Terminal saying there isn't enough room on your disk for the rest of it. Terminal will abort the receiving process if there isn't enough room, so make sure the disk you choose to store the file on has enough free space on it before you begin the transfer. If you forget to do this, you'll have to change disks or drives and start the process again.

USING THE FUNCTION KEYS TO CUT DOWN ON TYPING

Terminal has a feature that helps cut down on typing repetitive commands. This is a blessing when you're working online with systems that require that you type in the same information each time you log on to or interact with them. You can assign up to 32 different commands to your keyboard's function keys (four for each key from F1 to F8). When you press the key, the command is sent as though you typed it. It's just like a *macro* or the automatic key substitutions that programs like SmartKey, ProKey, and some word processors have built-in. However, since the basic function keys are used for other purposes (such as getting Help), you have to press Ctrl-Alt while using the function keys to get these results. There are two steps to using the keys: assigning the commands and executing them.

ASSIGNING THE FUNCTION KEY COMMANDS

To assign a command to a key:

1. Choose Settings ➤ Function Keys. This will pop up a dialog box, shown in Figure 10.9. Each key from F1 to F8 has two slots to type into. The key name is the name that will show up on the bottom of the screen when you elect to show the function-key settings. The command is what pressing the key will enter as if typed from the keyboard. If you don't name a key, it won't show up on the bottom of the screen.
2. Enter the key names and commands you want for each key.
3. If you want more than eight commands, click on Level 2 and enter more names and commands. Use Levels 3 and 4 if you want to. All told, you can enter as many as 32 key definitions.
4. Set the Keys Visible check box on if you want the keys to be automatically displayed at the bottom of the window when you open the .TRM file next time. This setting is saved with the file. (Normally keys are hidden until you choose Settings ➤ Show Function Keys.)
5. Save your settings with the File ➤ Save command.

FIGURE 10.9:

The Function Keys dialog box with examples. Each key can have a name that appears on the bottom of the screen.

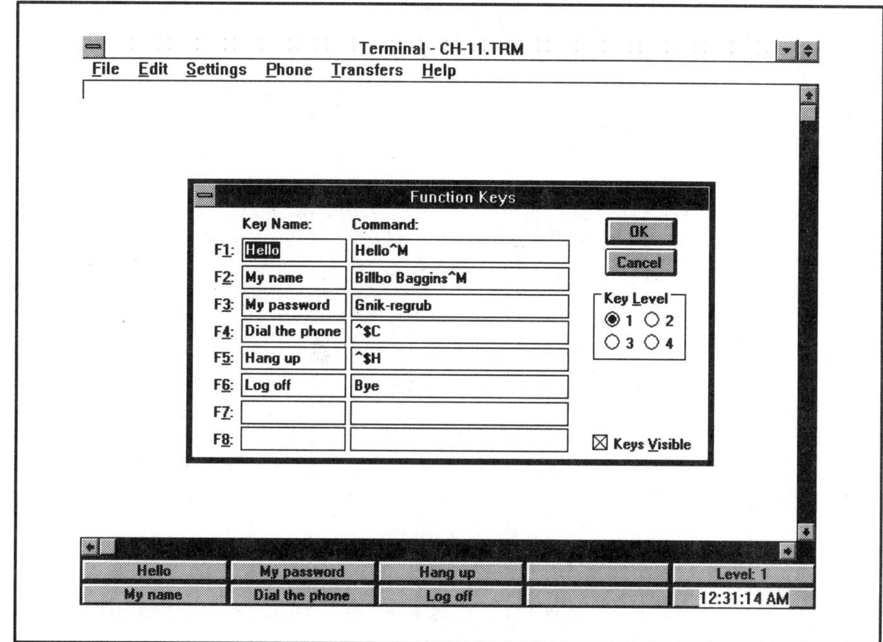

You'll typically assign just your name and password to function keys so you won't have to type them each time you log on to an information service. However, you may want to assign more than just text to function keys. You can also assign control-key commands, some menu commands, and the Enter key. Table 10.1 lists the special codes you can use to assign such actions to keys; these can be strung together and interspersed with normal text (enter the caret (^) with the shifted 6 key above the letter *T* on the keyboard). Here's an example of a complex command for one function key:

```
^$C^$D03^M$D03FJONES^M^$D03password^M
```

If you break it down, you'll see that it dials the number stored in the Phone Number dialog box, waits three seconds, executes an Enter command, types in *FJONES,* the user's name, waits three seconds again, enters the password, and executes another Enter command. This is a typical sign-on procedure for many services, such as MCI Mail. (You can increase the waiting periods if your commands seem to be issued too soon.)

TABLE 10.1: *Special Codes Assignable to Function Keys*

CONTROL CODE	EFFECT
^A–^Z	Sends Ctrl-A through Ctrl-Z
^$D*p*	Causes Terminal to delay for *p* seconds before continuing
^$B	Causes Terminal to transmit a 117-millisecond Break code. (Some computers stop a process in midstream when they receive the Break code.)
^$C	Has the same effect as choosing Phone ➤ Dial
^$H	Has the same effect as choosing Phone ➤ Hangup
^$L1–^$L4	Changes to key level 1 through 4

USING THE FUNCTION KEYS

When you want to use the function keys, bring them up on-screen by choosing Settings ➤ Show Function Keys, if the keys aren't displayed already. To switch to another level of commands, click on the Level button. The level will be switched, and the command names will change. (If there's only one level of settings, the button will be grayed). Click on the button representing the command or words you want transmitted to the other computer. To hide the buttons again, choose Settings ➤ Hide Function Keys.

As an alternative to clicking on the key, you can press Ctrl-Alt and a function key on the keyboard. (F1 through F4 correspond to the buttons on the top line of the display; F5 through F8 correspond to those on the bottom line.)

MANIPULATING TEXT FROM THE DOCUMENT WINDOW

You can manipulate the text in the document window in various ways while in a Terminal session. You can

- copy it to the Clipboard
- transmit selected text or the Clipboard's contents to the other computer as though you were typing it

- print incoming or selected text
- clear all the text in the window

Copying Text to the Clipboard

Any text you can see on-screen can be copied to the Clipboard. Once there, it can be pasted into other applications or sent to the other system:

1. Select text with the mouse, just as in any other program, such as Write or Notepad. (Refer to Chapter 9 for exact instructions on selecting text in Write.) To copy the entire document (i.e., all the text that's in the buffer) choose Edit ➤ Select All.
2. Choose Edit ➤ Copy. The text is now on the Clipboard.

Transmitting Text

Sometimes you'll want to send text from a different application to the other computer. If the document is in another window, this is very easy. You don't have to create and send a new file. Just follow these steps:

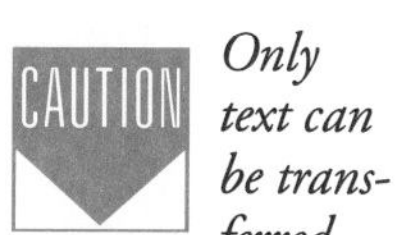

Only text can be transferred in this way. If a graphic is on the Clipboard, you cannot paste it.

1. Copy the text to the Clipboard. It can be text from a Terminal window or any other application window, such as Microsoft Word, Excel, Write, Ami Pro, PageMaker, etc.
2. Switch back to the Terminal window and choose Edit ➤ Paste. The contents of the Clipboard will be sent to the other computer, unchanged. If the other computer is using Windows, the user could then select the information, copy it to the Clipboard, and paste it into another document.

You can also transmit selected text from the Terminal window without having to copy it to the Clipboard. This is a quick way to repeat a command you've typed in once already:

1. Select the text.
2. Choose Edit ➤ Send.

Printing Incoming Text

If you want to print text as it comes onto your screen from the remote computer, follow these steps:

1. Set up your printer and put it online. Select the correct printer from File ➤ Printer Setup.
2. Choose Settings ➤ Printer Echo. A check mark will appear next to the menu selection. All received text will be printed. (If Local Echo is set on from the Terminal Preferences dialog box, everything you type will be printed too.)
3. Choose Settings ➤ Printer Echo again to turn it off.

Printing Selected Text

You can't print selected text directly from Terminal. However, here are two ways you can print what's come over the line:

- Select the text you want to print and copy it onto the Clipboard. Then open Write, Notepad, or another word processor and paste the text into the document, edit it, and print it as usual.
- Save the incoming text as a file, as explained in the earlier section "Capturing Text." Exit Terminal and then open the text file in a word processor and print it.

RUNNING MULTIPLE COMMUNICATIONS SESSIONS

There probably aren't too many times that you'd want to run multiple communications sessions, but it is possible to have two sessions connected at the same time. To do this, run Terminal a second time and open a new communications document while you still have the first one open. Set the parameters and connect as usual. You must *not* use the same communications port as you're using for the first session. From the Communications dialog box you'll have to select the unused COM channel (1 or 2) as the port for the second session. Of course, you'll need another modem (or cable in the case of direct connection) connected to the second port, as well. By using the Pause command wisely and jumping between windows, you could juggle the two communications sessions.

ENDING A COMMUNICATIONS SESSION

Once you've finished your work (or play) during a session, you should end it by following some simple rules:

1. If you want to save the settings you've made, choose File ➤ Save and name the file.
2. If you are logged on to an information service, electronic mail, or BBS, follow the system's instructions for signing off. This may be important to free up a connection for other users or to ensure that the service will cease billing you for connect time.
3. Choose Phone ➤ Hangup.
4. Close Terminal by double-clicking its Control box.

TROUBLESHOOTING

Despite great strides in the field of communications, mostly due to conveniences spurred by the personal computer market, communications is still a bit of a black art. Chances are good that you'll run into some problem or other while transferring files, sending mail, or whatever it is you end up doing with Terminal. Don't worry—the fault will not necessarily lie with Terminal (or yourself), but much more likely will be the result of improper wiring, faulty modems, noisy telephone lines, incorrect log-on procedures, or incompatible software on the other end of the line. Chapter 19 includes a number of troubleshooting tips that may solve your problems, should you have any. Look for the section on tips for Terminal in that chapter for likely cures to your communications woes.

FAST TRACK

CHAPTER

11

FAST TRACK

simply run Paintbrush by double clicking its icon in the Accessories group. If already running, just choose File➤ New.

choose File ➤ Open and choose the file from the dialog box. The file must be an *.msp, .pcx,* or *.bmp* file.

choose Options ➤ Image Attributes. Enter the width and height desired and units of measurement. Choose Color or Black and White. The changes don't go into effect until you open a new document.

click at the bottom of the screen on the color palette. Clicking the right mouse button sets the background color. Clicking the left button sets the foreground color. A new background color won't take effect until you open a new document or erase the current background color with one of the tools.

To use any of the tools in the Toolbox, ... 363

1. Click on the tool you want to use. This selects the tool.
2. Position the cursor where you want to start drawing, selecting, or erasing, and then click and hold the mouse button.
3. Begin drawing by moving the mouse. Release when you are through.

To paste down items you've added to the drawing, ... 365

1. Reselect the current tool.
2. Select a new tool, resize the window, or use the scroll bars. Once pasted down, an item can't be deleted without affecting the background.

To add text to the drawing, ... 380

click on the text tool (abc). Then position the cursor, click, and release. Start typing.

CHAPTER 11

FEATURING

Editing Existing Bit-Mapped Files

Choosing Foreground and Background Colors

Using the Drawing Tools

Adding Text

Manipulating Your Drawing

Pixel Editing

Using Paintbrush

aintbrush is a drawing program similar to a number of other graphics drawing programs on the market. The most popular of these are PC Paintbrush, Mouse Paint, and PC Paint. Although Paintbrush, like Write, isn't a top-of-the-line product in its class, the price is right and it's not bad. In fact, it has some unique features.

In the personal-computer world there are two basic classes of graphics programs—*bit-mapped* and *object-oriented.* With bit-mapped programs, you create a painting or drawing on the computer screen as if you were painting a picture on a canvas with paint. Paint you apply to the canvas irreversibly covers up the underlying surface.

Object-oriented programs create a drawing or graphic in a manner more analogous to a collage or like those felt boards used in grade school. Each item you place (lines, circles, text, etc.) retains its identity as a separate object. These objects can later be moved, sized, cut, copied, and otherwise altered without affecting anything else in the picture.

Paintbrush is of the first variety. Rather than being defined by objects, a Paintbrush bit-mapped drawing consists of a series of dots. Your computer's screen is divided into very small dots (*pixels* or *pels*) that are controlled by the smallest division of computer information—bits. A *bit map* is a collection of bits of information that creates an image when assigned ("mapped") to dots on the screen (or on paper). This is similar to a sports scoreboard that can display the score, a message, or even a picture by turning on and off specific light bulbs in a grid.

In the simplest of bit maps, one bit controls one dot. Since a bit is like a light switch in a computer and can either be on or off, each dot on the screen can either be on or off. So a drawing is created by a matrix of dots that are on or off. When you create a graphic with a bit-mapped drawing program, what you are doing is determining which dots are on and which are off. If the program uses color (as Paintbrush does) or gray-scaling, additional bits are required to store the color information for each dot, but that's another story. Anyway, the basic theory remains the same. Though this may seem academic now, it will make more sense later when you learn about editing the bit map with the Zoom command.

Enough theory. With Paintbrush, you can

- create signs
- create computer art
- create technical drawings
- create illustrations for printed matter
- create images for use in other Windows programs such as Cardfile
- design invitations
- enhance digitized images or photographs
- draw maps
- make wallpaper images for your Windows Desktop

STARTING A NEW DOCUMENT

To bring up Paintbrush:

1. Open the Accessories group and double-click on the Paintbrush icon.
2. The Paintbrush window appears. Maximize the window. Figure 11.1 shows the Paintbrush window and its component parts.

The work area is where you do your drawing. You use the tools selected from the Toolbox along with selections from the Palette and Linesize box to create your drawings.

The size of the drawing is determined by the amount of memory you have in your computer. While you're working on it, the entire picture is contained in RAM. If you have only a small amount of memory available, because other programs are open or you're simply short on RAM, the size of

FIGURE 11.1:

The Paintbrush screen

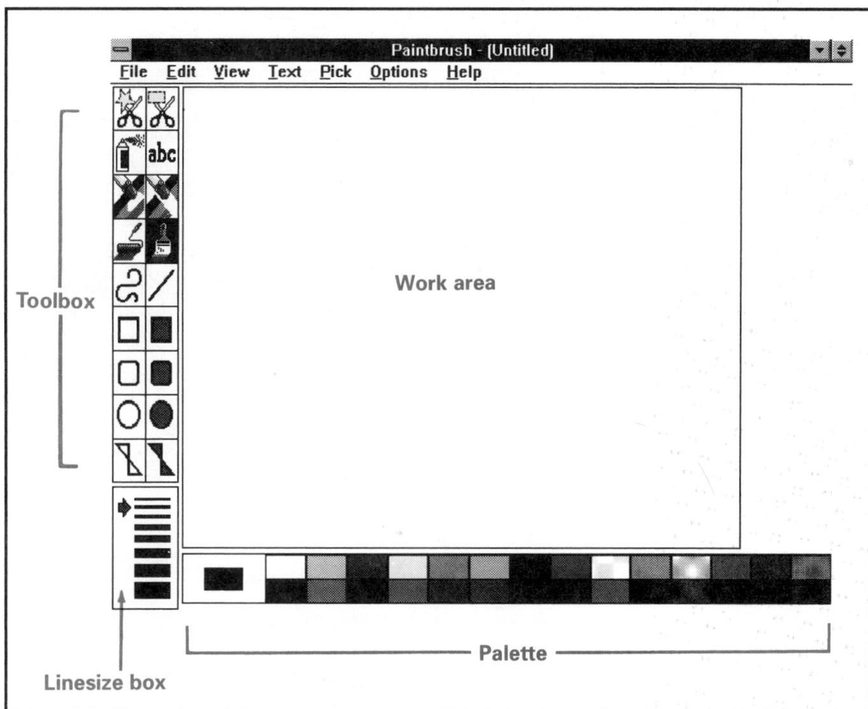

your drawing will be limited. You will be alerted if there is too little RAM to load a large picture.

LOADING AN EXISTING DRAWING

To load an existing picture, do the following:

1. Choose File ➤ Open.
2. Select the file name from the file and directory boxes. Figure 11.2 shows the CHESS.BMP file loaded. (If you upgraded from Windows 3.0, you will have this file in your Windows directory. If you didn't upgrade, you won't. Use another file instead.)

Now you can edit the file and save it under a new name, or copy a part of it to the Clipboard for use with other programs.

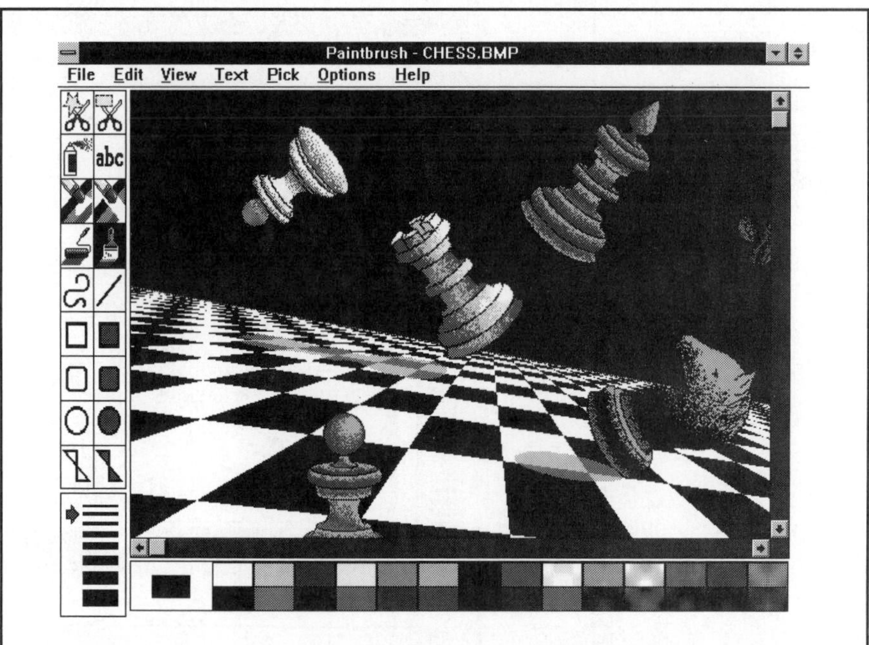

FIGURE 11.2: *Opening a file loads it into the work area*

SEEING MORE OF THE DRAWING

Sometimes the entire drawing is larger than the work area. If it is not too much larger, you may be able to see and work with the entire picture at one time. In any case, you can increase the viewing area in several ways:

- Choose View ➤ Tools and Linesize. The Toolbox and Linesize box along the left margin disappear and are replaced by more of the picture. You still have the scroll bars, Palette, and menu options onscreen, however, and whatever tool you're working with (we'll discuss tools later in this chapter).
- Choose View ➤ Palette. The Palette disappears, with similar advantage, as described above.
- Choose View ➤ View Picture. This shows as much of the picture as will fit on the screen at one time, though not necessarily the entire picture. However, this is only for checking your work, and doesn't allow you to work on the drawing. Clicking anywhere on the screen or pressing any key returns you to the working screen.
- To see the entire picture, even the space where you haven't drawn anything, choose View ➤ Zoom Out. Paintbrush will shrink the image to fit within the work area. The size of the image displayed is based on the size you declare in the Image Attributes dialog box (described in the next section). Though you can cut, copy, and paste in this zoomed-out mode, you can't draw anything new until you choose View ➤ Zoom In.

Double-clicking on the Pick tool (the one with the scissors and dotted box) has the same effect as choosing View ➤ View Picture.

It's more likely that you'll want the Toolbox on and the Palette off if you need to see more of the drawing, since the tools are used more frequently. To return to the Toolbox and the Palette, just choose these commands again from the View menu; they are toggles.

ALTERING THE SIZE OF THE DRAWING

The first thing you should determine when starting a new document is the size of the final drawing you're trying to create. When Paintbrush is run the first time on your system, it examines the video display you have and the amount of RAM in your computer. On the basis of these factors, it determines an appropriate drawing size. However, it's likely you're going to want to change this for some drawings. You set the drawing size in the Image Attributes dialog box reached from the Options menu:

1. Choose Options ➤ Image Attributes. The dialog box you see below appears.

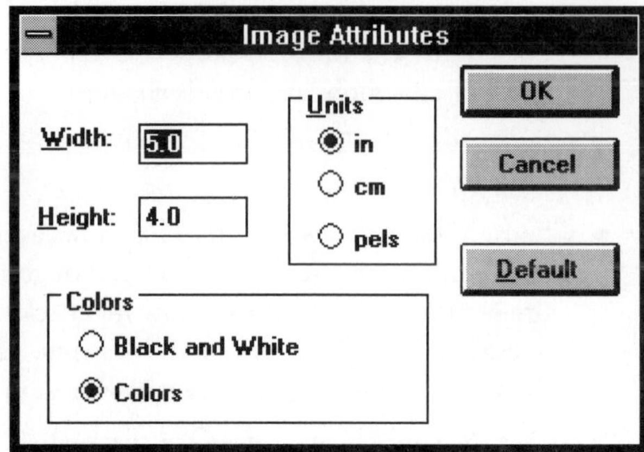

2. Enter the new width and height for your drawing and click on OK.

You can change other options from this box, too, as follows:

Units: determines the units for entering the width and height. The default is inches, though you can choose centimeters or *pels*. Pels are virtually the same as pixels, or bits. That is, each pel is equal to a dot on the screen.

Colors: determines whether your picture is created in black-and-white or in color.

Default: resets the drawing size to the amount Paintbrush originally figured as optimum for your system, though not necessarily the size you want.

Once you make these settings, they are stored and used each time you run Paintbrush. The thing to remember is that the settings won't affect the drawing you're currently working on. You have to change the settings *before* you start drawing a picture, and then choose File ➤ New.

If you make the settings too high (e.g., 200 inches by 200 inches), you may get a message the next time you run Paintbrush, saying there isn't enough memory in your system to edit a picture.

Here are some points to keep in mind when altering the image size:

- You can print the image in two resolutions—screen and printer. Printer resolution requires more memory than screen resolution.
- If you plan to print at printer resolution, you should enter the exact size in pixels of the final printed image.
- The dimensions you enter should be in proportion to those of the screen image of the drawing to avoid distortion of the image when printed.

SETTING THE BACKGROUND AND FOREGROUND COLORS OR PATTERNS

After setting the drawing size, the next step in creating a new picture or even modifying an existing one is to set the foreground and background colors selected from the Palette. The term *color* describes either a color or a colored pattern selected from the color Palette. If you are using a black-and-white screen, colors in the Palette may appear as shades of gray or varying densities of dot patterns.

The foreground color is the color you want a new item to be. For example, when you draw an item such as a circle, you'll want to assign a specific color to it. It's like deciding which color of paint to put on the brush before painting a stroke.

The background color determines the overall color of the canvas or backdrop for the picture. This is its primary function. It also has some effect on the drawing tools, determining the outline color of circles, squares, and enclosed polygons, and the color of text shading and outlining.

The current setting of the foreground and background colors is shown at the left side of the palette. The box in the middle shows the foreground color. The frame around it shows the background color. The default colors are black on white and always come up that way when you run Paintbrush:

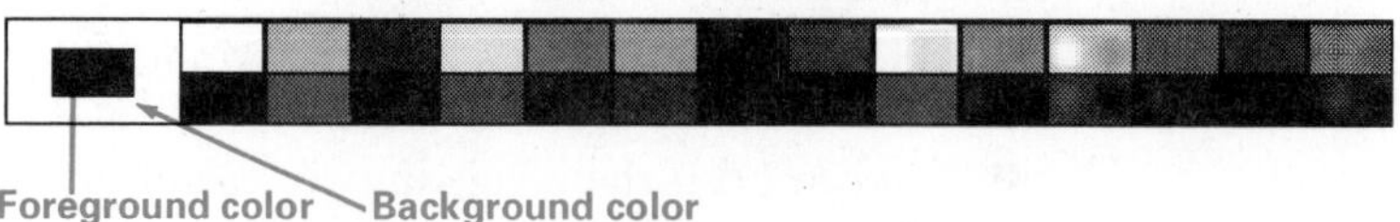

Setting the Background Color

To set the background color or pattern for the entire background of a new drawing:

1. Point to the color or pattern in the palette and click the *right* mouse button.
2. Choose File ➤ New. The new document will have the assigned background.

To change the assigned background color after starting a new drawing, just follow Step 1. This will not change the background color of the drawing itself, but it will affect the tools as explained above.

You can only determine the overall background color for a drawing once. If you want to change it later, you'll have to paint the new color on top of the old one with one of the tools.

Setting the Foreground Color

Set the foreground color as follows:

1. Point to the color or pattern you want.
2. Click the *left* mouse button. Now whatever you draw with the tools will appear in this color until you change it.

Typically, you'll change the foreground color very frequently if you're creating a drawing to be viewed onscreen. If you didn't, everything would have the same color, which is pretty boring. If you're drawing a picture to be printed on a black-and-white printer (which is likely, since color printers are relatively expensive at this point), you won't have much latitude in this regard. Paintbrush does try to render colors in shades of gray, though it doesn't do this as well as some other programs do. You may want to experiment a bit with your printer to determine what happens when you try to print colors. If the results aren't satisfactory, stick with the default foreground and background colors of black on white.

SETTING THE LINE, BORDER, AND BRUSH WIDTH

Probably the next thing you'll want to set is the line width for the drawing tools. The line width determines how thin or fat lines are. This includes lines around boxes and circles, curvy lines, and so on. To change it, click on the width you want in the Linesize box. This becomes the default until you choose a new size.

Note that if you don't specify a background color as different from the drawing's background, the lines around items you draw won't show up because they'll be the same color as the background. If this happens, change the background color and draw again.

USING THE TOOLS

TO USE ANY OF THE TOOLS IN THE TOOLBOX,

1. **Click on the tool you want to use. This selects the tool.**
2. **Position the cursor where you want to start drawing, selecting, or erasing, and then click and hold the mouse button.**
3. **Move into the work area and begin drawing. Move the mouse. Release when you are through.**

Once the preliminaries are out of the way, you can begin working. Unlike with the other programs supplied with Windows, using Paintbrush is largely a matter of trial and error, just as if someone gave you a brush and some paint and said "go to it." All you really need to know is the basics of each tool, a few tricks with menu options, and how to save the file and print it. The rest is up to you and your imagination.

In this section I'll explain each of the tools and suggest some tips and tricks for them. You might want to sit at your computer and work with each of the tools as you read, changing colors (if you have color), and line widths along the way. Start by creating a new file so you don't ruin one of the supplied ones. (Choose File ➤ New.) Then begin experimenting. Pretty soon you'll have a good high-tech mess on your screen, at which point you can just choose File ➤ New again to clear it and be ready for more experimentation. (When asked about saving the thing you created, click No unless you really like it.)

Figure 11.3 shows the tools icons and their names. To choose a tool, you simply click on its icon in the Toolbox. The tool is then activated (and highlighted), and the cursor changes shape when you move back into the work area. The tool stays selected until you choose another one, zoom out, or use the Paste From command. The following sections will describe each

FIGURE 11.3:

The Paintbrush Toolbox with its many tools, shown as icons

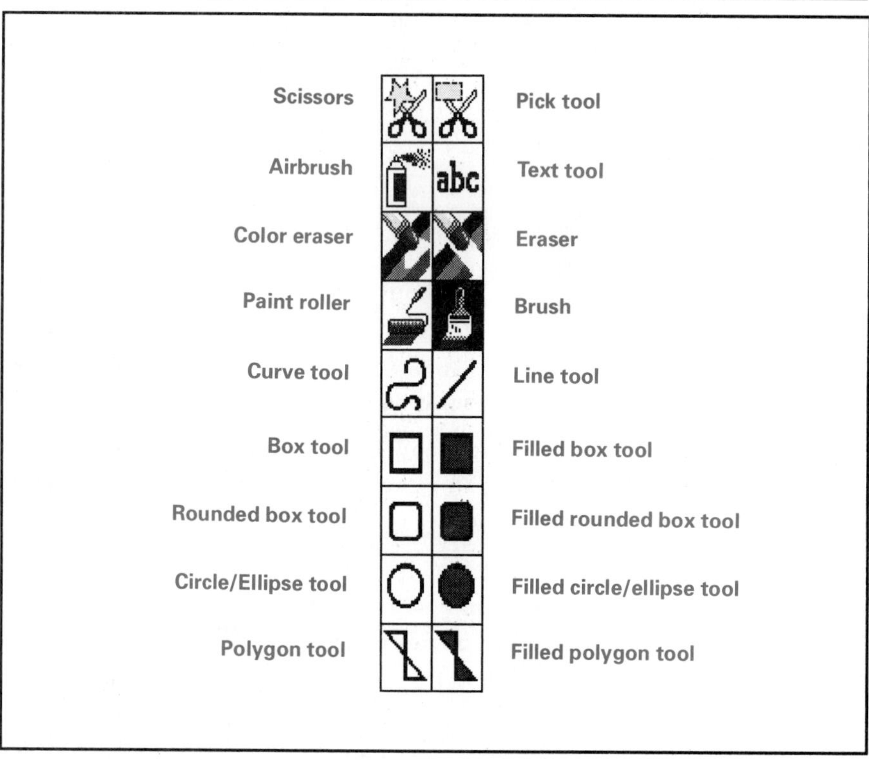

of the tools, referring to the names in the figure.

About Pasting Down

TO PASTE DOWN ITEMS YOU'VE ADDED TO THE DRAWING,

- **Reselect the current tool.**
- **Select a new tool, resize the window, or use the scroll bars. Once pasted down, an item can't be deleted without affecting the background.**

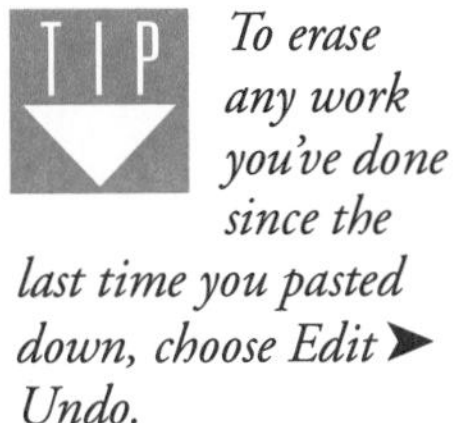

To erase any work you've done since the last time you pasted down, choose Edit ➤ Undo.

One thing you should know before moving on has to do with "pasting down" items that you draw. A nice feature of Paintbrush is that items that you add to the drawing don't immediately stick to the surface and become an irreversible part of it until you switch to another tool, use a scroll bar, open another application, or resize the window. Once you do any of these things, the new addition to the drawing gets pasted down, and what was behind it can't be reclaimed.

On the other hand, until you take any of the actions that paste down the new material, you can erase or modify what you've done with the Undo command or the Backspace key. You can make a major mistake and still not mess up your picture. Try experimenting with these options as you work with the tools.

To selectively erase some of the work you've done since the last time things were pasted down, press Backspace. The cursor will change to a box with an arrow in it. (You can adjust the size of the box by choosing a different line size.) The box is a selective eraser that erases only the unpasted material (lines, circles, airbrushing, etc.) but leaves what's behind it intact.

The Cutout Tools

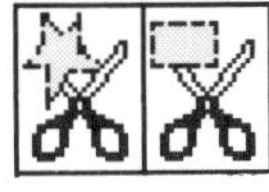

There are two tools for selecting portions of a drawing. In Paintbrush, a selection of the drawing that you cut or copy is called a *cutout.* Thus, the tools are called *cutout tools.* To differentiate them, the left one is called the Scissors tool and the right one the Pick tool (why *Pick,* I don't know).

The Scissors

The Scissors tool lets you do a free-form selection of a portion of the screen, as if using a pair of scissors, by drawing a line around the portion of the picture you want to cut or copy. It's useful because it lets you select a very specific area that can conform to the shape of an object. If you plan to paste objects together in proximity to each other, use this tool rather than the Pick tool to do the cutting. It will help to ensure that the edges of pasted items don't overlap each other.

To use the Scissors, select the tool and move to the spot where you want to start cutting. Draw a line completely around the object or area you want to cut out or alter. If you make a mistake, press the right mouse button and make the selection again.

You can move the object by dragging it with the mouse, cut or copy it, or perform other manipulations on it from the Pick menu (which are all explained in the section "Manipulating Portions of a Drawing" later in this chapter), such as inverting its colors or rotating it. The cutout area will be marked by a dotted line, as shown in Figure 11.4.

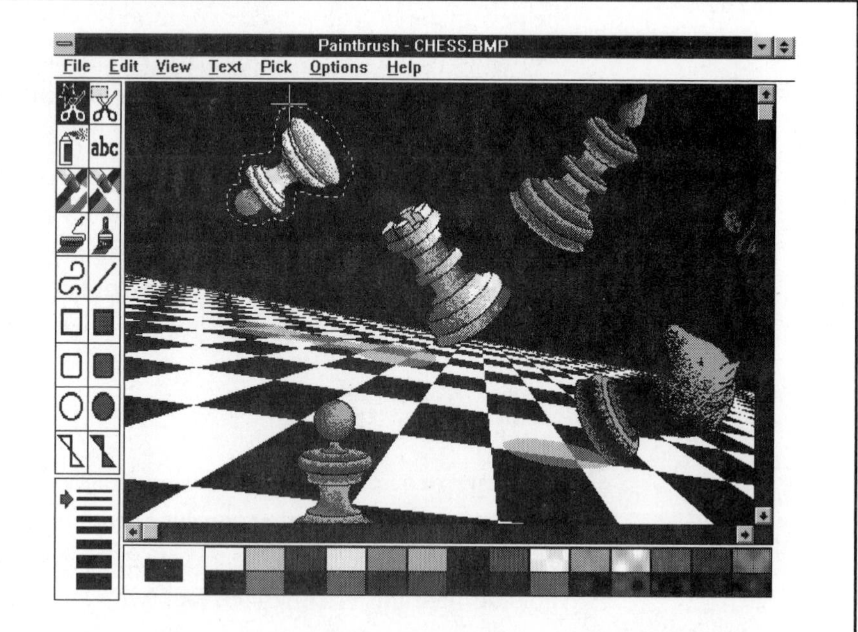

FIGURE 11.4: *You select a nonuniform cutout area with the Scissors tool. A dotted line indicates the cutout.*

The Pick Tool

The only difference between the Pick tool and the Scissors is that the Pick tool selects a rectangular area. It's faster to use, since you just drag the mouse to define a boxed area. You can easily select the entire drawing if you need to:

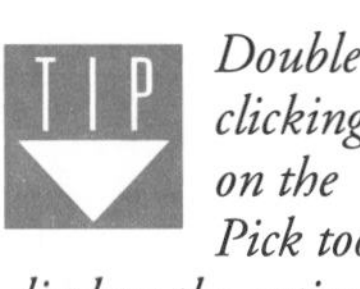

Double-clicking on the Pick tool displays the entire drawing, even portions outside the window. Click again to bring back the Paintbrush window.

1. Select the Pick tool.
2. Move to the upper-left corner of the boxed area you want to select. Click and hold the left mouse button.
3. Drag the mouse down and to the right. Release the button. A dotted line indicates the area of cutout. Once again, you can cut, copy, or drag the cutout, or use the commands on the Pick menu.

Figure 11.5 shows the results of copying and dragging.

If you hold the Shift key while dragging any cutout, the original cutout will be left in place. This is similar to copying and pasting, but easier. If you press the right mouse button when dragging, the image will be copied opaquely. That is, the background and image in the cutout will overlay and

FIGURE 11.5:
Once a cutout is defined, you can manipulate it in a variety of ways. Here you see chess pieces from the CHESS.BMP file copied and placed across the drawing.

obscure what's behind it. If you drag using the left button, the image will be copied transparently (any background color and image behind the selection will show through), assuming that the background of the cutout and the current selected background color are the same. By selecting an area, then shift-dragging, releasing the button, and shift-dragging again and again, you can create a repeated pattern of the same image.

If you drag the cutout, the background color is what shows through from behind. If you change the background color and then drag another selection, the background color for the second hole will be different from the first, even though the background color for the entire drawing does not change.

Saving and Retrieving a Cutout

You can save a cutout on a disk file for later use. Using this technique, you can create a stockpile of little graphics (like clip-art) which you can call up from disk to drop into new drawings. Here are the steps to save and retrieve a cutout:

1. Select the cutout with either of the cutout tools.
2. Choose Edit ➤ Copy To. A file box pops up. Name the file as you wish.
3. When you want to reload the cutout, choose Edit ➤ Load From, choose the cutout or picture file from the file box. It will land into the upper-left corner of the current drawing onscreen.
4. Reposition the cutout by dragging it.

The Airbrush

Here's a tool that's a legal outlet for repressed graffiti artists. The Airbrush works like a can of spray paint. It uses the selected foreground color, and as long as you hold the mouse button down, it sprays away. Think of the mouse button as the button on the top of the spray can:

1. Click on the color or pattern you want the Airbrush to spray.

You can make selective corrections to new items by hitting Backspace and moving the eraser square over your new material. This is particularly useful for touching up after the Airbrush.

2. Click on the line width that you want the spray to have.
3. Position the cursor in the work area and press the left mouse button.
4. Move the mouse around and spray the color onto the work area. Note that the speed of movement affects the density of the spray, just as it does with a real spray can: moving the mouse quickly results in a finer mist, while letting it sit still or moving very slowly plasters the paint on solid.

Figure 11.6 shows an example of some airbrushed writing.

The Eraser

As its icon suggests, the Eraser works like the eraser on a pencil—only you don't have to rub. Just passing it across an area erases whatever it touches, leaving nothing but the background color behind. Use the Eraser when you want to obliterate something that's already pasted down or when you want

FIGURE 11.6:
The Airbrush works like a spray can. Just point and spray.

to touch up some stray dots or lines:

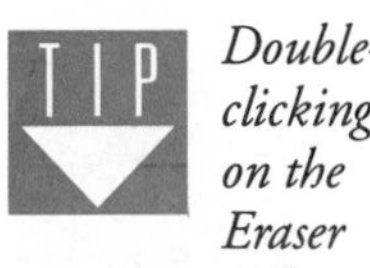

Double-clicking on the Eraser opens a new document. If you've modified the current file, you'll first be asked to save it.

1. Select the Eraser. The cursor will change to a hollow box when moved into the work area.
2. Set the background color to the same color as the area you're erasing in. If you don't, the object you erase will disappear, but it will be replaced by another background color.
3. Set the line width to determine the width of the Eraser. For fine work, use the thinnest setting.
4. Drag the mouse over the material you want to erase. Hold the Shift key down while moving the mouse if you want to constrict the mouse pointer's movement to just the vertical or horizontal direction.

Figure 11.7 shows the effect of dragging the Eraser over the TARTAN.BMP drawing. Notice that all colors have been replaced with the background color. Selecting a nonmatching background color and then using the Eraser with the line width set to maximum is a fast way of drawing really fat swaths

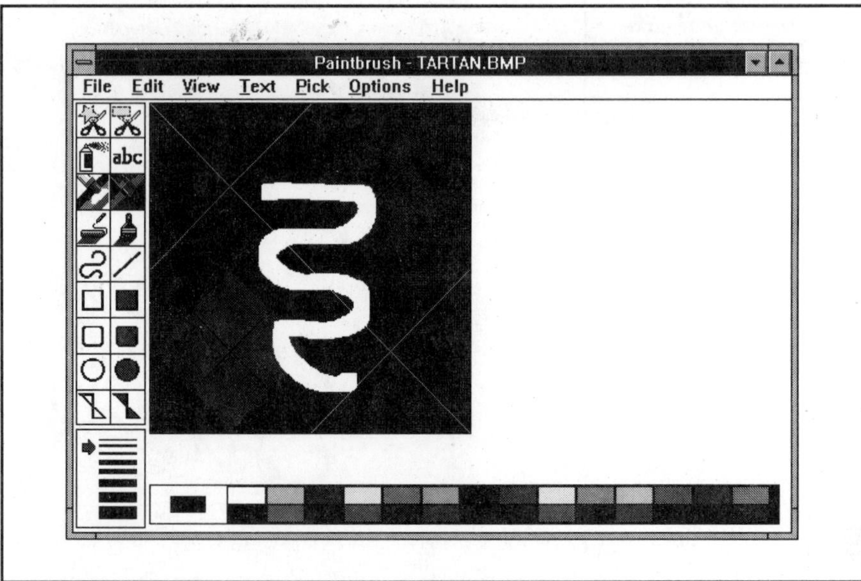

FIGURE 11.7: *Use the Eraser to remove any part of the drawing. The current background color will show through.*

of any color. Just keep changing the background color and then erasing another section of the screen. The lines of color are wider than those available with the Brush or the Airbrush.

THE COLOR ERASER

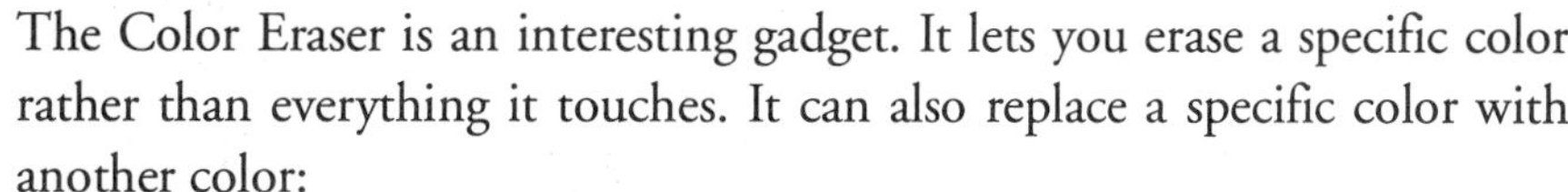

The Color Eraser is an interesting gadget. It lets you erase a specific color rather than everything it touches. It can also replace a specific color with another color:

1. Select the Color Eraser (it's the eraser on the left). The cursor changes to a box with a plus sign in it when moved into the work area.

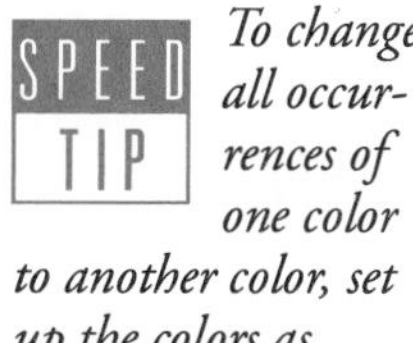

To change all occurrences of one color to another color, set up the colors as described and double-click on the Color Eraser.

2. Choose the color you want to erase by clicking in the Palette with the left button.
3. Choose the color you want to replace the erased color with by clicking in the Palette with the right button. (What you're really doing here is assigning the background color.)
4. Set the line width to adjust the size of the eraser.
5. Press the mouse button and move the eraser over the area to be erased. If you have set the backgound color to match the pre-existing background, the effect of erasing will be to neutralize the color. If you have set it to another color, the effect will be that of replacing the existing color with a new color. This is a great feature that makes changing the color scheme of a drawing really easy.

Figure 11.8 shows the effect of dragging the Color Eraser over the TARTAN.BMP drawing. Notice that only the selected (foreground) color has been replaced with the background color. The Color Eraser was set to the largest line width in this instance.

THE BRUSH

The Brush works like a paint brush, pen, or marker. Use this tool to create freehand drawings:

1. Choose the Brush icon.

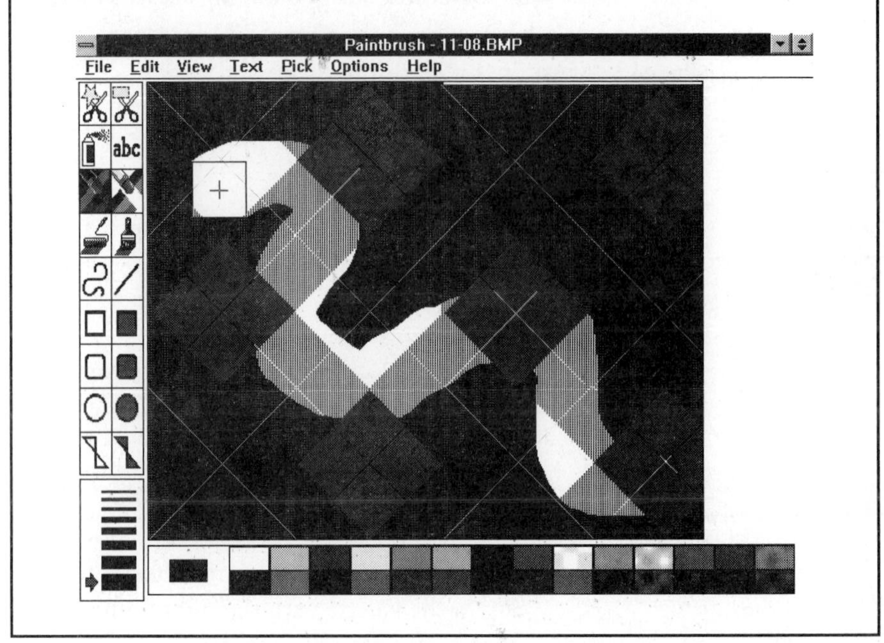

FIGURE 11.8:

Use the Color Eraser to remove a specific color or replace that color with a new one.

You can open the Brush Shapes box quickly by double-clicking on the Brush icon.

2. Select the color and width.
3. Press the left button and start drawing. Hold the button down as long as you want to continue the line. Release the button when you want to stop drawing the line. Repeat the process to draw another line.

If you hold the Shift key down while using the brush, only horizontal or vertical lines will result. You can change the brush shape if you want for special effects. Choose Options ➤ Brush Shapes. The following dialog box will appear:

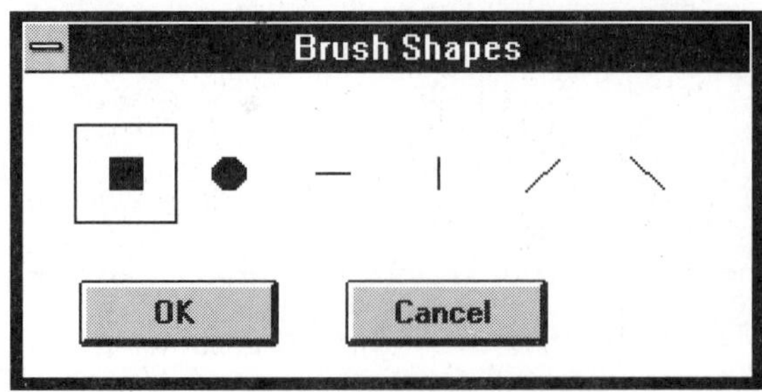

Choose the shape you want and click on OK. All subsequent drawings will use the shape. Figure 11.9 shows a simple brush drawing.

The Line Tool

Use the Line tool to draw straight lines:

1. Select the tool.
2. Select the color and width.
3. Move into the work area. The cursor becomes a cross hair.
4. Press and hold the left button, and move the mouse. A straight line will appear between the beginning (anchor) point and the end point.
5. Move the end point around until you are satisfied with its location, even in a circle around the anchor point.
6. Release the button when you want to stop drawing the line.

TIP *Hold the Shift key down to constrain the line to be vertical, horizontal, or at 45 degrees.*

Figure 11.10 shows an example of a drawing made up only of lines.

FIGURE 11.9:
A freehand drawing made with the brush

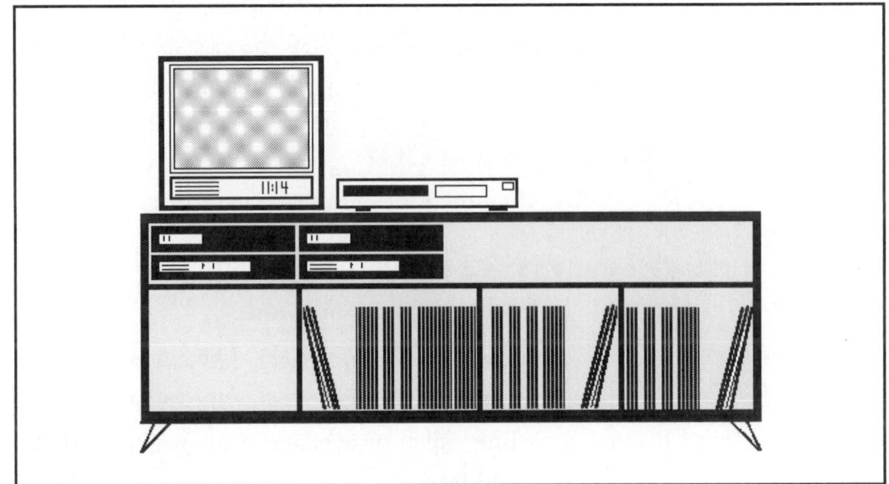

FIGURE 11.10:

You can create drawings such as this with only the line tool and the Shift key. (You could, however, shorten the task with the Box tool.)

To help you align objects such as lines, choose View ➤ Cursor Position. The column and row of the current position will then be displayed in the upper-right corner of the window. The units of measurement are determined by the Image Attributes dialog box.

Here's another tip: If you want to erase a line quickly and start over without having to use Undo, Backspace, or the Eraser, *don't* release the left button. Keep it down and press the right button, too. This will erase only the line you are drawing. (Remember, Undo erases everything not pasted down.) This also applies to the Curve, Box, Filled Box, Rounded Box, Filled Rounded Box, Circle/Ellipse, Filled Circle/Ellipse, Polygon, and Filled Polygon tools.

The Curve Tool

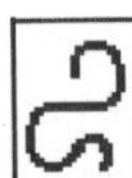

The Curve is a strange tool. It works like the line initially, but then allows you two chances to "pull" the line you've drawn—once from one location, and then once from another—to make a curved line. The result might be something of a semicircle, or it might be more like an S shape:

1. Choose the Curve tool and use the same techniques as for drawing a line.

2. Once the line is drawn, release the mouse button.
3. Move the cursor to one side of the line, hold down the left mouse button, and drag the cursor away from or towards the line. As you do so, the line will stretch like a rubber band. Release the button when the bend is correct.
4. If you don't want to add another bend to the line, click on the endpoint (not the anchor-point end).
5. If you want to add another bend, move near another position on the line, such as on the other side of it, and drag the cursor again. The line will again stretch like a rubber band. When you are satisfied with the final line shape, release the mouse button. The color and width will then be added to the line.

Figure 11.11 shows the process of drawing a curve.

FIGURE 11.11:

The three steps in creating a curved line: draw a straight line, bend it one way, then bend it another

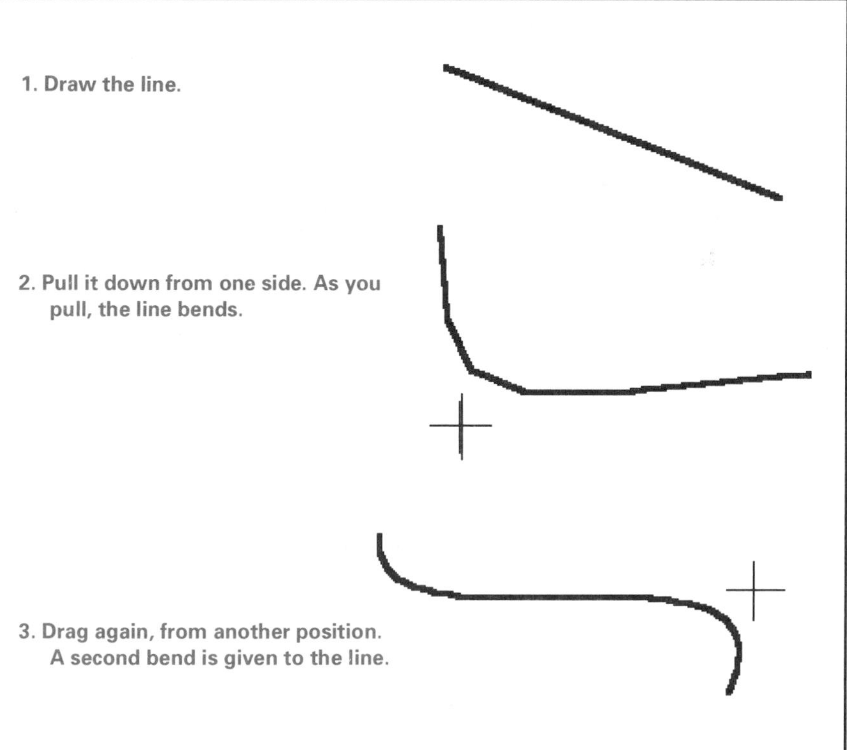

The Box and Filled Box Tools

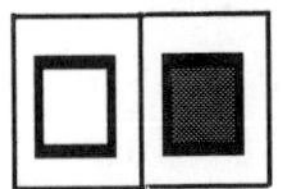

The Box tool draws boxes and rectangles. The boxes are hollow and the box's border appears in the foreground color:

1. Select the tool.
2. Set the color and line width.
3. Click where you want one corner of the box to start. This sets the anchor.
4. Drag the cross hair down and to one side. As you do, a flexible frame will appear.
5. Release the mouse button when the size is correct. (You can erase the box you've just drawn by pressing the left and right mouse buttons.)

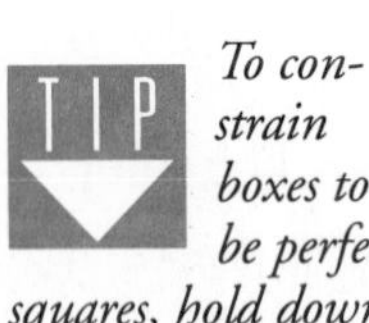

To constrain boxes to be perfect squares, hold down the Shift key as you draw. This applies to filled boxes as well as to hollow ones.

The filled box works the same way. However, the filled box uses the foreground color for its insides and the background color for its border. Set both colors before drawing. If you want a solid box of a single color, set the foreground and background to the same color.

The Rounded Box and Filled Rounded Box Tools

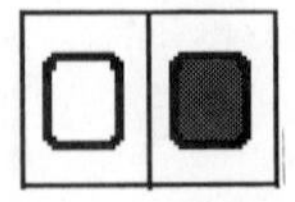

These two tools are identical in operation to the Box and Filled Box. The only difference lies in their appearance—their corners are rounded instead of having sharp 90-degree angles.

The Circle/Ellipse and Filled Circle/Ellipse Tools

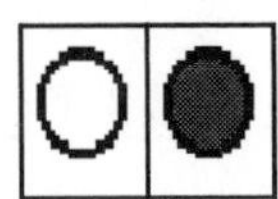

These two tools again work in much the same way as the Box, only they create circles and ellipses (ovals). Use the same basic drawing technique. The rules regarding the fill and border colors of boxes apply to ellipses, too. Figure 11.12 shows a healthy population of bubble-like objects created with the Filled Circle ➤ Ellipse tool and the Shift key. The Shift key was used to constrain ellipses to be perfect circles.

FIGURE 11.12: *Perfect circles are created with the Shift key and the Circle/ Ellipse or Filled Circle/Ellipse tools.*

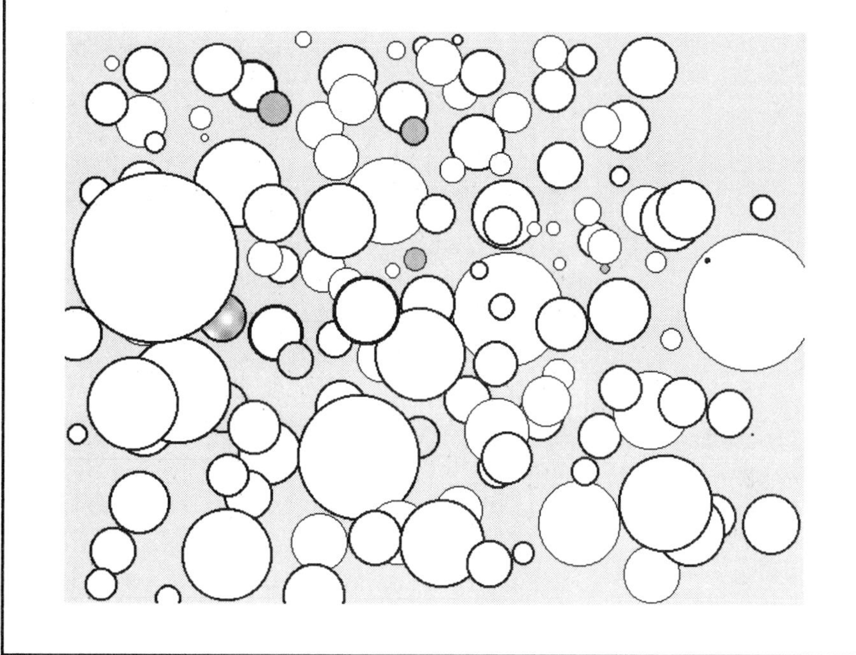

THE POLYGON AND FILLED POLYGON TOOLS

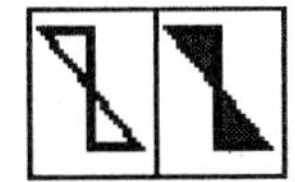

The Polygon and Filled Polygon tools are similar to the Line tool, except that you can keep adding more and more endpoints. Paintbrush then connects them all. With these tools, you can create an endless variety of polygonal shapes, and they come in handy for quickly creating irregularly shaped objects. You could draw them by hand with the brush, but it's usually easier with the Polygon tools. The filled polygon is even more fun because of the way it fills:

TIP *To constrain the lines of the polygon to be vertical, at 45 degrees, or horizontal only, hold down the Shift key as you draw.*

1. Select the tool.
2. Select the color and line width.
3. Click where you want the first anchor point to be and hold the button down.
4. Move to the point you want a straight line drawn to and release. A line will appear, sort of "connecting the dots." This defines the first side of the polygon.

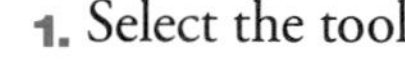

5. Move to the next point and click again. Another line will be drawn. Continue this until you have drawn all the lines in your polygon. When you want to stop the drawing, double-click. (The last and first points will be connected by Paintbrush if you don't line them up.)

Note that a polygon's sides can cross each other, as in the tool's icon. The polygons don't have to be symmetrically shaped the way hexagons or octagons are. You can haphazardly click all over the screen and, until you double-click, Paintbrush will keep connecting the dots.

The filled polygon is created the same way. Only in this case, Paintbrush will fill the inside of the polygon with the foreground color. (The background color, just as with filled circles and boxes, determines the border color.)

Here's a tip: If you want to see the lines as you are drawing them (as opposed to when you click), modify the technique a bit by clicking and holding as if drawing a normal line. When you reach the desired endpoint for the first line, release the button. Then, keeping the mouse still, click and hold again while drawing the next line.

You can create a cubist artistic effect with this tool because of the way Paintbrush calculates an "enclosed" area. It starts at the top of the screen and begins filling areas. If your polygon has lots of enclosed areas from multiple lines overlapping, Paintbrush alternates the fills. Thus adjacent enclosed areas will not all be filled. Using the tool with the cutout tools and the Inverse command can lead to some rather interesting geometrical designs. (Inverting is covered next in "Manipulating Portions of a Drawing.") Figure 11.13 shows an example of what can be done with this tool.

THE PAINT ROLLER

I've put off discussing the Paint Roller since using it requires understanding the other tools a bit. The Roller will fill in any enclosed area with the foreground color, unless the area has already been filled with one of the colors that has a grainy texture (any of the last 12 colors on the right side of the Palette). An *enclosed area* can be defined by any lines or curves in the drawing area. So three separate lines set up to form a triangle constitute an enclosed

FIGURE 11.13:

A geometric design created with the Filled Polygon tool

space just as much as a box's border does. Since the entire drawing area is also considered an enclosed space, you can use the roller to change the background of the drawing. Letters you create with the Text tool (discussed next) can be filled, too:

1. Select the tool.
2. Choose the foreground color for the fill.
3. Point the Roller's sharp edge at the item to be filled and click. The enclosed area will be filled with the foreground color.

Note that the color flows to fill the entire enclosed area. If there is a leak in what you thought was an enclosed area, the "paint" will seep through the crack, so to speak, and fill everything until it is stopped by a complete boundary. You may accidentally fill the entire work area. If this happens, just choose Undo.

The Text Tool

The Text tool lets you put characters on your creations. This is convenient when designing flyers, invitations, maps, instructions, and the like. The fonts and sizes of text you can use are determined by the printer you have installed:

1. Choose the Text tool.
2. Choose the style of type from the Text menu. Note that Regular turns off all the other options. Bold, Italic, and Underline can all be on at one time. Only one of Outline or Shadow can be on at a time.
3. Choose the color for the text via the Palette. Shadows and Outlines use the background color, while the text itself will appear in the foreground color.
4. Pick the type size and typeface you want to use via the Text ➤ Fonts dialog box. This is a standard Font box like that in Write and other applications.
5. Place the cursor where you want to start typing and click.

This marks the insertion point's position. There isn't any word-wrapping, so you'll have to use the Enter key to break a long line. You can erase mistakes with the Backspace key until you paste the text down. You can also change the style, size, font, and color of text until you paste the text down. (See "About Pasting Down" earlier in this chapter.) After text is pasted down, you'll have to use the Eraser or the cutout tools to delete it. Figure 11.14 shows some of the type styles available on my system. Yours may differ, depending on your printer.

MANIPULATING PORTIONS OF A DRAWING

So much for the tools. Now for the goodies. All the major goodies except for one are on the Pick menu. The Pick menu is dimmed until you select a cutout area. Once you do, you can open the menu and select commands from it. The following sections describe these commands.

FIGURE 11.14:

Some type styles produced with the Text tool on my system. They may differ from yours.

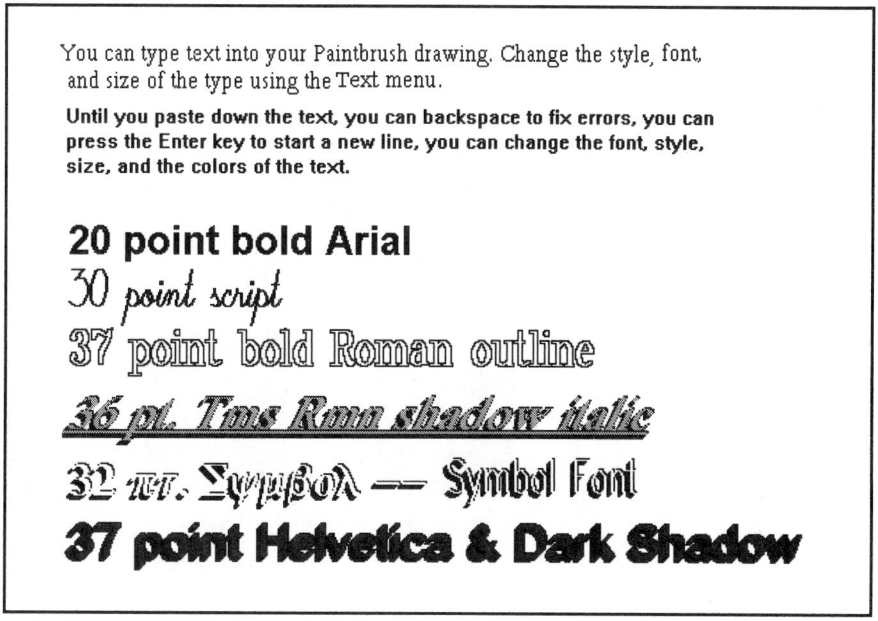

You can type text into your Paintbrush drawing. Change the style, font, and size of the type using the Text menu.

Until you paste down the text, you can backspace to fix errors, you can press the Enter key to start a new line, you can change the font, style, size, and the colors of the text.

20 point bold Arial

30 point script

37 point bold Roman outline

36 pt. Tms Rmn shadow italic

32 πτ. Σψμβολ — Symbol Font

37 point Helvetica & Dark Shadow

Flip Horizontal and Flip Vertical

Flip Horizontal and Flip Vertical are simple commands. They just flip the selected cutout around, just as if you took a color slide out of a projector, turned it over, and put it back in. The picture is reversed, either horizontally or vertically. You can use this command to create symmetrical drawings and patterns by defining a cutout of an existing shape, copying the cutout, pasting it into the same picture, flipping it, and repositioning it. This way, you don't have to draw the shape several times in different directions. Figure 11.15 shows an example.

To try the Flip commands,

1. Select the cutout with one of the cutout tools.
2. Copy and paste the cutout if you want. When you paste, the pasted material is automatically selected as the cutout, so commands will only affect *it*, not the original.
3. Choose Pick ➤ Flip Horizontal or Pick ➤ Flip Vertical. The selected cutout will be flipped appropriately.

FIGURE 11.15:

Cutouts flipped horizontally and vertically

Inverse

Inverse reverses the color in the cutout. Thus black will turn to white and white will turn to black. If you're working in color, the colors will turn to their complements. *Complementary colors* are defined here as being the color on the opposite side of the RGB (Red, Green, Blue) color wheel. This is a really fun tool. Try selecting several slightly overlapping squares of a picture and inverting them in sequence. An example is shown in Figure 11.16.

To try this,

1. Select the area to have its colors inverted.
2. Choose Pick ➤ Inverse.

Shrink and Grow

Shrink and Grow is a command that lets you increase or decrease the size of a selected area. Suppose you drew a section of a diagram too small. Rather than erasing it and drawing it again, you could increase its size with this command. You can also use this command to repeat patterns or shapes by copying and pasting in various sizes of the drawing.

To maintain the exact proportions of the cutout, hold down the Shift key while selecting it. This selects it in a perfect square. Then hold down Shift while creating each new box.

To try this command:

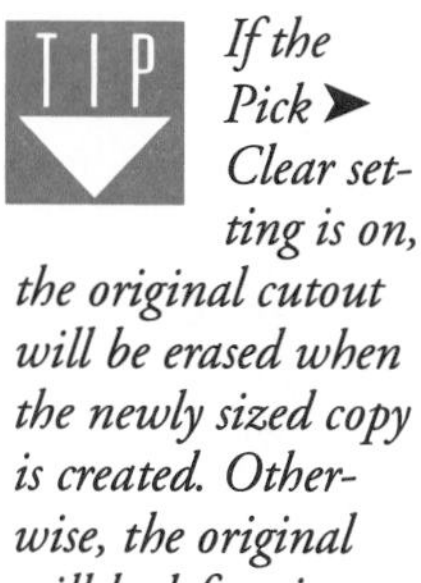

If the Pick ➤ Clear setting is on, the original cutout will be erased when the newly sized copy is created. Otherwise, the original will be left as is.

1. Select the cutout area to be enlarged or shrunk.
2. Select Pick ➤ Shrink and Grow.
3. With the cross-hair cursor, draw a box roughly approximating the size at which you want the cutout to appear. When you release the mouse button, the cutout appears in the box in its new size.
4. Repeat the last step as many times as you want, replicating the cutout in a variety of sizes. You can distort the image's proportions by drawing boxes that are substantially different in proportion from the original cutout. See Figure 11.17.

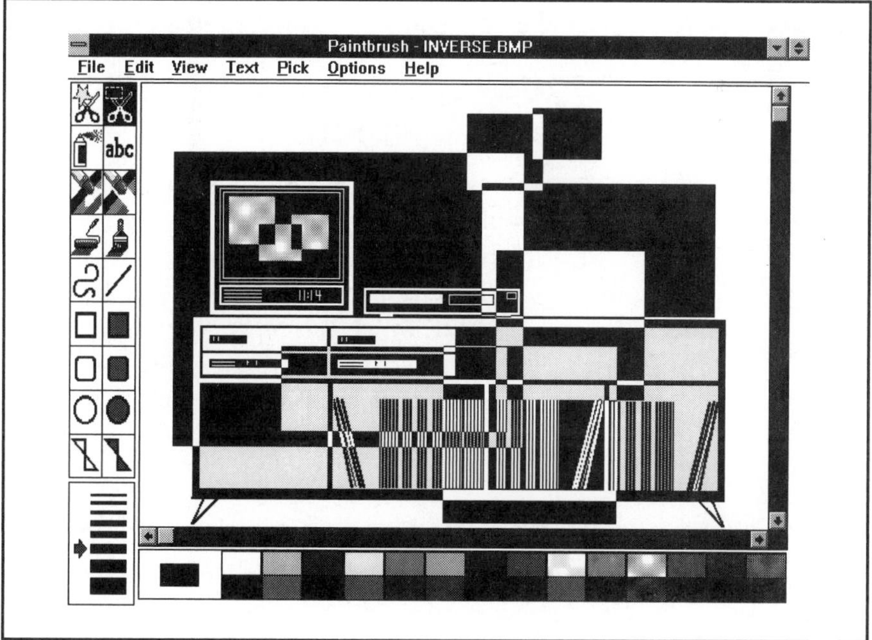

FIGURE 11.16:

Inverting a section of a drawing by selecting the cutout area and then choosing Pick ➤ Inverse

FIGURE 11.17:

Stretched and shrunken rooks

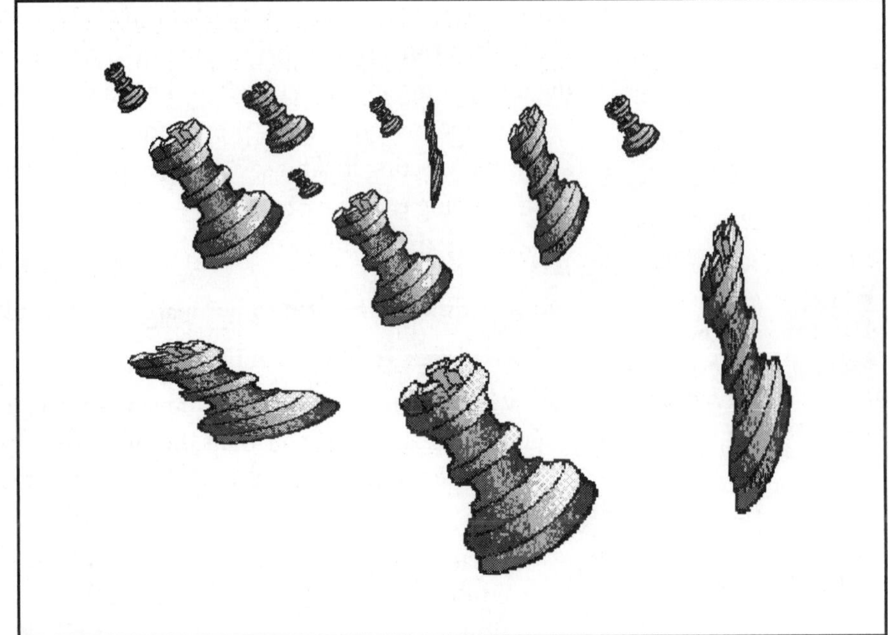

TILT

If the Pick ➤ Clear setting is on, the original cutout will be erased when the newly tilted copy is created. Otherwise, the original will be left as is.

The Tilt command lets you stretch a cutout on a slant:

1. Select a cutout area.
2. Choose Pick ➤ Tilt.
3. Move the cursor to a new location and then click and hold down the mouse button. A box the exact size of the cutout area will appear. Keep the mouse button down and move the mouse left and right. The box will tilt like a parallelogram about the anchor point, which is its upper-left corner. Release the button when the box is tilted the way you want. You'll probably have to experiment a few times to get it to look the way you want it.

If you position the cursor close to the same location as the original anchor point of the cutout, the tilted version will overlay the original, as you see at the bottom of Figure 11.18.

FIGURE 11.18:

Examples of tilting. Notice that tilting can grossly distort an object and can also give text that "Star Wars" movie-credits look.

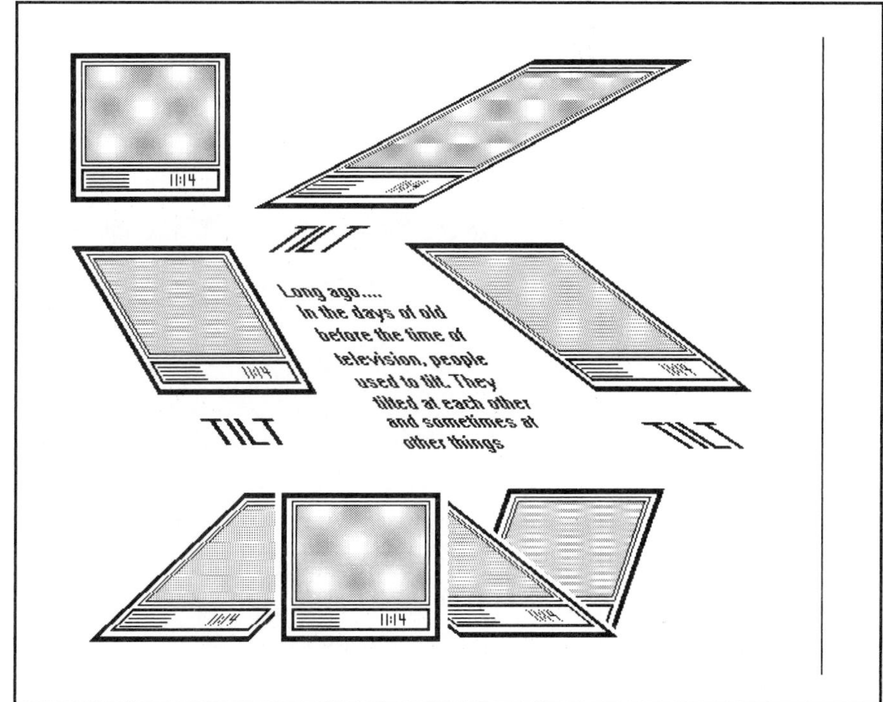

SWEEPING

Sweeping a cutout is a neat trick that smears numerous copies of the cutout across the drawing area as you move the mouse. You can use this technique to suggest motion of an object or to create interesting artistic effects.

To try it,

1. Select a cutout area.
2. Drag the cutout area while holding the Shift key down. Copies of the cutout are made as you drag the cursor around.

As with copying, you can do opaque or transparent sweeping. Transparent sweeping lets the images in the background show through the cutout you're sweeping. Opaque sweeping overlays them. Press the right mouse button when dragging to create opaque sweeping, or the left button for transparent. The background color of the cutout and the current background color have to be the same for transparent sweeping to work. Figure 11.19 shows an example of sweeping.

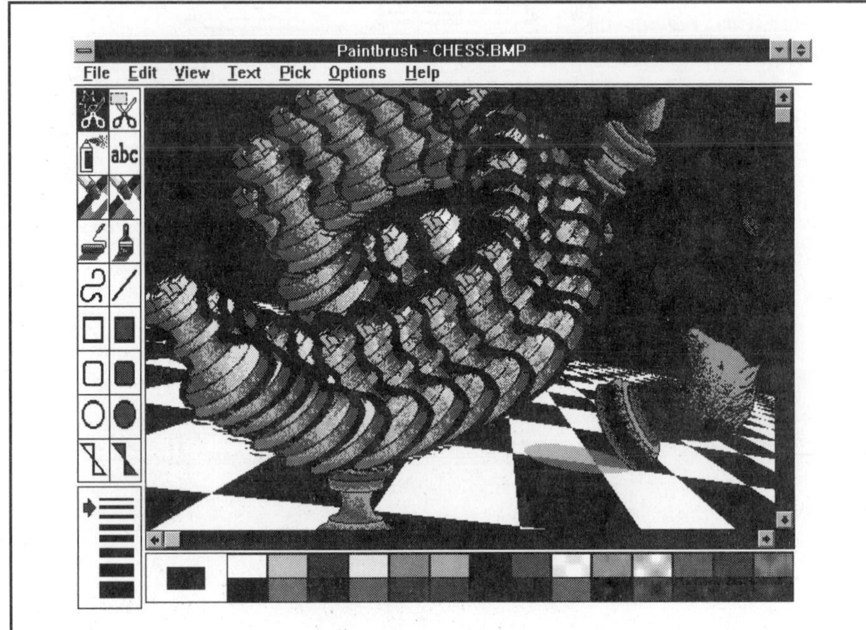

FIGURE 11.19:

Sweeping a cutout makes numerous copies on a single sweep of the mouse.

PIXEL EDITING

Pixel editing lets you blow up a portion of the drawing to do "microsurgery" on it. In this mode, the pixels in your drawing seem to become quite large, so that you can fine-tune them. This is useful for smoothing out lines, creating highlights on objects, creating minute patterns, and so forth.

To edit the pixels of an image,

1. Choose View ➤ Zoom In. The cursor becomes a box on the screen. (If it doesn't, you were zoomed out. Choose Zoom In again.)
2. Position the box over the area you want to fine tune and click. The screen changes dramatically, showing a closeup of the section. The normally sized section you're working with is displayed in the upper-left corner of the work area and will reflect any changes you make. The cursor becomes a pointer. Figure 11.20 shows an example.
3. Each time you click on a little box with the left button (which represents a pixel in normal size), the selected foreground color is assigned to it. Use the right button to assign the background color to the pixel. Basically, you just paint in the picture, dot by dot. Change the colors assigned to the mouse buttons whenever you want. You can use the Roller while pixel editing, too.
4. When you're happy with the state of things, choose View ➤ Zoom Out.

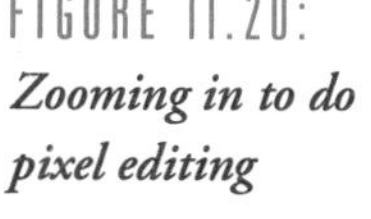
FIGURE 11.20:
Zooming in to do pixel editing

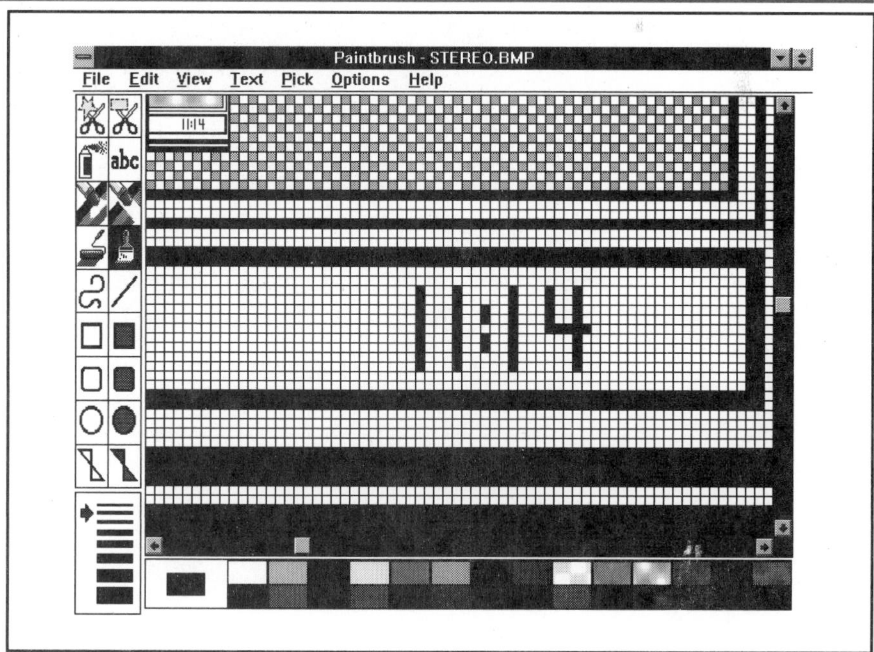

EDITING THE COLORS

Double-click on a color in the Palette to open the Edit Colors dialog box for that color.

If you are working in color, you may want to create custom colors. If you are working in black-and-white, you may want to create a new pattern. To do either,

1. Select a color or pattern you want to fine tune (or even radically change, say, if you never use it).
2. Choose Options ➤ Edit Colors.
3. The dialog box you see below will appear. Move the sliders. As you do this, the resulting color or pattern is displayed in the box to the right of the sliders. If you are working in black-and-white, the sliders all move together, changing from lighter to darker patterns. You can't adjust them individually. When you are satisfied, click on OK. Click Cancel to drop the changes or Reset to put the sliders back in their original positions to begin again. (Note that the changes you make do not affect any drawing you did with that color or pattern previously.)

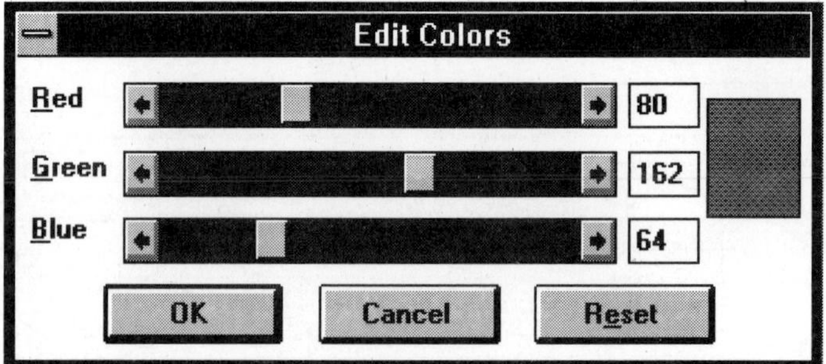

Save the color settings for a drawing with the Options ➤ Save Colors command. You can also load a color-settings file with the Options ➤ Get Colors command. Your colors will be used until you reload Paintbrush or change them again in the same session. Paintbrush uses the default colors unless you load a specific color set.

SAVING YOUR WORK

As you work, you'll want to remember two things. The first is that you should paste something down whenever you don't want to lose it. The easiest way to do this is to select another tool, or even the same tool you're using. By pasting down work you're satisfied with, you won't accidentally lose it when you press Backspace or issue the Undo command. Second, you should save your work to disk occasionally.

SAVING FILES

You can save files in a variety of formats. Normally, however, you can just let Paintbrush take care of the saving process.

When you open, edit, and then close a file, Paintbrush uses the same format it was created in. When you save a file for the first time, Paintbrush uses the Windows bit-mapped format, unless you stipulate otherwise by clicking on options. Here are the formats and their descriptions:

PCX: Paintbrush format. This is a graphics file format that can be used by many graphics programs. Originated by Paintbrush.

Monochrome Bitmap: For non-color Paintbrush bit maps.

16-Color Bitmap: Use when you have 16 colors or fewer in your picture.

256-Color Bitmap: Use when you have more than 16 and fewer than 257 colors in your picture.

24-bit Bitmap: Use when you have more than 256 colors in the picture. (This is highly unlikely.)

Microsoft suggests using the bit-mapped formats over other formats so that you can be assured of using the pictures with later versions of Windows. However, many more programs use PCX files than the proprietary Windows bit-mapped formats at this time. It's up to you. Decide which other programs you'll use the files with. Note that the more colors you save, the larger the files become, and the more disk and RAM space they'll need. Sixteen-color bitmapped files are roughly eight times larger than PCX files of the same drawing. (Incidentally, you cannot save a file in Microsoft Paint format.)

LOADING FILES

When you open a file, the default extension is .BMP. If you want to load a .PCX file or .MSP (Microsoft Paint) file, click on the appropriate button in the File ➤ Open dialog box. The file box will then show only files with the correct extension. Find the file using the boxes or type in its name. If you are loading an .MSP file, Paintbrush will ask if you want to convert it. *Once you convert it you won't be able to get it back to MSP format.*

If you want to scan in a printed image or photograph, use software and hardware that produce .BMP, .MSP, or .PCX files. Unfortunately, Paintbrush doesn't read .TIF files, so loading in a gray-scaled image is not possible. Incidentally, Paste From gives you more flexibility than Open, because you can determine the overall drawing size and reposition the pasted image. If you just open a drawing, it's likely to be stuck in the upper-left corner.

PRINTING YOUR PICTURE

Finally, you might want to print out your work! Here's how you do it:

1. Open the file.
2. Prepare the printer.
3. Choose File ➤ Page Setup. Set up the margins and headers and footers (if you want them).
4. Choose File ➤ Printer Setup and make sure the right printer is connected.

5. Choose File ➤ Print. The Print dialog box will appear, as you see below:

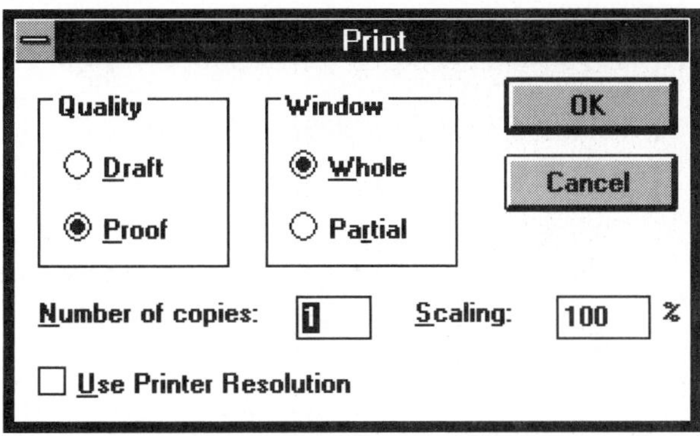

Make the settings as follows:

Quality: *Draft* prints in the fastest possible mode for your printer. *Proof* (the default) prints in the highest resolution.

Window: *Whole* prints the whole drawing. *Partial,* when selected, displays the whole drawing on the screen when you click on OK. From there you define a section to print by drawing a box.

Number of Copies: Type in the number of copies you want printed.

Use Printer Resolution: You can print in screen or printer resolution. If you use printer resolution, the picture will probably be more detailed, but it will take longer to print. You might also get some distortion in the printed output if you use printer resolution, since the height-to-width ratio may be different for the printer than for the screen, and Paintbrush doesn't compensate for this.

Scaling: If you want to increase the size of the picture, choose a percentage above 100. Percentages below 100 shrink the picture. Large scaling changes can have unpredictable effects on some printers. Experimentation is the key to success, here, I'm afraid. Remember that the size of the picture is best determined in the first step of creating it—setting the image attributes. And don't forget that you can scale a drawing with the Shrink and Grow command. Just select the whole drawing and stretch or shrink it.

You can add explanatory text, page numbers, the file name, and page numbers on your printed pages. You can also control the alignment of the header and footer.

To print a header or footer on a drawing,

1. Choose File ➤ Page Setup. The Page Setup dialog box appears.
2. In the Header and/or Footer box, enter the text you want to use as a header or footer, along with any of the codes that can be used in these boxes, as shown below. If your text exceeds the length of the box, the text area in the box will scroll.
3. Click on OK.

Table 11.1 shows the codes you can type in the Header and Footer boxes. You can include any combination of these codes in your headers or footers. Regardless of how margins are set, headers always print out at the top of the page (in the margin) and footers always print out at the bottom of the page (in the margin).

TABLE 11.1: *Codes to add to headers and footers*

CODE	EFFECT
&d	The current system date
&p	Page numbers
&f	The drawing's file name
&l	Header or Footer text (following this code) will be left aligned
&r	Header or Footer text (following the code) will be right aligned
&c	Header or Footer text (following the code) will be centered (default)
&t	The current time

FAST TRACK

CHAPTER

12

FAST TRACK

About the Notepad: 398

It's an ASCII text editor. Use it to create and edit nonformatted text files, including system files such as AUTOEXEC.BAT and CONFIG.SYS. Files can be up to 50K. Double-click on the Notepad icon in the Accessories group to run it.

To search for text in a Notepad file, ... 402

choose Search ➤ Find. Type in the text you want to search for and choose Forward or Backward to determine the search direction.

About the Cardfile: 403

It lets you keep track of small scraps of information on cards. Each card has an index line and a section for your notes. To run the Cardfile, double-click on the Cardfile icon in the Accessories group.

To add a Cardfile card, ... 404

press F6 to enter your first card. For subsequent cards, press F7. Type an identifying word or phrase into the Index dialog box. Click OK. Type the data into the information area of the card.

To search for a specific card (by index line), ... 406

choose Search ➤ Go To or press F4. Type in two letters or more and click OK. Press Ctrl and the cursor jumps to the index line of a card that starts with that letter.

To search through the text on all cards, ... 408

choose Search ➤ Find. Type in the search text and click on OK. Choose Search ➤ Find Next to find the next card.

About the Calendar: 414

It's a utility that keeps track of your appointments. Double-click on Calendar in the accessories group to run it. Type in your appointments next to the times. To change the time increments, choose Options ➤ Day Settings. See the whole month by choosing View ➤ Month. Click on the scroll buttons to move between days and months.

About the Recorder: 421

It's a macro recording and playback utility. It can record all keyboard and mouse actions. Double-click on the Recorder icon in the Accessories group to run it.

To record a macro, ... 421

position the cursor where you want the macro to begin and switch to the Recorder window. Choose Macro ➤ Record. Fill in the macro name and a shortcut key. Click on OK. Perform the actions you want to record. Press Ctrl-Break to stop recording.

To play back a macro, ... 425

press the assigned shortcut key or double-click on the macro's name in the Recorder window.

CHAPTER 12

FEATURING

Using Notepad, Cardfile, Calendar, Calculator, Clock, Recorder, and Character Map

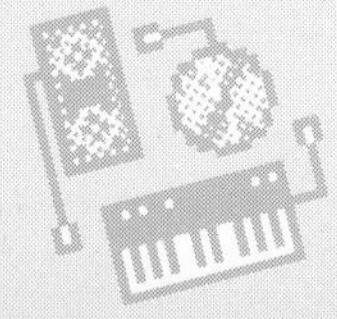

The Other Accessories

There are a few Windows accessories that I haven't discussed yet. They're not terribly complicated programs, and you may already have figured out how to use them just through experimentation or by running them and reading their Help screens. They are the following:

Notepad: for reading and writing short to medium-length text files

Cardfile: for recording and looking up short bits of information, something like a Rolodex or box of index cards

Calendar: for keeping track of appointments and organizing your daily schedule

Calculator: for performing standard arithmetic as well as scientific computations

Clock: for displaying the time and, if desired, the date on your Desktop

Recorder: for memorizing your typing and mouse movements and automating them for you; it's also used for creating automatic demonstrations of Windows programs

Character Map: for easily inserting characters into your document that aren't on your keyboard

Four other programs are discussed in subsequent chapters. The PIF Editor is discussed in Chapter 13. The File Associations Editor and Packager are discussed in Chapter 14 since they deal with DDE and OLE. Sysedit is discussed in Chapter 14. Media Player and Sound Recorder are covered in Chapter 15. The two supplied games—Solitaire and Minesweeper—are discussed in Chapter 20.

JOTTING DOWN NOTES WITH NOTEPAD

Think of Notepad as a scaled-down version of Write. It works similarly, but sports few frills. When you want to jot down some fairly lengthy notes, type up a quick memo with no fancy formatting, or read or print an existing text file (straight ASCII only), this is the tool for the job. (It's a bit like the notepad in Sidekick, if you've ever used that.) It's handy and uses relatively little RAM (about 13K plus any file you open with it). Since it's purely an ASCII editor, the files created have no special codes in them that would confuse other ASCII editors or programs that might need clean ASCII files. Thus, you can create or edit your CONFIG.SYS or AUTOEXEC.BAT files with Notepad.

If you keep Notepad open and on your Desktop, you can then easily switch to it when you have something to jot down. If you only want to jot down a few notes about something, consider using the Cardfile instead.

Notepad has the following limitations:

- It has no paragraph or character formatting capability. It will wrap lines of text to fit the size of the window, however, which is a nice feature.
- Files are limited to text only. WordStar, Microsoft Word, Word for Windows, WordPerfect, and other non-ASCII files won't load into the Notepad properly.

- Files are limited in size to about 50K. This is fairly large, accommodating approximately 15 pages of solid single-spaced text, or 20 or so pages of regularly spaced material.
- It doesn't have any fancy pagination options, though it will print with headers and footers via the Page Setup dialog box.

Running Notepad

TIP *If you have several Notepad files that you use regularly, you might want to put them into a program group for easy access—even into your StartUp group so they are loaded when you start up Windows—and assign each one a shortcut key for rapid access.*

To run Notepad, double-click on the Notepad icon, as you might expect. It's in the Accessories group. If you try to load a file that is too large, Notepad will warn you with the message:

```
File XXXX.XXX is too large for Notepad;
use another editor to change the file.
```

If you try to load a file of the wrong format, it may load and look like garbage, or it may not load at all and you will see a message:

```
XXXX.XXX is not a valid Notepad file;
ensure the file is a text file.
```

Entering and Editing Text

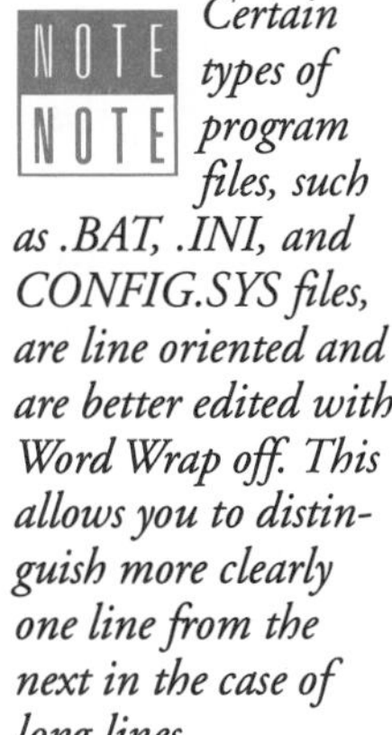

NOTE *Certain types of program files, such as .BAT, .INI, and CONFIG.SYS files, are line oriented and are better edited with Word Wrap off. This allows you to distinguish more clearly one line from the next in the case of long lines.*

You can enter and edit text in Notepad as you would expect, with a few exceptions. To enter text, just start typing. The insertion point will move, just as it does in Write. However, as you reach the end of the window, the text will not wrap. The window will pan to the right, shifting the insertion point to about the middle of the window. This is a rather inconvenient way to enter your text, since you can't see much of what you just typed. Each paragraph will keep scrolling to the right. When you press Enter, the window will pan back to the far left again, ready for the next line of text. Figure 12.1 shows an example of text in this state.

Choosing Edit ➤ Word Wrap causes the text to wrap within the constraints of the window. This doesn't affect the text file itself, however. That is, Notepad does not insert line feeds or carriage returns at the points where the lines wrap. If you resize the window, the text will rewrap to fit the available space. Figure 12.2 shows the same long line of text reformatted with Word Wrap turned on.

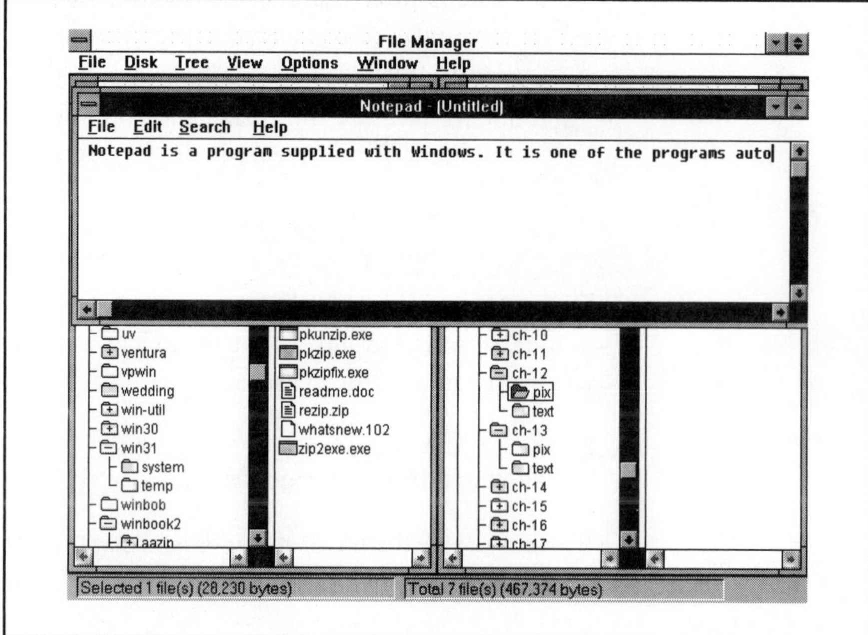

FIGURE 12.1: *Each paragraph of text will normally stay on one long line unless Word Wrap is turned on.*

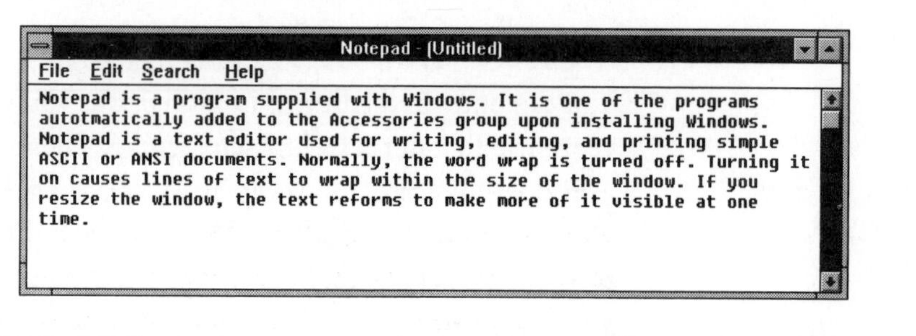

FIGURE 12.2: *Text will wrap within a window if Word Wrap is turned on.*

To edit your text, just move the cursor to the point you want to change. You can select, cut, copy, and paste text with the mouse, using the same techniques described in Chapter 9. To select all of the text in the file, choose Edit ➤ Select All.

To move around in the text, you can use the scroll bars, of course. You can also use the following keys:

KEY	MOVES INSERTION POINT TO
Home	Start of the line
End	End of the line
Ctrl-Home	Start of the file
Ctrl-End	End of the file

Entering the Time and Date into Your Text

A common use of a notepad-type program is to take notes pertaining to important phone conversations or meetings with clients or colleagues, or to type up memos. Typically, you'll want to incorporate the current time and date into your notes to document developments as they happen. The Time/Date command on the Edit menu does this quickly.

To enter the time and date at the cursor:

1. Position the insertion point where you want the time and date inserted.
2. Choose Edit ➤ Time/Date or press F5.

Another option is to have the time and date automatically added to the bottom of the file whenever you open it. This is useful for creating a time log of entries—for example, when taking orders by phone or logging scientific observations of some type:

1. At the top of the file (first line, first column) add the letters **.LOG** in all capital letters.
2. When you open the file next, a blank line and the time and date should be added to the bottom of the file. The insertion point will be on the next line waiting for you to enter new text.

Searching for Text

You can search for specific text in a Notepad file, but you can't replace it automatically. Follow these steps to search:

1. Choose Search ➤ Find. The dialog box shown below will appear:

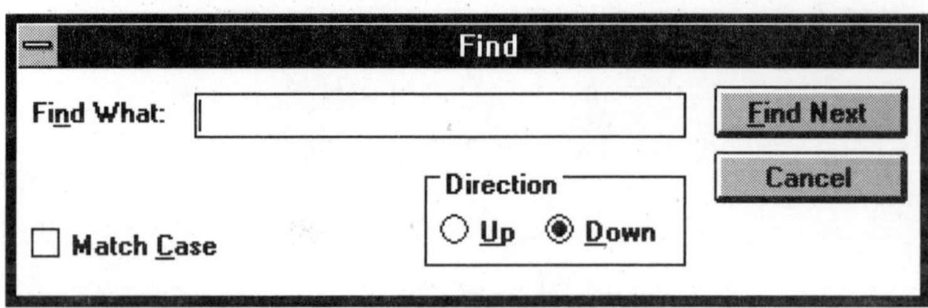

2. Type in the text you want to search for.
3. Check the Match Case box if you don't want the search to ignore capitalization.
4. Click on Up if you want to search the portion of text above the current insertion point. Down is the default setting—the Notepad searches from the insertion point to the end of the file and stops. Unlike Write, the search does not wrap around to the top of the file and continue down to the insertion point.
5. If you want to search again for the same word, choose Search ➤ Find Next or press F3.

Printing a Notepad File

To print a Notepad file, do the following:

1. Make sure the correct printer is currently selected.
2. Alter the headers and footers and page margins from the File ➤ Page Setup command, if necessary.

If you want to add some indents to the left and right sides of the page, increase the margin settings. The screen won't reflect the changes, but the printed page will. As for the headers and footers, the defaults will print the file name at the top of the page and the page number at the bottom. Here are the other options you could enter:

NOTE *These special header and footer codes can be used in the header and footer dialog boxes of many of the supplied accessory programs.*

CODE	EFFECT
&d	Includes the current date
&p	Includes the page number
&f	Includes the file's name
&l	Makes the subsequent text left-aligned at the margin
&r	Makes the subsequent text right-aligned at the margin
&c	Centers the subsequent text
&t	Includes the time of the printing

You can enter as many of these codes as you like.

FILING INFORMATION WITH CARDFILE

Cardfile is one of my favorite accessory programs. I use it all the time to keep track of people's phone numbers, make notes about things I have to do, and store bits of information about pending projects. For example, I have a Cardfile file in which I've added tips and tricks about Windows to put into this book.

Cardfile works like a Rolodex or box of index cards. Each card has a title line (called the *index line*) and room on it for up to 11 lines of text. The index line is used for identification, just so you can quickly see the topic of each card in the list when they are cascaded or listed on the screen. Cardfile automatically alphabetizes the cards according to the index line, so this line is also used to keep them in order. Obviously this is perfect for keeping people's phone numbers and addresses in order, since you can add and delete cards and leave the realphabetizing to Cardfile.

The number of cards you can have in a file depends on the amount of RAM in your computer, the number of other programs running, and the amount of information on the cards. If you have graphics on a card, it will take up more memory than a card containing just text.

Running Cardfile

TO ADD A CARDFILE CARD,

press F6 to enter your first card. For subsequent cards, press F7. Type an identifying word or phrase into the Index dialog box. Click on OK. Type the data into the information area of the card.

To run Cardfile, simply double-click on the Cardfile icon in the Accessories group. The program comes up with a new card file that has only one card in it, as shown in Figure 12.3.

For the first card, you have to use a command to enter the index-line information. (On subsequent cards, the dialog box opens automatically.) There

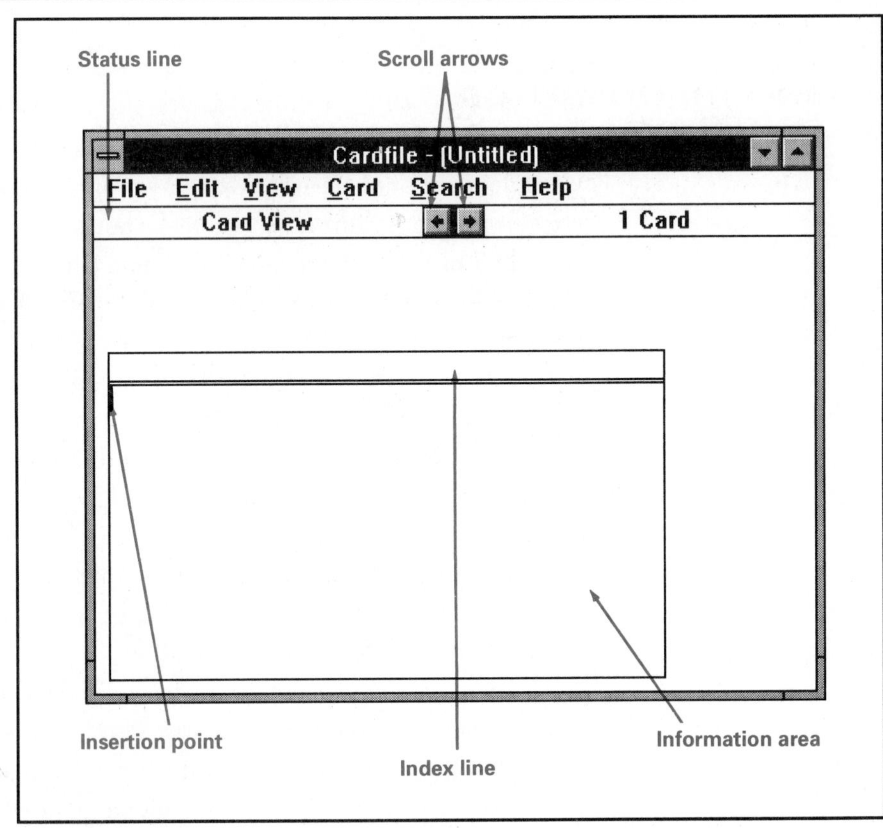

FIGURE 12.3: *A new Cardfile document and its component parts*

are three ways to open the index dialog box:

- Double-click on the index line of the card.
- Choose Edit ➤ Index.
- Press F6.

Once you do one of these, the Index dialog box opens, as shown below:

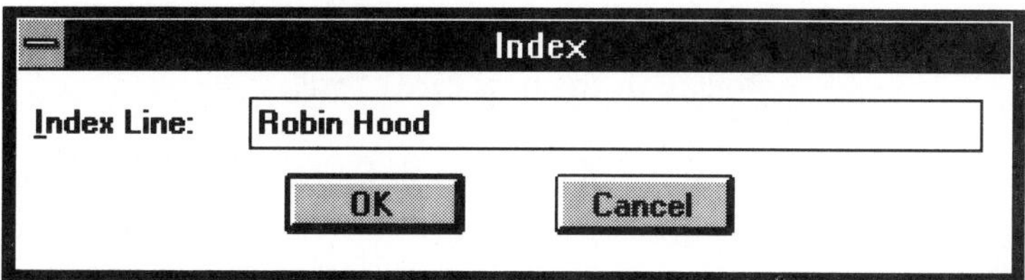

Type in something about the card's contents that will help you remember what it's about. Then click on OK. What you type will be displayed in the card's index line.

Now the insertion point drops to the information area, ready for you to enter the text for the card. As you type, the text will wrap. When you reach the end of the card, you'll hear a beep and you won't be able to type in any more characters. You can edit the text with Cut, Copy, Paste, Backspace, Delete, the arrow keys, and Undo. Double-clicking a word selects it. Add blank lines by pressing Enter.

When you run out of room on a card, it can be frustrating. The first thing to do is try editing the information down. Be more concise or use abbreviations. If that won't do, add a new card with the same index line but with a number as a suffix, such as

Robin Hood 2

Cardfile will keep them next to each other in the stack. Actually, you can use the same index line again and again for new cards, but then it's hard to tell the order of the series when you're looking up information later.

Adding Another Card

Adding a new card is simple:

1. Choose Card ➤ Add or press F7.
2. The Add dialog box appears. It's really the same one as the Index dialog box. Just type in the new index line for the card and click on OK. Your new card is added to the pile of cards and the stack is realphabetized.
3. Fill in the new card's text.

Continue filling in cards for each item of information. As you add new cards, they are cascaded, just like windows, only from right to left instead of from left to right. The number of cards is indicated at the side of the status line.

Editing the Index Line

You may need to edit the index line of a card. To do so,

1. Double-click on its index line, press F6, or choose Edit ➤ Index.
2. Enter or edit the index line. To edit, click somewhere in the line first or press one of the arrow keys. This deselects the text so that it isn't all erased when you start typing.

Viewing the Cards

Once you have a bunch of cards entered, it's easy to retrieve the information on them. You've probably already figured out at least one way, but there are several:

- The easiest way is to click on any part of the card. The list will quickly rotate: The stack stays in order, but the cards in front will move to the back and the selected card will scroll forward to the front.
- You can scroll through the list, card by card, until you get to the one you want. Press the PgDn or PgUp key, or click on the scroll arrows at the top of the box. Press Ctrl-End to go to the last card or Ctrl-Home to go to the first.

- You can choose Search ➤ Go To or press F4 and type at least two letters into the resulting dialog box. (Capitalization doesn't matter.)
- The keyboard shortcut is to press Ctrl and the first letter of the card you want. The first card beginning with that letter will pop to the front. This will at least get you close to the card you want, possibly bringing it into view. Then click on the card or scroll to it using the scroll arrows or the PgDn key.

There's another way to view the cards that you might find helpful. It's called the List View. As opposed to Card View, in which you see the stack of cards and the information on the front of the first card, List View displays only the index lines. The advantage is that you can see more index lines in this view than in Card View (see Figure 12.4). Notice that the status line indicates you're in List View. Use the scroll bars and arrow keys to move through the list if there is more than a windowful.

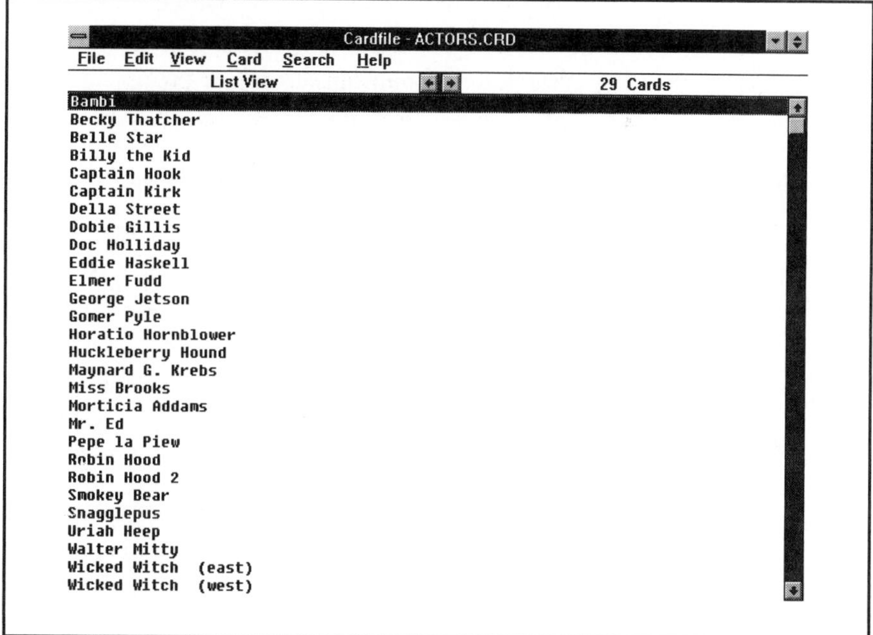

FIGURE 12.4:

You can view cards with their index lines arranged in a list. Choose View ➤ List to switch to this view.

Once the cards are displayed in a list, you can do two things with them:

- Edit the index line of any card line by first double-clicking it, then making the changes in the Index dialog box.
- Read and edit the card's information by clicking on its index line and then choosing View ➤ Card.

Searching for Text in a Stack of Cards

TO SEARCH THROUGH THE TEXT ON ALL CARDS,

choose Search ➤ Find. Type in the search text and click on OK. Choose Search ➤ Find Next to find the next card.

One terrific feature of Cardfile is that it can find a needle in a haystack. Once you have lots of notes on cards, it's likely that you'll forget where some little gem of information is located.

Suppose you're a casting director for movies and you'd like to look up someone in your list of actors who has a specific talent. If you had included a description of each actor's special talents on their cards, you could easily search for such information. For example, say you want to find out who can play the bongo drums. Here's how to perform the search:

1. Choose Search ➤ Find. The Find dialog box will appear.
2. Type in **bongos** and press Enter or click on OK. The Cardfile will display the next card containing any words matching the description, and will highlight the found text. In my case, it is Maynard's card, as shown in Figure 12.5.
3. If you want to repeat the search to see if there are other matches, choose Search ➤ Find Next. If no other matches are found, the Cardfile will let you know about it in a dialog box.

Incidentally, searching starts from the current card to the end of the file, then jumps to the beginning of the file, and continues until the starting point is reached again.

FIGURE 12.5:

To search for a particular card on the basis of text in its information area, choose Search ➤ Find. The card jumps to the front with the text highlighted.

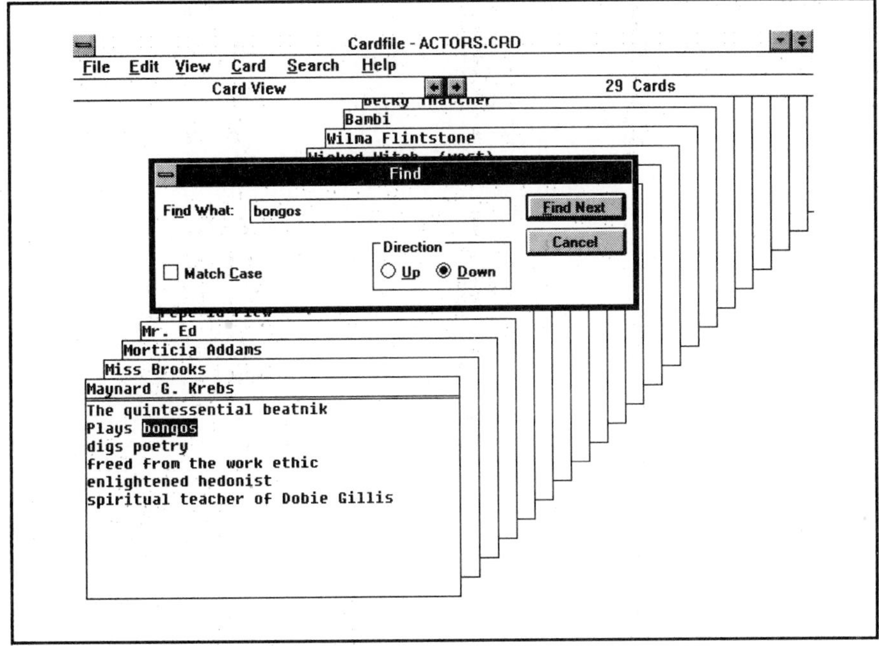

Making Copies of Cards

You can duplicate cards if you need to. This is useful in cases where several cards will have primarily the same information on them:

Make up the first card and bring it to the front of the stack.

Choose Card ➤ Duplicate. A duplicate card will be made and will appear at the front of the card stack.

Edit the card as necessary.

Deleting a Card

If you want to remove a card from a stack for some reason,

1. Bring the card to the front of the stack through a search or any other method.
2. Choose Card ➤ Delete. A dialog box will ask for confirmation.

Be careful with this command since deleted cards can't be restored.

Copying, Cutting, and Pasting Text, Graphics, and Sounds

You can copy and cut text between cards with the Clipboard. You can also pull graphics and sound bites onto a card, which is a pretty nifty feature for illustrating your cards or integrating multimedia effects into them.

To copy or cut text between cards, simply select the text in question and choose the Cut or Copy commands from the Edit menu. Then move to the card to be pasted to, position the cursor, and choose Edit ➤ Paste.

Pasting graphics or sounds from another program onto a card can be very useful. For example, a police department might want to make up a card file with scanned photographs of every person in a most wanted list. Each card could contain the photo and relevant information on the person. Or as an educational aid for children, you could make up a "flash card" stack by drawing pictures of items whose names you are teaching. The items' names could be shown below the pictures, or you could put the names on the following cards, thereby requiring a press of the PgDn key to see the answer.

Pasting graphics and sounds can be done via simple pasting or by the more elaborate embedding or linking. Simple pasting is covered here. For normal pasting, you have to create the graphic or sound in another program, cut or copy it to the Clipboard, and then switch to Cardfile.

To copy a graphic onto a card, using the normal pasting method:

1. Move the destination card to the front of the stack.
2. Choose Edit ➤ Picture. This puts Cardfile in Picture mode, in which you can work with graphics.
3. Choose Edit ➤ Paste. The Clipboard's contents will be placed into the card's upper-left corner.
4. Drag the picture to the desired location. If the picture is too big to fit on the card, only a portion will show. To adjust the part of the picture that will show, use the arrow keys on the keyboard.
5. When the graphic is adjusted to your satisfaction, choose Edit ➤ Text. This pastes down the graphic and returns to Text mode.

To copy a sound, put it on the Clipboard from the sound program you're using, then switch to Cardfile, move to the desired card, and choose Edit ➤ Paste. The microphone icon will be inserted onto the card. Double-clicking it will cause the sound to play (see Chapter 15).

If you later want to move the graphic or cut it from the card, just get into Picture mode again and drag the picture or choose Edit ➤ Cut.

A card can only have one graphic on it, so if you try to add a second picture, the first one will be replaced. The resolution of the graphics on your cards (and in all Windows programs) is determined by the resolution of your screen. If you need to incorporate more detailed pictures into your cards, consider using a higher resolution screen that supports Windows 3.1.

You can also use Object Linking and Embedding to insert a drawing or sound effects on a card. Linked and embedded graphics and sounds can be conveniently edited in Cardfile, unlike drawings that are pasted into Cardfile by the more conventional method. See Chapter 14 for more information about linking and embedding.

Undoing Changes to a Card

If you have second thoughts about changes you've made to a card, you can back out and undo them with the Restore command. However, this is only possible if you do it before bringing another card to the front of the stack.

To restore a card, choose Edit ➤ Restore. The card will be returned to its previous state, prior to any edits that were made since it was brought to the front of the stack.

If you want to undo only the last action which you took, choose Edit ➤ Undo.

Dialing a Phone Number from a Card

If you have a phone number on a card and a Hayes-compatible modem hooked up, you can have Cardfile dial the number for you. If you do lots of phone calling, this may be a boon, unless you're already using a program such as Prodex or Hotline, which manage phone numbers and calls for you. This is a sort of bare-bones approach, but it will certainly suffice. Once the call is made, you can take notes on the card, too. Here are the steps required:

1. Make sure your modem is on and hooked up.

2. Move to the card you want to dial from. It should have a phone number on it. The number can have an area code in it, too. Acceptable number formats are the same as those for the Terminal program. (Refer to Chapter 10 for the particulars on that.) Cardfile assumes that any number containing four digits or more is the one you want to dial. If other numbers appear on the card before the phone number, that's what Cardfile will dial, even if it's a street address or the serial number of your computer. Therefore, if you're going to use Autodial to call people, it will save you time to type the most frequently dialed phone number above any other numbers on the card. However, you can have Cardfile dial any number on the card. Simply select the number using one of the usual text selection techniques.

3. Choose Card ➤ Autodial. The following dialog box will appear (with a different phone number, of course):

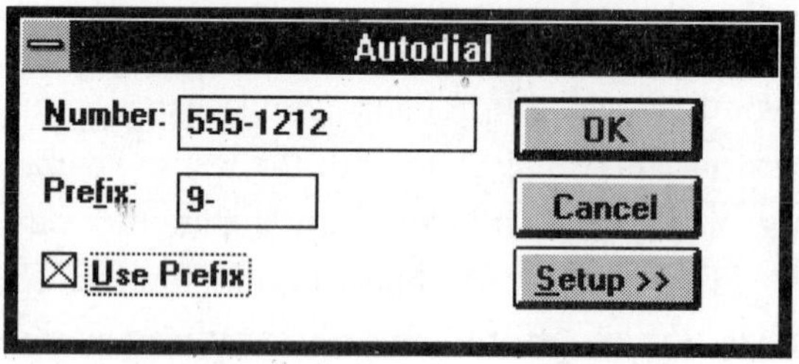

Autodial
Number: 555-1212
Prefix: 9-
☒ Use Prefix
OK
Cancel
Setup >>

4. If you need a prefix such as 9 for an outside line or *70 to block call waiting, enter it and click on Use Prefix. (The prefix will precede the phone number itself when Cardfile dials for you.) Leave the check box off if you don't need the prefix dialed.

5. You can also type in an area code in the prefix section, or commas, if you need them. Each comma tells the modem to wait two seconds before sending the next part of the number. You may have to add a comma after a prefix if your phone system requires a second or two to switch to an outside line and dial tone. Typically you would use

   9,

   as a prefix (assuming 9 is the outside line access number).

6. Click on OK. Cardfile will dial the phone number, then a dialog box will tell you to pick up the phone to talk.
7. Pick up the phone and then click on OK. This tells the modem to hang up so that you and the modem aren't on the line simultaneously.

If dialing doesn't work, you might want to check the modem setup. Try to dial again, and then choose Setup from the Autodial box. Set the COM port, baud rate, and dialing type (tone or pulse) to match your modem's switches and type of phone service.

Merging Card Files

Sometimes I wind up with a few card files that aren't really that different in overall concept and should probably be joined together. As a typical example, I recently found I had an Odds & Ends file, a Miscellaneous file, and a General file. These all contained general information, so I decided to join them into one card file. That way I wouldn't have to remember which one to use each time I wanted to record or retrieve some general piece of information. Cardfile lets you join files together:

1. Open one of the files that you want to combine.
2. Choose File ➤ Merge.
3. The File Merge dialog box comes up. Choose the file you want to merge with the currently open file and click on OK. Repeat this process for each file you want to merge. As you merge files, the new cards will be added and the whole lot will be realphabetized.
4. Either save the file as it now stands or—if you want to keep the original file as it was—use File ➤ Save As to save the file under a new name.

Note that merging doesn't affect the files you select; it only pulls a copy of their data into the cardfile you've got open on your screen.

Printing Your Cards

Add oft-used Cardfile document icons to a program group for quick access—possibly in the StartUp group.

Occasionally you may want to print your cards. Here's how:

1. Set up the printer as usual.
2. Switch to Card View if you're not already in it.
3. To print the current card, choose File ➤ Print. To print all the cards, choose File ➤ Print All.

The cards can be printed four cards to an 8½-by-11-inch page in portrait layout (three if you use the default one-inch margin). In landscape layout, two cards are printed per page.

SCHEDULING APPOINTMENTS WITH THE CALENDAR

The Calendar program is an electronic version of a paper calendar. You can keep track of your time, schedule appointments, and so forth, just as you would on a calendar or electronic pocket scheduler. The Calendar also has an alarm function that will alert you to upcoming appointments, if you wish. This program has an internal "perpetual" calendar formula to calculate the layout of every month for any year between 1980 and 2099.

Starting the Calendar

To start the Calendar, double-click on its icon in the Accessories group. A blank calendar will appear, as shown in Figure 12.6. On your system, the current day will be shown (if it isn't, correct the system's date from the Control Panel). This is the Day view, one of two calendar views. The other one shows the whole month. Double-click on the status line, press F9, or choose View ➤ Month to switch to the Month view. Figure 12.7 shows an example of this.

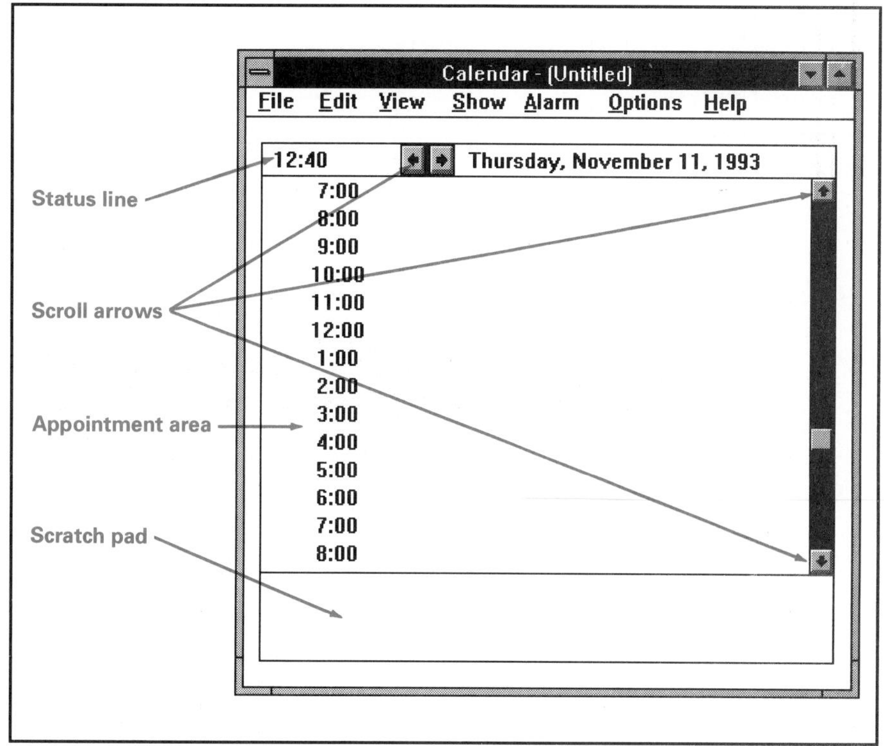

FIGURE 12.6:
A blank new calendar. This is the Day view.

Moving through the Calendar

It's simple to move from month to month and day to day. In Day view, click the right and left scroll buttons. Each click moves one day forward or backward. The scroll bars move through the day's appointment times. In Month view, the scroll buttons move from one month to the next. In both Day and Month view, Ctrl-PgUp and Ctrl-PgDn also move you to the previous and next day or month. Double-clicking on a day's square in the month view quickly brings up that day's appointment list (the Day view). Or you can press F8 to return to the Day view.

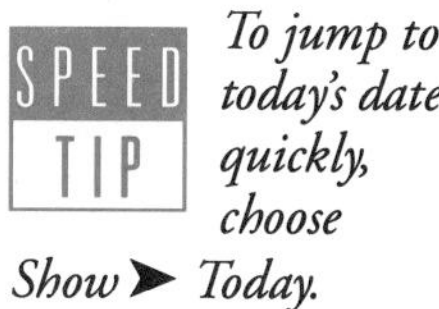

To jump to today's date quickly, choose Show ➤ Today.

To get to a specific date directly, choose Show ➤ Date or press F4. Then type in the date. Use the form 3/6/93 or 3–6–93. Leading zeros aren't necessary. The full year must be entered for dates beyond 12/31/99.

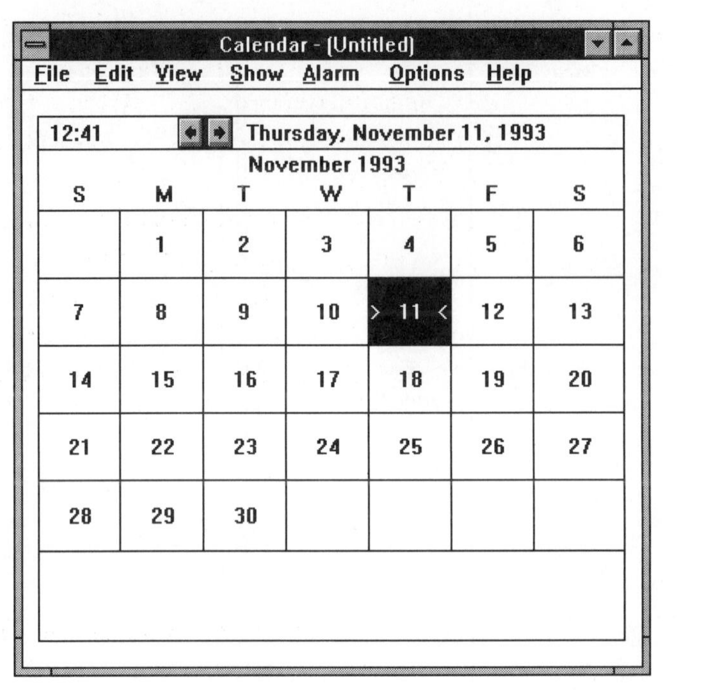

FIGURE 12.7:
The Month view. The current date is marked with angle brackets: >11<.

To move around within a day's calendar, press Enter or the down arrow to get to the next listed time. Move to the previous time with the up arrow. Ctrl-Home takes you to the starting time and Ctrl-End to twelve hours after that.

Entering Appointments

As a default, a new calendar will have time increments set to the hour. You may want to use half-hour or quarter-hour intervals, however. Choose Options ➤ Day Settings to alter this according to your needs. The resulting dialog box also lets you change the time you want each day's appointment list to begin, and whether you want the time displayed on a 12- or 24-hour day. The default starting time is 7:00 AM. Change any settings and type in the new starting time. Click OK when the settings are how you want them.

To actually enter appointments, click to the right of the time and begin typing. You can enter up to 80 characters. To add an appointment at a time that doesn't fall exactly on one of the listed times, choose Option ➤ Special Time or press F7. Type in the new time and click Insert. You can later delete the special time with the same box (although getting in a regular routine of spending special time with family members is a good idea).

Each day has room at the bottom of the window for up to three lines of notes. (You may have to enlarge the window to see it.) This area is called the Scratch Pad. Enter text here as you do in Notepad.

Setting the Alarm

You can set an alarm as a reminder as many times in the day as you like. To set an alarm for a specific time:

Alarms will be inactive if the Calendar is not running. Remember to run Calendar upon booting up your computer.

1. Position the cursor on the time in your calendar when you want the alarm to sound.
2. Choose Alarm ➤ Set or press F5. A small bell will appear to the left of the alarm time.
3. When that date and time arrive, you will be alerted by four beeps. If the Calendar window is active, a dialog box will also appear. If it's inactive, its title bar and borders will flash (though you might not see it if it's concealed by another window). If it's iconized, the icon will flash.
4. The flashing will continue until you double-click on the window or icon and click OK in the dialog box that reports the appointment.

You can turn off the beeper for all alarm settings or set your alarms to ring up to ten minutes early by Choosing Alarm ➤ Controls and setting the options in the dialog box.

REMOVING APPOINTMENTS

From time to time you may want to reduce the size of your calendar file by removing old appointments. This will delete everything during a range of dates that you specify in a dialog box. To remove appointments,

1. Choose Edit ➤ Remove.
2. In the dialog box, enter the starting and ending dates of the time period whose appointments you want to remove.
3. Click on OK.

PRINTING YOUR APPOINTMENTS

To print your appointments, do the following:

1. Set up the printer.
2. Choose File ➤ Page Setup to set the margins, headers, and footers if you want to alter them from the defaults. You can use the special headers and footers codes listed in the Notepad section of this chapter.
3. Choose File ➤ Print. A dialog box will appear, asking you for the dates you want to print. The current day, as selected in the month or day view, will be typed into the dialog box for you.
4. If you only want that day, just press Enter or click OK. If you want more than the current day, enter the date range, then press Enter or click OK.

PERFORMING CALCULATIONS WITH THE CALCULATOR

The Calculator is modest in appearance, but it's quite a sophisticated accessory. It's a pop-up tool that you can use to perform simple or complex calculations. There are really two calculators in one—a Standard Calculator and a more complex Scientific Calculator for use by statisticians, engineers, computer programmers, and business professionals.

To run the Calculator, click on its icon, as you would expect. A reasonable facsimile of a hand-held calculator will appear on your screen, as shown in Figure 12.8. If your Calculator looks larger, it's the Scientific one. Choose View ➤ Standard to switch back to the basic calculator. The program always remembers which type was used last and comes up in that mode.

1. Clear the calculator's display by pressing Esc or clicking on the C button.
2. Enter the first value in the calculation by clicking on the numbers or using the keyboard. (If you set the keypad's Num Lock setting on, you can use it to enter the numbers and the four mathematical operators. This is easier than using the number keys across the top of the keyboard.) You can use the Backspace key to fix mistakes, click C to clear the calculator and start again, or CE to clear the present entry.
3. After entering the first number, click on the mathematical operator you want to use. (The asterisk represents multiplication, SQRT calculates the square root, and 1/*x* calculates the reciprocal. The others are self-evident.)
4. Enter any additional numbers followed by the desired operators.

FIGURE 12.8:
The Standard Calculator

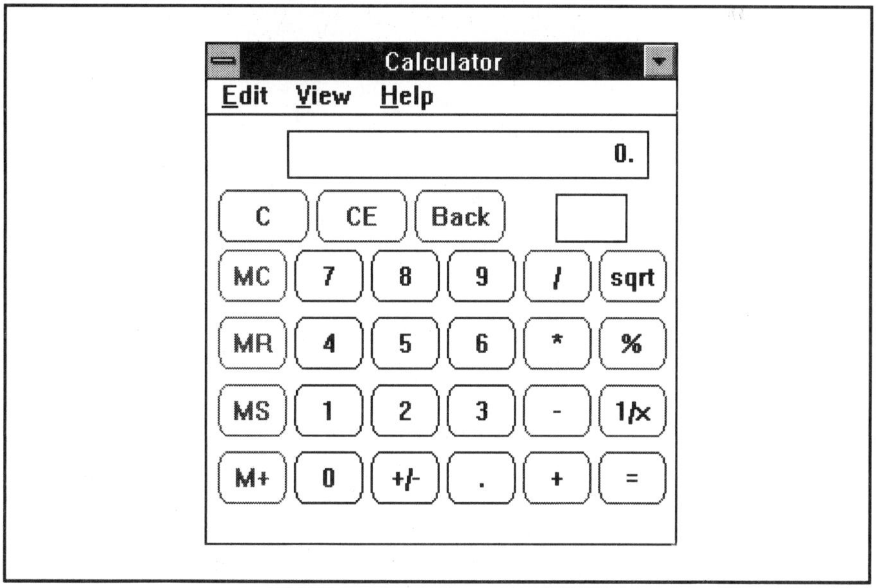

5. Press Enter or click on the calculator's equals (=) button. The answer appears in the display. (You can use the Enter key on the numeric keypad, if you want.)

You can also use the memory keys just as on a standard calculator. MS stores the displayed number in memory, MR recalls the memory value to the display for use in calculations, M+ adds the current display value to the existing memory value, and MC clears out the memory, resetting it to zero.

Among the myriad options you have while using the calculator is a useful feature that cuts down on typing and typos when you're entering numbers into reports or memos. Just use the Calculator for your computations, and then, when the result you want is in the display, choose Edit ➤ Copy (or press Ctrl-Ins). The figure will be copied to the Clipboard. Then switch back to your document, position the cursor where you want the result, and paste it in.

KEEPING TIME WITH THE CLOCK

As with other windows, the Clock has a Control menu as well as the Settings menu that you see below the title bar. Besides all the usual commands in the Control menu, there is one that you won't see anywhere else. It's called Always on Top, and it's last in the list. When you select Always on Top, the clock will stay on top of whatever you're working on. Even if you iconize it, it will never be covered up by any document or window. To hide it, just turn the command off. If you are using a Microsoft Windows screen saver, however, the clock *will* be concealed by it until you clear the screen to get back to work. If you are using the After Dark screen saver (from Berkeley Systems), the clock will stay visible.

From the Settings menu you can choose to show the date, change between digital and analog display, and select the font for the digital display. You can also turn off the title and menu bars so that all you see is the clock. To restore the title so you can use the menus, just double-click on the clock face.

CREATING MACROS WITH THE RECORDER

TO RECORD A MACRO,

position the cursor where you want the macro to begin and switch to the Recorder window. Choose Macro ➤ Record. Fill in the macro name and a shortcut key. Click on OK. Perform the actions you want to record. Press Ctrl-Break to stop recording.

The Recorder falls into a category of programs in the computer world known as *macro editors*. Macro editors help automate your work and cut down on the keystrokes you have to enter. They do this by "memorizing" a series of words or letters you type and then playing them back at a predetermined time, or whenever you press specific keys.

For example, I've used a macro program to type the word *Windows* throughout this book. All I type is Alt-W and the macro program does the rest. If you're a seasoned PC user, you've probably used a macro program such as Tempo, SuperKey, SmartKey, or others. Some of the more popular macro programs will also respond to a program's prompts, entering information automatically, but not before the application is ready for it. This allows for unattended automation of such things as telecommunications sessions in which files are uploaded or downloaded during the night when phone costs are lower.

The Windows Recorder does all this, with the exception of running unattended at a predetermined time. However, it has one feature that makes it particularly useful with Windows applications: it can record mouse movements. Thus, with Recorder, you can simulate a person using a Windows program, complete with key presses, mouse movements, dragging, clicking, and so forth. This is particularly useful for unattended demonstrations of Windows applications, though it obviously has everyday utility for anyone using Windows.

For example, you could:

- cut down on the typing of recurring phrases within a word-processing document.
- quickly repeat complex calculations or a series of commands while using a spreadsheet.

- amaze your friends when your computer automatically draws a picture with Paintbrush.

To record a sequence of actions,

1. Position the windows so that the application you want to automate and the Recorder window are both visible. My suggestion is to resize the Recorder window to a small strip at the bottom of the screen, with just the menu bar showing.
2. Place the application's cursor (such as its text cursor) in the position from which you want to start recording. If it doesn't have a cursor other than the mouse pointer, skip this step.
3. Switch to the Recorder window and choose Macro ➤ Record. The dialog box shown in Figure 12.9 will appear. The default settings will be fine for most macro work. However, when you have lots of windows on the screen, macros can get a little hairy, and they might not work as planned. If this happens, you should try adjusting some of the settings, as explained in the section "Other Options" below.

FIGURE 12.9:

Check and/or change the macro options from this dialog box before beginning the recording process.

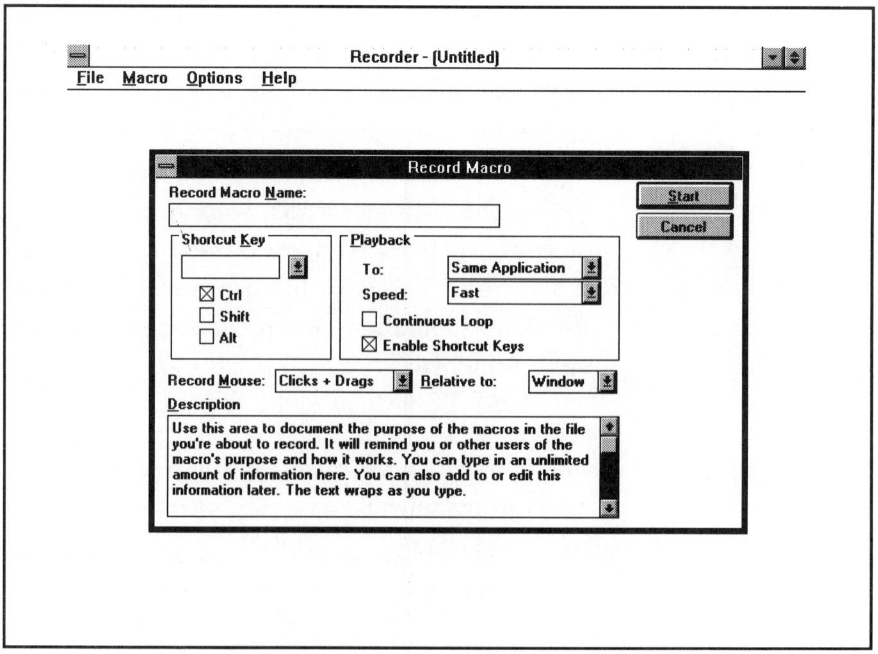

4. In the Record Macro Name area, type in a name for the macro. You can use up to 40 characters. Make it descriptive so you can later remember what it's for.
5. Enter the Shortcut Key that you will later want to use to trigger the macro. This is optional but recommended. You can start a macro with the mouse, but a key is much faster. If you want to use Ctrl-A, check the Ctrl box and type **A** in the text box. If you want to use other common keys besides letters and numbers (such as Space, Delete, Backspace, etc.), choose them from the drop-down list provided. You can use Ctrl, Shift, and Alt individually or in combination (which greatly increases the number of macros you can define). Avoid using Alt alone, since Alt-key combinations are used for Windows menu selections.
6. Click on Start. The Recorder window automatically becomes iconized and the icon blinks as long as you are recording.
7. Reactivate the application window and type in your text, or make whatever mouse movements or menu selections you want to record. It's best to keep mouse movements to a minimum, since they often screw up later when you play them back.
8. When you are finished recording, click on the icon. If you can't see it because it's covered up by a window, press Ctrl-Break. A dialog box will appear, asking what you want to do now.
9. Make sure that the Save Macro option is selected and click on OK. The macro will be saved. (If you want to resume the recording to add more actions to the macro, or cancel the recording, click the appropriate option button and then click on OK.)

Repeat the above steps to add each new macro to a file. For example, you might want shortcut keys for all the repetitive phrases you use while typing (this is the most common application). Just keep opening the Recorder window, choosing Macro ➤ Record, and following the above steps. As you record new macros, each time you open the Recorder window you will see additional macro names and their associated shortcut keys listed. This is a quick way of seeing which shortcuts you have already used. Figure 12.10 shows an example of macros I have created to cut down on my typing.

FIGURE 12.10:

Macros you create are listed in the Recorder window. These are all the Ctrl-key combinations that type recurring phrases or words in this book.

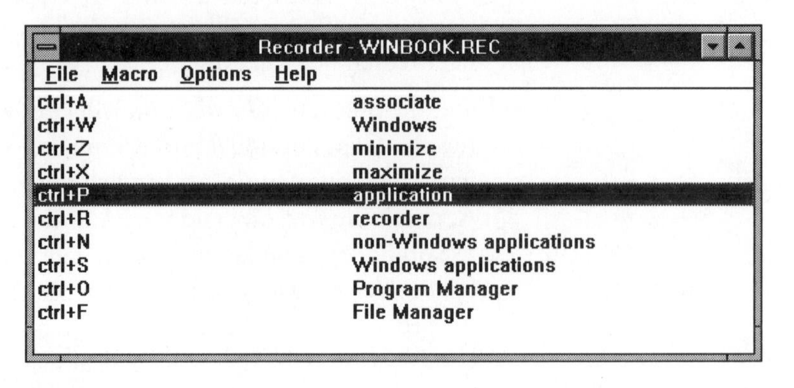

Saving and Loading Macro Files

Macros, once created, can be saved in a file. You can have files of macros for different applications and load them whenever you wish. You can only have one set of macros open and functional at a time, though, or they might conflict. To save your macros, choose File ➤ Save or File ➤ Save As. The extension .REC is added to the name you choose.

You load Recorder files as you might expect: Run the Recorder, choose File ➤ Open, and choose the name. As a quicker alternative to running a macro you use a lot, add a macro document icon to a Program Manager group. (Drag the .REC file from a File Manager window into the destination Program Manager group window.) Then you can just double-click on it to run the Recorder and open the file.

Using a Macro

NOTE *You don't have to save a macro file before using it. If you don't want to use a macro again, don't bother saving the file.*

Once you have created a macro, you can use, or *trigger,* it in three ways:

- Open the Recorder window and double-click the macro you want to run.
- Highlight the macro you want to run and choose Macro ➤ Run.
- Press the shortcut key from any location.

When you do any of the above, the window belonging to the application in which the macro was created is activated, and the macro is played in it. You don't have to worry about activating the window. Recorder does that for you.

If you run the macro while working in an application window other than the one in which you created the macro, Recorder will activate the correct window. Using my example, if I press Ctrl-W while in a Notepad document, the word *Windows* will not be typed into it. Rather, the Write document currently open will be automatically activated, I'll hear an insistent beep, and *Windows* will be typed at the cursor location in the Write document. This is because I created the macro while in Write.

If you try to run a macro when the application where it is used is iconized, you'll hear the same warning beep and get a rather ominous error-message dialog box entitled

Recorder Playback Aborted!

This box contains three lines of information pinpointing the source of the error, the gist of which is that the active pointer is outside the playback window. If the macro's application isn't even running when you try to use it, you'll get a warning message similar to the above, though slightly less emphatic. The upshot of all this is to make sure you have the application running and its window open before invoking the macro.

To stop the execution of a macro, press Esc.

Other Options

As you probably noticed in the Record Macro dialog box, there are lots of options that can affect how macros are recorded and played back. These are detailed below.

Playing Back Macros in Other Applications

If you want a macro to work with any application, you can change the Playback To setting in the Record Macro dialog box either when you make the macro or afterward. To change it afterward, select the macro by clicking on its line. Then choose Macro ➤ Properties. The Macro Properties dialog box will appear (this is almost the same box used for recording). Open the To drop-down list box and select Any Application. Then click OK. Now the macro will work on any application.

The macro may not always work correctly in another application, of course, since the keystrokes or mouse movements may be inappropriate for some programs, but you'll have to determine that by experimentation.

Keeping the Macro Window Open When Playing Back a Macro

Normally the recorder's window is minimized when a macro runs. You can keep it open if you choose Options ➤ Minimize on Use to remove the check mark in the Options menu.

Recording Every Mouse Movement or No Mouse Movements

Normally, only mouse clicks and drags are recorded. This is because other motions are probably irrelevant and take up space in a macro. However, some programs may make use of mouse movement on the screen even when the buttons aren't clicked. To record these types of movements, open the Record Mouse drop-down list box in the Record Macro dialog box and choose Everything.

If you are recording "everything," you should use Ctrl-Break to end your recording session. Otherwise, even the mouse movement to the Recorder icon will be recorded, and this could cause problems when running your macro later (if screen or window variations alter the position of the icon).

If you want the Recorder to ignore all mouse movements (this saves space in the macro file), choose Ignore Mouse from this list. Use this setting when you don't know what kind of computer the macro is going to be played on. If it has a different type of screen (e.g., CGA instead of VGA), the mouse motions won't work anyway, so it's better to avoid them.

Recording Relative to the Window or Screen

The Relative To setting in the Record Macro dialog box determines whether the mouse activity is tracked relative to the position of the window's edge or the screen's edge. Even if you expect to be changing the size and location of the playback window, recording relative to the window works fine. The Recorder compensates for these adjustments during playback. This is the default setting.

If you are working with applications that run full-screen, however, and are having trouble getting a macro to line up its activities in the window, try recording relative to the screen. Unfortunately, this is a parameter that can't be changed after the fact. You have to decide when you record the macro. Once again, experimentation is the key.

Preventing Macros within Macros

Normally, you can have a macro run another macro. That is, you can create a macro that uses a shortcut key that's assigned to another macro. With this technique you can combine predefined macros in a vast variety of ways. Each macro can contain up to five levels of nested macros (including the first).

You can disable the use of nested macros while recording. You might need to do this when an application uses key sequences that would otherwise run other macros. To do this, turn off the Enable Shortcut Keys check box in the Record Macro dialog box.

Running a Macro in a Continuous Loop

For demos or instructional macros, you may want to have a macro run non-stop. This way, people passing a booth at a trade show or in a store, or learning a program, will always see the demo in motion. Set the Continuous Loop check box on for this type of operation. You can do this before recording the macro or from the Macro Properties dialog box afterward.

You may also want to slow down the speed of the playback to more closely simulate the real operation of a program. Do this by setting the Playback Speed in the Record or Properties dialog box to Recorded Speed.

If you want to prevent someone from interrupting your continuous macro playback, you can disable the Ctrl-Break function. To do this, choose Options ➤ Ctrl+Break Checking to set the check mark on. When this is set on, you'll have to restart your computer with Ctrl-Alt-Del to stop the macro's execution.

Deleting Macros

You can delete a macro from a file by highlighting it and choosing Macro ➤ Delete. You'll then be asked to confirm the deletion.

Merging Macro Files

As explained above, you can save your macro files to disk and load them again later. Keep in mind that the reason for having a series of macros in one file is so that they can be loaded together, all available for use at one time, usually with a specific application.

And just as you can merge Cardfile files, you can also merge your macro files. Say you have developed two sets of macros that you'd like to have available for a single application, such as Microsoft Excel. By merging these two files, you'll be able to load and use both sets of macros at the same time.

To merge two files, open the first one and choose File ➤ Merge. Then in the Merge dialog box, choose the second file and click on OK. If you want to keep the original file unsullied, use File ➤ Save As to save the new merged file under a different name.

Changing Recorder Default Settings

The Recorder always returns to the original defaults when you record a new macro. To change the defaults so that you don't have to modify the settings in the Record Macro dialog box each time, choose Options ➤ Preferences. Make the changes there, then click OK. The new defaults will take effect with the next macro you record.

The Recorder is a useful tool, but it's a bit finicky. With so many variables—such as screen resolution, window sizing and placements, and different applications—this is not surprising. You'll no doubt have to rely on some trial and error to debug your macros after they're created. Unfortunately, there is no editing feature that lets you examine a macro's operation step by step. Still, when an error is encountered, it's reported in a dialog box. With some experience, you'll be able to catch the drift of the error messages and possibly avoid them next time. See Chapter 19 for tips on the Recorder.

ENTERING SPECIAL SYMBOLS WITH CHARACTER MAP

The purpose of Character Map is to allow you to choose and insert into your documents those oddball characters such as foreign alphabetic and currency symbols, and characters from specialized fonts such as Symbol and Zapf-Dingbats. Character Map lets you easily view and insert these symbols even though there aren't keys for them on your keyboard.

Here are some everyday examples. Suppose that instead of default straight quotes (like "this") you'd prefer to use real open and close quotes (like “this”) for a more professional-looking document. Or perhaps you regularly use the symbols for Trademark (™), Registered Trademark (®), Copyright (©); Greek symbols such as π, δ, γ, etc.; or the arrow symbols ↑, ↓, ←, and → that we use in this book. These, as well as fractions and foreign language accents and the like, are included in your Windows fonts, and can most likely be printed on your printer.

Character Map is a small dialog box which displays all the normal and special symbols available for each font. You select the symbol(s) you want, and Character Map puts them on the Clipboard for pasting into your document. Figure 12.11 displays some examples of special characters.

USING CHARACTER MAP

Here's how to use it:

1. Run Character Map or switch to it if it's already running (it's in the Accessories group). The Character Map table comes up, showing 224 characters included in the default font set:

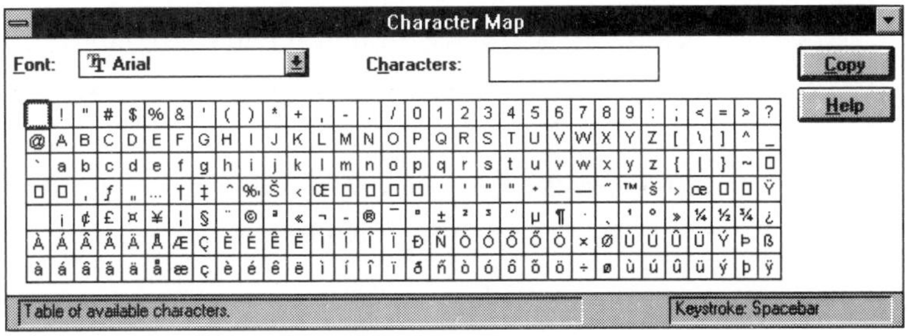

Character Map
Font: Arial
Characters:
Copy
Help
Table of available characters.
Keystroke: Spacebar

FIGURE 12.11:

Sample characters inserted into a Write document using Character Map

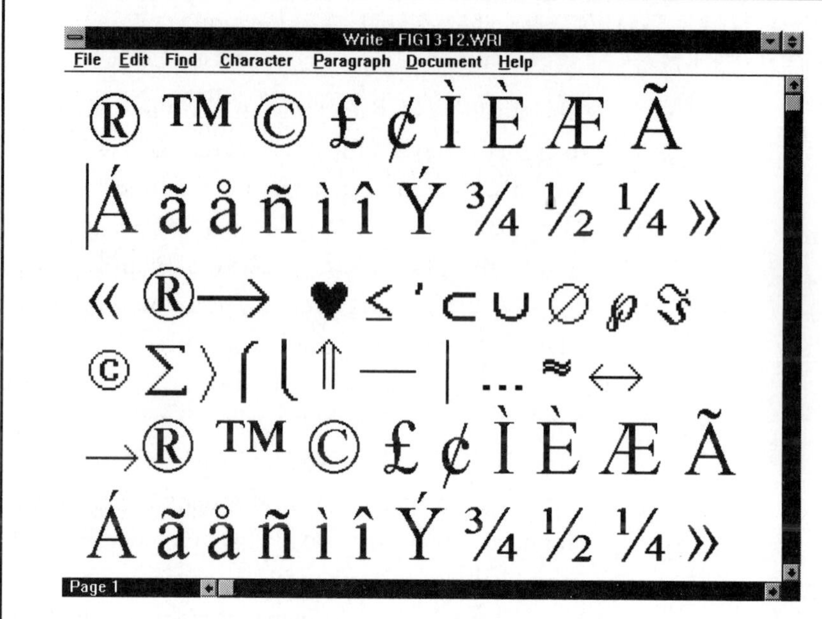

2. Choose the font you want to work with. Most of the fonts have the same characters, but some special characters, such as math and Greek symbols, are only included in the Symbol font.
3. Double-click on the character you want. This places it in the Characters box.
4. If you click on a character box and hold the mouse button down, or move to the box using the arrow keys, the character is displayed in a larger size for ease of viewing. If you use the arrow keys, pressing the spacebar selects the character.
5. If you want to grab more than one character, keep adding them in the same way. The additional characters will be added to the Characters box.
6. Click the Copy button. This puts everything displayed in the Characters box on the Clipboard.

7. Switch back to your destination application and use the Paste command (typically on the application's Edit menu) to insert the characters into your document. You may then have to select the inserted characters and choose the correct font to format the characters correctly.

Some off-beat, high-resolution screens may not be able to display certain alternate characters such as the Symbol character set unless high-resolution screen fonts were supplied to you by the manufacturer.

Entering Alternate Characters from the Keyboard

Notice that the bottom of the Character Map dialog box includes a line that reads

Keystroke:

When you click on a character in Character Map, this line displays the keys you would have to press to enter the character directly from the keyboard, not from Character Map. For example, say you wanted to enter the Copyright symbol (©) into a Windows application document. Instead of using the Character Map, you could do the following:

1. Press Num Lock to activate the numeric keypad on your keyboard, if the keypad is not already active.
2. Press Alt-0169 (i.e., hold down Alt and press 0, 1, 6, and 9, in that order). Upon releasing the Alt key, a character will be dropped into the document.
3. Change its font and size if you need to.

Not all Windows application programs accept characters in this way, but it's worth a try as a shortcut to using the Character Map.

Character Sets: ANSI vs. IBM

Normally you'll be using Character Map with Windows applications. However, you may have some success dropping special characters into non-Windows applications. You'll have to run the application in a window (this requires 386-Enhanced mode) and paste the Clipboard contents into your application using the application's Control menus via Edit ➤ Paste. (The techniques for pasting into non-Windows applications are explained in Chapter 8.) Check your non-Windows application's manual to see if it includes information about entering non-keyboard characters from the keyboard.

Windows uses the American National Standards Institute (ANSI) character set to display characters on the screen and assign them to the keyboard. This includes 256 characters, numbered 0 to 255. Your PC has another character set called the IBM extended character set. There are differences between the two. Most PCs have the same codes for characters numbered between 0 and 127, which correspond to the letters, numbers, and symbols on a standard U.S. keyboard. PCs will sometimes differ, however, in the characters displayed by codes 128 to 255. For example, in ANSI the British pound symbol (£) is 163, whereas in the IBM extended character set the symbol is 156.

The bottom line is this: If you want to enter a symbol that is included in your computer's character set and is between 128 and 255, you may or may not be able to do so. If it's a symbol that's included in the ANSI character set used by Windows, Windows will do the translation of the code automatically, dropping the correct symbol into your document. If the symbol doesn't exist in the ANSI character set, this won't work; you'll get a different character instead.

Here's how to try it:

1. Look up the Alt code for the extended character set symbol you want to insert. This would be listed in your computer's manual or your DOS manual.
2. Press Num Lock to activate the numeric keypad on your keyboard, if the keypad is not already active.
3. Enter the code, omitting the initial 0 used the in the example above (e.g. Alt-156 for the Pound symbol—*not* Alt-0156). The symbol is inserted. Windows does the translation to the ANSI character.

If you later edit the file with an application (such as a non-Windows one) that does not use the ANSI character set, you may see strange, unwanted characters on the screen in place of the ones you inserted.

Likewise, if you import a non-Windows application file that contains extended characters other than those included in the ANSI character set, those characters will be represented by small solid or hollow boxes. If the file is a text file, you might try using Write as a translation medium. Load the file into Write and allow it to convert the file to Write format. Write will attempt to translate the extended codes into ANSI codes for you. Before trying this process, make sure that the destination Windows application can read one of the formats that Write can save to. If it can't, try importing the file into another application that can read and convert the source file's character set. Check the documentation supplied with your word-processing or other program for hints on foreign, symbol, or IBM extended character sets. Most full-fledged word processors and desktop publishing programs can deal with such contingencies.

PART THREE

Advanced Topics

Part III deals with somewhat more esoteric aspects of Windows. Chapter 13 covers memory management, multitasking operations, and running batch files, memory-resident programs, and non-Windows applications. Chapter 14 discusses techniques for sophisticated data sharing between programs using DDE and OLE. Chapter 15 introduces you to the multimedia extensions, with discussions about adding sound, CD-ROM, MIDI, and video to your system. Chapter 16 explains a variety of approaches for increasing the speed and improving other performance factors of your Windows setup. Chapter 17 is about running Windows on a network. Chapter 18 offers a detailed discussion of font management and TrueType fonts.

FAST TRACK CHAPTER 13

FAST TRACK

About PIFs: 441

A PIF, or Program Information File, is an optional, auxiliary file that controls how Windows will run a specific, non-Windows application. PIFs contain settings that pertain to memory usage, multitasking options, video modes, keyboard shortcut keys, foreground and background processing, and full-screen or windowing operations. When there isn't a PIF for a non-Windows program, Windows uses its own defaults.

To create a PIF, ... 443

1. Open the Main group and double-click the PIF Editor icon.
2. Open the Mode menu and select the mode for which you are assigning the PIF settings.
3. Make your settings, as described later.
4. Choose File ➤ Save and save the file with the same first name as the application but with .PIF as the extension.

To edit an existing PIF, ... 443

choose File ➤ Open to load the PIF. Make the changes you desire and save the file. To make several PIFs for a program, each of which has different settings, save them under different names.

To run the PIF Editor, ... 444

open the Main group and double-click the PIF Editor icon. The window you see will be determined by the mode you are running in. Standard mode has one dialog box, while 386-Enhanced mode has another type. You can change the mode for which you are assigning the PIF settings by opening the mode menu and choosing the mode you want. Since PIF files store settings for each mode, you can declare settings for Standard mode and 386-Enhanced mode separately. The settings used when you run the programs will be determined by the mode Windows is running in at the time.

make sure you have opened the dialog box for the correct mode. Fill in the settings you want to alter. The Program Filename is required. Others are optional. Refer to the explanations in this chapter or use the Help system if you don't understand the meaning of a setting. Then save the PIF with the File ➤ Save command. Save the file with the same first name as the application but *.pif* as the extension.

run the program from within Windows, as you would any non-Windows application. If the hot-key for the program conflicts with Windows, create a PIF for the pop-up program that reserves the shortcut keys for it.

add their commands to the *config.sys* or *autoexec.bat* file just as you normally would. If only a particular non-Windows application needs the memory-resident driver, create a batch file that loads it and then runs the program. Run the batch file as you would any non-Windows application. The application and memory-resident driver will be removed from memory when you quit the program.

CHAPTER 13

FEATURING

Using the PIF Editor

Creating PIFs for Batch Files

Altering Default PIF Settings

Running Memory-Resident Programs

Fine-Tuning Your Non-Windows Applications with PIFs

This chapter covers non-Windows applications. The first section examines the PIF Editor and explains how and when to use it. The next section explains how to make memory-resident and pop-up programs work properly within Windows, and provides tips about running such non-Windows programs. If you are having problems running programs, you should read this, Chapter 16, and Chapter 19. Chapter 16 covers RAM management. (PIFs and RAM management are interdependent.) You should also read the online documents README.WRI, WININI.WRI, SYSINI.WRI, and NETWORKS.WRI for tips about specific programs and hardware.

THE PIF EDITOR

Windows is a sophisticated graphical operating environment that attempts to make the best of a bad situation. The bad situation is that there are still (despite the enormous popularity of Windows) many more non-Windows applications than Windows applications written to run on IBM PCs and compatibles.

To accommodate this application mix, Windows has to be rather ingenious in managing your computer's hardware resources, scoping out what types of programs it's running, and operating accordingly. This is primarily because of the discrepancies between Windows and non-Windows applications.

Windows applications are designed to coexist peacefully while running simultaneously in the same computer. Windows manages the distribution of your system's resources such as RAM space and CPU time so that well-written applications will rarely clobber each other or tie up more memory than is needed. When you switch between windows, RAM is reallocated to give the current application as much memory as possible in order to maximize the number of programs and documents that can be open at once. Windows sometimes uses hard-disk space as a temporary buffer (a form of virtual memory) in this process. All this happens rather seamlessly (though sometimes slowly), without much fuss, and behind the scenes.

Non-Windows applications, on the other hand, were designed to run one at a time, and are usually memory hogs. They often need at least 640K of RAM, and some may require expanded or extended memory to perform well. When you switch from one non-Windows application to another in Windows, memory is not reallocated. This leaves potentially large amounts of memory tied up even when a program isn't actively in use, with little or no remaining room for additional programs. Running a non-Windows program with several other programs (particularly *other* non-Windows programs) is conceptually like bringing a bunch of ill-mannered guests to a formal dinner.

The moral of all this is simply that Windows has a lot of housekeeping to do in order to keep non-Windows applications happy. In essence, what Windows is doing when running non-Windows applications is giving each of them a simulated PC to work in. The applications don't really "know" that other applications are running, and they expect to have direct access to all the computer's resources such as RAM, printer, communications ports, screen, and so on.

In most cases, Windows 3.1 does pretty well at faking out the application without your help, using various default settings and its own memory-management strategies. (This was not the case with versions before Windows 3.0, which regularly ran out of memory.) However, even Windows 3.1 isn't omniscient, and you may occasionally experience the ungracious locking up of a program, or see messages about the "system integrity" having been corrupted.

In dealing with such problems, the more you know about how Windows manages vital resources for your non-Windows programs, the better you can make them run. This is because Windows lets you fine-tune your applications by storing relevant settings in what are called *PIFs* (Program Information Files). PIFs help Windows successfully run non-Windows programs. The correct PIF settings help an application to take advantage of Windows' considerable conveniences, hopefully saving you from unnecessary aggravation when your program crashes, runs too slowly, or exhibits some other annoying anomaly.

Eventually, problems such as these will diminish as more and more application programs comply with Windows specifications. Since the release of Windows 3.0, hundreds of such applications have become available for the Windows environment and, as this is being written, one magazine reports that approximately 200 more will be released shortly. In the meantime, however, when running DOS applications in Windows, you may have to use the PIF Editor to make and edit your own PIFs.

About PIFs

First off, PIFs are only used with non-Windows applications. (Windows applications already know what to do with Windows.) PIFs are short files stored on disk, usually in the same directory as the application or in the Windows directory. They contain settings Windows will use when running a particular application. These settings affect many aspects of the application's operation, such as, but not limited to:

- the file name and directory
- the directory that becomes active once an application starts

- conventional memory usage
- expanded or extended memory usage
- multitasking priority levels
- video adaptor modes
- the use of keyboard shortcut keys
- foreground and background processing
- full-screen or windowed operation

PIFs generally have the same first name as the application, but have .PIF as the extension. Thus, the PIF for WordStar (WS.EXE) would typically be WS.PIF, though you can name it whatever you like.

Only directories listed in the search path as set up by your AUTOEXEC.BAT file are examined for PIFs.

When you run a non-Windows application from Windows (using any technique), Windows first searches through your files in hopes of finding a PIF for it. If a PIF is found, Windows uses the settings contained in it to run your application. (If you chose to have Setup install applications for you when you installed Windows, it may have created some PIFs for you. Therefore, you might have some PIFs on your hard disk that you don't even know about.) If no PIF is found, Windows uses default settings stored in a file named _DEFAULT.PIF. Microsoft claims these will work with most applications. However, there are notable exceptions to this, particularly among programs that expect or prefer to use expanded memory.

You can run a program directly from its PIF. Just double-click on its name in a File Manager window, add it to a group as a program icon and double-click that, or type its full name into the File ➤ Run dialog box. (This is the same technique as for running any program.) Running directly from a PIF is useful when the PIF isn't in the current search path, or when you have more than one PIF for an application, each with its own settings.

Using PIFs Supplied with Programs

Some programs come supplied with PIFs. When you want to use such a program in Windows, you should copy its PIF to the appropriate directory and drive. The PIF might be identified in the program's manual as designed for IBM's TopView rather than for Windows, but it will work with Windows. The install program for the application might copy the PIF over to your hard disk or it might not. Consult the supplied manual for this.

Use the File Manager to copy the PIF from the floppy disk onto the directory in which the program is located if the install program doesn't do this for you. For example, if WS.EXE is in the C:\WS directory, put the PIF there, too. Then add the PIF to a Program Manager group as you would any other program. When you double-click on the icon to start the program, the PIF will then be found and used.

USING THE PIF EDITOR

TO CREATE A PIF,

1. **Open the Main group and double-click the PIF Editor icon.**
2. **Open the Mode menu and select the mode for which you are assigning the PIF settings.**
3. **Make your settings, as described later.**
4. **Choose File ➤ Save and save the file with the same first name as the application but with .PIF as the extension.**

TO EDIT AN EXISTING PIF,

choose File ➤ Open to load the PIF. Make the changes you desire and save the file. To make several PIFs for a program, each of which has different settings, save them under different names.

Okay, now for the PIF Editor itself. You'll find it in the Main group. It is simple to use once you understand how it works. Essentially it presents you with a dialog box from which you choose or enter settings. Then you save the settings as a PIF.

Every PIF can have two complete groups of settings—one for Standard mode and one for 386-Enhanced mode. The different settings are required since Windows manages system resources differently in the two modes. The 386-Enhanced mode settings additionally include those needed for advanced options such as multitasking and expanded memory use. When creating a new PIF for an application, you can choose which mode you want to make the settings for. Then when you run the application, Windows uses the settings that go with the mode in which you're currently running Windows.

To bring up the PIF Editor,

1. Open the Main group and double-click on the PIF Editor icon. A new PIF is opened. If you are in Standard mode, you will see the box displayed in Figure 13.1. If you are in 386-Enhanced mode, you will see a different dialog box, as we will discuss in the section "The 386-Enhanced Mode Settings." The new PIF has the default settings already filled in, so if you are curious, you can see the settings that Windows uses for applications that don't have PIFs.
2. The options you'll see displayed are the ones for the mode you're now running in. If you want to change the options for another mode, you can do that by opening the Mode menu and choosing it. You'll be alerted to the fact that you're trying to alter settings for the wrong mode. Just click on OK.

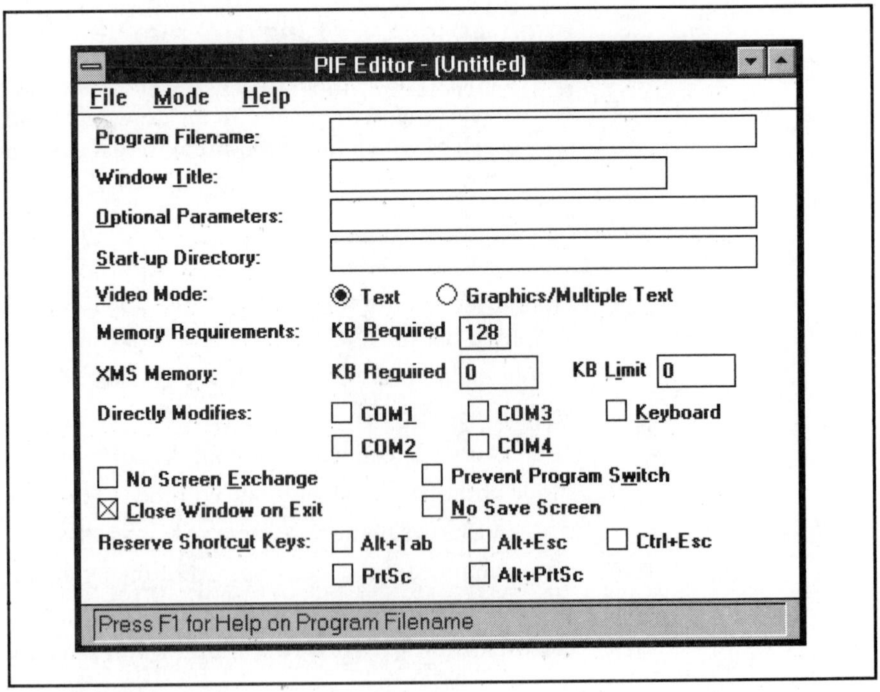

FIGURE 13.1:

The PIF Editor as it appears for making Standard mode settings

PIF Editor - (Untitled)

File Mode Help

Program Filename:

Window Title:

Optional Parameters:

Start-up Directory:

Video Mode: ◉ Text ○ Graphics/Multiple Text

Memory Requirements: KB Required 128

XMS Memory: KB Required 0 KB Limit 0

Directly Modifies: ☐ COM1 ☐ COM3 ☐ Keyboard ☐ COM2 ☐ COM4

☐ No Screen Exchange ☐ Prevent Program Switch

☒ Close Window on Exit ☐ No Save Screen

Reserve Shortcut Keys: ☐ Alt+Tab ☐ Alt+Esc ☐ Ctrl+Esc ☐ PrtSc ☐ Alt+PrtSc

Press F1 for Help on Program Filename

3. When the correct PIF options are displayed, go ahead and make the changes to the default settings as you deem fit, either from your knowledge of the needs of the particular application or from information in the application's manual. (The meaning of all the options for each mode are described on the following pages.)

4. Save the PIF as you would any other file (with File ➤ Save or File ➤ Save As). It should have the same first name as the application it works with and should be stored in the Windows directory or in the application's directory. This way it is sure to be found when you run the application. You edit a PIF by reloading it into the PIF Editor with the File ➤ Open command.

The Standard Mode Settings

In this section, I'll explain each of the Standard mode settings. The 386-Enhanced settings are covered next.

Program Filename

Type in the name of the application that the PIF goes with. Be sure to include the complete path name of the file and its extension, too—for example, C:\WP\WP.EXE. The file can be a .COM, .EXE, or .BAT file. You have to fill in this box or the PIF won't work.

Window Title (Optional)

This is the name that will show up in the title bar for the window (if running in 386 mode) and under the program's icon. Make it descriptive if you like, such as "Joe's Lotus 1-2-3." If you leave this blank, the PIF will still work. Windows will use the program's name instead.

Optional Parameters

In this space, you enter any parameters you want to pass to the program as it starts up. For example, you might want to tell a program to start up in a specific mode or to load a particular file. Whatever information you type in here will be added to the program's line as if you entered it at the DOS command line. For example, say you wanted the PIF to run its application and open the file LETTER.DOC. You'd enter

LETTER.DOC

on this line. Windows takes care of inserting one space between the command name and the parameter. Some parameters require a slash (/) before them. If you normally use a slash when typing your command at the DOS prompt, make sure to enter it here, too. Parameters can be up to 62 characters long. If you enter nothing but a question mark in the box, you'll be prompted for parameters when you run the PIF. This is handy when you want your application to immediately open a file of your choice each time you run it.

Start-up Directory

After the application has started, which drive and directory do you want to be the default? Often you'll enter the directory which contains the application. This is the safest approach, since your application may need to use support files, such as spelling dictionaries or overlays, that are stored in that directory. Having a different directory on this line may leave your application unable to find its files unless the program uses the DOS search path when looking for them (and the search path includes the directory that holds the necessary support files). If it *will* use the search path, then you can use the start-up directory setting to have Windows switch to the directory with the data files you want to have access to. If it *won't* use the search path, it still may be okay to specify a different start-up directory as long as the program doesn't need access to support files. (Many programs don't). If all else fails, and the program does use support files, and it doesn't use the search path to find them, then you either have to put all your data files for that program in the same directory as the program itself or use the program's own commands for switching directories after it starts up.

Video Mode

There are two video modes that an application can use. One shows only text, the other text and graphics. The setting you make here tells Windows how much memory to set aside for storage of a program's screen when you switch to another program. By saving the program's screen in memory, it can restore it quickly when you switch back to it:

Text Choose this option for programs that you know only use text characters on the screen. dBASE, Crosstalk, WordStar, and XTree are just a few examples of text-only programs. Even though there may be lines or boxes on a program's screen, it may still be "character-based," using only the accepted IBM text characters (which include lines and boxes, smiley faces, and so on). This setting uses less system memory to store the screen image, and so is preferable to the graphics setting, since memory used to store the screen diminishes the memory available for the application. But don't use this setting if you think your program might use graphics mode. Some applications, such as Microsoft Word in graphics mode, use graphics to display text attributes such as underlining and italics.

Graphics/Multiple Text Choose this setting for programs that use the screen's graphics mode or that use more than one page of the video controller's memory to store more than a page of text at a time. If you're unsure of the setting you should use, this is the better bet. It will prevent you from getting locked into an application's window with no escape but to terminate the program.

Memory Requirements

In this text box, type in the minimum number of kilobytes the program needs in order to run (refer to its manual). When you run the application, Windows will then compare this amount with what's available to determine if the program will run. If extra memory is available, Windows will give it to the application, so don't worry about that. You might have to do some experimentation to figure out the amount of memory really needed for the application, since manuals are often inaccurate on the topic and typically include the amount of memory needed for DOS, device drivers, and buffers in their estimates.

XMS Memory

XMS memory is extended memory that conforms with the Lotus-Intel-Microsoft-AST standard. Not many applications use this standard, so it's not a big deal. You can probably leave these two settings alone (set at 0) for most applications, unless you're using Lotus 1-2-3 Release 3—which *does* use extended memory—or you know that your program expects some extended memory:

KB Required Enter the amount of XMS required for your program to run at all. If more is available, Windows will allot it, but if less is available, you'll get a message saying that the program won't run because of an XMS memory shortage. Leave this setting at 0 if your program doesn't require or use extended memory. When applications use extended memory, your system will slow down.

KB Limit Enter the maximum amount that should be allotted to the application. Keep this number as low as possible, since Windows needs as much extended memory as it can get to run efficiently. If you enter −1 in this box, all available extended memory will be given to the application, but it may slow Windows to a crawl.

Directly Modifies

Some programs directly control the hardware in your computer, while others use the operating system to do this. Using the operating system to control such things as the keyboard or screen usually guarantees higher compatibility with other programs and machines, but sacrifices potential speed improvements. Some software makers write their programs to control certain parts of the machinery directly, so as to increase the efficiency of the program. In other cases, there is no choice on the programmer's part but to do so. Regardless of the reason, Windows needs to know whether your application expects to monopolize the COM ports or the keyboard, so that it doesn't allow other programs to have access to them, which would cause problems:

COM1, COM2, COM3, COM4 If your program uses one of these ports, click in the check box for the port. Communications programs typically use COM1 or COM2. The other two are rarely used.

Keyboard Some programs directly control the keyboard, rather than going through the BIOS and operating system. Check this box if your application does this. When programs take over the keyboard in this way, you can't control Windows with the normal Ctrl- and Alt- key combinations. As a result, you can't switch between windows or copy parts of the screen onto the Clipboard. (You won't be returned to Windows until you exit the program.) If you check this setting, Windows will take this as a sign that it can give your application memory that it would otherwise use to store the screen display for switching purposes, since it assumes you won't be needing it.

No Screen Exchange

Setting this on prevents you from copying portions of the screen (or all of it) to the Clipboard with the PrtScr and Alt-PrtScr keys. If you don't expect to be making copies of your application's screen, set this option on, since this will give your application some additional memory.

Prevent Program Switch

Setting this on prevents you from switching out of the non-Windows application until you exit the program. This also gives the application more memory, since Windows assumes you won't need RAM to store the screen's contents during switching.

Close Window on Exit

If you want the program's window to disappear and dump you back into Windows when you exit the program, set this box on. Otherwise, the remains of the application stay on the screen when you quit and nothing happens. You will then have to press any key to return to Windows. In most cases you'll want this box set on.

No Save Screen

Choose this option when the application can redraw its own screen when you return to it. This will free up memory for the application to use. If this option is not set on, Windows will allocate some memory for temporary storage of the screen image when you briefly switch to another application.

Reserve Shortcut Keys

These options let you specify which Alt- and Ctrl-key combinations your application needs to use. Specifying these keys prevents a conflict between your application and Windows when you press the keys. When a box is checked, Windows relinquishes use of the key (and its normal functioning with Windows) and allows your application to use it. Check one or more of these boxes only when your application needs the key combination(s).

Basic 386-Enhanced Mode Settings

In 386-Enhanced mode, the PIF Editor comes up with a slightly different dialog window, as shown in Figure 13.2. These are the basic settings. You can get to additional settings by clicking on the Advanced button, but I'll cover them after explaining all the basic settings. (Program Filename, Window Title, Start-up Directory, and Close Window on Exit all have the same meanings and explanations as for the Standard mode settings above.)

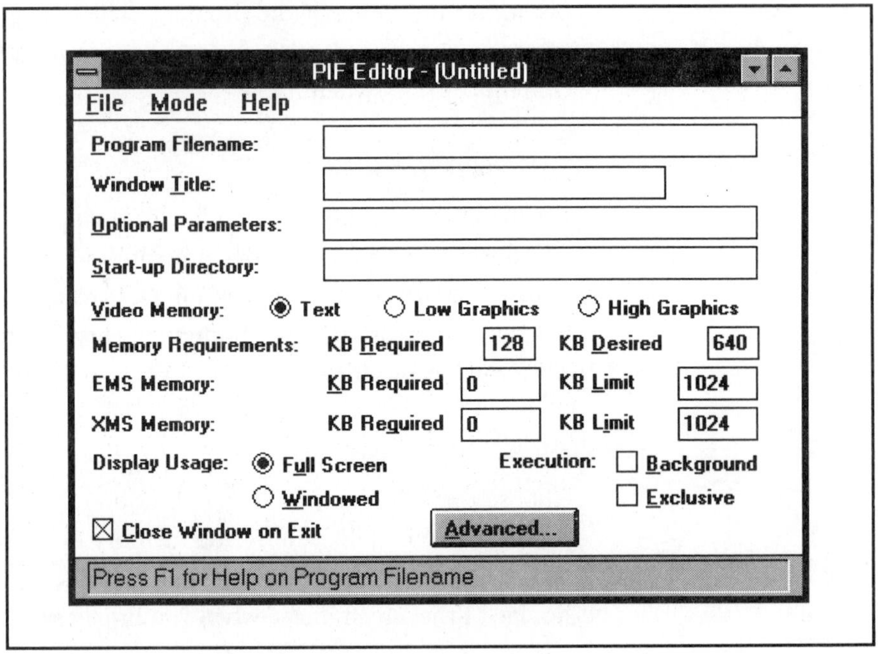

PIF Editor - (Untitled)
File Mode Help
Program Filename:
Window Title:
Optional Parameters:
Start-up Directory:
Video Memory: Text Low Graphics High Graphics
Memory Requirements: KB Required 128 KB Desired 640
EMS Memory: KB Required 0 KB Limit 1024
XMS Memory: KB Required 0 KB Limit 1024
Display Usage: Full Screen Execution: Background
Windowed Exclusive
Close Window on Exit Advanced...
Press F1 for Help on Program Filename

FIGURE 13.2: *The default settings for 386-Enhanced mode PIFs*

Optional Parameters

The description of these settings is the same as for Standard mode, but parameters are stored separately for each of the two modes. Because of this, you can have one parameter for Standard mode and another for 386-Enhanced mode. Which parameter is used will depend on which mode Windows is running in at the time you run the application. You might find saving two sets of parameters useful with programs that you want to behave differently in 386-Enhanced mode. For example, some programs let you dictate in the command line what kind and amount of extended or expanded memory they can use. Since only in 386-Enhanced mode can an application use expanded memory, you would want to use a different parameter for that mode than in Standard mode, where only extended memory is available.

Video Memory

This determines how much system memory Windows allocates for saving the application's screen image when you switch away from the application. Choosing Text mode allocates about 16K, Low Graphics 32K, and High Graphics 128K. Windows can adjust the amount later as you switch modes, calling on available memory for storing the screen image, should you switch away from the application. If you choose a mode that's too low for your screen's and application's needs, however, your screen may be only partially restored or may go blank when you switch back to the application. But using too high a mode uses up more memory. As a rule of thumb, CGA screens only use Text and Low Graphics. VGA and EGA screens often use High Graphics. If in doubt, experiment by running the PIF with different settings and see what happens. If you've chosen too low a setting, your application's window will be partially or totally missing. If you want to ensure that there's always enough memory available for the application's screen, choose High Graphics and turn on the Retain Video Memory option. Retain Video Memory prevents windows from releasing memory to other applications when that memory is not being used as temporary storage for your display. You choose this option from the Advanced Settings dialog box as explained in the section below, "Advanced 386-Enhanced Mode Settings."

Memory Requirements

This controls the amount of conventional memory given to the application:

KB Required See the same section under Standard mode for an explanation of the KB Required box. Setting this to –1 gives the application as much conventional memory as is available.

KB Desired This sets the ceiling for the amount of conventional memory the application can have: 640K is the maximum. If you want other applications to have some memory, set this amount lower than that. A setting of –1 allocates as much as possible, up to 640K.

EMS Memory

EMS is *expanded memory.* Not to be confused with *extended memory,* this is another form of memory above the normal 640K DOS limit. Some programs (Ventura for example) can use expanded memory to improve their performace greatly. One of the big advantages of running Windows in 386-Enhanced mode is that it gives your applications access to expanded memory. Though Windows requires that you set up any memory above 640K in your computer as extended memory, and uses it as such, it can simulate expanded memory for programs that need it. It does this on the fly, by loading an expanded memory manager and giving up some of its system memory normally used for Windows applications.

There are two settings for EMS memory. These work just like the settings for conventional and XMS memory:

KB Required This setting tells Windows how much has to be available before even trying to run the application. If it isn't available, you'll see a message telling you to free up some memory and then try running the application again. Set this to zero to indicate that none is required for the application to run, even though it might benefit from having some.

KB Limit This setting prevents the application from taking all the available EMS (which it will do unless told otherwise). If you want some EMS left for other applications, enter a number in here that is less than the total EMS but more than the Required amount. A zero entered here prevents Windows from assigning any EMS to the program.

XMS Memory

Same as in Standard Mode.

Display Usage

The 386-Enhanced mode lets you run a non-Windows application either full-screen or in a window. This setting determines which of those two ways your application will initially come up. Of course, as explained earlier in this book, you can toggle between these two views with Alt-Enter. Note that in full-screen display, the mouse is surrendered to the application. When the application is running in a window, Windows takes over the mouse. Then it can only be used for Windows operations. When running in a window, the application also uses more memory.

Execution

This section determines whether the application will run when it's not in the foreground. It also determines whether other programs will be allowed to run in the background:

NOTE *See Chapter 5 for information about device contention and background and foreground prioritizing.*

Background When checked, this box tells Windows to keep running the application (such as a database doing a sort or a spreadsheet calculating) even when it's inactive or iconized and you're using another program. Otherwise, the application stops running until you activate the window again. Theoretically, a communications program could also be assigned to continue working in the background, sending or receiving data, though you should experiment with it just to see whether any received data are lost. Your computer may not be able to keep up with the incoming data while servicing other programs that you are running.

Exclusive When checked, this box tells Windows not to work on other programs while this application is active, even if the other programs are set to work in the background. This gives the program more CPU time, and more memory. For maximum memory advantage, also run the program full-screen.

Advanced 386-Enhanced Mode Settings

If you need to get into the real nitty-gritty of your applications in 386-Enhanced mode, Windows will certainly let you. When you click on Advanced in the 386-Enhanced PIF Editor dialog box, a bigger, more intimidating dialog box with 29 more settings comes up, as shown in Figure 13.3. (And we were told Windows made everything easy!) Well, at least you'll typically only have to deal with the second section, because it covers expanded and extended memory usage.

Multitasking Options

This section determines the allocation of CPU time to the application under three different circumstances:

Background Priority The number you type here determines the relative amount of CPU time the application gets when running in the background (in arbitrary units). This number doesn't have any effect unless the

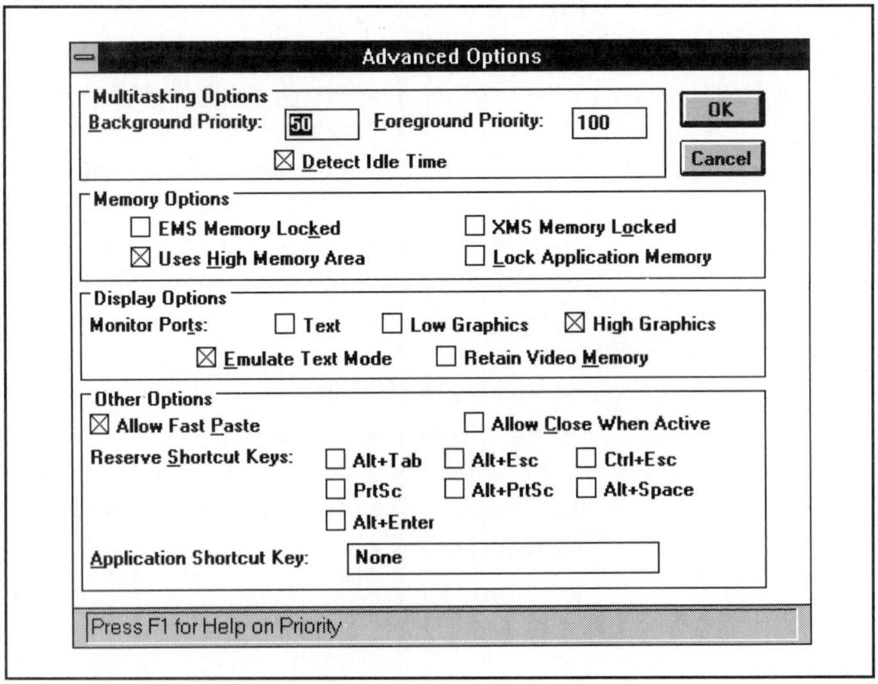

FIGURE 13.3:
Advanced PIF settings for 386-Enhanced mode

Advanced Options

Multitasking Options
Background Priority: 50 Foreground Priority: 100
☒ Detect Idle Time
OK
Cancel

Memory Options
☐ EMS Memory Locked ☐ XMS Memory Locked
☒ Uses High Memory Area ☐ Lock Application Memory

Display Options
Monitor Ports: ☐ Text ☐ Low Graphics ☒ High Graphics
☒ Emulate Text Mode ☐ Retain Video Memory

Other Options
☒ Allow Fast Paste ☐ Allow Close When Active
Reserve Shortcut Keys: ☐ Alt+Tab ☐ Alt+Esc ☐ Ctrl+Esc
☐ PrtSc ☐ Alt+PrtSc ☐ Alt+Space
☐ Alt+Enter
Application Shortcut Key: None

Press F1 for Help on Priority

application's background operation is enabled, as described earlier. The number can range from 0 to 10,000, and the default is 50. Since all applications are normally set to a background priority of 50, they all get equal amounts of CPU time when in the background. If they were all set to 10,000, they would still get equal amounts of time, since the setting is a relative figure. If you want one program to have more CPU time when in the background, increase its number. Remember that the program in the foreground (the active application program) also takes CPU time.

Foreground Priority This determines how much CPU time the application gets when it's active (in the foreground), relative to other applications' settings. The default is 100. Normally you'll want to set this number higher than the background setting, so the application works faster when the window is active and slower when inactive or iconized. There might be instances when you would want this number to be relatively low compared to other programs, though. For example, some programs, such as simple word processors, need only a little CPU time to keep working fairly smoothly. If you want to give more CPU time to your background programs, try lowering the settings (both foreground and background) for the foreground program.

Detect Idle Time When this option is set on, Windows will stop giving CPU time to an application when it senses that the application isn't doing anything new. Applications often sit around waiting for you to type something on the keyboard. So instead of continually checking to see whether you've typed something, the CPU can do more productive things like working on background applications. This option is set on by default and should probably be left that way.

Memory Options

Now for the dreaded memory options. This is where things can get a little sticky. Make sure you understand how your application works vis-à-vis memory. Does it use expanded or extended memory? What are its minimum requirements and maximum limits? How much do you really need for the work you do? My advice is to answer these questions *before* you start tinkering with the memory settings. If you are sketchy about distinctions between EMS and XMS, you might want to refer to the next chapter as well as to the discussion below:

EMS Memory Locked When on, this option will prevent Windows from swapping your application's EMS data to hard disk when other applications need it, or to simulate more EMS than is physically there using virtual memory management. Locking the EMS cuts down on the EMS available but increases overall performance of the application, since disk swapping takes time.

XMS Memory Locked The locking option has the same effect as described immediately above, but affects XMS memory instead.

Uses High Memory Area When checked, this box tells Windows that the application can use the first 64K of extended memory (just above the 1 megabyte boundary). This area is called the High Memory Area or HMA and lots of programs use it as a way of avoiding RAM shortages. For example, many memory-resident utilities, BIOS "shadowing" programs, and network drivers use this area. If your application expects to use this area, set the check box on.

If no other program is using the HMA when you boot up Windows, Windows will let other programs use it. If it's already in use, say, for a network driver, Windows will note this and won't let any programs use the HMA, even if their PIFs are set to use it.

Also, Windows is smart enough to prevent contention between multiple programs that use HMA. So you can have more than one program using HMA at a time in Windows, whereas under DOS this is impossible. Windows does this by swapping the 64K of HMA in and out as you switch between programs.

If you don't know whether your program uses the HMA, leave this box checked. If you want to prevent the program from using HMA, turn the setting off.

Lock Application Memory This is similar to the lock options for EMS and XMS memory, but it applies to conventional memory only. It prevents Windows from swapping out your application's memory to hard disk when you switch to another application, as long as your application is running. Checking this could speed up the application, but it will probably reduce the efficiency of Windows in general, since it may make Windows do more swapping of other applications than it would normally have to.

Display Options

This section of the Advanced PIF options affects the way Windows controls your screen and the memory it uses to store the screen image when switching between windows:

Monitor Ports If your application directly writes to the display adapter's hardware (the card in your PC), you might have to use one or more of these options. Windows assumes applications use acceptable means (DOS and the BIOS) to write to the screen. Some programs don't, however. (An example is Microsoft Flight Simulator, which writes directly to the screen.) Use these options to tell Windows to "monitor," or watch, what your application is doing to your display card, so that the screen reappears correctly when you switch away from the program and return to it. Note that these settings are irrelevant to IBM VGA and some other adapters. Most applications require the High Graphics setting, so it's the default. Few require monitoring in Text and Low Graphics modes.

For most applications, you can leave these settings as they are. However, if the screen does not properly restore when switching back to it, and you have tried assigning a higher mode (such as High Graphics) to it in the main PIF Editor dialog box, try altering these settings by choosing the setting that correponds to the video mode that the application runs in.

If you notice that your application is running too slowly because of sluggish screen updating, try turning off all monitoring check boxes. This may speed up operation of the application. However, it may prevent your returning to the application from Windows. The only solution is to quit the application before switching back to Windows.

Note that these settings have no effect when your application is running in a window.

Emulate Text Mode If you see garbage characters on the screen when your application is running, if the cursor is in the wrong location, or if the application won't run at all, try turning this setting off. Normally it is on and speeds up text display.

Retain Video Memory See "Video Memory" above.

Other Options

This section contains some odds and ends about such sundries as shortcut keys and pasting information into your application:

Allow Fast Paste Normally this option is on. If you have trouble pasting information into your application from the Clipboard, quit the application, modify its PIF by turning this off, and try again. The pasting will be slower, but it might work.

Reserve Shortcut Keys Same as in Standard mode.

Allow Close When Active When checked, this box lets you exit Windows or close the application's window without actually terminating the application itself. This is a risky option, because you would lose data if you didn't manually close the files you were working on with the application. Only use this option if you know the application uses DOS file handles to flag which files are open. Windows will ensure that they are closed when it closes the application. If you're in doubt, don't use this option!

Application Shortcut Key The key combination you enter here will cause your application to jump to the foreground. Whenever the application is running, the shortcut key will work. Otherwise it's deactivated. This is a great feature because it means you don't have to use the Task List, or click on the application's window, or press Alt-Esc to get to an application. By giving each one a special shortcut key, you can switch between them quite easily. To enter the shortcut key, click on the text area for the key and press the key combination you want to assign to the application. It has to include the Alt or Ctrl key, or both. You can use function keys in the combination as well. Three keys are okay, too, such as Shift-Ctrl-F8, or Alt-Ctrl-Z. Don't set a shortcut key to be a combination that other programs might use, such as Alt-F (which many Windows applications use to open their File menu), since the shortcut keys are assigned exclusively to the application that the PIF is for. Also, you can't use Esc, Enter, Tab, the spacebar, PrtScr, or Backspace. Choose OK after entering the key. To erase a shortcut key, click on the text area and press Shift-Backspace.

CHANGING SETTINGS WHILE A PROGRAM IS RUNNING

You can change some PIF settings while a program is running in 386-Enhanced mode. (Other modes don't allow this.) There are four changes you can make. You can:

- change the display from full-screen to windowed or vice-versa.
- change the foreground and background priorities.
- change the multitasking options to turn on or off background processing and/or make the program the exclusive task.
- terminate the non-Windows program (in case it bombed or you somehow lost control of it).

To change the settings, first make sure the non-Windows application is running in a window by pressing Alt-Enter while in full-screen mode. Then open the Control box of the application's window and choose Settings. The dialog box such as the one shown in Figure 13.4 will appear. The application's name will be in the window's title bar. In this case, it's WordStar Professional, since that's the program that was running in the window.

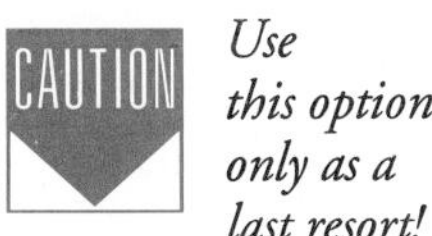

Use this option only as a last resort!

The settings are identical to the ones in the PIF dialog boxes, with the exception of the Terminate option. Use the Terminate button as the *last resort* when a non-Windows application *bombs* (crashes, hangs, unexpectedly terminates, or whatever you like to call it) in Windows. This might result from a bug in the application, a bug in Windows, or simply a bad relationship between the two. With so many variables, it's hard to know the cause of a crash.

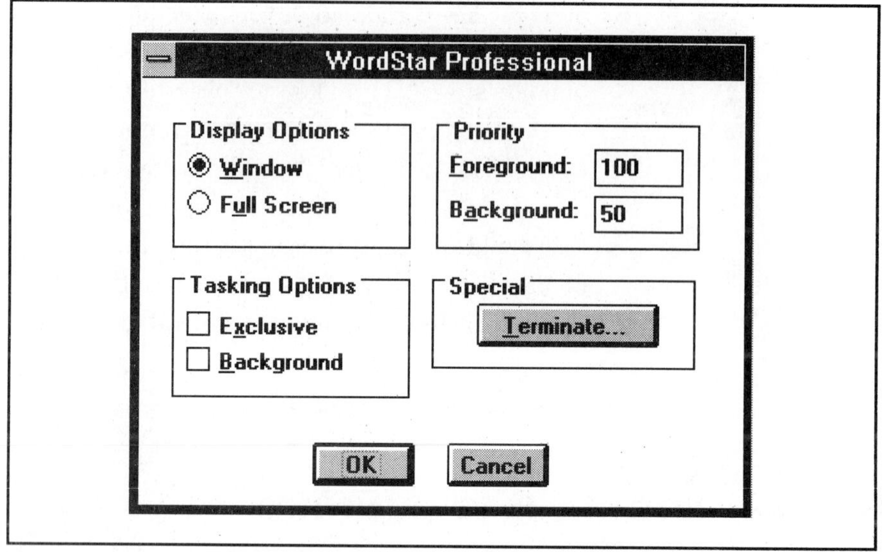

FIGURE 13.4: *You can change a few PIF settings for a running DOS application from this box. You open it by windowing the application and choosing Settings from the Control box.*

As you experiment with PIFs, you're likely to come up with a few crashes, so get used to this option. The good news is that instead of rebooting your computer, which could have adverse affects on the programs you're running, Windows lets you close the bombed application, save any other open files, close applications, exit Windows, and *then* reboot your computer. Do reboot, so that DOS and everything else is reloaded. Don't just rerun Windows, since DOS or the device drivers might have been corrupted when you terminated the application program!

PIFS FOR BATCH FILES

Though it might sound strange at first, you can create a PIF for a batch file rather than just for applications per se. Using a PIF for a batch file lets you set the various PIF parameters for it. When the batch file is run from its PIF, all the settings come into play and they will affect all the programs in the batch file. (A *batch file* is a group of commands that executes DOS in sequence for you, without your having to type them in.) A typical batch file might switch directories, load a memory-resident program, and then run an application.

For example, I have a batch file for running Ventura Publisher called V.BAT that looks like this:

```
CD\WYSE
NSCREEN GRAPHICS
VPPROF
```

I have to load the program for my screen to work with Ventura. If I don't load it, Ventura bombs. Therefore, I can't start Ventura the usual way with VPPROF (which, incidentally, is also a batch file). What do I do? Well, I could run NSCREEN first and then run Ventura, but that's a pain because it means going through the motions of running two programs instead of one. Or I could just run my batch file from Ventura too, as I would any other program. But here's the catch: When executing a batch file, Windows doesn't look for the PIF file that goes with each application in the list. It only looks for the PIF file with the *batch file's* name. Thus, when I run V.BAT, it looks for V.PIF. Even if VPPROF.PIF exists and has all the necessary PIF settings in it, they won't go into effect! This is really dumb on Windows' part. Ventura needs special PIF settings since it uses expanded memory, so I had to create a PIF file called V.PIF with all the same settings I'd normally use for Ventura.

The moral is this: If you use a batch file to run an application that needs a PIF, make sure you have a PIF for the batch file, too. Put the same settings in the batch file's PIF that you'd put in the application's PIF.

If the batch file runs multiple applications that normally use different PIF settings, try to concoct a PIF containing settings that will accommodate the needs of all the programs. In other words, make it as generous as possible in assigning memory, screen modes, and so on.

If the applications require radically different settings, such as lots of expanded memory for one, and lots of extended memory for the other, you're out of luck. This is just a limitation of Windows that you will have to live with. You'll have to run the applications separately, or perhaps use a utility such as a fancy macro program that can run applications sequentially from within Windows.

ALTERING THE DEFAULT PIF SETTINGS

As mentioned earlier, each time you run a program that doesn't have a PIF, Windows uses default settings for the application. (To see what the defaults are, open a new PIF file and examine it.) If you want to change the default settings, you can. This might be useful if you want all the programs without PIFs to run a particular way, such as full-screen with exclusive attention of the CPU.

NOTE *These settings don't affect the default settings you see in a new PIF.*

To do this, just create a PIF called _DEFAULT.PIF. (Note that the first character in the name is the underline character.) Leave the Window Title box empty, but type any valid program name in the Program Filename box. (C:\COMMAND.COM is a good choice.) Windows will ignore the program name when it uses the PIF as a default, but the PIF Editor needs a file name or it won't save the file. When you run any program that doesn't have a PIF, these _DEFAULT.PIF settings will go into effect.

RUNNING MEMORY-RESIDENT PROGRAMS

A special class of programs called *memory-resident programs* deserves specific attention when used from Windows. These programs include "pop-up programs," such as Borland's Sidekick, and memory-resident utilities that don't pop up, such as keyboard enhancers like SmartKey (No Brainer Software). Disk-enhancement programs such as SMARTDrive and Stacker are also examples of memory-resident programs, as are CD-ROM or tape backup device drivers. Sometimes these programs are called TSRs for *terminate and stay resident.* Memory-resident programs hang out invisibly in the background until reactivated by a precipitating event. For example, Sidekick comes to life when you press Ctrl-Alt.

Though you're likely to have success running these programs in Windows, just as you always have from DOS, a little more understanding of them may help you to get the most out of them, while minimizing the impact on Windows' performance.

Here's an example of how you can run such a program. Suppose you like to use Lotus 1-2-3 and have Sidekick available as a pop-up program. There are several ways to do this. Most simply, you can run a DOS session by double-clicking the MS-DOS Prompt icon in Program Manager. Then run Sidekick, followed by Lotus 1-2-3, both from the DOS prompt. Sidekick and Lotus 1-2-3 will then work just as if they were run from "normal" DOS. Pretty straightforward. Another way to do it is to create a batch file that runs both programs, then give the batch file an icon and add it to a Program Manager group.

Likewise, if you just want to run a DOS session and have Sidekick available while doing so, simply run Sidekick in whichever way you like (DOS prompt, Program Manager, File Manager, Run command, etc.).

Regardless of the technique you use, once a memory-resident program is loaded, Windows will confirm that it has been installed by issuing a message on your screen. If it's a pop-up program, then pressing the relevant keys that normally bring it up (such as Ctrl-Alt for Sidekick) will work as expected. If the pop-up program uses keys that conflict with keys used by Windows or Windows programs, make a PIF for it and reserve its pop-up key by clicking one of the Reserve Shortcut Keys checkboxes.

Any memory-resident program will stay active until the DOS session it is running in is closed. Typically that happens when you type **EXIT** at the DOS prompt. If you run your memory-resident program from a batch file, though, the DOS session will close only after the last line of the batch file finishes executing.

If you want every DOS session you run from Windows to have the advantage of a particular memory-resident program by default, load that program *before* you run Windows. For example, suppose you want every DOS session to have Sidekick available automatically: you should load Sidekick before running Windows.

However, loading it this way will take up precious conventional memory from all other programs, including Windows (as is the case with device drivers, discussed below). For this reason, if you don't need the memory-resident program for all your DOS sessions, economize on your system's conventional memory by loading the memory-resident program only in the DOS session with which you plan to use it.

For a discussion of the impact of memory-resident programs on conventional memory, and techniques for loading them most efficiently, see Chapter 16.

Using Device Drivers

If all the programs you intend to run need a certain device driver, just add it to the CONFIG.SYS or AUTOEXEC.BAT program. This is how manufacturers usually tell you to install their drivers.

If only a particular non-Windows application needs the driver, then create a batch file with the utility in it (it has to be an .EXE or .COM file, though—not a .SYS file), followed by the related program. The Ventura batch file I explained earlier is a good example of this. It loads a screen driver and then Ventura:

```
NSCREEN GRAPHICS
VPPROF
```

If you're running in 386-Enhanced mode, you can install a driver that affects only Windows applications. To do this, just add the driver name to the WINSTART.BAT file. Then only Windows applications will have access to the driver.

FAST TRACK CHAPTER 14

FAST TRACK

To embed an object in a Write document, ... 472

1. Load both files.
2. Determine the insertion point in the text for the object.
3. Choose Edit ➤ Insert Object.
4. Select the program and click OK.
5. Choose File ➤ Update.
6. Choose File ➤ Exit & Return to….

To edit an embedded object, ... 474

1. Double-click on the embedded object.
2. Make changes to the object in its original application.
3. Choose File ➤ Update.
4. Close the application.

To link an object to a Write file, ... 476

1. Copy the object in its original application to the Clipboard.
2. Open Write and determine the insertion point.
3. Choose Edit ➤ Paste Link.

To edit a linked object, ... 478

1. Double-click on the linked object.
2. Edit the object in its original application.
3. Close the application.

To set a link for manual updating in Write, ... 485

1. Select the object in Write.
2. Choose Edit ➤ Links.
3. Select the Manual option button and click on OK.

To update the link manually, ... 490

1. Select the object in Write.
2. Choose Edit ➤ Links.
3. Click on the Update Now button and click on OK.

To package a file, ... 490

1. Run Object Packager.
2. Choose File ➤ Import.
3. Select the file to package.
4. Choose Edit ➤ Copy Package.

To package part of a file, ... 495

1. Select part of the source document and choose Edit ➤ Copy.
2. Run Object Packager and choose Edit ➤ Paste or Edit ➤ Paste Link.
3. Choose Edit ➤ Copy Package.
4. Determine the insertion point in the destination document.
5. Choose Edit ➤ Paste.

CHAPTER 14

FEATURING

Embedding and Linking Objects into Documents

Packaging Objects and Applications with Documents

Sharing Information among Applications

ne of Windows' greatest advantages is the ability it gives you to use two or more separate programs in concert, almost as if they were designed as a single piece of software. You've already learned how you can use the Clipboard to freely pass information—text, numeric data, drawings, charts, and so on—from one program to another. But Windows can do better yet, providing a new information-sharing system that allows the information passed to other programs to remain "linked" to the program from which it came. Microsoft calls this new-and-improved feature OLE, for *Object Linking and Embedding.*

How does OLE (pronounced *olé*) benefit you? Take a classic business example. Say you're starting a new enterprise and want to put together a convincing, professional-looking business plan with your Windows word processor. Of course, you'll need to substantiate the projections in the plan with financial data taken from a spreadsheet. But rather than simply place a set of numbers into your document, you can link the "live" spreadsheet directly to it. That way, if you get new information and must change the numbers in the spreadsheet, they'll automatically change in your business plan as well. Figure 14.1 shows a Microsoft Excel spreadsheet linked to a Microsoft Word document, where it appears in identical form.

When it's time to enter new data, you don't have to locate and open the spreadsheet program yourself. Since Windows knows which program the numbers came from, you just click on the copy of the spreadsheet in your word-processor document to bring up the spreadsheet software on your screen, with the correct file loaded.

It's easy to think of other uses for this sort of "smart," sophisticated information sharing. With OLE, you can link charts, graphics, and even sounds created in one program to documents you're working on in another.

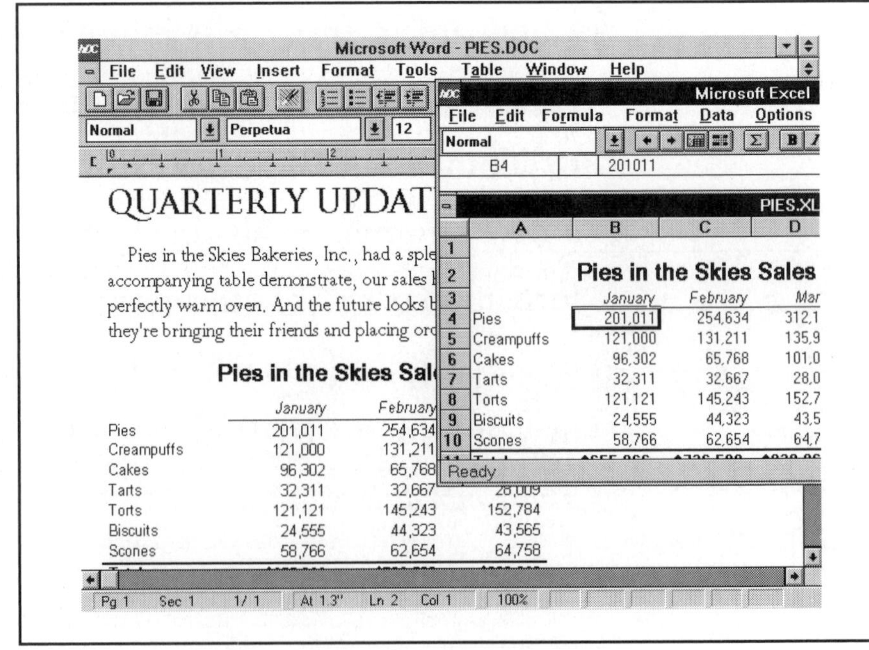

FIGURE 14.1:

In this illustration, the Excel spreadsheet on the right has been linked to a Microsoft Word document behind it. Once the link has been made, any changes made in the spreadsheet automatically appear in the Word document.

You might want to add a chart from that same spreadsheet program to your business plan to communicate the numeric information graphically. Again, you'd want the chart to be redrawn automatically to reflect any changes in the underlying data.

Or perhaps you're using a presentation graphics package to prepare slides and speaker's notes for an upcoming sales tour. You plan to fine-tune your spiel for each audience by including some references to the local geography, cuisine, and so on. With OLE, you can edit the text of your talk with your favorite word processor and let Windows see to it that the changes show up in your speaker's notes automatically.

Windows 3.1 provides a number of methods for taking advantage of OLE, allowing you to choose the technique that's best suited to each specific situation. There are several ways to link or embed information from one application directly to or in another. In addition, a special utility program called the Object Packager provides a kind of "way station" between the original application and the destination program. All of these techniques are described in this chapter.

UNDERSTANDING WINDOWS' INFORMATION-SHARING FEATURES

As the latest of Windows' built-in systems for sharing information between programs, OLE is easier to use and more powerful than the two earlier ones, the Clipboard and Dynamic Data Exchange. Still, Windows continues to provide the older information-sharing features, and you'll want to be familiar with them.

The Clipboard was the first information-sharing feature and it is covered in Chapter 8. It continues to be a convenient way to transfer information between programs. In addition, many OLE activities rely on the Clipboard.

With previous versions of Windows, you could achieve some of the same benefits you get with OLE, using a technique called *Dynamic Data Exchange,* or DDE. One drawback of DDE is that it leaves much of the work of sharing information to each individual program. Thus, you must use a different method to link documents with DDE for every program—you have to consult the program's manual for instructions. Still, since some earlier programs haven't yet been upgraded to work with OLE, DDE can be an extremely useful tool for sharing information between programs.

USING OLE TO SHARE INFORMATION

At this point, the benefits of OLE probably sound a little abstract. To get a feeling for how OLE really works and to get a sense of its inherent limitations, let's try a couple of actual examples.

In the process of working with OLE, you'll be learning some new terminology. Like OLE itself, most of the OLE terms may sound a bit obscure at first, at least to those of us who aren't already computer professionals. But since you'll be seeing a lot of these terms, it will pay to acquaint yourself with them now.

Two OLE terms that are fairly self-explanatory refer to the documents with which an object is associated: the *source document* is the one in which an object is originally created, while a *destination* document is the one into which you place the object.

OLE makes possible two separate types of information sharing: *embedding* and *linking*. Embedding is the simpler of the two.

EMBEDDING A PAINTBRUSH PICTURE IN A WRITE DOCUMENT

TO EMBED AN OBJECT IN A WRITE DOCUMENT,

1. **Load both files.**
2. **Determine the insertion point in the text for the object.**
3. **Choose Edit ➤ Insert Object.**
4. **Select the program and click OK.**
5. **Choose File ➤ Update.**
6. **Choose File ➤ Exit & Return to....**

Many of the applications included with Windows have been designed with OLE in mind. For your first experience with OLE, you'll use Paintbrush and Write to produce an illustrated report by embedding a Paintbrush picture in a Write document.

Begin by starting Windows and opening Write. Type a paragraph or two of text, or open an existing text file. Save the document as EMBED.WRI. With the text of your dummy report in place, you're ready to embed a Paintbrush picture in the document:

1. Find a point in the text where you'd like an illustration to appear and move the insertion point there.
2. Choose Insert Object from the Edit menu. In OLE's jargon, an *object* is any chunk of information passed as a bundle between one program and another. It can consist of as little as a single spreadsheet cell, database field, or graphic element, or as much as an entire spreadsheet, database, or—as in this example—a complete picture. You'll see the Insert Object dialog box, which lists all the programs installed on your hard disk that have been designed to use OLE.
3. Select Paintbrush Picture and choose OK. Paintbrush opens.
4. Draw something in the workspace. Alternatively, you can choose Paste From on Paintbrush's Edit menu to open an existing Paintbrush file.
5. Choose Update on Paintbrush's File menu. This transfers a copy of your drawing into the Write document, while keeping you in Paintbrush.
6. From the File menu, choose Exit & Return to EMBED.WRI. Windows sends you back to Write where you'll see the drawing at the previous insertion point (see Figure 14.2). You can continue editing the text if you like.

So what exactly does it mean to embed an object? Embedding an object means that you place a copy of the object into a document in another program, much as you would with the Clipboard. As with Clipboard transfers, once the object is embedded, there's no longer a connection between it and the source document.

FIGURE 14.2:

The embedded picture in the destination document

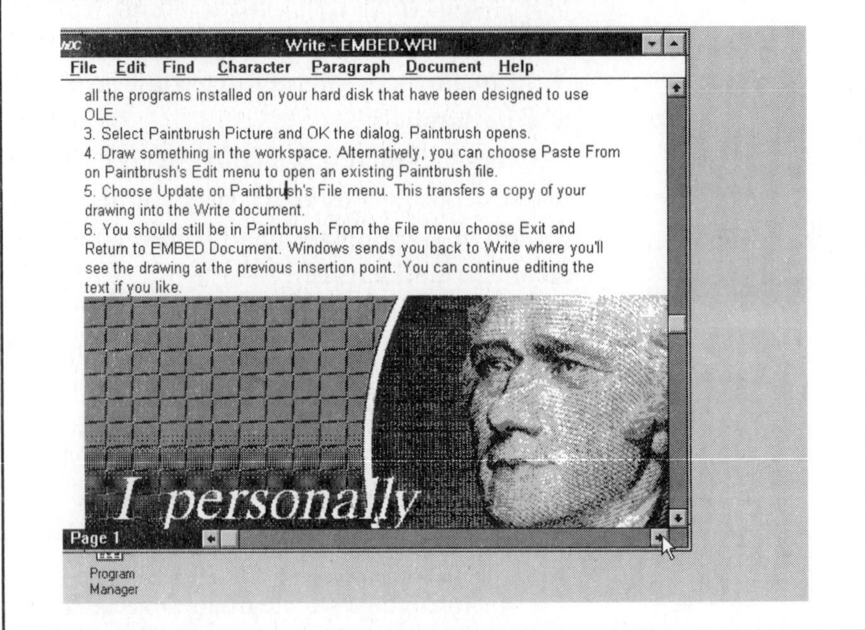

Editing an Embedded Picture

TO EDIT AN EMBEDDED OBJECT,

1. **Double-click on the embedded object.**
2. **Make changes to the object in its original application.**
3. **Choose File ➤ Update.**
4. **Close the application.**

There's an important advantage to embedding the object rather than copying it with the Clipboard. The embedding process forges a "trail" between the two programs, allowing you to open the program that created the object and edit the object by simply selecting it in the destination document. However, since the embedded object is no longer connected to the original source document, any changes you make now won't appear in the original. Likewise, if you open and edit the original source document separately, the changes you make won't show up in the destination document.

You should use embedding only if you think you might need to edit an object after placing it in the destination document, but you don't plan to keep the original copy of the object for other purposes, such as placing it in other documents. (Linking, on the other hand, preserves the connection between the object and its source document—but we'll cover linking a little later.)

To see how all this works, try making a change to the picture you just embedded in your Write document:

1. If necessary, scroll the Write document so that you can see at least a part of the embedded picture.
2. Double-click anywhere on the picture. Alternatively, you can click on the picture and open the Edit menu. You'll see a choice called Edit Paintbrush Picture Object, which you should choose. Either way, Paintbrush should automatically open, displaying your picture.
3. Make whatever changes you like in the picture.
4. Choose Update from Paintbrush's File menu.
5. From the File menu in Paintbrush, choose Exit & Return to EMBED.WRI. Paintbrush closes and Windows sends you back to your Write document. The picture should display the changes you've just made.

Embedding a Sound File in a Cardfile Card

Embedding allows you to place a copy of any sound file stored on your system in a destination document created in Write, Cardfile, or other applications. After embedding, you'll see a microphone icon representing the sound file in the destination document. You can then play the sound simply by double-clicking on the icon.

Let's see how this works. In the process, you'll learn a second major technique for embedding that's even simpler than the first: simply copy the object from the source document and paste it into the destination:

1. Start Sound Recorder and open the sound file you want to embed. Make any changes you want.
2. Choose Edit ➤ Copy.
3. Switch to the Program Manager and start Cardfile.
4. In Cardfile, choose Edit ➤ Paste. The microphone icon appears in the upper-left corner of the current card.
5. To play the sound you've just embedded, double-click on it. You can accomplish the same thing by choosing Edit ➤ Sound Object ➤ Play.

Just like the embedding method you learned first, this copy-paste technique works only when both applications are designed for OLE. Otherwise you'll simply move the information without any connection to the original application.

To edit the embedded sound from Cardfile:

1. Choose Edit ➤ Sound Object ➤ Edit. Sound Recorder starts and loads the embedded sound file.
2. Make your changes to the sound.
3. Open Sound Recorder's File menu and choose Update.
4. Choose File ➤ Exit to close Sound Recorder and return to Cardfile. The embedded sound has been updated with the changes you made.

This same technique works for embedding pictures from Paintbrush into both Cardfile cards and Write documents. Starting from Paintbrush, you cut or copy the part of the picture you want to embed. You then switch to Cardfile or Write and choose Edit ➤ Paste. That's all there is to it.

Linking a Paintbrush Picture to Write and Cardfile Documents

TO LINK AN OBJECT TO A WRITE FILE,

1. **Copy the object in its original application to the Clipboard.**
2. **Open Write and determine the insertion point.**
3. **Choose Edit ➤ Paste Link.**

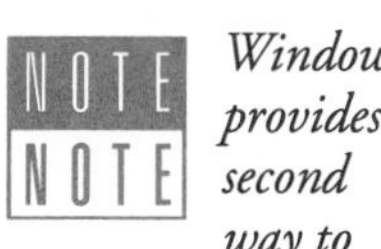

Windows provides a second way to embed or link objects, using a utility program called Object Packager, discussed later in the chapter.

Though the procedure for linking an object is similar to the one for embedding, there is an important difference: linking keeps alive the connection between the object and a source document. Instead of copying the object's data to the destination document, you're establishing a link in the destination document back to the source document. That is, you're telling the destination document where it can find the object.

As with embedding, you can call up the program which originally created the object directly from the destination document. This time, however, editing the object *will* change the source document. Likewise, if you open and edit the source document the ordinary way—independently of the link process—any changes you make will automatically appear in the destination document the next time you open it (if you wish, you can have the changes appear only when you want them to).

Finally, you can link the same object to more than one destination document. Whenever you change the object in the source document, the changes will appear in all the destination documents. Linking is the technique to use when you want to use data that must always be identical in two or more documents.

You can practice linking using Paintbrush, Write, and Cardfile. First create a picture to link and copy it to the Clipboard:

1. Start by opening Paintbrush. Paint and save a new picture. Alternatively, you can open an existing picture of your choice, but if you make any changes in the document, be sure to save it before you go on.
2. Select the drawing by clicking on it.
3. Choose Copy from the Edit menu to copy the picture onto the Clipboard.

Now you're ready to link the picture to a Write document:

1. Start Write and open or create a document.
2. When your text is ready, move the insertion point to the place where you want to put the picture.
3. From the Edit menu, choose Paste Link.
4. Save the Write document.

Establish a second link, this time to a card in Cardfile:

1. Open Cardfile and select the card into which you want to link the drawing. It doesn't matter where the insertion point is, since linked pictures automatically go into the upper-left corner of the card.
2. Choose Picture from the Edit menu. The picture should appear in the card.
3. Save the card.

EDITING A LINKED DRAWING

TO EDIT A LINKED OBJECT,

1. **Double-click on the linked object.**
2. **Edit the object in its original application.**
3. **Close the application.**

Once you've linked an object to one or more destination documents, you can edit the object in its original source document starting from any of the destinations. As you'll see, the technique is exactly the same as editing an embedded object. The outcome, however, is different—changes you make to a linked object appear in all the documents to which you've linked it.

To prove this to yourself, start from Cardfile and proceed as follows:

1. Double-click on the linked drawing or choose Edit Paintbrush Picture Object from the Edit menu. (In Cardfile, you don't have to worry about where the insertion point is when you choose this command.) Paintbrush opens and displays the document containing the linked picture. You'll see the entire Paintbrush document; if the linked picture is only part of the document, a border will surround it.
2. Add a fancy title to the picture (see Figure 14.3).
3. From Paintbrush's File menu, choose Save, then Exit. When Paintbrush closes, Windows returns you to Cardfile where you can verify that your title appears in the linked copy of the picture.

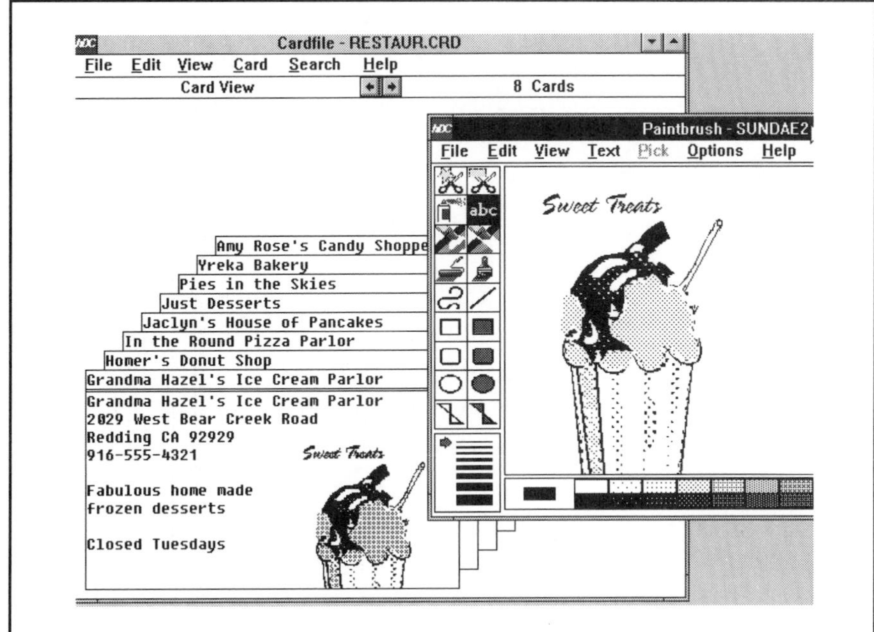

FIGURE 14.3: *Because the picture is linked rather than embedded, changes you make in the original Paintbrush document appear immediately in the destination document. In this case, some text newly typed into the Paintbrush picture appears in the linked card in Cardfile.*

4. Switch back to the Write document containing the linked picture. You'll see that the changes you made have been carried over to the Write document as well.

Copying Links from One Document to Another

There's yet another way to place a linked object in more than one destination document—by copying the link, not the object itself, from one document to another using the Clipboard. Try it, using a second Write document:

1. Starting from Cardfile, click on the linked picture to select it.
2. Choose Copy from the Cardfile's Edit menu to place a copy of the link onto the Clipboard.
3. Open a new Write document and put the insertion point where you want the picture to appear.
4. Choose Paste from Write's Edit menu. A third copy of the linked picture should appear in your document.

Changing the Format of Clipboard Information

The Clipboard provides a simple way to transfer chunks of information from program to program. However, the problem you'll sometimes face is that different applications use different formats to store similar kinds of information. For example, you could create identical-looking pictures using two separate programs, the Paintbrush program that comes with Windows and PC Paintbrush, a more sophisticated painting program. Behind the scenes, however, Paintbrush stores the picture in the BMP format, while PC Paintbrush uses the PCX format.

How does that affect your work with the Clipboard? If two programs use different information formats, you won't be able to transfer a selection between them. As Windows applications get smarter, however, more and more of them are being designed to assist in the translation process from format to format. When you copy or cut a selection to the Clipboard, many programs will place the information on the Clipboard in more than one format. When you then paste the information into a second program, the destination program can choose the format it prefers.

Windows offers a command called Paste Special that lets you control which format the destination application will receive. This is useful when you know that the destination application will select a format other than the one you want. Paste Special works with both standard Clipboard transfers and paste links.

NOTE *The Paste Special command is available only in programs that have been specifically designed to provide it, so it may not appear on the Edit menu in some of your applications.*

Paste Special also lets you control whether the information you're transferring will be embedded, linked, or simply copied in the destination document. In fact, one important reason to use Paste Special is to place information from the Clipboard into your document *without* embedding it, that is, without establishing a connection to the originating application. When the information on the Clipboard comes from an OLE application, the standard Paste command automatically embeds the information into the destination document. If you want to paste the information in the destination document without embedding it, choose Paste Special and then select the desired format for the information, avoiding choices that list the originating application's name.

For example, if you've copied part of a Paintbrush picture to the Clipboard and want to paste it into a Write document without embedding it, you'd choose Paste Special, then select Bitmap or Picture as the paste format, but not Paintbrush Picture.

Here's how to select the information format with Paste Special:

1. Cut or Copy the information onto the Clipboard.
2. Open the destination document.
3. Ready the destination document to receive the information. In Write, place the insertion point where you want to paste the information. In Cardfile, choose Picture from the Edit menu.
4. Choose Edit ➤ Paste Special. You'll see the Paste Special dialog box.
5. The Paste Special dialog box displays the available formats for the information now on the Clipboard in the Data Type list box. Select the format you prefer.
6. Choose Paste to embed the object if you've chosen an application-specific format from the Data Type list, or to simply transfer the information into your destination document if you've chosen a format that does not refer to a specific application. Choose Paste Link to link the object. The Paste Link button will be inactive if the program used to create the object is not an OLE server, if the object on the Clipboard hasn't been saved in a file, or if the format isn't application-specific.

Using OLE with Other Applications

TO LINK AN EXCEL SPREADSHEET TO A WORD DOCUMENT,

1. **Select a portion of the spreadsheet to link.**
2. **Choose Edit ➤ Copy.**
3. **Move to Word and determine the insertion point.**
4. **Choose Edit ➤ Paste Special.**
5. **Choose the data type from the dialog box and click on either Paste or Paste Special.**

TO LINK AN EXCEL SPREADSHEET TO A VENTURA DOCUMENT,

1. **Create and select an empty frame in Ventura.**
2. **Remain in Frame mode and choose Edit ➤ Paste Link.**
3. **Enter a name for the Ventura file to store the linked data.**
4. **Save the file.**

Aside from the programs that come with Windows, such as Write, Paintbrush, and Cardfile, few applications have yet been adapted to work with OLE. What's more, each application that *does* provide OLE differs a little in the way its features work. All this is to be expected since OLE is so new—it first appeared with Windows 3.1—and since software developers are free to enhance it in their programs. But it does mean you may have to adjust the way you work with OLE a bit from application to application, at least until OLE becomes better established.

Take the example used at the beginning of the chapter of linking an Excel worksheet to a Microsoft Word document (see Figure 14.1). To establish the link, create a worksheet in Excel and save it on disk, or open a previously saved worksheet file. Select the portion of the worksheet you want to link and choose Edit ➤ Copy. Now move to the Word document and place the insertion point where you want the worksheet data to appear.

So far, the procedure has been exactly like that of linking a Paintbrush picture to a Write document. From here on, however, you'll notice some differences. In Word, choose Edit ➤ Paste Special (Word has no Paste Link command on the Edit menu). When the Paste Special dialog box appears, you'll have five different options for the data type you want to paste: Excel Worksheet Object, Formatted Text (RTF), Unformatted Text, Picture, and Bitmap. The second choice is already highlighted for you.

If you accept the Formatted Text data type and click on the Paste Link button, Word will place the worksheet data into a Word table automatically, with each cell of the worksheet in its own table cell. The fonts used in the original worksheet are preserved as well. From this point on, you can reformat the table to suit your document, changing attributes such as fonts, column width, and row height. However, if you change the structure of the table by merging cells or deleting rows or columns, these changes will be lost when the link is updated each time you open the Word document or save the worksheet file from Excel.

If you select Excel Worksheet Object as the data type in the Paste Special dialog box, you'll notice that the Paste Links button becomes inactive. In other words, this option allows you to embed (paste) the data, but not to link them. On the other hand, the remaining three choices in the Paste Special dialog box *do* permit linking. If you choose Unformatted Text ➤ Paste Link, the worksheet data will enter your document as ordinary text in the font currently active in Word. You can format the numbers and text as you like, and you can copy them to other parts of the document. However, you'll lose any editing changes you make in the pasted worksheet data each time the link gets updated.

The two remaining data-type choices in the Paste Special dialog box, Picture and Bitmap, both link an image of the worksheet data to your Word document. The image looks just like a real Excel worksheet, complete with the gray row and column headings (if you haven't turned off their display in Excel). Here you can't change the contents of the linked data in Word, even temporarily. You can, however, resize the image to suit your needs by clicking on it and dragging one of the resizing handles. The difference between the Picture and Bitmap choices is simple: You can resize a picture without losing clarity of the numbers and letters; however, if you change a bitmap's size, the text in the worksheet image will become difficult to read.

If you're in Text mode when you choose Paste Link, the worksheet data will enter your Ventura document as ordinary text, as if you'd chosen Paste, and no link will actually be established. Tabs will separate the data from each cell of the original worksheet.

Ventura Publisher 4 (Ventura Software) is another major application that offers OLE features. Again, we'll use the example of linking an Excel worksheet to explore Ventura's OLE capabilities. Unlike Word, Ventura has a Paste Link command on the Edit menu. To use this command, you must first create and select an empty frame to receive the linked data. Remain in Frame mode. When you then choose Paste Link, a dialog box will appear, asking you to enter a name for the file in which Ventura should store the linked data. (It goes into a separate file, which is typical of the components of a Ventura document.)

After you've saved the file, an image of the linked portion of the worksheet appears in the frame. This image is just like the Picture format in Microsoft Word—it includes row and column headings from the worksheet, and you can resize it without losing resolution, but you can't otherwise format the information it displays.

Several choices are available in Ventura's Paste Special dialog box when you're working with Excel data on the Clipboard. Selecting the Linked Object option, then clicking the Paste Link button, is identical to choosing Paste Link on the Edit menu, while selecting Embedded Object and clicking the Paste button embeds rather than links the worksheet data. The ASCII Text choice simply allows you to paste the data as ordinary text, without any connection to the worksheet. The Windows Metafile and Device Dependent Bitmap choices place graphical images of the worksheet into Ventura—but again, these lack any connection to the original worksheet file.

Understanding Some OLE Concepts

By now you're probably beginning to catch on to some of OLE's fine points. For one thing, you've surely noticed that there are two distinct roles to play in the process of sharing information via OLE: one program originates the object that is to be embedded or linked, while the other program accepts the object. In OLE's terminology, a program that creates an object is called a *server,* while a program into which an object can be linked or embedded is a *client.*

What's important here is that the typical program functions either as a server or a client, but not both. For example, Paintbrush and Sound Recorder are servers only—they can originate objects for linking or embedding, but they can't accept them. On the other hand, Write and Cardfile function only as clients—they are unable to originate objects but they can accept them.

Of course, there's nothing to prevent a software developer from designing a program to work as both a server and client. Microsoft Excel is such a program: it originates chart and spreadsheet objects that can be placed into documents prepared in a word processor or desktop publisher, but it also accepts linked or embedded database objects.

You've probably guessed what all this implies about OLE in general: a program must be specifically designed to use OLE. Windows offers built-in features to facilitate data transfers from program to program via OLE, but Windows programs can't take advantage of these features automatically. The software developer must add the necessary menu choices, dialog boxes, and behind-the-scenes processing.

Another point you may have noticed is that there can be slight variations in the way you work with OLE in different applications. Recall that in Cardfile you don't have to place the cursor over a linked picture before you edit it, since Cardfile knows the picture is in the upper-left corner. Similarly, since you play a linked or embedded sound object in a destination document by double-clicking it, you can't use the double-click method to edit the object—instead, you must open the Edit menu, choose Sound Object to display a special cascading menu, and then choose Edit.

Manually Updating a Linked Object

TO SET A LINK FOR MANUAL UPDATING IN WRITE,

1. **Select the object in Write.**
2. **Choose Edit ➤ Links.**
3. **Select the Manual option button and click on OK.**

TO UPDATE THE LINK MANUALLY,

1. **Select the object in Write.**
2. **Choose Edit ➤ Links.**
3. **Click on the Update Now button and click on OK.**

Normally, any changes you make to the original version of a linked object automatically appear in all the linked copies of that object in other documents. When circumstances dictate, however, you can set up any link so that the changes appear in the destination document only when you want them to. This is termed *manual updating.*

For example, imagine that you've developed a spreadsheet that compares monthly and total payments on several loan packages, calculating these figures on the basis of loan amount, interest rate, and term. In preparation for discussing the available loan options at a company meeting, you've filled in the spreadsheet with the pertinent values for each loan and linked it to a report discussing the pros and cons of the choices available.

As the meeting date approaches, market conditions are changing rapidly. You want to be able to keep tabs on the loans you're considering by revising the figures in the spreadsheet as often as necessary. But you don't want the linked copy to change automatically, since the report draft you've written is based on the specific numbers it contains.

The night before the meeting, you're ready to prepare the final copy of your report. After checking to make sure that all the loan figures in your spreadsheet are current, you switch to your word-processor document and carry out a manual update of the linked information, then proceed to make whatever revisions are necessary in the report.

While the spreadsheet/word processor scenario is probably more relevant to what you'll be doing in real life, you can practice setting up a manually updated link using links you've already established between Paintbrush and Write:

1. Open one of the Write documents that contains a linked picture.
2. Click on the picture to select it.
3. Choose Links from the Edit menu. You'll see the Links dialog box which presents you with a list of the current links in this document, identifying each link by the source document file name (see Figure 14.4). Notice that the link for your picture is already selected because you selected the picture prior to opening the Links dialog box. (Actually, unless you've added other links, this will be the only link in the list).
4. Select the Manual option button at the bottom of the Links dialog box and choose OK.

If the Links dialog box lists two or more links, hold down the Shift key while clicking with the mouse to select consecutive links. You can also press Ctrl to select non-consecutive multiple links.

You can return to automatic updating for any link whenever you like. Repeat the process just described, only select the Automatic option button in the Links dialog box.

Now that you've specified a manual link, the painting shown in your Write document will remain as it is, even if you change the original object, until you manually update it. To see for yourself, open the document containing the original object by double-clicking on the picture in your Write document. When Paintbrush appears on the screen, make any changes you like in the picture, then save it. Now switch back to Write, and notice that the changes you just made haven't affected the picture there.

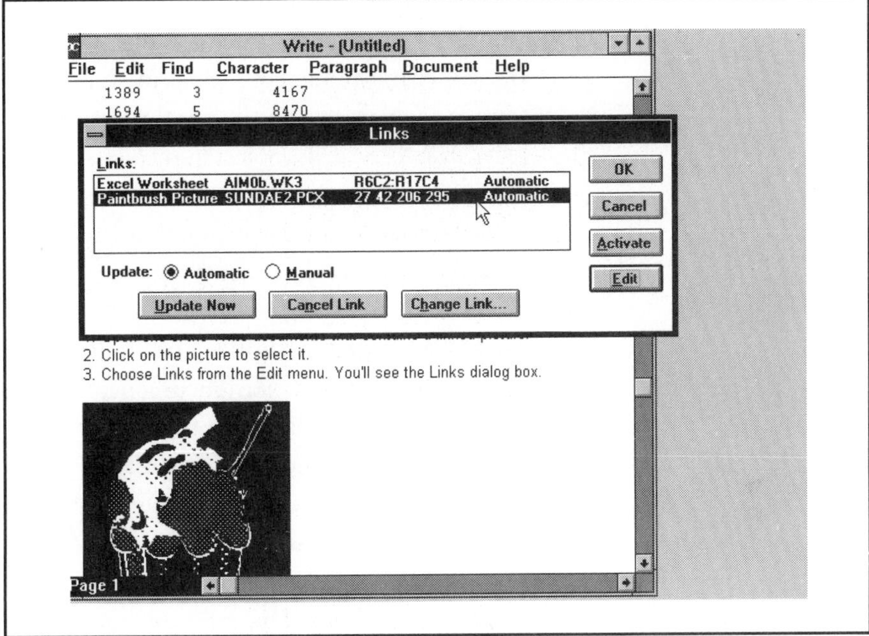

FIGURE 14.4:

The Links dialog box as seen in Write. The document shown contains two links, and you must select the one you want to work with before going further.

Now you're ready to update the linked picture manually:

1. With your Write document still active, open the Edit menu and choose Links. The Links dialog box appears.
2. Select the link for your picture.
3. Click the Update Now button, then click OK.

Managing Links

Besides specifying and manually updating links, you can break or delete links, fix broken links, and alter existing links to refer to different source documents.

Canceling and Deleting Links

When you *break* a link, you destroy the connection between the source and destination documents. Although the object still appears in the destination document, you can't edit it from within that document—you can't, for example, double-click on a picture in Write to open the object in Paintbrush. Instead, two separate copies of the picture now exist, one in the source document, one in the destination.

You can still revise the object in the destination document, but you must do so manually, by copying it to the Clipboard and pasting it back into the originating program. The only time you'd want to break a link is if you're fairly certain you'll never be revising the object as it appears in the destination document.

By contrast, deleting a link not only cuts the cord, but actually removes the object from the destination document. If you delete a link to a picture in Write, the picture will disappear from the Write document. Of course, the picture in the source document isn't affected.

Starting from the program that contains the object with the link you want to break or delete, select the object and choose Links from the Edit menu to bring up the Links dialog box with the object you selected highlighted in the list of links. To cancel the link, click the Cancel Link button. To delete the link, press the Del key.

Fixing Broken Links

There's another way to break a link: accidentally, by changing the name of the source document containing the linked objects. Since Windows relies on the document's file name to locate the original object, it won't know where to look if you change it. However, you can reestablish the link:

1. Open the document containing the object with the broken link.
2. After selecting the object, choose Links from the Edit menu. The Links dialog box appears with the object already highlighted in the list of links.
3. Click the Change Link button. The Change Link dialog box appears.
4. In its File Name list box, select the file name of the source document that contains the original object.

5. Choose OK. The Links dialog box reappears, showing the new name of the source document as the selected link.
6. Choose OK. When the Links dialog box closes—assuming the link is set for automatic updating—the current version of the linked object will appear in the destination document.

You can also use Change Link to replace one link with a completely different one. Just select a different file name for the source document—say, a different Paintbrush document. Assuming the source document contains a linkable object, that object will now be linked to the destination document in place of the old one.

LINKING AND EMBEDDING WITH PACKAGES

So far, you've practiced embedding and linking objects by placing the objects themselves into destination documents. But this is only one of the two methods Windows gives you for embedding or linking. As an alternative, you can embed or link an object in the form of an icon that represents the object.

NOTE *Packages can contain linked or embedded objects, but packages themselves are always embedded. A package has the same properties as any embedded object, meaning that you can make changes only from the destination document.*

This special type of icon is called a *package*. You can create packages with a special utility that comes with Windows, called the Object Packager, found in the Accessories window. (The File Manager is used, too.) When you activate a package embedded in a destination document, the object contained in the package opens in the application that created it (or, in the case of sound or animation objects, the object plays).

Why use packages instead of the ordinary embedding and linking method? Packages are an extremely simple but remarkably powerful way to provide access to supplemental information in documents that are designed to be used primarily on the screen, rather than printed out. Instead of cluttering up a document with every picture, chart, or table that might interest a user of your document, you can add these objects in the form of packages. If you label each package with a good description (such as "For details on gray whale migration in 1993, activate this package"), users of your document can decide for themselves whether and when to open the package and examine its contents.

A package can contain an entire document or just a selected portion, but the methods you use to prepare these two types of packages will be different. Likewise, a package can contain either an embedded or a linked object. Object Packager can only package embedded objects; to package a linked object, you must use the File Manager.

A package can also contain a DOS command line that you can execute in the destination document (see "Packaging a DOS Command-Line Command" later in this chapter). That's not possible with ordinary embedding or linking.

One more point on terminology: the process of *packaging* an object not only encompasses preparation of the package, but also includes placing that package into a destination document.

PACKAGING AN ENTIRE DOCUMENT

TO PACKAGE A FILE,

1. **Run Object Packager.**
2. **Choose File ➤ Import.**
3. **Select the file to package.**
4. **Choose Edit ➤ Copy Package.**

TO PLACE THE PACKAGE IN A DOCUMENT,

1. **Determine the insertion point.**
2. **Choose Edit ➤ Paste.**
3. **Double-click on the icon to run the package.**

To become familiar with using the Object Packager to package complete documents, try your hand at embedding a Paintbrush picture object in a

Write document again, but this time as a package. Before you begin, be sure you have saved a Paintbrush document to work with:

NOTE *Whenever you create a new package, Object Packager automatically uses the icon of the application that created the source document as the icon for the package. As you'll see later, you can select another icon instead.*

1. Click on the Packager icon in the Accessories group window to open the Object Packager. Object Packager has two windows, labeled Content and Appearance.
2. Select the Content window either by clicking the window or pressing Tab. (It may already be selected.)
3. Open the File menu and choose Import to display the Import dialog box.
4. Move to the directory containing the picture document you want to package, then choose the document's file name.
5. Click OK. At this point, you'll see the file name of the document you chose in the Content window and the icon for the Paintbrush application in the Appearance window, as shown below.

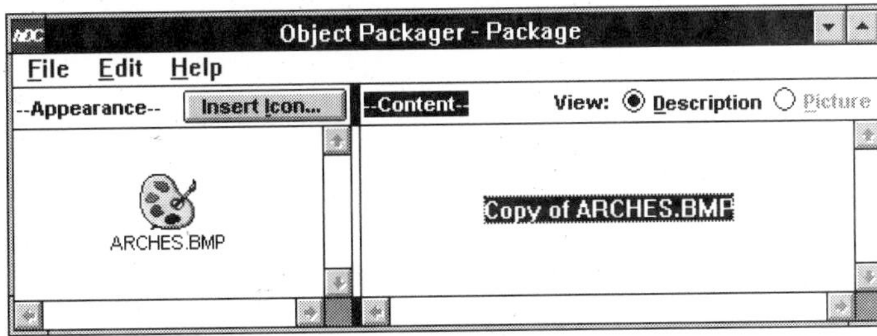

6. Choose Copy Package from the Edit menu, then close the Object Packager.

Now you're ready to place the package into your Write document. The rest of the procedure is just like ordinary embedding:

1. Start Write and open the destination document.
2. Position the insertion point where you want to place the package.
3. Open Write's Edit menu and choose Paste. The package appears in the document in the form of the Paintbrush program icon, labeled with the document's file name (see Figure 14.5).

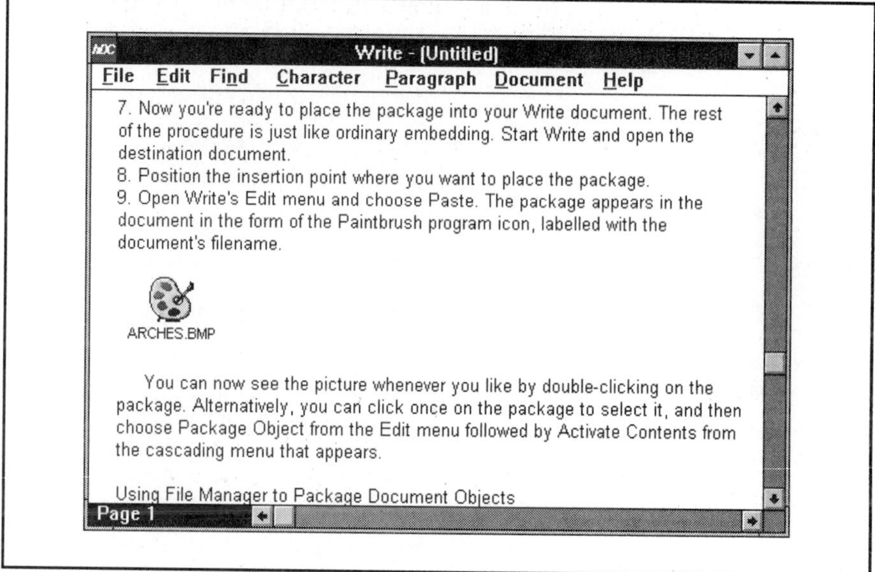

FIGURE 14.5:

The package created in Object Packager has been embedded into a Write document; you see the Paintbrush icon in the document with the name of the original Paintbrush file.

You can now see the picture whenever you like by double-clicking on the package. Alternatively, you can click once on the package to select it, then choose Edit ➤ Package Object ➤ Activate Contents. (If you want to change the package itself, choose Edit ➤ Package Object ➤ Edit Package instead.)

USING FILE MANAGER TO PACKAGE DOCUMENT OBJECTS

File Manager can also package complete document objects, and in fact it does so more flexibly than the Object Packager. If you routinely keep File Manager open, it may be simpler to bypass the Object Packager and rely on the File Manager. Also, using File Manager is the only way to prepare packages containing linked objects.

You can choose from among three ways to package documents with File Manager, although all three won't be available with all your programs:

- Use the Clipboard to copy the document from the File Manager, pasting it into the destination document as a package.

- Use the mouse to drag the document icon to the destination document.
- Use the Clipboard to copy the document from the File Manager to the Object Packager, from which you can copy it to the destination document and paste it as a package.

Packaging an Entire Document Using the File Manager and the Clipboard

Here's how to use the File Manager in concert with the Clipboard to package an entire document:

1. In the File Manager, open the directory containing the document you want to package.
2. Highlight the document's file name.
3. Open the File menu and choose Copy. The Copy dialog box appears.
4. Choose Copy To Clipboard and click on OK.
5. Open the destination document.
6. If necessary, position the cursor or insertion point where you want to place the package.
7. Choose Paste Link from the Edit menu to place the document package as a linked object; choose Paste to place the package as an embedded object.

Packaging an Entire Document from the File Manager Using the Mouse

You can also create packages in the File Manager by dragging documents to their destination with the mouse. Here are the steps:

1. In the File Manager, open the directory that contains the source document.
2. Open the destination document.

3. Arrange the File Manager and destination document windows so that you can see the source document icon and the spot in the destination document where you want to place the package.
4. In the destination document window, move the cursor to the spot where the package should go.
5. To place the document package as an embedded object, drag the icon of the source document into the destination document window. To place the package as a linked object, press Ctrl-Shift while dragging the source document icon into the destination window. As you drag, the mouse pointer will change to the file icon.
6. Release the mouse button to place the package at the insertion point.

Creating a Package Using the File Manager and Object Packager

Finally, you can transfer a document from the File Manager to Object Packager and then to the destination document. Use this method when you find it difficult to position both the File Manager and destination windows on the screen at the same time. By the way, this method also lets you use Object Packager to create linked packages:

1. In the File Manager, open the directory containing the source document.
2. Select the source document's file name.
3. Choose Copy from the File menu. You'll see the Copy dialog box.
4. Choose Copy To Clipboard and click on OK.
5. Open Object Packager and select the Content window.
6. From the Edit menu, choose Paste Link to create a linked document package; choose Paste to create an embedded document package. When you do, the file name of the source document should show up in the Content window. Simultaneously, the Appearance window should display the icon of the application that created the document.
7. Open the Edit menu and choose Copy Package.

8. Open the destination document, move the cursor to the location where you want to insert the package, and choose Paste from the Edit menu. The package will appear in the document.

Packaging an Application

You can place a package containing an application into a destination document just as easily as you can insert a document package. For example, you might place a package containing Calculator into a spreadsheet document. That way, the person who uses the document will be able to call up the calculator directly from the document to do "scratch-pad" math without having to switch first to the Program Manager.

You can use any of the techniques you've learned for packaging documents to insert an application package into a document. Just be sure that you select the file name or icon of the application itself during the process. You'll end up with the application's icon in the destination document labeled with the program's full file name. Activating the package starts the packaged application. When you exit the application, Windows returns you to the original document.

Packaging Part of a Document

TO PACKAGE PART OF A FILE,

1. **Select part of the source document and choose Edit ➤ Copy.**
2. **Run Object Packager and choose Edit ➤ Paste or Edit ➤ Paste Link.**
3. **Choose Edit ➤ Copy Package.**
4. **Determine the insertion point in the destination document.**
5. **Choose Edit ➤ Paste.**

The main reason to use the Object Packager rather than the File Manager for packaging objects is so that you can limit the package to contain only a specific portion of the source document. You might, for example, want to package a single paragraph of text taken from a larger word-processor document. You could insert this paragraph package into a chart you've prepared with your presentation graphics software to provide additional background information on a specific topic illustrated in the chart. Anyone who views the chart could then read the paragraph by clicking on the package icon.

Here's how to package a particular portion of a document as an embedded or linked object:

1. Create or open the source document. In this case, the object must have been created by an OLE server—that is, an application designed to originate linked or embedded objects. As always, if you want to link the object rather than embed it, you must first save the source document on disk.
2. Select the particular object you want to package, whether it's a block of text, a chart, a portion of a picture, or what have you.
3. Choose Copy from the Edit menu.
4. Now open the Object Packager and select the Content window if it's not already selected.
5. Open the Object Packager's Edit menu and choose Paste if you want to embed the object, or Paste Link if you want to link it. The Content window will display the path and file name for the source document, while the Appearance window will show the icon of the application used to create the document.
6. From Open Packager's Edit menu, choose Copy Package.
7. Open the destination document. Position the insertion point or cursor where you want to insert the package, then choose Paste from the Edit menu. You'll see the icon representing the package in the document.

Now whenever you want to see the package contents, all you have to do is activate the package. In some programs, you double-click the object, while in others, you select the package by clicking on it, then choosing Edit ➤ Package Object ➤ Play.

Packaging a DOS Command-Line Command

Object Packager has a special feature for generating a package containing a DOS command-line command which you can then insert into a destination document. A packaged command line might run a batch file (batch program) or start a non-Windows application. Although you could manage the same trick using the standard techniques for packaging an application, it's easier with Object Packager's special command.

Here are the steps you'll follow:

1. In Object Packager, choose Command Line from the Edit menu.
2. Type a DOS command in the little dialog box that appears. If you are typing the name of a batch or program file, enter the full path.
3. Click OK. The command you entered will show up in the Content window.
4. Before you can package the command, you must assign an icon to it. Choose the Insert Icon button in the Appearance window. The Insert Icon dialog box pops up.
5. Select an icon of your choice from the scrolling display. To see a different set of icons, choose the Browse button and select the program file containing the icons you want to display. Click OK.
6. Click OK in the Insert Icon box. The Appearance window should now be displaying the icon you selected.
7. Choose Edit ➤ Copy Package.
8. Insert the new package into your destination document in the standard way.

You can now execute the command line directly from the destination document simply by activating the package.

Changing a Package Icon or Label

Windows automatically supplies two visual cues for every package you create, an icon and a label. After you've inserted the package into the destination document, the icon and label help you remember what the package contains.

The standard icon is the one showing the program that created the source document. The label consists either of the source document's file name, if you packaged an entire document, or a description of the object (such as "Excel Chart" or "Paintbrush Picture") if the package contains only part of the document. To make a package's icon or label more meaningful to the person who uses the destination document, you can change it to one of your choice.

You make these changes using Object Packager either before or after you place the package in the destination document. If you're using Object Packager to create a new package, you can change the icon or label as soon as you've pasted the embedded or linked object into the Content window. If you're working with a package that you've already inserted in a document, you select the package by clicking on it and then choosing Package Object from the application's Edit menu to return to Object Packager and make your changes.

From this point, the procedure is the same until the very last step:

- To select a different icon for the package, choose the Insert Icon button, located at the top of Object Packager's Appearance window. The Insert Icon dialog box appears. Icons are stored in executable program files as well as in special icon files. To find the file containing the icon you wish to use, select the Browse button. If you see more than one icon in the Current Icon box (some program files contain multiple icons), select the icon you want to use. When you click OK, you'll see the new icon in the Appearance window.
- To modify the existing icon in the Appearance window or to design a new one from scratch, select the Appearance window and choose Copy from the Edit menu. Now open Paintbrush and paste the icon into the document. Make whatever changes you like, copy the new icon to the Clipboard, return to the Object Packager, and paste it back into the Appearance window.
- To change the package label, choose Label from Packager's Edit menu to bring up the Label dialog box. Type the text for the new label and click OK.

Once you're happy with the package's icon and label, your next step depends on whether you're creating a new package or modifying an existing one. If this is a new package, insert it in the destination document by choosing Copy Package from Packager's Edit menu, switching to the destination document, and pasting the package in. If you're working with an existing package, just choose Modify from Packager's File menu—the new icon and label will appear in the destination document.

That concludes your tour of the capabilities of OLE, Windows' smart information-sharing feature. With these flexible tools, you'll be able to set up all your favorite applications to work together for maximum efficiency.

FAST TRACK

CHAPTER 15

FAST TRACK

1. Open the Conrol Panel and choose Drivers.
2. Click on Add.
3. Choose a driver from the list and click on OK.
4. If the driver you want isn't on the list, choose Unlisted or Updated Driver. Click on OK and specify the location of the driver.
5. Make additional settings, if necessary, then exit Windows and reboot.

1. Open the Control Panel and choose Drivers.
2. Select the driver.
3. Click on Remove. Click on OK, then reboot.

1. From the Control Panel, choose Sound.
2. Choose the event.
3. Choose the sound you want to assign.
4. Repeat Steps 2 and 3 for other events you want to modify.
5. Click on OK.

To play a multimedia file, ... 516

1. Ensure that the correct driver is installed.
2. Run Media Player.
3. Choose the correct device from the Device menu.
4. Choose the desired file from a dialog box (only required for compound devices).
5. Use VCR-like buttons to control the playback.

To use Sound Recorder, ... 519

1. Run the Sound Recorder.
2. Load in a sound via File ➤ Open.
3. Use the VCR-like buttons to control the playback.
4. To record, click on the microphone button (a sound board is required).
5. To edit, move, or stop the play head in the desired location, choose the appropriate command from the Edit menu.
6. To add effects, use commands from the Effects menu.

CHAPTER 15

FEATURING

A Discussion of Multimedia

Managing Multimedia Drivers

Recording, Assigning, and Editing Sounds

Using MIDI Mapper

Multimedia Information Sources

All About Windows Multimedia

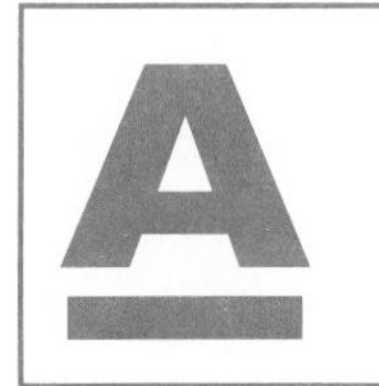

s you may be aware by now, one supposedly significant advantage of Windows 3.1 over its predecessor is that it incorporates the fundamentals of a forthcoming new wave of so-called *multimedia applications.* If you're new to the multimedia thing, discussions of its finer points have probably gone in one ear and out the other. What is multimedia anyway, you ask, and who cares?

WHAT IS MULTIMEDIA?

The term *multimedia*—alias "interactive media" or "hypermedia"—is difficult to define, which accounts for much of the general confusion. At the simplest level, in today's use of the term, it simply means adding sound to your applications. At the most advanced level, it is the amalgamation of animation, graphics, video, digitally recorded sounds, and text—with all of these presentation media controlled by a single PC.

Some multimedia applications are *interactive.* That is, through keyboard, mouse, voice, or external controller—such as a Musical Instrument Digital Interface (MIDI) keyboard—you interact with the system to control aspects of the presentation. Most of today's computers are based on text display only, perhaps supplemented by simple graphics. With the added capabilites of stereo sound, animation, and video, multimedia computing offers a much richer and more efficient means for conveying information. Multimedia enables the fast dissemination of information in ways not possible with text-only systems.

For example, consider the simple interactive tutorial that comes with Windows, the one that demonstrates Windows fundamentals and illustrates how to use the mouse. You may have run it shortly after installing Windows. That tutorial is rudimentary multimedia, integrating moving images and text. Now imagine expanding such a tutorial to include spoken instructions, music, realistic animation, and moving video images just as if you were watching TV. Animators, musicians, designers, writers, programmers, audio engineers, industry experts, and video producers are beginning to join forces to create multimedia applications such as:

- a WordPerfect document that lets you paste in video clips (with audio) from a VCR tape. Instead of displaying just a still graphic, the document will be "alive" with sight and sound.
- a music-education program on a CD-ROM from Microsoft that plays Beethoven's Ninth Symphony, while displaying informative and educational text about each passage and about the composer.
- a dictionary, thesaurus, book of quotations, and encyclopedia on a CD-ROM from Microsoft that not only contain a huge amount of textual information, but actually pronounce the dictionary entries; read quotations aloud in the voices of Robert Frost, Carl Sandburg, T.S. Eliot, e.e. cummings, Dylan Thomas, and JFK; and illustrate scientific phenomena with animation.
- programs that teach you how to play the piano, using a MIDI keyboard connected to your PC. The computer senses whether you play the lesson correctly and responds accordingly with a recorded high-quality voice. Similar programs teach music theory.

- multimedia magazines on CD-ROM that let you choose what news topics you want to read. News is displayed like television, with high-fidelity sound and video.
- interactive company annual reports, product demonstrations, presentations, or corporate training manuals for new employees.
- interactive real-time video conferencing ("videotel conferencing") on your desktop computer, where you can see your colleagues at several remote office locations while working interactively on your company's newsletter, also displayed on the screen.
- "moving catalogs" from mail-order houses, displaying everything from cars to coats via high-quality video and audio.
- an interactive geography test used at the National Geographic Society Explorer's Hall in Washington, D.C.
- interactive high-speed, random-access books, newspapers, or catalogs for the blind, using high-quality voice synthesis or recorded voices.
- interactive training for hard-to-teach professions such as medical diagnosis, surgery, auto-mechanics, and machinery operation.
- complex interactive games that incorporate stereo sound effects, flashy visuals, speech synthesis, and speech recognition, where you interact with the game by speaking.

Some of these applications (often called "multimedia titles" or "information titles") already exist. Others are still in the making.

General Multimedia Developments

Apple Computer has a recognized presence in the multimedia field with CD-ROM, sound, and animation programs that have been available on the Macintosh for several years. More recently, industry giants like Intel and IBM—and somewhat smaller, innovative companies such as Commodore and NeXT—have bounded into the fray as well, hoping to stake their claim in the potentially very profitable multimedia arena. Looking to benefit from Apple's background in multimedia, IBM has united with the Macintosh's maker to form a multimedia software company called Kaleida, whose mandate is to develop new multimedia applications and titles.

Though some other machines, such as the NeXT, Amiga, or Macintosh come better equipped for multimedia work than do IBMs and compatibles, the mere existence of 15 million PCs of AT-class or higher represents fertile turf for a potential multimedia revolution. Other manufacturers have realized this as well. The result? Numerous multimedia hardware and software upgrades for IBM compatibles at affordable prices are becoming readily available.

Recognizing the desire for a more thorough blending of media on PCs, Microsoft has been a very strong advocate of multimedia, pushing the CD-ROM for several years now, with major press and technical conferences on the topic. Microsoft developed its own Windows 3.0 "multimedia extensions"—software driver add-ins you purchased separately to give your Windows 3.0 computer some multimedia capability. Now Microsoft has further strengthened its position as a contender in the multimedia scene with Windows 3.1, which includes the necessary hooks that programmers need for writing multimedia applications that work in the Windows environment.

In its desire to spawn further development, Microsoft has spearheaded a consortium of 11 hardware companies called the Multimedia PC Marketing Council to define multimedia standards and design multimedia workstations called Multimedia Personal Computers (MPCs). As a result, you'll be seeing multimedia applications like those described above in the next few years, and a high degree of hardware and software compatibility between machines, applications, and add-in cards.

Advances in the field are occurring so quickly that it's difficult to keep up-to-date (and certainly impossible to be so in a book). To help you find current information, I've listed some information sources at the end of this chapter, including names and addresses of the MPC Marketing Council.

Is Multimedia Hype?

Some industry pundits argue that multimedia is just more computer-hype aimed at creating another profitable PC aftermarket. After all, how many media are there? Until your computer is capable of stimulating the sense of smell or touch, we're left with visual and auditory input alone. Breaking down the visual half, what do you have? Text and graphics. Many applications already present both text and graphics (e.g., any word processor or desktop publishing program capable of integrating the two). Also, some applications, notably ones for the Macintosh, already record and reproduce sound. So what's the big deal?

The big deal is the quality of video, animation, and sound from a variety of sources, and their seamless integration to create single applications and documents on Windows machines. In my opinion, there is, in fact, a revolution of sorts going on, which could be called PC-based multimedia. As standards for encoding, embedding, and replaying high-quality animated graphics, video, and digitized sound take hold, we'll see an expansion of application capabilities that will have significant impact in education, business, and entertainment.

Consider the desktop publishing revolution that brought typesetting abilities to our personal computers. Now numerous desktop publishing features have been incorporated into popular word-processing programs to the point where the term has lost some of its panache. I wouldn't be surprised if five years from now the term *multimedia* meets the same fate after the new flashy "look and sound" becomes commonplace. You'll simply regard any computer lacking color animation, video, music, and speech as a dinosaur.

THE SUPPLIED MULTIMEDIA APPLICATIONS AND UTILITIES

With Windows 3.0, working with multimedia required purchasing Microsoft's Multimedia upgrade kit or buying an MPC (*multimedia PC*). MPCs are manufactured by some of the vendors listed at the end of this chapter. Whether upgrading an exisiting computer or buying an MPC, the results were about the same: you got the Microsoft multimedia "extensions" (drivers), a CD-ROM drive, audio card, and a good VGA video card.

Either solution was pricey, often amounting to thousands of dollars. Some people didn't want to shell out for the hardware because they had it already or because they only needed a specific hardware addition, such as a sound card. More often than not, people just wanted the software drivers. In response to this interest, Microsoft decided to bundle some popular drivers and a couple of utility programs with the Windows 3.1 package in the hopes that this would accelerate the development of multimedia Windows applications. Microsoft also included the programming *hooks* (called APIs, for Application Programming Interface) in Windows 3.1 that allow multimedia applications to run on it.

A variety of multimedia applications, utilities, and hardware is becoming prevalent now that the extensions have been included with Windows 3.1. Obviously, I can't cover the entire gamut here, just as this book doesn't have room to cover details of particular printers or of Windows applications such as WordPerfect or Lotus 1-2-3. Instead, let's look at what's supplied with Windows, what classes of hardware and software additions you might consider, and why you might want to bother.

Here's what you get in the way of multimedia programs and utilities with Windows 3.1:

Drivers A utility in the Control Panel lets you install drivers for many add-in cards and devices such as CD-ROMs, MIDI interface cards, and video-disk controllers. Drivers for popular sound boards such as the Sound Blaster (from Creative Labs, Inc.) and Ad Lib (Ad Lib, Inc.), and popular MIDI boards such as the Roland MPU-401 (Roland Digital Group) are supplied. Other drivers can be installed from manufacturer-supplied disks using this option. Even if your hardware is physically installed, it won't work unless the proper driver is loaded.

Sound Settings This Control Panel utility lets you assign specific sound files (stored in the .WAV format) to Windows "system events" such as error messages, information dialog boxes, and when starting and exiting Windows.

MIDI Mapper If you've installed a sound driver that supports the MIDI protocol, this icon appears in the Control Panel, letting you declare settings for your MIDI device, such as channel assignment, key remapping, and patch number reassignment.

Media Player This application program lets you play a variety of multimedia files on their respective target hardware. In the case of a device that contains data, such as a CD-ROM or video disk, Media Player sends commands to the hardware, playing back the sound or video therein. If the data are stored on your hard disk (as are MIDI sequences, animation, and sound files) Media Player will send them to the appropriate piece of hardware such as a sound board or MIDI keyboard or device.

Sound Recorder This is a little application for recording sounds from a microphone and then editing them. Once recorded, sound files can be used with other programs through OLE, or can be used to replace the generic "beeps" your computer makes to alert you to dialog boxes, errors, etc. Sound Recorder also allows editing of .WAV files, some of which are supplied with Windows.

WHAT YOU DON'T GET WITH WINDOWS 3.1

As of this writing, there are few multimedia components you don't get with Windows 3.1. Those things that aren't included amount to little programs and some drivers that were included previously with the Multimedia Extensions version 1.0, and will be available from other sources such as hardware vendors and possibly from Microsoft. There's even a likelihood that one or two of these have been bundled with Windows 3.1 by the time you read this. Here's the list of missing items and what they do:

MUSICBOX.EXE	Controls playing of audio CD's in a computer CD-ROM drive
ALARMCLK.EXE	A clock program that lets you assign sounds to alarm clock time settings.
MCICDA.DRV	MCI driver for CD-ROM drives that allows Media Player and other MCI applications to play CD audio disks. At the 11th hour, this driver was actually shipped with Windows 3.1, but it isn't installed by default. You have to use the Driver utility in the Control Panel to install it.

MCIPIONR.DRV	This is an MCI driver for the Pioneer LD-V4200 videodisk player. This driver will be included in the Windows Driver Library available from Microsoft.
DISPDIB.DLL	A dynamic link library (DLL) that allows VGA screens to switch modes to MCGA mode.
MCGA256.DRV	300 x 200 x 8 resolution video driver.
VGAPAL.DRV	Palettized VGA driver.
SCRNSVR.CPL	Screen saver program that is now part of the Control Panel's Desktop dialog box.

MANAGING MULTIMEDIA DRIVERS

If you're updating a driver, you have to remove the old one first. See "Removing Old Drivers" later in this section.

When you add a new piece of hardware to your system, such as a sound board, CD-ROM controller, MIDI board, or other piece of paraphernalia, you'll have to alert Windows to this fact by installing the correct software device driver for the job. Some drivers simply control an external player as though you were pushing the buttons on the device's control panel by hand. These types of devices are called Media Control Interface (MCI) devices and include audio CD players, video disc players, and MIDI instruments. Other drivers actually send the sound or video data to the playback card or hardware, as well as control the playback speed and other parameters.

You use the Drivers option in the Control Panel to install the device driver. As I mentioned, drivers for popular multimedia items are included with Windows. Others you'll have to get from the manufacturer or from Microsoft. (Incidentally, Microsoft always has new device drivers on CompuServe as they are developed, which you can download.) Usually a hardware item comes with a disk containing a Windows device driver.

Installing New Drivers

TO INSTALL A NEW DRIVER,

1. **Open the Conrol Panel and choose Drivers.**
2. **Click on Add.**
3. **Choose a driver from the list and click on OK.**
4. **If the driver you want isn't on the list, choose Unlisted or Updated Driver. Click on OK and specify the location of the driver.**
5. **Make additional settings, if necessary, then exit Windows and reboot.**

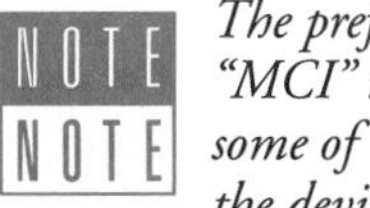

The prefix "MCI" in some of the device names stands for Media Control Interface, Windows' software "layer" for accessing multimedia devices.

You use the Drivers utility in the Control Panel to install new drivers. If you've purchased a board or other hardware add-in, read the supplied manual for details about the installation procedure. Then you might want to take a look at the drivers that came with your copy of Windows 3.1 to see if there's one for your device. Here's how:

1. Run Control Panel.
2. Double-click on Drivers. You'll see the Drivers dialog box as shown below, listing the drivers already installed on your system:

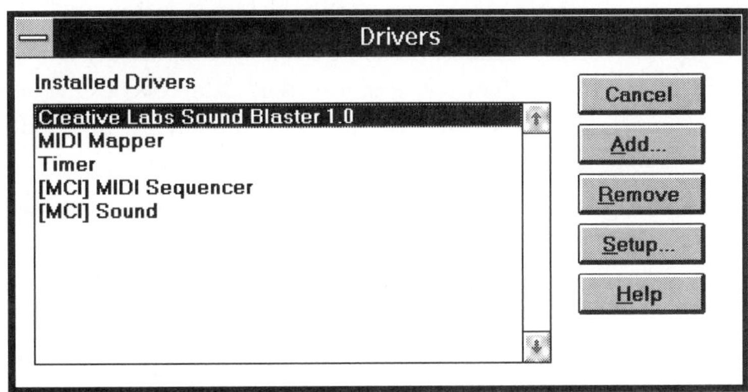

3. Note the drivers already installed. Is there one you need? If not, click on Add. Another dialog box will appear, listing the drivers that came with Windows.
4. Check out the list to see whether what you need is there. If it's there, highlight it. If it isn't, click on Unlisted or Updated Driver.
5. Click on OK.
6. You'll be instructed to specify a path where the driver can be found, just as when installing a printer or screen driver. Follow the normal procedure and on-screen prompts to add the new driver to your list. However, don't type the file name for the driver, just its path. Usually this will be just **A:** or **B:**. If it's on a hard disk and you don't know the drive letter or directory, click the Browse button to select the source drive and directory.
7. Some drivers need you to make additional settings. A typical example is the Sound Blaster card driver, which requires you to set the port address and interrupts for the board. If a setup dialog box appears for the driver, fill it in appropriately, using the board's supplied manual for guidance. (You won't get any hardware-specific help from Windows.) Make sure your settings don't conflict with other boards or devices already installed in your PC. How do you know this? To be frank, if you're not sure which ports and interrupts your other boards are using, use the old trial-and-error technique. For example, I installed a Sound Blaster card recently and used the default settings. But I kept getting dialog box error messages from Windows, indicating that there was some conflict. I repeatedly adjusted the IRQ and port settings until it worked. With two COM ports, a parallel port, and a hard disk, you'll most likely use port 220 and interrupt 7 with success.
8. When you are finished selecting any necessary settings, click the OK button. Some drivers install several additional, related drivers which might need you to make settings too, so more dialog boxes might pop up. Just fill them in as prompted.
9. New drivers won't work until you reboot Windows. So either wait until your next Windows session or close any files you're working on and rerun Windows if you want to get the device working immediately.

Changing a Driver's Settings

Occassionally you'll have to change a driver's settings. A case in point is when you use the trial-and-error method of making the settings, as I suggested above:

1. Double-click on Drivers in the Control Panel.
2. Highlight the driver in question.
3. Click on Setup. The relevant dialog box will appear, from which you can make the settings. If Setup is dimmed, you've selected a device that doesn't have or require settings.
4. Don't forget that you have to reboot Windows for the driver changes to take effect.

If you're having trouble with a driver/device combination, consider whether:

- you selected or installed the wrong driver for the hardware
- you need an updated driver
- there's something else wrong, such as a hardware conflict

Check out any little switches or jumpers on the card you just installed. Read the card's manual, too. This kind of sleuthing gets tricky if you have five different cards that compete for interrupt (IRQ) lines, but that's life in PC land where things don't always work together like we would hope.

Removing Old Drivers

TO REMOVE AN OLD DRIVER,

1. **Open the Control Panel and choose Drivers.**
2. **Select the driver.**
3. **Click on Remove. Click on OK, then reboot.**

When you remove a device such as a card or CD-ROM from your system, you should remove the old driver from your Windows system. Drivers take up memory in your Windows setup, so leaving old ones installed will impair your system's efficiency and ability to run more programs simultaneously.

You should also remove an old driver before installing an updated version of the same one.

Removing a driver from your system list doesn't actually eliminate it from the disk—which is both good and bad. The bad part is that drivers take up disk space. If you're short on disk space you'll want to eliminate the driver and associated files (see the device's manual) if you don't intend to use it later. However, the good part is this: If you think you'll want to use the driver later, it'll be there when you go to install it the next time. So just specify C:\WINDOWS\SYSTEM as the path for the driver when you install it as explained in the section above.

Be careful when removing driver files, though. Windows needs *some* of them just to work. All the drivers that showed up in the Drivers dialog box the first time you opened it are the ones that Windows must have. As a rule of thumb, don't remove a driver you didn't install, and make sure that any other files you erase from your disk aren't used by one of the supplied drivers.

Steps for removing a driver are similar to those for installing one:

1. Run Control Panel and choose Drivers.
2. From the list of installed drivers, select the driver you want to remove.
3. Click on Remove.
4. Confirm the removal in the resulting dialog box.
5. Restart Windows to have the removal take effect immediately.

ASSIGNING SOUNDS WITH THE CONTROL PANEL'S SOUND UTILITY

TO ASSIGN SOUNDS TO SYSTEM EVENTS,

1. **From the Control Panel, choose Sound.**
2. **Choose the event to assign a sound to.**
3. **Choose the sound you want to give it.**
4. **Repeat Steps 2 and 3 for other events you want to modify.**
5. **Click on OK.**

The Control Panel's Sound utility is for designating sounds to system events, such as warning dialog boxes, error messages when you click in the wrong place, and so on. Once you've installed a sound board, you can personalize your computer's beep to something more exciting than just "beep." Aside from making life more interesting, having different sounds for different types of events is also more informative. You know when you've made an error as opposed to when an application is acknowledging your actions, for example.

To add basic sounds to your Windows setup, you need a sound card that is MPC compatible; that is, it must conform to the Multimedia Personal Computer specification. Sounds must be stored on disk in the .WAV format to be used. The Sound Recorder program explained later in the chapter records sounds in this format. Windows comes with a few sound files that are OK, but not great. You'll probably want to make more interesting ones yourself, but you'll need a sound board such as Sound Blaster or other digital sampler board to record your own sounds. I have messages in my own voice, such as, "You made a stupid mistake, you fool," which—for a short time—seemed preferable to the mindless chime. Tired of self-flagellation, I moved on to acoustic guitar riffs and ditties off of CDs. Incidentally, you can also map system events to a MIDI device such as a synthesizer, but that's covered later in this chapter in the section on the MIDI Mapper.

Once you're set up for sound and have some .WAV files, you assign them to specific events. These events have names which you'll see in the Sound dialog box. Here's what you do:

1. Open the Control Panel and run Sound. The following dialog box appears:

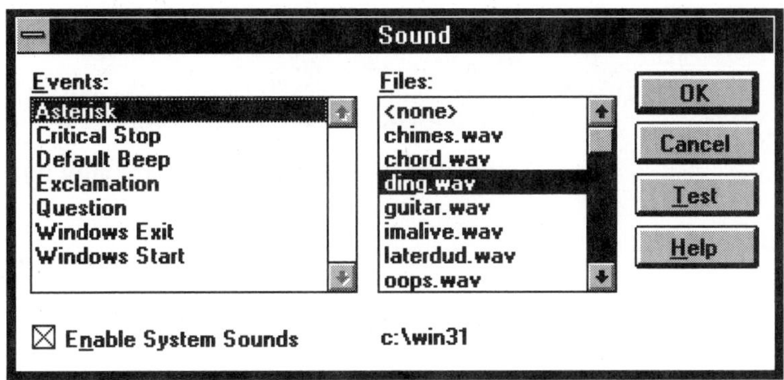

2. Choose an event in the left list box to which you want to assign a sound. When you click on it or highlight it, the sound file (.WAV file) assigned to that event will be highlighted.
3. In the right list box, choose the sound file you want for that event. Click the Test button if you want to hear the sound before finalizing your choice. Change the drive and directory to choose .WAV files that are stored elsewhere by scrolling to the bottom of the Files list box. Choosing <none> has the obvious effect; no sound will occur. Assigning all events to <none> will effectively silence your computer for use in a library, church, etc. You can also do this for all sounds except Windows Start and Windows Exit by turning off the Enable System Sounds check box. To mute the remaining two, you have to assign them manually to <none>.
4. Repeat the process for other events to which you want to assign or reassign sounds.
5. Click on OK.

Keep in mind that different applications will use event sounds differently. You'll have to do some experimenting to see when your applications use the default beep, as opposed to the Asterisk, Question, or the Exclamation.

PLAYING MULTIMEDIA FILES WITH MEDIA PLAYER

TO PLAY A MULTIMEDIA FILE,

1. **Ensure that the correct driver is installed.**
2. **Run Media Player.**
3. **Choose the correct device from the Device menu.**
4. **Choose the desired file from a dialog box (only required for compound devices).**
5. **Use VCR-like buttons to control the playback.**

Media Player is a little application that plays multimedia files, such as digitized sounds, MIDI music files, and animated graphics. It can also send control information to multimedia devices such as audio CD players or video disk players, determining which tracks to play and when to pause, when to activate slow motion, and so on.

You can only use Media Player on devices installed in your system and for which you've installed the correct device drivers (see "Installing New Drivers," above), so first see to that task. Then follow these instructions for playing a multimedia file:

1. Run Media Player from the Accessories group. The Media Player's control panel appears, as shown in Figure 15.1.
2. Open the Device menu and choose the type of device that's going to receive the information.
3. If the type of device you've chosen has an ellipsis (...) after it, a File Open dialog box will appear, asking for the name of the file you want played and displaying the files with the correct extension for the selected device. This only happens with devices that play a file that's stored in a disk file. (This type of device is called a *compound* device, incidentally.) Choose the file you want played. If the device you selected has no ellipsis after it, it's a *simple* device. This means the data to be played are already in the drive, as in

FIGURE 15.1:
Media Player plays back a variety of multimedia files and can also control external devices like audio CDs and video disks.

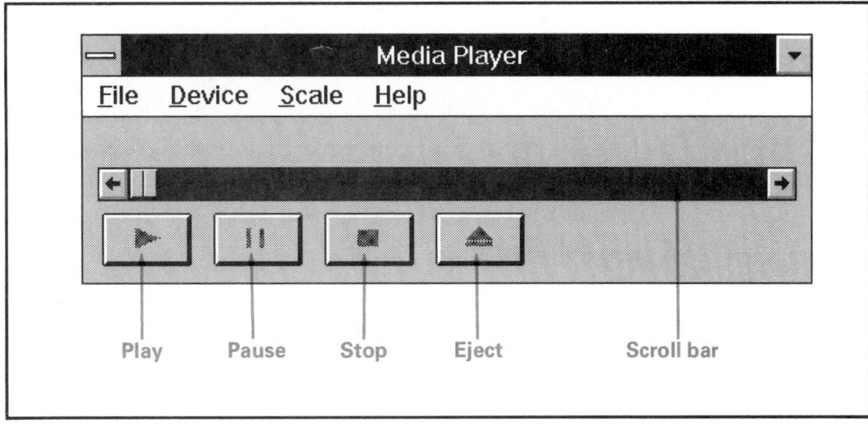

the case of a CD-ROM or video disk, and don't have to be chosen (no File Open box will appear). When you load a file for a compound device, the Media Player's appearance will change slightly to display a scale and tick marks indicating the length of the item:

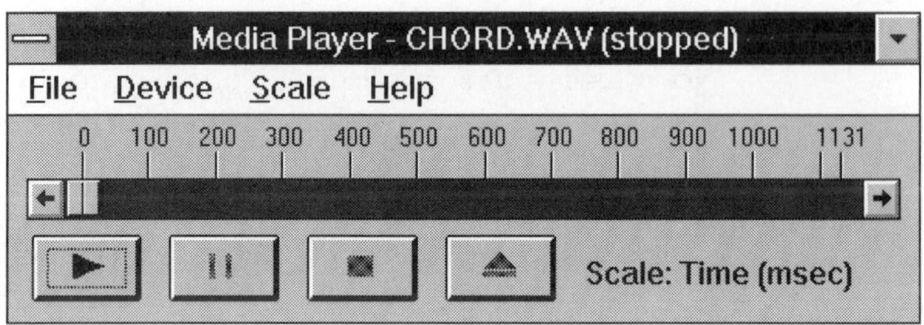

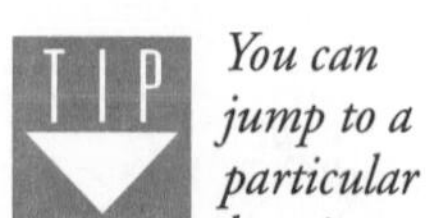

You can jump to a particular location in the piece by dragging the scroll button, clicking at the desired point in the scroll bar, or with ↑, ↓, ←, →, PgUp, and PgDn.

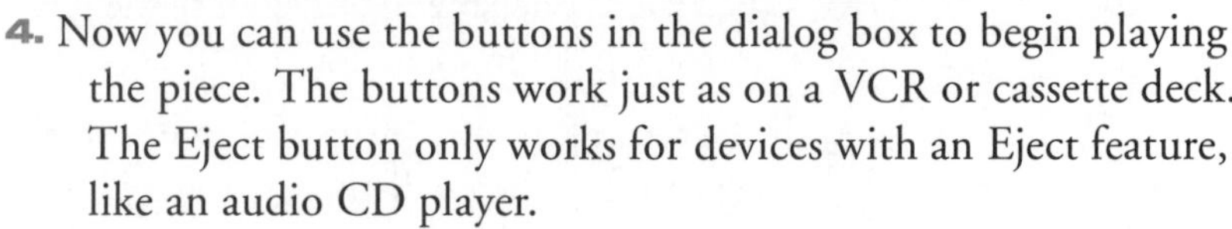

4. Now you can use the buttons in the dialog box to begin playing the piece. The buttons work just as on a VCR or cassette deck. The Eject button only works for devices with an Eject feature, like an audio CD player.
5. If you want to open another file for the same device (in the case of compound devices), use the File ➤ Open command to do so. If you want to play a file intended for another device, you'll have to change the device type first from the Device menu, then use the File ➤ Open command.
6. You can change the scale (tick marks) above the scroll bar to show *tracks* instead of time. Track display may be useful when you're playing audio CDs or video disks arranged by track. Do this from the Scale menu. Track tick marks will then replace the time tick marks. To change tracks, drag the scroll bar, click on the scroll buttons, or use →, ←, PgUp, and PgDn.
7. When you're done playing, close the application from the Exit menu.

Compound devices will stop as soon as you quit Media Player; simple devices will continue to play.

RECORDING AND EDITING SOUNDS WITH SOUND RECORDER

TO USE SOUND RECORDER,

1. **Run the Sound Recorder.**
2. **Load in a sound via File ➤ Open.**
3. **Use the VCR-like buttons to control the playback.**
4. **To record, click on the microphone button (a sound board is required).**
5. **To edit, move, or stop the play head in the desired location, choose the appropriate command from the Edit menu.**
6. **To add effects, use commands from the Effects menu.**

NOTE *For crude sound production, you can use the PC speaker driver available from Microsoft. In that case, no sound board is necessary.*

Sound Recorder is a nifty little program that lets you record your own sounds and create .WAV files. To make it work, you have to have a digital sampling card such as the Sound Blaster with a microphone. The program also lets you do some editing and manipulation of any .WAV files you might have on disk. You can do this even if you don't have a microphone.

The resulting .WAV files can be put to a variety of tasks, including assigning them to system events or using them with other multimedia applications, such as Media Player. Once a file is recorded, you can edit it by removing portions of it. Unfortunately, you cannot edit from one arbitrary spot to another, only from one spot to either the beginning or the end of the file. You can also add an echo effect to a sample, play it backwards, change the playback speed (and resulting pitch), and alter the playback volume.

PLAYING A SOUND FILE

Follow the steps below to play a sound file:

1. Make sure you've installed the correct driver and that your sound board works.
2. Run Sound Recorder (it's in the Accessories group). The Sound Recorder window will appear, as shown in Figure 15.2.

3. Choose File ➤ Open and choose the file you want to play. Notice that the length of the sound appears at the right of the window and the current position of the "play head" appears on the left.
4. Click on the Play button or press Enter to play the sound. As it plays, the wave box displays the sound, oscilloscope style. The status bar also says Playing. When the sound is over, Sound Recorder stops and the status bar says Stopped. Press Enter again to replay the sound. You can click on Stop during a playback to pause the sound, then click on Play to continue.
5. Drag the scroll button around (see below) and notice how the wave box displays a facsimile of the frequency and amplitude of the sample over time.

FIGURE 15.2: *Sound Recorder lets you record and edit .WAV sound files.*

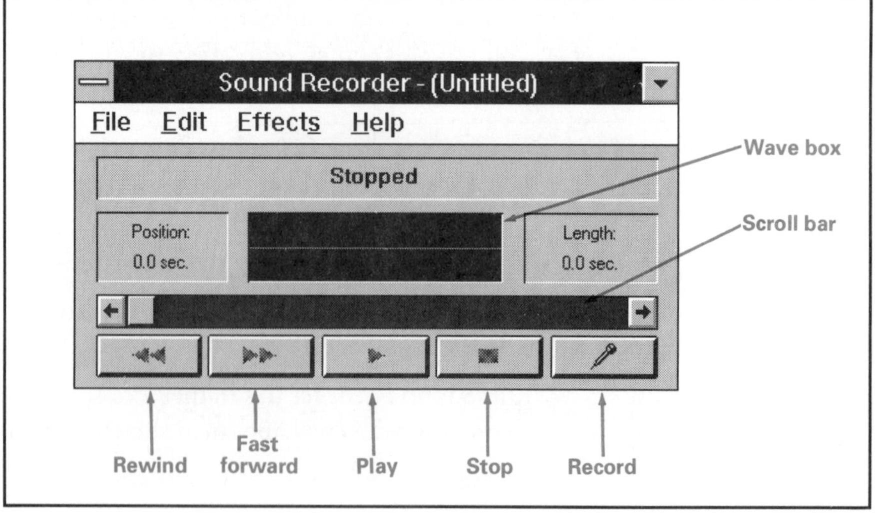

You can also click on the rewind and fast-forward buttons to move to the start and end of the sample, or press the PgUp and PgDn keys to jump the "play head" forward or backward in longer increments.

Recording a New Sound

This is the fun part, so get your microphone ready. Suppose you want to make up your own sounds, perhaps to put into an OLE-capable application document such as Write, Word, Excel, or Cardfile so that it talks when clicked on. Here's how:

1. Choose File ➤ New. The Record button (microphone icon) becomes active.
2. Click on the Record button. The clock starts ticking, counting the passing time. Begin talking, playing music, or whatever into the microphone. You can record for up to one minute. Be cautious about the length of your sounds, since they tend to take up a large amount of disk space. For example, a one-second sample is about 20K in size.
3. Click on Stop when you are finished recording.
4. Play back the file to see if you like it.
5. Save the file with File ➤ Save As. Be sure to enter the .WAV extension or your file won't show up in future listings with the File ➤ Open command.

Make sure to speak loudly and clearly, particularly if you notice that playback is muffled or buried in noise.

Editing Sounds

You can edit your own sound files or those that you've acquired in several ways. For instance, you can:

- add echo to a sample
- reverse a sample
- mix two samples together
- remove unwanted parts of a sample

- increase or decrease the volume
- increase or decrease the speed and pitch

To edit a sound file:

You may run out of memory if your file becomes very long, due to inserting files into one another. The amount of free memory determines the maximum size of any sound file.

1. Open the sound file from the File menu.
2. Open the Effects menu to add echo, reverse the sound, increase or decrease volume, or increase or decrease speed. All the settings except echo are undoable, so you can experiment without worry. You undo a setting by choosing its complementary setting from the menu (e.g., Increase Volume vs. Decrease Volume) or by choosing Reverse.
3. To cut out the beginning or ending of a sound—i.e., to eliminate the lag time it took you to get to the microphone or hit the Stop button—start and stop the sound several times to determine the beginning and ending points of the sound. Get to the actual starting position of the sound and choose Edit ➤ Delete Before Current Position. Then move the scroll button to the end of the desired portion of the sample and choose Edit ➤ Delete After Current Position.
4. To mix two existing sounds, position the cursor where you'd like to begin the mix, choose Edit ➤ Mix with File and choose the file name. This can create some very interesting effects that are much richer than single sounds.
5. To insert a file into a predetermined spot, move to the spot with the scroll bar, choose Edit ➤ Insert File, and choose the file name.
6. To put a sound on the Clipboard for pasting elsewhere, use Edit ➤Copy.
7. To return your sound to its original, last-saved state, choose File ➤ Revert.

Note that not all sound boards have the same features. Some won't let you record into certain types of sound files. Also, the quality of the sound differs from board to board. Some boards sound "grainy," others less so. This is determined by the sampling rate, the quality of the digital-to-analog converters (DAC), and so forth.

HANDLING NONSTANDARD MIDI HARDWARE WITH MIDI MAPPER

MIDI Mapper is a Control Panel utility used to create or modify settings that affect Windows' interaction with MIDI instruments, such as synthesizers. If you don't have a MIDI-equipped sound board or interface (such as the Roland MPU-401 or Sound Blaster with MIDI attachment) and a MIDI instrument or device, this section won't apply to you and the icon won't show up on the Control Panel—so you can skip it. If you *do* have a MIDI setup, however, and a basic working knowledge of the MIDI specification and concepts, read on for a general description of what MIDI Mapper does and how to begin using it. At the least, if you are using an application such as Media Player that plays sound files through a MIDI port or plug-in card like the Ad Lib card, you need to use MIDI Mapper to select the correct MIDI setup for the synthesizer that will be playing the file.

Because of the technical detail involved in reassigning channels, patches, and key maps, the exact procedures for doing so aren't covered here. Use the MIDI Mapper Help system and Windows Users Guide for explicit instructions.

WHAT IS MIDI MAPPER?

MIDI Mapper is analogous to one of those old-style telephone operator's switchboards that has lots of plug-in cables. What it does is create a table of settings that link, or *map,* MIDI events in your multimedia files to MIDI commands sent to your synthesizer, board, or other MIDI device. Such a device is typically an instrument, but not always. MIDI is used nowadays for some computer-controlled professional theatre lighting equipment, automated sound mixers, and a variety of other machinery. In any case, you can think of MIDI Mapper as a translator of sorts that lets you define how incoming commands are transformed before being passed on to the destination hardware.

One of the strengths of MIDI is that it allows for easy translation between event types. Many commercially-available MIDI Mapper programs or stand-alone MIDI Mapper boxes give you tremendous control over MIDI event translation in just this way. (MIDI Mapper is just a Windows implementation with the proper hooks for Windows applications.) For example, say you want to control velocity from the modulation wheel of your synthesizer keyboard instead of from the normal source, which is the speed of your key presses. You would remap a portion of your MIDI data stream to translate mod wheel data into velocity data. This is just one example, but the possible number of combinations is considerable, since the MIDI specification is so extensive and flexible.

For the MIDI implementation to work from Windows, your MIDI files must meet Microsoft's MIDI specs. Since Microsoft adheres to the "General MIDI" specification for channel settings, instrument patch settings, and key assignments, most files created by other programs should work acceptably with MIDI Mapper and play accurately.

When you install Windows, MIDI Mapper configuration files (MIDIMAP.CFG) are added for the popular interface boards, so remapping shouldn't even have to be done for these. The two reasons for using the mapper are as follows:

- if your board doesn't comply with the General MIDI standard
- if you want to select a different MIDI setup, create a new setup, or creatively edit your patch, channel, or key mappings for an existing setup

In the case of a synthesizer or sound board that doesn't comply with General MIDI, you may, in particular, have to remap the patch and key assignments used by your synthesizer.

Check with the manufacturer of the board for the availability of a configuration file before going through the hassle of creating one from scratch. They might have one for Windows 3.1 that you can acquire. Put it in the Windows directory, then run MIDI Mapper.

The Three MIDI Mapper Modes

When you bring up MIDI Mapper from the Control Panel, you see this box:

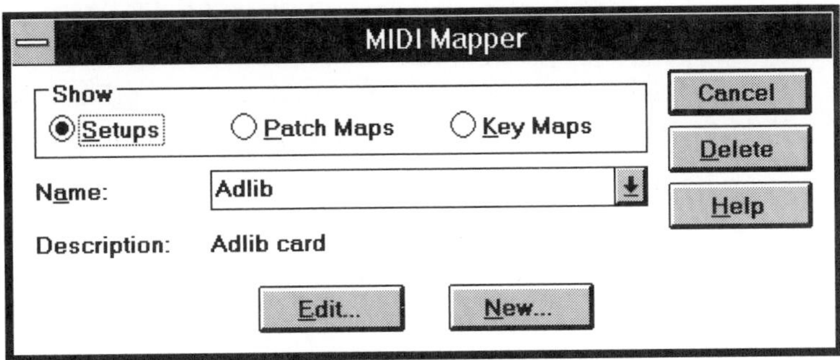

There are three modes that MIDI Mapper runs in, chosen from the Show section of the MIDI Mapper window. Here is a brief discussion of each of these modes:

Setups Use this mode to set up channel mapping for specific synthesizer or synthesizer/board combinations. Each MIDI channel in the setup edited in this mode can be ported to a different MIDI device, and can have a different patch map assigned to it. Setups for several popular synthesizers are supported, such as the EMU Proteus/1, Roland MT-35, and Roland SC-55, but you can create your own setups.

Patch Maps Once the setup is correct, you use Patch Map mode to correct for weird patch-numbering schemes that some synthesizers use. For example, the MIDI file you're playing may contain commands that select a particular patch. (A *patch* is a preset "voice" or sound, such as piano, violin, bass, etc.—and patches have numbers.) The General MIDI implementation stipulates the patch-change numbering scheme for all synthesizers. Even though the MIDI file is sending correct patch numbers, your device may be interpreting them incorrectly because it wasn't designed to comply with the same MIDI specifications. The result is that your device switches to the wrong patch right in the middle of a song—so you get a violin when you wanted a snare drum. Using the Patch Map editor, you establish a lookup or cross-reference table that translates patch numbers in the MIDI file into patch numbers your synthesizer understands.

Key Maps Each key has a number. Sometimes you'll want to change this, particularly in the case where you've got a MIDI sequence for percussion. Typically, each percussion instrument is assigned to a key on your synthesizer, or—if you're using a nonkeyboard synthesizer module—each sound is assigned to a key number. If the allocation of percussion sounds in the synthesizer doesn't match the key numbers encoded in the MIDI sequence file, then the instruments get mixed up—so the tom-tom plays when you expected the castanets, the bass drum when you wanted the high hat, etc. Using the Key Map editor, you establish a lookup or cross-reference table that translates key numbers in the MIDI sequence file into the right key numbers on your synthesizer.

The General Reassignment Procedure

The general procedure for editing channel, patch, and key maps is as follows:

1. Choose the correct synthesizer or synthesizer/card combination from the Name drop-down list. If your synthesizer or card isn't on the list, and the one you're using isn't similar to any of those that are there, then click on New. You'll be prompted to type in a name and description for your new setup, followed by the channel-mapping box in which you'll organize the basic setup for the new device.
2. Choose the correct mode from the Show section of the dialog box.
3. Click on Edit to edit the settings for the selected mode. A large dialog box will come up, such as the MIDI Patch Map dialog box in Figure 15.3.
4. Click in a cell (as shown) and use the small up and down arrow keys and drop-down list boxes to edit the assignments for each channel, patch, or key (depending on which mode you're editing in.)
5. OK the box and subsequent confirmation to save the settings.
6. Exit MIDI Mapper.

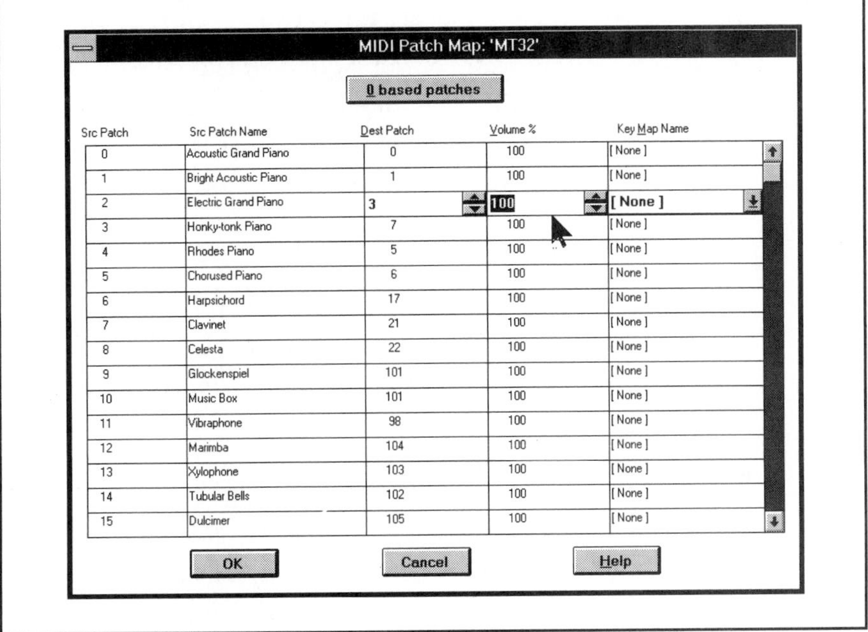

Src Patch	Src Patch Name	Dest Patch	Volume %	Key Map Name
0	Acoustic Grand Piano	0	100	[None]
1	Bright Acoustic Piano	1	100	[None]
2	Electric Grand Piano	3	100	[None]
3	Honky-tonk Piano	7	100	[None]
4	Rhodes Piano	5	100	[None]
5	Chorused Piano	6	100	[None]
6	Harpsichord	17	100	[None]
7	Clavinet	21	100	[None]
8	Celesta	22	100	[None]
9	Glockenspiel	101	100	[None]
10	Music Box	101	100	[None]
11	Vibraphone	98	100	[None]
12	Marimba	104	100	[None]
13	Xylophone	103	100	[None]
14	Tubular Bells	102	100	[None]
15	Dulcimer	105	100	[None]

FIGURE 15.3: *The MIDI Patch Map editor. Use it to edit or create a patch map if your synthesizer's patch list differs from the general MIDI patch assignments.*

INFORMATION SOURCES

See also Chapter 21 for a list of Windows information sources.

Magazines are great sources of information about the quickly changing computer product market. Visit your local smoke shop or magazine rack to look for multimedia intelligence. One new magazine speaks directly to the issues herein—*MPC World,* available nationwide.

For online assistance, files, and general chitchat on multimedia, try CompuServe's Multimedia Forum (GO MULTIMEDIA) and Multimedia Vendor Forum (GO MULTIVEN); they contain the latest gossip, hints, trivia, and tips on the subject. Also try the Windows Advanced Forum (GO WINADV).

The Windows Information Manager (WIM) is a disk-based periodical that's offered in a hypertext multimedia format, incorporating sound and animation. From R & R Development Corporation: (212) 929-2206.

Finally, there is at least one book that looks at Microsoft's multimedia development tools and discusses processes that are involved in integrating image, sound, and text within a multimedia title. *Microsoft Windows Multimedia Authoring and Tools Guide*, available from Microsoft Press, is intended for publishers, managers, and developers who are considering writing their own multimedia titles. It doesn't touch on other vendor's authoring languages (of course). Still, it should be required reading when planning and preparing your sound, MIDI, graphics, animation, text, and CD-ROM data for use with any authoring language front-end. Logistics of project planning and coordination are also covered.

Some Multimedia Sound and Animation Products

Below are some listings of multimedia sound and animation products:

Sound Products

SoundEngine-Media FX Add concert hall sound to your PC. This card combination uses 16-bit stereo CD-quality sampling to add music and sound to your system. MIDI compatible, with 213 preset sampled sounds. It's fairly expensive, however. Call Video Seven at (510) 623-7857.

Desktop Stereo Add a stereo FM receiver to your computer. Tuning, volume, treble, bass, and other functions are controlled by the software. From Optronics Technology at (503) 488-5040.

Sound Palette, Sound Booster Record and play back sounds on your PC's speaker, so you don't have to install a sound board. Includes a library of 50 sounds. Optional parallel port connector allows connection to external amplifier and speakers. Macros for adding sound to ToolBook, Word, and Excel included. From M.P. Technologies, Inc. at (301) 907-0042.

Wired for Sound Similar to the product above, but more popular. It allows sounds to be attached to any dialog box, but does not record sounds. It includes a talking clock. From Aristosoft, Inc., at (800) 338-2629.

Sound Blaster, Sound Blaster Pro Very popular, fairly inexpensive sound boards. They contain an on-board synthesizer, microphone input, digital voice input and output, stereo amplifier, and MIDI interface. From Creative Labs, Inc., at (408) 986-1461.

Video/TV Products

Watch TV in Windows on a VGA screen: 122 channels with a 4 Watt audio amplifier. Videomail has a number of products that integrate video information and hi-fi sound with Windows. Call them at (408) 747-0233.

Hauppauge Computer Works is a competing company in the TV/-Windows field that offers similar products. Their number is (516) 434-1600.

Digital Still Images

Fotoman This low-cost digital camera takes pictures that you can show on your computer screen and integrate into Windows documents and applications. Creates TIFF, PCX, BMP, and EPS files. No film necessary. Built-in flash. Stores 32 pictures. You can edit the pictures later. The editor is called Fototouch. From Logitech at (510) 795-8500.

Authoring Languages/Environments

Build applications containing all the elements of multimedia, even if you aren't a "creative type" at using these programming or multimedia *authoring products:*

Animation Works, by Gold Disk, Inc., (310) 320-5080

Autodesk Multimedia Explorer, by Autodesk Multimedia, (800) 228-3601

Asymetrix Toolbook and Multimedia Resource Kit, by Asymetrix, (206) 637-1500

Music Products

Composer Quest Explore music, history, and the arts from the year 1600. What was happening in the world when Chopin wrote the Minute Waltz? What do paintings by Monet, Turner, and Rembrandt look like? CD-quality sound makes this crash course in history and art pretty interesting. Requires an MPC-compatible setup. Call Dr. T's Music Software at (617) 455-1460.

X-oR Need a MIDI librarian/editor that includes the kitchen sink? X-oR gets, sends, loads, and saves patches and banks of patches from any MIDI instrument. You edit them with sliders. Change envelopes, randomize patches, do MIDI merging, rechannelize, and play music with your mouse. Also from Dr. T's Music Software.

Miscellaneous Multimedia Products

Get yourself 40 interface graphics, 75 animations, 25 digitized video clips, 100 sound effects, and 25 digitized musical selections for dropping into your multimedia creation. Call MacroMind Paracomp at (415) 442-0200.

Microsoft has three "entertainment packs" that include tons of animated games. They are cheap. Each pack is $40. Microsoft's number is (206) 882-8080.

Audio Tracks Libraries Contains a large library of digital sounds, effects, and music for Sound Blaster cards. Get it at HSC Software at (310) 392-8441.

Power Japanese Want to read and write Japanese in 15 minutes? Animated writing and sound teaches Japanese quickly. From Bayware at (800) 538-8867.

Multimedia PC Marketing Council

These are the companies involved in establishing multimedia standards for PCs. They also market multimedia products and are good sources of information on MPC systems and software:

AT&T Computer Systems
1 Speedwell Ave.
Morristown, NJ 07960

CompuAdd Corp.
12303 Technology Blvd.
Austin, TX 78727

Creative Labs, Inc.
2050 Duane Ave.
Santa Clara, CA 95054

Media Vision, Inc.
47221 Fremont Blvd.
Fremont, CA 94538

Microsoft Corp.
1 Microsoft Way
Redmond, WA 98052-6399

NEW Technologies Inc.
1255 Michael Drive
Wood Dale, IL 60191

Olivetti
Via Jervis 77
10015 Ivrea, Italy

Phillips Consumer Electronics Co.
1 Phillips Drive
P.O. Box 14810
Knoxville, TN 37914

Software Publishers Association
1730 M St. N.W.
Suite 700
Washington, DC 20036

Tandy Corp.
700 One Tandy Center
Fort Worth, TX 76102

Video Seven
46221 Landing Parkway
Fremont, CA 94538

Zenith Data Systems
2150 East Lake Cook Road
Buffalo Grove, IL 60089

FAST TRACK

CHAPTER

16

FAST TRACK

To speed up Windows' overall performance, ... 538
upgrade an older computer by installing a new microprocessor.

To run Windows optimally on your system, ... 543
be sure that the memory is configured properly. On an 80286, 80386, or 80486, configure all additional memory as extended, except for whatever amount of expanded memory is demanded by your specific programs.

To give Windows plenty of space for programs and their data, ... 545
install as much memory as you can afford, but be careful to match it to your computer's microprocessor.

To speed up Windows' screens, ... 546
install a graphics board equipped with a coprocessor.

To fine-tune the DOS software settings for your needs, ... 549
edit your CONFIG.SYS and AUTOEXEC.BAT files.

To create additional room on your hard disk, ... 550
delete all unnecessary files, including any temporary files left over from earlier sessions.

To run your hard disk at maximum speed, ... 559
use a defragmenting utility to streamline your disk so that all files are located in unbroken blocks. Also, use an interleaving utility to adjust the disk interleave to the optimum setting.

To speed up your hard disk dramatically, ... 565
install the SMARTDrive disk-caching utility, and set it for a minimum cache size of 256K.

To get the fastest possible performance with 386-Enhanced mode, ... 569
set up a permanent swap file on your hard disk.

To run Windows and DOS on the same computer, ... 576
create separate pairs of CONFIG.SYS and AUTOEXEC.BAT files, one for each environment.

To fine-tune the Windows software settings for your needs, ... 577
edit your WIN.INI and SYSTEM.INI files.

CHAPTER 16

FEATURING

A Discussion of What Determines Windows' Performance

Supercharging Your System Files

Supercharging Your Hard Disk

Using SMARTDrive

Optimizing Swap Files

Supercharging Your System for Windows

The Setup program does an excellent job of automatically tailoring Windows for your particular computer and its accessories. To run Windows at its best, however, you may need to get your hands dirty and do some customizing of your own.

Supercharging Windows has two main goals: increasing speed and boosting memory capacity. Obviously, you want your programs and Windows itself to run as fast as possible, so you don't have to wait unnecessarily while you work or when you switch from program to program. You also want to be sure you have enough memory to run all the programs you use at the same time, with enough left over for all the data your programs keep in memory.

The easiest way to achieve both goals is to upgrade your computer hardware with a faster processor, more memory, a bigger hard disk, and a faster graphics adapter. I'll mention some of the things you should consider when choosing new hardware for a high-performance Windows system a little later in the chapter.

Almost as important as upgrading your hardware is the art of "tweaking" various system software settings to make the best use of the hardware you have available. That's the main focus of this chapter. Even if you have a state-of-the-art computer loaded with memory, you'll want to squeeze every ounce of performance out of your expensive investment by making a few custom adjustments.

WHAT DETERMINES WINDOWS' PERFORMANCE?

Before you can begin supercharging, you need to understand the major factors that affect the performance of Windows. The most important of these are your computer's memory, hard disk, graphics adapter, and microprocessor. Microsoft refers to the first two items, memory and disk space, as your *system resources,* but the capabilities of your graphics adapter and microprocessor also have a telling impact on performance. Together, these four components determine which programs you can run, how many of them you can run at the same time, and how fast they run.

YOUR COMPUTER'S MICROPROCESSOR

Windows 3.1 will run on many different makes and models of computers. The only absolute requirements are an 80286, 80386, or 80486 microprocessor and full compatibility with the IBM line of personal computers. However, the type of microprocessor in your system and the speed at which it's set to run have a major impact on Windows' own speed and capabilities.

If money were no object, you'd get yourself a new Windows machine with an 80486 processor running at the fastest possible rate (33 megahertz or better, in the case of an 80486). Most people, though, can't afford to junk their present computers, slow as they may be. A compromise that works well for some owners of 80286 computers is to keep the old machine and upgrade the microprocessor.

For as little as $200 or so, you can drop an add-in board containing an 80386 chip into almost any 80286 system. While your upgraded computer might not be quite as fast as a whole new machine, performance will be at least as good as before. And you'll be able to run Windows in 386-Enhanced mode.

Unless you have an 80486 computer, another way to boost performance in some situations is to add a math coprocessor to your system board (an 80486DX has its own built-in math coprocessor). A math coprocessor is a special-purpose calculating chip that handles mathematical computations far faster than the regular microprocessor. Depending on the type of computer you have, the right math coprocessor for your machine may be the 80287 or 80387.

Although Windows itself doesn't take advantage of a math coprocessor, many Windows and non-Windows programs do. Examples include Microsoft Excel (a spreadsheet program), Arts & Letters Graphics Editor by Computer Support (a sophisticated graphic-design program), Pixie by Zenographics (a business charting package), and even Publisher's Type Foundry by ZSoft (which lets you design your own fonts). All will run much faster if your system has a math coprocessor on board.

Understanding Memory

Your computer's memory (RAM) serves as the temporary work space for everything you do with your system. To run any program—or Windows itself for that matter—your computer must first load the program into memory from disk. In turn, your programs need memory to store the information with which they're actively working.

The amount and type of memory you have will directly affect Windows' performance in several ways. Obviously, the size of the programs you can run and how many you can run at the same time depend on how much memory you have. In just the same way, the amount of memory determines how much data your programs can work with at a time; in practical terms, that can mean that the size of your spreadsheets or the complexity of your graphics will be limited by how much memory you've installed.

The memory available in your system doesn't necessarily put an absolute limit on the number of programs you can run or the size of their files. Many programs are designed to work with just the parts of a file that can fit in memory. When this kind of program finishes working on, say, part of a spreadsheet or graphic, it stores that section of the file on disk and then loads the next section into memory. As we'll see, Windows itself can use a similar technique to run more programs and store more data than will fit into memory. But even though this method lets you work around memory limitations, the amount of memory you have still has an impact on your system's performance. The more memory in your system, the less time will be wasted on the relatively slow process of transferring data back and forth between memory and your hard disk.

Types of Memory

IBM-compatible computers can be equipped with three types of memory: *conventional, extended,* and *expanded.*

Conventional Memory This is the fundamental type of memory found on all computers that run DOS, no matter what microprocessor is installed. Conventional memory provides a maximum of one megabyte of memory, although your programs can use only a portion of that total.

The first 640K of conventional memory is the portion that is always available. Here your computer keeps all or part of DOS itself, any device drivers or memory resident (pop-up) utilities you install, and your application software and its data. You must have a full 640K of this usable portion of conventional memory to run Windows.

Extended Memory Most 80286, 80386, and 80486 computers come with at least 1MB of memory. Almost everything beyond the first 640K of conventional memory in these systems is extended memory. So if you have a 286, 386, or 486 system equipped with 1MB of memory total, it has 640K of conventional memory and 384K of extended memory (1MB is equal to 1024K).

Extended memory works almost as quickly as conventional memory, so it's the ideal kind to use. However, there was a hitch before Windows 3.X came out. Extended memory is designed for the advanced memory-accessing capabilities introduced with the 80286 microprocessor. Unfortunately, DOS was developed before the 80286 chip was. For this reason, DOS simply won't allow programs to take advantage of extended memory, even when you run them on an 80286 or 80386 computer. Since Windows is based on DOS, that posed a problem. (By contrast, IBM's operating system, OS/2, was designed specifically for the 80286 processor and uses extended memory fully.)

The problem was solved when several software developers came up with a way to let specially designed DOS programs use extended memory. These techniques are called *DOS extenders.* True to form, Windows 3.1 has a cutting-edge DOS extender built right in and can make full use of extended memory. Programs developed specifically for Windows can take advantage of Windows' DOS extender as well. The practical upshot is simple: give Windows as much extended memory as you can.

Since DOS wasn't designed for extended memory, you must run a special piece of software called an *extended memory manager* to see to it that Windows and all your programs coexist peaceably in the available extended memory. Windows comes with an extended memory manager called HIMEM.SYS, which was installed for you when you set up Windows (if your system has extended memory). Third-party memory management products such as QEMM (Quarterdeck Office Systems), Netroom (Helix Software), and 386Max (Qualitas), discussed in more detail later, can take the place of HIMEM.SYS.

Expanded Memory Before the DOS extenders came along, expanded memory or EMS was the only place to turn for programs needing more memory for larger files. Lotus 1-2-3, the all-time, best-selling spreadsheet, and Ventura Publisher (the GEM version) are just two of many DOS programs that utilize expanded memory. Some older Windows applications also use expanded memory.

Expanded memory works by creating a small "window" in conventional memory through which the microprocessor can access large amounts of memory it would normally be unable to address. In order to make this trickery work, you must install a piece of software called an *expanded memory manager,* which serves as the go-between for a program and the memory it needs, supplying additional memory through the window as the program asks for it.

Expanded memory is slower than extended memory. The reason is simple: the expanded memory window is small. As you work with programs or data stored in different parts of expanded memory, the expanded memory manager has to keep shifting the window to view different areas of memory, and this slows things down. For this reason, Windows does not use expanded memory for its own operations.

Though not used by Windows internally, Windows can supply expanded memory to programs that need it. If you plan to run such programs, the method you must use to provide expanded memory in Windows depends on the type of computer you have and the Windows mode you're running in:

- With very few exceptions, 80286-based computers require that you buy a special add-on expanded memory board. You must then install the expanded memory manager supplied with the board. When shopping for an expanded memory board, look for one that is fully compatible with the LIM EMS 4.0 standard. That way, any programs that use expanded memory will find it.
- In 386-Enhanced mode you don't need any special hardware or even a separate expanded memory manager—Windows itself exploits the special memory capabilities of the 386 and 486 microprocessors to simulate expanded memory for non-Windows programs that need it. (Setting a non-Windows program's PIF to request the use of this expanded memory manager is explained in Chapter 13.) However, you may still want to consider installing an expanded memory manager such as QEMM, 386Max, or the one that comes with DOS 5, to increase your available conventional memory (see "Running Memory-Resident Programs" in Chapter 13).
- If you own a 386 or 486 machine and for some reason wish to run Windows in Standard mode, you'll have to install an expanded memory manager, but you won't need to buy a special expanded memory board. The memory manager can convert as much of your existing extended memory into expanded memory as you tell it to. Windows comes with an expanded memory manager called EMM386, but you may also use a third-party memory

manager instead (such as QEMM or 386Max) to take advantage of its additional features.

Table 16.1 lays out the memory and memory management considerations for each mode and CPU type.

Buying More Memory

Windows craves memory—the more memory you have, the better your system will run. So my basic advice is simple: buy as much memory as you can afford. What kind of memory should you buy, extended or expanded? The answer depends on the kind of microprocessor you have and the software you plan to run.

TABLE 16.1:

Memory requirements and considerations for each CPU type and Windows mode

CPU MODE	STANDARD	386-ENHANCED
80286	640K conventional memory and 256K XMS required. If EMS is required by your application, install your own EMS driver at bootup. If your applications do not use EMS, configure all extra RAM as XMS and make sure that the HIMEM.SYS file is in the CONFIG.SYS file (described later). Windows and its applications will use XMS. Your non-Windows applications may be able to access the XMS too, if they are compatible with the HIMEM.SYS driver supplied with Windows 3.1. The amount of XMS available depends on how much EMS was requested by your EMS driver when it loads. Whatever is left can be used as XMS.	Not possible

TABLE 16.1: *Memory requirements and considerations for each CPU type and Windows mode (continued)*

CPU MODE	STANDARD	386-ENHANCED
80386, 80386SX, 80486, 80486SX	640K conventional memory and 256K XMS required. If EMS is required by your application, you must load the Windows- supplied EMM-386.SYS file or a Windows 3.1-compatible expanded memory driver at boot time. If applications need extended memory see note directly above (286 in Standard mode) about XMS and HIMEM.SYS.	640K conventional memory and 1024K extended memory required. Windows will automatically allocate EMS and XMS as needed to Windows applications. In the case of non-Windows applications, Windows will automatically allocate as much as 1024K of XMS or EMS in an attempt to accommodate the needs of the program. If your application needs more than 1024K of XMS or EMS, configure a PIF requesting it.

Note: XMS means Extended Memory; EMS means Expanded Memory

If you have an 80386 or 80486 computer, you'll definitely want to buy extended memory. Generally speaking, you can do this by plugging more memory chips into your main system board rather than buying costly add-in memory boards. This method also gives you the most direct connection between your microprocessor and memory, ensuring the fastest operation possible.

Extended memory is generally the best type to buy for 80286 computers as well. Keep in mind, however, that you can't convert extended memory to expanded on this type of machine. If you plan to run programs that require expanded memory you'll want to buy that as well. With rare exceptions, you'll have to buy an add-in expanded memory board for this purpose. Just be sure that the board you choose lets you configure its memory as either expanded or extended, or some of each, for maximum flexibility—as your needs change.

No matter which type of computer you have, you'll want to make sure that the speed of the memory you buy matches the speed of your microprocessor. If the memory is too slow, it may not work reliably, or your microprocessor will waste time twiddling its thumbs waiting for the memory to ready itself. But don't buy memory that's faster than the computer can take advantage of. After a certain point, faster memory doesn't do anything to speed up your system—in this case, the microprocessor (or motherboard circuitry) becomes the bottleneck—yet you'll be paying a premium.

Memory speed is specified in nanoseconds (a *nanosecond* is one billionth of a second). Seventy-nanosecond (70-ns) memory is very fast and relatively costly. Even if you have a 12 MHz AT or clone, you'll probably be fine with chips slower than that, such as 150 or 100 ns. To be certain, take a look at the computer's manual. There may be some indication of the minimum speed of RAM chips you add. If there is, buy that speed and don't bother buying faster chips unless you intend to put them later into a faster machine.

The Importance of Hard-Disk Space

You probably think of your hard disk as the place where you store your programs and files when you're not using them and where they stay when your computer is turned off. And that's certainly one of the disk's major functions. But your hard disk also has another important role as a temporary parking place for programs that Windows is running and for program data. As a result, the amount of free space on your hard disk—that is, the amount of space still available after all your programs and files are accounted for—can have a direct bearing on the performance of Windows.

The way Windows uses free disk space depends on which Windows mode you're running in. In 386-Enhanced mode, Windows can perform some sophisticated tricks with your hard disk. In particular, Windows uses the extra room on your disk as "virtual" memory for your system when you run out of the real thing. It does this by swapping information stored in memory to a temporary storage file on the disk, thus freeing up memory for use by another program. Your programs don't know that the swapping has occurred; when a program needs to work with a portion of memory that has been swapped to the hard disk, Windows reloads that information automatically after first swapping it with whatever had been occupying its place in memory.

Obviously, the more free space you have on your hard disk, the larger the swap file that Windows can store and the more virtual memory your system can have. If you know how much memory your system has, you can quickly see for yourself how much more Windows has added with the smoke-and-mirrors swapping technique. (You can check the free memory space by choosing Help ➤ About Program Manager from the Program Manager.)

Windows isn't quite as clever when running in Standard mode, but free disk space still has a big impact on how quickly you use up available memory if you're running non-Windows programs. In Standard mode, Windows creates a swap file for every non-Windows program you run. Every time you switch from a non-Windows program, Windows conserves memory by parking some or all of the program in its swap file. Again, the more free disk space available, the more swap files you can have and the more non-Windows programs you can run.

In both modes, Windows programs often use temporary files stored on your hard disk to hold program sections or data that don't fit in memory, or to hold information currently in use. Some programs won't run if they can't create a temporary file because you've used up all the space on your hard disk.

SPEEDING UP VIDEO PERFORMANCE

Even if you run Windows on a computer equipped with the fastest microprocessor around, and even if you fit your machine with plenty of memory and a big, fast hard disk, there will still be a noticeable time lag every time you change anything on a Windows screen. To make Windows snappier on the screen, consider upgrading your video hardware, software, or both.

Unlike standard DOS, Windows relies on graphics mode to display everything you see on the screen. In graphics mode, each screen dot must be individually drawn on your monitor. Even the text you see on a Windows screen must be generated one dot at a time. Whenever you scroll a window, change a graphic, or open a menu, Windows must redraw hundreds or thousands of tiny dots that make up the part of the screen you've changed. Drawing all those dots takes time. What's more, the higher the resolution of your screen, the more dots there are and the greater the drag on your system's performance.

If your system is equipped with an ordinary graphics adapter such as an EGA, VGA, or even a Super VGA board, the computer's main microprocessor is directly in charge of drawing the dots that make up the screen image. But the central processor wasn't designed for this job and it isn't very fast at it, relatively speaking. Besides, the main microprocessor has better things to do, such as calculating your spreadsheets and sorting your databases—in short, running your applications. But as long as the processor is drawing dots on the screen, it's not available to run your programs, so they run more slowly than they otherwise would.

One way to speed up your system dramatically is to add a graphics board equipped with a microprocessor of its own that's designed specifically for graphics display functions. Such a board relieves your computer's main processor of the job of drawing screen dots individually. Instead, the main processor can simply tell the board, say, where a line should appear on the screen. The board takes over the task of actually drawing the line, allowing the main processor to get back much sooner to its real work of running your programs.

Graphics speedup boards come in two versions, depending on the type of microprocessor they contain. *Graphics accelerators* such as Graphics Vantage (ATI Technologies, Inc.) have processors that are permanently programmed for specific display functions. Because their capabilities are fixed, graphics accelerators can be relatively inexpensive ($600 or so) yet deliver stunning performance. By contrast, the microprocessors on *coprocessor boards* are fully programmable, making them theoretically more flexible. As a result, however, they are more expensive than the graphics accelerators (up to $3500). Moreover, they may not run Windows any faster. For most people, graphics accelerators make better sense.

No matter what sort of graphics board you decide on—standard, accelerator, or coprocessor—it'll pay you to do some comparison shopping between models of that type. In each category, some boards are significantly faster than others.

Keep in mind, however, that the quality of the software driver that communicates between Windows and the board is critical in determining the actual display performance you get. Boards with dazzling speed on lab tests may give only mediocre showings under real-life conditions if the accompanying drivers fall short.

In fact, if funds are limited, you may want to consider sticking with a standard Super VGA board and upgrading to a faster driver. WinSpeed is an optimized replacement driver that works with many of the Super VGA boards on the market, boosting their performance by two to five times, the manufacturer claims. According to published reviews, the speedup is most noticeable on computers with 80286 and slower 80386 microprocessors. WinSpeed is available from Panacea, Inc. at (800) 729-7420.

SUPERCHARGING YOUR SYSTEM FILES

Windows' performance depends almost as much on proper software setup as it does on your computer's hardware components. Fortunately, Windows does most of the work for you when you install it onto your hard disk. The Setup program analyzes your system in detail and makes decisions about what configuration settings to use based on factors such as your computer's microprocessor, the amount of memory you have, and how much space is available on your hard disk. However, the choices Setup makes for you may not be ideal for the software you plan to run. To ensure top-flight performance, you'll need to manually check the settings for each element of your system.

Two files are critical to optimizing your system for Windows. The first is CONFIG.SYS, a unique file containing special instructions executed each time you start your computer. It's used to install *device drivers,* small programs that control the way your system interacts with various hardware components. For example, device drivers are often necessary for managing memory, CD-ROM players, and special graphics displays, as well as many other parts of your system. Other entries in the CONFIG.SYS file control a variety of important system settings, such as the number of disk files that can be open at any one time.

Unlike CONFIG.SYS, AUTOEXEC.BAT is an ordinary DOS batch file. Like all batch files, it can execute a series of standard DOS commands in turn. However, AUTOEXEC.BAT does have one special characteristic: your system automatically runs it each time you start the computer, immediately after carrying out the instructions in CONFIG.SYS.

When you install Windows for the first time, the Setup program will automatically add or change a number of commands in both the CONFIG.SYS and AUTOEXEC.BAT files as needed by Windows. But Setup leaves many of the commands that are already present alone, and it doesn't always add all the commands that you may need. As a result, you may have to edit these files yourself to ensure optimum Windows performance.

Editing Your CONFIG.SYS and AUTOEXEC.BAT Files

In this section, I'll outline the basic steps you should take to edit your CONFIG.SYS and AUTOEXEC.BAT files for top performance with Windows. In the sections that follow, you'll get detailed advice on what to add, what to change, and what to take out when you edit these two files.

Before you make any changes in your existing CONFIG.SYS and AUTOEXEC.BAT files, save copies of the files as backups. If you make a mistake while editing or if you want to switch back to your previous setup (see "Using Windows and DOS on the Same Computer" later in the chapter), you'll have the old files at hand. To make the backup copies, just use the DOS COPY command to copy the files to another directory on your hard disk or to a backup floppy disk.

The easiest way to edit the files is to use the Sysedit program that comes with Windows. You can also use a word processor or text editor that can save files in standard ASCII format (also known as the DOS text format) without the formatting codes usually added to most word processor files.

If Sysedit hasn't been included in a Windows group, you can add it with the New command on the Program Manager's File menu or by running Windows Setup from the Main group and choosing Options ➤ Set Up Applications. Sysedit should be located in the WINDOWS\SYSTEM directory. Alternatively, you can start it with the Run command on the File menu or from the File Manager (move to the SYSTEM subdirectory in your Windows directory, then double-click on the program name SYSEDIT.EXE).

You could also choose the Run command from the File menu in the Program Manager. In the dialog box that appears, type in

SYSEDIT

and press Enter.

When you start Sysedit, the program automatically opens WIN.INI, SYSTEM.INI, CONFIG.SYS, and AUTOEXEC.BAT in four cascading windows. To edit one of these files, click on its window to bring it to the top of the stack and then add, change, or delete text just as you would in Notepad. After you've made the recommended changes, exit Sysedit, saving the files as you go. Then exit Windows.

Your changes won't take effect until you restart your computer. Do so by pressing Ctrl-Alt-Del (all three keys simultaneously). The computer will run the edited CONFIG.SYS and AUTOEXEC.BAT files. If you've made any errors in editing the files, note the messages you receive from DOS as the system starts (if you can read them fast enough). Then go back and edit the files again to correct the mistakes. If you make any really serious errors, you can start over by copying the original versions of the files from the directory or disk where you stored them.

I'll go over the changes you should make to your CONFIG.SYS file on the next several pages. You'll find tips on editing your AUTOEXEC.BAT file later.

Removing Unnecessary Commands from CONFIG.SYS

The first step in editing your CONFIG.SYS file for Windows is to strip it of any commands that Windows doesn't need. By consuming memory, these commands may be a serious drag on Windows' performance.

After you've opened CONFIG.SYS, scroll through the file to locate any lines used to install device drivers that Windows can do without. The preferred way to eliminate the installation of an unneeded device driver is simply to insert the statement REM (for "remark") at the beginning of the line for that driver.

For example, Windows has a built-in mouse driver which even works with DOS applications that you might run full-screen from Windows, so unless you'll be using your mouse outside of Windows, you don't need the standard mouse driver in your CONFIG.SYS file. If you have a line that reads something like:

```
DEVICE=MOUSE.SYS
```

change it to

```
REM DEVICE=MOUSE.SYS.
```

Similarly, since Windows and Windows programs rely on extended rather than expanded memory, you may not need your expanded memory manager any more. If that's the case, add the REM statement to the beginning of the line in CONFIG.SYS that starts your expanded-memory manager.

If you're running any subvariety of DOS version 3 (such as 3.1, 3.2, or 3.3), a REM statement in your CONFIG.SYS file will result in the on-screen message `Unrecognized command in CONFIG.SYS` whenever your computer starts up. Don't panic. The message is harmless and nothing untoward has happened. Unfortunately, you'll see the same message if you mistype a CONFIG.SYS command. You'll just have to count the number of times the message appears to be sure it's the same as the number of REM statements in the file. If the error messages bother you, you can shut them off by deleting all the lines with REM statements after you've verified that the CONFIG.SYS file is working right. DOS versions 4.0 and above recognize REM statements properly.

Adding Windows Commands to CONFIG.SYS

Once you've taken out the unnecessary and unwanted lines from CONFIG.SYS, it's time to add the commands that Windows needs. The specific lines you should add depend on the type of computer you have. The optimal entries in your CONFIG.SYS file also depend on how much memory is installed, the kinds of programs you'll be running, and other details about your system. I'll discuss the various CONFIG.SYS options in brief in the sections on each type of computer below. Many of these options are covered in greater depth in later sections as well.

To add new commands to your CONFIG.SYS file, just type them in as you would any other text. Each command must be placed on a separate line. If a statement is similar to one that's already present in the file, just edit the existing statement to match the version recommended for Windows.

Setting Up 80386 and 80486 Computers

With enough memory, 80386 and 80486 computers can run Windows 3.1 in either of its modes, Standard or 386-Enhanced. Each time you start Windows, it figures out how much memory your system has and selects the best mode accordingly (you can override Windows' choice if you wish, as explained in Chapter 2).

Windows can run in Enhanced mode only if you have at least 2MB of total system memory (640K of conventional memory, the rest extended). You need 640K of conventional memory and at least 256K of extended memory to run in Standard mode.

If you have a memory board in your system that can be configured either as extended or expanded memory, set it up as extended memory according to the manufacturer's instructions.

To configure your computer, edit your CONFIG.SYS file so that it contains the lines described below, where appropriate (in each case the proposed line appears first, followed by its description).

This FILES statement tells DOS how many files can be open at once and sets aside the necessary memory:

```
FILES=30
```

The BUFFERS statement below tells DOS how many disk buffers to create and sets aside the necessary memory. Assuming you're using SMARTDrive, the Windows disk-caching utility, you should set up ten buffers as shown here:

```
BUFFERS=10
```

If you're not using SMARTDrive, you should define no more than 20 buffers (30 if you're using DOS 5). Later in this chapter, you'll find details on when to use SMARTDrive and how to set it up.

This next line loads the HIMEM.SYS extended memory manager. You can substitute any Windows 3.1-compatible extended memory manager that you prefer:

```
DEVICE=C:\HIMEM.SYS
```

Use the next line only if you have DOS 5:

```
DOS=HIGH
```

This loads part of DOS itself into the *high memory area* (HMA), the first portion of extended memory. By moving DOS into the HMA, you free up a significant chunk of conventional memory, the first 640K of RAM. This lets larger Windows programs run faster and may allow you to run larger non-Windows programs that otherwise would not fit in the available conventional memory. If you plan to use upper memory for loading device drivers or memory-resident programs, as described in "Making the Most of Conventional Memory" later in the chapter, the line should instead read:

```
DOS=HIGH,UMB
```

The next line loads a portion of the SMARTDrive disk cache. SMARTDrive dramatically improves Windows' speed when it reads or writes information on your hard disk. You load the main portion of SMARTDrive from the DOS command line; you need the line shown here in your CONFIG.SYS file only if you have an older computer (see "Using SMARTDrive" for details):

```
DEVICE=C:\WINDOWS\SMARTDRV.EXE
```

The STACKS statement below can free up memory if your system is running DOS version 3.3 or later. You can omit it if your system is running DOS 3.1 or 3.2:

```
STACKS=0,0
```

The above setting works on most computers capable of running Windows. On certain systems, however, it will cause trouble. If your computer locks up when you try to run Windows, remove the above command and see if that solves the problem.

The next line activates Windows' expanded memory manager, which converts extended memory in 80386 and 80486 computers into expanded memory. Use this line in either of the following situations: if you're running Windows in Standard mode, and then only if you will be running programs that require expanded memory; or if you're running in 386-Enhanced mode with DOS 5 and you wish to load memory-resident programs into upper memory—otherwise, a separate expanded memory manager isn't necessary. If you use a third-party expanded memory manager such as QEMM or 386Max, substitute the correct line for the one shown here:

```
DEVICE=C:\WINDOWS\EMM386.EXE
```

This next line loads the extended memory manager for an add-in memory board. You need this line only if you've installed a third-party extended memory board in your computer:

DEVICE=[*name of extended memory manager*]

The line below loads the expanded memory manager for an add-in memory board. You should use this line only if the memory board can't be reconfigured as extended memory or if you wish to use the expanded memory on the board for loading memory-resident programs (again, see "Making the Most of Conventional Memory"):

DEVICE=[*name of expanded memory manager file*]

This line activates the Windows RAM disk, RAMDrive, which emulates a disk drive in memory. Although a RAM disk can be useful for speeding up programs that store temporary files, your system will usually run faster overall if you let the SMARTDrive disk cache have the memory:

DEVICE=C:\WINDOWS\RAMDRIVE.SYS [*size of RAM disk in kilobytes*]

Add the line below if you have an EGA monitor and you're using Windows to run non-Windows programs in Standard mode. In other words, you don't need this line if you're not running non-Windows programs or if you're working in 386-Enhanced mode:

```
DEVICE=C:\WINDOWS\EGA.SYS
```

If you're running Windows with a special display such as a large screen monitor, you may need to add a line that activates the driver for the display to your CONFIG.SYS file. Consult the manufacturer's instructions for details:

DEVICE=[*name of display driver*]

Setting Up 80286 Computers

Computers with 80286 microprocessors can run only in Standard mode. You must have a minimum of 1MB of memory installed in your system, which must consist of 640K of conventional memory and at least 256K of extended memory. Expanded memory doesn't count toward the 1MB total needed for Standard mode.

Note, though, that Windows can't use extended memory to simulate expanded memory in Standard mode. For this reason, your system must also have enough expanded memory as required by the programs you plan to run. On most 80286 computers, the only way to provide expanded memory is by installing an expanded-memory board.

If you *do* have a memory board in your system that can be configured either as extended or expanded memory, divide the available memory between the two types as the needs of your software dictate. Use the manufacturer's instructions to set aside only as much expanded memory as your programs require and configure as much as possible as extended memory. Edit your CONFIG.SYS file as follows.

This FILES statement tells DOS how many files can be open at once and sets aside the necessary memory:

```
FILES=30
```

The BUFFERS statement below tells DOS how many disk buffers to create and sets aside the necessary memory. Assuming you're using SMARTDrive, you should set up ten buffers as shown here:

```
BUFFERS=10
```

If you're not using SMARTDrive, you should define no more than 20 buffers (30 if you're using DOS 5). (You'll find details on when to use SMARTDrive and how to set it up later in this chapter.)

This line loads the HIMEM.SYS extended memory manager supplied with Windows. Memory management products such as QEMM and 386Max can perform the same duties as HIMEM.SYS; if you use one of these products, substitute the line that activates it:

```
DEVICE=C:\HIMEM.SYS
```

This line loads a portion of the SMARTDrive disk cache. You need this line in your CONFIG.SYS file only if you have an older computer (see "Using SMARTDrive" for more information):

```
DEVICE=C:\WINDOWS\SMARTDRV.EXE
```

This STACKS statement can free up memory if your system is running DOS version 3.3 or later. You can omit it if your system is running DOS 3.1 or 3.2:

```
STACKS=0,0
```

The above setting works on most computers capable of running Windows. On certain systems, however, it will cause trouble. If your computer locks up when you try to run Windows, remove the above command and see if that solves the problem.

This line loads the extended memory manager for an add-in memory board. You need this line only if you've installed a third-party extended memory board in your computer:

DEVICE=[*name of extended memory manager*]

This next line loads the expanded memory manager for an add-in memory board. If you can configure the board's memory as either expanded or extended, choose expanded only if you need expanded memory for the programs you plan to run or for loading memory-resident programs (see "Making the Most of Conventional Memory"):

DEVICE=[*name of expanded memory manager file*]

This line activates the Windows RAM disk, RAMDrive, which emulates a disk drive in memory. Although a RAM disk can be useful for speeding up programs that store temporary files, your system will usually run faster overall if you let the SMARTDrive disk cache have the memory:

DEVICE=C:\WINDOWS\RAMDRIVE.SYS [*size of RAM disk in kilobytes*]

Add this line if you have an EGA monitor and you're using Windows to run non-Windows programs in Standard mode. In other words, you don't need this line if you're not running non-Windows programs:

DEVICE=C:\WINDOWS\EGA.SYS

If you're running Windows with a special display such as a large-screen monitor, you may need to add a line that activates the driver for the display to your CONFIG.SYS file. Consult the manufacturer's instructions for details:

DEVICE=[*name of display driver*]

Other Changes to Make in Your CONFIG.SYS File

No matter what type of computer you have, you may want to make one or two additional changes to the existing commands in your CONFIG.SYS file in the interest of saving memory. Your CONFIG.SYS file may not include these commands, but if it does, here are the possibilities:

- You can change the disk-drive letter name following the LASTDRIVE command to a letter earlier in the alphabet. LASTDRIVE is used to specify the last valid disk-drive letter name accessible to your computer. Working in alphabetical order, the LASTDRIVE command reserves a small amount of memory for each drive up to and including the one you name in the command. The downside of making this change is that you will not be able to access disk drives designated by letters later in the alphabet.

- You can reduce the size of the DOS "environment" space by editing the SHELL command. You'll have less room for environment variables, but you'll save a little more memory (see your DOS manual for more information about the SHELL and LASTDRIVE commands).

Altering Your AUTOEXEC.BAT File

When you've finished with CONFIG.SYS it's time to tackle your AUTOEXEC.BAT file. Don't worry; this part is a lot simpler. Switch to the AUTOEXEC.BAT file window in Sysedit—or load AUTOEXEC.BAT into your text editor—and edit it as follows:

Be sure that your Windows directory has been added to the PATH statement. Setup should have done this automatically if you let it, but you should double-check. The PATH statement should look something like this:

```
PATH=C:\WINDOWS
```

or

```
PATH=C:\;C:\DOS;C:\WINDOWS...
```

If not, edit the path statement appropriately.

Remove all the commands that start memory-resident programs (except ones that you want available to all the programs—including DOS programs—you run in Windows). They just hog good memory and can cause problems like "hanging" your system (causing memory address conflicts). If you want to use them some of the time, see "Using Windows and DOS on the Same Computer" at the end of this chapter, and "Running Memory-Resident Programs" in Chapter 13.

Designate a directory where your programs should store their temporary files. When a program wants to read or write a temporary file, it uses the directory designated by the TEMP environment variable. If you decide to park temporary files in the PARK directory on your hard disk, type in the line

```
SET TEMP=C:\PARK
```

When you install Windows, it creates by default a WINDOWS\TEMP directory and modifies your AUTOEXEC.BAT file accordingly. Thus, your file probably reads

```
SET TEMP=C:\WINDOWS\TEMP
```

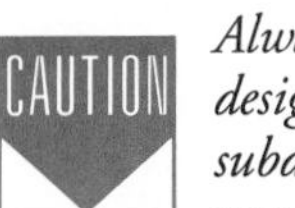

Always designate a subdirectory as your temporary directory, never the root directory. Since DOS limits the number of files that can occupy a root directory, it's a remote possibility that you could run into that limit.

If you have plenty of spare memory, you may want to set up a RAM disk for your temporary files—RAM disks are much faster than hard disks. In this case, you have to create the temporary files directory, and then designate it. If your RAM disk is drive D and your temporary directory will be PARK, you should add the following two lines to your AUTOEXEC.BAT file after the RAM disk is set up:

```
MKDIR D:\PARK
SET TEMP=D:\PARK
```

Leave undisturbed commands that set basic system functions, such as PROMPT, DATE, and TIME. Likewise, don't change any commands that have to do with your computer's functioning on a network.

SUPERCHARGING YOUR HARD DISK

No matter how big and fast your hard disk is, Windows will make you wish it was bigger and faster still. In this section, you'll learn tips for freeing up space on your hard disk and making it run as fast as it possibly can. See Chapter 19 for additional tips.

Deleting Files You Don't Need

On a big hard disk, it's easy to build up a huge collection of files you just don't need anymore. There may be multiple backup versions of letters and reports long outdated, electronic junk mail you read but forgot to delete, demo copies of programs you decided not to buy, readme files ad nauseam, and miscellaneous magnetic flotsam and jetsam of all types. Before you know it, you're down to a megabyte or two of free space on that 80MB hard disk you thought would never fill up, and that's not enough for Windows to operate at its best.

Get rid of those useless files! Make it a point to occasionally sift through all the data files dated a month ago or earlier. Copy the ones you think you're going to need again to a floppy disk and then delete the whole lot of them from the hard disk.

Windows itself installs many files you may not need on your hard disk. Delete all those pretty Windows wallpaper patterns you're not using—if you really want to switch wallpaper later on, you can save the files on a floppy first. To free up really big chunks of disk space, you might even consider deleting some of the Windows programs you use only occasionally. For example, you can free up over 500K by deleting the Windows programs Paintbrush (PBRUSH.EXE and PBRUSH.HLP) and Write (WRITE.EXE and WRITE.HLP).

Deleting Temporary Files

Temporary files are supposed to occupy space on your hard disk only while the program that created them is running, but they have a way of getting left behind. This almost always happens when the program or Windows itself comes to a halt without the proper exit procedures, usually when you lose power or your system hangs up for whatever reason—that is, when it bombs.

Leftover temporary files never get used again and your system may not delete them, yet they're often very large and a few can easily consume several megabytes of disk space with their worthless data. You can delete them without fear. You'll find them in the directory you've specified with the SET TEMP command in your AUTOEXEC.BAT file, as outlined in "Altering

Your AUTOEXEC.BAT File" above. Their names begin with ~ and end with the extension .TMP. To delete these files, exit Windows, switch to the temporary file directory, and enter the DOS command **DEL ~*.TMP**.

Another class of temporary files are the swap files used by your programs and Windows itself. With one exception, you should also delete any swap files left over after you've exited Windows. (If you run in 386-Enhanced mode, you have the option of setting up a "permanent" swap file, which you don't want to delete!)

Program swap files start with ~WOA, and they're normally stored in the same directory as Windows itself (but you can change this, as detailed in the section "Optimizing Windows Swap Files," below). The temporary swap file for 386-Enhanced mode is called WIN386.SWP and is stored in the WINDOWS directory; you can delete it as well without ill effect after you exit Windows. Just don't touch the permanent swap files, called 386SPART.PAR and SPART.PAR.

Delete temporary and swap files only from DOS when you're not running Windows or any other programs on a network. If Windows or one or more programs is running, some of the files will probably be in use.

To give yourself a clean slate automatically each time you boot up, you can include a line or two in your AUTOEXEC.BAT file to do the job for you. Let's assume you've specified the WINDOWS\TEMP directory on drive C as the storage site for your temporary files. In this case, to have DOS automatically delete all your temporary and swap files for you, add these lines to the AUTOEXEC.BAT file:

```
DEL C:\WINDOWS\TEMP\~*.TMP
DEL C:\WINDOWS\TEMP\~WOA*.*
DEL C:\WINDOWS\WIN386.SWP
```

Depending on what files are around and what mode you've been running in, there may or may not be files to erase when you boot up. It doesn't matter if there aren't. DOS will just skip over the commands and continue the boot procedure.

Note that some non-Windows applications use temporary files but may not store them in the temporary directory specified with the SET command. In this case, add a line deleting the appropriate files.

Running CHKDSK

Once in a while, chunks of information lose their moorings and wind up on your disk taking up space, but not as part of a real file. The errant data usually come from files that a program was using when it shut down abnormally because of a power failure or system error, although sometimes DOS just seems to garble a file accidentally. In either case, you can use the DOS program CHKDSK to turn the lost information into files again. You can review the contents of these files to make sure they're not vital, and then delete them.

To use CHKDSK to find and recover lost information, exit Windows, switch to your DOS directory, and enter **CHKDSK /F** at the DOS prompt. If the program finds any lost data, it will ask you whether to convert the data to files. At this point, if you know that the data is inconsequential, type **N** to have CHKDSK delete it immediately. If you want a chance to review the data before you delete it, type **Y** instead. In response, CHKDSK will save the data into one or more files named FILE0000.CHK, FILE-0001.CHK, FILE0002.CHK, and so on. You can then view these files and extract information from them with an editor.

Run CHK-DSK /F only after exiting Windows completely, never from within Windows!

DEFRAGMENTING YOUR HARD DISK

Once you've freed up as much space as you can on your hard disk, you're ready to speed up the disk by defragmenting the files that remain. In normal operation, DOS often stores files in separate pieces on your hard disk. Fragmented files take longer to read than do files that are stored in one long stretch, because the disk head has to jump around from place to place on the disk.

The solution is a disk defragmenting or compacting utility program that collects all the fragments of files and copies them to continuous sections of the disk. Good defragmenting utilities are smart enough to move all the files in each directory to one area of the disk and to put the files you use most often closest to the disk head for fastest possible access. They can also protect your files should a power failure or other glitch occur during the defragmentation process.

ADJUSTING YOUR HARD-DISK INTERLEAVE

Another way to speed up your hard disk is to make sure that its interleave is set at the optimum value for your system. *Interleave* refers to the numerical ordering of the disk's sectors, the sections of the disk into which data on hard disks are organized. Disk-drive controllers read one sector of data at a time. Since some controllers read data more slowly than the disk spins, the sectors on many hard disks must be laid down out of numeric order. An interleave of 2:1 means that the controller skips over every other sector. If the disk is set to a 3:1 interleave, the controller skips over two sectors at a time. If your hard disk controller is fast enough, the most efficient interleave would be 1:1, so that the sectors fall in true numeric order—in other words, no interleave at all.

On many computers, the interleave setting is higher than it needs to be. That is, your controller can actually read data faster than the interleave setting permits it to. With a good hard-disk utility, you can test your system to determine the optimum interleave value and then reorder the sectors to match, without disturbing the data on your disk. This can often speed up the disk by 50 percent or more. If you don't already have a utility of this type, I recommend Power Disk (Multisoft Corp.), SpinRite II (Gibson Research), or OPTune (Gazelle Systems).

USING SMARTDRIVE

SMARTDrive, the Windows disk-caching utility, is one of the key elements in any Windows speedup program. Fine-tuning SMARTDrive for your system can noticeably improve the overall performance of Windows. SMARTDrive's job is to boost the apparent speed of your hard disk. No matter how fast your hard disk is, it can't compare with the blazing performance of your system memory. Of course, you need a hard disk, since you can't store all your programs and files in memory. But SMARTDrive provides a way to make hard-disk data available at the speed of system memory much of the time.

What SMARTDrive does is make a copy of the information your system reads from the hard disk in a reserved area of extended or expanded memory called a *cache*. The next time your system wants to read from the disk, SMARTDrive checks the cache to see whether the requested information is there. If it is, there's no need to use the hard disk again—SMARTDrive turns the information over to the system immediately at the speed of system memory. If not, as the system reads the new information from the hard disk, SMARTDrive gets involved, either adding it to the data already in the cache if there's room, or replacing the existing cache data with the new information. Over time, SMARTDrive adjusts the contents of the cache so that it contains the disk information you're accessing most frequently.

SMARTDrive also intervenes when your system tries to write information on the hard disk, parking it in the cache instead. Then, whenever SMARTDrive detects that your system is idle, it sends some of the information to the disk. This way, you don't have to wait as long to get back control of your computer when saving files. The problem with this write-caching technique is that you have to worry about losing data. If a power failure or other glitch shuts down your system before SMARTDrive finishes copying the cached information to your disk, whatever remains in the cache is lost forever. As you'll see later, you must shut caching off for your hard disks altogether to avoid any possibility of such data loss.

Incidentally, SMARTDrive performs the same disk-speedup magic when you're not running Windows. Unless you have another disk-caching program you prefer, leave SMARTDrive installed when you're using DOS without Windows.

Though the price is right for SMARTDrive (it's included with Windows), there are other disk-caching programs that outperform it. One in particular is Super PC-Kwik Disk Accelerator from Multisoft. If you are intent on squeezing every nanosecond out of your Windows setup, do some research on the latest disk-caching programs and their comparative performances. Before purchasing, be sure the package is compatible with Windows.

Fine-Tuning Smartdrive

The best SMARTDrive setup depends on your system and the way you work. It's pretty obvious that the bigger the cache, the more disk information SMARTDrive can park there and the more often Windows' performance will benefit. On the other hand, the memory you reserve for SMARTDrive will be unavailable for use elsewhere, and the number of programs you can run and the maximum size of their files will be reduced.

Actually, though, SMARTDrive has considerable flexibility here: It can adjust the size of the cache as Windows' own memory needs change, within limits. If Windows requires additional memory to run a new program or load a larger file, SMARTDrive gives up some of the memory in the cache. Later, once Windows has finished with the "loaned" memory, SMARTDrive reclaims it.

When you first run SMARTDrive, you can specify how big a cache you want at the outset, before Windows starts, and you can also specify a minimum cache size that SMARTDrive will reserve no matter what Windows demands. Fortunately, SMARTDrive is smart enough to choose initial and minimum cache sizes itself, on the basis of the amount of memory it detects in your system. Yet, although SMARTDrive's choices work well, you may be able to squeeze out a few extra percentage points of performance by experimenting with its settings.

Starting SMARTDrive

To ensure that SMARTDrive automatically runs each time you turn on your computer, place the command

```
C:\WINDOWS\SMARTDRV.EXE
```

in your AUTOEXEC.BAT file. The Setup program should have done this for you when you installed Windows, if you let it. Alternatively, type **SMARTDRV** at the DOS prompt prior to starting Windows.

Setting SMARTDrive Cache Sizes

To set the size of the SMARTDrive cache, type the number of kilobytes you want for the initial cache size followed by the number of kilobytes you want in the cache at a minimum. For example, to create a cache that is 2MB (2048K) to start with and a minimum of 256K while Windows is running, you would type

```
SMARTDRV.EXE 2048 256
```

You only need to type the initial and minimum cache sizes if you want to change the settings that SMARTDrive chooses automatically. Table 16.2 shows SMARTDrive's default cache sizes, which are based on how much extended memory your system contains.

Specifying Other SMARTDrive Options

You can control several SMARTDrive options by typing additional entries at the DOS command line when you start the program. Once SMARTDrive is running, you can alter its operations by entering **SMARTDRV** again, followed by additional commands at the DOS prompt. I'll cover the most important of these commands here.

Default cache sizes of SMARTDrive

EXTENDED MEMORY	INITIAL CACHE SIZE	MINIMUM CACHE SIZE
<1MB	No caching	No caching
≥1MB but <2MB	1MB	256K
≥2MB but <4MB	1MB	512K
≥4MB but <6MB	2MB	1MB
≥6MB	2MB	2MB

For example, you can turn caching on or off for any disk drive on your system by typing the letter name of the drive followed by + or –. If for some reason you wanted SMARTDrive to ignore drive D, you would type the following command:

```
SMARTDRV D–
```

You can specify as many different drives as you like with one command. In addition, you can use this command repeatedly, whenever you need to change the caching status for one or more drives.

The + and – commands turn on both read and write caching for the specified drive. Since SMARTDrive ordinarily provides read caching only for floppy drives and other drives with removable media, this gives you a way to turn on write caching for these drives. Once you've turned on write caching for a floppy drive, you can only turn it off while leaving read caching on by typing the drive letter alone, without a + or –, as in **SMARTDRV B**.

Unfortunately, you can't turn off write caching for your hard disk without also disabling read caching. Remember, write caching can occasionally lead to data loss. When you're working with supercritical data, you may decide not to risk that possibility, by turning off all caching for the hard disk. Luckily, SMARTDrive provides a command-line switch that ensures that all the data in the cache get written to disk. Type **SMARTDRV /C** *after* you exit Windows to execute this command. Once the disk lights stop flickering and the sounds of disk activity cease, it's safe to turn off your computer.

However, this command won't help if your computer shuts down on its own because of a software error or power failure.

Two other SMARTDrive command-line switches provide information about the program. Type **SMARTDRV /S** to see the size settings of the cache, a summary of the *hit rate* (how many times your system found the information it sought in the cache), and the caching status for each disk drive in your system. Type **SMARTDRV /?** to display a help screen listing all the switches you can use with SMARTDrive.

Using SMARTDrive with Older PCs

Depending on your computer's design, you may need to activate SMARTDrive twice every time you use it: once via your CONFIG.SYS file and a second time via the AUTOEXEC.BAT file or the DOS command line (the ordinary way). In fact, because many systems require this double-buffering technique, the Setup program automatically places a line such as

```
DEVICE=C:\WINDOWS\SMARTDRV.EXE
```

in your CONFIG.SYS file when you install Windows.

However, since double buffering consumes a little memory and slows your system down a bit, you shouldn't use it unless you have to. As a rule of thumb, you'll need to use double buffering if your computer's internal operating program, or BIOS, is more than three years old. But the only way to tell for sure is by checking on SMARTDrive's operation after you've started Windows.

To do this, open a DOS window by double-clicking on the MS-DOS Prompt icon. When the DOS prompt appears, type **SMARTDRV /S**. You'll see a screen of information on SMARTDrive's operations. Find the column labeled buffering. If the entry for any line in this column is yes, your system requires double buffering. If all the lines say no, you don't need double buffering and you should take the line **DEVICE=SMARTDRV.EXE** out of your CONFIG.SYS file.

OPTIMIZING WINDOWS SWAP FILES

In 386-Enhanced mode, Windows can give you more memory than actually exists in your computer by storing programs and parts of Windows itself not currently in use in a temporary swap file on your hard disk. You can control the way Windows configures its swap file for best results with your system. In Standard mode, Windows creates separate swap files for each non-Windows application you run. In this case, your swap file settings are less important, but can make some difference in performance and convenience.

No matter which mode you run in, you need plenty of free hard disk space to get the most out of your swap files. Keep your hard disk free of all unnecessary files by using the techniques described earlier.

TEMPORARY VS. PERMANENT SWAP FILES

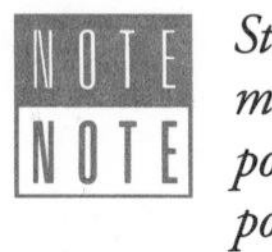

Standard mode supports temporary swap files only.

The important decision you must make about your swap files in 386-Enhanced mode is whether they should be temporary or permanent. The trade-offs are pretty straightforward. You'll get top performance with a permanent swap file, primarily because a permanent swap file occupies an unbroken stretch on your hard disk for quick access, but also because Windows doesn't need to create it afresh for each session. By reserving space for a permanent swap file, you also ensure that Windows never runs out of disk space for the swap file, so you can count on a given amount of virtual memory for programs and data.

On the other hand, a permanent swap file cuts down the disk space that's free when Windows isn't running. If you use programs outside of Windows that need a place to store temporary files, they may not have enough room.

TIP *When electing to use a temporary swap file, always ensure there is ample free space on your hard disk, at least several megabytes.*

The alternative is to let Windows create a temporary swap file during each session. A temporary swap file doesn't need to reside in an unfragmented, contiguous section of your hard disk. Also, Windows deletes it automatically when you exit, freeing up disk space for other temporary uses. The downside to a temporary swap file is simply that it makes Windows run slowly.

Just because the temporary swap file is deleted when you exit from Windows doesn't mean you need any less free disk space than you would for a permanent swap file. If you fill up your hard disk with other files, Windows won't have room to create the temporary swap file and you won't have the extra memory capacity it would have provided.

To determine which type of swap file you're currently using, load the Control Panel and click on the 386 Enhanced icon. When the dialog box appears, click the Virtual Memory button. You'll see a little window of information, listing the swap-file type, size, and location.

Setting Up Swap Files for Enhanced Mode

Standard mode handles its swap files for non-Windows applications automatically. In 386-Enhanced mode, however, you have more control. You can choose whether or not a swap file is used at all—and if so, whether it is temporary or permanent and how large it is. If you decide to go with a permanent swap file, be sure to defragment your hard disk before you set up the file.

Since a permanent swap file requires a contiguous block of your hard disk, you'll unnecessarily limit the size of the swap file if your other files are scattered in random fragments all across the disk. Correct this problem by optimizing the disk first with a compacting utility, as described earlier, to create the largest possible contiguous stretch of free disk space.

You set up your 386-Enhanced mode swap file from within the Virtual Memory dialog box. Open the Control Panel, double-click on the 386 Enhanced icon, and click the Virtual Memory button. This displays the Virtual Memory dialog box, showing the current swap-file settings. To make changes in the swap-file setup, click on Change. The dialog box enlarges, giving you new options. You can select the type of swap file you want (temporary, permanent, or none) from a drop-down list box. Another list box lets you choose the drive on which you want the swap file to reside. Be aware that you can't install a permanent swap file on a network drive, so network drives won't show up in the list if you've chosen a permanent swap file.

In the New Size text box you tell Windows how big to make the swap file. For a permanent swap file, your entry here, in kilobytes, determines the fixed size of the file. For a temporary swap file, this is its maximum size, meaning that Windows will never use more disk space than this for temporary swapping. By setting a limit on the temporary swap file size, you can ensure that there will always be some disk space remaining for storing your own files.

To help you decide how large to make your swap file, the Virtual Memory dialog box reports the space available for the type of swap file you've chosen on the selected drive. If you've selected a permanent swap file, you'll see both a Maximum Size, indicating the largest contiguous space available on the disk, and a Recommended Size, which is never more than half of the total free space on the disk. If you've chosen a temporary swap file, you're presented with a Recommended Maximum Size, indicating Windows' guess as to the best compromise between swap file size and free space for your own files.

Using FastDisk to Speed Up Your Permanent Swap File

If your system's disk controller card meets certain specifications and you're running in 386-Enhanced mode, you'll see an option in the expanded Virtual Memory dialog box called Use 32-Bit Disk Access. When activated, this option (often called *FastDisk*) does several things to crank up your system's performance:

- speeds up all disk access under Enhanced-mode Windows
- allows you to run more DOS applications at once, instead of getting an "out of memory" message even when Program Manager reports you have gobs of memory available
- speeds up overall system performance when running DOS applications in the background

Turning on the option kicks in an advanced software driver that lets Windows access your hard disk directly, circumnavigating your system's BIOS (basic input output system) and DOS. The result is much zippier disk access and generally faster operation of Windows all around.

You'll also be able to run more DOS sessions when this option is activated, because the driver lets Windows run DOS sessions in virtual memory, swapping portions of them to disk when RAM is needed by other applications. This normally isn't possible when Windows uses the BIOS and DOS to access your drive. In those cases, the entire DOS program you're running has to fit into RAM at one time.

Unfortunately FastDisk doesn't work with every computer. You'll have the check box only if your system's hard disk and controller hardware seems to perform correctly with the FastDisk driver. (Windows performs an automatic test during installation to check for compatibility.) Even then, the option won't be turned on by default. You'll have to activate it manually.

To get a little more technical, the driver supplied by Microsoft is compatible with most Western-Digital 1003-compatible controllers only. If your controller isn't WD-1003-compatible, check with the hard disk's manufacturer to see if they have a FastDisk-compatible driver for Windows 3.1. Microsoft is encouraging all hard disk manufacturers to write such drivers. Since the benefits are significant, I suspect drivers should be appearing on the market shortly after the release of Windows 3.1.

One caution about this option is worth considering. Direct disk access can, in certain instances, screw up the data on your hard disk. Most notably, this can happen with laptops and portables that turn off the hard disk to conserve battery power. Often these machines don't inform the operating system or Windows that the hard disk has powered down. This can confuse the FastDisk driver and lead to serious data loss when the drive comes back online. For this reason, you shouldn't activate this option on portables that power down the hard disk unless the computer's manufacturer insists that FastDisk works acceptably with it, or unless you can disable the hard disk from powering down by changing a software or switch setting.

USING (OR NOT USING) RAMDRIVE

Windows comes with a special utility program called RAMDrive that can make a portion of your computer's memory act just like a disk drive. In other words, you can copy files to and from this RAM disk just as you would with your hard disk or a floppy. Of course, there's one big difference between a RAM disk and a regular magnetic disk: the contents of the RAM disk disappear every time you turn off the computer.

The reason to create a RAM disk is to speed up disk operations. Since memory operates many times faster than a mechanical disk drive, your programs can store and retrieve data from a RAM disk in far less time than from even the fastest hard disk. Besides the fact that you lose your RAM disk data every time the power goes off, the only real drawback of a RAM disk is the fact that it consumes memory that would be better used for other purposes.

If you had an infinite supply of memory, or at least enough for a RAM disk that could hold all the files on your hard disk, you would notice a tremendous speedup in all disk functions. But if your memory supply isn't that big, only the particular files you put in the RAM disk will benefit. Even if you create a fairly sizeable RAM disk—say several megabytes—you won't have room for all the disk files that Windows and your programs will need during a session. You'll only get the benefit of the RAM disk some of the time, but you'll have given up a lot of precious memory that could be used to run programs.

A better alternative is to let the SMARTDrive disk-caching utility shuttle disk information back and forth to temporary storage in a memory cache. On average, Windows' overall performance with a relatively small SMART-Drive cache (about one megabyte) will be about the same as with a RAM disk several times larger.

About the only time it makes sense to use RAMDrive is when you're running Windows on a networked computer that lacks its own disk drive. In this situation, the RAM disk would cut down on RAM available for Windows and the active applications.

If you decide to install RAMDrive, set it up by adding an appropriate line to your CONFIG.SYS file. Use the techniques for editing your CONFIG.SYS file described earlier to open the file. Then, following the lines that start HIMEM.SYS and your expanded-memory manager, if any, add a line that looks similar to this example:

```
DEVICE=C:\WINDOWS\RAMDRIVE.SYS 1024 /E
```

In your own CONFIG.SYS file, replace C:\WINDOWS in the example with the disk-drive letter and directory where you stored the RAMDRIVE.SYS driver. (Unless you've moved the file, it will be in the same directory as Windows itself.) Next, enter the size in kilobytes of the RAM disk you want. The RAM disk created by the example would be 1024K, or one megabyte.

You can configure RAMDrive to store the RAM disk in either extended or expanded memory. Add /E at the end of the line for extended memory, as in the example. Add /A, instead, for an expanded-memory RAM disk.

MAKING THE MOST OF CONVENTIONAL MEMORY

Although Windows programs are freed from the DOS-imposed 640K limit on accessible memory, managing that first 640K conventional memory space can still be important. For one thing, larger Windows programs run faster when there's more conventional memory available. For another, the amount of conventional memory that's free when you start Windows determines how much memory each non-Windows program has to work with. If there's not enough conventional memory, large non-Windows programs simply won't run or there won't be enough room for your data.

To maximize the amount of free, available conventional memory, you just have to avoid filling it with other programs before you start Windows. Every device driver or memory-resident program (TSR) you install, including DOS itself, takes up room in memory.

You can use two main strategies to free up more conventional memory. The simplest approach is just to get rid of as many TSRs and device drivers as possible. You can either simply do without them or, in the case of memory-resident programs, wait to load them until *after* you start Windows. Remember, you can start multiple, separate copies of the DOS prompt from Windows by double-clicking on the MS-DOS Prompt icon for each copy you want to run. In each of these DOS sessions, you can run as many TSRs as will fit. Keep in mind, however, that the programs you run in one DOS session will be available only in that session. If you need a given memory-resident program in two or more sessions, you must either run it independently in each separate session—which isn't always possible—or run it before loading Windows.

In this situation, a better solution would be to run the memory-resident program before you start Windows—it will then be available in every DOS session you launch. But then you're back to where you started: using up too much conventional memory. However, there is a way you can have your cake and eat it too—by moving TSRs and device drivers into upper memory, out of the conventional memory space.

LOADING MEMORY-RESIDENT PROGRAMS INTO UPPER MEMORY

You'll recall from our earlier discussion of the different types of memory that there is an area in memory between the 640K top of conventional memory and the start of extended memory at 1MB. Although this upper-memory area is set aside for the software built into your computer and into your add-in boards, the built-in software doesn't use up all of the upper-memory area. If you have the right computer hardware, you can borrow chunks of extended memory, making them appear to your system as if they were located in upper memory. You can then load memory-resident programs and device drivers in these upper-memory blocks (UMBs). As a result, you can continue to use your memory-resident programs and device drivers, yet you've freed up the conventional memory that they would have occupied.

This technique works for many, but not all, memory-resident programs and device drivers. Some are simply too large to fit into the available upper-memory blocks. Others weren't designed to run from upper memory and so don't work—or worse yet, they cause your system to shut down unceremoniously. You'll have to experiment to find out which programs and drivers do work.

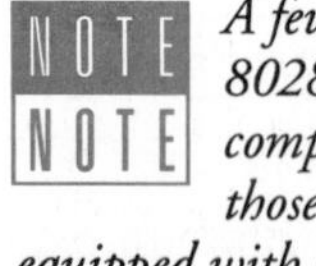

A few 80286 computers, those equipped with certain types of "shadow RAM," also permit you to access the upper-memory area.

To use upper memory for this purpose, you must have the following:

- an 80386 or 80486 computer
- an expanded memory emulator to convert extended memory in your system into usable upper memory
- a special utility program to load your memory-resident programs and device drivers into upper memory

Aside from providing expanded memory to applications that require it—a function that you don't need when running Windows in Enhanced mode—expanded memory managers can perform the memory tricks needed to make upper memory available to your programs and drivers. Earlier, we touched on how to load the expanded memory emulator that comes with Windows, EMM386, from your CONFIG.SYS file. EMM386 provides upper memory, but *only* if you're running DOS 5. It's always best to use the version of EMM386 that came with the copy of Windows you're currently running.

To review, you load EMM386 with a line similar to this in your CONFIG.SYS file:

```
DEVICE=C:\WINDOWS\EMM386.EXE 640
```

You must place this line after the one that starts HIMEM.SYS, but before any commands that require expanded memory. The number at the end of the line tells EMM386 how much extended memory (in kilobytes) to convert to expanded memory.

In addition, you must tell DOS to make the upper-memory area available. Unless you have a specific reason not to, you should also load DOS into the high-memory area (a part of extended memory distinct from upper memory); this will save a considerable amount of conventional memory. Add the following command to your CONFIG.SYS file (it can come before or after the line that starts EMM386):

```
DOS=HIGH,UMB
```

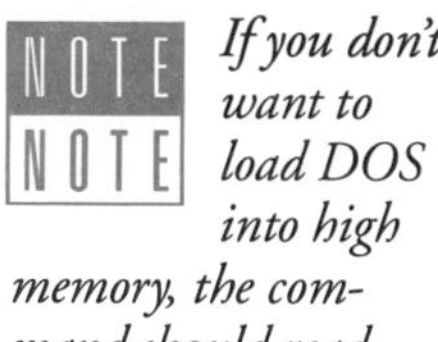

If you don't want to load DOS into high memory, the command should read **DOS=UMB**.

After you've loaded EMM386 and activated upper memory via this command, you can place device drivers and memory-resident programs into upper memory with DOS 5 commands. To load a device driver into high memory, use the command **DEVICEHIGH=** in your CONFIG.SYS file, rather than the standard **DEVICE=** command. For example, to load a CD-ROM driver into upper memory, you'd use a command like the following in your CONFIG.SYS file:

```
DEVICEHIGH=C:\SCSI\CDROM.SYS
```

To load memory-resident programs into upper memory, start each program from the DOS prompt or a batch file with the LOADHIGH command. For example, to load Sidekick into upper memory, you might type the following at the DOS prompt:

```
LOADHIGH C:\SK\SK
```

As an alternative to EMM386, you can use third-party Windows-compatible expanded memory managers such as QEMM, 386Max, and Netroom. These products work with earlier versions of DOS as well as DOS 5, and they frequently create more available upper memory than EMM386 does.

They replace HIMEM.SYS as well as EMM386. These products supply their own utilities to load programs and device drivers into the upper memory they create. Just be sure the expanded memory manager you buy is fully compatible with Windows 3.1.

USING WINDOWS AND DOS ON THE SAME COMPUTER

Unless you use your computer exclusively for Windows, don't be surprised if you cause yourself new headaches by configuring your system for optimal Windows performance. The problem? Almost always, the system configuration that's ideal for ordinary DOS programs running without Windows is very different from the ideal Windows setup.

With Windows out of the picture, you'd probably like to run several memory-resident utilities before you start your main program, and you might want to install an expanded-memory manager or a driver that lets you switch from program to program at the press of a key. The trouble is that all these kinds of software conflict with Windows. When you load ordinary memory-resident programs from DOS, they consume some of the precious 640K of conventional memory; Windows requires as much conventional memory as possible for top performance and may not even run at all if you load too many memory-resident programs. And since very few Windows programs require expanded memory, an expanded memory manager may be worse than useless to you, since it consumes memory itself.

You may be happy running all your DOS programs under Windows, possibly using specialized PIFs. If not, what you need is a way to switch between two different system configurations, one for Windows and one for DOS.

Unfortunately, there's no easy method for doing this. If you've been running Windows and you want to switch to plain DOS, or vice versa, you have to change the system files (CONFIG.SYS and AUTOEXEC.BAT) and then restart your computer. To make this cumbersome process as painless as possible, do it this way:

1. Edit your CONFIG.SYS and AUTOEXEC.BAT files so that they contain the optimal configuration settings for Windows as outlined earlier in this chapter. When you're finished, make copies of

this pair of files on your hard disk as one CONFIG.WIN and AUTOEXEC.WIN.

2. Create a second pair of system files containing the ideal settings for your DOS programs. Save these files as CONFIG.DOS and AUTOEXEC.DOS.
3. Create two short batch files and store them in the root directory of the hard disk from which you boot your system. Call the first batch file WINGO.BAT. It should contain these two lines:

```
COPY C:\CONFIG.WIN C:\CONFIG.SYS
COPY C:\AUTOEXEC.WIN C:\AUTOEXEC.BAT
```

4. Call the second batch file DOSGO.BAT and put these lines in it:

```
COPY C:\CONFIG.DOS C:\CONFIG.SYS
COPY C:\AUTOEXEC.DOS C:\AUTOEXEC.BAT
```

5. If you've been using Windows and want to switch to DOS, exit Windows and enter **DOSGO** at the DOS prompt. Then restart your computer by pressing Ctrl-Alt-Del. To switch from DOS to the Windows configuration, enter **WINGO** at the DOS prompt and then restart the computer.

As an alternative to creating your own batch files, a much better solution to the problem of incompatible entries in the CONFIG.SYS and AUTO-EXEC.BAT files is to use a utility program called Bootcon, which lets you create one CONFIG.SYS file containing two or more different system configurations. Each time you start your computer, a menu appears allowing you to select which of these setups you want to use for this session. The menu selection you make can also determine which of several alternate sets of commands in your AUTOEXEC.BAT file are executed. Bootcon is available from Modular Software Systems. Call them at (818) 440-9104.

EDITING THE WIN.INI AND SYSTEM.INI FILES

Windows stores important system settings in two files, WIN.INI and SYS-TEM.INI, located in your Windows directory. Windows reads the settings in these files each time it starts up to determine how to configure itself. By altering these files, you can fine-tune your Windows setup in a number of useful ways.

The WIN.INI and SYSTEM.INI files are divided into sections of related settings. The code words for the sections and settings can be a bit cryptic, but they're readable, as in this excerpt from WIN.INI:

```
[windows]
load=
run=cmdpost.exe
Beep=yes
Spooler=yes
NullPort=None
device=PostScript (Micrografx),MGXPS,LPT1:
BorderWidth=3
KeyboardSpeed=31
```

Each section in the WIN.INI and SYSTEM.INI files starts with a section name in brackets. Individual settings are then listed in the format keyname=value where *keyname* is the setting's name and *value* may be words or a number, depending on the setting.

The settings in SYSTEM.INI relate mainly to the specific hardware components of your system. The file tells Windows which drivers to use for your display, mouse, network, and so on, and how to set up non-Windows applications, Standard mode, and 386-Enhanced mode.

The WIN.INI file, on the other hand, mainly controls various aspects of Windows operation according to your personal preferences. For example, WIN.INI settings in the excerpt above determine which programs start automatically when you start Windows, whether Windows beeps at you when you make a mistake, and so on. Individual Windows programs also store their own settings in WIN.INI. CorelDRAW (Corel Systems), a popular drawing program, uses WIN.INI to keep track of which fonts and file-import utilities are installed, among other things.

Don't bother looking for information on WIN.INI and SYSTEM.INI in the Windows User's Guide—it's not there. Instead, a series of files in your Windows directory explain how WIN.INI and SYSTEM.INI work and describe each of the individual settings in detail. These files are named WININI.WRI and SYSINI.WRI, and they can be read in Write.

Because Windows maintains key settings in ordinary text files, you can easily check the files to ensure that the settings are correct and change them to your liking using any old text editor. But don't start changing things until you know what you're doing—it's fairly easy to accidentally alter or erase a key setting in a way that could foul up Windows' operation.

You can edit WIN.INI and SYS.INI with any text editor that can read and save plain, unformatted ASCII text files. The easiest way, though, is with Sysedit.

When you've finished making changes, save the files and close Sysedit. The changes won't take effect until the next time you start Windows.

MAINTAINING YOUR WIN.INI FILE TO IMPROVE WINDOWS PERFORMANCE

As you've just learned, almost every Windows application you install adds something to your WIN.INI file. As your collection of Windows programs grows, WIN.INI gets longer and longer. As a result, because Windows must process all the information in the WIN.INI file each time it starts, Windows begins to slow down a bit. In addition, if you've learned to edit the WIN.INI file manually, you'll find it harder and harder to find what you're looking for in the file.

It might seem that deleting unused programs with Windows Setup would be an easy way to restore efficiency to your WIN.INI file. Unfortunately, however, deleting a program does not automatically remove its entries from WIN.INI. They remain there, cluttering up the file and busying Windows needlessly.

In addition to deleting a program, then, you must delete its entries in WIN.INI yourself. Open WIN.INI using a text editor (Sysedit or Notepad are good choices) and find the section labeled [Extensions]. Look for and delete the line corresponding to the file name extension used by the program you're removing. For example, if you're removing Write, the line you want is

```
wri=write.exe ^.wri
```

Then comb through the file to find the section devoted to that program—it begins with the program name in brackets, like this:

```
[MSWrite]
```

or

```
[CorelDraw]
```

Delete everything that follows this title up to the next bracketed title. This may consist of many lines of settings.

FAST TRACK

CHAPTER 17

FAST TRACK

1. Choose Disk➤Network Connections or Connect Network Drive from the File Manager (depending on your type of network).
2. Specify the information you are prompted for (such as name of the drive, drive letter, and optional password), or click on Previous to see past connections or on Browse to look through available drives.
3. Click on Connect.

1. Choose Disk➤Connect Network Drive. A dialog box will appear. It allows you to choose the letter name you want to assign to the drive. Normally, this is the next available letter. Change it from the drop-down list if you want.
2. Type the path of the drive in the Network Path text area.
3. Type in the password for the drive if it's required.
4. Click on Connect and the drive should be added to your directory tree.

1. Choose Disk➤Network Connections.
2. In the Network Connections dialog box, select the network drive you want to disconnect.
3. Click on Disconnect.
4. Click on Close or OK.

To disconnect from a network drive (with the Disconnect command): 593

1. Choose Disk ➤Disconnect Network Drive.
2. The Disconnect Network Drive dialog box will then appear. Select the drive you want to disconnect.
3. Confirm the choice.
4. Click on OK. The drive will be disconnected.

To connect to a network printer, ... 594

1. Run the Control Panel.
2. Choose Printers.
3. Choose Connect.
4. Choose the Network button.

To ensure efficient networking, ... 596

go for higher speed throughput—at least 10 Mbit/sec. Research your network O/S carefully and compare it to Novell Netware. Use a high-speed server, preferably a 486DX with a considerable amount of RAM. Insist on a fast, high-capacity hard disk and large disk-cache. Finally, include a backup system to prevent data loss.

CHAPTER 17

FEATURING

Two Approaches to Windows Networking

Working with Network Drives

Handling Problems with Network Applications

Network Installation and Maintenance Tips

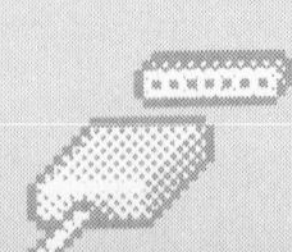

Using Windows on a Network

The evolution of local area networking on Windows has been a gradual one. Windows 2 left a great deal to be desired in this regard. In that version, sharing network devices while running Windows was problematic at best, and you had to make all your connections to printers and network servers prior to running Windows. Then, if you were lucky, Windows recognized the connections you had made. In addition, since Windows 2 used memory far less efficiently, you often wouldn't have much room for your application after DOS, the network shell, and Windows were all loaded onto your computer.

Large strides were made with Windows 3.0. That version *did* recognize a variety of networks, allowed you to log on to network drives, and, possibly, send E-mail and use network printers. However, with 3.0, users complained of unexplained system crashes, *UAEs* (unrecoverable application errors), and other unpredictable anomalies.

Version 3.1 resolves much of this. By working closely with network developers, Microsoft has added numerous support files, device drivers, and sundry utility software that will enable Windows to behave more smoothly with many popular networks. Installation has also been simplified in Windows 3.1. In addition, UAE dialog box messages now tend to provide more useful suggestions as to how problems can be resolved.

If memory shortages have been an issue when running networks and Windows, version 3.1 may offer a solution in that area as well, since Windows 3.1 is compatible with memory managers that are more intelligent than those supplied by Microsoft, such as QEMM by Quarterdeck. As a result, with Windows 3.1 you'll likely be able to recover a little more RAM space for applications without having to sacrifice either Windows or your network drivers.

Finally, necessary setup information for the more popular networking systems, such as Novell NetWare, Microsoft LAN Manager, and Banyan Vines, is included with Windows 3.1, decreasing the amount of "tweaking" that system administrators have had to perform to get a Windows-based network up and running.

Installation issues aside, if you are using one of the networks that is well supported by Windows 3.1, you'll have simple-to-use dialog boxes from which to choose a variety of network options. As a result, you can make changes to your network setup without exiting to DOS and typing in commands, as is required with networks running in the DOS environment. Also, since the dialog boxes are easier to understand and control than their text-based counterparts, Windows can actually render a network easier to use. Thus, you might consider Windows a friendly "front-end" to the network.

Appendix C of this book discusses Windows for Workgroups, a new peer-to-peer network version of Windows.

In fact, Microsoft's eventual plans are to make using a Windows network so easy that typical users won't know they're using a network at all. All resources such as printers and disks will appear as if they are local devices, directly attached to the user's computer rather than across the hall or across the country, connected by a network. One Windows 3.1 feature to this end causes each network station to automatically reconnect to all the printers and network drives that were in use in the previous session, rather than forcing the user to connect to them manually each time the workstation is booted up.

Networking under Windows still isn't as seamless as it could be, but there are some utilities from other companies that can help. Be sure to see Chapter 19 for a discussion of some of these. It's a common misconception, though, that Windows isn't ready for prime time when it comes to networking. With a little know-how, reading the supplied online text files (particularly NETWORKS.WRI), and doing some experimenting, you'll find that Windows networking can actually be fast and easy. More about that later in this chapter.

First, here's some general discussion about using Windows on a network, from the user's point of view. Later in this chapter, I'll discuss general networking strategy for administrators. Nowhere in this book will I discuss nitty-gritty details of WIN.INI settings for each of the networks, so if that's what you're looking for, refer to NETWORKS.WRI instead. It will be more up-to-date than anything we could put in a book, since it changes with each new mini-update of Windows.

WHICH NETWORKS ARE SUPPORTED?

The number of networks that is supported by Windows is constantly increasing. The best way to determine whether your network is supported is to read the file NETWORKS.WRI that came with your copy of Windows. It should be in the directory into which you installed Windows (typically, C:\WINDOWS). You can avoid confusion and problems by reading this file, since it contains information pertinent to each network brand.

As of this writing, the networks supported by Windows are the following:

Novell NetWare

Banyan Vines

3Com 3+Open and 3+Share

IBM PC LAN

Microsoft LAN Manager and MS-Net derivatives

If you have another brand of network, contact the manufacturer for Windows 3.1-compatibility information. They may have a network driver for you. Many networks emulate one of the above brands, particularly LAN Manager or IBM PC LAN, so it may be possible to use one of the network drivers above for yours.

TWO APPROACHES TO WINDOWS NETWORKING

There are two basic ways that you can run Windows with a network:

- from a copy of Windows that you install on each user's machine
- from a copy of Windows that is installed on a network file server

Which approach you choose depends on your system needs, the number of users, the type of workstations on the network, and your approach to network security and backups. Some network administrators prefer to keep all programs and files on a central file server. This simplifies the process of backing up important files and reduces the possibility of accidental data and program losses. As long as regular backups are made of the file server's hard disk, you're pretty well insured against catastrophic loss of data. Some network administrators even go so far as to use workstations that have no hard or floppy disks. It is then assured that all files will be kept on the file server's hard disk.

Keep in mind, however, that running Windows over a network will slow the network somewhat. Windows does a lot of disk swapping (reading and writing data to and from the hard disk), and this may prove problematic in some setups. It could turn into a bottleneck, tying up your network, particularly if it's a relatively slow one. In cases where you may have many users on a network, or a significantly high amount of data traffic on the network for other reasons, you might want to install Windows on the network users' hard disks instead of in a central location.

Unfortunately, considering the number of permutations of network topologies and the plethora of applications programs possible, making recommendations about where you should install your copy of Windows would be pure speculation. This is one of those areas where you'll just have to experiment. Try it both ways and see which approach offers the greater advantages.

The instructions for installing Windows on a network server are rather complex, requiring the system administrator to create custom settings files for each workstation. The settings file contains information reflecting the hardware setup of each workstation, and options that can limit a user's access to program groups, directories, and so on. You should refer to the *Microsoft Windows 3.1 System Administrator's Guide* for information about this. The alternative is to install Windows on each workstation, running it on each one as described in this book. The only differences pertain to how you use the resources of the network, such as disk drives and printers.

The sections below explain special network procedures and possible problems you might encounter when using Windows on the network.

USING SETUP ON A COPY OF WINDOWS ON A NETWORK SERVER

If you or your network administrator decided to put a single, shared copy of Windows on the network server, you would then use the Setup program to install it for your workstation, stipulating the configuration of your system. Setup then stores some of the Windows files (such as WIN.INI and SYSTEM.INI) on your system's disk so that when you run Windows from your machine, the hardware and software settings you've chosen will be used. Another user may have different settings, which will be stored on that user's disk in similar fashion.

To set up your own copy of Windows from a network server,

1. Log on to the network server's hard disk and directory where Windows is installed.
2. At the DOS prompt, enter the command

   SETUP /N

   and press Enter.
3. Setup will run similarly to the way it runs when it installs Windows on a local machine (see Appendix A). When asked which drive

and directory you want to install on, specify a directory on the hard disk in your computer. This way the files that customize Windows for your use will be stored in your machine.

SPECIAL CONSIDERATIONS WHEN RUNNING FROM A NETWORK

This section explains some aspects of running Windows on a network that you should consider. To run a shared version of Windows from a workstation, you issue the WIN command from the DOS prompt (or from a batch file) just as you would for a local version of Windows. However, there's a difference in how Windows is actually found and loaded. The startup files that Setup stored in your local directory (or in a personal directory on the server in the case of a diskless workstation) direct your computer to load Windows from the server disk drive and directory rather than from your local drive. So far, this is all automatic. However, there are two important things to remember; otherwise, Windows won't be found, and therefore won't run:

- Make sure the network and your workstation's connection to it are up and running before you try to run Windows.
- Make sure that your workstation is connected to the network drive that contains Windows, and that you have assigned that drive the same letter name it was assigned when you ran Setup. If it was drive E when you ran setup, it must be designated E when you run Windows. This is because Setup recorded the drive letter in the startup file during installation and uses that letter each time it starts Windows.

Windows does not offer any special protection for files that are being shared by users on the network. The network operating system takes care of this. If you are storing your document files in directories to which other users have access, make sure the files are locked appropriately to prevent accidental modification by them. Confer with your network administrator (if there is one) or refer to the network software's manual.

USING NETWORK DRIVES

Assuming your network works with Windows, you'll have two options in the File Manager's Disk menu that let you connect to and disconnect from drives on the network.

CONNECTING TO A NETWORK DRIVE

TO CONNECT TO A NETWORK DRIVE,

1. **Choose Disk ➤ Network Connections or Connect Network Drive from the File Manager (depending on your type of network).**
2. **Specify the information you are prompted for (such as name of the drive, drive letter, and optional password), or click on Previous to see past connections or on Browse to look through available drives.**
3. **Click on Connect.**

Network drives have their own style of icon, similar to the hard-disk icon. (They say NET on them.) Depending on whether you connected to a network drive before running Windows or not, your File Manager's directory tree may or may not show any network drives when you first open it. If the drive you want to access is not showing, you can connect to it if you know its path name and password. Once connected, Windows will remember the connection when you quit and restart Windows. If you don't want the connection maintained each time you start up Windows again, run Control Panel and choose Network. Make the appropriate settings from the dialog box to prevent the reconnection.

You make and break connections to network drives from the File Manager. Depending on the type of network you have, you'll have either one or two commands on the File Manager's Disk menu in addition to the ones that are normally there. Either you'll have

Network Connections

or

Connect Network Drive
Disconnect Network Drive

If you only have the Network Connections command, use these steps to connect to a network drive:

1. Choose Disk ➤ Network Connections.
2. From the resulting Network Connections dialog box, specify the name of the network drive, drive letter, and password, if required. You may have a Browse button or feature, depending on the network, for viewing a list of available drives.
3. If you have connected to a network before (in another session, for example), the Previous button can be used to reselect a network drive you have used before. This saves you the hassle of searching the network to find the drive you want.
4. Click on the Connect button in the Network Connections dialog box.
5. Repeat Steps 1–3 to make more network connections.
6. Click on Close.

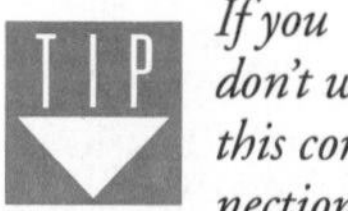

If you don't want this connection to be made when you restart Windows, press and hold down Shift when you click the Connect button.

If your File Manager gives you the Connect and Disconnect choices on the Disk menu, connect to a network drive using the following commands:

1. Choose Disk ➤ Connect Network Drive. A dialog box will appear. It allows you to choose the letter name you want to assign to the drive. Normally this is the next available letter. Change it from the drop-down list if you want.
2. Type in the path of the drive in the Network Path text area.
3. Type in the password for the drive if it's required.
4. Click on Connect and the drive should be added to your directory tree.

Windows keeps a list of previous connections you have made, assuming the Add to Previous List check box was set on when you made those connections. Instead of having to type in the path name and password each time, you just have to make the connection once. Then you can use the Previous button in the dialog box to see a list of previous connections. Choose the connection you want to make from the list.

Depending on the network, the Connect Network Drive dialog box may have an option for browsing through available drives. This lets you choose which drive you want before you actually connect to it. The resulting dialog box will differ depending on the brand of network.

Disconnecting from a Network Drive

If your File Manager's Disk menu has only the Network Connections command, you use the following steps to disconnect a network drive:

1. Choose Disk ➤ Network Connections.
2. In the Network Connections dialog box, select the network drive you want to disconnect.
3. Click on Disconnect.
4. Click on Close or OK.

If your File Manager's Disk menu has the Disconnect Network Drive option on it, you disconnect from a network drive like this:

1. Choose Disk ➤ Disconnect Network Drive.
2. The Disconnect Network Drive dialog box will then appear. Select the drive you want to disconnect.
3. Confirm the choice.
4. Click on OK. The drive will be disconnected.

Note that if you connected to the drive prior to running Windows, you may not be able to disconnect in this way. Also note that some non-Windows applications let you connect and disconnect to and from network drives while in the application. If you use this technique to connect to a drive, you should disconnect from the drive before leaving the application.

Using Long File Names

Some networks support a feature that lets you use file names that are longer than the eight characters allowed by DOS. If you're connected to such a network, you'll be allowed to use the longer names with some limitations.

For example, files with long names will show up in File Manager displaying their complete names, and you'll be able to copy and move them freely between directories that support longer names. However, you'll not be allowed to run the programs or open the documents from the File Manager; you'll have to run them from an application that supports the longer names.

If you try to copy the files to a directory that doesn't support long file names, you'll see a dialog box in which Windows alerts you and suggests a shorter name.

Connecting to a Network Printer

You connect to a network printer using the Control Panel, just as you would connect to any other printer:

1. Run the Control Panel.
2. Choose Printers.
3. Choose Connect.
4. Choose the Network button.

Refer to Chapter 6 for more details regarding printer setup and connection.

Note that every time you connect to a network printer, you should make a point of using the same port for that printer. This is because the Control Panel saves the settings for a printer in a file on disk. This file contains the port settings as well as the name and type of printer. Changing the port will cause a conflict with the recorded settings. You'll have to use the Control Panel's Printer option to reset the port if it's necessary to do so.

PROBLEMS WITH NETWORK APPLICATIONS

This section discusses some problems you may have while using Windows on a network. When installing your copy of Windows, the Setup program may at first seem to recognize that you are connected to a network, listing its correct name and version in the system configuration box. But then when you continue with the installation, Windows may not actually connect to the network. If this happens, you will know because the Control Panel will not show the Network icon, nor will other network options—such as connecting to a network drive from the File Manager—be available. If you're having trouble getting a network to function with Windows, you may not have the latest version of some of the network's drivers. Read the NETWORK.TXT file for the latest information on Windows compatibility for your type of network. You might be able to download the latest driver from an information service such as CompuServe or get it from the manufacturer.

If you can't get a network driver that supports Windows 3.1, then making a few modifications to your setup may still allow Windows to run. If you're having trouble running in 386-Enhanced mode, or if you can't seem to get non-Windows applications to run over the network, try Standard mode when on the network.

Another possible solution is to avoid switching between applications (i.e., quit one application before switching to another). Also, try setting the program's PIF for exclusive operation (you can do this in 386-Enhanced mode only).

If you can't seem to connect to a network drive or printer while in Windows, exit Windows and then try connecting to the drive or printer from DOS or whatever network utilities you normally use for the purpose. Then rerun Windows.

NETWORK INSTALLATION AND MAINTENANCE TIPS

This section describes strategies and techniques that may be useful to systems administrators during setup and maintenance of their particular LAN. It particularly addresses questions which arise when considering whether to migrate to the Windows environment—and if so, how to realize the migration as effortlessly as possible.

The first thing you should consider is the condition of the hardware you have at hand. As you probably know, Windows makes great demands on hardware, particularly memory and processor speed. On the bright side, the Windows installation program is pretty intelligent. It will recognize what's available in a given machine and install the necessary drivers and make the necessary settings to match the machine's available memory, screen, mouse, etc.

Take an inventory of all your machines before switching to a Windows-based network. Judging from opinions of associates and clients, as well as reports from publications and corporations, it's generally agreed upon that a 386DX with 4MB of RAM is the optimal machine to use as a workstation on a Windows network. Of course, lower configurations are workable, too, such as a 386SX with 2MB RAM. As a rule, upgrade memory first, then the processor.

If your inventory consists of 286 machines, or a mix of 286 and 386 machines, remember that some users will be running Windows in Standard mode. If those users aren't used to working in Windows, consider what impact slower operation, particularly in the area of screen updates, will have on them.

NOTES ON NETWORK HARDWARE AND SOFTWARE

TO ENSURE EFFICIENT NETWORKING,

go for higher speed throughput—at least 10 Mbit/sec. Research your network O/S carefully and compare it to Novell Netware. Use a high-speed server, preferably a 486DX with a considerable amount of RAM. Insist on a fast, high-capacity hard disk and large disk-cache. Finally, include a backup system to prevent data loss.

If you decide to install the bulk of Windows on a network server (see the discussion at the beginning of this chapter), pay special attention to the network hardware/software combination and the server's efficiency, just as you would with any server-based network (as opposed to a distributed server network where every workstation is a server). Pay particular attention to the following:

- In general, if you haven't already purchased the network cards, cabling, and software, choose the highest-speed Windows-compatible configuration you can afford. Speed is rated in millions of bits per second (megabits/sec) and refers to the rate at which data travel along the network wiring. (An acceptable speed is 10 Mbit/sec.) Then choose a well-respected brand of network software. It should include all the features you want, and then some. Leave room for growth. You should be able to add workstations as you please, in a variety of topologies (not just along a straight line, but more like tree branches). As far as software goes, you can't go wrong with one of the Novell NetWare products. A reasonably high-performance/medium-cost combination is Novell NetWare on off-brand (clone) 16-bit Ethernet cards. Clone Ethernet cards that will work with NetWare are available pretty cheaply (about $100 per card) from computer-supply stores and through magazine ads. Of course, you can buy brand names too, if you want extra technical support and possibly better warranties.
- The server should be as high-speed as you can afford. With prices dropping as they have, it shouldn't be difficult to afford at least a 33 MHz 386DX. Use a 25 MHz 486DX or better if you can. Remember that SXs are slower than DXs even if the clock speed (25 MHz, 33 MHz, etc.) is the same.
- Though the bulk of today's machines use the old tried-and-true ISA (Industry Standard Architecture) 16-bit AT-style bus, many 486s are available with some EISA (Extended Industry Standard Architecture) 32-bit slots. Data transfer across the server's bus will be doubled using such a machine. This can be relevant to your networking throughput, but only if you use such a machine in concert with an EISA hard disk controller card and/or an EISA network-interface card in the server. If not, save your money and buy an ISA-based machine.

- The server should have a very fast hard disk. That is, it should have somewhere in the range of an 18 ms (millisecond) access time. Your workstations can have slower access times, such as today's typical speeds of 20–30 ms. Obviously, if you intend to allow network users to store applications and documents in their own directories on the hard disk, its storage capacity should be considerable, or you'll have to purge files more often than you'd like. With reliable and fast 200MB hard drives becoming affordable, consider one. If you can't afford it, buy a lower capacity drive (~100MB) and then use a hard disk compression-decompression utility program such as Stacker (Stack Electronics) to approximately double the drive's capacity. (Check with the network software manufacturer to ensure that the utility program works with the network software first.) Also, insist on a fast hard disk controller, one capable of a one-to-one interleave, and which has a fast transfer rate, such as an IDE or SCSI type—but not an MFM.
- Don't overlook purchasing backup software and hardware. Regular backups of network server hard disks are a must. Backing up to floppies isn't practical on a network. A tape backup unit capable of storing 250MB on a single $25 tape will run about $350 if you shop carefully. Units that I have had success with are the Everex Systems and Colorado Memory Systems tape backup units. Both come with software. For higher capacity or higher speed backups, consider optomagnetic units.
- Server RAM is crucial. The server should have tons of it. The strategy is to avoid disk access on the server as much as possible. Even though you may have paid a lot of money for a high-speed drive, any disk access is going to be slower than RAM access. So you want to have a large disk-cache in the server. Depending on the network workload, this may mean somewhere between 4–8MB of server disk-cache RAM. For a network to attain optimal throughput, you'll want to have enough cache so that over a typical day the hard drive is actually accessed on only about 5 percent of all disk reads. Consult the network software's documentation for information on network caching.

Configuration File Tips

There are numerous tips and tricks for customizing the SYSTEM.INI, CONFIG.SYS, and AUTOEXEC.BAT files for each network workstation. Settings will vary depending on the workstation hardware and user preferences, of course, so this is a difficult topic to cover in a book of this range. Don't overlook digging into these files to cure what may appear to be the fault of Windows itself, or to set up some preference that will satisfy a user's needs. Contrary to popular belief, Windows can run almost as quickly across a network as it can on a stand-alone computer.

Here I discuss two settings in particular from these files. If you notice an excruciatingly slow startup of Windows across a network, this may be the result of a setting in the SYSTEM.INI file. Here's why: When a workstation attempts to start up in 386-Enhanced mode, Windows examines the network drive for room to create "virtual memory." That is, unless you've used the Control Panel's 386 option to set up a permanent swap file on a local drive or other location, Windows looks for an appropriate space on the server's disk to create a temporary swap file. This swap file is used when the workstation runs too many programs to actually fit in RAM. In the process of calculating the location and optimal size of the swap file, Windows checks out the entire network hard disk. On a network server's drive, that's typically several hundred megabytes. It then can mistakenly allocate much too large a swap file, taking up disk space which should be left free for use by other workstations. All of this can take upwards of a minute to accomplish.

You can prevent this error by adding the following two lines in each user's SYSTEM.INI file under the [386Enh] section:

```
PagingDrive=n
MaxPaging FileSize=1024
```

where *n* is the letter of the drive on which you want the temporary file. (Don't stipulate a directory.) These lines tell Windows which drive to use for virtual memory and what the maximum size of the swap file should be. If you want a larger swap file, enlarge the number. As a rule, don't use a swap file (either temporary or permanent) that's under 512K in size, as this will slow down Windows considerably.

Another common problem has to do with Windows not detecting add-in boards that occupy memory space in the HMA (High Memory Area—between 640K and 1MB). More often than not, Windows will detect boards and programs that occupy this area. Some enhanced video boards' ROM BIOS memory locations are not detected accurately by Windows, however. If you are having unexplainable system crashes, memory conflicts may be the cause. You can add commands to the SYSTEM.INI file to reserve any memory spaces you like for use with other programs, boards, and so forth. Try excluding the 32K area that your video boards might be tying up by adding this line in the [386Enh] area of the SYSTEM.INI file:

```
EMMExclude=C000-C7FF
```

FAST TRACK

CHAPTER 18

FAST TRACK

- bit-mapped fonts
- vector fonts
- scalable fonts

- roman (also called regular or normal)
- bold
- bold italic
- italic

- Allow plenty of space between lines.
- Don't mix too many fonts in one document.
- If you use two or more font sizes, be sure that they contrast adequately.
- Use italics or bold face type to indicate emphasis.
- Make your margins generous.

CHAPTER 18

FEATURING

Which Fonts You Should Use

How Windows Uses Fonts

Building and Maintaining a Font Collection

Guidelines for Using Fonts in Documents

Using Fonts Effectively

For many people, one of the most compelling reasons to adopt and stick with Windows is the convenience of having a single system for displaying and printing text that works with all programs. An increasing number of ordinary DOS programs can display and print high-quality fonts, but they rely on a bewildering hodgepodge of different printer drivers and font formats. By contrast, all Windows programs can take advantage of a single printer driver and one set of fonts.

In Chapter 5 you learned about the nuts and bolts of working with fonts in Windows. Here you'll learn how Windows uses fonts and get some advice about the choices you'll face in selecting fonts and managing your font library.

WHICH FONTS SHOULD YOU USE?

As you know, you can install three main types of fonts into Windows: bit-mapped fonts, vector fonts, and scalable fonts (such as TrueType). But as long as your printer can print graphics and is not a plotter, you should stick to scalable fonts and ignore bit-mapped and vector fonts entirely—in fact, you can remove them from your system, as discussed later.

Bit-mapped fonts look good on your screen, but only at the particular size they're designed for; when you display them at another size, they appear distorted and jagged. In addition, bit-mapped font files are large, requiring too much disk space. Since you need one file for every size of a given typeface you want to display, one set of bit-mapped fonts can consume a great deal of valuable territory on your hard disk. It's also inconvenient to keep track of all the files involved.

Vector fonts are worth using only if your output device is a plotter. While the files aren't overly large, and while you can print vector fonts at any size, they have an unattractive, noticeably angular appearance. One plus: vector font files are quite small.

TrueType and other scalable fonts, by contrast, look great when displayed or printed at any size. If you decide that a particular document requires, say, a 13.5-point rendition of Times, all you have to do is request it and Windows will generate it automatically. Although TrueType font files are fairly large, typically around 60K, you only need one file for each typeface. Font files of other scalable font formats such as Type 1 PostScript and FaceLift tend to be somewhat smaller.

THE CHARACTERISTICS OF A FONT

Fonts are also described in terms of style and size. Windows recognizes four basic font styles: roman (also called regular or normal), bold, bold italic, and italic.

Font size is usually expressed in points. One point is approximately 1/72 of an inch. A twelve-point character would therefore be about 1/6 of an inch. Be careful not to confuse point size with pitch, a term commonly used to describe the size of a fixed-width font in terms of characters per inch.

HOW WINDOWS USES FONTS

Most Windows programs that print text let you specify the font you want. In some cases, as in most word-processing programs, you can change fonts with every text character, while other programs restrict you to one font for each block of text or field.

Ideally, Windows should let you select only from the fonts your printer can actually print. Unfortunately, this isn't always the case if you install more than one printer driver. In this situation, many Windows programs offer you all the fonts available with every installed printer driver, leaving it to you to figure out which ones are appropriate for your printer.

Once you've chosen a font, what you see on the screen depends on the kind of font you're using. If you've selected a TrueType or other scalable font, Windows will generate the appropriate screen font for you, so you'll always get a close match between the screen and the final printout. On the other hand, if you're using a nonscalable font, Windows must look for a screen font that corresponds to the one you'll be printing with. If it can't find a match, Windows will substitute the most similar screen font it can find. Depending on the font you've chosen and your screen font collection, this substitute screen font may not look anything like the printed version. Nevertheless, at least the line lengths and page breaks you see on your screen will be accurate.

When you print the document, Windows checks your printer driver file and the WIN.INI file, looking for the fonts you specified. If the fonts exist, Windows will know whether they're already "resident" in the printer or must be scaled or downloaded from the hard disk. If a font is missing, Windows will again make an effort to substitute a similar one.

BUILDING A FONT COLLECTION

Windows comes already with a set of very attractive TrueType fonts that will serve you well in most situations, whether you're writing letters, preparing reports or grant proposals, or adding text to charts or graphics. So why buy more fonts?

Broadly stated, the reason to enlarge your font collection is simple: to improve your ability to communicate. Typographers claim that the fonts you use can influence the impact of your message on your readers, even if they're not consciously aware of their reactions. With more fonts to work with, you'll be better able to select ones that suit the mood of whatever document you're preparing. Some fonts, such as Bodoni or Times New Roman, have a decidedly formal appearance, ideal for serious business correspondence. But these same fonts are just too stuffy for a letter to a friend; for this you'd be better off using a font with a casual look, such as Dom Casual or Tekton.

In addition, looking beyond the stock Windows fonts helps you create an identifiable style for your printed documents. Like a logo, the typefaces you choose become associated with you or your business in the minds of those who read your documents regularly. Using the same typeface that everyone else does will make it harder to establish your own typographic identity.

Scalable-Font Options

TrueType fonts are the most convenient kind of scalable fonts for anyone who uses Windows, since TrueType technology is built right into the Windows environment. However, you have several other choices in scalable-font formats you might want to consider.

PostScript fonts used with Adobe Type Manager are referred to as Type 1 fonts to distinguish them from another PostScript font format, Type 3. Don't get Type 3 fonts unless you have a PostScript printer or a way to convert them to Type 1.

TrueType's biggest competitor is the Type 1 or PostScript format. Type 1 fonts produce very high-quality screen fonts and printed output. Vast numbers of fonts are available in the Type 1 format from many different manufacturers, including some of the most respected typographic houses, and they cover an extremely wide range of beautiful designs.

By comparison, the selection of TrueType fonts is limited at the moment, though this is changing rapidly as Windows 3.1 becomes established. But there is at least one other reason to consider using Type 1 fonts instead of TrueType fonts: PostScript is still the established standard for very high resolution typesetting devices used in professional publishing. If you stick with Type 1 fonts, you can use the exact same fonts for printing drafts on a desktop laser printer and outputting final typeset copy on a Linotronic or other digital typesetter. This means you can be confident that, aside from lower resolution, your draft will look exactly like your final document.

To use Type 1 fonts to your best advantage, you need a utility program called Adobe Type Manager. ATM performs the process of scaling Type 1 fonts to the requested size faster than Windows does. It also provides a number of useful options for handling the fonts that you don't get with Windows' built-in font manager.

Other scalable font choices for Windows are less attractive, though you might want to consider them in special circumstances. If you have access to a library of fonts in another scalable font format, it may make sense to purchase a font-scaling utility that allows you to use your font collection with Windows. Like ATM, other font-scaling utilities take over from Windows the job of creating the correctly-sized final fonts for the screen and printer.

The runner-up font-scaling utility with the broadest appeal for Windows users is probably Intellifont-for-Windows (by Hewlett-Packard). It works with the Intellifont scalable-font format designed for the LaserJet III family of printers. If you have a LaserJet III, IIID, or IIISi and use Intellifont fonts with your non-Windows programs, it may make sense to use Intellifont-for-Windows and stick with a single set of fonts.

Another choice is Bitstream's FaceLift. Although FaceLift produces high-quality output, the only reason to prefer it to TrueType is if you have already purchased a large FaceLift font library for use with the non-Windows programs that require this format.

SuperPrint (by Zenographics) is the Rosetta stone of font-scaling utilities. It works interchangeably with most of the major font formats, including Type 1, FaceLift, Intellifont, Fontware, and Nimbus Q—although reviews have judged output quality to be lower than that from ATM or FaceLift. As a bonus, SuperPrint speeds up Windows graphics printing significantly and allows you to print sophisticated graphics on non-PostScript printers.

Finally, if you have a limited font budget, consider Publisher's Powerpak for Windows (by Atech Software) and MoreFonts (by MicroLogic Software, Inc.). The fonts that work with them are much, much less expensive than most TrueType, Type 1, and FaceLift fonts.

Choosing Specific Fonts

Technically, "typeface" is the correct term for the design of an entire set of characters; the term "font" traditionally refers to a specific size of a given typeface. With the advent of scalable type, the two terms have become interchangeable.

Once you've settled on the font format you're going to use, your next task is to decide on which specific fonts to buy. The number of typeface designs available for Windows totals in the thousands and is still growing. With that much variety, selecting a set of fonts that's right for you can be a daunting proposition.

For this reason, it makes sense to stick to the tried-and-true favorites of typographic professionals when you're just getting started in building a font library. Figure 18.1 offers a few suggestions; you can't go wrong with any of the fonts shown here. Another simple solution is to buy one of the font sets available from vendors such as Adobe Systems and Monotype. Each of these packages comes with several fonts chosen for a specific type of document, along with design tips for using the fonts appropriately.

Understanding Fonts

As Figure 18.1 suggests, fonts can be classified in various ways. Even if you choose from the fonts in that figure, a basic understanding of the classifications is a good idea before you start buying fonts.

FIGURE 18.1:

The faces in the top two groups are proven designs that work well in many types of documents. To be safe, start with these faces. It's more difficult to recommend display faces, since you must choose them carefully for the particular mood you want to convey. Still, they are high-quality designs, popular among professional designers, and they cover a considerable range of moods.

Serif typefaces for body text

Baskerville Caslon
Garamond Palatino

Sans-serif faces for general use

Futura Gill Sans
Optima Univers

Display and decorative faces

Benguiat Bernhard Modern
LITHOS PEIGNOT

The simplest division in the font kingdom is between serif and sans-serif designs. As a look at the table will show you, serifs are the little bars or lines that extend out from the main parts of the characters. A sans-serif font such as Gill Sans lacks serifs. It's important to choose a few fonts from each category, since almost any combination of a serif and a sans-serif font will look good together, but two sans-serif or two serif fonts will clash.

Another simple classification for fonts depends on the space allotted to each character. In a monospaced font, every character occupies the same amount of space in the horizontal dimension. That is, an *i* takes up just as much room on a line of text as a *w*. Proportionally spaced fonts, by contrast, vary the space given to each character. Proportional fonts are easier to read and allow you to fit more text in a given space. (The typefaces in this book are proportional.) The only reason to use monospaced fonts is when you're printing reports or tables in which the alignment of columns is determined by spaces (space characters).

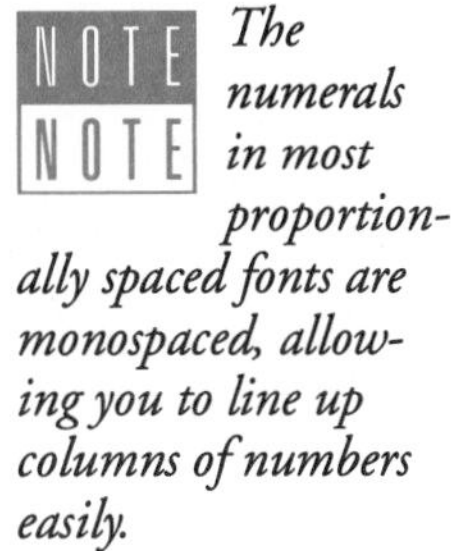

The numerals in most proportionally spaced fonts are monospaced, allowing you to line up columns of numbers easily.

Still another way to classify fonts has to do with their intended purpose: for body text, headlines, ornamental special effects, or nonalphabetic symbols. Body fonts have highly legible characters and work well for long blocks of text. Although any body-text font can be used for titles and headlines, display or headline fonts are specifically meant for that purpose (such as those used in this book). They boast stronger, more attention-getting designs, but for that reason don't work well for body text.

The two remaining font types aren't shown in Figure 18.1 because they don't have universal application. The distinction between ornamental or novelty fonts and display fonts is arbitrary. Still, the idea is that an ornamental font is so highly stylized that it might distract the reader's attention from your message. Use ornamental fonts with care when you want to set a special mood. Symbol or pi fonts contain special symbols such as musical notes, map symbols, or decorations, instead of letters, numbers, and punctuation marks. Figure 18.2 shows several examples of ornamental and symbol fonts.

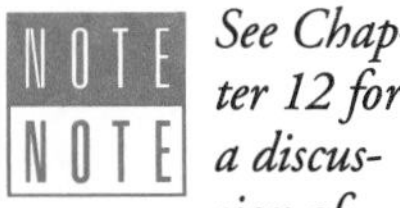

See Chapter 12 for a discussion of Character Map, a program for inserting symbols into documents.

WHERE TO BUY FONTS

The explosion of interest in typography generated by desktop publishing technology has, in turn, resulted in a proliferation of font vendors. Figure 18.2 lists some of the many sources of TrueType and Type 1 fonts. In addition to the large, well-known font publishers, you'll find several smaller vendors offering unique, attractive font designs in this list.

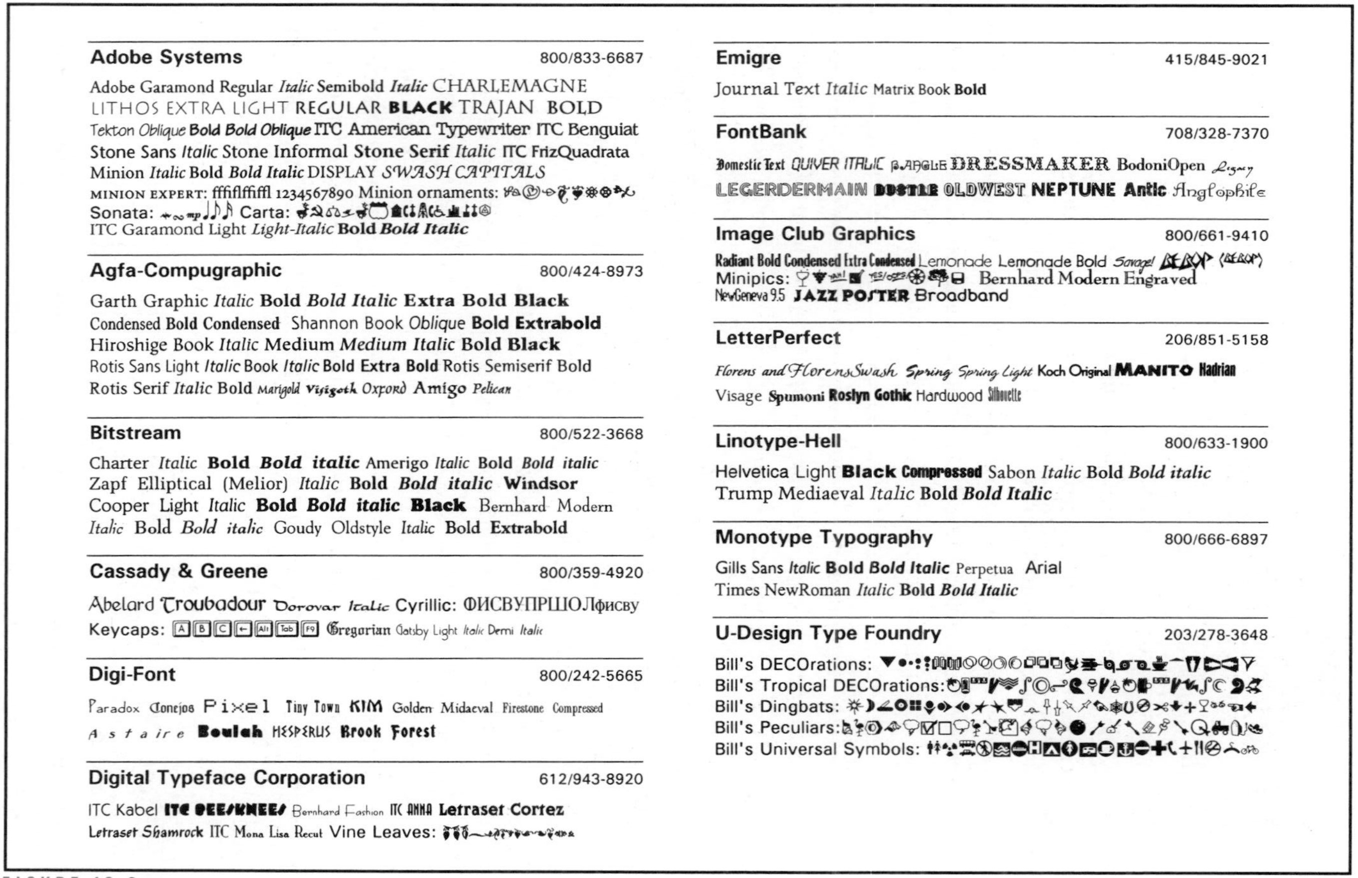

Adobe Systems 800/833-6687

Adobe Garamond Regular *Italic* Semibold *Italic* CHARLEMAGNE
LITHOS EXTRA LIGHT REGULAR **BLACK** TRAJAN BOLD
Tekton *Oblique* **Bold** ***Bold Oblique*** ITC American Typewriter ITC Benguiat
Stone Sans *Italic* Stone Informal **Stone Serif** *Italic* ITC FrizQuadrata
Minion *Italic* **Bold** ***Bold Italic*** DISPLAY *SWASH CAPITALS*
MINION EXPERT: ffifflffiffl 1234567890 Minion ornaments:
Sonata: Carta:
ITC Garamond Light *Light-Italic* **Bold** ***Bold Italic***

Agfa-Compugraphic 800/424-8973

Garth Graphic *Italic* **Bold** ***Bold Italic*** **Extra Bold Black**
Condensed **Bold Condensed** Shannon Book *Oblique* **Bold Extrabold**
Hiroshige Book *Italic* Medium *Medium Italic* **Bold Black**
Rotis Sans Light *Italic* Book *Italic* **Bold Extra Bold** Rotis Semiserif Bold
Rotis Serif *Italic* Bold Marigold Visigoth Oxford Amigo *Pelican*

Bitstream 800/522-3668

Charter *Italic* **Bold** ***Bold italic*** Amerigo *Italic* Bold *Bold italic*
Zapf Elliptical (Melior) *Italic* **Bold** ***Bold italic*** **Windsor**
Cooper Light *Italic* **Bold** ***Bold italic*** **Black** Bernhard Modern
Italic Bold *Bold italic* Goudy Oldstyle *Italic* Bold **Extrabold**

Cassady & Greene 800/359-4920

Abelard Troubadour Dorovar *Italic* Cyrillic: ФИСВУПРШОЛфисву
Keycaps: Gregorian Gatsby Light *Italic* Demi *Italic*

Digi-Font 800/242-5665

Paradox Conejos Pixel Tiny Town KIM Golden Midaeval Firestone Compressed
Astaire **Boulah** HESPERUS **Brook** **Forest**

Digital Typeface Corporation 612/943-8920

ITC Kabel **ITC BEESKNEES** Bernhard Fashion ITC ANNA **Letraset Cortez**
Letraset Shamrock ITC Mona Lisa Recut Vine Leaves:

Emigre 415/845-9021

Journal Text *Italic* Matrix Book **Bold**

FontBank 708/328-7370

Domestic Text *QUIVER ITALIC* BANGLE DRESSMAKER BodoniOpen Legacy
LEGERDERMAIN **BUSTLE** OLDWEST **NEPTUNE** **Antic** Anglophile

Image Club Graphics 800/661-9410

Radiant Bold Condensed Extra Condensed Lemonade Lemonade Bold *Savage!* BEBOP (BEBOP)
Minipics: Bernhard Modern Engraved
NewGeneva 9.5 **JAZZ POSTER** Broadband

LetterPerfect 206/851-5158

Florens and *FlorensSwash* *Spring* *Spring Light* Koch Original **MANITO** **Hadrian**
Visage **Spumoni** **Roslyn Gothic** Hardwood Silhouette

Linotype-Hell 800/633-1900

Helvetica Light **Black** **Compressed** Sabon *Italic* **Bold** ***Bold italic***
Trump Mediaeval *Italic* **Bold** ***Bold Italic***

Monotype Typography 800/666-6897

Gills Sans *Italic* **Bold** ***Bold Italic*** Perpetua Arial
Times NewRoman *Italic* **Bold** ***Bold Italic***

U-Design Type Foundry 203/278-3648

Bill's DECOrations:
Bill's Tropical DECOrations:
Bill's Dingbats:
Bill's Peculiars:
Bill's Universal Symbols:

FIGURE 18.2:

Here's a sampler of Type 1 and TrueType fonts you can buy for Windows. Currently, many of the fonts shown here are not yet available in the TrueType format, but this should change rapidly as Windows 3.1 is widely distributed. In most cases, the fonts shown in each vendor's section were designed by that vendor. Be aware, however, that you can buy most of these fonts from several different vendors. Also, some font vendors copy the font designs of other vendors, selling them under different names.

SOME BASIC GUIDELINES FOR USING FONTS

Whether you rely on the fonts supplied with Windows or put together a sizeable font collection, you should follow a few simple guidelines when formatting your documents. Attractive fonts by themselves aren't enough—the chief goal is readability:

- Allow plenty of space between lines. The space between two lines of text should be about 20 percent greater than the size of the font. Thus, if you're using a 12-point font, you should set the line spacing or leading to 14 points. This guideline doesn't hold true for headlines, in which the line spacing should usually be about the same as the font size.
- Don't mix too many fonts in one document. It's often best to stick with one font for the main body of your text and a larger, bold version of the same font for headlines. If you want to mix fonts, use a serif font for the body of your text and a sans serif for the headlines, or vice versa. You can get away with using a third font for sidebar text, but you'll run the risk of clashing font designs.
- If you use two or more font sizes, be sure that they contrast adequately. If your main text is in 12-point Times New Roman, use at least 14-point type for the subheadings.
- Use italics or boldface type to indicate emphasis. Avoid underlining and capitalizing letters, both of which make it harder to read your text.
- Make your margins generous. One of the most common mistakes that causes an amateurish-looking document is text that crowds too closely to the edge of the paper. Allow plenty of space between columns as well.

Following these few guidelines will help you avoid the most glaring errors of document layout. For more detailed advice, consult books such as *Understanding Desktop Publishing,* by Robert W. Harris (SYBEX).

DELETING FONT FILES FROM YOUR HARD DISK

While a variety of high-quality fonts can definitely lend a professionally-typeset look to your printed documents and make it easier to understand the information on your screen, a big font collection isn't necessary to run Windows. In fact, you don't even need all the fonts that come with Windows.

There are only three critical "system" fonts that you must have on your hard disk, because without them, Windows simply won't work (your specific system fonts depend on the type of screen you have). In addition to the system fonts, you also need at least one and as many as four additional fonts if you plan to run non-Windows programs in color text mode. But if disk space is at a premium and if the appearance of your text isn't critical for the work you do with Windows, you can remove all the other fonts from your Windows setup, saving up to 200K on your disk in the process. Even if disk space isn't a big concern, I recommend that you remove all but one of the bit-mapped fonts and all of the vector fonts so their names won't get in the way when you're choosing fonts for a document.

NOTE *Bit-mapped and vector fonts are stored on disk in files with the extension .FON; TrueType font files have the extension .TTF.*

To prepare for deleting the unneeded fonts, back up all of your Windows font files for safekeeping by copying all the .FON and .TTF files in your Windows and System directories to another disk. For safety's sake, it's also a good idea to determine which three fonts your system requires before you start deleting font files from your disk. To find out their file names, examine the SYSTEM.INI file found in your Windows directory by opening it with Notepad or Sysedit. In the very first section of the file you'll see three lines that look something like this:

```
FIXEDFON.FON=VGAFIX.FON
OEMFONTS.FON=VGAOEM.FON
FONTS.FON=VGASYS.FON
```

The first part of each line, up to and including the equal sign, is the generic name for one of the system fonts. This is the same no matter what type of screen you have. Take note of the part of each line following the equal sign—this is the name of the specific font file used for that system font by your Windows installation. The example above shows the required system font files for VGA screens, but your copy of SYSTEM.INI will list different font files if you use another type of screen. The fonts needed to run non-Windows programs in color text mode are stored in files named CGA40WOA.FON, CGA80WOA.FON, EGA40WOA.FON, and EGA80WOA.FON.

Then, using the Control Panel, you can remove all the fonts you find unnecessary from your Windows installation and delete their files on disk at the same time. The procedure is detailed in "Removing Fonts" in Chapter 5. You can remove all the fonts listed in the Control Panel Fonts dialog box. Fortunately, the Control Panel won't let you delete those vital system fonts, since they're not even listed there. However, I recommend you keep the font listed as MS Sans Serif in the dialog box since Program Manager and File Manager, among other programs, use it extensively. If you remove this font, whose file name is SERIF.FON, these programs will substitute a system font that you may find harder to read.

After removing all the fonts from the Control Panel list, you can then check your disk for any remaining .FON or .TTF files. You should keep your three system fonts, the fonts for non-Windows program, and SERIF.FON (if you're saving it), but you can delete all the other font files.

WHAT IS TRUETYPE?

One of the most important advancements in Windows 3.1 is the addition of support for TrueType fonts. For the first time, Windows provides, without the addition of any third-party software, typefaces that can be scaled to any size and displayed or printed accurately on virtually all displays and printers.

TrueType is important primarily because it enables true What-You-See-Is-What-You-Get (WYSIWYG) font capabilities. Because Windows uses the same typeface to display text as it does to print text, you can be assured that your document will look the same on paper as it does on screen. Furthermore, you no longer have to ensure that you have fonts in your printer that match the fonts on-screen.

In the past, if you used a printer like the LaserJet II, you might have been limited only to the two fonts that come standard with that printer (Courier and Line Printer). If you wanted to print any other fonts, you had to buy a cartridge containing a few additional fonts, or you had to buy "soft fonts"—fonts that could be stored on your computer's hard disk and downloaded into your printer's memory. These fonts had to be individually rendered by the vendor in each size that might be required. This could be costly and require a tremendous amount of hard disk space. If you wanted to display the fonts on-screen, you had to create yet another set of screen fonts that matched the printer fonts. Even if you could create and format a document in TmsRmn or Helv, if your printer didn't contain an appropriate substitute for them, you couldn't print the document using those fonts.

With TrueType, any printer that can print graphics can print the full range of TrueType fonts—all orchestrated by Windows 3.1. And the results will look more or less the same on different printers. Although different printers provide different resolutions, the essential characteristics of a TrueType font will remain consistent whether it is printed on a 9-pin dot matrix printer or a high-resolution imagesetter.

TrueType also allows users of different computer systems to maintain compatibility across platforms. Because TrueType is also integrated into System 7, the Macintosh operating system, a document formatted on a Macintosh using TrueType fonts will look exactly the same on a Windows 3.1-equipped PC.

Finally, because TrueType is an integrated component of Windows 3.1, any Windows application can make use of TrueType fonts. These fonts can easily be scaled (increased or decreased in size), rotated, or altered—all by Windows itself.

You can only use TrueType fonts if you have a Windows 3.1-specific printer driver. When an application asks Windows for a list of fonts, it polls the printer driver. If the driver doesn't know about TrueType, it will only respond with fonts specific to your printer.

You may run into difficulties if you use a LaserJet III or compatible printer. Windows communicates with the LaserJet III family through a language called PCL5 (Printer Control Language Level 5). When Windows 3.0 shipped, the PCL5 driver had a number of bugs. Microsoft tried to correct this by having applications like Word for Windows install a new PCL5 driver—but Word puts the driver in its own directory rather than in Windows' SYSTEM directory.

If you use Word for Windows 2.0 with any member of the LaserJet III family or any compatible printer, make sure that there is no file called HPPCL5A.DRV in your WINWORD directory. If there is—delete it! Word for Windows looks first in its own directory for a printer driver before looking at Windows' directories. Once the WINWORD version of the driver is gone, you'll be able to access TrueType fonts normally.

Comparing TrueType Fonts to Bit-Mapped and Vector Fonts

Although TrueType fonts are new in Windows 3.1, font support has been around since the first release of Windows. Windows 3.1 provides support for two different types of fonts: screen fonts and printer fonts. Screen fonts are designed specifically to be displayed. Printer fonts are those installed in or downloaded to your printer.

There are two types of screen fonts: bit-mapped and vector. Each is quite different from the other; each serves a distinct purpose. Bit-mapped fonts are essentially a collection of bitmaps. These bitmaps cover the entire character set and range of styles for a particular typeface in a limited number of sizes.

Examples of bit-mapped fonts in Windows 3.1 are Courier, MS Serif (formerly called TmsRmn), MS Sans Serif (formerly called Helv), Small Fonts, and Symbol. When you install Windows, these fonts are automatically selected and copied to Windows' SYSTEM directory by Setup. Windows comes with a number of versions of these fonts. Based on the resolution of your video adapter, Windows chooses the font files that take best advantage of your particular display. Figure 18.3 shows a character map of a bit-mapped font (MS Serif).

Because a bit-mapped font is dependent upon the bitmaps included in its font file, you cannot display these fonts in sizes other than those provided. Windows can only scale bit-mapped fonts to exact multiples of their original sizes. For example, MS Serif for VGA resolution includes bitmaps for display at 8, 10, 12, 14, 18, and 24 points. However, Windows can also scale 10-point MS Serif to 20, 30, or even 40 points, although with results that will not look as good as a TrueType font at the same size.

Vector fonts are more suitable for devices like plotters that can't use bit-mapped characters. Vector fonts are a series of mathematical formulas that describe a series of lines and curves. They can be scaled to any size, but because of the process involved in computing the shape and direction of the curves, these fonts can be quite time-consuming to generate. Examples of vector fonts are Modern, Roman, and Script. Figure 18.4 shows a character map of a vector font (Roman).

There are also several different types of printer fonts—device fonts, printable screen fonts, and downloadable soft fonts. Device fonts are those fonts installed in your printer, either factory defaults or members of a font cartridge collection. Printable screen fonts are bit-mapped and vector fonts that can be sent to the printer. Downloadable soft fonts are fonts that, like TrueType, are stored on your PC's hard disk and can be sent to the printer as needed. Unlike TrueType fonts, though, they are specific to your printer and are generally provided in limited styles and sizes.

FIGURE 18.3:
A bit-mapped font

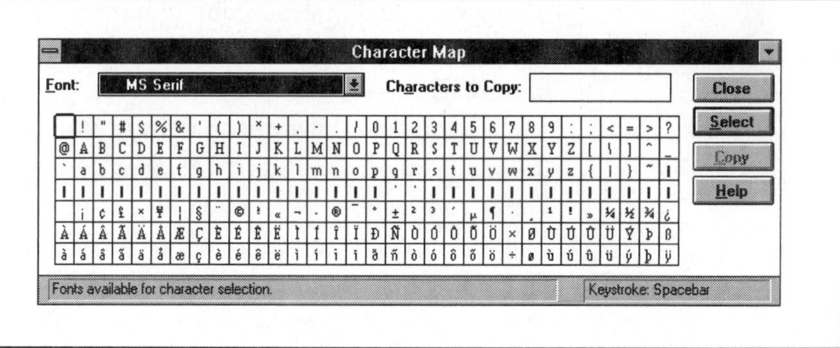

FIGURE 18.4:
A vector font

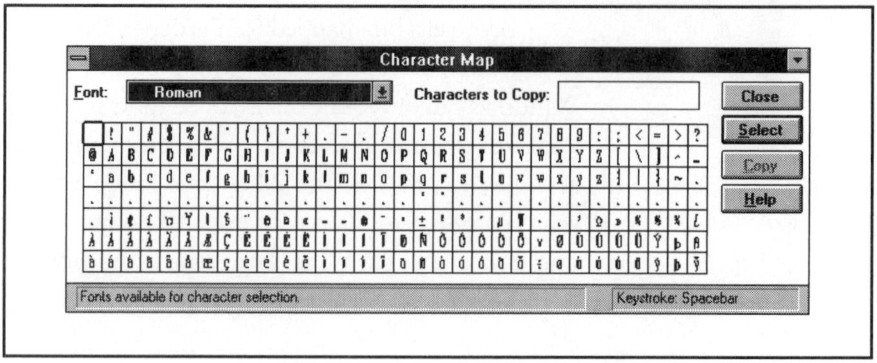

How Does TrueType Work?

TrueType fonts are similar to both bit-mapped and vector fonts. They contain a description of the series of lines and curves for the typeface—like a vector font. When you press a key in a Windows word processor, for example, that application asks Windows to generate the bitmap of the appropriate character in the right font and size at a particular spot on screen. Windows' Graphical Device Interface (GDI) creates a bitmap in memory that best represents that character. But the job of creating the character is only half done.

Like bit-mapped fonts, TrueType fonts include a number of bitmapped "hints" that help Windows when rendering the font in smaller point sizes. Hints are an extremely important element of TrueType. Because the resolution of a VGA monitor is considerably less than that of a 300-dpi laser printer, many fonts simply don't look right on screen. There just aren't enough pixels to accurately reproduce the font at smaller point sizes.

When Windows displays a character at a small point size, it uses the hinting instructions located in a TrueType font to "cheat" a bit by reshaping the character so that lines or curves aren't missing or misshapen. But hints are not just important for screen display. Look closely at a page of small text generated by your printer. If it prints 300 dots per inch, chances are you'll notice slight imperfections in characters. An *O* may not be perfectly round; the slant of a *W* may not be truly straight. Hinting ensures the highest possible quality of fonts despite the resolution limits of today's most common output devices.

You may notice that when you select a different font or a new point size that Windows pauses for a moment. During this delay, it creates bitmaps for the entire character set in the new size or style. This happens only once during a Windows session. After first generating the bitmaps, Windows places them into a memory cache where they can quickly be accessed the next time they are required.

If you have a number of documents you created using fonts that you no longer have, you don't need to go through the documents and change your formatting. You can force Windows to substitute appropriate replacements. Load WIN.INI into an editor like Notepad. If you look at the [FontSubstitutes] section of the file, you'll notice lines like "TmsRmn=MS Serif."

Add any associations you like, keeping the old name on the left of the equation and the new name on the right. Windows will automatically fill requests for the old font with the new font.

ELEMENTS OF TRUETYPE TYPOGRAPHY

As discussed earlier, the term "font" is now used freely to describe a number of different typographical elements. Font is often used to mean the same things as "typeface," a group of fonts that are closely related in design. Technically, a font is a specific set of characters, each of which shares the same basic characteristics. For example, Arial is a typeface. In turn, Arial comprises the fonts Arial, Arial Bold, Arial Bold Italic, and Arial Italic. When you pick Arial from your word processor's font dialog box and then choose to italicize text, you are selecting the font Arial Italic.

As with other types of fonts, all TrueType fonts can be generalized into font families. These are a group of typefaces with similar characteristics, but are much more loosely related than the members of a typeface. Windows recognizes five font families: Decorative, Modern, Roman, Script, and Swiss.

The most common of these families are Roman and Swiss. The Roman font family contains the majority of serif fonts. Sans-serif fonts like Arial are generally members of the Swiss family. Figure 18.5 shows fonts from the Roman and Swiss families.

SPECIAL CHARACTERS

Each TrueType font contains a number of special characters like Trademark (™) and Yen (¥), punctuation such as the em dash (—) and curly quotes ("), and foreign (ñ) and accented (é) characters. But Windows 3.1 also includes two special fonts you should become familiar with: Symbol and WingDings.

Symbol contains a number of mathematical symbols such as not-equal-to (≠) and sum (Σ). It also contains a complete Greek alphabet for scientific notation.

WingDings is quite a bit more versatile. It contains a wide range of symbols and characters that can be used to add special impact to documents. Instead of printing "Tel." next to your phone number, why not place a

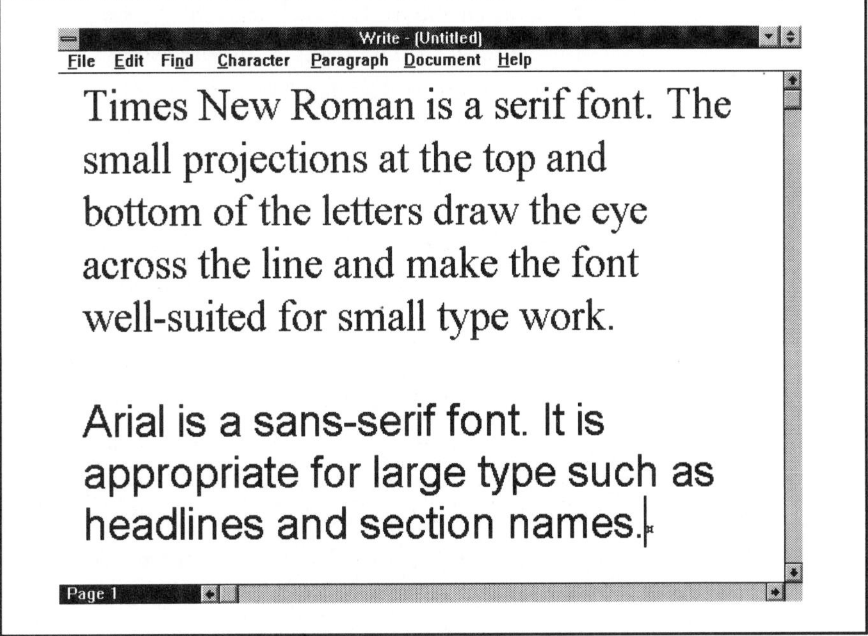

FIGURE 18.5: *A Roman font (Times New Roman) and a Swiss font (Arial)*

telephone symbol? WingDings includes several religious symbols including a cross, a Star of David, and a crescent and star, as well as several zodiac signs.

You can access these special characters in several different ways. The easiest is to select WingDings or Symbol in any TrueType-compatible application. Then, type characters from the keyboard. For example, the universal symbol for "airport" corresponds to a capital Q in WingDings. This method requires a bit of memorization or a handy reference chart to keep the associations straight. Microsoft Word for Windows 2.0 now ships with a macro called CharacterSet that will allow you to print all characters in a given font. CharacterSet can be found in the file PSS.DOC. (If you don't have this file, call Microsoft and ask for release 2.0a of Word for Windows.)

Alternately, you can enter keys by using the Alt key with your numeric key pad. Each character in a font is associated with a numeric value between 0 and 255. By holding down the Alt key while entering that number, you can insert the appropriate character. For example, to insert an em dash (—), hold down the Alt key and press the numbers 0151 on the keypad. This will not work with the "regular" number keys at the top of your keyboard, and you must remember to preface the number with a 0. Again, you will need a reference chart for the particular font you're using in order to take advantage of this method.

Many word processors include a function called Insert Symbol. This feature allows you to choose a character from a table of all the characters in a particular font. You just highlight the character you want and click OK (or double-click the character), and it appears instantly in your document. This is not the quickest way to enter a symbol, but it is the easiest if your word processor offers it. Figure 18.6 shows the Insert Symbol table in Word for Windows 2.0.

If your application lacks an Insert Symbol feature, you can open the Character Map accessory discussed in chapter 12 and copy the symbols you want to the clipboard. Then switch back to your application and paste the symbols where you want them. While not the easiest way to insert symbols, this method is adequate for most uses.

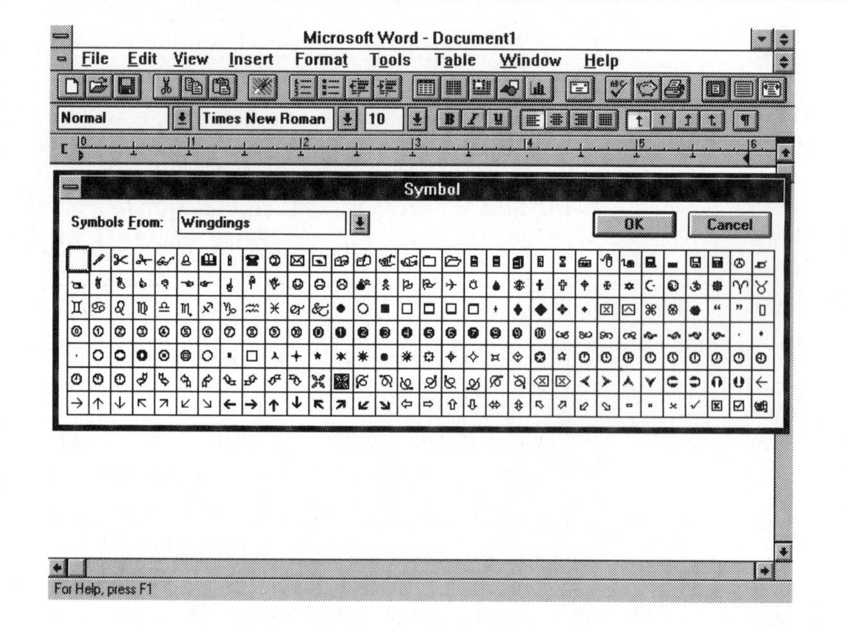

FIGURE 18.6: *A typical Insert Symbol table in a word-processing application*

Font Embedding

But what if you get a document from a friend or a business associate that was formatted with TrueType fonts you don't have on your system? One of the most important new features of Windows 3.1 is its ability to *embed* TrueType fonts in documents. So when you send a document to someone else, the fonts you use go with it. But beware: although Windows itself supports embedded TrueType fonts, as of the summer of 1992, most Windows applications do not.

When you load a document that contains embedded TrueType fonts, Windows copies those fonts into memory temporarily. They can then be used in conjunction with that document specifically. Depending on the attributes set by the font vendor, a font can have one of three embedding options—read-only embedding, read-write embedding, or no embedding at all.

The most common type of font will most likely be "read-only." If you load a document containing read-only fonts—and you don't have those fonts yourself—you will only be able to print or view the document. You won't be able to alter it. This prevents non-owners of a font from using it without paying for it.

However, the fonts supplied by Microsoft in Windows 3.1 as well as those in the TrueType Font Pack are "read-write" fonts. Documents containing these fonts can be printed, viewed, and edited regardless of whether the fonts themselves are installed on the system. Also, Windows provides the ability to save the fonts themselves for use with future documents. Obviously, this approach will not be popular with commercial developers who make their livings selling their fonts, but a quick scan of public domain TrueType fonts that have popped up on on-line services like CompuServe and GEnie shows that most free fonts are read-write enabled.

On the other end of the spectrum, vendors may choose to disallow embedding of their fonts. If you try to save a document that contains one of these typefaces, your word processor will simply not include the fonts. Essentially, this would create documents similar to those used today that contain no font information other than the name of the original font.

TrueType's greatest advantage is that it ensures that the fonts you see on-screen are the fonts you get on paper. Embedded TrueType takes this one step further by ensuring that the fonts used to create a document are the ones used to view, edit, and print it.

So Where Do I Get These Fonts?

A number of leading font vendors have jumped on the TrueType bandwagon, and as a result, several really good values have emerged. Of course, Microsoft is offering its TrueType Font Pack as part of its Windows 3.1 upgrade path. This $99 collection of 44 fonts was designed by the same group that produced Arial, Courier New, and Times New Roman—the TrueType fonts included with Windows 3.1.

Other leading font vendors, including Bitstream, and SWFTE have brought out TrueType versions of their font collections. You can find these in most software stores.

If you're looking for fonts on the cheap side, check out one of your local bulletin-board systems or an on-line service like CompuServe or GEnie. The Windows sections of these networks hold a number of free fonts that are yours for the taking. Many of the fonts are PostScript Type 1 fonts that have been converted to TrueType. The quality of these fonts is generally not as good as the commercial fonts, but in most cases, you'll be hard-pressed to notice the difference.

Do-It-Yourself Fonts

Another great way to build a huge library of TrueType fonts is to create your own fonts or convert an existing library. If you've used type managers like Adobe Type Manager, you probably have a number of PostScript fonts that you use frequently. If you own a copy of CorelDraw, you have more than a hundred fonts at your disposal. Why not convert your fonts to TrueType and use them in any Windows application? Consider one of the following conversion tools to salvage your font investment.

AllType for DOS and Windows

AllType is the first commerical utility for the PC to convert fonts to and from TrueType. It lets you move fonts from one format to another with little perceptible change in quality. AllType currently supports eight font types, including TrueType, Hewlett-Packard Laserjet III format, the Intellifont format from AGFA, Atech's own FastFont format, the lesser-know Royal and Nimbus Q fonts, and—most importantly—PostScript Type 1 and Type 3 fonts.

Until recently, AllType was available only as a DOS application. However, Atech now packages both a DOS and a Windows version of the program in the same box. During installation, you can choose to install one or the other—or both if you want.

Operation of the program is smooth and intuitive. The main AllType menu screen has two main areas—Source Fonts and Destination Fonts (Figure 18.7). On the Source Fonts side, you choose the format of the source fonts and the directory in which they can be found. On the Destination Fonts side, you enter the desired format of the fonts to be created as well as the directory in which they will be stored.

On both sides of the screen, AllType displays the names of the fonts it finds in the source and destination directories. It uses the internal font naming schemes of the various formats to do so (for example, TIMESBI.TTF is displayed as [Times New Roman Bold Italic]), making selection of the right font a snap.

An interesting feature of AllType is its ability to automatically install fonts in a variety of applications, including GeoWorks, WordPerfect, CorelDraw, Microsoft Word, and Windows 3.1. When you select one of the

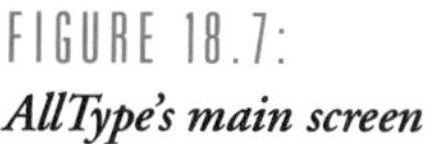

FIGURE 18.7:

AllType's main screen

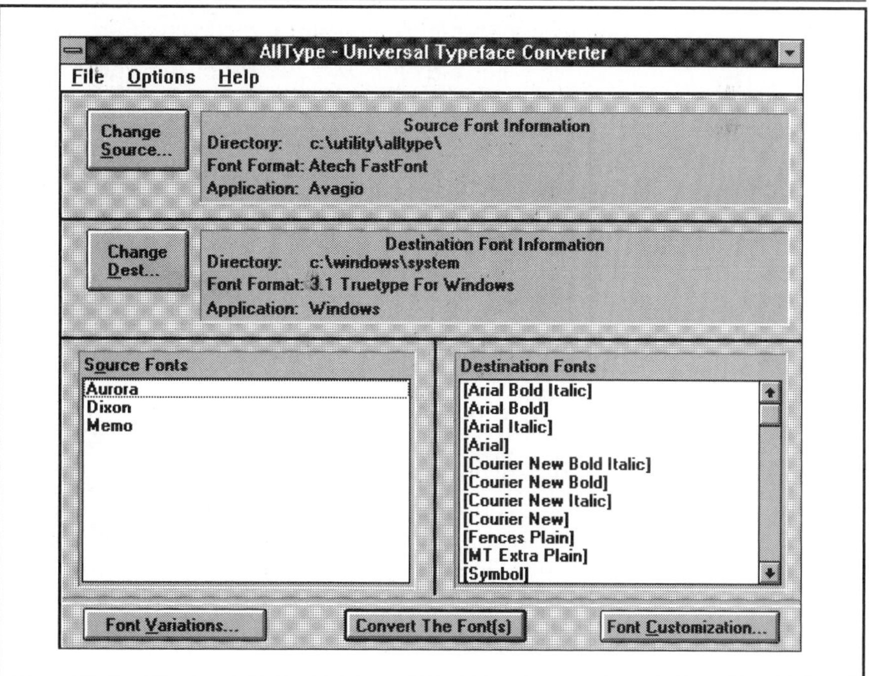

proposed applications on the Destination side, AllType saves you the bother of getting your program to recognize the existence of the new fonts. In Windows, this means you would no longer have to open the Control Panel and add the new fonts individually—a great timesaver. This feature, however, is optional. If desired, AllType will just create and save the fonts.

Also, AllType allows the user to customize fonts during the conversion process, creating a variety of effects in the new font. Available effects include bold, hollow, italic, thin, and condensed. Other options allow modification of the angle of the font, its leading, pitch, or weight.

The conversion process is fast—about two minutes per font, including installation of the fonts in the selected application. The anticipated conversion time and disk space requirements is displayed when the conversion process begins. The size of the fonts created is generally right in line with the size of similar fonts which had been created in the destination font format in the first place.

However, the process is not entirely perfect in its conversion. Because of the differences in capabilities among the various formats, a font converted from, say, PostScript Type 1 to TrueType and then back to Type 1 would not be the same as the original Type 1 font. However, the difference between the two Type 1 fonts would be imperceptible. Just as there are several ways to express a thought, there are several ways to describe a font.

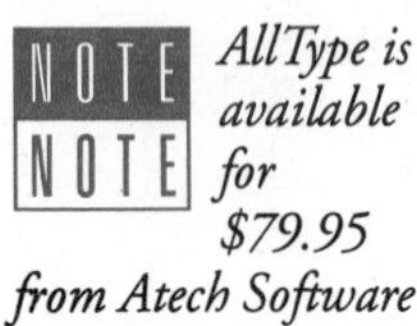

AllType is available for $79.95 from Atech Software in Carlsbad, California. Call 800-748-5657.

The only major drawback of AllType is its lack of an on-screen preview of the converted fonts. There is no way of knowing what a font will look like until it is brought up in the destination application. This hampers efforts to select fonts by sight rather than by name. Who can remember what a font looks like by name, anyway?

At a suggested list price of $79.95, AllType is a great bargain. And the savings associated with converting just one of your fonts will more than pay for the package the first time you use it.

FontMonger for Windows

Like AllType, FontMonger can convert fonts—and it does a great job at it. It also provides support for TrueType, PostScript Type 1 and Type 3, Nimbus Q, and Intellifont, as well as CorelDraw WFN and LaserMaster formats.

But FontMonger goes far beyond simple format conversion. FontMonger is a full-featured type-manipulation and editing tool. It becomes clear after just a few minutes with the product that format conversion is just a side benefit of FontMonger.

FontMonger was originally developed for the Macintosh, where fonts are a passion of the highest order. FontMonger's interface shows a great deal of thought and attention to detail, in contrast with the sparse, functional interface of AllType for Windows.

Fonts can be converted by FontMonger as a batch, or individually. When you select File ➤ Convert Batch, you are presented with a batch list containing the names of fonts in your last conversion batch (Figure 18.8). When you press the Find button, FontMonger will scan the directories you specify for all the font types it knows. You just select the files you want to convert, tell FontMonger what format to convert them into, and off it goes.

As simple as it is to convert a batch of files, the time and effort you put into converting each font individually will prove to be well worthwhile. To

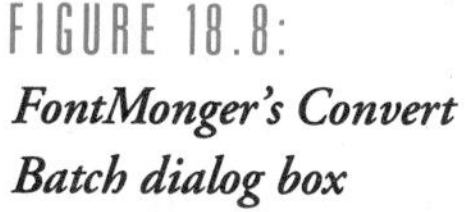

FIGURE 18.8: *FontMonger's Convert Batch dialog box*

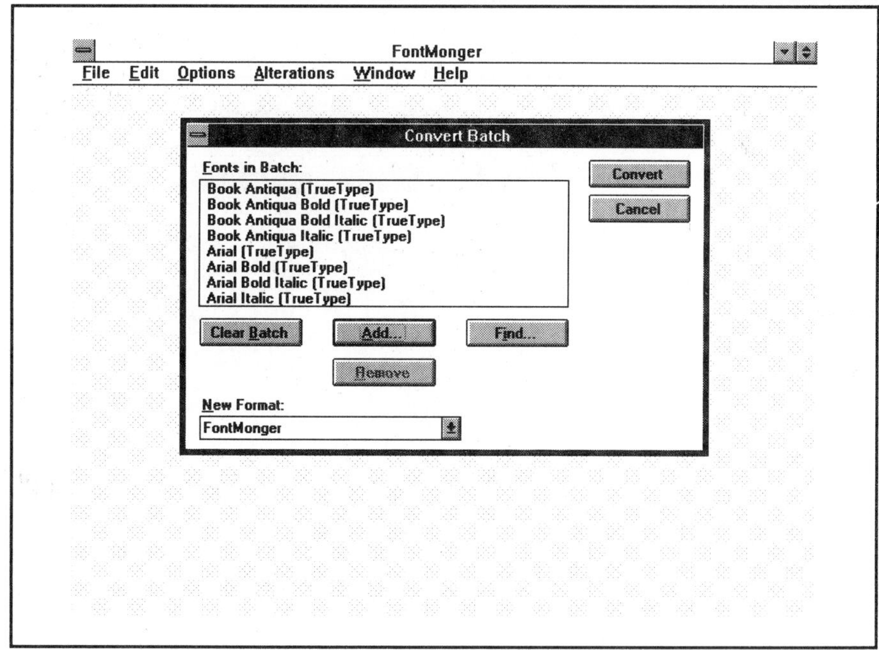

convert an individual file, you first open a font file. When you do, Font-Monger renders small versions of each character on an on-screen keyboard (Figure 18.9). You can refer to the keyboard for a quick overview of the font. Alternately, you can view the font from a Character Chart that displays the full complement of characters.

FontMonger provides facilities to set font information such as font name and family relationship (normal, bold, italic, bold italic, or other). Once you've set the selections appropriately, you can set the font protection level (meaning whether your font should have read-only or read-write embedding). Unless you want to customize further, you can then choose File ➤ Build Font to create a new font. Select the new format for the font and you're done.

The main difference between the conversion features found in AllType and those in FontMonger, besides the ability to select font settings, is its ability to re-hint fonts. AllType uses the hinting information found in the source font. In contrast, FontMonger looks at the font itself and generates new hinting rules based on the characteristics of the font. The result is clean, crisp-looking screen fonts that can be recognized as distinct designs even at

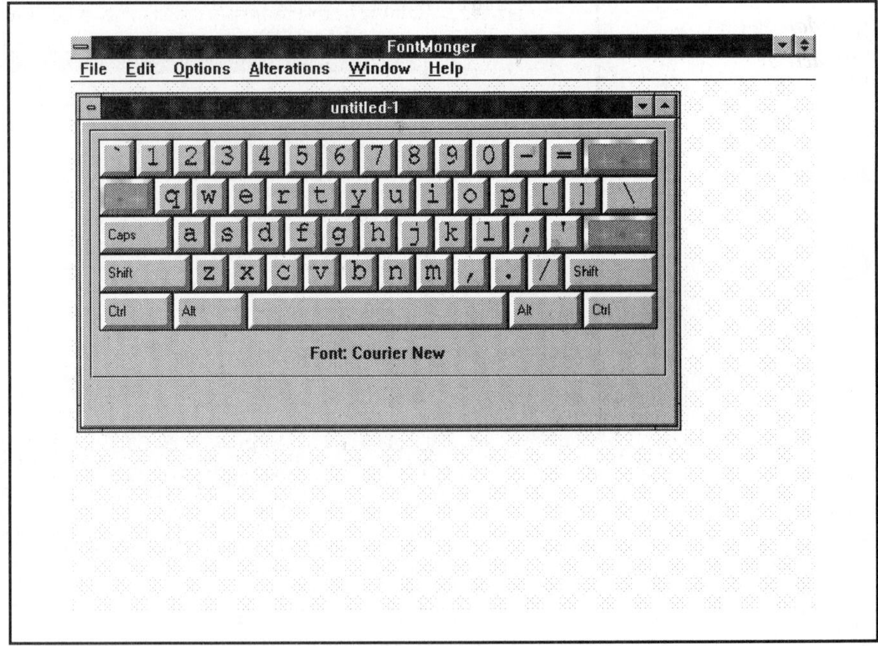

FIGURE 18.9:

FontMonger's keyboard display

small point sizes. Additionally, the time it takes to convert a font is a bit less than the time it takes AllType to do the same.

But the real strength of FontMonger is its full complement of font-editing tools. FontMonger will easily perform a number of alterations to a font based on selections under its Alterations menu. The default alterations include Small Caps, Slant (italicize), Superior (superscript), and Inferior (subscript). You can even create your own custom alterations. However, the most useful of these alterations is the Alter Character(s) selection.

Double-clicking a character on the on-screen keyboard—or highlighting the character and selecting Alterations ➤ Alter Character(s)—brings up an editing window, as shown in Figure 18.10. Here, you can view a character's outlines and the lines and curves of the design of the character. It is a simple matter to drag and move lines, or draw entirely new curves.

Font-Monger is available for about $149 from Ares Software in Foster City, California. Call 415-578-9090.

FontMonger also lets you import characters designed in Adobe Illustrator or saved in Encapsulated PostScript. You can develop a logo or symbol in a drawing package such as Illustrator, Micrografx Designer, or CorelDraw, and assign your logo to a key in a standard font.

FIGURE 18.10:

FontMonger's Alter Character window

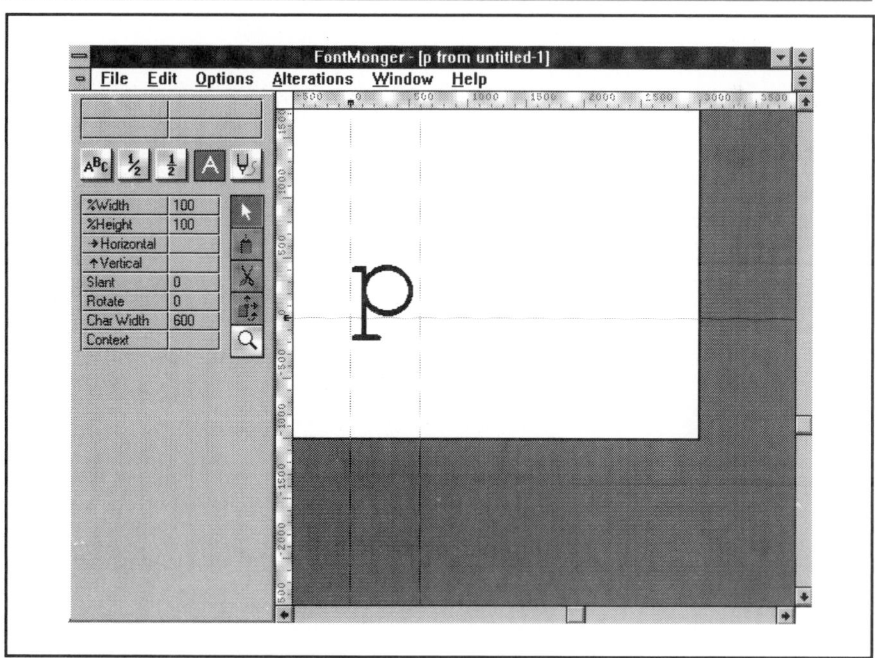

All in all, FontMonger is a sensational package. If you have more than a passing interest in fonts and fontography, FontMonger is well worth its \$149 suggested retail price. If you just want to convert fonts, the \$79.95 price of AllType makes it a great value and a strong performer.

PART FOUR

Troubleshooting, Tips & Tricks, and Products

art IV contains a lot of Windows information. Ranging from essential Windows survival skills to interesting and entertaining trivia, you'll find the information in this section well worth reading. Part IV is divided into three chapters:

- Chapter 19 contains troubleshooting information to help you discern and cure various forms of Windows misconduct such as system crashes, bungled communications sessions, and memory shortages. Included are explanations as to why these events occur and suggestions to prevent them.
- Chapter 20 contains Windows tips, tricks, and time-savers to help you get more out of Windows with less hassle.
- Chapter 21 covers Windows-related products, such as alternatives to the Windows Program Manager and File Manager; how to run Windows on a laptop computer; minireviews of handy Windows utilities; and Windows information sources and product manufacturers.

CHAPTER 19

FEATURING

Avoiding Memory Shortages

Curing Printer Problems

Solving Communications Glitches

Mouse Maladies

Miscellaneous Troubleshooting

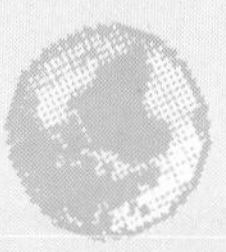

Troubleshooting

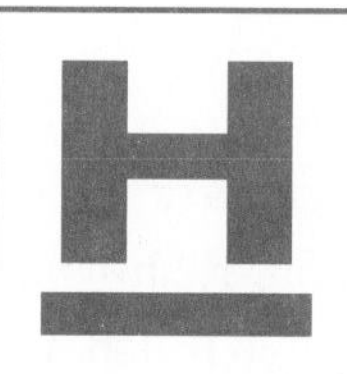

aving trouble with Windows? Don't worry, you're not alone. Though Windows has developed into a terrific graphical user interface, there's so much going on under the surface and so many hardware and software combinations possible that Murphy's Law is bound to kick in once in a while, with a system crash here and there or some other annoying anomaly whose cause isn't immediately apparent.

In hopes of detecting and correcting problems before each new version of Windows goes to market, Microsoft sends pre-release ("beta") versions of Windows to "beta testers" such as myself for months of testing and feedback. When errors such as system crashes crop up, they are saved on disk in a log file and sent to Microsoft to work on. Suggestions for improvements are registered as well, through voice, modem, and fax.

As vigilant as everyone tries to be, there are always undetected bugs or calculated decisions about known ones. At some point, the show must go on, so the product is shipped. Windows 3.1 is significantly more "stable" and "robust" than version 3.0, but you're still going to see error messages on your screen from time to time about memory shortages, missing files, or combinations of software that just don't seem to work. And, of course, there will be times when your system crashes of its own volition.

Below you will find a list of the most common Windows-related ailments and their most likely solutions. These are based on my own experiences and on those of my colleagues and clients. The first section deals with installation. Other sections deal with memory shortages, printer problems, modem problems, and more.

HAVING TROUBLE INSTALLING WINDOWS?

Though the installation procedure has improved markedly since version 3.0, there are still times when Setup will bomb for no obvious reason. Removing memory-resident programs is one good place to start. But since so much file copying and module building goes on behind the scenes during installation, it's hard to know what's really going on. All you know is that the hard and floppy disk lights are on non-stop. One last resort is to run the install program with the /L switch:

```
SETUP /L
```

This tells Windows to create a "log" of the installation process, recording each successful step, and writing it to disk.

Another problem you might have is "Out of memory" messages with first-time Setup. If you have trouble installing Windows for the first time, the most likely cause is a lack of sufficient memory. You may have too many memory-hogging device drivers and other TSR's incorporated into your startup files (CONFIG.SYS and AUTOEXEC.BAT). Rather than undergoing the hassle of redoing them and possibly losing your time-tested settings, try booting up a simple, unencumbered DOS. That way, more conventional memory will be available to the Windows Setup program, and it may load without coughing. Start by making a system disk:

1. Insert a disk you don't mind formatting in drive A.
2. Get to the DOS prompt and type

   ```
   FORMAT A: /S
   ```

3. When the formatting is done, leave the disk in and reboot your computer with the new disk in drive A. DOS should come up, possibly asking for the time and date.
4. Remove the DOS disk, and insert Windows disk 1. Now try running the Setup program again.

WHAT TO DO WHEN YOU RUN OUT OF MEMORY

It's not unlikely that you'll get an "insufficient memory to run application" message from Windows at some point. This usually happens immediately after you try to run a program. More often than not, it will be a non-Windows application rather than a Windows one.

When you run a program, Windows first checks to see whether there are enough memory and *system resources* available for the program. If there aren't, it aborts the process of launching the application and gives you an error message. There are several tricks you can try before attempting to run the program again. If these approaches don't work, and if it's a non-Windows application, then you'll have to create or modify a PIF for the application.

The first thing to do is to check the amount of available memory. Do this by opening the Program Manager's Help menu and choosing About Program Manager. (Many other application's Help menus have an About choice on their Help menus too, which will display similar information.) You'll see a box reporting the amount of free memory and system resources (explained below). Note that Windows includes the size of any existing swap file in the remaining ("free") memory figure. So you're likely to see a figure that exceeds the size of your actual hardware RAM. For example, if you have 4MB of RAM and a 10MB swapfile, and you're running in 386-Enhanced mode, Windows may report something like 12MB of free memory with no programs other than the Program Manager running. (DOS, Windows, SMARTDrive, mouse drivers, TSRs, device drivers, and other operating-system components typically consume a couple of megabytes.) The amount of free RAM may suggest that you should have plenty to run the application that is causing the out-of-memory message. Unfortunately, the "gas gauge" isn't always accurate; it also doesn't represent the complete story. (More about that in the next section.)

TROUBLESHOOTING AND TIPS & TRICKS

Other things you can do when you run out of memory are as follows:

- Close any applications you don't need to have open. You may only have to close one of them to get enough space for your application to run.
- Try running your larger applications first and your smaller ones last. Running programs this way allows the smaller programs to fit into memory nooks and crannies that larger ones can't fit into. To see how large a program is, look at its .EXE file size in File Manager, or select Help ➤ About Program Manager (or Help ➤ About File Manager, depending on where you are) before and after running each application.
- If you have any wallpaper loaded, change it to a different pattern. A pattern of 50% Gray or None uses the least amount of memory.
- If you don't need what's on the Clipboard, clear it (see Chapter 8). If you have something large on it, it could be taking up enough RAM to prevent your application from loading.
- Run non-Windows programs full-screen instead of windowed.
- Iconize any Windows programs that you want to keep open; otherwise close them. They use less memory when iconized.
- Check your CONFIG.SYS and AUTOEXEC.BAT files for RAM-resident programs that you don't need. Windows can only offer as much memory to programs as is initially available when Windows starts up. If you have lots of memory-resident software loaded when you boot up, it will decrease what Windows has to work with, which affects all applications. Even though memory-resident programs adversely affect non-Windows applications more than Windows applications, memory shortages have, at the least, a slowing effect on Windows' overall performance.
- Clean up your WIN.INI file as described in Chapter 16 to remove any obsolete or duplicate application settings.
- Remove unused fonts from your system using the Control Panel. (See Chapters 5 and 18 for information about fonts.)
- If you are running Adobe Type Manager or another font manager that allows you to adjust the size of the font cache, try reducing the cache size. This will slow down screen redrawing, but will free up some RAM.

- Decrease the size of your disk cache. Check the SMARTDrive settings (or those of any other disk-cache program if you're using one) in your CONFIG.SYS or AUTOEXEC.BAT file. Apportioning less RAM to the cache frees up some for Windows to use. As a rule, don't decrease the cache to less than 512K, however, unless you can live with significantly slower overall Windows performance. A 1MB cache performs plenty well on most systems.
- Try upgrading to DOS 5 if you are using an earlier version. DOS 5 makes more conventional memory available to your programs. The memory managers included with DOS 5 (HIMEM.SYS and EMM386.EXE) allow DOS 5 to free up more conventional memory for application use by moving parts of DOS, some device drivers, and memory-resident programs into the High Memory Area (HMA) between 640K and 1MB of your system's RAM.
- Read the sections below for more tips.

About System Resource Shortages

Windows may present an out-of-memory message even when there is plenty of memory left. These so-called memory shortages are often caused not by a RAM shortage, but by a system resource shortage, the other commodity shown in the About Program Manager (or other application) dialog box. Windows programs call upon a collection of predefined functions called Application Programming Interfaces (APIs), which ensure that Windows applications will run on any computer that can run Windows. System resources consist of two classes of APIs, called the Graphics Display Interface (GDI) and the User Library. These APIs are used to draw functional objects on the screen, such as menus, icons, option buttons, windows, word-processing "rulers," tool bars, and so forth.

Unfortunately, because of a limitation in DOS, only 128K of RAM can be used for such objects. Even with nothing but the Program Manager running, system resources are tied up. With more and more applications using tool bars (such as Lotus 1-2-3's SmartIcons and WordPerfect for Windows' Button Bar), system resources can become a scarce commodity quickly when you run multiple applications simultaneously. If you appear to have plenty of memory available but still can't run an application, perhaps you're out of resources.

Eliminating bit-mapped wallpaper and extra fonts from your system won't free up resources, so the techniques listed above won't help, nor will adding RAM to your system. However, if you follow the tips below, you'll be better able to conserve this limited resource:

- Keep the number of simultaneously open applications and documents to a dull roar: Only open those you need.
- Most applications allow you to open multiple documents with only a single instance of the application running. If you need access to a number of documents simultaneously, use this approach, rather than run additional instances of the same program.
- If you must have many programs running at once, keep application windows iconized when you're not using them. This way they're still running, but not using as many resources. To switch to another application, first iconize the one you're using, then bring up the Task List and choose the application you want to switch to, or get to the Desktop and double-click the icon of the next application or document you want to use.
- If you have multiple document windows open within an application, minimize resource-gobbling options in each window. Turn off tool bars, SmartIcons, etc., if not needed.
- If the application allows complex menus, "rulers," or "ribbons" (such as with Microsoft Word for Windows), turn these off when not needed.
- Some poorly written programs don't free up system resources the way they should after being closed. Check the remaining resources (by choosing Help ➤ About Program Manager) before and after running the application to see if they are reclaimed. If not, the application is to blame.

More Elaborate Techniques for Freeing Up Memory

If none of the above techniques work, well, then you may have to get creative. There's probably a fix that will work, but it'll take some experimenting.

To be frank, even though the Windows manual doesn't state this in so many words, if you're having lots of out-of-memory problems, you may just have to buy more memory. Having a couple of megabytes of extended memory really helps speed up Windows and eliminates many of those annoying messages.

Before giving up and buying the memory, though, consider this: Are you having problems only when you run non-Windows applications? If so, which ones? Perhaps Windows isn't meeting the memory or display requirements of the application. You may have success by creating or modifying the PIF(s) for the application(s) you're attempting to run, particularly if your low-memory message is coming from the application itself.

For example, Ventura Publisher Professional (version 2.0 that runs under GEM) puts its own dialog box up on the screen when you run it in a system that is short on memory. Ventura, like certain versions of Lotus 1-2-3 and some other non-Windows applications, requires expanded memory, so I had to create a PIF requesting it.

Here are some PIF settings to consider altering, since they affect memory usage (see Chapter 13 for detailed information on these settings and on how to edit PIFs):

Memory Requirements: Try decreasing the number in the Memory Required section of the application's PIF. It's likely the application doesn't need as much memory as its manual states, anyway. Also, set the XMS or EMS (386-Enhanced mode only) memory requirements to zero unless the program needs it. In other words, you may be getting an out-of-memory message not because there isn't enough memory available for the application, but because the application has a PIF that's requesting more than is really needed and Windows can't supply that much.

Program Switch: By turning off the program-switching ability, Windows relinquishes memory it would otherwise use to store the screen display when you switch out of the application. Try turning this option on.

Video Mode: Select the video mode that uses the least amount of memory—which is text mode. If the application doesn't run with this setting, change it back. If the application uses text mode when it initially starts up, this technique should work at least to get the program running. However, if the application changes to a higher mode later to display some graphics, Windows might not let you switch out of the program until you close it or until you return to text mode.

Tasking Options (386-Enhanced mode only): Set the application to exclusive tasking.

Retain Video Memory (386-Enhanced mode only): Clear this setting.

You might want to try making these changes one at a time, rather than using the shotgun method. Save the PIF, making sure to close the PIF Editor (since it takes up memory too), and rerun the application.

If after making all the possible changes you're still short on memory, change the PIF settings of other running non-Windows applications. If you're not running any other applications at the same time as the one you're having trouble with, you've got a real problem. Check the amount of free memory via the Help ➤ About Program Manager command. If it says that you have tons of memory and the application still won't run, make sure you're assigning the right kind of memory. Maybe your application needs expanded or extended memory.

When Non-Windows Applications Crash (Low Environment Space)

If you are receiving UAEs (Unrecoverable Application Errors) or messages from DOS indicating low "environment" space or "not enough memory to run program" when you try to run a non-Windows application, there may not be enough DOS environment space for the application. Of course, you might not have enough free memory in general, or you might not have requested enough memory in the PIF for the application. But those problems have been discussed earlier. Here's another slant on a solution, particularly if you have reason to believe you're running out of DOS environment space.

As many experienced DOS tweakers know, the /E variable in the DOS SHELL command determines the amount of environment space for DOS sessions. (The DOS environment is an area of memory reserved for storing variables and pointers and is normally 265 bytes in size.)

Windows, however, uses its own default settings for running DOS sessions, instead of this variable entered into your CONFIG.SYS.

Perhaps one or more non-Windows applications you want to run under Windows require a larger environment size. If there isn't enough space available, programs may accidentally try using space not allotted for environment information, causing a crash.

Unfortunately, just increasing the /E:*xxxx* parameter in the SHELL command will not do the trick. Here's how to handle the problem:

1. Create a PIF that runs COMMAND.COM (enter COMMAND.COM in the Program Filename field).
2. Declare a larger size parameter in the Optional Parameters field of the PIF Editor (e.g., /E:1024).
3. Modify other parameters of the PIF as you like and save it.
4. Make an icon for the PIF and add it to a Program Manager group. Call it something to indicate the larger environment, such as DOS /E 1024.
5. Run the PIF to get a DOS prompt, then manually enter the name of the program you want to run.

If you want the PIF to run a program after invoking COMMAND.COM and setting the environment size, add /C (with a space before and after it) and the program's name (and path, if necessary) in the Optional Parameters field, like this:

```
/E:1024 /C C:\WP5\WP.EXE
```

You Get the Message "A20 Line Already Enabled"

This message means that your system is experiencing a conflict between extended memory managers or between HIMEM.SYS and a device driver that uses extended memory. Check to see that you only have one extended memory manager (I recommend the version of HIMEM.SYS that came with your version of Windows), and check that it loads *before* any device drivers that need access to extended memory.

Once, when installing Windows on a laptop (an ALR Venture 386SX), I received the following message:

```
A20 Line Unavailable (or not enabled)
```

This is sort of the reverse problem of that explained above. After trying everything else, I found a brief explanation in the computer's manual about a setting within the computer that had to be changed before extended memory was accessible. After altering the setting, which required running a utility program supplied with the computer, everything was fine.

PRINTER PROBLEM SOLVING

The computer printing process is fraught with maladies and pitfalls. The veracities of Murphy's Law sometimes seem undeniably confirmed when you're struggling to achieve even the simplest of hard-copy renderings.

Printing is problematic because there are so many variables to contend with. In fact, things have much improved since the days when you had to make the cable and write the driver yourself. Printers probably work right about 90 percent of the time these days. But setting up the Windows printer driver alone requires more dialog boxes than you can shake a stick at. Compound the possible errors made while setting the boxes with the zillions of available printers and computers, the varieties of cables to connect them (cables both correctly and incorrectly configured—especially the ones for serial printers), and the wide variety of applications programs (many of which don't explain printing in detail), and you have all the ingredients for major frustration. On the other hand, if you're lucky, all will go well the first time because your computer is really IBM-compatible, your printer is really supported by a Windows driver (or a manufacturer-supplied one that is well designed and tested), and the application program is well designed.

Unfortunately, there isn't room here—or in any book—for all the tips and tricks you'd need to resolve every problem that can crop up in the software-computer-printer chain. So I'll just outline the basic problem areas and their most likely remedies instead. Chances are good that you'll weed out the culprit and be printing correctly in short order.

Some of the solutions apply to problems other than those listed under the specific headings. These are the most common causes of printer problems:

- Be sure you've installed the correct printer driver, port, and printer name. Refer to Chapter 6 and the online Help information.
- Check the cable between your printer and your computer. Is it secure? Is it the correct type of cable?
- Check the switch settings and power to your printer.

IF NOTHING PRINTS

If nothing prints at all, there may be a fast fix, because it means something's *really* wrong. Here are some possibilities:

- Is the printer actually turned on and plugged in?
- Is the printer connected to the computer? Check to see that the cables are tight.
- Does the printer have paper?
- Is the printer online? Check the switches. Try turning the printer off and then on again to reset it.
- Is there an error light or indicator that would alert you to a problem with the printer? If so, check the manual to see what it means and try to correct the problem. It could be a paper jam, a ribbon that's dead, or a font cartridge that has to be plugged in.
- Is the correct printer selected from the application's Printer Setup dialog box? If the application doesn't have a Setup dialog box, it assumes you want to use the default printer. Check to see that the default printer is the one you're trying to print to. (See Chapter 6 for information about setting the default printer via the Control Panel.)
- Is the printer driver set up to print to the correct port? Check the Configure dialog box. (Again, see Chapter 6 for details.)
- If the printer is connected to a serial port (COM1 through COM4), are the communications settings correct? They must be the same on both sides (printer/computer). Set them using the Ports icon on the Control Panel.

- Does the printer work with any application? Does it work outside of Windows? If it does, then the problem is with your Windows setup.

If Your Printer Prints Garbage

Another common problem is printing garbage. *This* is garbage:

!^&*(ghAU"YW*%^#$!!

If you get something like it, read the following:

- Severe garbage invariably results when a serial printer's communications settings are configured incorrectly (though it could have other causes). Check the Ports settings from the Control Panel and the switches on the printer. Baud rate, stop bits, and parity must all be set identically for the printer and computer. Try running at a slower baud rate.
- On a serial printer, if everything prints okay for a while (a few lines or a couple of pages) and *then* goes bananas, the "flow control" (sometimes called *handshaking*) is not correct. The printer is telling the computer to stop sending data, in order to catch up, but the computer doesn't get the message—and keeps sending. That's when the garbage starts. Check the flow control for the printer's COM port by double-clicking the Ports icon in the Control Panel, then clicking on the Settings button. The setting is called Flow Control in that dialog box. The Xon/Xoff method is software flow control. The Hardware method uses voltages on specific wires in your cable to control handshaking. Your printer and Windows have to be using the same flow-control method, so make sure the handshaking method for the printer matches that for the port. (See your printer manual for the default settings.) For additional help, click the Help button in the Settings dialog box.
- It's possible that your serial printer cable is wired incorrectly and isn't relaying the handshaking information to the right pin on the computer's serial port. Check that the cable is intended for use with an IBM PC and that your serial interface card is configured correctly (with the correct port and handshaking).

- Try another printer driver that's similar.
- Try another printer name that's similar (from the Options settings, as explained in Chapter 6).
- Try the Generic/Text Only printer driver.
- Turn your printer off and on again. There may have been leftover data in the buffer.
- Try another cable.
- Is the printer in the correct mode? It may be set to emulate another type of printer. For example, Apple LaserWriters and some other PostScript printers can be in HP mode or Diablo mode. Check the manual.
- Try the printer's self-test if it has one. Maybe the printer is defective.
- Try printing from DOS. At the DOS prompt, enter

  copy *filename.txt port*

  where *filename.txt* is an ASCII text file and *port* is LPT1:, LPT2:, COM1:, COM2:, etc.

If the Page Formatting Looks Wrong

If the margins, page breaks, indents, tabs, or line spacing don't match what you see on the screen, one of the following may be wrong:

- Did you choose the correct printer before printing? One printer may act very differently from another, particularly when it comes to formatting. The letters may still print, but formatting codes will not be interpreted correctly.
- If the application didn't let you choose the printer, is the correct default printer selected? (See Chapter 6.)
- Is the printer in the correct mode? It may be emulating another type of printer. Check the manual.
- Check the switches on the printer. They may accidentally be set to override the printer driver, creating a specific page length, character width, or lines per inch. In general, settings should be as "generic" (plain) as possible. This allows the printer driver to control formatting. If in doubt, check the other points in this list, then come back to this point, and try changing some of the

printer's internal formatting settings if it has them. The most common problem is a switch that causes an automatic line feed when a carriage return is received. This should be turned off.

- Check that you installed the correct printer driver for your printer. (See Chapter 6.)
- Check that you installed the correct printer name from the driver you installed. (See Chapter 6.)
- Check that the printer is set up for the correct paper source.

If Downloaded Fonts or Cartridge Fonts Don't Print

If you try to use fonts that you've downloaded to a printer or fonts that are in a plug-in cartridge and they don't print, check the following:

- Did you install the fonts properly? There should be installation instructions supplied with the fonts.
- If the fonts were downloaded into the printer's RAM (sometimes called making the fonts *permanent*), they will be lost when the printer's power is turned off. You will have to download them again if the power was turned off at any time subsequent to the downloading. (They're not *really* permanent!)
- If you are using cartridge fonts, the cartridge may not be plugged in firmly. Turn off the printer's power and push the cartridge in all the way. Then power up again.
- Did you set the options for your printer correctly, as covered in Chapter 6?
- Printers that accept downloaded fonts have a finite amount of RAM space for holding them. It is possible to completely fill the RAM font space, after which no more fonts can be accepted by the printer. Perhaps you downloaded more fonts than it can handle, so the last few fonts weren't actually installed. Some printers come with utility programs that will print out a list of the installed fonts. An example is PS Exec, supplied with some PostScript printers. Try running one of these to see if the fonts are really getting to the printer.

◆ Some printers cannot print high-quality fonts in landscape orientation because they cannot successfully rotate the fonts the required 90 degrees. If your printout appears in a cruder font than you expected, such as Courier, try printing in portrait orientation. If this works, you've found the problem.

If a TrueType Font Prints Incorrectly

Some users have noted that when working with True Type fonts, they sometimes don't print as expected. For example, one version of a Garamond-like font that was downloaded from a BBS (dial-up Bulletin Board Service) failed to behave when asked to print certain characters such as an apostrophe or upper-ASCII characters including Greek letters, accents, and symbols. Instead of printing an apostrophe, this public-domain font printed a period. Underlines didn't print correctly in WordPerfect for Windows. And so on. What gives with these freebie fonts?

Good fonts take a lot of time to design correctly. Unfortunately, though one might look good at first blush, inner details of a font may not prove worth the time it took to download it. If on your printout you get a period instead of an expected character, this means the designer of the font didn't create that particular character. Typically, a period will appear in your printout to indicate the missing character. You can view which characters in a font are extant or vacant using the Character Map accessory in the Accessories Group. (See Chapter 12 for a discussion of Character Map).

Another problem you might encounter with cheaper fonts is uneven spacing. Since most TrueType fonts are proportionally-spaced fonts, creating a typeface isn't a matter of just designing attractive letters, numbers, and punctuation marks. Considerable know-how and aesthetic judgement calls go into the design of proper character kerning and spacing. You get what you pay for. If you're particularly fond of a given typeface and plan to do serious work such as desktop publishing with it, consider buying it from one of the better sources such as Adobe, Bitstream, or Agfa-Compugraphic. Although getting fonts from a BBS can be fun, and the price is right, they often don't measure up to those that are professionally crafted.

If Only Part of a Graphics Page Prints

If only a portion of a page prints when you're printing graphics, consider the following:

- Some laser or ink-jet printers have limited internal RAM that prevents them from printing a whole page of graphics in the highest resolution. Select a lower resolution and try printing again.
- If your printer lets you add memory and it's likely that you've run into a memory limitation, install more memory. Typical laser printers have as much as 4.5 MB of memory. This can handle extra fonts and full pages of graphics easily. If you do a lot of complex printing, it's worth the price.
- Does the paper size selected in the printer's setup box match the paper you're using? Check and adjust it if necessary.

SOLVING GLITCHES WHEN USING TERMINAL

Chances are good that you'll run into some problem or other while transferring files, sending mail, or whatever it is you end up doing with Terminal. The fault will not necessarily lie with Terminal, but much more likely will be the result of improper wiring, faulty modems, noisy telephone lines, incorrect log-on procedures, or incompatible software on the other end of the line. Here's a small list of tips and possible cures in the event of trouble.

Communication Doesn't Even Begin

- Check to see that the modem is on.
- If you're using an external modem, make sure it is connected to the correct serial port.
- Check to make sure you selected the correct port from the Settings ➤ Communications dialog box.

TIP *If your Hayes-compatible modem (external type) answers the phone even when you don't want it to, open the modem and set switch 5 to the down position. This disables automatic answering.*

- If you're using an internal-type modem, did you select the correct port assignment (COM1 or COM2)? Make sure there are no conflicts with other equipment, such as printer ports, a serial mouse, or others. Only one device can be assigned to a port. You may have to switch to COM2 if COM1 is being used by another device.
- Test the link between your computer and modem this way: If you are using a Hayes-compatible modem, type **AT** (uppercase) and press Enter. The modem should respond with OK on your screen. If it doesn't, there may be something wrong with the wiring, the modem, or the port selection.
- If you and the person on the other end of the line see garbage on the screen, such as

  !!!12#()))) @(#^&**(&@#%^,

  when you type in terminal mode, most likely you are transmitting at different baud rates. Hang up, call the other person, agree on a baud rate, and try again. (Also check the number of data bits and stop bits.)
- If your Hayes-compatible modem doesn't answer the phone, try this: With the communications session running, type **AT** and press Enter. You should see an OK message issued from the modem in return. Now type

  AT S0=1

  (that's S-zero). This turns on auto-answer. When you're done with your session, type

  AT S0=0

  to disable auto-answer unless you want to leave it on. If you leave it on, your computer may take a call that was intended for human consumption.

You Can't Log On to an Information Service or BBS

- Try pressing Enter or Ctrl-C upon seeing a prompt from the host computer.

- Did you type the log-on, password, and so on *exactly* as they are supposed to be typed? Uppercase and lowercase letters are often distinguished by remote systems.

You Have Difficulty Transferring a File

- If you're using XModem, you will have to start both computers (sending and receiving) at roughly the same time; otherwise they will time out. XModem programs will completely abort the transmission process after a time out. Terminal only waits about one minute before aborting an XModem sending or receiving attempt, after which you will have to begin the process again. I have the greatest success with XModem binary-transfers if the receiving computer is set up first, then the sending computer. The other order tends to cause timeout problems.
- If you're using Send Text or Capture Text and characters at the beginning of each line are lost in the process, increase the end-of-line delay of the sending computer. If the sending computer is the PC running Terminal, you do this from the Transfer/Send Text dialog box.
- If you need to perform many file transfers between a Macintosh and your PC, you may want to consider other alternatives, such as hardware/software products devised specifically for that purpose. TOPS, an inter-operating system local area network from Sitka Corp. in Alameda, California ((510) 769-9669) is one example. Also, some Macintoshes can now directly read and write $3\frac{1}{2}$-inch floppy disks from a PC, and software is available for PCs to read Mac disks.

Your Communications Sessions are Terminated Unexpectedly

If while running a communications session you are abruptly cut off, the culprit may be "call waiting." You know you were cut off because the screen will probably say something like

```
NO CARRIER
```

when the other party didn't really hang up on you. Call waiting allows you to be interrupted by a new incoming call when you're already talking to someone. However, modems don't like call waiting at all. (They're even less forgiving of it than some of my friends.) When the second call comes in, the modem's carrier tones are interrupted and they think the party's over, so they unceremoniously hang up the phone. The solution is either to use a line that doesn't have call waiting or to see if you can turn it off. In Berkeley, California, for example, where I live, I can turn off call waiting by dialing *70, waiting for a second, and then dialing the number. Call waiting is then disabled until I hang up. If I'm concerned about being interrupted in a communications session, I'll tell the other person that *I'll* call so that I can turn off my call waiting first. (If he or she calls me first, I can't.) I also use the *70 command in front of any phone numbers I enter into the Terminal phone settings, like this:

```
*70,510-555-1212
```

SOLVING PROBLEMS WITH NON-WINDOWS COMMUNICATIONS PROGRAMS

As you probably remember, pressing Alt-Enter while running a non- Windows application full screen will put it into a window. In addition, pressing Alt-Spacebar will quickly window it and open the Control Menu. This is useful for making temporary adjustments that affect multitasking priority options. Why would you want to do this? Some non-Windows applications require more CPU slices than others, and may misbehave if they are under-attended by your CPU.

A good example of this scenario is sometimes encountered with communications programs. If you are running your communications program as a background task and find that it isn't keeping up with incoming data from your modem, it may be because the CPU does not have enough time to process the incoming data quickly enough. The Settings option on the

Control menu may be the solution. (Other examples are non-Windows applications that just seem to be running too slowly while sorting a database, recalculating a spreadsheet, or spooling data to a printer.) In any of these cases, here's the general procedure for stepping up performance on a one-time basis (use PIF settings for the application to permanently alter the CPU priority—see Chapter 13).

1. Switch to the non-Windows application that's misbehaving.
2. Press Alt-Spacebar.
3. Choose Settings from the Control menu. The following box appears:

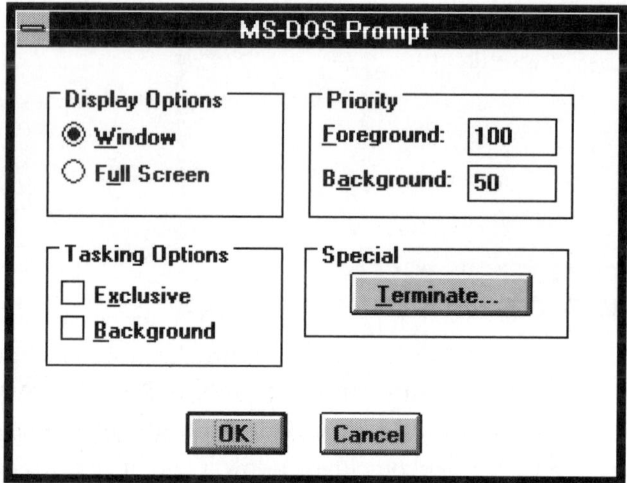

4. Foreground and background priority settings are the ones to pay attention to. If the problem has been occuring when the application is running in the background, increase that number. If the problem occurs when the program is running in the foreground (as the active window), increase that number. As explained in Chapter 13, the values are relative to other applications that are running, so absolute interpretation of the values is difficult. The values can range from 0 to 10,000.

OTHER TYPES OF PROBLEMS

The following items have been known to cause problems with Windows in some situations. If you're having problems running Windows, you might try some of the following solutions:

TIP *Consider online information services such as CompuServe and Prodigy as good sources of tips and tricks about Windows. As new Windows programs come out and people discover bugs and solutions to them, they're likely to be written up for public access on these services. Other sources are listed at the end of Chapter 20.*

- On some machines you have to specify both a minimum and a maximum size for SMARTDRV.SYS. Consult your Windows User's Guide and Chapter 16 of this book for information on SMARTDrive.
- For some reason, Windows seems to perform better when it is placed toward the front of your search path. Edit your AUTOEXEC.BAT's path statement with Sysedit or a text editor and make sure the Windows directory is listed as one of the first few directories in the PATH statement.
- When running Windows, you should not use the following DOS utilities:

  APPEND
  FASTOPEN
  JOIN
  SUBST

Below I discuss other types of problems you might encounter while running Windows. Some of the problems apply to Windows programs, while others apply to non-Windows programs. Each problem is described briefly and followed by possible solutions:

Windows Won't Start

If you have trouble getting Windows to start, load the file WIN.INI in Windows' directory into a text editor and check the lines that start with LOAD= or RUN=. These lines tell Windows the names of any programs that should be loaded when Windows starts. Try removing the file names and restarting Windows.

Creating a Log File of the Windows Bootup Process

If you still can't get Windows to start, you can pinpoint the cause of the conflict by running Windows with the following command:

```
WIN /B
```

This forces Windows to create a file called BOOTLOG.TXT when it starts. BOOTLOG.TXT contains a list of each Windows module as it loads and the result of loading the module up to the point at which Windows failed. For example, if the file USER.EXE is corrupt or missing, you might see the following line at the end of BOOTLOG.TXT:

```
LoadFail = USER.EXE Failure code is 02
```

Once you find the source of your problem, you can either use the information when calling Microsoft's technical support department, or you can try copying a new version of the corrupt file from your original distribution disks.

Resolving System Conflicts

A common and recommended practice for resolving system conflicts is to create bare-bones versions of your CONFIG.SYS and AUTOEXEC.BAT files. Of course, you should first make sure that you have copies of the original files in a safe place. Remove references to any programs or device drivers that are not absolutely necessary. Then reboot your computer and again attempt whatever operation caused the conflict. If you are successful, try adding programs and drivers back in, one by one, until one of them fails. At that point, you will know the cause of your conflict and can work at resolving it. Microsoft Technical Support can help: (206) 637-7098.

Garbage Appears When You're Running Terminal

If garbage characters appear on the screen when you're running Terminal or another communications program, try setting the COM port from the Control Panel's Ports window. The baud, stop bits, and parity may not match that of the modem. Check to see that no other applications are using the same port at the same time.

You Get a UAE While Assigning an Icon

Unrecoverable Application Errors can actually be caused by improperly created icon files. If you trigger repeated UAEs when assigning an icon to an application as you're adding it to Program Manager, try using another icon. Just using another icon that's internally acceptable to Windows may curtail further difficulty. If you don't want to give your application a different icon, try editing the icon with an icon editor such as the one from hDC. In most cases, just opening and saving the file will clear up any problems with the icon.

Icons Remain Misaligned

If, after you choose the Arrange Icons command from the Program Manager, the icons are still misaligned, close all the group windows. As long as a group window is open, the Arrange Icons command only arranges the program icons in the current group, not the group icons.

Not All Running Programs Are Visible

If, after you use the Tile command from the Task List, you can still see only some of the running programs (and some are missing), iconize the Program Manager. It is obscuring the programs that seem to be missing.

You're Told an Application Is Active When You Try to Exit Windows

The active program's icon will be highlighted, so you'll know what the offending program is. Open the program's window and quit that program. If you can't quit because a program is hung (crashed), read the tip below.

An Application Crashes and You Can't Terminate It

If a DOS or Windows application has crashed and you can't terminate it, try pressing Ctrl-C, Ctrl-Break, or Esc. If those don't bring the application to its senses, open the Task List by pressing Ctrl-Esc. Make sure the program's name is highlighted and then choose End Task. This should close any Windows application. If it's a non-Windows application and the program's PIF (if it has one) has the Close When Active setting set on, you'll then see a warning message about how terminating in this way is a last resort. Go ahead and terminate the program. Close other programs and then quit Windows. You should reboot after that to reload DOS. If the application's Close When Active setting in its PIF isn't on, then you won't be allowed to quit the application this way. So press Ctrl-Alt-Del. Windows will intercept the three-key reset and ask whether you want to reboot totally, just terminate the current program, or change your mind with a message such as the one shown in Figure 19.1 (this one for a non-Windows application). Press Enter to kill the program. Windows should continue to run properly. If you want to be super safe, exit Windows and reboot, just in case the crashed application also messed up DOS, Windows, or other applications when it died. If the crashed program was a non-Windows application in a window and you're running in 386-Enhanced mode, you can terminate the program from the window's Control box; just choose Settings and click on Terminate. You do not have to reboot. You'll then see the warning box in Figure 19.2. Click on OK.

Your Mouse Doesn't Work with a Non-Windows Program

Windows 3.0 didn't allow a mouse to work with a DOS program running windowed; the mouse was reserved just for Windows operations, such as selecting portions of the DOS window for copying to the Clipboard. Windows 3.1 *does* support mouse operations in DOS windows. However, it will

FIGURE 19.1:

To kill an application that crashed while you were using it, press Ctrl-Alt-Del, followed by Enter.

```
                              DOS

You pressed CTRL-ALT-DEL in this non-Windows application

* Press ESC to cancel and return to Windows.
* Press CTRL-ALT-DEL again to restart the system.
* Press ENTER to close an application that is not responding.

          Press ENTER for OK or ESC to cancel
```

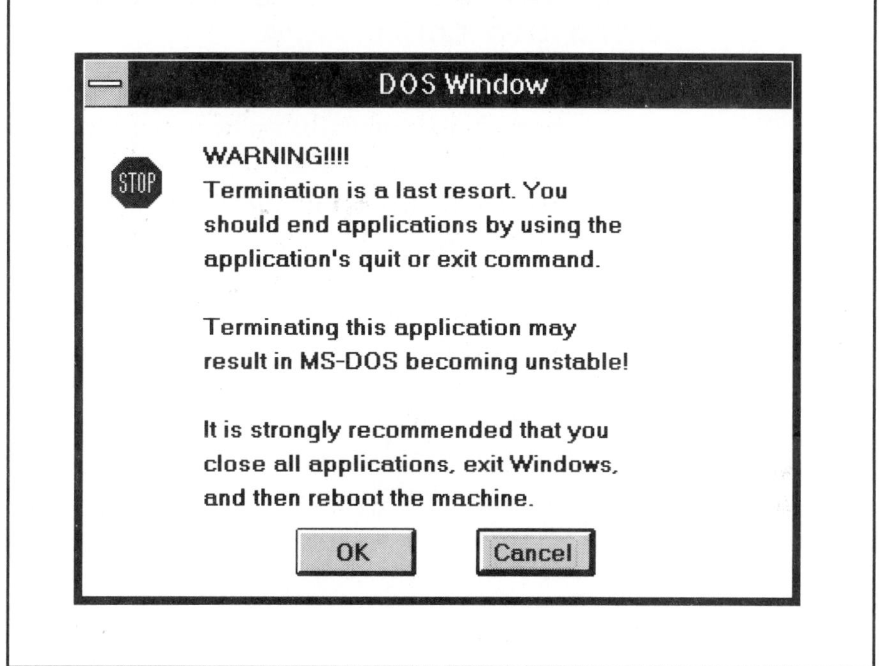

FIGURE 19.2: *To kill a non-Windows application that is running in a window, open the Control box and choose Settings. Then click on the Terminate button.*

only work if the mouse and screen drivers are ones supplied with Windows 3.1 or are specifically claimed to be compatible with these features of 3.1 (check with the manufacturer). If you're running a DOS program whose mouse works properly in full-screen mode, but isn't working correctly windowed, try checking the mouse driver command and/or path in your AUTOEXEC.BAT or CONFIG.SYS files. Typically the command will be

```
C:\MOUSE.COM
```

in the AUTOEXEC.BAT file or

```
DEVICE=C:\MOUSE.SYS
```

in the CONFIG.SYS file. If the mouse driver you want to use (preferably one supplied with Windows) is in another directory, change the path statements appropriately.

You Can't Copy the Screen onto the Clipboard

If you can't copy the screen onto the Clipboard, the application's PIF may have the No Screen Exchange setting enabled. Edit the application's PIF to turn this setting off. Also, make sure the keys you're using to capture the screen aren't reserved for other applications that are running. Check their Reserve Shortcut Keys setting or the current application's Application Shortcut Key setting for a conflict.

PIF Changes Don't Take Effect

If you keep changing a PIF but the changes don't seem to take effect, put the PIF in the same directory as the program or in the Windows directory. Give it the same first name as the application. Try running the program from its PIF instead of from the program itself. Ensure that you're doing this by opening a File Manager window and clicking on the PIF's name.

You Can't Return to Windows

If, after you finish a non-Windows program, the screen doesn't clear and you are not returned to Windows, do the following: Edit the application's PIF and turn on the Close Window on Exit setting to prevent this in the future. Sometimes simply pressing a key, clicking the mouse, or—if the application is in a window—double-clicking the window's Control box will return you to Windows. Pressing Ctrl-Tab works sometimes, too.

You Can't Switch out of a Non-Windows Application

If you can't switch out of a non-Windows application while it's running, check the application's PIF to see that the Prevent Program Switch option isn't set on. Check that the Reserve Video Memory setting is set on. Check that the shortcut keys used for switching aren't being reserved by the Reserve Shortcut Keys settings in the PIF. Make sure the correct video mode is selected in the PIF, too. Perhaps the program is using a high-resolution video mode that Windows doesn't support. This could be the case with programs that supply their own screen drivers, such as desktop publishing programs like Ventura. You'll have to exit the program before you can return to Windows. This is required because Windows knows that it can't restore the screen for you to switch back. Finally, some PIFs are designed to prevent your switching out of the application. If you make changes to the PIF that would allow switching, other problems might arise. If all else fails, call the program's manufacturer to get the PIF settings for Windows 3.1.

A DOS Application Isn't Working

If the non-Windows application is displayed in a Window, but suddenly it isn't working at all—you can't interact with it—look at the title bar. If it says Select, Mark, or Scroll, it thinks you're trying to copy information to the Clipboard. This happens when you use the mouse in a windowed non-Windows application. Press Esc to return to normal functioning. If that doesn't clear up the problem, switch the program back to full-screen mode. Some programs just can't run properly in a window, even in 386-Enhanced mode.

A Key Combination Doesn't Work Properly

If you press a key combination that the program should respond to and Windows does something else instead, such as switching programs, check the PIF for the application. Chances are good that you need to reserve shortcut keys for the application or clear them for use by Windows. Refer to Chapter 13 for a discussion of shortcut keys. If you're running Windows in 386- Enhanced mode and pressing a key combination constantly switches you back to a particular program, examine *that program's* PIF for the Application Shortcut Key setting. It may be set to the combination you're trying to use in your other application. Clear the setting or close the application. Also check the program icon's shortcut key by highlighting the icon in Program Manager and pressing Alt-Enter. The icon's shortcut key overrides the PIF's shortcut key.

Your System Is Slow When Running a Non-Windows Application

If only a particular non-Windows application is slow, try setting its PIF to *exclusive tasking* or, if you're in 386-Enhanced mode, do this temporarily by windowing the application (pressing Alt-Enter), opening the Control box, and choosing Settings. Also, look at the hard-disk light (or listen to the drive). Is the disk being used like mad every time you do the slightest thing?

If so, your system is really short of memory. See the discussion above about memory. Also read Chapter 16 for other optimizing tips. Try turning off the Detect Idle Time setting in the application's PIF. If the application takes too much time doing internal operations when you're not typing, Windows might mistakenly suspend the application.

Your System Is Slow When Print Manager Is Running

If, while Print Manager is printing a document, your other applications seem extremely sluggish, check Print Manager's priority option. This can be set to High, Medium, or Low. High priority settings may significantly affect the speed of other applications in the system while Print Manager is operating in the background. In most cases, Medium priority is best.

Windows or Your Application Crashes

If Windows or your application crashes for no apparent reason, perhaps you're trying to run an older Windows program. Check the application's manual for Windows compatibility information. If it was designed for Windows 2, you can't run it under Windows 3.1. You could run it under Windows 3.0 in Real mode, if you happen to have Windows 3.0. (You start up Windows 3.0 in Real mode with the command **WIN /R**.) But you're better off getting an update of the program designed for Windows 3.1, if there is one.

Perhaps your program is a bad copy of the original. Try installing another copy.

NOTE *If all else fails, call the Microsoft technical support line at (206) 454-2030.*

Many Windows programs come with auxiliary files called Dynamic Link Libraries (DLLs for short). If a needed DLL is missing from the directory in which it's expected by the application, the application will often bomb. Perhaps you'll see a message indicating which file is missing. Windows programs also often put an .INI file in the Windows directory. The .INI file stores settings and directory information for the application. For example, Lotus 1-2-3 for Windows has an .INI file called 123W.INI. Sometimes if a program's .INI file is missing, the program won't run. Try reinstalling the program, or search around on the program's original floppy disks or on your hard disk (using File Manager's File ➤ Search command) to attempt to find misplaced files and relocate them properly.

You may have some incompatible hardware, such as a screen or network. Check the hardware and software compatibility lists that came with Windows or call Microsoft.

Maybe your hard disk is messed up. Check it with a good hard-disk diagnostic program such as Disk Technician Gold (Prime Solutions, Inc.) or SpinRite II (Gibson Research Corp.).

Perhaps your copy of Windows somehow got bungled. Try reinstalling Windows from scratch. This is a last resort, mind you, since it's time consuming and you run the risk of deleting some files you might need. If when you try to run the Setup program again, Windows says you don't have enough room on your disk, you'll have to erase all the files in your WINDOWS and WINDOWS\SYSTEM directories. *Before you do this:*

1. *Back up any files you've created and stored there!* In addition to any documents such as text and graphics files you might have saved, make a temporary directory and copy all the .INI, .GRP, and .PIF files to it.
2. Reinstall Windows.
3. Setup should retain your .INI, .GRP, and .PIF files. If it didn't (i.e., if your groups don't have the correct icons), copy the backed-up files back into the WINDOWS directory. (The .GRP files store the information about your program groups. The .INI files store all the startup information such as the screen colors, as discussed in Chapter 16. The .PIF files store information about non- Windows applications.)

Your New Video Board Seems to Crash Windows or Cause UAEs

Correctly installing video boards and their software drivers (and optionally supplied fonts) is a particularly engaging black art and one of those favored by veteran Windows hackers who like a good challenge. Aside from the usual display issues such as resolution, refresh rate, color depth, VGA passthrough circuitry, VRAM, and so forth, there are the tastier issues for hard-core VDT fiddlers. Among these are how much system RAM the board will occupy, where in the computer's address the board's RAM and ROM will reside, whether there will be BIOS conflicts, and whether the board will coexist peaceably with other programs such as memory managers, TSRs, device drivers, and DOS.

When you are troubleshooting a Windows setup, keep in mind that a significant number of UAEs occur as a result of such video conflicts. Highly intelligent memory manager programs such as QEMM are pretty good at detecting what memory is free before carefully tucking TSRs, DOS, and device drivers into upper memory, but they can't always be accurate, since many cards shift their memory-mapping requirements with changes of resolution modes. Your system could boot up fine, and then crash when you switch to a higher resolution that uses more upper memory area.

If you are lucky, your display adaptor will come with instructions telling you what EXCLUDE lines to put into your CONFIG.SYS to instruct your memory manager to correctly prevent this type of collision. If you're having trouble, don't hesitate to call the maker of your video board to ensure that your memory manager and video card aren't walking on top of each other.

Your Mouse Dies in the Middle of a Windows Session

Once in a while your mouse will croak for no obvious reason. The breakdown could be a hardware problem, but more likely it's due to a software bug. Mice seem to die more frequently for me when I'm using non-Windows applications a lot, some of which use the mouse, or when I've installed some cursor enhancement program and am testing new applications with it. Whatever the cause of your mouse's sudden demise, follow these steps to remedy the situation without losing your work.

1. If you've made changes to the file, save them by first pressing Alt-Tab (or use the Task List via Ctrl-Esc) to activate the application's window and then using the appropriate Save command for the given application. In most Windows applications, the command will be Alt-F to open the File menu, then S to save the file. For non-Windows applications, the commands will vary widely, of course. Just use the Save command you normally employ. If the non-Windows application is mouse-driven, there's probably a pop-up menu that can be keyboard activated. Try to remember what the keystrokes are. For example, in Microsoft Works (DOS version), pressing Alt or F10 activates the menu bar. Then use the

arrow keys or press the highlighted letters to open the appropriate menus.

2. Switch to Program Manager with Alt-Tab or the Task List.
3. Press Alt-F to open the Program Manager's File menu.
4. Press X to exit Windows. When the dialog box about exiting Windows appears, press Enter to OK the box.
5. Now reboot your computer. This will ensure that DOS and any drivers you use are reloaded and that any port your mouse is connected to is reinitialized.
6. Rerun Windows if it doesn't normally come up automatically. If your mouse doesn't work now, check its connector or clean the mouse mechanism.

Your Mouse Is Acting Jumpy

Make sure to check the cabling on the mouse. Loose connections are the most common cause of computer problems. If your mouse acts just a little weird, meaning it's just slightly difficult to control, then try cleaning it. It's innards—ball and rollers—probably have some built-up crud on them. Figure out how to remove the ball (on a Logitech mouse you rotate a little disk in the direction shown by the arrows, on most Microsoft mice you slide a little door forward). Then clean any lint off the ball. Then look inside for little rollers. CAREFULLY remove any junk from the rollers. Reassemble. If you still have trouble, make sure your mouse work surface is smooth and clean. Note that some very smooth surfaces, such as glass, don't work well with a mouse.

Your Mouse Freezes Up

If your mouse repeatedly freezes when running a non-Windows application as a window, check the Advanced settings of the application's PIF file. From the PIF Editor, select Advanced, then Display Options, and select all three Monitor Ports check boxes. This may correct the problem.

You Have Trouble Accessing Your CD-ROM Drive under Windows

Try installing a file called LANMAN10.386, which comes on one of the Windows distribution disks. Expand the file and copy it to your Windows system directory and add the following line to the [386Enh] section of SYSTEM.INI:

```
DEVICE=LANMAN10.386
```

In many cases, this will clear up the problem.

CHAPTER 20

FEATURING

Program Manager Tips

File Manager Tips

Tips for Running Applications

Printing Tips

Hard Disk Speed Up and Maintenance Tips

Buying and Fine-Tuning Your Video Setup

Troubleshooting Strategies

Tips & Tricks

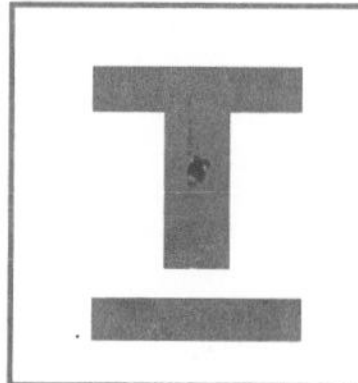

This chapter contains Windows tips and tricks that I've discovered or collected. Tips are organized according to application. Those that are not application-specific are broken out according to general topic. Each tip is presented with a minimum of discussion so you can get down to work without having to wade through too much explanation of why it works.

GENERAL TIPS

Tip 1: General Warning about Why You Should Use Share

You may have heard that the DOS program Share should not be listed in your AUTOEXEC.BAT or CONFIG.SYS files if you intend to run Windows. This is not true, and is a misinterpretation of something in the Windows documentation. You will be well advised to use Share as it will help to safeguard your valuable documents.

Share is a DOS program whose job is to prevent the simultaneous use of document files (such as that budget spreadsheet you're working on) by more than one program. This is particularly important in networking environments where two people could inadvertently be trying to modify the same data file at the same time. The unfortunate result of such a situation is often clobbered data, or, at best, a case where the last person to save the file wins out. Any previous saves are written over.

It is true that Share should be unloaded or disabled prior to running Windows Setup. This is because it can interfere with the installation process. So you should remove any lines in your CONFIG.SYS or AUTOEXEC.BAT files that refer to SHARE before running Setup for the first time. For example:

```
INSTALL=C:\DOS\SHARE.EXE
```

or

```
C:\DOS\SHARE.EXE
```

Just add the word REM (for REMark) in front of either of these two statements to disable the line, save the file, and reboot. For example:

```
REM INSTALL=C:\DOS\SHARE.EXE
```

or

```
REM C:\DOS\SHARE.EXE
```

Note that SHARE can be loaded either way—in AUTOEXEC.BAT or CONFIG.SYS, so check both files.

Once Windows is installed, you should reenable SHARE by removing the REM statement in whatever file was loading SHARE, or adding to one of the two files if it never was there to begin with. It doesn't matter which way you load the program, just so it's loaded at boot time.

One additional point about SHARE is germane to DOS 4.0 users. In that version of DOS, SHARE has the additional job of ensuring that hard disks over 32M in size work properly with older DOS programs. Without SHARE, older DOS programs that use FCSs (File Control Blocks) could corrupt your hard disk's data. If you are using DOS 4.0, have a disk that's larger than 32M (pretty likely these days), and run DOS programs, you should absolutely make sure that SHARE loads when you boot up.

TIP 2: Adding Sound without Buying a Sound Board

If you haven't yet added a sound card to your PC, don't worry: You can still enjoy some of Windows 3.1's multimedia enhancements. The PC Speaker driver (available as part of Microsoft's Windows Drivers Library and on many on-line services) lets you play WAV files through your system's built-in speaker. This won't provide the quality of a full-featured sound card, but the price is certainly right.

NOTE *Drivers are installed in the Control Panel using the Drivers option (double-click the Drivers icon).*

When you install the driver according to its accompanying instructions, you will probably want to stay with the default settings. The driver automatically determines these settings on the basis of the speed of your CPU. The only settings you may want to modify (in the PC Speaker Setup dialog box) are volume and the maximum length of playback (referred to as Seconds to limit playback).

Microsoft did not distribute the PC Speaker driver with Windows 3.1 because the technique it relies on to produce sound requires full control of the CPU. As a result, whenever you play a sound using the PC Speaker driver, the system pauses until that sound is complete. This is why you may want to limit the sample lengths to an adequate length. You can compromise with Windows by checking the box marked Enable interrupts during playback. This allows Windows to interrupt and return to playback, but it will do so at considerable expense to sound quality.

TIP 3: More Help with Windows Help

Whenever you need to learn more about Windows and other Windows applications you have, Help is at hand. You may have already noticed that almost all Windows programs come with Help files to assist new users. These files have the .HLP extension and can be accessed through their respective application menu systems. But what if you want to learn about several programs at once, or wish to browse several Help files one after another without running their respective programs?

There is a program in your Windows directory called WINHELP.EXE that lets you do this. Launch this program by using the Program Manager or File Manager's File ➤ Run command, entering **WINHELP**, and pressing Enter. Or you can double-click on the WINHELP.EXE file in File Manager. The Windows Help Engine will then appear, as shown in Figure 20.1. Choose File ➤ Open. WINHELP lists all of the Help files in the current directory. Choose the file you want to read. When you're through, you can continue reading Help files by selecting Open from the current Help file's File menu and choosing another file. Or you can close the file and WINHELP with File ➤ Exit.

TIP 4: Changing Colors on Help Screens

Ever wanted to change the colors of the hot spots on Help screens? I was having trouble seeing the dotted-underlined words (definitions) and the solid-underlined hot spot words (the ones you click on to jump to another topic) on my LCD display. When I use the Windows Default color scheme

FIGURE 20.1:
Windows Help Engine opening screen

(green on a color monitor), these screen elements display in a light-gray. None of the color settings from Control Panel affect these elements on the Help screens you get when you press F1 from Windows programs such as Program Manager, File Manager, and so on.

As it turns out, there are two undocumented keywords that control these colors. You can add these keywords to the [Windows Help] section of WIN.INI, as follows:

```
JumpColor=000 000 000
PopUpColor=000 000 000
```

The JumpColor= command controls the text you click on to go to another topic. PopUpColor= controls the dotted-underline items that produce a pop-up box of information.

When you add these lines, you'll need to change the numbers to represent colors of your choice. To determine the numbers, study the [Colors] section of WIN.INI. Compare those settings to the current screen colors of each element (button face, shadow, and so on). The numbers following each of the color components are the Red, Green, and Blue (RGB) values of the color. For example, 0 0 0 means no color at all, resulting in the color black. The value 255 255 255 means the highest values for Red, Green, and Blue in equal measure, resulting in white.

To solve my problem, I set both commands to 255 255 255 (white). Now I can clearly see the dotted-underlined keywords and the solid-underlined keywords on my LCD screen. (Since I have my Toshiba LCD set to reverse colors, a white setting results in a black display.)

TIP 5: Rolling the Windows Development Team Credits

Ever wonder who, exactly, is behind the development of Windows? To find out, try doing the following:

Through all of the following steps, hold down the Ctrl, Alt, and Shift keys.

1. In Program Manager, select Help and then About Program Manager.

2. Double-click on the Windows icon in the upper-left corner of the About Program Manager dialog box.
3. Click on OK.
4. Again, select Help and About Program Manager.
5. Double-click on the Windows icon. This time, you will see a little tribute to the Windows development team.
6. Click on OK.
7. One last time, select Help and About Program Manager.
8. Double-click on the Windows icon. Then sit back and watch the credits roll.
9. When you're finished, click on OK.

Who are those people? Well, they're the Microsoft employees who worked on Windows 3.1, but the names are electronic mail addresses. Everyone at Microsoft has an account on the companywide electronic mail system. For example, BRADSI refers to Brad Silverberg, the head of the Windows team. Further down on the list you'll find a special thanks to BILLG who is, of course, Bill Gates, CEO of Microsoft.

And the figure gesturing at the names? If you try this trick more than once, you'll find that the face on the figure changes randomly each time. The bearded figure is Brad Silverberg. The man with light-colored hair is Bill Gates. The balding man is Steve Ballmer, head of Microsoft's Systems Division, under whom Windows was developed. And the bear was a mascot of the Windows 3.1 development team, an in-joke referring to a creature who supposedly punished programmers for introducing bugs into the program code.

TIP 6: Using the Scientific Calculator

Most people don't realize that the Calculator utility that comes with Windows has two modes: Standard and Scientific. In its default (Standard) mode, the Calculator looks like an ordinary desk calculator. But choose Scientific from the program's View menu and you'll see a supercharged version with complex trigonometric functions such as sine, cosine, and tangent, as well as some helpful advanced features such as factorial (n!) and logarithm.

TIP 7: Playing Music CDs on Your CD-ROM Drive

Most CD-ROM drives can also play regular audio CDs—but not without the MCI CD Audio driver that comes with Windows 3.1. Run Control Panel and select Drivers. If you don't see an entry for CD Audio, choose Add... and then select [MCI] CD Audio. Click OK and follow the on-screen directions to install the driver.

Once you've installed the driver, you can use any of a number of shareware CD audio utilities available on most BBSs and on-line services. (For more about installing multimedia drivers, see Chapter 15.)

TIP 8: What's Missing in 3.1? MS-DOS Executive and Reversi!

Two programs from past versions of Windows failed to make it into Windows 3.1: Executive and Reversi. But both are available from Microsoft in the Windows Driver Library.

Before Windows 3.0, Executive was the Windows interface. A cross between Program Manager and File Manager, it worked much the same as the MS-DOS 5.0 DOS Shell. For quick access to frequently used functions, many Windows power users prefer Executive's all-in-one approach over the Windows environment.

Reversi is Microsoft's implementation of the age-old game of Go. It was superseded in Windows 3.1 with Minesweeper. If you upgraded from Windows 3.0 to Windows 3.1, Reversi will still be on your system, but if you're just starting out with Windows 3.1, Reversi is a game worth seeking out.

TIP 9: Some Secret Windows 3.1 Programs

Microsoft "hides" a few secret programs that are copied to your hard disk when you install Windows but aren't put into any Program Manager groups. These programs can be of tremendous help when you're trying to track down some bug or incompatability.

Dr. Watson: This program (DRWATSON.EXE) can be found in your Windows directory. It will keep an eye on your system. If an application malfunctions, it saves certain information to a file called DRWATSON.LOG. You can send this information to Microsoft in order to facilitate troubleshooting. If your Windows system is manifesting mysterious maladies, add Dr. Watson to your Startup group. When a serious bug occurs, a small Dr. Watson window pops up, asking you to type in a few notes about what you just did. Your notes are combined with data about what was happening inside Windows at the time of the accident. Here's how to add Dr. Watson:

1. Get into Program Manager and select the Startup group.
2. Choose File ➤ New ➤ Program Item and click on OK.
3. In the Command line, type C:\WINDOWS\DRWATSON.EXE. You can leave the other lines blank.
4. Click OK, and Dr. Watson is added to your system.

Try running Dr. Watson if you want, just as you'd run any program. You don't have to restart Windows. Nothing appears to happen, except that Dr. Watson now appears in the Task List and as an icon on the Desktop. If you switch to it via the Task List, you'll see the message "No faults detected." A text window will appear only when Dr. Watson detects an internal problem that adversely affects the stability or integrity of Windows.

SysEdit: The next program that doesn't make it into Program Manager but is referenced throughout this book is the System Configuration Editor, known as SysEdit (SYSEDIT.EXE). SysEdit lives in the \WINDOWS\SYSTEM subdirectory. In case you don't yet know, this is a text editor like Notepad—but with a difference. SysEdit automatically loads the four essential system files: CONFIG.SYS, AUTOEXEC.BAT, WIN.INI, and SYSTEM.INI. These files each have their own window within SysEdit; the windows can be tiled or cascaded (see Figure 20.2) for easy reference when you're trying to find the source of a conflict . Put this one in your Accessories group.

Microsoft Diagnostics: This program (MSD.EXE) reports a wealth of information about your system—its video adapter, CPU, and memory. Diagnostics also reports everything it knows about the way DOS and Windows are operating in the system. This program works best if you run it outside of Windows, so:

1. Exit Windows.

FIGURE 20.2:
The System Configuration Editor (SysEdit)

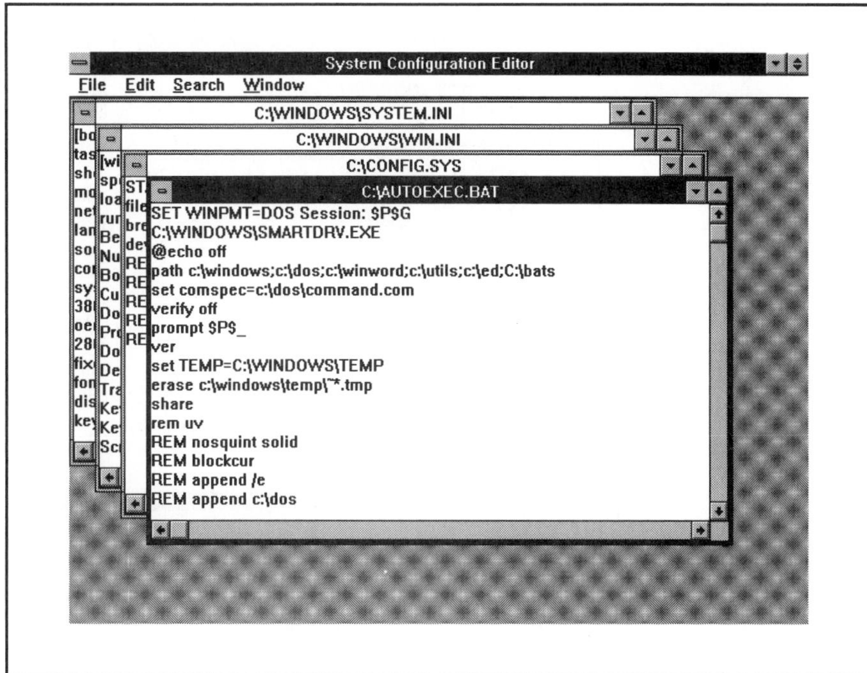

2. Switch to your Windows directory and enter Diagnostics by entering these lines at the C: prompt:

```
cd\windows
msd [Enter]
```

3. Your screen changes to a display similar to that in Figure 20.3.

TIP 10: Three-Key Resets

One of the nicest features of Windows 3.1 is the ability to selectively terminate applications that are misbehaving. When an application begins to act strangely or refuses to respond to input, press Ctrl-Alt-Delete. Instead of rebooting, Windows will pop up a message asking if you want to end the active application. If you press Enter, the application will be shut down. This works equally well with Windows and non-Windows applications.

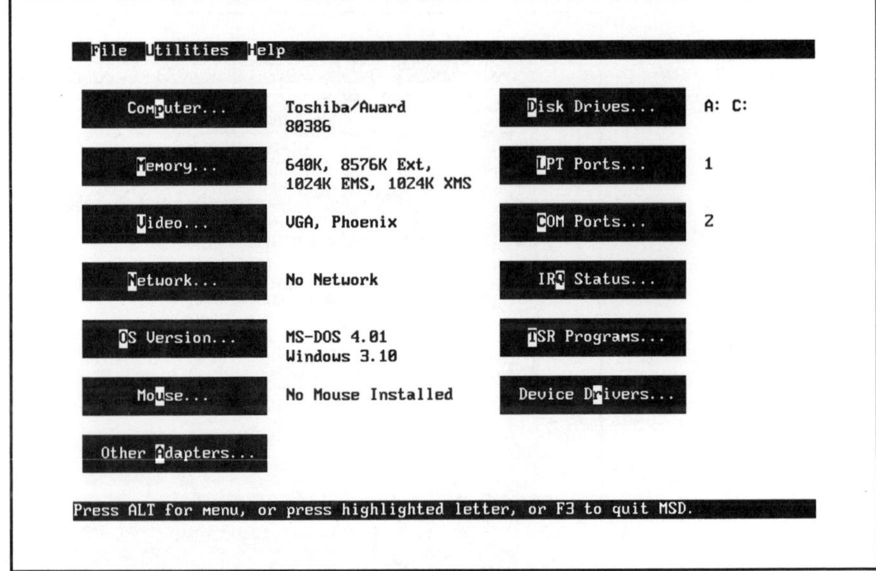

FIGURE 20.3: *Microsoft Diagnostics display*

But before shutting down an application, keep in mind the following:

- This feature only works in Enhanced mode; in Standard mode, the entire system will reboot.
- You cannot terminate an application that is locked up just because it is waiting for network response. Although the application may be unstable, the system itself must be stable.
- You may need to add the following line to the [386Enh] section of your SYSTEM.INI file:

  LocalReboot=ON

TIP 11: Editing .INI Files

Caution: If you edit text-based data files such as WINDOWS.INI and SYSTEM.INI using Windows Write, it is extremely important to choose "No Conversion" when you load the file. Otherwise, the file will be saved in Write's special binary format, making it unusable by Windows.

TIP 12: Getting Help with Your SYSTEM.INI and WIN.INI Files

A number of tips I discuss in this chapter refer to the SYSTEM.INI and WIN.INI files. (You'll also encounter suggestions for working with these files on bulletin boards, and in other books and magazine articles.) These are complex files, teeming with arcane settings and options that Windows uses when it starts up. A great deal of textual information about these files actually comes with Windows, but isn't in the manual—you have to look for it in Write files that Setup puts on your hard disk when you install Windows. Read the files called SYSINI.WRI and WININI.WRI in your \WINDOWS directory for descriptions about every parameter in these files, including their purpose and suggested means of adjusting their values. Open the relevant .WRI file by double-clicking on it in File Manager. It's kind of weighty stuff, but you'll find it interesting if you are a technical type, and it may provide information applicable to your particular system.

TIP 13: Preventing Sharing Violations

Sometimes when you're trying to open a document, or move a file, or delete or otherwise modify a file, you'll receive an error message like one of these:

Or, if you're running a DOS application, you might see the message,

```
Sharing violation reading drive C
Abort, Retry, Fail?
```

Messages like this may appear when you try to access a file that is already in use by another application. For example, say you open a text file with Notepad and begin working on it. Then you might switch to another program and try to open the file again, forgetting that it was already in use by Notepad. That's when you'll see the file sharing violation or other access denial message. In a nutshell, Windows knows when a file is open, and unless the file is marked for sharing between applications (as is the case with most documents and applications designed for sharing between network workstations), an error will pop up whenever an attempt is made to use the file elsewhere.

Most often the solution to this problem is to first determine what other application is currently using the file. Then you need to close that document and try again.

INSTALLATION TIPS

TIP 14: Expanding Individual Files from the Windows Master Disks

Occasionally you will trash one of the Windows system or accessory files on your hard disk and will need to copy it from an original Windows installation disk. Files on the master disks are stored in compressed format and must be expanded (decompressed) before they can be used, so it isn't as easy as you might think to recover one of these files. Here's how to do it.

First you have to figure out which file you need. There are an intimidating number of support files in your Windows directory; however, a little study will save you the hassle of reinstalling Windows from scratch. So consider whether you have lost a screen, mouse, or printer driver—these you can quickly install with Windows Setup. Ditto for most of the accessories, help files, games, screen savers, and wallpaper. This Tip is for when you need to recover something else.

Once you've determined the file you need and located which disk it's on, insert the disk and find the file. (Compressed files typically have an underline or some other character as their last character, as in MOUSE.CO_.)

During Windows installation, a utility called EXPAND.EXE was copied to your Windows directory. You'll now use this to expand the file you want. From the Windows directory, enter a command in the following syntax:

```
EXPAND A:\MOUSE.CO_ MOUSE.COM
```

Note that you've specified the source file and directory first, followed by the destination file name. Since the destination drive and directory aren't specified, EXPAND assumes you want to use the default directory—the one from which you're currently working, which is the Windows drive and directory.

You can't expect Windows to automatically work with driver files you add to the directory in this way. When you install drivers with the Drivers option in Control Panel or through Setup, your SYSTEM.INI and WIN.INI files are updated to reflect changes to your Windows environment. Only when you copy in driver files already familiar to Windows will the procedure work automatically. If you're adding a new driver, you'll have to modify your WIN.INI or SYSTEM.INI files yourself, or use the Setup program.

TIP 15: Is Setup Crashing?

Some users have reported an inability to install Windows 3.1 for the first time. If Setup locks up inexplicably or you can't run it at all, try running it with the SETUP /I command. The /I option forces Setup to skip its detection of incompatible hardware, which is often the source of the lock-up.

If this doesn't work, try SETUP /L. The /L option creates a log of each step that Setup can successfully complete. You can then read the last few lines of the log file to Microsoft Technical Support, and they may be able to quickly figure out the source of your problem.

TIP 16: Avoid Multiple Versions of Windows

If you choose to save an older version of Windows when upgrading to version 3.1, make sure that the directory containing the version you plan to use most often comes first on DOS's directory path. Otherwise, you may find yourself running the wrong version of your applications. In general, it is not a good idea to have more than one version of Windows installed.

TIPS FOR CUSTOMIZING YOUR WINDOWS 3.1 SYSTEM

TIP 17: Customizing the Windows Sign-on Logo

See also the descriptions of the hDC Micro Apps in Chapter 21.

Instead of having the Windows logo come up when you run Windows, how about displaying your own company logo, or a picture of your choice? When you install Windows for a VGA monitor, the Setup program looks for a file called VGALOGO.RLE (assuming you have a VGA monitor) in the WINDOWS\SYSTEM directory, and incorporates it into the video driver. To change the sign-on screen,

1. Find or create your custom picture and save it in 4-bit RLE format (similar to GIF files). Many graphics programs will convert other formats, such as PCX and TIF, to RLE files.
2. Make a backup copy of VGALOGO.RLE in another directory, or under a different name (such as VGALOGO.BAK)—in case you want to go back to the old logo.
3. Now you have to run Setup to get it to properly associate the VGA screen driver and the new logo picture. To run Setup from Windows, double-click the Windows Setup icon in the Main program group, or you can select File ➤ Run in the Program Manager. To run Setup from DOS, do not use the MS-DOS icon. First exit Windows, change to the WINDOWS directory, and then run Setup. (Otherwise, Setup won't find the details of your setup and thinks you want to install Windows from scratch.)
4. Note the current display type, and change it to one of the other VGA choices—something other than the one you're already using—to trick Windows into using the new logo. You may be asked to plug in a disk so Setup can get the driver.

5. After the new driver is installed, don't reboot Windows, since the new screen driver may not work with your screen. Instead, run Setup again and change back to the original display. When asked about using the existing driver, choose to do so. (It'll save you the hassle of plugging in the Windows floppy disk again.)

TIP 18: More on Customizing the Windows Sign-On Logo

For those of you who want to know even more about how Windows puts up its sign-on logo, and how to change it, here's some more detail, and another approach to altering it.

When you install Windows, Setup creates a file called WIN.COM in the Windows directory. WIN.COM is the program that runs when you type WIN to load Windows. This file consists of three smaller files sandwiched together. These files can be found in the Windows System subdirectory.

The first file, WIN.CNF, performs the bulk of the work. It examines your system environment, sets up a few variables, displays the title screen, and launches Windows. The second file may be called VGALOGO.LGO, EGALOGO.LGO, or CGALOGO.LGO, depending on your video adapter. It is a subroutine called by WIN.CNF that displays the image contained in the third file, which is either VGALOGO.RLE, EGALOGO.RLE, or CGALOGO.RLE. This last file is a compressed .BMP file.

To replace the title screen, follow these steps:

1. Create a .BMP file in Paintbrush or any other package that can produce BMP images.
2. Use a utility such as WINGIF (a shareware utility available on most BBSs or on-line services) to convert your .BMP file to RLE-4 format. Save the converted file in the Windows System subdirectory (most likely, C:\WINDOWS\SYSTEM). Give it a name like MYTITLE.RLE.
3. Exit Windows, and create a backup of WIN.COM, which can be found in your Windows directory. Rename it to something like WIN.OLD. (If you run into trouble, you can always copy WIN.OLD back to WIN.COM.)
4. Switch to the System subdirectory.

5. Enter the following command exactly as shown here:

   COPY /B WIN.CNF + VGALOGO.LGO + MYTITLE.RLE C:\WIN-DOWS\WIN.COM

   Note: If you have an EGA video card, you'll need to replace VGALOGO.LGO with EGALOGO.LGO in the foregoing command.

6. Run Windows.

TIP 19: Skip the Windows Sign-on Screen

Tired of looking at the Windows sign-on screen when you start Windows? You don't have to. Just start Windows by typing WIN : and pressing Enter. Adding the colon prevents the sign-on screen from displaying. Be sure to precede the colon with a space.

There has been a lot of talk about how much time you'll save by using this tip. Much has been made of this, and no one has ever said just how much difference it will make, but one is generally left with the impression that it could be measured in hours. After some scientific experimentation, I can assure you that there is no discernible difference between starting Windows with the sign-on screen or starting Windows without it.

TIP 20: Bypass Startup Screen and Launch an Application

You probably just read the foregoing tip about bypassing the startup screen that Windows displays by entering a space and a colon after WIN when you start up the program. Another way to bypass the startup screen is to go right into a specific Windows program. If you typically run only one program, such as WordPerfect or 1-2-3, you might want to try this trick.

As an example, suppose you want to run File Manager just to do some disk housekeeping, and you don't have File Manager in the Startup group. Just run Windows with the application name on the command line, like this:

```
WIN WINFILE.EXE
```

Windows will skip over its title screen and run File Manager. (WINFILE is the File Manager's program name.)

TIP 21: "Dedicating" Windows to One Application

Before Windows 3.0, Microsoft used to distribute a "run-time" version of Windows that allowed users to run only one Windows application. When using this version, you wouldn't have access to other Windows commands and accessories.

You can still achieve the same effect in Windows 3.0 and 3.1. To create a "dedicated" version of Windows, load SYSTEM.INI into a text editor, go to the [Boot] section, and find the following line:

```
SHELL=PROGMAN.EXE
```

(If you are using a Program Manager replacement such as Norton Desktop, the name of the program after shell= may be something other than progman.exe.)

Change progman.exe to the name of the Windows application you want to run exclusively. From now on, when you start Windows, it will run only that application. When you exit the application, you will also exit Windows.

TIPS FOR IMPROVING YOUR DESKTOP

TIP 22: Solid Color Desktop

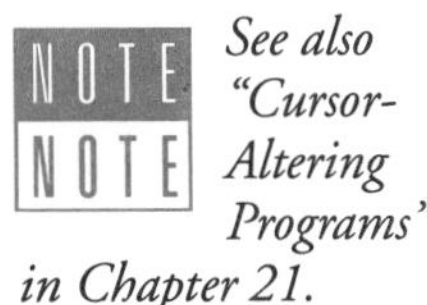

See also "Cursor-Altering Programs" in Chapter 21.

Want to create a solid color for your Desktop? The Control Panel's Desktop utility lets you assign patterns, black, and 50 percent gray, but no other solid colors. Here's how you can do it yourself:

1. Run Paintbrush.
2. Fill the workspace with a solid color using the Paint Roller.
3. Save the file in the normal way (as a .BMP file), putting it in your Windows directory (typically C:\WIN).
4. Select Desktop from the Control Panel and open the File drop-down list box in the Wallpaper section. Choose the file you just created, then set the Tile option on so the color fills the whole screen.

TIP 23: Make Desktop Icon Names More Visible

Certain Desktop patterns prevent you from seeing icon names clearly, particularly on laptops and other grayscale screens. If you can't read the icon names, change the background to a solid color (as explained above in Tip 22).

TIP 24: Prevent Icon Name Overlap

Are the icon names overlapping each other? In Windows 3.0 there was no way around this except to space the icons farther apart from one another or keep the names short. In Windows 3.1, you can elect to have the icon names wrap to a second line. This is the default setting, but if it's turned off, here's how to reactivate name-wrapping:

1. Run Control Panel.
2. Double-click on Desktop.
3. Choose Wrap Title in the Icons section.

TIP 25: Increasing the Width of Borders to Ease Grabbing

The border of a window may seem of little consequence to the vast majority of Windows users. This is not true! If you're like me, you alter the size of a window many times a day. So the size of the window border makes a difference in how easy or hard it is to grab the border for resizing—because once the border is wider, the double-headed arrow mouse pointer that indicates you are in position to resize the window will stay visible longer.

From the Control Panel application, double-click on the Desktop icon. In the lower-left portion of the dialog box you'll see a parameter called Border Width. The default setting is 3. Increase the size of the border to 5 or 6 to make grabbing it easier.

TIP 26: Accelerating Submenus

Have you noticed that cascading menus open and close too slowly? (Cascading menus are the ones that appear when you pull down a menu and choose an option that has a small right-pointing arrow in it, such as Edit ➤ in the Control menu of windowed DOS sessions.)

For you speed demons out there who work frequently with multi-leveled cascading menus, here's a tip that will speed things up. You can add two lines to the [Windows] section of your WIN.INI file, like these:

```
MenuShowDelay=0
MenuHideDelay=0
```

These two parameters determine how quickly cascading menus pop up and how quickly they disappear.

TIP 27: Adding Space between Icons

If your icons are too close together, it may be difficult to quickly select the one you want. You can change the amount of space between icons: Run Control Panel and choose the Desktop icon. Increase the value for Icon Spacing and see if it helps.

TIP 28: Screen Saver with Sound

Several vendors have released screen savers for Windows. These generally provide more modules than the screen savers included with Windows 3.1. Often, they also supply sound support. While your system sits idle, you can be treated to both visual and audible shows.

An interesting feature of Intermission, by ICOM Simulations, is that it includes drivers to run screen-saver modules (the animated picture files) designed for other screen savers, including After Dark and the ones that come with Windows 3.1. Check computer magazines for ads.

TIP 29: Screen Saver in Full-Screen Non-Windows Applications

The Windows built-in screen saver will not operate over a full-screen non-Windows application. If you want the screen saver to function properly, make sure that you switch back to Windows before leaving your computer.

TIPS FOR USING THE MOUSE

TIP 30: Can't See Your Mouse?

If you have trouble seeing your mouse cursor when it moves (this is particularly troublesome for laptop users), go into Control Panel and double-click the Mouse icon. Turn on the Mouse Trails option, as illustrated below. This forces Windows to display the progression of the cursor as it moves across the screen.

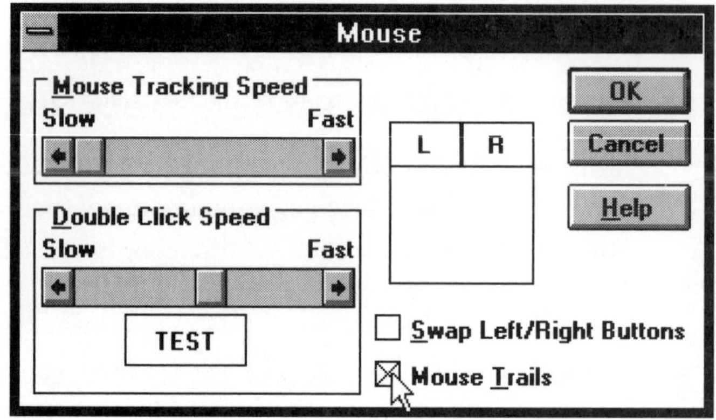

TIP 31: Having Trouble Double-Clicking?

New Windows users often have trouble mastering the art of double-clicking. The secret is to hold the mouse extremely steady when you double-click. If you move the mouse when clicking, Windows assumes either that you're attempting to drag-and-drop, or that you've single-clicked twice.

To make it easier to get the hang of this mouse operation, edit your WIN.INI file and add the following two lines anywhere in the [Windows] section:

```
DoubleClickHeight=10
DoubleClickWidth=10
```

These variables determine how much the mouse can move between clicks and still register a double-click. The default is 4. Once you get more confident of your double-clicking ability, you can remove these lines.

By the way, for more about editing WIN.INI, see Tip 9, which tells you how to use SysEdit for editing system configuration files. Also, read the section "Editing Your CONFIG.SYS and AUTOEXEC.BAT files" in Chapter 16.

TIP 32: Suggestions for Using Drag-and-Drop

Drag-and-drop is an important new feature in Windows 3.1. You simply select an item by moving the mouse cursor to the item, and clicking and holding the left mouse button. Then you drag the object to another location by moving the mouse while you're still holding the left button down.

Here are some reminders and suggestions for using drag-and-drop:

- *Moving or copying files among directories or drives in File Manager.* If you drag-and-drop from one directory to another on the same drive, the file is moved; that is, the file disappears from its old location. If you drag-and-drop from one disk to another, the file is copied and appears in both locations. To copy a file from directory to directory, hold down the Ctrl key while dragging. You'll notice a + sign appears on the mouse pointer. To move a file from drive to drive, hold down the Alt key while dragging.
- *Placing files into Program Manager groups.* Open File Manager and select the file you want to add to an existing group. If necessary, resize or move File Manager so that you can see the target group. Drag the file and drop it into the group; the group can be either open or iconized.
- *Moving icons from group to group in Program Manager.* To move an icon, drag it from one group into another. The destination group can be open or iconized. To copy an icon, hold down the Ctrl key while dragging. You'll notice that a black-and-white duplicate icon appears while you are dragging the icon to a new or duplicate group.
- *Printing or editing a file.* Several Windows accessories, including Print Manager, Write, Notepad, and Paintbrush, as well as applications such as Excel and Word, are "drop targets." Try it: Load and minimize Print Manager. Then drop a file on Print

Manager's icon; this causes the file to be printed. Drop the file on the minimized icon of one of the other applications to simultaneously open the program and load the file that you dropped.

TIP 33: Using a Mouse with Non-Windows Applications

Mouse activities in most non-Windows applications that have mouse support will work as expected when run under Windows 3.1. However, for the mouse to work when you're running the non-Windows application full screen, you must load the mouse driver before running Windows.

To get the mouse to work properly with the non-Windows application when the application is windowed, you *must* be using a mouse driver supplied with Windows 3.1, or one that is compatible with 3.1. Windows 3.1 does its best to automatically update your mouse driver file with a compatible one during installation. For a Microsoft or compatible mouse, a driver file named MOUSE.SYS or MOUSE.COM is supplied with Windows 3.1. One or the other is automatically put into your Windows directory (depending on which file was in your Windows 3.0 installation). There's a file called LMOUSE.COM or LMOUSE.SYS for Logitech mice.

- If you intend to use mouse-compatible non-Windows applications while in Windows, add a line to either your AUTOEXEC.BAT or CONFIG.SYS file (refer to your mouse documentation if you're not sure which) to load your Windows 3.1-compatible mouse driver whenever you boot your system.
- If you don't intend to use a mouse in non-Windows applications, removing any mouse commands from your AUTOEXEC.BAT or CONFIG.SYS file will give your non-Windows applications more room to run in. As mentioned in Chapter 16, since Windows takes care of its own mouse driver now, you can also remove mouse commands from your CONFIG.SYS file (unless you want to use the mouse outside of Windows).

If your mouse doesn't seem to work with a particular non-Windows application, make sure the application does support a mouse. If it does, try running full screen. If a driver is properly installed, try adding the following line to the [NonWindowsApp] section of SYSTEM.INI:

```
MouseInDosBox=1
```

This setting should force Windows to enable the function.

If this doesn't work, you may have to run the mouse driver (the .COM file only, not the .SYS file) within a DOS session prior to running the application. That is, select the MS DOS prompt option from Program Manager, and then issue the appropriate mouse command, either MOUSE <Enter> or LMOUSE, followed by the name of the non-Windows application on the next line. As an alternative, you can create a batch file that loads the mouse driver and then the application. For example, to load a mouse driver and then dBASE, enter (in the DOS session)

```
MOUSE
DBASE
```

Then create an icon to run the batch file.

As a final note to understanding how a mouse works with non-Windows applications, be aware that when running a mouse-capable non-Windows application in a window, certain domains (areas) of the window are interpreted as Windows territory, and others are left to the application. The title bar, scroll bars, and so forth will respond as in any Windows screen. Inside the work area, mouse activities are passed to the application.

PROGRAM MANAGER TIPS

TIP 34: Saving Your Program Manager Settings without Exiting Windows

NOTE *See also "Program Manager and File Manager Replacements" in Chapter 21.*

How many times have you arranged your Program Manager group windows just the way you want them, then had Windows crash before the settings are saved? When you restart Windows, everything is as cluttered as it was before you rearranged things. This happens because Windows saves the arrangement to disk only when you exit Windows and return to DOS. The long way to save your setup in case an application or Windows bombs is to exit Windows and then restart it. (Make sure the Options ➤ Save Settings on Exit command is first set on.) The shortcut to saving without exiting Windows is this:

1. Check the Options menu to see that Save Settings on Exit is turned on.
2. Choose File ➤ Exit Windows (Alt-F4).
3. When the This will end your Windows session message comes up, choose Cancel. The settings are saved before the dialog box comes up. Cancelling then returns you to Windows.

TIP 35: Oops! Don't Save Those Settings!

If you happen to have screwed up the arrangement of your group windows by using a command such as Tile or Cascade when you didn't mean it and don't want to save the revised setup when you exit Windows, be sure to turn off Options ➤ Save Settings on Exit before exiting. When you rerun Windows, the settings will be as they were.

TIP 36: Opening Program Manager's Window at Startup

It can be annoying each time you boot up Windows and open the Program Manager window that it doesn't come up maximized. Here's the easiest way to make sure that the Program Manager window always comes up maximized:

1. Maximize the Program Manager window.
2. Turn on Options ➤ Save Settings on Exit.
3. Exit Windows by double-clicking the Control box or pressing Alt-F4.
4. Rerun Windows.
5. Turn off Options ➤ Save Settings on Exit.

TIP 37: Jump to Program Manager Fast!

The quickest way (except for using a shortcut key) to jump to the Program Manager at any time is to press Ctrl-Esc, then **P**, then Enter. If there is another program running that starts with *P*, press **P** until Program Manager is highlighted in the Task List. (See Tip 52 for how to establish a shortcut key for the Program Manager.)

TIP 38: Protect Group Setups from Unwanted Changes

To safeguard your groups and all their settings, you can set the associated .GRP file for the group to Read Only:

1. Highlight the group icon in Program Manager.
2. Press Alt-Enter. In the dialog box, note the file name used for the group.
3. Move to File Manager and find the file (it's probably in the Windows directory).
4. Highlight the file name and press Alt-Enter or choose File ➤ Properties.
5. Set the Read Only check box on.

This will prevent anyone from changing any aspect of your group's icons, such as their arrangement, properties, and so on. Programs can still be run, but you won't be allowed to delete or add icons, or delete the group from the Program Manager. This is particularly useful if a number of people regularly use your computer. It's quite inconvenient when someone accidentally deletes a group icon, taking with it all your program and document icons.

TIP 39: Quickly Changing a Group Name

Changing the name of a Program Manager group is easy when you know how. Select the group to be renamed by first minimizing it to an icon and then clicking once. You will see a Control menu for that group. Click on any blank area in the Program Manager window to make the menu disappear. The name of the group will still be highlighted. Next, choose Properties from Program Manager's File menu and enter a new name in the Description field. Click on OK to confirm the change.

TIP 40: More Icon Shapes to Choose From

Windows 3.1 includes many icons you may not know about. Each Windows application can contain as many icons as it requires. The two largest repositories of icons are Program Manager (PROGMAN.EXE) and a file called MORICONS.DLL.

You can change any icon in any group window in Program Manager. Open the group window, select the icon you want to change, and choose File ➤ Properties. Click the Change Icon button and enter the name of the file you want to look at (PROGMAN.EXE or MORICONS.DLL). You will see a number of icons in the bar below the file name. Use the scroll arrows to move through the choices. When you see one you like, click on it and then click on OK. Click OK again and you'll see the new icon replace the old one.

TIP 41: Quickly Adding Icons to Groups

An easy way to add applications and data files to Program Manager groups is to use File Manager's drag-and-drop features in conjunction with Program Manager. Open File Manager, and make sure its window does not cover the Program Manager group you want to change. Select the program or file you want to add by positioning the cursor over the file name and pressing the left mouse button. Holding down the mouse button, move the cursor to the spot in the Program Manager group where you'd like the new icon to be. Release the button, and you have an instant icon.

TIP 42: Saving Program Manager Settings without Exiting Windows

Have you ever discovered, after you've carefully set up all the window sizes, locations, icon arrangements, and DOS window font size preferences for your group windows, that the settings mysteriously revert to a previous state the next time you run Windows? Suddenly it dawns on you: You forgot to save the settings by choosing Options ➤ Save Settings on Exit. Next time, you remember to activate the setting and exit properly—but eventually you realize that even then you still need to remember to turn it off, so that next time you move things around and exit Windows, you haven't saved things in the wrong location. This means setting things up, turning on Save Settings, exiting, starting Windows again, and turning off Save Settings. What a hassle! There is a better way:

1. Turn off the Save Settings on Exit option.
2. Arrange everything the way you want it—window locations, sizes, icon arrangments, and so forth.
3. Hold down the Shift key.
4. From Program Manager, choose File ➤ Exit Windows. There will be some hard disk activity in a second or two, but Windows won't terminate. You've successfully saved your settings without leaving Windows.

The next time you make some Program Manager changes you want to save, just repeat steps 3 and 4. (Incidentally, the same technique works for File Manager.)

TIP 43: Easily Copying Icons

You might know that it's easy to move a program icon from one group window to another by dragging the icon from the old group to the new one. But did you know that you can also copy the icon, by holding down the Ctrl key while dragging?

TIP 44: Tiling Your Windows

Often, you may find that you have more Windows applications running than you want to keep track of. A handy way to create a "dashboard" of Windows programs is to tile them. Press Ctrl-Esc to bring up the Task List, and press the Tile button. Each application will take up a small amount of screen space, and each will be in full view.

TIP 45: Automatically Minimize Your StartUp Applications

Applications in the StartUp group can be set to run minimized automatically. Open the StartUp group and select the program you want to set up. Choose File ➤ Properties from the Program Manager menu bar. Click on the box marked Run Minimized to mark it with an *X*, and then click on OK. From now on, Windows will start that program up as an icon.

TIP 46: Automatically Load Frequently Used Documents

Program Manager lets you add icons for data files as well as applications. For example, if you frequently work on a Write file called MYBOOK.WRI, you can create an icon that will launch Write and load MYBOOK.WRI into it automatically.

1. Choose File ➤ New from Program Manager.
2. In the New area of the dialog box, select Program Item and click on OK.
3. In the Command line text box, enter the name of the data file you want to load along with the application. Be sure to begin the file name with the full path, including the directory name.
4. Click OK, and Program Manager will create the appropriate icon for Write, with the name of the document below it.

Note: This will only work if the file has an extension that has been associated with an application. To make associations, you select File ➤ Associate from within File Manager (see Chapter 4 for details).

TIP 47: Any Group Can Be Your Startup Group

A little-known fact about Program Manager is that any group can be your startup group; it doesn't have to be Startup. If you already have a group of applications set up that would make a perfect startup group, don't duplicate it, but rather do this:

1. Load PROGMAN.INI into a text editor, such as Notepad.
2. Add a line like the following line to the [Settings] section:

   ```
   Startup="Applications"
   ```

   Of course, you should replace "Applications" with the name of your desired startup group. You must put the name between quotation marks, and make sure that this is the same name that appears beneath the group's icon or on its menu bar.
3. Save the file. Next time you run Windows, the new group's applications will open as your startup group.

TIP 48: Mouseless Application Minimizer

As you know, holding down the Shift key while double-clicking a program icon causes the application to launch and immediately be minimized to an icon. But did you know that this works even if you don't have a mouse? Just select the program you want to run, and hold the Shift key down when you press Enter.

TIPS FOR RUNNING WINDOWS APPLICATIONS

TIP 49: Use Shortcut Keys

Don't overlook using shortcut keys to launch and jump to applications or to open documents quickly. For example, I can press Ctrl-Shift-T to open the TIPS.TXT Notepad file in which I collected these tips. *Note that the first time you use a shortcut key to run a program you have to do it with the Program Manager window active.* Once the application is running, its shortcut key works from anywhere, even within another program. I always have File Manager running with Alt-Ctrl-F as its key. Whenever I want to move or copy a file, it's there waiting.

TIP 50: Quickly Creating Shortcut Keys

To quickly set up a shortcut key for a program or document:

1. Highlight the program's icon in the Program Manager.
2. Press Alt-Enter. This opens the Program Item Properties dialog box.
3. Enter the shortcut key as detailed in Chapter 13. You can use numbers, function keys, and punctuation marks in your shortcut key combinations.

If you assign a shortcut key to an icon while the application is already running, you'll find that the shortcut key doesn't work. You have to close the application and then rerun it before the key takes effect. Even if you follow the advice in the tip above, a shortcut key may not work within certain applications. This can be caused by a conflict between the application and Program

Manager. Work around this by creating a shortcut key for Program Manager as explained in the tip below. Switch to Program Manager, then do the shortcut key.

You can't use the same shortcut key for two different applications. If you try to assign a key combination that's already in use, the Program Manager will alert you to this fact, informing you of the application that's already using that combination—a thoughtful feature.

TIP 51: Remembering Shortcut Keys

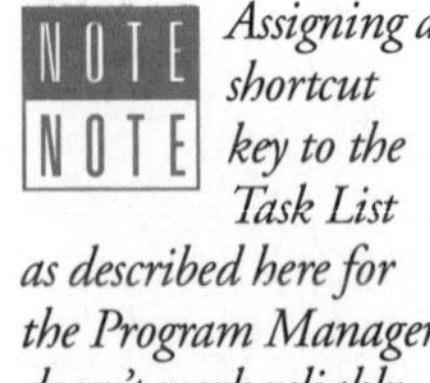
Assigning a shortcut key to the Task List as described here for the Program Manager doesn't work reliably. Use Ctrl-Esc instead.

How do you remember the shortcut keys for all your programs? Easy. Make a small list and store it next to your keyboard, or make a Notepad document called CODES. Create an icon for it and assign it Ctrl-Alt-C (for *codes* or Ctrl-Alt-K for *keys*, or something similar that you'll remember). Put the document icon in your StartUp group. When you forget your shortcut code for a program, just press Alt-Ctrl-C and up they'll come.

TIP 52: Assigning a Shortcut Key to Program Manager

The fastest way in the West (or East, North, or South for that matter) for getting to Program Manager: Assign a shortcut key combination. Yes, you can set up a shortcut key for Program Manager even though it isn't an application that you normally have an icon for in any of the Program Manager groups. Here's how:

1. Using File ➤ New, add a new program item to a group. I added mine to StartUp, so this shortcut key is activated as soon as Windows runs.
2. Name it whatever you want. I called mine *Program Manager.*
3. For the program name, enter **\WINDOWS\PROGMAN.EXE**.
4. Assign a shortcut key. I use Alt-Ctrl-P since it's easy to remember.

Now when you want to get to the Program Manager, just press Alt-Ctrl-P from anywhere. Don't worry about having an additional PROGMAN file running on top of the one that loads when you boot Windows. Only one instance (as a running version of a program is called) of PROGMAN can run at a time. All that gets loaded by having the icon in the StartUp group is its shortcut key setting.

TIP 53: PIF vs. Properties Shortcut Keys

The Properties dialog box and PIFs both allow the assigning of shortcut keys. The setting in the Properties box takes precedence in the cases of a conflict between shortcut key assignments for an application.

TIP 54: Run and Iconize a Program in One Swell Foop

Here's a little speed tip I'll bet you didn't know. If you press Shift while double-clicking an icon in the Program Manager or File Manager, the program or document will run and be immediately iconized. This is useful if you want to load several programs or files quickly, without having to wait for them to come up full-screen and clutter your Desktop.

TIP 55: Quickly Jump to a Program Icon

Can't find a program or document icon in a group window because there are too many to show at once? You could scroll the window using the scroll bars, but that's tedious. Just press the first letter of the icon you want and it will pop into view. If there are two or more with the same first letter, press again until the one you want appears.

TIP 56: Quickly Tidy Up Group Windows

Can't find a particular group window because of clutter in the Program Manager? Quickly arrange all open Program Manager group windows by pressing Shift-F5 (to tile) or Shift-F4 (to cascade). All open windows will reorganize.

TIP 57: Fast Maximize or Restore

Double-clicking on an application's title bar alternately maximizes and restores the window to its previous size. You don't have to aim for the Maximize or Restore buttons anymore.

TIP 58: Alt-Tab Backwards through Running Applications

Switch *backwards* between applications with Alt-Shift-Tab. If you're running lots of applications at once, Alt-Tab is a quick way to switch between them. However, it's really easy to Alt-Tab your way right past the application you want to stop on. Then you have to go around the whole circle of application names again to get the one you want, and hope you stop in the right place. It's a bit like trying to set the time on a digital clock without overshooting. Try pressing Alt-Shift-Tab the next time you've "gone too far." Each press backs you up one application.

RUNNING WINDOWS APPLICATIONS

TIP 59: Auto-Starting Documents

Applications aren't the only things that you can include in a Program Manager group. If you have a word processing document or spreadsheet you access frequently, you can add it to a group, too. The file must be associated with an application. Select File ➤ New ➤ Program Item, and then click on OK. In the Command Line field, enter the name of the data file and click on OK. Program Manager will take care of the icon and description for you (and you can change them if you want, in the Program Item Properties dialog box).

TIP 60: Loading a Program Minimized

Sometimes it's helpful to have a program loaded and ready to run—even if you're not ready for it yet. Rather than running and then minimizing an application, try holding the Shift key down when you double-click on the program's icon. The program will appear as an icon at the bottom of the screen, ready to click when you're ready.

TIP 61: Preventing the StartUp Group from Executing

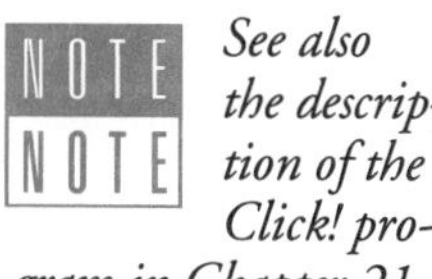

See also the description of the Click! program in Chapter 21.

Having all the programs in the Startup group run whenever you start Windows can sometimes be a real annoyance. I have about ten programs in my Startup group, but sometimes I just want to start Windows and quickly print a letter or look up an address—without starting up all those programs. Luckily, you can suppress the automatic execution of the Startup group's programs. After you type WIN and press Enter, just press and hold the Shift key while Windows starts up.

TIP 62: Auto-Starting the Programs in a Group Other Than StartUp

If you are new at making changes to your SYSTEM.INI file, make a backup copy of it first before editing it. If you make a mistake and Windows refuses to run as expected, copy the backup file into the Windows directory.

As you know, any programs included in your Startup group run automatically when you start Windows. But what if you want another group—say one called Writing Tools—to start up automatically instead? You can set this up by editing the PROGMAN.INI file in your Windows directory. Locate the [Settings] section of the PROGMAN.INI file, and a line similar to the following:

```
Startup="Writing Tools"
```

When you start Windows, all the programs in the Writing Tools group will load and run, instead of the Startup group.

TIP 63: Assigning Another Program to the Desktop Double-Click

See also the description of the Straight-Line program in Chapter 21.

As you know, double-clicking on the desktop (or pressing Ctrl-Esc) brings up the Task List. When you do either of these things, a setting stored in your SYSTEM.INI file contains a pointer that tells Windows what program to run. Normally that pointer sends Windows off to execute a program called TASKMAN.EXE. You can change this pointer by editing your SYSTEM.INI file, so that double-clicking on the desktop or pressing Ctrl-Esc brings up a program of your choice. (I almost never use Task List myself, relying on Alt-Tab to switch between applications.)

Suppose you use Sysedit a lot, and want to have it pop up instead of Task List. Here's how you do it:

1. Open your SYSTEM.INI file with Sysedit or Notepad.
2. Look for these lines

   ```
   [boot]
   taskman.exe=taskman.exe
   ```

   near the top of the file, and change the second line to

   ```
   taskman.exe=sysedit.exe
   ```

   If there is no taskman.exe= line in your file, add one. Put it right under the [boot] label.
3. Save the edited SYSTEM.INI file, exit Windows, and restart it. Now when you double-click the desktop or press Ctrl-Esc, you'll see the Sysedit program instead of Task List.

If you want to trigger another program instead, such as Control Panel, just figure out the file name of the application you want, and type it after the tasksman.exe= line in SYSTEM.INI. In the case of Control Panel, it's CONTROL.EXE. Other possible choices for you might be a task-switching utility program such as Salvation (reviewed in this special section), a game, or a Windows accessory such as Notepad.

TIP 64: Powerpoint Printing Problems

If you use Powerpoint and find that your output to a laser printer looks horrible, that's because Powerpoint keeps its own printer information. Even though you've set up Windows to use your laser printer at 300 dpi (dots per inch), Powerpoint will use a default setting of 70 dpi. You must set it to 300 dpi, and then it will use this as a default the next time you start the program.

TIP 65: The Word for Windows "Do It Again" Key

The Word for Windows pull-down menus and icon bar are great, but if you need to repeat what you have just done, it is a chore to click the commands over and over. Happily, there is a quick solution: the F4 key, Repeat Command. It lets you bypass the extra keystrokes for almost any editing and formatting actions. With F4 you can repeatedly cut, copy, or paste anything in the Clipboard, apply a style without having to scroll through the list of available styles, and execute macros repeatedly without having to assign them shortcut keys.

TIP 66: Word for Windows—Quick Block Moves

Here's a great feature in Word for Windows 1.1 you might not know about. (If you're using version 2.0, don't bother reading this.) Moving a block of text doesn't require the usual three steps of marking it, cutting it, and pasting it. Instead, just do this:

1. Select the text any way you want.
2. Position the mouse over the target destination.
3. Click the *right* mouse button. Voilà! The text is moved.

TIP 67: The Word for Windows Dictionary

If you have changed from Word for DOS to Word for Windows, you don't have to abandon the DOS version's user dictionary to which you have painstakingly added your own words. Here's how to make it usable for Word for Windows:

1. Copy the old Word user dictionary (UPDAT-AM.CMP) to the directory where Word for Windows is stored (usually \WINWORD).
2. Delete (or rename) STDUSER.DIC.
3. Rename UPDAT-AM.CMP to STDUSER.DIC.

If your old dictionary contains foreign characters, use the following procedure to translate them properly for use with Word for Windows:

1. Start Word for Windows and open the file UPDAT-AM.CMP (or STDUSER.DOC if you've renamed it already) via the File ➤ Open command.
2. If asked, choose to open the file as text. This converts the foreign characters from ASCII characters to ANSI characters.

3. Save the file as STDUSER.DIC. Select the plain text option, and save the file in the directory containing the Word for Windows user dictionary.

TIP 68: Changing Some Word for Windows Defaults

When you start Word for Windows, it reads your WIN.INI file and looks for a section called [Microsoft Word]. There it finds settings pertaining to your copy of Word for Windows. Most of these settings have to do with the conversion DLLs (Dynamic Link Libraries) you may have opted to install when you set up Word for Windows from the master disks. However, you can add the following lines in this section of the file to control some of Word for Windows's defaults—notably ones that pertain to where the program looks for files.

[Microsoft Word]

DOT-PATH=*pathname*	To indicate the location of document templates
INI-PATH=*pathname*	To indicate the location of WINWORD.INI
UTIL-PATH=*pathname*	To indicate the location of Spelling, Hyphenation, Thesaurus, and Help files
BAK-EXTENSION=*extension*	To change the default file name extension for Word for Windows backup documents
DOC-EXTENSION=*extension*	To change the default file name extension for Word for Windows documents
DOT-EXTENSION=*extension*	To change the default file name extension for Word for Windows document templates

For example:

```
[Microsoft Word]
DOC-EXTENSION=W4W
DOT-PATH=C:\WINWORD\TEMPLATE
```

or whatever you want the extension to be.

TIP 69: Changing Word for Windows 1.1's File ➤ Open Extension Default

When you are saving documents, you can easily save them with almost any extension. But to retrieve them later is a pain, because when you choose File ➤ Open, the dialog box always defaults to the *.DOC files—which in many cases are not what you want. I typically want to see all the files in the directory, so I have to type *.* into the File Name text box and press Enter to get a relisting of available files.

You can change this default if you want, right from Word for Windows. For instance, if you want to have *.* (all files) displayed as the default when you go to open a file, do this:

1. Start Word for Windows.
2. Choose Macro ➤ Edit.
3. When the Macro Edit dialog box appears, look for the FileOpen macro. (Make sure that the Show All option is set on, or you won't see this macro.)
4. Double-click the FileOpen macro, which will bring up the macro editor. The FileOpen macro will look like this:

```
Sub MAIN
Dim dlg As FileOpen
GetCurValues dlg
Dialog dlg
Super FileOpen dlg
End Sub
```

5. To change the macro to get it to display all the files (*.*), add these new lines to the code:

```
Sub MAIN
On Error Goto ENDER
Dim dlg As FileOpen
GetCurValues dlg
  dlg.NAME = "*.*"
Dialog dlg
Super FileOpen dlg
ENDER:
End Sub
```

6. Close the file, and answer Yes to the prompt about saving it.

7. Exit Word for Windows. A message box appears, asking if you want to save global changes to the glossary and commands. Answer Yes.

8. When you reenter Word for Windows and choose File ➤ Open, you will see your changes in effect.

The On Error Goto ENDER line you added will eliminate the annoying "WORDBasic err=102" or "WORDBasic Err=114" error box that appears when you cancel the File Open dialog box without choosing a file.

TIP 70: Word for Windows—Returning to Normal Typestyle

When you use any of the Ctrl-key combinations in Word for Windows to apply boldface, italic, underline, and other formatting attributes, there are three quick ways to terminate the special format and return your typestyle to the normal font. Try them:

- Press Ctrl-Spacebar.
- At the end of the formatted text you've just entered, press the Right Arrow key. This moves the cursor out of the area (or mode) you have defined with the special attribute, and into normal formatting again. (In Word for Windows 2.0, this also moves you to the next line.) You may find this the easiest method.
- Toggle the particular format off by entering its shortcut key again (for instance, press Ctrl-B again to terminate boldface formatting).

TIP 71: Cutting Down on Print Time with Some Windows Applications

Some applications are not smart enough to figure out that, when you are printing multiple copies of a document using downloadable soft fonts, you really only need to send down one copy of the fonts and print the multiple copies with the same set of fonts.

These applications (among them Word for Windows) send down the soft fonts before each copy of the document, wasting valuable print time. There is a way around this problem: Use the Copies box in the Printer Setup dialog box, which is usually available via File ➤ Printer Setup. If not, it can be reached through the Printer icon in the Control Panel.

> **NOTE** *If you are using resident fonts—fonts permanantly stored in the printer or on an installed cartridge—this tip isn't applicable, because downloading of the fonts doesn't occur. For example, if you are printing a document formatted in one of the fonts already in your PostScript printer (or your PostScript printer setup substitutes PostScript fonts for TrueType fonts), Windows doesn't have to download soft fonts.*

If you are printing multiple copies of large documents, this trick will not make much difference. If you are printing multiple copies of smaller documents, however, you'll save a good amount of time, because the ratio of font download time to print time is that much greater. Here's what to do:

1. Within the application from which you're printing, choose File ➤ Printer Setup.
2. If there isn't a Copies box on the resulting dialog box, there's probably a Setup button. Click on that to bring up a more detailed box.
3. Print your document (in some rare cases you may also have to enter the number of copies you want into this dialog box).
4. Follow steps 1 and 2 again to reset the Copies number back to 1 for future print jobs, or you'll have to watch unwanted extra copies roll out the next time you print.

If you're in doubt about whether fonts are being downloaded with each print job, try the following experiment:

1. Run Print Manager, and adjust your windows so you can see both Print Manager and the application from which you're printing.
2. Follow the steps of the foregoing procedure, and print two copies of a file.

3. Notice the file sizes as reported in Print Manager and see whether the second file is smaller than the first. If it is, soft fonts are being downloaded, and you should use the procedure in this tip in the future. If the two files are the same size, just go ahead and print as you normally do, using only the regular Copies box in the File ➤ Print dialog box.

TIP 72: Word for Windows Missing Fonts

Have you installed new fonts only to find that Word for Windows doesn't seem to make them available even though other programs do? Here's the scoop. Word for Windows looks to your printer driver for information about what fonts are in your system. But it only does this when it has some reason to believe the fonts have changed, not every time you run Word. You have to initiate some communication between Word and your printer driver before Word gets the message that fonts have changed:

1. From Word for Windows, choose File ➤ Printer Setup.
2. Make sure the correct printer is selected.
3. Click on Setup to get the Setup dialog box.
4. In the Setup dialog box, click OK.
5. Click OK again to return to Word for Windows. The list of currently installed system fonts will be updated internally by Word for Windows.
6. Check your font list now via the Format ➤ Character dialog box. It should include your newly installed fonts.

TIP 73: Ami Pro—Better ASCII Files

If you want to make an ASCII file from an Ami Professional formatted document, for exporting to a desktop or other system, you may obtain better results by not using Ami's ASCII file filter or the Windows TTY file-print driver. Both methods may retain margins, centering, and indents that you may not want in your conversion; also, you may get extra spaces that you will then have to remove. Try this instead:

1. Choose File ➤ Save. (If you have already saved the file to disk, use the File ➤ Save As command.)

2. Type in the name of the file. Check the ASCII format check box, or select ASCII in the File Type drop-down list.
3. Invoke the ASCII Option menu. Leave CR/LF at Lines (the default) selected. This creates an ASCII file with each line ending in a carriage return/line feed and a blank line between each paragraph. Also, formatting will be stripped out.

TIP 74: Ami Pro—Newsletter Layouts

Ami Pro will not let you put more than one page layout on a page. This can pose a problem if you want to create a newsletter with a single swath of text at the top of the page for headlines or opening text, and multicolumn text below. But you can work around this by using Ami's "frame" feature. Create your newsletter document with a multicolumn layout, then place a frame at the top of the page and make it as wide as the page. You are now free to put text or graphics into this frame. The frame will push down any text in the columns below, making room for whatever you put in the frame.

TIP 75: Volkswriter

If you're running Volkswriter 4, you'll notice that the bottom status line turns yellow when it runs in a window. That's because Windows doesn't do a great job of translating the colors when going into graphics mode. To solve this, run the VW4 setup program (it's a file called SETUP in the VW4 directory). Tell VW4 that you have a color monitor, and then change the status line background color from brown to red. The best way to see the results is to run the setup program in a window.

TIP 76: Excel—Two Views of the Same Data

Here's how to view formulas and values for the same worksheet at the same time:

1. Open a second window into your worksheet by issuing the Window ➤ New Window command.
2. Then use the appropriate Window ➤ Arrange command to tile both Windows on the screen at the same time. The first window will show the values.

3. To show the formulas in the other window, first activate the window. Select Options ➤ Display. Click in the Formulas check box and then on OK.

Excel will automatically double the width of all columns and display all formulas. Because both windows are displaying the same worksheet, a formula change in one window will immediately cause the values to be updated in the other window.

TIP 77: PageMaker—Closing Dialog Boxes Fast

There are many dialog boxes in PageMaker 4.0 that are opened and closed from other dialog boxes. You will often have a whole string of "nested" dialog boxes up on screen in the process of getting to the one setting you have to change. Then you have to close all the dialog boxes by clicking on OK in each box. Take heart—there's a faster way. To close all open dialog boxes at once, hold down the Alt key as you click OK or Cancel. This shortcut is equal to clicking on either the OK or Cancel button in every open dialog box.

TIP 78: Changing Notepad's File ➤ Open Default to *.*

This tip originally appeared in the September 1991 issue of *The GUI Gazette*, the monthly newsletter of the Windows on the Rockies Users Group (WRUG). I've modified it for use with Notepad version 3.1.

Use this trick carefully; it's sneaky and could be dangerous to your Notepad program.

Notepad is a handy ASCII text editor, but whenever you choose File➤ Open, the file box shows the default extension to be .TXT. If you frequently edit files of different types with Notepad, such as .BAT files, this is a nuisance. You have to type in *.BAT and hit Enter before you see the files you want. Or you have to type in the name of a specific file, complete with path.

Luckily there's an easy way to edit your Notepad .EXE file to change this default. What's really surprising is that you can edit it using Write. Here's what to do. (*Note:* This is for version 3.1 of Notepad, not version 3.0.)

1. Operate within a copy of Notepad, rather than in the original. To do this, use File Manager to make a copy of the NOTEPAD.EXE file in the Windows directory. Name the copy NOTEPAD2.EXE.

2. Run Write from Program Manager, and choose File ➤ Open.
3. Type in the name of the Notepad copy, **NOTEPAD2.EXE**, and press Enter.
4. Next you'll see a dialog box asking the question, "Convert Text to Write format?" You don't want to change the contents of the NOTEPAD.EXE file to Write's format, so click once on the No Conversion button. A lot of strange characters will then appear on the screen. (What you're looking at are the innards of a compiled Windows program.)
5. Choose Find ➤ Replace and type ***.TXT** in the Find What text box. Enter *.* followed by two spaces in the Replace With text box. These two spaces MUST follow the second asterisk in order to replace all characters of the .TXT entry that was there previously. This is very important! Any changes made in the .EXE code must be replaced with a string of the exact same size.
6. Click on Find Next or press Alt-F. This finds the first occurrence of *.TXT—DON'T REPLACE THIS ONE!
7. Again, click on Find Next or press Alt-F. This jumps you to the second occurrence of *.TXT, as shown in Figure 20.4.
8. Click on Replace. This replaces *.TXT with *.* (and two spaces). Click Close to close the Replace dialog box.
9. Choose File ➤ Save. *Do not* use the Save As command, because this will change the size of the file and impair execution of Notepad. Then Close Write.
10. Run NOTEPAD2 and choose File ➤ Open. The new default file extension listed in the Filename text box is now *.*, and all of the files in the current subdirectory appear in the Files list box.

If the foregoing procedure didn't work, erase the NOTEPAD2.EXE file, make another copy of the original Notepad .EXE file, and try it again. This time, be careful not to change anything except the *second* occurrence of *.TXT, revising it to *.* followed by two spaces.

FIGURE 20.4:

Making changes to NOTEPAD2.EXE

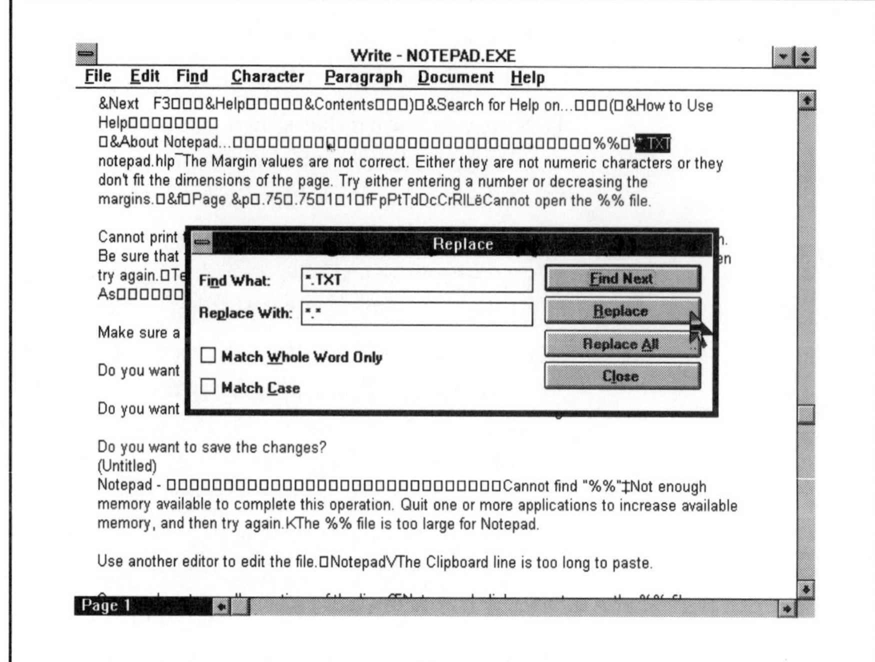

TIPS FOR RUNNING DOS SESSIONS AND NON-WINDOWS APPLICATIONS

TIP 79: Shortcut to a DOS Session

Do you use DOS a lot? Give it a shortcut key. I've added a DOS Prompt icon to my StartUp group. (I copied it from the Main group.) Then I gave it a shortcut key of Alt-Ctrl-D. When I boot up Windows, a DOS session is automatically loaded and waiting. I just press Alt-Ctrl-D to jump to the prompt.

TIP 80: Changing the Font Size for DOS Windows

Want to change the font size in a running DOS window? As of version 3.1, you can (only in 386-Enhanced mode, of course). With DOS running in a window, open the Control box. Choose Settings ➤ Font, then choose one of the font sizes. Note, however, that you won't have the Fonts option if your screen driver does not support this feature.

TIP 81: Force DOS to Always Come Up Windowed

Why does DOS always come up full-screen? Because there isn't a PIF for the DOS prompt. When Windows can't find a PIF for a DOS program (and the DOS prompt *is* a DOS program, called COMMAND.COM), it uses default PIF settings stored in a file called _DEFAULT.PIF. This PIF has the screen size set to full-screen. If you want DOS to come up in a window when you run it, follow these steps. They'll create an icon called DOS Window and a PIF for it. Then running the DOS Window icon (or running COMMAND.COM from the File menu in File Manager or Program Manager) will result in a windowed session of DOS. This tip works only in 386-Enhanced mode:

1. Run the PIF Editor and fill in the PIF as you see in Figure 20.5. In the Program Filename line, enter **C:\COMMAND.COM** (use another path if COMMAND.COM is located in a different directory or on another drive).

FIGURE 20.5:

Use these settings to make DOS always come up in a window.

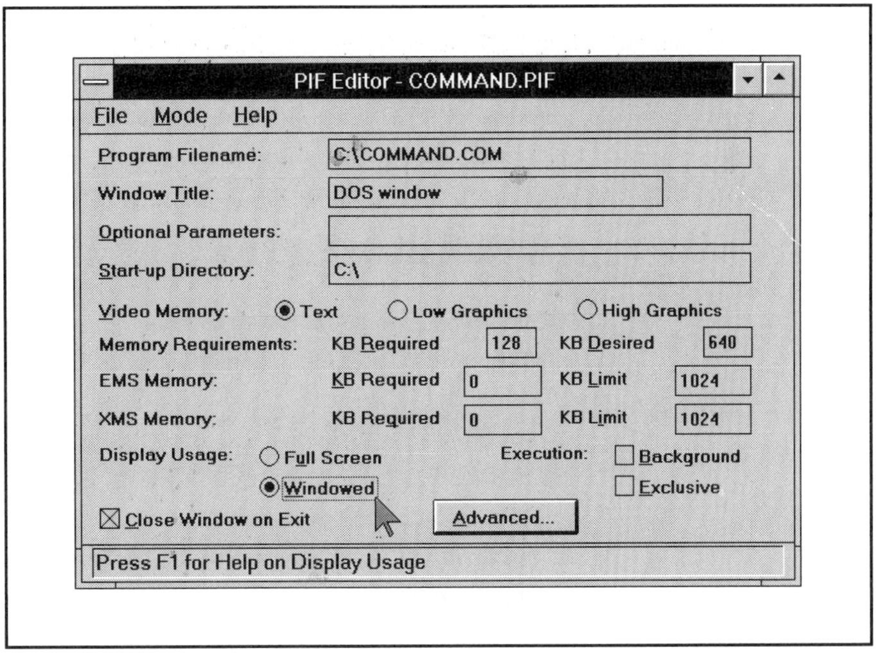

2. Save the PIF with File ➤ Save As and name it \WINDOWS\COMMAND.PIF.
3. Add a program icon to your Main group called **DOS Window** (or another name if you prefer), whose properties are as shown below:

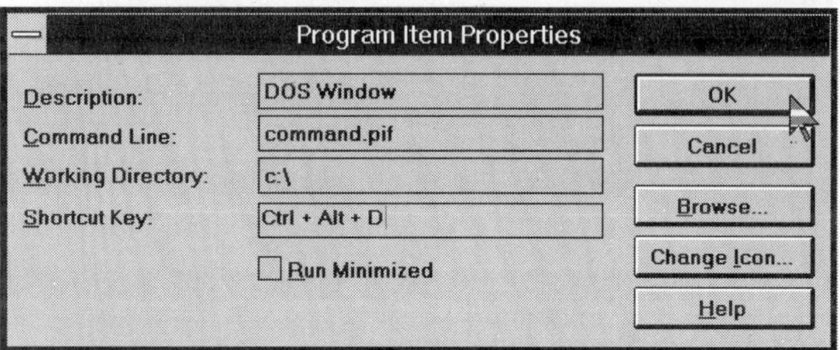

Notice that I've given it a shortcut key of Ctrl-Alt-D (the D is for DOS), but you might want to assign another key combination or none at all.

4. Change the icon if you want to, or just click OK and it'll be given the standard DOS Prompt icon.

Now you'll have two DOS Prompt icons in the Main group: one for full-screen and one for a windowed version of DOS. Note that this technique of creating a PIF with a windowed setting will work for any DOS program you want to be windowed automatically, rather than full-screen, when run.

TIP 82: Window Your Non-Windows Applications Automatically

Do you wish there was a way to make all your iconized non-Windows applications come up in windows when you run them? As explained in Tip 81, Windows handles non-Windows applications on the basis of the settings in a file called _DEFAULT.PIF. (This only works for applications that don't have .PIF files.) So if a non-Windows application for which you've created a Program Manager icon doesn't have a PIF, use the Tip 81 instructions to force it into a window at startup, whether run from File Manager or from Program Manager.

On the other hand, if either you or Windows Setup has already created a PIF for an application and you turn on Windowed for the PIF Editor's Display Usage option, the .PIF file rather than the application will come up in a window. (Windows Setup knows about a large number of applications and the PIF settings that work with them.) To fix this, look in the Program Item Properties box for the icon in question (highlight it and press Alt-Enter) to see if a PIF is part of the command line. Then use File Manager to look for a .PIF file with the same first name as the program. Edit the PIF as explained in Tip 81 to turn on a windowed display.

TIP 83: Running Non-Windows Graphics Programs in a Window

Sometimes you'll see the following message when you try to run a non-Windows graphics program in a window:

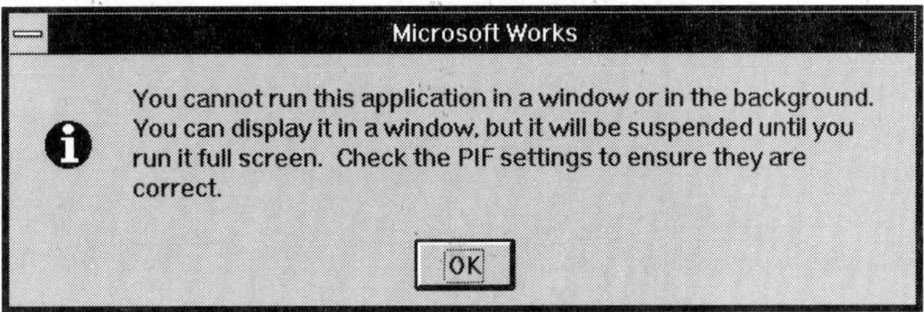

With some displays (notably those with proprietary drivers) you can't run a non-Windows program in a window if it uses high-resolution graphics. It can only be run in a window if it uses "text mode." The example above resulted from running Microsoft Works (for DOS) in graphics mode on a 1024×768 WYSE 7500 display monitor, then trying to window it with Alt-Enter. Similar results would occur with any other DOS-based graphics mode program such as Microsoft Word for DOS in graphics mode, Flight Simulator, or DOS versions of Lotus 1-2-3 when displaying a graph. If you really want to run it in a window, refer to the program's manual to find out how to switch it to text mode. Otherwise only run it full-screen. For example, in the case of Works, you choose Options ➤ Works Settings ➤ Text. Then it will run in a window.

TIP 84: Remember to Close DOS Windows

When you're finished running a non-Windows application or a DOS session within Windows, and you no longer need to have the window available, you should close the window. This frees up precious memory, as well as makes more CPU time available for other activities.

Once your DOS session is finished, type **EXIT** and press Enter to close the session and return to Windows.

TIP 85: Using Alt-Spacebar with Non-Windows Applications

Normally, pressing Alt-Spacebar causes a full-screen non-Windows application to be windowed, and then opens the window's Control Menu. Some applications, however, such as Microsoft Word (for DOS), use Alt-Spacebar for other purposes, and you won't want the window-with-Control-Panel arrangement to override the application's assigned operation. To get back to full-screen operation after such an occurrence, press Alt-Enter; or you can do the following:

1. Choose Settings from the Control Menu.
2. Choose Full-Screen from the Display Options section in the dialog box.
3. Press Enter or click on OK.

Then, to prevent Windows from conflicting with the desired Alt-Spacebar action, reserve the key-combination your program uses in its PIF. Refer to Chapter 13 for information about reserving keys with PIFs.

TIP 86: Allowing Various Ways of Starting Up a Non-Windows Application

Do you have a non-Windows application that you need to run in various ways from time to time? For example, you may want to set up an icon that runs the program and passes it a specific parameter pertinent to the application, such as how much extended or expanded memory it will have, or what template to use (as in WordPerfect), or whether it will run in graphics or character mode (as in Word), or what drivers to load (as in Lotus 1-2-3).

Another icon might be used to run the application and automatically open a particular data file. With a third icon, you might run the application and execute a macro. The capabilities of the application will, of course, vary, but in any case you can achieve these and similar effects by creating a different .PIF file for each icon, as follows:

NOTE *Windows may already have a PIF for your non-Windows application. All PIFs for programs Windows knows about are stored in the APPS.INF file in the WINDOWS\SYSTEM subdirectory.*

1. Using the PIF Editor, create a .PIF file for your basic working version of the progam, and save it (see Chapter 13 for details).
2. Now modify the PIF for each variation of the program you want to run. Typically, you'll need to change the Window Title, Optional Parameters, Startup Directory, memory requirements, and whether the program is run full screen or windowed. If you want the PIF to prompt you for a parameter upon starting up the application, enter a question mark as the first character in the Optional Parameters line.
3. As you finish each setup for the application, save the .PIF file under a new name for that setup. For example, you might create files called WORD-1.PIF, WORD-2.PIF, and WORD-3.PIF to run three different arrangements of Microsoft Word for DOS.
4. Once the PIFs are saved to disk, create Program Manager program icons for running them. Or, if you want, you can execute the PIFs via the Run command in File Manager or Program Manager. Just remember to type the full name of the .PIF file, complete with path, in the Command Line text box.

TIP 87: Protect Your File Allocation Table

As briefly mentioned earler in the book, non-Windows programs that modify your hard disk's file allocation table (FAT) shouldn't be run from within Windows. If you do run this type of program, you're running the chance of corrupting your hard disk's directory—the information that tells DOS and Windows where programs and data are stored on the disk. Programs that modify your FAT are hard disk compacting or defragmenting utilities, programs that unerase files, CHKDSK with the F option (CHKDSK /f), and so forth. Running such a program from within Windows may even wipe out temporary files that Windows is using, causing

Windows to lock up and requiring a three-key reset. Unless a defragmenting or unerase program is specifically guaranteed to be Windows-compatible, always run these programs from the DOS prompt, *after* exiting Windows.

TIP 88: DOS Commands That Wreak Havoc with Windows

As mentioned in Chapter 19, the DOS commands FASTOPEN, APPEND, ASSIGN, SUBT, and JOIN should be avoided when running DOS from Windows. These commands can cause trouble with your file allocation tables (FATs).

TIP 89: Are You in DOS or Windows?

Wouldn't it be nice if you could easily know whether you're in a DOS session running under Windows or actually in DOS itself, outside of Windows? Fortunately, Windows provides a little-known trick for doing just that. Add the following line near the beginning of your AUTOEXEC.BAT file:

```
SET WINPMT=DOS Session: $P$G
```

This sets a DOS variable called WINPMT—the prompt Windows uses in each DOS session—without modifying your actual DOS prompt. When you're in a Windows DOS session, the prompt will say

```
DOS Session: C:\Windows
```

(or C:\ and another directory name). When you're in DOS outside of Windows, the prompt will be the usual C:\ prompt.

TIP 90: Multitasking Non-Windows Applications

Even if you aren't a Windows fan, or don't always use Windows, do use it as a task switcher for your non-Windows applications. On a 386 machine in 386-Enhanced mode, Windows does a good job of allowing you to run multiple DOS sessions in "virtual machines"—simulations of stand-alone PCs, each running a copy of DOS. Simply open several non-Windows applications (using PIFs as necessary to reserve the needed memory, shortcut keys, and graphics options), and switch between them using Alt-Tab or the Task Manager. Windows does the job of reassigning memory and managing the hardware.

Windows also manages the sharing of CPU time so that each non-Windows program will continue working when in the background. You may want to have one of these programs working in the background, but with less processing time allocated to it as compared with other running applications (perhaps because you've noticed that it's slowing down your foreground application). Just decrease the Background Priority value in the MultiTasking Options area of the Advanced Options dialog box of the 386-Enhanced PIF settings for the application. Or you can temporarily window the application (press Alt-Enter), open its Control Menu, choose Settings, and decrease the Background Priority there. (By the way, you can temporarily window the application and simultaneously open its Control Menu by pressing Alt-Spacebar.)

As an alternative, you can increase the Foreground Priority if you find the program running there is running too slowly when non-Windows applications are running in the backgound. Remember that the numbers are relative, and don't mean anything absolute. If you want an application to have all the CPU time it needs while in the foreground, give it a value of 10,000.

When you want the application to have all the CPU, select the Execution Exclusive option check box in the PIF Editor dialog box.

TIP 91: Switching among Non-Windows Applications

You can use Alt-Tab to switch among non-Windows applications. When you press Alt-Tab while running a non-Windows application full screen, you see the name of the next application on a line near the top of the screen, rather than in the middle as you do when using Alt-Tab in a Windows application. Here's how you can switch applications: As long as you don't release the Alt key while a Windows application name (such as Program Manager) is displayed, and only release Alt when a non-Windows application name is displayed, you'll switch among only non-Windows applications. By switching once between two non-Windows applications, you can then toggle between them by pressing Alt-Tab once and releasing. Windows only displays one line on the screen in an effort to speed up the switching process, since less screen rewriting time is needed to display a name rather than the whole screen for each application.

TIP 92: Pasting Data into WordPerfect, Excel, and Lotus 1-2-3

As explained in Chapter 8 about the Clipboard, you can copy data to and from non-Windows applications when they are windowed. However, there are some tricks to doing this. One involves the line feeds and carriage returns at the end of lines when you are pasting multiple lines of text.

Every line of text has an invisible carriage return/line feed pair at the end of it. When you copy multiple lines into a WordPerfect file or Excel spreadsheet, these characters are nicely handled. In WordPerfect, each line of text is entered on a new line in the file, as expected. With Excel, each line of text or numbers is copied into a new cell. In 1-2-3 for DOS, however, all the lines are dumped on top of each other into one cell. To successfully copy multiple lines of text or numbers into separate 1-2-3 cells, you'll have to select each line from the source application, copy it to the Clipboard, and then paste it into the destination cell.

TIP 93: Copying Text from Non-Windows to Windows Applications

As discussed in Chapter 8, you can copy text from non-Windows applications to the Clipboard, from whence it can be pasted into Windows applications. First window the non-Windows application. Choose Edit ➤ Mark in the non-Windows application Control Menu, select the text with the mouse, and then choose Edit ➤ Copy or press Enter.

Problems often occur when copying columns of text from non-Windows applications into most Windows applications. Columns of text that line up neatly in the non-Windows application may not align properly in the Windows application. This happens because most DOS fonts are monospaced fonts, whereas most Windows fonts are proportionally spaced. The easiest solution is to select all the text you copied and reformat it with the Courier or Courier New font, both of which are monospaced. Another solution is to insert tabs before each column (if the non-Windows application you're working with accepts tabs). You may then have to adjust the tab locations to make this work.

Note that if you bring the text into Notepad, the copied text is automatically given a monospaced font and will align properly from the start.

TIP 94: Altering Text Font Size in Non-Windows Applications

There's no need to squint at small, barely-readable text when you run a windowed non-Windows application. From the application's Control Menu, select Fonts to open the font selection dialog box. Experiment with the different font settings until you find the one that works best for you. Once you click OK, the settings will be stored permanently for use with each future session in that application.

Keep in mind that this only affects font settings for non-Windows applications that operate in text mode. Text characters that are actually displayed as graphic images (as when running Microsoft Word for DOS in graphics mode) will not be affected by this setting.

If you don't see a Fonts option on a non-Windows application's Control Menu, you may be using a video driver that hasn't been updated for Windows 3.1. Ask the video card manufacturer for a driver designed to work with Windows 3.1. In the meantime, try adding this line to the [NonWindowsApp] section of SYSTEM.INI:

```
FontChangeEnable=1
```

This forces Windows to offer font selection for non-Windows applications. But be aware that this setting may wreak havoc with the application's windows.

TIP 95: Standard vs. 386-Enhanced Mode with Non-Windows Applications

Windows can run in two modes: Standard and 386-Enhanced. Non-Windows applications run differently in these modes. In Standard mode, non-Windows applications can only run full screen. In 386-Enhanced mode, they can run in a window. In Standard mode, only one non-Windows application can be actually running at a time. As soon as you switch away from one, its activity is suspended and no more CPU time is given to it. When you switch back to it, it continues to run, but all other programs, including all Windows applications, become suspended.

In contrast, in 386-Enhanced mode, all programs (Windows and non-Windows) can run simultaneously, even when in the background. Windows can do the job of distributing memory and CPU time among them all, and of managing the hardware. However, by default, this isn't the case. Non-Windows applications are normally set with background tasking turned off. To activate background tasking for an application, you'll have to either make a PIF for that application, or window the application, open the window's Control Menu, choose Settings, and mark the Background checkbox in the Tasking Options area of the Settings dialog box. (By the way, you can simultaneously window an application and open its Control Menu by pressing Alt-Spacebar.)

Another consideration is the amount of available memory for non-Windows applications in the two modes. In Standard mode you'll often run out of memory when trying to run multiple non-Windows applications, and switching is slower because Windows uses swap files on disk for each of these applications. In 386-Enhanced mode, Windows pools all conventional, extended, and virtual (disk-based) memory, assigning it to non-Windows applications as needed, on a first-come-first-served basis. As a result, you'll be able to run more non-Windows applications in this mode, and switching is often faster. If you don't need to run non-Windows applications, some sources report that you'll probably be better off running in Standard mode. Your Windows applications will still multitask, and efficiency will likely be increased.

TIP 96: Keep a DOS Batch File from Disappearing

You may have noticed that when you run a DOS batch file to load TSRs for use during a DOS session, the batch file loads the TSRs and then returns to Windows, closing the DOS session. For example, assume that for DOS work you like to load Sidekick, DOSEDIT, and Turbo Lightning, then want to return to the DOS prompt to run a variety of programs. The usual batch file from DOS would look like this:

```
SK
DOSEDIT
LIGHT
```

Unfortunately, running this batch file from Windows opens the DOS session, loads the TSRs, and quits the DOS session. This is because no "real" program is loaded—only background and pop-up programs. The solution is to end the batch file with COMMAND.COM to invoke DOS after the TSRs are loaded, like this:

```
SK
DOSEDIT
LIGHT
COMMAND.COM
```

TIP 97: Trimming Down Your PATH Statement

Many applications add their own directories to your DOS PATH statement in AUTOEXEC.BAT, without telling you or with only a mention that they will be making the changes. Intelligently designed installation routines allow you to view the current AUTOEXEC.BAT and the proposed new version. You can then make an informed judgment about whether you want the changes incorporated. Since your path statement is restricted to a maximum length of 127 characters, you run the risk of its becoming too long as you install new programs over time. When this happens, some of the PATH statement becomes nonfunctional, possibly causing programs to bomb when they can't find required files.

NOTE *See Chapter 3 for a discussion of the Program Item Properties dialog box, and Chapter 13 on the use of the PIF Editor. See Chapter 16 for more on the PATH statement.*

Generally, Windows applications do not require an entry in the PATH, so you can save space there by omitting or removing them. If you are diligent about entering the command line and working directory of programs in the Program Item Properties dialog box in Program Manager, Windows will ensure this information is passed to the application.

If you are working in DOS, the path to a particular application may be important, but not always. Depending on the program, you may be able to just enter the path in the Command Line and Working Directory text boxes in the Program Item Properties dialog box, or in the PIF's Program Filename and Start-up Directory lines. Other DOS programs, notably those that draw upon several directories for support files, may need a bona fide PATH statement to function without choking.

One other time when a PATH statement may be needed is when you're opening files from the File Manager by double-clicking on a document file name. When you open files this way, Windows checks the [Extensions] section of your WIN.INI file for an associated .EXE file to match the document type. If the associated .EXE file isn't on the DOS PATH, then it must be listed as part of the entry in the [Extensions] association list, or you'll get an error message and the document won't open.

The moral here is this: If you want to keep the search PATH from growing too long, be prepared to edit your WIN.INI file to include paths in the [Extensions] section when a document doesn't want to open. Or, clean up the PATH statement, and add a directory to the PATH list only when a program or file won't open.

TIP 98: A Quick but Dangerous DOS Killer

A handy PIF setting that is often overlooked is Close When Active. By selecting this option when you're editing a PIF in the PIF Editor, you can terminate a non-Windows application the same way you would a Windows program—by double-clicking the control bar or pressing Alt-F4. But beware: most non-Windows applications do not expect to be abruptly terminated. By exiting a non-Windows program in this way, you may lose any work that you haven't yet saved.

TIP 99: Running Copy-Protected Software

Some older programs rely on disk-based copy protection schemes that can be thrown off by the presence of SMARTDrive. (Programs that require you to uninstall them in order to remove them from your hard disk usually have this type of copy-protection.) If you have problems with a program that you know or suspect to have some kind of disk-based copy protection scheme, try removing SMARTDrive temporarily. Here's how:

1. Run SysEdit.

2. Edit your AUTOEXEC.BAT file and place a REM statement in front of the SMARTDRIVE line, like this:

   ```
   rem C:\WINDOWS\SMARTDRV.EXE
   ```

3. Exit Windows.
4. Reboot your computer, rerun Windows, and try the application again.

TIP 100: Checking Your Mode/Getting into 386-Enhanced Mode

Having trouble getting your non-Windows applications to run in the background? You may not be running in 386-Enhanced mode. To check on which mode of Windows is executing, from Program Manager select Help ➤ About Program Manager. This handy dialog box tells you a lot more than the copyright date of Windows. It also reports Windows's mode (Standard or 386-Enhanced), the amount of free RAM, and the percentage of free system resources currently available for things like icons and bit-maps.

If you *should* be running in 386-Enhanced mode but aren't, try restarting Windows with this command:

```
WIN /3
```

Tip 101: About Converting Files across Formats

NOTE *See also "Converting Files across Platforms" in Chapter 21.*

While the Clipboard allows for the sharing of relatively small portions of text and graphics between applications, and DDE and OLE facilitate dynamic links between certain applications, none of these vehicles addresses the need to share or transport complete files between applications and operating systems. Though not part of the immediate domain of Windows operations, knowledge of the various data file formats and conversion possibilities is relevant to your everyday use of Windows. Let's take a look at some general information, and then I'll give you some helpful tips.

You'll likely, at some point, be faced with the task of converting a data file (such as a word processing, spreadsheet, or database file) from its native format created by a non-Windows application, to a format usable by a Windows application. Though less likely, the reverse of this task—converting a file created in a Windows application so it's usable in a non-Windows application—may also be necessary, as the number of available Windows-compatible applications increases. Many modern programs can read and write data files stored in a variety of common formats, so data conversion is less of a headache than it used to be. Still, you should have some idea about when to keep files in their native formats, when to use one of the popular intermediary formats, and when file compatibility is out of the question.

People often come to me with a disk containing a letter or resume they want me to print out on my laser printer. When I ask what program was used to create the file, their eyes usually glaze over and they say they're "not sure...." With the magic of Windows, there is often an incorrect assumption that all data files can be easily shared.

Unfortunately, virtually all applications encode their data files in unique, proprietary formats before the files are stored on your hard disk. For example, though a WordPerfect file and Microsoft Word file might print out absolutely identically, their formats stored on disk are not at all identical. Examine their files on the disk, and you'll discover numerous technical differences. Information about the font size, page margins, tabs, indents, and so forth is ferreted away via proprietary codes that vary radically from manufacturer to manufacturer. The same disparity in format applies to database, spreadsheet, and graphics files. And now with multimedia on the rise, we're beginning to see new incompatibilities, in competing formats for audio, compressed video, and MIDI files.

Obviously, your best bet when working with a "foreign" file is to use the program that created it. Simply find out what type of file it is, and use the appropriate program to edit, print, or view it. If you don't know what program was used to create it, sometimes the file's extension provides a clue. Use the Windows File Manager or the DOS DIR command to examine the file's name. If the file name extension (the last three letters after the period) is WKS or WK3, it's likely the file is a Lotus 1-2-3 file. Microsoft Word creates DOC files, and dBASE creates DBF database... You get the idea. The list of common file name extensions is quite long, and there are some inconsistencies within the industry. Also, be aware that just because a file has, say, a .DBF extension, it isn't necessarily actually a dBASE file. Anyone can change a file name extension by simply using the DOS RENAME command, or the Windows File Manager. Unfortunately, just changing the extension does not alter the file's format or make it readable in another program.

If you don't have or can't get the creating program, your next step is to figure out if you have a program that can "import" the file in question. For example, I often use Microsoft Word for Windows to import text files from a number of sources. Word for Windows is a perfect tool for this because it recognizes a plethora of text file formats—WordPerfect, WordStar, Windows Write, MultiMate, Works, and others. Other major word processing programs such as WordPerfect, and typesetting programs such as Ventura Publisher do equally well at importing foreign files. In like manner, many database programs will read other database file formats; many spreadsheet programs will read Excel, Quattro Pro, and 1-2-3 files; and many graphics programs will read PCX files, TIFF, and BMP files.

When the file you're trying to read isn't stored in one of the more popular formats, and can't be successfully imported into the application you want to use, then you have to go to plan C: finding a common language, or lingua franca, that will serve as a translation medium. Several standards have been developed for this purpose as the PC industry has begun to acknowledge users' needs for passing dissimilar data files between programs. Nowadays most good applications will import and export at least one of the following common formats:

- *Delimited, or CSV (Comma Separated Values).* These are database, mail-merge, and spreadsheet data files stored in plain ASCII, where fields or cells are separated by a *delimiter*, typically a comma. Some programs, such as dBASE, allow you to assign an arbitrary delimiter, such as quotation marks, when exporting and importing files, but commas are more popular. The other common delimiter is the tab character. Field data is aligned in vertical columns, with each line of several fields representing a record. A carriage return terminates the record. When separated by tabs, field data typically cannot exceed a predefined maximum length.

- *.TXT and ASCII.* Many .TXT (text) files are stored in text or ASCII (American Standard for Information Interchange) format, though in Windows, ANSI text files are often used. Text stored in this format typically does not have formatting information—margins, headers, footers, font data—stored in the file, but the bulk of the text will be there. Some variations on text files, such as "TXT with breaks," also exist. Such variations refer to the way carriage returns and line feeds at the end of each line are stored in the file. As a rule, if you know you're going to transfer a file to another party using TXT or ASCII format, don't bother spending much time on fancy formatting.
- *TIFF.* These are graphics files.
- *PCX.* These are graphics files originally introduced by the Windows Paintbrush accessory.
- *DIF.* This is an acronym for Data Interchange Format, which is used typically for transferring data and text between spreadsheet programs.
- *RTF.* The Rich Text Format was developed by several companies to allow sharing of formatted text between dissimilar word processors.
- *RTF-DCA.* This is IBM's version of RTF. This format is used to transfer IBM word processing files between programs.

For additional information about using Write to convert files and strip out unwanted hard carriage returns, see "Opening Documents Stored in Other Formats," in Chapter 9.

To successfully copy material between dissimilar applications, then, be they DOS or Windows applications, you'll first need to determine a common format both programs can understand. Then, in the creating application, save the file in the acceptable format, and import it into the target application by specifying that format.

If all else fails, one approach that almost always works is to "print" the source data to a disk file. (Refer to the creating application's manual for how to do this.) As an example, you can tell dBASE to print a report or an entire database to a disk file instead of to the printer, using the Set Alternate To or Copy To commands. The resulting data file will be in ASCII format. With some programs, you'll have to install a "dumb," "generic," or TTY (Teletype) printer driver for this trick to work; it won't on a laser printer.

If you're moving data in the other direction, from a Windows to a non-Windows application, and can't find a common file format, save your document as an ASCII file. If the file type called Text Only (*.txt) is available in your application, select it to get your ASCII-format file. If you don't have this option, you may be able to "print" your document directly to a file; this creates a file in ASCII format. In this case, in the dialog box called Print (or something similar), you'll see an option such as Print to File. Select this, and specify any other print options for this document. After you click OK, you'll have the opportunity to name your file (include a path if you want one); finally, click OK to "print" your document into an ASCII-format file.

TIP 102: Dropping an Excel Chart into a WordPerfect for DOS Document

Here's another way to get around file format dissimilarities. Suppose you have a nice chart created in Excel and want it to appear in a WordPerfect for DOS document. (If you have WordPerfect for Windows, you can use the Clipboard or OLE to move the chart.)

1. First, make sure you have installed the HP 7550A Plotter as one of your printers. Do this from the Control Panel. (See Chapter 6 for details on printer installation.) Select Printers, then Connect, and in the Connect dialog box, choose FILE: for the port. Also, be sure to uncheck the Draft option in the Setup box.
2. Next, if you haven't already done this, create the chart in Excel and save it.
3. Print the chart. It will be "printed" to a file (you'll be prompted for the file name) and stored on disk as an HPGL (Hewlett-Packard Graphics Language) file.
4. Run WordPerfect for DOS, and use the graphics import commands to read in the HPGL file and place the chart appropriately.

FILE MANAGER TIPS

TIP 103: Accelerate File Manager by Turning Off Branch Display

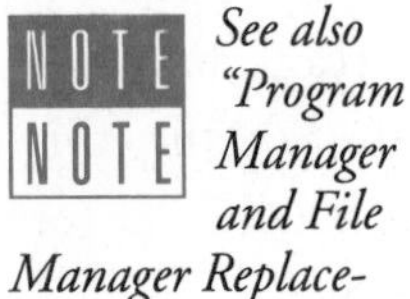

See also "Program Manager and File Manager Replacement" in Chapter 21.

The delay you experience in order for File Manager to load, to display new drives, or to refresh the current drive (by pressing F5) will be decreased if you elect to eliminate the display of expandable directories in the tree pane. Open the Tree menu and set Indicate Expandable Branches off. If you still want to be able to see the names of subdirectories of the current directory, choose View ➤ By File Type and set Directories on.

TIP 104: Turn On Branch Display for Reorganizing Your Disk

If you regularly drag files around between directories to reorganize your hard disk, do the reverse of the tip above. That is, have Indicate Expandable Branches set on and turn off the display of directory folders in the file pane.

TIP 105: Use File Manager as Document Manager

Is there an easy way to work on a bunch of document files without having to create icons for them in the Program Manager? Yes. Here's an example: I didn't bother making document icons for each chapter of this book. Instead, I had them neatly organized in directories called CH-1, CH-2, and so forth. When I wanted to open one of the chapters to edit it, I just pressed my shortcut key for File Manager, moved to the correct directory, and double-clicked on the document name in the file pane.

Since the File Manager is in my StartUp group, and I save File Manager with the desired directory displayed whenever I close it, bringing it up immediately shows me the files I've been working with. Just make sure there is an association already set up for the file's extension. In the example above, the .DOC extension is associated with Microsoft Word for Windows. (Refer to Chapter 4 for information on associations.)

TIP 106: Quick Extension Change for Easy Document Viewing

Sometimes you'll just want to view (or perhaps edit) a file that doesn't have an association. I've found that the quickest way to do this is to change the file's extension temporarily to an extension that has an appropriate association. For example, I often write letters using an ASCII text editor (PC-Write by Quicksoft, Inc.). I often don't give my files any extension (e.g., DIANE). So double-clicking on such a file in the File Manager results in the following message:

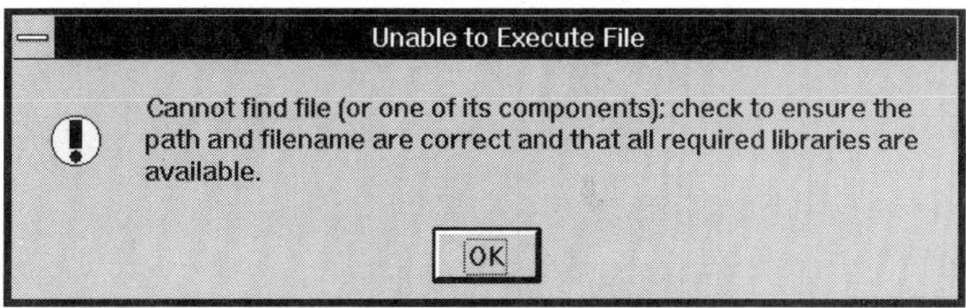

Since I know the file is an ASCII file which could be read by Notepad, I just temporarily change the file's name to DIANE.TXT by quickly highlighting it, pressing Alt-F, then N (for File ➤ Rename), typing *DIANE.TXT,* and hitting Enter. Then I press Enter again to open the file in Notepad and view or edit it.

Notepad will only read normal, unformatted text files correctly, so I can't use this technique on documents created with other programs such as Write, WordStar, WordPerfect for Windows, Word, Ami Pro, etc. If I have documents created with a sophisticated program such as these and want to view it quickly, I often change the name to a DOC extension, which is associated with Word for Windows. When Word for Windows tries to open the file, it recognizes it as a foreign format and gives me a list of word-processing filters to choose from. Usually the correct one is highlighted, so I can simply press Enter to open and view (or edit) the file. When I'm finished looking at or editing the file, I may or may not decide to change the extension back to its original name, depending on which program I intend to use it with next time. (See the discussion of Norton Desktop for Windows in Chapter 21 for another workaround for painless file viewing.)

TIP 107: Opening a New Window

When you double-click on a drive icon, File Manager assumes that you want to open a new window so that you can see the new drive information as well as the old drive's information. To see only the new drive window, click just once on the drive icon.

TIP 108: Quickly Open Another Drive

Need to display a different drive window in a hurry? While holding down the Ctrl key, press the letter of the drive you want to see. This replaces the current drive window with the new one. So to quickly see drive A, press Ctrl-A; for drive D, press Ctrl-D.

TIP 109: Opening Two Copies of the Same Directory

Holding down the Ctrl and Shift keys while double-clicking on a directory in the directory pane side of the File Manager window gives you a second window for that directory. The second window contains only the file list, not the directory pane, and is a bit easier to read.

TIP 110: Quickly Find a File on Your Hard Disk

A handy feature of File Manager is its ability to locate files you may have lost track of on your hard drive. Choose File ➤ Search and tell File Manager as much as you know about the name of the file you're looking for. For example, to find all files with the extension .DOC, enter *.DOC in the Search For text box. If you remember that the file started with WIN but aren't sure of the rest, type in WIN*.*. File Manager also needs to know where to start looking. If you aren't sure, your best strategy is to enter the root directory (C:\ in most cases) in the Start From box, and check the Search All Subdirectories check box. Click on OK, and File Manager will then look across your entire hard drive to find your file.

TIP 111: Combatting Visual Overload

In a directory full of files, File Manager's display can be somewhat confusing. To narrow down the range of files displayed, choose View ➤ By File Type. Check only the types of files you want to see (for example, just directories, or program files, or documents). Then you'll be able to more easily pick out the files you're looking for.

TIP 112: Turn Off Confirmation

You can speed up File Manager activities by turning off the settings found in the Options ➤ Confirmation dialog box. But be careful! With this option turned off, File Manager does not ask you to confirm your commands and selections.

TIP 113: Quick File Selection

To deselect all files but your most recent selection, press the | key (hold down Shift while pressing the Backslash key). This is handy when you're working with multiple files.

TIP 114: Quick Keyboard Selection of Noncontiguous Files

A little-known but very powerful feature of File Manager is the Selection Cursor, which lets you quickly select a number of files using only the keyboard. To use it, position the cursor over the first file you want, and hold down the Shift key while pressing F8. Notice that the border around the highlighted file name begins to pulsate. Use the arrow keys to move to the next file you want to select, and press the Spacebar. Now that file is highlighted as well. Using this feature, you can rapidly choose any number of noncontiguous files.

TIP 115: File Missing?

When you save a file in an application you launched from File Manager, you might not see the file listed when you return to File Manager. Don't worry—just press F5 to refresh the view. File Manager might be just a step behind.

TIP 116: Determining Your Existing Associations

As explained in Chapter 4, setting up associations gives you the wonderful convenience of starting an application and opening a specific file all at once. Just point and click on the document in the File Manager, or choose File ➤ Run and then type in the document name, such as README.TXT. As long as the file's extension has an association set up for it, Windows will run the associated .EXE file, pass it the file name parameter, and you're into the document. So what else is new, right?

Well, if you've been using Windows for some time, you probably have lots of associations set up by now. For example, I have one for viewing gray-scale .TIF files of screen shots I take for the computer books I write; I have another one for Wordstar (.WS) files. The more associations, the easier it is to forget which ones you've created. To complicate matters, some programs set up their own associations during their install procedures.

Unfortunately, File Manager doesn't display a list of your personal associations in the File ➤ Associate dialog box. Only the basic Windows associations will appear. If you explicitly type in a file name extension, any association you've set up will display. An easier way to see all the existing associations (both supplied and created) is to check out your WIN.INI file. Look for the [Extensions] section, in which you'll see a series of lines like the ones shown in Figure 20.6. (I've highlighted the [Extensions] section for clarity.)

At the far left margin are file name extensions for data files that are associated. On the right side of the equals sign is the name of the application that'll run when you double-click a file with that extension from File Manager, or when you enter the name of a file with that extension in the File ➤ Run dialog box.

TIP 117: Using Wildcards with File ➤ Commands

If you're an old DOS hand, chances are you often prefer typing in commands rather than using Windows's graphical approach when it comes to copying, moving, or deleting files. Luckily, File Manager dialog boxes are designed to

FIGURE 20.6:

Using the WIN.INI file to locate associated files

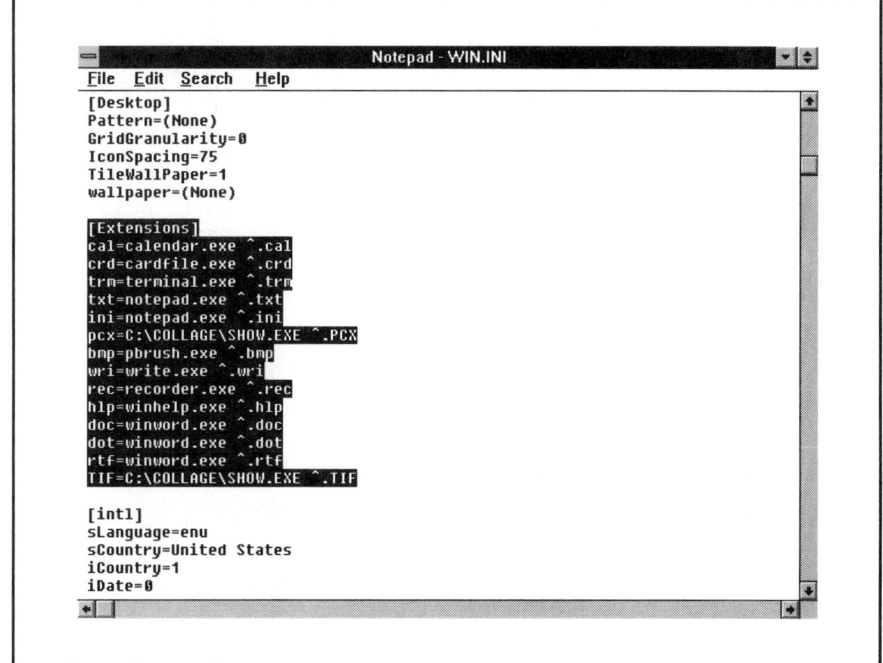
Notepad - WIN.INI

File Edit Search Help

```
[Desktop]
Pattern=(None)
GridGranularity=0
IconSpacing=75
TileWallPaper=1
wallpaper=(None)

[Extensions]
cal=calendar.exe ^.cal
crd=cardfile.exe ^.crd
trm=terminal.exe ^.trm
txt=notepad.exe ^.txt
ini=notepad.exe ^.ini
pcx=C:\COLLAGE\SHOW.EXE ^.PCX
bmp=pbrush.exe ^.bmp
wri=write.exe ^.wri
rec=recorder.exe ^.rec
hlp=winhelp.exe ^.hlp
doc=winword.exe ^.doc
dot=winword.exe ^.dot
rtf=winword.exe ^.rtf
TIF=C:\COLLAGE\SHOW.EXE ^.TIF

[intl]
sLanguage=enu
sCountry=United States
iCountry=1
iDate=0
```

let you do just that. Of course, you can always get to a DOS prompt and type in commands such as COPY A:*.* C:\WINDOWS. But if you've already got File Manager running, and are using its helpful tools for dragging files around from directory to directory, quickly running applications, and easily opening documents, why not take advantage of some of its less well known capabilities?

Did you know that you can enter DOS-type wildcard characters into some of File Manager's dialog boxes? You can save the time otherwise required to locate files, open and adjust a window or two, select the files with the mouse, and choose the correct command. Suppose you want to copy all of your .WKS files from drive A's root directory to your \123 directory on drive C. Here's how you can quickly do it, keyboard fashion, from File Manager:

1. Switch to File Manager. Forget about what directory or drive windows are showing—it doesn't matter.
2. Choose File ➤ Copy.

TROUBLESHOOTING AND TIPS & TRICKS

3. Fill in the dialog box as shown here:

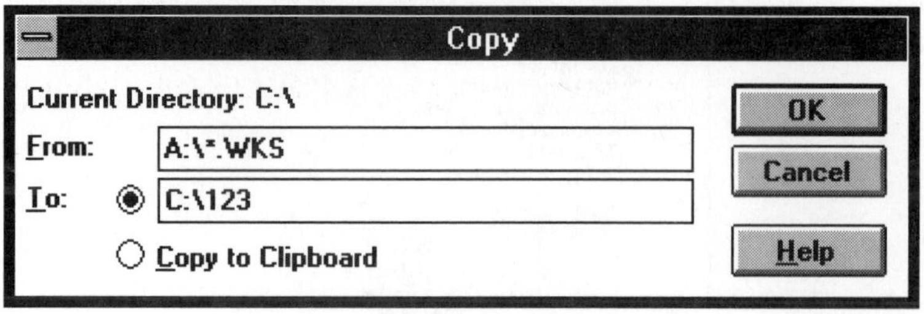

Copy

Current Directory: C:\

From: A:*.WKS

To: (•) C:\123

( ) Copy to Clipboard

OK | Cancel | Help

4. OK the box. Respond to the subsequent prompts as necessary, depending on your Confirmation settings.

That's it. File Manager does the rest. You can use the same approach for moving, deleting, or renaming files, too.

Rather than using DOS wildcards (* and ?), you can type in a string of file names for File Manager to process. Just separate the file names with a space.

If what you want to do is move, copy, or delete an entire directory of files, you can stipulate the directory name in the dialog box and File Manager will accept that. For example, to make backup copies of all the files in your \123 directory, storing them in a new directory called \123\BACKUP, choose File ➤ Copy and type in the source and destination directories as you see them shown below. File Manager will create the target directory (if necessary) and any associated subdirectories, and then copy in the files for you.

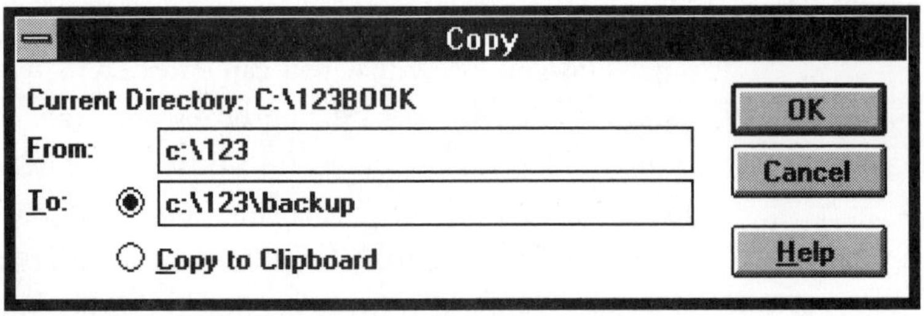

Copy

Current Directory: C:\123BOOK

From: c:\123

To: (•) c:\123\backup

( ) Copy to Clipboard

OK | Cancel | Help

Of course, you can drag an entire directory fairly easily with the mouse to achieve the same effect, but you'd have to create the directory first, using the File ➤ Create Directory command. What's more, if you wanted to apply wildcards to filter the copying process (as for copying only .WKS files), the graphical-and-mouse approach would require using the View ➤ By File Type command first, then selecting all the .WKS files from the file window using the mouse or keyboard...all in all, a hassle compared to typing in a few lines of text.

TIP 118: Add Your Own Commands to File Manager and Control Panel

Attention power users: Microsoft has opened up two new avenues to you for extending Windows. You can put new functions into File Manager by adding a section called [AddOns] into WINFILE.INI. Here's an example:

```
[AddOns]
Test=TEST.DLL
```

This [AddOns] command adds a Test item to File Manager's menu bar. Selecting Test will run the functions found in a program called TEST.DLL. (No DLLs (Dynamic Link Libraries) are included with Windows 3.1, but full details are available in the Windows 3.1 SDK (Software Development Kit).

You can also add new functionality to Control Panel by writing a compliant application with the extension .CPL.

TIPS FOR THE CLOCK

TIP 119: Keep Clock Always on Screen

Want the Clock always visible? Open its Control box and set Always on Top ON. Now size and position the Clock out of the way, such as the upper- or lower-right corner of the screen.

TIP 120: Prevent Clock from Burning Your Screen

As mentioned above, the Clock can be set to be always on top of other applications via its Control box. However, when this is the case, even screen savers won't blank the Clock, so it could burn a spot on your monitor's screen if left on all the time and not moved around. Here's a workaround: Assign a shortcut key for the Clock, such as Alt-Ctrl-C. When you want to see the time, just press the assigned key; a quick press of Alt-Tab will return you to your work.

TIP 121: Keep Clock Handy

Another great way to make sure you always know what time it is—without taking up a lot of screen space—is to keep the Clock running as an icon. Even minimized like this, the Clock will display the current time. You can facilitate this by putting the Clock in your Startup group.

TIP 122: Change Clock's Face Color

Want to change the Clock's color? The Clock's face color is the same as the Button Face color, which is alterable:

1. Run the Control Panel.
2. Double-click on Colors.
3. Click on Color Palette.
4. Choose Button Face from the Screen Element list.
5. Click on the color square containing the color you want your Clock to be.
6. Click on OK and exit Control Panel.

Of course, this will affect the color of all buttons in all Windows programs, and a few other odds and ends (a good many programs use this color setting for screen elements), but by lowering the brightness of this color assignment, you may avoid screen burning caused by having the Clock always on top.

TIP 123: 24-Hour vs. 12-Hour Display

You don't like 24-hour time when viewing the Clock in digital format? Change it to 12-hour time:

1. Run the Control Panel.
2. Double-click on International.
3. Click on the Change button in the Time Format section.

4. Choose 12 hour and make any other changes you wish.
5. Click on OK and exit Control Panel.

The Clock will now show 12-hour digital time.

TIP 124: Changing the Clock's Font

If you like the digital look, you might want to try changing the Clock's font from time to time. Choose Settings ➤ Set Font to see a list of available fonts for the Clock. Some look quite nice, particularly Times New Roman.

TIP 125: Remove Clock's Title and Menu Bars

Double-clicking on the face of the Clock alternately removes and restores the menu and title bars. Removing them renders the Clock more attractive.

TIP 126: Running More Than One Clock at a Time

Windows 3.0's Clock program had a cool feature that allowed you to run more than one Clock at a time. Version 3.1's Clock doesn't let you do this. But if you like to have more than one Clock running (because you use a large virtual screen with a number of desktops, for example) you can use the 3.0 Clock to do so. The 3.0 Clock isn't quite as attractive as 3.1's, but at least you can run it more than once.

First you'll need to procure the Windows 3.0 Clock program (it's called CLOCK.EXE, just like the 3.1 version). Copy it from someone who has Windows 3.0, or, if you elected to keep 3.0 when you upgraded to 3.1, copy it from your Windows 3.0 directory. You will also need to copy the font file for the old Clock, called DIGITAL.FON; the old Clock won't work right without it. You can also copy CLOCK.EXE from your Windows 3.0 installation disk 2, and both CLOCK.EXE and DIGITAL.FON will need to be expanded (see Tip 14). If you installed Windows 3.1 over 3.0, DIGITAL.FON is already in the Windows directory.

1. Once you have a copy of the 3.0 version of CLOCK.EXE, rename it to something like OLDCLOCK.EXE or CLOCK3-0.EXE. Then copy it to your Windows 3.1 directory (and DIGITAL.FON, too, if it's not already there).

2. Create a program icon for the old Clock and put it in the Accessories group right next to the new Clock. Now you can run it as you did in Windows 3.0, as many times as you like.

TIPS FOR THE MACRO RECORDER

TIP 127: Close Unused Windows

The Recorder only works with Windows applications.

When recording, close any unneeded windows. If left open, they may complicate matters.

TIP 128: Use Keyboard Commands, Not the Mouse

Avoid overusing the mouse. It tends to cause problems. So choose menu commands with the keyboard whenever possible.

TIP 129: Don't Move Windows Around

Avoid moving a window on the screen as part of a macro. The next time the macro moves the window, the macro may bomb, saying the pointer is outside the screen boundaries.

TIP 130: International Keyboard Conflicts

Recording and playing macros with computers set up for different countries (on the Control Panel's International setting) can cause keyboard incompatibility problems, such as typing the wrong letters or commands when the macro is run.

TIP 131: Know Your Target Application

Make sure other settings in the application won't prevent the macro from operating correctly. Such things as incorrect margin settings in Write, foreground and background color selections in Paint, or files set to Read Only may interfere with proper macro execution. Become familiar with the application that you're designing the macro for, in order to preclude such conflicts.

TIP 132: Give a Macro an Icon!

Assign a program icon to a macro to run it easily. A highly underestimated little program, Recorder can automate many repetitive tasks. For example, suppose you regularly have to reconfigure your serial ports to specific settings for use with a variety of external hardware. Or perhaps you like to change your screen colors from one set of saved colors to another. These operations would normally require running Control Panel and making several selections. Why bother, when you can assign them to Recorder files and give the files icons in Program Manager?

1. Record a macro for each task and save it as a separate .REC file.
2. Create a new group in Program Manager (or use an existing one) and add icons for each .REC file.
3. Select each macro's icon and press Alt-Enter to bring up its properties box. In the Command Line text box enter the following:

   RECORDER.EXE –H *shortcut-key FILENAME.REC*

(The –H tells Recorder to execute the macro assigned to the shortcut immediately upon running.) Replace *shortcut-key* with the key you assigned to the macro and replace *FILENAME.REC* with the name of the macro file you created. You have to use special codes to indicate Ctrl, Alt, and Shift in the shortcut key:

Ctrl	%
Alt	^^
Shift	++

Thus, to load a macro file called COLOR1.REC and run a macro assigned to Ctrl-Alt-Shift-Z, you'd use the following line:

RECORDER.EXE –H %^+Z COLOR1.REC

TIP 133: Automate Complex Startup Tasks

Suppose you want several operations to occur as soon as Windows comes on. In many cases this could be achieved through the StartUp group and standard program or document icons. But not always. StartUp is good for running a program or opening a document. Typically though, nothing truly automated will result from this, unless the application that runs has a macro function in it. As an example, some communications or tape-backup programs can be set to perform unattended duties during the wee hours. But if you want something more specific—such as to instruct Terminal to come on as soon as you boot up Windows, open a specific .TRM file, and dial a phone number—just create a macro as described above in Tip 132 and put the icon in the StartUp group.

TIP 134: If Recorder Doesn't Cut the Mustard

For creating elaborate macros beyond the scope of the Recorder accessory, there are three products to consider: Tempo for Windows, PubTech BatchWorks, and Bridge ToolKit. Bridge ToolKit has received high marks by users, though it is a bit more expensive than the other two. However, its scripting language lets you easily create your own menus and dialog boxes, as well as automate tasks the way Recorder does. For product information on Bridge ToolKit, call Softbridge, Inc., at (800) 955-9190. For more information on PubTech BatchWorks, call Publishing Technologies, Inc., at (800) 782-8324. For information on Tempo for Windows, call Affinity Microsystems, Ltd., at (800) 367-6771. Prices range from $100–175.

TIPS FOR TERMINAL

TIP 135: Using Two Modems Simultaneously

Do you have two modems and two phone lines that you'd like to use simultaneously? If you have two free COM ports in your computer, you can. Every Terminal .TRM file stores COM port, baud rate, and other settings in it. So you can create two such files, each with its own port-settings mode, by selecting Settings ➤ Communications. Save the files (File ➤ Save As), naming them something memorable like COM1 and COM2, install the modems for each line, and you're in business.

TIP 136: Automating Terminal Sessions

Terminal doesn't have a scripting language. If you need to perform automated downloading and uploading of files at regular times, you still may be able to do it with Terminal using Recorder, as long as you don't have to sign on to the remote computer in an interactive manner.

TIP 137: A Communications Program with Scripting

If you need to do automated downloading that requires logging on to a system, typing in a password, executing commands, and so forth, consider a more comprehensive communications program such as Crosstalk for Windows by Crosstalk Communications/DCA. Their number is (800) 241-6393.

TIP 138: Changing Terminal's Default Settings

If you frequently use the same settings with Terminal, you can change the defaults that the program starts up with. By doing so, even if you don't open a Terminal .TRM file, your preferred settings will be in effect. Here's how to do it: Simply save your preferred settings in a file named TERMINAL.TRM in the Windows directory; the Terminal program always looks there for a file with this name. The next time you run Terminal, it will find the settings stored there and put them into effect.

TIP 139: Monitoring Communications with Terminal or Other Communications Programs

Online information services and BBSs are often busy, and it's frustrating to have to keep dialing up the service again and again. Terminal has a Redial command that will wait a specified amount of time and then redial. Other programs have a similar feature. You don't really have to sit around and wait for your program to connect. Just switch to another window and go back to work while the communications program keeps trying to connect. Most programs will sound a beep when they've finally established contact with the remote modem. Depending on the application, you may have to iconize it for this to work.

TROUBLESHOOTING AND TIPS & TRICKS

Similarly, once you're logged on and sending or receiving files, you may not need to closely monitor the progress of the transmission. Most communications programs will sound a beep when a binary file transmission is successfully completed.

Here's another way of keeping tabs on file transmission; it works with Terminal, and may work with other communications programs you may have, as well. Start sending your binary file. Iconize Terminal and keep it within view at the bottom of the screen. Switch to another task and go back to work, adjusting your windows so you can keep an eye on the Terminal icon. The icon's background slowly fills up with another color, indicating the progress of the transmission. When sending is finished, the background will be completely colored. Just glancing at the icon occasionally will keep you posted on progress, and you'll know when you need to restore the window to continue an interactive session.

TIP 140: Printing Text Already Received in Terminal

One of the biggest oversights in Terminal's design is its apparent inability to print text that has already been received. Certainly you can toggle incoming text to flow directly to the printer, but once the text is received, it may seem to be "gone." Not so!

Highlight the text you want to print, and select Copy from the Edit menu. Next, start up and switch to Notepad. Paste the text into Notepad, and then select File ➤ Print. This may seem a roundabout, but it works!

TIPS FOR CALENDAR

TIP 141: Using More Than One Calendar File

NOTE *See also the description of the Almanac shareware program in Chapter 21.*

If you have a need for more than one Calendar file, it's no problem—you can create as many as you like, and save them under different names. Just use Calendar's File menu to save the file, and to open it again when you want to use it. Give your Calendar files names that will prod your memory, such as JOE.CAL or WORK.CAL.

TIP 142: Ensuring Alarm Settings Are Activated When You Boot Up

If you like to use the alarm function in Calendar, you'll have to make sure the Calendar program is running. The easiest way to do this is to automatically load Calendar when you start Windows. Add your Calendar file to your Startup group by dragging it from File Manager, or by using File ➤ New ➤ Program Item in Program Manager. Now, when you start Windows, your Calendar file will load and the alarms will be activated.

If you need a refresher on creating items in Program Manager, see Chapter 3.

TIP 143: Ensuring Accurate Alarm Times

The Calendar program relies on your computer's internal clock for the correct time and date. If your computer's internal clock isn't set correctly, your carefully set alarms will go off at the wrong time. To check the accuracy of your system's time and date, you can use the Clock program.

1. If the date isn't showing, turn it on by choosing Settings ➤ Date.
2. If the Clock shows an incorrect date or time, correct it by running Control Panel and double-clicking on Date/Time.
3. Change the date or time settings as needed, click on OK, and close the Control Panel.

TIP 144: To Quickly Jump to a Given Appointment Day

Even if you are in Day view in Calendar, it's easy to view your schedule for some other day. Try this:

1. If you have Calendar in Day view, double-click on the Calendar's status line. This switches Calendar to Month view. (See Chapter 12 if you need help finding the Calendar's status line.)
2. Double-click on the the day whose schedule you want to see, and it will appear.

TIPS FOR CARDFILE

TIP 145: Jumping to a Card in Cardfile

To jump to the first card in a Cardfile whose name begins with a particular letter, hold down Ctrl and Shift and press that letter key.

TIP 146: Importing Text to Cardfile

Although it isn't possible to directly import a text file into Cardfile, a shareware tool called WinCard lets you convert from text to Cardfile format and vice versa. WinCard is available on many BBSs or on-line services.

PRINTING TIPS

TIP 147: LaserMaster's WinPrinter Accelerates Print Jobs

If your copy of Windows was acquired outside the U.S., your package should include an information card that lists BBSs from which you can obtain updated device drivers. This card should also list local telephone numbers you can call to obtain drivers if no BBS is available or you cannot access a BBS.

If you print large quantities of documents, such as company reports, spreadsheets, or graphics from Windows, you may have noticed it can be slower than you'd like. Consider a product from LaserMaster Technologies, Inc., called the WinPrinter 800. This is an 800 dpi (dots per inch) laser printer with accompanying software based on LaserMaster's clone of Microsoft's TrueImage page-description language (which is, in turn, a clone of Adobe's PostScript language.) The system is compatible with Adobe PostScript, HP's Printer Control Language, and also includes a "direct Windows" mode, which prints from Windows programs very quickly using the same graphical display commands that Windows uses to paint your screen's image. The package is based on a 4 ppm (page per minute) laser printer engine and includes several additional Windows speedup programs. For product information, call LaserMaster at (612) 944-6069. It lists for $1795.

TIP 148: Printing with Drag-and-Drop

Printing lots of documents in a batch? You can quickly and conveniently print documents from the File Manager by dragging files into an iconized or windowed Print Manager (see Chapter 4 for details).

TIP 149: Hey! Driver!

In addition to device drivers supplied with Windows 3.1, Microsoft also has a Windows Driver Library (WDL) that contains device drivers made available after Windows version 3.1 was released. Printer, screen, and other types of device drivers are added to the WDL as they become available. If you have a modem, you can download WDL device drivers from network services including CompuServe, GEnie, MS OnLine, various user-group bulletin board services (BBSs on the APCUG network), and the electronic downloading service maintained by Microsoft ((206) 637-9009). If you don't have a modem you can purchase disks by calling Microsoft Customer Support Services at (800) 426-9400.

TIP 150: Speeding Up the Print Manager

As shipped from Microsoft, the Windows Print Manager doesn't get highest priority relative to other applications you might be using while a print job is in progress. On Print Manager's Options menu, the default priority is Medium. Depending on what other applications you are running and printing from, and how fast your printer can actually print, increasing this setting to High may accelerate Print Manager's operations. (It can also, sometimes, slow down other applications; see Chapter 19.) If you don't mind suspending all other work while Windows prints out a document, you can even turn off Print Manager altogether, which will also speed up printing. Here's how to turn off Print Manager:

1. Run Control Panel.
2. Choose Printers.
3. Highlight the correct printer.

4. Unmark the Use Print Manager check box in the bottom of the dialog box, as shown here:

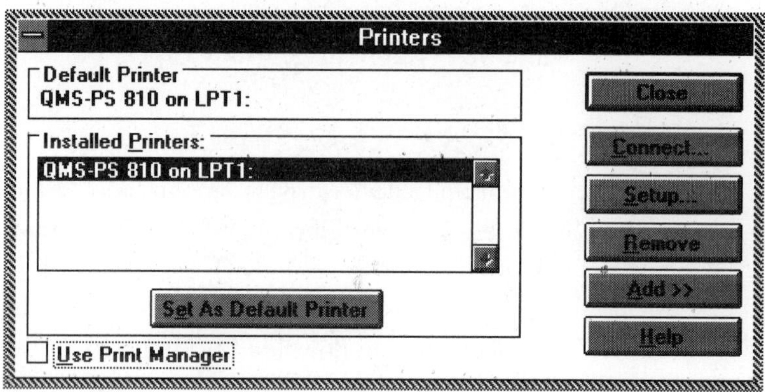

5. Close the dialog box.

Now any printouts from the selected printer will go directly on to the printer port.

TIP 151: Printing from Non-Windows Applications within Windows

You'll recall that printing from non-Windows applications doesn't take advantage of the Print Manager. The virtual machine that Windows creates to simulate a DOS computer acts just like a normal PC. The problem is that there's only one printer port on your computer. If you try to print from two non-Windows applications at the same time, or from a mix of Windows and non-Windows applications, you'll create a data collision at the printer port, resulting in a trashed printout.

As a rule, it's wise to suspend all other print jobs when you print from a non-Windows application under Windows. Another solution is to use a utility program that intercepts non-Windows application printing, shunting it to the Print Manager. With such a program, in addition to avoiding data collisions, you get all the advantages of printing with a spooler, such as the ability to queue your print jobs and get back to work while your printing progresses in the background. An example of this type of utility is Win-DOS from Celtic Software in Pittsburgh, PA, (800) 2-CELTIC.

TIP 152: Getting a Printout of a Windows Screen

Have you ever needed to print a copy of a Windows display? If you press the Print Screen key, Windows copies the entire contents of the screen to its Clipboard as a bit-mapped image. You can then paste the image into any Windows application, including Write or Paintbrush. From there, it's an easy job to print the screen.

If you hold down the Alt key when pressing Print Screen, Windows saves just the active window to the Clipboard.

TIP 153: Capturing a DOS Screen

Tip 152 also works when running a non-Windows application, but with a twist. If you press Print Screen when your DOS program is displaying graphics, the screen is saved as a bit-map. But if the DOS session is in text mode, Windows copies the screen to its Clipboard as text that can be pasted into any text editor or word processor.

FONT TIPS

TIP 154: TrueType Problems

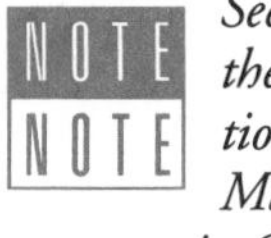

See also the description of the MakeUp program in Chapter 21.

The error message "Invalid TrueType Font" may be caused by a corrupted font file. If you see this message when you select a TrueType font, you'll have to make another copy of the original font file. Get out your original distribution disks and go into the Fonts section of Control Panel. Select the button marked Add... and insert the first disk into the appropriate drive. Select that drive, and see if the offending font appears in the Select Font box. If it doesn't, insert the next disk and double-click on the folder icon in the directories list. Continue until you find the right font. Highlight it and click on OK.

TIP 155: Font Substitutions

An interesting section of the Windows WIN.INI file is [FontSubstitutes]. Under this heading, Windows allows the creation of "synonyms" for fonts. By including these lines in the [FontSubstitutes] section,

```
Tms Rmn=MS Serif
Helv=MS Sans Serif
```

Windows ensures compatability with older applications that relied on the Helvetica and Times Roman fonts—these fonts have since been renamed.

Using this technique, you can make sure that documents created for PostScript printers refer to equivalent TrueType fonts included in Microsoft's TrueType Font Pack. If you have installed these additional fonts, add the following lines to the [FontSubstitutes] section of WIN.INI:

```
AvantGarde=Century Gothic
Bookman=Bookman Old Style
Courier=Courier New
Helvetica-Narrow=Arial Narrow
NewCenturySchlbk=Century Schoolbook
Palatino=Book Antiqua
ZapfChancery=Monotype Corsica
ZapfDingbats=Monotype Sorts
```

TIP 156: Changing the Font Used in Labels under Icons

If you find the titles of icons—the labels located immediately below them—difficult to read, you can change the font used to display these labels by adding two lines to the [Desktop] section of WIN.INI. To change the font itself, add this line:

IconTitleFaceName=*fontname*

where *fontname* is the name of the font you want to use—for example, Times New Roman. (The default is MS Sans Serif.) To change the size of the font, add this line:

IconTitleSize=*number*

where *number* is the size. (The default number is 8.)

TIP 157: Key-Cap Fonts

If you write computer user documentation, you may have a need for characters that look like the keys on a computer keyboard (called key-caps). Cassady & Greene makes such a font, as shown in Chapter 18, Figure 18.2. There are also similar font files available on BBSs. One such freebie key-cap font is obtainable from the Windows Online Information Database Service (see Chapter 21 for the phone numbers). This zipped TrueType font file is called DBKCTT.ZIP.

TIP 158: When Word for Windows Doesn't Show Your New Fonts

If, after you've added new fonts to your Windows system (particularly Adobe fonts when running Adobe Type Manager), the new fonts don't appear as choices within Microsoft Word for Windows (version 1.1), then you have to do the following:

1. From Word for Windows, choose File ➤ Printer Setup.
2. Make sure the correct printer is selected.
3. Click on Setup to get the Setup dialog box.
4. In the Setup dialog box, click OK.
5. Click OK again to return to Word for Windows. The list of currently installed system fonts will be updated internally by Word for Windows.
6. Check your font list now via the Format ➤ Character dialog box. It should include your newly installed fonts.

Now you should be able to see the new fonts in the Ribbon or in the Character dialog box. You must do this every time you add a new ATM (or any) font—it's just the way Word for Windows updates its own .INI file.

TIP 159: Printer Speed vs. Fonts

If you use several printers or are considering a new printer to buy for use with Windows, I recommend one with font scaling capabilities. This will give you faster performance if you frequently use a number of different fonts and font sizes. Popular printers that have this capability are PostScript laser printers (such as the QMS PS series and Apple LaserWriters), and the Hewlett-Packard HP LaserJet III.

When printing on a printer with built-in font scaling, the increase in speed occurs because the printer does the scaling using its own CPU. On normal printers, Windows and the TrueType font manager (or some other font manager, such as ATM) do the calculating. Since printers with font scaling are optimized for this type of work, printing is more efficient. When Windows must do the work, the resulting file that is sent to the printer is much larger, because a graphical image of the page is transmitted—rather than just the text and the printer's instructions for size, style, typeface, and margins.

TIP 160: Application Can't Access Your TrueType Fonts?

One of the most significant new features of Windows 3.1 is TrueType fonts. Unfortunately, however, some programs are still a little buggy when it comes to using these new fonts. If you can't access your TrueType fonts from within a Windows application, try the following corrective measures.

1. Run Control Panel.
2. Select Fonts.
3. Choose TrueType....
4. Make sure that the box next to Enable TrueType Fonts is checked. If it isn't, click the box and then OK.
5. Click on Close to exit Fonts and close the Control Panel.

If this doesn't solve the problem, check with your printer's manufacturer to make sure that the printer driver is designed to work with Windows 3.1. Many older printer drivers may trick Windows applications into thinking that there are no TrueType fonts in the system.

Here's a quick way to see if your printer driver is current for Windows 3.1:

1. Run Control Panel.
2. Select Printers.

3. Make sure that your printer name is highlighted, and click Setup.
4. Click the About button to see information about the printer driver you have assigned to your printer.

The dialog box that opens will either say that the driver was designed for Windows 3.1, or that it has a copyright date of 1992 or later. If this is not the case, contact your printer manufacturer for a copy of the latest driver.

TIP 161: What TrueType Fonts Do You Have?

To see what TrueType fonts are installed in your system, run Control Panel and double-click the Fonts icon. A list of fonts will appear (Figure 20.7). Select any of the font names from this list, and you'll see a sample of the highlighted font in the Sample box. The TrueType fonts say [TrueType] after their names, and show only one size in the Sample box. Bit-mapped fonts show the available type sizes.

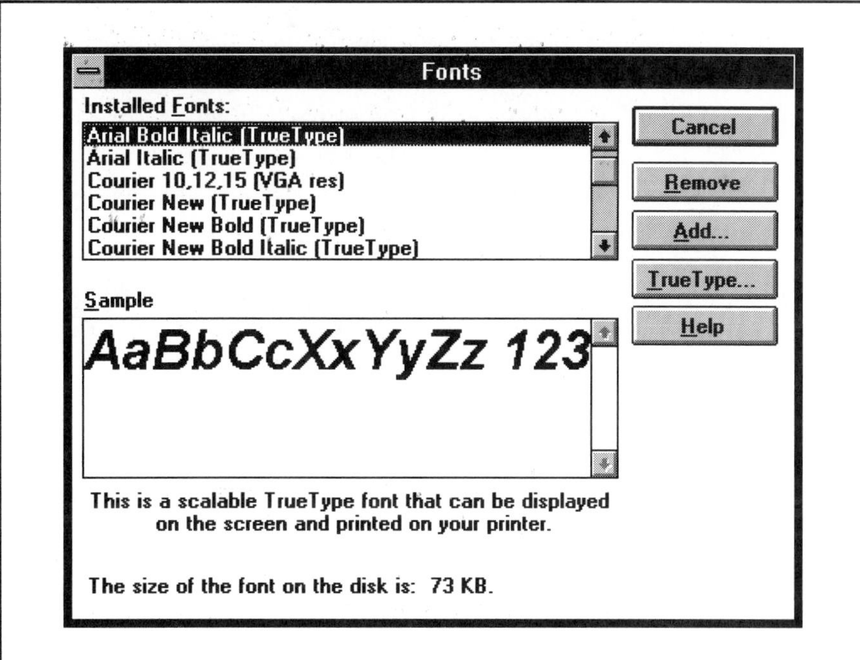

FIGURE 20.7: *A list of available fonts*

DISK SPEEDUP AND MAINTENANCE TIPS

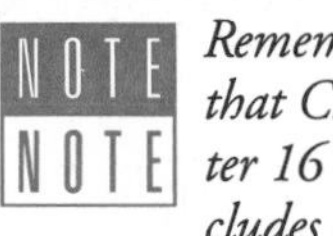

Remember that Chapter 16 includes more than 40 pages of tips for supercharging your Windows system.

In addition to those discussed in Chapter 16, here are a few additional tips to consider for speeding up your hard disk operations.

TIP 162: Preventing Disk Gridlock

Keep your hard disk cleaned up. Extra files waste space and can slow down Windows operations. Windows and Windows applications (and some Non-Windows applications as well) create temporary files that call on space when operating. One of my systems (a normally speedy 486) came to a crawl the other day. I figured I had enough disk space, so that couldn't be the problem. But when I checked, there was a scant 230K left on the 205MB drive. There was no warning message, but the application I was running went into snail mode so severely that I had to take a coffee break. I removed some unwanted files, providing a couple megabytes of space—and voilà, everything returned to normal. So remove unwanted and/or duplicate files on a regular basis. If you've already done so and are still pressed for space, consider eliminating some of Windows' files that you don't use. Table 20.1 lists files you might remove and the commensurate space you'll regain. The total from all these programs and help files is 1,470,056 bytes. Not a humongous amount, but it's a start—and even more significant if you're running on a 20MB drive, which many laptops have. If you've loaded other components such as network server and workstation modules, and you're not working on or serving a network anymore, you should also remove network-related files.

TABLE 20.1: *Non-Essential Windows Files*

FILE NAME	SIZE (IN BYTES)	PURPOSE
Readme Files (total=313,166)		
README.WRI	99,584	General windows information
NETWORKS.WRI	68,096	Networks information
PRINTERS.WRI	44,928	Printers information
WININI.WRI	31,104	WIN.INI information
SYSINI.WRI	53,760	SYSTEM.INI information

TABLE 20.1: *Non-Essential Windows Files (continued)*

FILE NAME	SIZE (IN BYTES)	PURPOSE
Help Files (total=783,946)		
APPS.HLP	15,695	Application compatibility help
CALC.HLP	18,076	Calculator help
CALENDAR. HLP	20,656	Calendar help
CARDFILE.HLP	24,810	Cardfile help
CHARMAP.HLP	10,797	Character map help
CLIPBRD.HLP	13,071	Clipboard viewer help
CONTROL.HLP	121,672	Control Panel help
GLOSSARY.HLP	46,570	Glossary of Windows terms
MPLAYER.HLP	12,896	Media Player help
NOTEPAD.HLP	13,894	Notepad help
PACKAGER.HLP	21,156	Packager accessory help
PBRUSH.HLP	40,269	Paintbrush help
PIFEDIT.HLP	33,270	PIF Editor help
PRINTMAN.HLP	40,880	Print Manager help
PROGMAN.HLP	30,911	Program Manager help
RECORDER.HLP	18,200	Recorder help
REGEDIT.HLP	22,681	Registration Editor help
REGEDITV.HLP	15,731	Advanced Registration Editor help
SETUP.HLP	41,453	Windows Setup program help
SOL.HLP	13,753	Solitaire help
SOUNDREC.HLP	17,686	Sound Recorder help
TERMINAL.HLP	36,279	Terminal help
WINFILE.HLP	76,855	File Manager help
WINHELP.HLP	26,960	Help about Help

TABLE 20.1: *Non-Essential Windows Files (continued)*

FILE NAME	SIZE (IN BYTES)	PURPOSE
WINMINE.HLP	12,754	Mine Sweeper help
WRITE.HLP	36,971	Write help
Accessories (total=1,746,716)		
CALENDAR.EXE	59,824	Calendar program
CALC.EXE	43,072	Calculator program
CARDFILE.EXE	93,184	Cardfile program
CLOCK.EXE	16,416	Clock program
CHARMAP.EXE	22,016	Character Map program
DRWATSON.EXE	26,864	Dr. Watson bug reporting program
EXPAND.EXE	15,285	File expansion utility program
MPLAYER.EXE	33,312	Multimedia controller program
NOTEPAD.EXE	32,736	Notepad text editor program
PACKAGER.EXE	76,480	Packager program for OLE-related activities
PBRUSH.EXE	183,376	Paintbrush drawing program
PIFEDIT.EXE	55,168	PIF Editor program
RECORDER.EXE	39,152	Macro recorder program
RECORDER.DLL	10,414	Recorder support file
REGEDIT.EXE	32,336	Registration editor program
SOUNDREC.EXE	51,305	Sound recorder program
TERMINAL.EXE	148,160	Modem communications program
WINTUTOR.EXE	124,416	Windows tutorial program
WINFILE.EXE	146,864	File Manager program. Careful. Unless you're using Norton or another file manager, you might want to keep this around.

TABLE 20.1: *Non-Essential Windows Files (continued)*

FILE NAME	SIZE (IN BYTES)	PURPOSE
WRITE.EXE	244,976	Write word processing program
Games (total=208,864=or 234,971 with Help files)		
SOL.EXE	180,688	Solitaire game
WINMINE.EXE	27,776	Minesweeper game
Screen Savers (total=74,376) Deletable if you don't use a screen saver		
SCRNSAVE.SCR	5,328	Windows default screen saver
SSFLYWIN.SCR	16,160	Flying windows screen saver
SSMARQUE.SCR	16,896	Marquee screen saver
SSMYST.SCR	19,456	Mystify screen saver
SSSTARS.SCR	17,536	Stars screen saver
Wallpaper (total=139,306) (Deletable if you don't use a Desktop wallpaper background)		
26COLOR.BMP	5,078	(wallpaper bitmap file)
ARCADE.BMP	630	(wallpaper bitmap file)
ARCHES.BMP	10,358	(wallpaper bitmap file)
ARGYLE.BMP	630	(wallpaper bitmap file)
CARS.BMP	630	(wallpaper bitmap file)
CASTLE.BMP	778	(wallpaper bitmap file)
CHITZ.BMP	19,918	(wallpaper bitmap file)
EGYPT.BMP	630	(wallpaper bitmap file)
FLOCK.BMP	1,630	(wallpaper bitmap file)
HONEY.BMP	854	(wallpaper bitmap file)

TABLE 20.1: *Non-Essential Windows Files (continued)*

FILE NAME	SIZE (IN BYTES)	PURPOSE
LEAVES.BMP	15118	(wallpaper bitmap file)
MARBLE.BMP	27,646	(wallpaper bitmap file)
REDBRICK.BMP	630	(wallpaper bitmap file)
RIVETS.BMP	630	(wallpaper bitmap file)
SLASH.BMP	2,038	(wallpaper bitmap file)
SPOTS.BMP	4,558	(wallpaper bitmap file)
SQUARES.BMP	630	(wallpaper bitmap file)
STEEL.BMP	7,174	(wallpaper bitmap file)
THATCH.BMP	598	(wallpaper bitmap file)
WINLOGO.BMP	38,518	(wallpaper bitmap file)
ZIGZAG.BMP	630	(wallpaper bitmap file)
Miscellaneous Files (total=451,138) (some of these are in the\WINDOWS\SYSTEM directory)		
RAMDRIVE.SYS	5,873	RAM Disk driver. Eliminate if not using a RAM disk.
SMARTDRV.EXE	43,609	Windows disk-cache program. (Only eliminate if not in your AUTOEXEC.BAT!)
MORICONS.DLL	118,864	Collection of icons to assign to programs
MOUSE.COM	14,394	Only necessary for use with mouse-supported DOS programs. (Windows uses MOUSE.DRV.)
WIN386.PS2	852	Only necessary on PS/2 machines
MIDIMAP.CFG	34,522	Configuration file for sounds. Only required if sound driver installed

TABLE 20.1: *Non-Essential Windows Files (continued)*

FILE NAME	SIZE (IN BYTES)	PURPOSE
MIDIMAP.DRV MCISEQ.DRV MMSOUND.DRV MCIWAV.DRV	109,648	Sound board drivers. Can be eliminated if no sound board installed
MMTASK.TSK	1,104	Only needed with multimedia sound
COMMDLG.DLL	89,248	Library of commonly used dialog box (for programmers only). Can be eliminated if you are not writing Windows programs.
SYSEDIT.EXE	18,896	Text editor for modifying system files. (Stored in \WINDOWS\SYSTEM directory)
TOOLHLP.DLL	14,128	Debugging tool for Windows programmers only.

The Windows Setup program makes removing (and later adding if you change your mind) unnecessary programs, help files, network files, and other informative text ("readme") files a fairly simple task, saving you the hassle of digging around on your hard disk with File Manager, Norton Desktop, XTree, DOS commands, or whatever you use for hard-disk file management. Here's how to use Windows Setup to remove a class of unwanted files:

1. From Program Manager's Main group, run Windows Setup.
2. Choose Options ➤ Add/Remove Windows Components. You'll see the dialog box in Figure 20.8.
3. To remove a whole class of components, clear its check box. As you clear check boxes, you'll see the aggregate disk space that will be liberated.
4. Click on OK and the files will be erased.

TROUBLESHOOTING AND TIPS & TRICKS

FIGURE 20.8:

Erase entire classes of components by clearing check boxes from this dialog box.

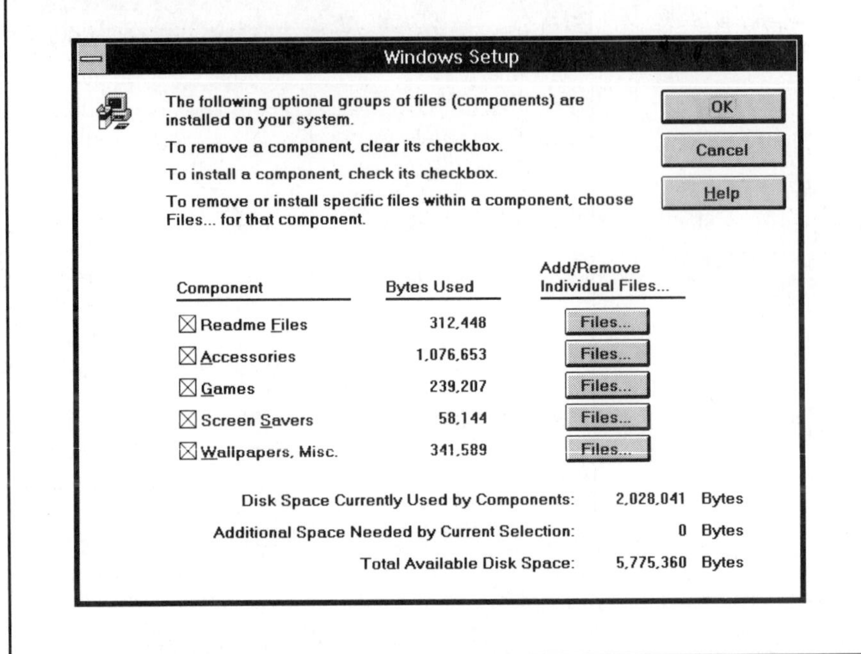

If you want to eliminate only specific files within a class of components:

1. Run Windows Setup.
2. Choose Options ➤ Add/Remove Windows Components.
3. Click on the Files button next to the class. You'll then see another dialog box, as shown in Figure 20.9. Here you see the name and size of each file.
4. Click on each file you want to trash.
5. Click on Remove as you see the pointer doing here. This moves the files to the left side of the box.
6. Click on OK to erase the files from your disk.

Note that these dialog boxes double for *adding* Windows components as well, if you elected not to do so during installation or if you've eliminated some since. When adding files, you'll be prompted to insert the relevant original Windows floppy disks.

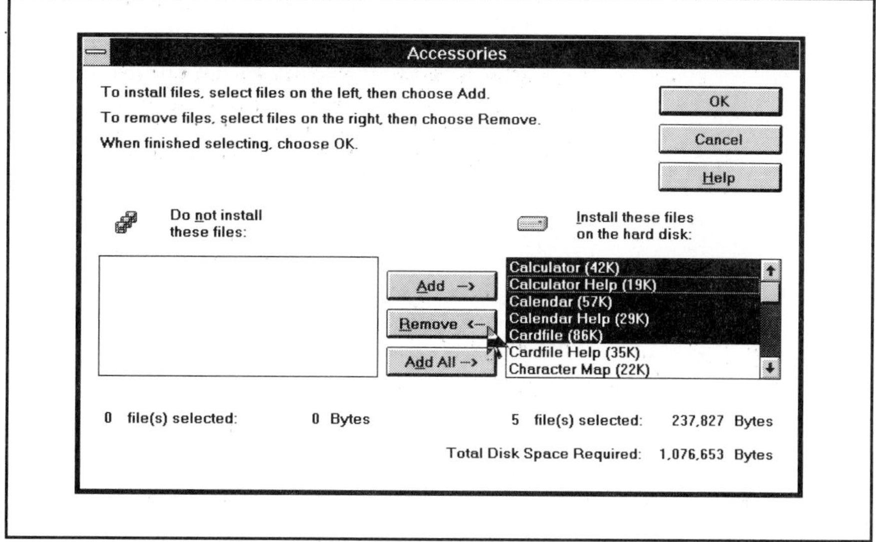

FIGURE 20.9: *To erase only certain files within a class (such as only one or two accessory programs), select them in the right list box and click on the Remove button.*

Because Setup doesn't display the actual file names, you won't know exactly which files you're deleting, or what they do. If you want more control over what's being deleted, use File Manager or the DOS ERASE command to delete files, using Table 20.1 as a guide. Before deleting a file, consider carefully whether you use it.

TIP 163: Keeping Your Sectors Together

Regularly use a defragmenting program to rearrange your files' sectors consecutively. This speeds reading and writing of files. DOS is designed to store files in any available sectors on your hard disk. Often there are not enough contiguous sectors free for storing a file you write to disk. DOS then must break up the sections into "fragments," scattering them across the disk. This forces the hard-disk heads to move around the disk's surface, much like the arm on a record player, to access the correct tracks and sectors. Obviously this slows down the reading and writing processes. When you or an application (such as DOS, Windows, or another program) requests the file later, the same thing happens in reverse. The hard disk must work overtime to retrieve the file. Regular use of an optimizing or defragmenting program reorganizes all the files into contiguous lumps of data, thus decreasing the time it takes to read and write files. After a few weeks of use, however, files will begin to become significantly fragmented again. One good defragmenting program is PC-Kwik Power Disk. Norton Utilities, Norton Desktop for Windows, PC Tools, and Mace Utilities all include defragmenters, as well.

Here's some product information on hard-disk utility programs. The number and type of disk utilities vary between products. Most include defragmenters, backup, and disk analyzers that repair or "map out" damaged sectors. Some can even resuscitate dead disks. For information on PC-Kwik Power Disk, call Multisoft Corp. at (800) 274-5945. For information on the Norton Utilities or Norton Desktop for Windows, call Symantec/Peter Norton Computing Group at (800) 441-7234. For information on PC Tools, call Central Point Software at (800) 445-4076. For information on Mace Utilities and Fastback Plus, call Fifth Generation Systems, Inc., at (800) 873-4384. For information on Disk Technician Gold, call Prime Solutions at (800) 847-5000. Prices range from $80–$180.

TIP 164: SMARTDrive vs. the Competition

As explained in Chapter 16, SMARTDrive is the disk-caching program supplied with Windows. Its purpose is to speed up disk access by loading frequently used sectors of hard-disk data into RAM. When the operating system wants to access information, it looks in the cache first. If it's there, the relatively slow process of finding and retrieving the data from the hard disk is avoided. SMARTDrive is an acceptably speedy disk-cache program, and it's certainly going to be compatible with Windows 3.1 since it's supplied by Microsoft along with Windows. The 3.0 version came under fire because it only cached disk reads, not writes. The version supplied with Windows 3.1 now does cache writes, preventing unnecessary slowdowns due to redundant disk writes. Though only marginally faster on most systems, there are still some nimbler caching programs out there that sport features that your system may need. I'll describe the notable ones.

Most caching programs rely on firmware code in your computer's ROM BIOS for access to the hard disk. This sometimes leads to conflicts when the BIOS isn't 100-percent compatible with the IBM standard. If you are having what appear to be compatibilty problems with SMARTDrive, consider a product called Power Cache Plus (by Intelligent Devices Corp.).

Its claim to fame is high compatibility with oddball computers and mass-storage devices based on ESDI, IDE, CD-ROM, and SCSI technology due to its use of DOS file I/O calls rather than BIOS calls.

Another program, HyperDisk (by Hyperware), has beaten out SMARTDrive in some performance tests, according to several magazines. This is probably the result of intelligent "staged writes" that write data to the disk only when your computer's CPU is twiddling its thumbs. The problem with staged writes is the potential for data loss if your computer or application bombs before the data are written. This probably isn't too likely, however, since idle CPU time during which writes would occur is fairly copious on most systems.

A popular caching program among DOS users is Super PC-Kwik Disk Accelerator (by Multisoft). Though not noted for its speed (SMARTDrive is faster), it offers the advantage of being bundled with several other programs from the same company, all of which work together: a keyboard accelerator, a screen accelerator, a print cache, and a RAM disk program. These utilities use RAM dynamically, reassigning it as needed. Unfortunately, only the disk cache works with Windows applications. But, if you use DOS sessions a lot (either from within Windows or outside of it), you may benefit by using the Super PC-Kwik package (called "PC-Kwik Power Pak"—I just hate that "k" thing) instead of SMARTDrive. Since Windows doesn't use Print Manager to queue DOS print jobs, using PC-Kwik's print cache could fill that gap when you do. The manual includes instructions written specifically for Windows users.

For information on Power Cache Plus, call Intelligent Devices Corp. at (714) 920-9551. For information on HyperDisk, call Hyperware at (615) 864-6868. For information on Super PC-Kwik, call Multisoft Corp. at (800) 759-5945. Prices range from $79–$130.

TIP 165: Optimal SMARTDrive Size

Some testers have noted that SMARTDrive reaches a point of diminishing returns with a size setting of about one megabyte. After that, allocating your extended memory into a large disk cache doesn't net you the additional speed advantages you'd expect. You're better off leaving the memory available for applications or for a RAM drive that Windows and applications can use for temporary files while running. Here's how to use the RAMDRIVE.SYS device driver that came with Windows for that purpose:

1. Edit your CONFIG.SYS file to include the following line:

   ```
   DEVICE=C:\WINDOWS\RAMDRIVE.SYS 1024 /E
   ```

2. Modify your AUTOEXEC.BAT file to include the following lines:

   ```
   MKDIR n:\TEMP
   SET TEMP=n:\TEMP
   ```

Step 1 creates a RAM drive of one megabyte and assigns it the next available drive letter name. If you have a C drive, but no D drive, it will then name it "D:." Step 2 makes a TEMP directory in the new drive and then sets the DOS environment variable that tells applications to store temporary files in the new RAM drive instead of on disk. *Make sure to change the* n *to the letter of your RAM disk.* This line won't work as written above!

Note that if you are using many applications that create temporary files, or some programs that create large temp files, 1MB of space may not be large enough for them. Normally, this will be an acceptable size, however. If you find you have problems with your programs after this alteration, remove these lines from your setup and go back to using your hard disk for temp files.

TIP 166: Standard Mode Can Be Faster

NOTE *Using 32-bit disk access improves 386-Enhanced mode performance, however.*

A little-known fact is that running in 386-Enhanced mode isn't necessarily the fastest way to run Windows. This mode does give you multitasking, expanded memory for applications that need it, and virtual memory, but all at the price of speed. Programs will run faster in Standard mode on a 386 or 486 machine and you'll still have access to extended memory above one megabyte. If you have enough extended memory, you'll still be able to run a good number of programs even without the virtual memory supplied by your hard disk in 386-Enhanced mode. If some of your applications need expanded memory, you can load an expanded memory driver via your CONFIG.SYS file at bootup; this will provide expanded memory to your non-Windows applications. In short, if you normally just switch between applications and don't mind if each is put in suspended-animation when not in the active window, you might try Standard mode for a speed boost. (Start Windows in Standard mode by typing **WIN /S** at the DOS prompt.) If you do run into low-memory messages, run fewer programs at one time, add more memory to your system, or go back to 386-Enhanced mode.

Be warned, however: In Standard mode you won't be able to use Windows 3.1's Ctrl-Alt-Del trick to kill individual malfunctioning applications.

TIP 167: Regarding Tip 166, or Standard Mode Revisited

Regarding Tip 166: You might also want to run in Standard mode if you have an 80386 computer with between 2MB of memory (640K conventional, 1024K extended) and 3MB of memory (640K conventional, 2096K extended), and if you do not use non-Windows applications within Windows. On such systems, Windows runs faster in Standard mode than in 386-Enhanced mode. Another call for Standard mode would be if you are having unexplained hardware compatibility problems when running in 386-Enhanced mode.

TIP 168: Clean Up Your INI Files for Faster Windows Load

Does Windows take too long to load? You can decrease the time it takes for Windows to load by eliminating blank lines from the SYSTEM.INI and WIN.INI files. Blank lines are added to make reading the files easier, separating sections of settings from one another. But if you don't care about that, edit these two files using Sysedit or a text editor and eliminate the blank lines. The next time you start up Windows it will load faster. Don't forget about cleaning out your WIN.INI file from time to time, as explained in Chapter 16. Also, remove unnecessary icons in your StartUp group, since each application loaded slows down the initial loading of Windows.

TIP 169: What Are All Those Files?

Have you ever wondered what all those files are in your WINDOWS and WINDOWS\SYSTEM directories? Comparing their extensions with Table 20.2 may help decide what to keep and what to throw away. This is a complete (as far as I know) alphabetized table of Windows-related files, and a few more just for reference.

TABLE 20.2: *Windows-Related Files, by Extension*

EXTENSION	FILE TYPE
.BAT	Batch DOS instruction
.BMP	Windows bit-mapped picture
.COM	Compiled machine code (program)
.CPL	Control Panel information file
.DAT	Program data
.DLL	Dynamic Link Library (data link)
.DRV	Windows device driver
.EPS	Encapsulated PostScript graphic
.EXE	Relocatable executable machine code (program)
.FON	System font
.FOT	Font table
.GRP	Program group
.HLP	Help text
.INF	User settings for a program
.INI	Windows program initialization parameter
.MID	MIDI sequencer file
.PCX	Paintbrush bit-mapped picture
.PIF	Program information file (executable)
.REC	Recorder macro
.SCR	Screen for screen saver
.SYS	Windows system driver
.TTH	TrueType font
.TXT	ANSI text
.WAV	MCI Waveform sound recording
.WPD	Windows printer driver
.WRI	Write document

TIP 170: How to Use ZIP and UNZIP in Windows

If you use file compressing and decompressing programs such as ZIP and UNZIP, PKZIP and PKUNZIP, ARC and UNARC, or any permutations of these, you probably wish there were an easy way to use them from within Windows. Well, there undoubtedly will be Windows versions of these products widely available in time. As of this writing, in fact, there are already some appearing. However, if you have the DOS versions, you don't have to go out and buy the Windows variety. Here are some tips for zipping and unzipping files using the File Manager and a simple batch file. Since I use the programs ZIP and UNZIP, I'll use those names in these examples. Substitute your program names if they're different.

Typically, you'll have downloaded a zipped file from a BBS, or a friend will have given it to you on disk. Here are the steps to unzip the file from File Manager:

1. Copy or move the zipped file into the directory containing the UNZIP program. You'll probably want to make sure there aren't other programs or files in there, since unzipping may create a lot of files, making it difficult to determine what's what. Also make sure you have enough disk space to hold the unzipped files.
2. Drag the UNZIP.EXE icon over the zipped file icon and release it. This tells File Manager to run UNZIP using the icon under it as the source file. File Manager now asks you:

   Are you sure you want to start UNZIP using FILE.ZIP as the initial file?
3. Click on Yes. A DOS session is run, UNZIP is run, the files are unzipped, and then you're returned to File Manager.
4. Press F5 to refresh the directory or you won't see the new files. You're done.

So much for unzipping. How about zipping things up? This isn't so easy, since passing the file name parameters to UNZIP can't be done directly by File Manager. You have to give it some help. Here are two techniques for zipping files. The first one does a single file at a time. The second approach zips all the files in a directory at once. Both approaches create a file called NAMEME.ZIP, reminding you to name the file after it's created.

For both techniques you have to create a DOS batch file called ZIP-UP.BAT with the following lines in it:

```
ZIP NAME-ME.ZIP %1
PAUSE
```

Make sure that ZIP.EXE is in a directory that is in your search PATH; if not, you'll need to add the name of your ZIP directory to the command in the batch file, like this:

```
C:\UTILS\ZIP NAME-ME.ZIP %1
PAUSE
```

Otherwise, when you try to ZIP a file, you'll get a message that ZIP.EXE couldn't be found.

The *PAUSE* line is optional, but it gives you a chance to see what's happened before the DOS session closes and File Manager reappears.

To zip a single file at a time:

1. Arrange your File Manager windows so you can see the ZIP-UP.BAT file and the file you want to zip.
2. Drag the file to be zipped over ZIP-UP.BAT and release it. A DOS session runs, the batch file runs, the file name parameter is passed to the batch file, and the file is zipped into a new file called NAME-ME.ZIP.
3. Press F5 to see the new file NAME-ME.ZIP in the directory.
4. Repeat Steps 1 and 2 until you've added all the files you want zipped. Each one will be added to the existing NAME-ME.ZIP file. If you only want one file in the .ZIP file, make sure to rename NAME-ME.ZIP, or else the next time you zip something, you'll unintentionally add it to the old archive file.

Here's how to zip up all the files in a specific directory. Use this method when you routinely have to crunch down whole directories of files, either to reclaim disk space temporarily, when preparing to send a group of files over a modem, or when performing a directory-by-directory backup:

1. Copy ZIP-UP.BAT into the directory whose contents you want to zip.

2. Double-click on the ZIP-UP.BAT file icon. This runs the ZIP program but doesn't give it a starting file name (parameter). The default response to having no parameter is to zip everything in sight, which means all files in the directory. This includes ZIP.BAT, but that's OK, since it's so small. A DOS session will run, with zipping progress reported on your screen. Then you'll be asked to press a key to return to File Manager.
3. Back at the File Manager, press F5 to refresh the directory. NAME-ME.ZIP should now contain an archive of all the files in the directory, in zipped format—that is, substantially crushed in size.
4. Rename NAME-ME.ZIP to something that will remind you of what's in the archive.
5. Decide what you want to do with the source files you just zipped. Erase them, move them into another directory, etc.

TIP 171: Doubling Your Hard Disk Space

Even with a large disk, you'll doubtless run out of space unless you're scrupulous about clearing out old files (nature abhors a vacuum, etc). One approach to deferring the inevitable can be found in the form of disk "companding" (compressing/expanding) programs. Such memory-resident programs compress data when written to the hard disk and reconstitute it on the fly when calling it back up, all with no significant speed penalty. This is possible because, once compressed in RAM, there are actually fewer data to store on the disk than there were before. The time spent compressing/decompressing the data is comparable to the amount of time it would have taken to read or write the data in a noncompressed form. The great news is that these compression techniques almost double your hard disk's capacity. A typical 40MB drive will swell to between 70–80MB in effective capacity once it's converted.

The most popular programs are Stacker, SuperStor, and Squish Plus. Stacker can be used either with or without a plug-in board that speeds its data processing. This is a good choice for laptops and seems to work fine with Windows. The fastest programs use an add-in card. One case in point is Expanz!. (Obviously this isn't a viable choice for laptop users since those machines may not have card slots.) If possible, you should install these programs *before* you have lots of files on your disk, since any existing files have to be compressed from and rewritten to the same disk. It's a bit like trying to walk while one foot is on top of the other. The procedure for setting up each of the programs varies, but SuperStor is the easiest to install on a hard disk already packed with data.

For product information on SuperStor, call AddStor, Inc., at (415) 688-0470. For information on Stacker, call Stac Electronics at (800) 522-7822. For information on Squish Plus, call Sundog Software Corp. at (718) 855-9141. Prices range from $100–130.

TIP 172: Accelerate Operations by Eliminating Your Swap File

As discussed in Chapter 16, a swap file allows Windows to juggle programs, shifting them to and from the disk during Windows sessions. Swap files "simulate" extended memory, giving the effect of additional RAM even if your system doesn't have it. Using a swap file is much less expensive than adding more RAM, but unfortunately, the swap file's performance is slower than RAM. Permanant swap files are faster than temporary ones, but speed is still limited by your hard drive's read/write electronics, seek time, and interleave.

If performance is your game and you're not addicted to running a bevy of programs in tandem, you can disable your swap file altogether. Once you do, if you only have a couple of megabytes extended RAM, you'll probably run into low-memory messages when you're running more than one non-Windows application, but since there won't be any disk paging (swapping), the speed improvement may be worth it. If you have more extended memory (say 4 to 8 megabytes), you shouldn't have trouble running a number of programs, and with some speed gain.

You can disable your swap file as an experiment to see how your application mix fares sans paging. Here's how:

1. Open the Control Panel and choose 386 Enhanced.
2. Click on the Virtual Memory button, and then click the Change button.
3. From the Type drop-down list, select None. Click on OK, and then click Yes to confirm the change.
4. Because you've changed your virtual memory setting, you must restart Windows for the change to take effect.

If you get more low-memory messages than what you'd like, reenable virtual memory. Repeat steps 1 and 2 above, and then select the drive, type, and size for the new swap file.

TIP 173: SMARTDrive Cache Sizes

How do you decide what size cache to use with Windows? If you have enough memory, and you are trying to decide how much memory to give Windows and how big to make your cache (for example, SMARTDrive), consider the following:

- Almost any size cache will be of great benefit. The larger the cache you give Windows, the more quickly Windows will be able to reload a program or file. In other words, consider whether Windows is reloading from fast memory (cache) or from your slower hard disk.
- If you typically open several applications and leave them open on your desktop, you'll need lots of memory and could afford to make your cache smaller in size.
- If you tend to open only a few applications at a time, and then close most of them and reopen them again a little later, then a cache will be of great benefit to your system. In this case, you will want to make your cache larger in size.

TIP 174: Caution When Powering Down

Always be sure to exit Windows before turning off power to your computer! Turning off the computer first may cause damage to files on your hard drive.

TIP 175: CHKDSK Warning Reminder!

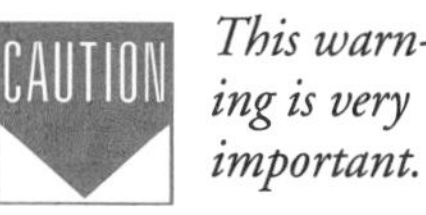

This warning is very important.

Never, never, never run the DOS CHKDSK command while in Windows! Using the /F option (CHKDSK /F) in a DOS session can corrupt your hard disk. (The version of CHKDSK included in DOS 5.0 won't let you use this command from within Windows.)

TIP 176: Stack Overflows

If you ever see the error message, "Internal Stack Overflow," load CONFIG.SYS into a text editor and make sure that the following line is included:

```
STACKS=9,256
```

If these numbers (9 and 256) are different, change the line. And don't forget the comma.

TIP 177: Only Use One Disk Cache

If you use the SMARTDrive disk cache utility provided with Windows 3.1, make sure that no other disk caches are loaded in CONFIG.SYS or AUTOEXEC.BAT. The use of more than one disk cache at a time may corrupt your hard disk or destroy valuable data.

If you want to run a third-party disk cache such as Super PC-Kwik or HyperDISK, remove the reference to SMARTDRV.EXE from your AUTOEXEC.BAT file.

If your hard disk uses a caching controller (a card with a RAM cache on board), then using SMARTDrive or any other software caching program is probably redundant. Why use up good extended memory on a disk cache when the card has dedicated RAM chips for just that purpose?

TIP 178: Disabling Virtual Memory Accelerates System Performance

In some cases, you may find that your system runs a bit faster if you disable the Virtual Memory feature.

1. From Control Panel, click on 386-Enhanced.
2. Select Virtual Memory, and click on Change.
3. Choose None for the type of virtual memory.
4. Click OK, and then Yes to confirm the change to your virtual memory settings.
5. You will be prompted to restart Windows for your change to take effect. Click Restart Windows.

Disabling Virtual Memory forces Windows to use only the actual memory installed in your system, rather than swapping inactive sections of RAM to your hard disk from time to time. If you have 4MB installed, you'll only be able to run 4MB of applications, and you will get out-of-memory messages much sooner. On the other hand, if you only run a few programs as a rule, then your system will run much faster. I have 9MB in my Toshiba T-2000SX laptop, and this is the way I run it—with no virtual memory. I get the fewest disk hits and fastest performance.

TIP 179: A Crash Course in Virtual Memory

Virtual Memory is an important feature of Windows 3.1. It allows sections of memory that are not in use to be swapped to the hard disk, freeing up more real memory for programs. It lets you run more applications, but at some cost in speed.

The most effective way to use this feature is to create as large a swap file as possible, as follows:

1. Use a program such as Norton Utilities Speed Disk or PC Tools Compress to defragment your hard drive. (The Windows swap file must be a contiguous block of disk space. When a utility defragments your hard drive, it creates a large, contiguous segment of disk space that's perfect for a swap file.)
2. Open Control Panel and select 386-Enhanced.
3. Click Change, and change the type of memory to Permanent. Make sure that the size of the swap file is the same as the Recommended size.

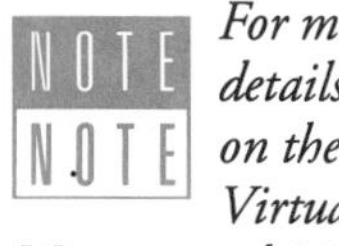

For more details on the Virtual Memory and 32-Bit Disk Access options, see Chapter 16.

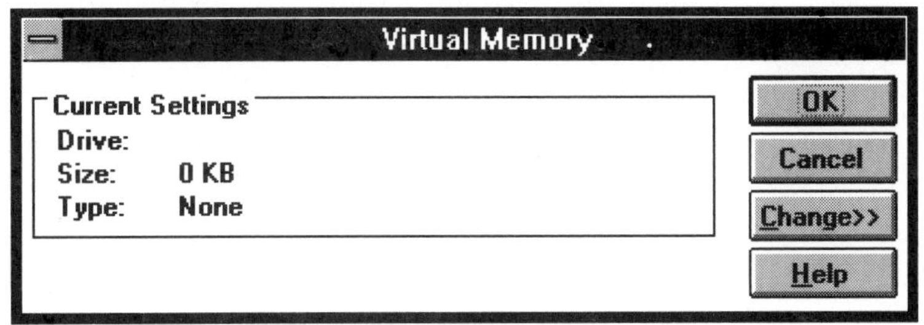

4. Finally, if the option exists, check Use 32-Bit Disk Access. This will accelerate Windows' access to the disk.

TIP 180: Speeding Up Hard Disk Backups

A piece of advice we're all tired of hearing is that we should back up our hard disks on a regular basis. But what a hassle! Not the least of the bother is the time the backups take—even if you're using a high-speed backup device such as a SCSI tape drive, rather than floppies. Doing "incremental" backups saves you time, of course, since only files that have changed since the last backup are archived.

Another trick is this: Don't bother backing up your permanent swap file, if you're using one. Since swap files can be planetary in size (often 2 to 10MB), backing up these files can be a real time waster—particularly since swap files are just placeholders on the disk for Windows to use as a temporary storage cache; they don't contain any useful data. Keep your eyes peeled for files called 386SPART.PAR and SPART.PAR in your root directory, and eliminate them from your list of files to back up. If you don't see these files, you may see \WINDOWS\WIN386.SWP (a temporary swap file); don't back this one up, either.

If you're backing up from within Windows and your backup program isn't smart enough to automatically avoid TEMP or hidden files, do it yourself by watching for files with a .TMP extension or starting with the characters ~WOA. These will typically be stored in your \WINDOWS\TEMP directory.

TIP 181: Preparing for a Windows Catastrophe

Once in a blue moon, Murphy's Law may collide with your good karma—resulting in your Windows setup or directories getting bollixed. If this happens, Windows typically then refuses to run (or acts supremely weird), and you're faced with the prospect of reinstalling from scratch, losing your precious WIN.INI and SYSTEM.INI information and numerous other settings, drivers, and application .INI files.

One way around this is to always have an exact replica of your \WINDOWS and \WINDOWS\SYSTEM directories on hand, tucked away on a backup tape, on floppies, or on your hard disk (preferably zipped to save space). Though this does work, it can take up a large amount of space, because your backup will include zillions of relatively unimportant files, such as accessories, Help files, vanilla-flavored fonts, and so forth. In my case, that is a total of 12MB of precious hard disk real estate!

Is there a novel backup technique for achieving somewhat the same result in less space? Yes—there is another approach. I mention it briefly in Appendix A of this book, and here it is again, in more detail. What you have to do is create a batch file to save all the truly important files in both your \WINDOWS and \WINDOWS\SYSTEM directories. These files are as follows:

\WINDOWS*.INI

\WINDOWS*.GRP

\WINDOWS*.PIF

\WINDOWS\SYSTEM*.INF

Have the batch file copy these files to a backup directory of your choice, such as \WINSAFE and \WINSAFE\SYSTEM, which of course you must create in advance. Next, add the batch file's name to your AUTOEXEC.BAT file, so that each time you turn on your computer, the files will be backed up.

If you ever have to reinstall Windows, after you're done with the reinstallation, exit Windows and use DOS to copy the backed-up files into their respective homes. When you start Windows again, things should be as they were.

If you are using off-beat hardware that requires special drivers (such as special display monitors, sound boards, printers, and so on), those drivers should still be in their respective directories—unless the situation got so out of hand that you had to erase everything in your Windows directories and truly start from scratch, or unless your original problem was that one of the drivers was somehow corrupted. Typically, after a Windows reinstallation, you should be able to get the special drivers up and running via Windows

Setup or Control Panel's Drivers icon. You'll want to specify your Windows directory as the repository of the manufacturer-supplied driver, so you don't have to hunt around for the floppy disk that came with your device.

One last suggestion for dealing with catastrophe: Whenever you do a normal reinstallation of Windows over an existing one (and you don't manually erase all the files in the Windows directories), Setup will recognize your personal Program Manager groups (.GRP files) and reinstate them into Program Manager. This is great. But be aware that three Windows-supplied groups, Main, Games, and Accessories, are exceptions to this, and will be overwritten during the reinstallation. So it's not a good idea to put new programs in these groups, because you'll lose them during reinstallation. As mentioned above, a way around this is to copy all your .GRP files into a temporary directory, then reinstall Windows, and finally copy those .GRP files back into your Windows directory.

TIPS FOR YOUR VIDEO SYSTEM

TIP 182: High-Resolution Primer

NOTE *See also the description of the WINSPEED product in Chapter 21.*

As discussed in Chapter 16, one of the biggest improvements you can make to your Windows setup is to move up to a higher-resolution screen. If you have a CGA, EGA, or Hercules screen, you should consider moving up to a VGA. You really need at least a VGA-compatible screen for Windows to look decent. Normal VGA offers you a 600 × 480 dot pattern on your screen. Most of the figures in this book were taken on a screen with that resolution. (Several were taken at 1024 × 768.) Unfortunately, even with normal VGA, you'll have to do a fair amount of scrolling around to see your work. After experimenting with many screen resolutions and sizes, I suggest that the serious Windows user move up to 800 × 600 or higher. It will increase your efficiency considerably.

Though there are several resolutions dubbed *Super VGA,* an industry consortium called Video Electronic Standards Association (VESA) has decided that Super VGA is 800 × 600. This resolution will give you roughly 50 percent more work space than standard VGA. However, the resolution I recommend for most Windows work, if you can afford it, is 1024 × 768 (sometimes called 8514/A or XGB). A screen with this resolution displays roughly twice the amount of information as a normal VGA. Though no laptops are available with either of these resolutions, it's not difficult to find desktop monitors that are. Consult the screen and video card's documentation to determine the correct Windows 3.1 driver to use with them.

Personally, I use a 19" gray scale monitor/card combo (the WYSE Technology WY7500) that displays 1280 × 1024 in 16 shades of gray. It's also capable of 1280 × 960, 1024 × 768, and 600 × 480 resolutions, and allows attachment of a color monitor as well. Unfortunately, it is not coprocessed, so it can be a bit slow at the higher resolutions. However, the image is almost flicker-free. More often than not I use it in the 1024 × 768 mode with Windows, simply because text is a bit too miniscule in the higher modes. When I do desktop publishing or CAD, I switch to a higher resolution.

Figures 20.10, 20.11, and 20.12 will give you an idea of the relative video "real estate" displayed on a 600 × 480, 1024 × 768, and 1280 × 1024 screen, respectively.

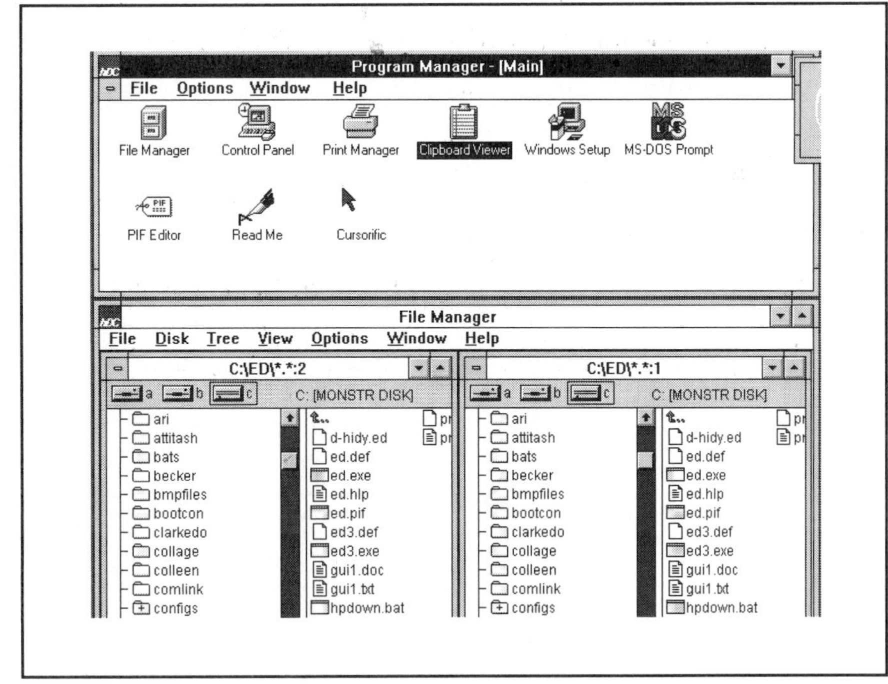

FIGURE 20.10: *600 × 480 VGA is standard VGA resolution. Here only two windows appear on-screen.*

FIGURE 20.11:

1024 × 768 resolution is becoming a popular compromise between high resolution and large enough text for everyday work. Here there's room for a third window and a row of icons along the bottom.

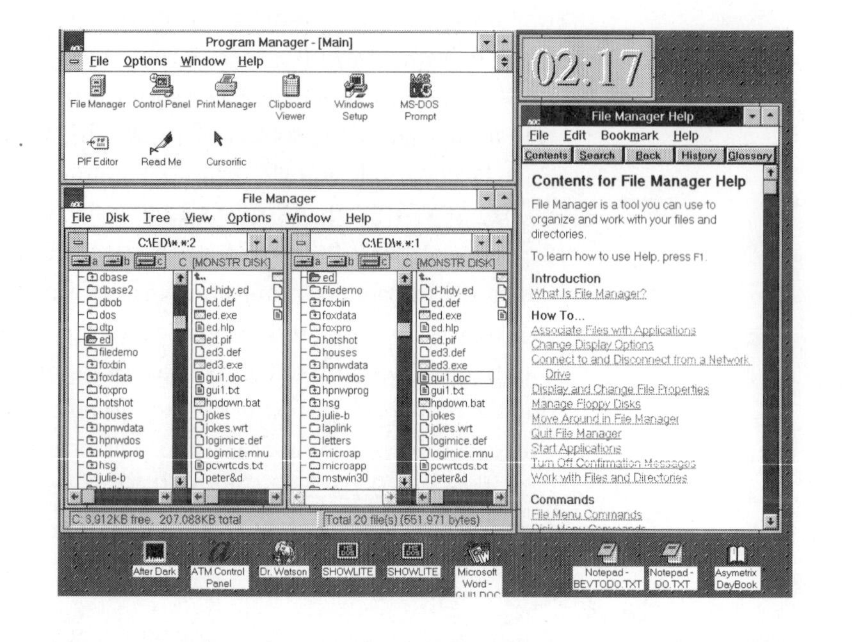

FIGURE 20.12:

1280 × 1024 resolution allows the maximum number of windows to be seen at one time. However, text can become very small.

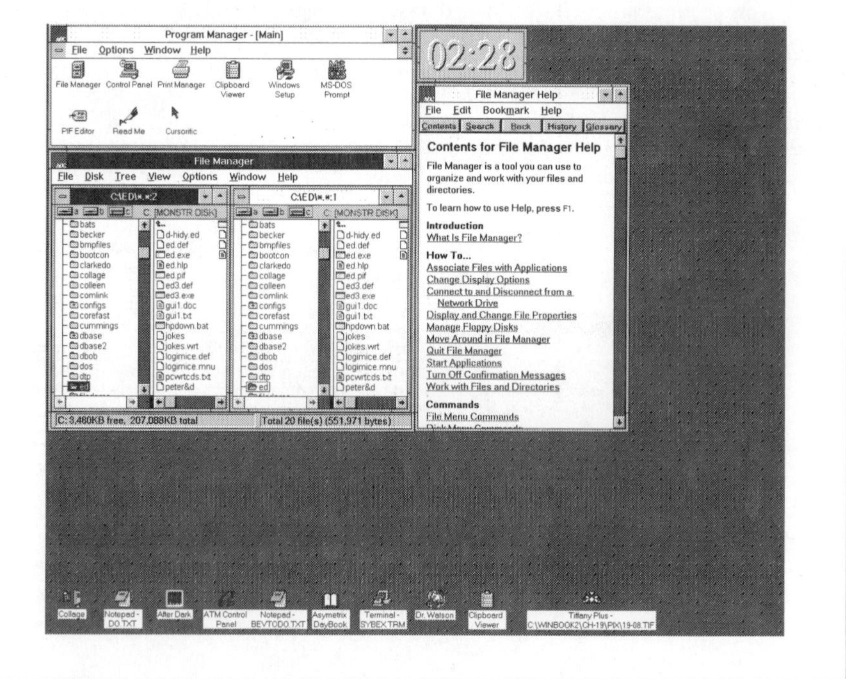

TIP 183: Get a Larger Monitor without the Hardware

Can't yet afford a new screen to increase your resolution? Here's an interim solution. Try one of the "virtual screen" software products that fakes Windows into thinking you have a bigger screen. That way, your existing screen becomes a window into the larger virtual screen. One such product is called MORE Windows from Aristosoft. It lets you create several different sizes of virtual screens, depending on your choice. You can even have a virtual screen as large as 1280 × 1024 using a standard VGA monitor. Moving the cursor to the edges of the screen quickly and smoothy scrolls the image around as though you were reading a newspaper with a magnifying glass. Depending on the applications you use, moving around with the mouse in this way may be preferable to using the scroll bars or the PgUp and PgDn keys all the time.

Another product, WideAngle, lets you create nine virtual desktops each with different arrangements of icons and windows. You switch easily between them using an on-screen number pad that looks like a telephone keypad. This program effectively helps you avoid the visual confusion created by overlapping windows, while still keeping many applications open at once. The program can be configured to open up assigned applications in their respective windows when you run Windows. I describe WideAngle in more detail later in this chapter under "Windows Utilities."

For product information on MORE Windows, call Aristosoft, Inc., at (800) 338-2629. It retails for $99. For information on WideAngle, call Attitash Software, Inc., at (800) 736-4198. It costs around $80.

TIP 184: How Old Is Your Driver?

Tests have shown that screen drivers (the software that controls the screen) can make a dramatic difference in your video system's performance. If you're using a driver supplied by the manufacturer of your screen, make sure you're using the latest version of that driver.

TIP 185: DRAM vs. VRAM

One of the big bottlenecks on the performance of higher-resolution video boards (above 800 × 600) is the relatively slow dynamic RAM (DRAM) chips used to store the screen image on the board. Video RAM (or VRAM), though more expensive, permits much faster operation by virtue of its ability to accept data from the computer at the same time as it's displaying it on the screen. DRAM allows only one of these processes at a time. If you're shopping for a high-resolution board, consider one with VRAM.

TIP 186: Lower Your Color Choices to Increase Video Speed

If you're using a noncoprocessed color card and monitor, you can increase your video system's speed between four to ten times by using a 16-color driver instead of a 256-color driver. If you don't need a precise selection of colors, give it a try.

TIP 187: No DOS Font Choices?

If you find you can't change the font in a non-Windows application running in a window, consider two possibilities. First, you have to be using a screen driver supplied with Windows, not from another manufacturer. So if you're using the vanilla VGA, Super VGA, CGA, EGA, or other on the supplied screen driver list, you should be fine. If you still aren't seeing the Fonts option in the Control menu of the windowed Non-Windows application, check your SYSTEM.INI file (the procedure for making alterations to SYSTEM.INI is explained in Chapter 16). In the section [NonWindowsApp] make sure you have the following line:

ChangeFontEnable=1

instead of

ChangeFontEnable=0

TIP 188: Health Hazards of VDTs

There is some concern among health professionals about video screen radiation. This is a personal interest of mine, one that I've followed and written about over the years. There are numerous unconfirmed studies suggesting that the low level ELF (Extremely Low Frequency) and VLF (Very Low Frequency) radiation emitted from video screens can lead to a variety of illnesses, ranging from cataracts to birth defects. The battle over this issue has been raging both in the laboratory and in the courts for years now, with no conclusive findings to date. However, if you are interested in taking the conservative approach, it is at least known that the subtle flickering and positive ions emitted from the surface of video screens are tiresome to the eyes. If you work with Windows a lot and are experiencing eye irritation, consider switching to a laptop computer with an LCD or gas plasma screen. Even though smaller, and probably not color, they are easier to focus on for long periods of time. They don't flicker—and they avoid the ELF and VLF radiation issue completely. If you wish to stay with a traditional screen, consider a brand that claims to meet the new SWEDAC low-emission standards now mandatory in some European countries. As of this writing, several NEC models meet this health requirement.

TIP 189: Run Setup from DOS

When you change monitor types (e.g., CGA to VGA or VGA to Super VGA), you'll have to tell Windows about it via the Windows Setup program. You can do this from within Windows or from DOS. I recommend doing it in DOS. Doing it from the Windows Setup icon in the Main group often prompts you to insert disks you really don't need. In DOS, however, you have to run the Setup program from the Windows directory or it won't find the current information about your system, most of which you want to retain (mouse, keyboard, etc.). Rather, it will think you want to install a new copy of Windows on your system. Here are the steps:

1. Exit Windows.
2. Install the new monitor or do whatever else is necessary to switch your monitor's mode to another resolution.
3. Switch to your Windows directory.
4. Type **SETUP** and press Enter.

5. Scroll up to the display line using the × key.
6. Press Enter to see a list of available screens. If the screen you're installing isn't on the menu, refer to the documentation that came with your new screen. Otherwise choose the correct screen or resolution types. Then follow instructions on the screen about confirming the setup, inserting disks, and which keys to press.
7. Run Windows. The new screen should work. Read the next tip too.

TIP 190: Use Drivers and Fonts Already Installed

Once you've installed a screen, the necessary driver and fonts for that screen are loaded into your Windows and System directories. You shouldn't have to load them again when you switch back to a previous screen or resolution, even though running Setup from within Windows will prompt you to do so. Run Setup as explained in Tip 189 above, and you won't have to feed disks into your computer just to change screen setups. Here's an example: Say you have a multisync color monitor capable of both standard VGA and 1024 × 768 Super VGA. Run Setup (from the Windows directory) and install for VGA. Then run Setup again and install for Super VGA. To change from one resolution to another, exit Windows and run Setup, choosing the correct screen resolution. You won't have to insert any Windows disks.

TIP 191: Buying a New Monitor?

If you are considering upgrading your monitor, here is a checklist of features to consider:

- The monitor should have a fine *dot pitch*, which is a measurement of the size of the dots on the screen. Dots that are too large result in a blurry image. A dot pitch of 0.25 is acceptable; a dot pitch of 0.30 is only marginal. Most magazine ads or supplied user manuals will list the dot pitch for a screen.
- Both the monitor and card that drives it should work in *noninterlaced* mode at the desired resolution. Noninterlacing reduces flickering considerably. *This is particularly important for 800 × 600*

and above. Look at the screen from the corner of your eye (using your peripheral vision). The amount of flicker will be more apparent when viewed this way. This is due to the retina's increased sensitivity to flicker outside of its central focal area.

- Look at the screen while running Windows and in full-screen DOS. Is the picture stable and clear? Could you look at it for hours? Is the left margin still on the screen? Are the sides and top of the image fairly straight or do they bend outward?
- Can you adjust the horizontal and vertical size of the image? You may want to be able to do this when switching from Non-Windows applications to Windows applications.
- Is there an antiglare coating on the screen?
- Is the casing made of plastic or metal? Metal will shield your body from electromagnetic radiation more effectively.
- Does the monitor have a flat picture tube or curved one? Flat ones usually give a truer image, though they are more expensive. Zenith and NEC are two manufacturers of flat tube monitors.
- Is it a multisync type monitor? Though more expensive, multisync monitors work with more types of computers and video cards than do other types of monitors. You can use them on CGA, MDA, EGA, VGA, and often on Super VGA cards.
- What is the *refresh rate* of the screen/card combination? Refresh rate greatly affects the perceivability of flicker. It's a measurement of how many times the screen is repainted per second. A refresh of 60 Hz or above (preferably 70 Hz) is acceptable.

TIP 192: Testing a Video Before You Buy

Wondering how you can test potential display monitors and cards for the best performance, before you buy? You can always read industry magazines to hear what testers have to say. As thorough as some reviews seem to be, however, you can't always count on them when it comes time for your final purchasing decision. Having written hundreds of reviews for the magazines, I can tell you that reviewers don't always have the space to report everything they discover, often don't have objective means of comparison, and aren't likely to have the same pet peeves and requirements that you have. So are there any tools available to help you test out potential products before you plunk down your thousands on that state-of-the-art, coprocessed, super-duper, hi-rez, tilt-and-swivel monitor/card combo?

It has come to my attention that the technical folks at one magazine have standardized a commercial video-testing program called DisplayMATE Video Display Utilities. According to some product evaluators, it's a great program. It comes with a large book (386 pages) about the tests that includes an in-depth discussion of common display problems. Be prepared to find out, though, that your prized display system doesn't cut the mustard. Some of the tests, though revealing, aren't very forgiving.

If you don't run Windows, and only use character-based programs in DOS, don't bother with this program. Your monitor probably performs about as well as any, since speed only becomes an issue when your system must move huge numbers of pixels around the screen—something character-based programs don't require.

But as dot density increases, so does the need for a testing program like this. So if you're running Windows and looking into a Super VGA (800 × 600) system or higher, then DisplayMATE can help. As this book goes to press, you can buy the program for around $149 from the publisher, Sonera Technologies, (800) 932-6323.

TIP 193: A Cheap, Fast VGA Board

Looking for an inexpensive VGA board designed for speed? Weitek Corp., maker of the Weitek math coprocessor chips used in many PCs, has come up with a high-speed VGA board capable of normal VGA and interlaced 1024 × 768. The list price for Weitek Power for Windows is only $299, so it will be available pretty cheaply once discounted. It's designed for the business user who is typically working with word processors and spreadsheets and doesn't need fancy features. The board uses Weitek's W5086 controller chip to speed up scrolling, pasting, page previewing, and window resizing and moving. If you work mostly with text, don't need more than 16 colors, and are on a tight budget, this is a good bet. Call Weitek Corp. at (408) 738-8400.

TIP 194: Increase Display Performance with Microsoft Drivers

NOTE *This is a tip directly from Microsoft and is included in the README file supplied with Windows 3.1.*

If you are using a video card and monitor (NEC Multisync 3D/4D/5D or other multifrequency monitor) capable of 800 × 600 16-color resolution with a VGA driver, a third-party Super VGA driver, or one of the following drivers provided in the Windows 3.1 Supplemental Driver Library:

ATI Mode 54h (800 × 600, 16 colors) version 2.00

CHIPS Super VGA 82C451 (800 × 600, 16 colors)

CHIPS Super VGA 82C452 (800 × 600, 16 colors)

Paradise VGA (800 × 600, 16 colors)

use the Super VGA (800 × 600, 16 colors) driver provided with Windows instead. If you do not update your driver, Windows may not work properly when running in 386-Enhanced mode. In addition, the 3.1 driver contains new features and performance enhancements. Also, you can obtain over 50 percent more screen space if you run Windows with a Super VGA driver instead of a VGA driver.

TIP 195: About Custom Video "Chip Sets" for Windows

As I mention in Chapter 16, a fast video board can help supercharge your Windows setup. (There I discuss some of the basic concepts of coprocessed and noncoprocessed video boards.) A slow board can bottleneck your work, even on a speed-demon computer. Recognizing this, some video board manufacturers have released boards they tout as being designed for Windows. As of this writing, a few have even begun releasing boards based on chip sets (custom computer video display chips) supposedly optimized for Windows. The primary advantage of chip sets is their ability to move portions of the screen around quickly, using a technique called bitblt (pronounced bit-blit). This stands for "bit-block transfer" and is what happens when, say, you reposition a window on the screen.

TIP 196: Color Isn't Necessarily Better

Color isn't necessarily better. Though most high-resolution screens are color these days, and Windows does some nice things in color, certain tasks lend themselves to monochrome (black-and-white) monitors. Desktop publishing (unless you're working in color a lot) is a case in point, as are word processing, CAD, spreadsheet work, and other engineering tasks. Monochrome screens tend to have superior focus and be less costly than color monitors of the same size. Many of the better monochrome monitors are called "gray-scale monitors," meaning they render colors as shades of gray. The screens in this book are indicative of what a gray-scale monitor looks like in Windows. Most VGA laptops use gray-scale screens, since color LCDs are so expensive at this moment.

TIP 197: Working with Display Drivers Not Updated for Windows 3.1

Windows 3.1 comes with a display driver that works with most VGA (480 × 640) and super-VGA (800 × 600) chip sets. For higher resolution or for off-beat monitors, however, you often have to use the drivers supplied with those monitors. Unfortunately, some OEMs (original equipment manufacturers) haven't yet updated their Windows 3.0 display drivers to accommodate Windows 3.1. You may be able to get around this by using the older driver disk, finding a file on it called SETUP.INF, and renaming it to OEMSETUP.INF. Then run Setup from the Windows directory (from the DOS prompt) or from the Main group's Windows Setup option, and choose Other for the display type. You'll be prompted to insert the driver disk.

TIPS TO IMPROVE YOUR SYSTEM'S PERFORMANCE

TIP 198: Three Performance Improvements

NOTE *See also the description of the WinSleuth Professional program in Chapter 21.*

Here are three suggestions that can be used in addition to those explained in Chapter 16, for supercharging your Windows setup.

- Turn off graphics port trapping. The speed of running non-Windows applications under 386-Enhanced mode can be noticeably improved by not selecting any of the Monitor Ports options in the Advanced section of the PIF Editor. The High Graphics option is on by default to provide compatibility with the widest range of non-Windows applications, but is not required for most of these applications.

- Turn off the FileSysChange= option in SYSTEM.INI. Windows 3.1's 386-Enhanced mode can monitor disk access by non-Windows applications and send directory update messages to the File Manager. This allows File Manager to be automatically updated by changes made to files or directories by non-Windows applications. However, it is not a necessity, and leaving this option turned off (the default) accelerates file access by non-Windows applications.

  To disable this feature, in the [386Enh] section of the SYSTEM.INI file, change the FileSysChange= setting to no or "off"; it should read FileSysChange=no. This is the default setting, but check it anyway just to make sure.

- Use the lowest common display driver. Using a display driver with a higher resolution or greater number of colors results in slower display performance. If you do not require the extra features of a particular display driver, use a driver with less capability. Usually this suggestion applies to display systems that are VGA-compatible but offer an extended mode driver, such as the Video Seven or 8514. Choosing the standard VGA driver instead, offers faster display performance but less resolution and/or color support.

TIP 199: Pruning Unnecessary Lines from Your WIN.INI File

We mentioned this in Chapter 16, but it's worth repeating: One of my biggest gripes with Windows is that many programs (including Microsoft products) use the WIN.INI file to store data. The disadvantage here is that when you remove programs from your Windows system (that is, icons from Program Manager) and even from your hard disk, the corresponding lists of settings for each program in your WIN.INI file are not removed. Rather, you must do this yourself. So the more settings you accumulate in that file, the longer it will take for Windows to load. This is especially true for those of you using Adobe Type Manager. As you install more and more fonts, Windows will take longer and longer to load. (If you install a couple of hundred fonts, it takes a *very* long time!)

Be diligent about cleaning up your WIN.INI file occasionally, as discussed at the end of Chapter 16.

TIP 200: Deleting Leftover Temporary Files

Temporary files sometimes remain on your hard disk when Windows or an application crashes and you don't exit the program or Windows normally. The result can be the unwelcome consumption of precious hard disk space by now-useless TEMP files. Until these dead TEMP files are erased, this space will not again be available for your general use. I explain a couple of techniques for manually or automatically scrubbing your disk of these files in Chapter 16, under the topic "Deleting Temporary Files." You may want to refer to that advice if the level of your available disk space has suddenly plummeted.

Note that you should do this outside of Windows, and that these temporary files are often hidden. You may have to use a program such as XTREE, or run DOSSHELL, that will display hidden files (a DOS DIR command won't do it).

TIP 201: Choosing Your Swap Disk for Standard Mode

If you are running Windows in 386-Enhanced mode, your swap disk (virtual disk) location and size are determined by the Control Panel's 386-Enhanced ➤ Virtual Memory setting. Your application's TEMP files are determined by the TEMP variable in AUTOEXEC.BAT.

When running in Standard mode, however, the drive/directory location for your swap files and application TEMP files are both determined by the TEMP variable in your AUTOEXEC.BAT file, for example:

```
SET TEMP=C:\WINDOWS\TEMP
```

For fastest performance when switching between programs, you should use your fastest hard disk for TEMP files (if you have more than one hard disk). Hard disks are rated according to step times and average access times. Check the documentation supplied with the disk or ask your dealer to determine which of your hard disks is fastest.

Note to Network Users: Using a network hard disk for your TEMP files is generally not a good idea because data will have to be sent back and forth across the network link each time you switch applications.

You can also set the TEMP file location by altering your SYSTEM.INI file. Locate the section called [NonWindowsApp] and add a line such as this:

```
SWAPDISK=D:\TEMP
```

where D: is the drive you want to use, and TEMP is the name of the target directory.

TIP 202: Using the RAM Drive for TEMP Files to Accelerate Windows on Older 286 Machines

NOTE *See the discussion in chapter 16 for additional details on setting up a RAM disk.*

If you are running Windows on an 80286, particularly one with an old, slow hard disk (65ms average access time, or thereabouts), you may notice an annoying sluggishness when switching to and from non-Windows applications. This is because non-Windows applications are always swapped out to TEMP files on disk when you switch away from them in Standard mode. On a slow computer or a slow hard disk, the swapping can take a few seconds. A trick that can accelerate this process is to create a 2MB RAM disk and tell Windows to use it for your TEMP files. Since Windows at boot time looks to the TEMP variable as established by your AUTOEXEC.BAT file, you just add the appropriate line there to steer Windows to the RAM drive. (You have to create the RAM drive before setting the TEMP variable.)

For example, if you've set up a RAM disk on F, you'd set your TEMP line to read as follows:

```
SET TEMP=F:\TEMP
```

Since a RAM disk is orders of magnitude faster than any hard disk, you will reduce system overhead dramatically during both file creation and access. The improvement in speed can be dramatic. If you have plenty of RAM, and have a 286 or run in Standard mode, you'll want to try this technique.

Always use a subdirectory (such as \TEMP) rather than the root directory as the target for the TEMP files (even on a hard disk). DOS limits the number of files that can be entered into a root directory; using a subdirectory prevents a possible system or application crash in the event there isn't room in the drive's FAT for all the files needed. You create the subdirectory, and then set the TEMP variable with commands like this in your AUTOEXEC.BAT:

```
MD F:\TEMP
SET TEMP=F:\TEMP
```

Note that some applications will crash if they run out of space on any disk. RAM disks are usually much smaller than the available space on a hard disk, so you are more likely to encounter problems if you don't make your RAM disk large enough. According to Microsoft, you should at least have 2MB. Then keep an eye out for erratic behavior, and occasionally check to see how much space is free on the RAM disk, using the DOS DIR command, the File Manager, or some other utility.

TIP 203: DOS File Handles for Windows

Make sure that you allocate sufficient DOS file handles for Windows. When a program like Windows needs to open a file, it uses a file handle—a special section of memory DOS uses to keep track of open files. File handles are set in CONFIG.SYS. Look for a line like this:

```
FILES=50
```

Make sure that the FILES= number in your CONFIG.SYS file is at least 35. Some applications will increase the number when they are installed. There is some consumption of conventional memory (below 640K) as this number is increased. However, this small loss is worth it when you don't have to run into this message from DOS: "Too many files open"—the telltale sign of a less-than-adequate FILES= allotment.

For a one-time fix, without changing your CONFIG.SYS file, just close an application or two and then again try running the application that caused the error message.

TIPS ON MEMORY MANAGEMENT AND MEMORY SHORTAGES

TIP 204: Changing the Order of Running Applications

If Windows informs you that you're running low on memory and can't load another program, try closing all your applications and then reopening the large programs before the smaller ones. By doing so, the small programs may fit into the "gaps" left between the larger ones.

TIP 205: Using DOS 5 to Make More Conventional Memory Available

When running Windows in Standard mode, non-Windows applications are temporarily stored in a swap file on disk whenever you switch back to Windows. Each non-Windows application is given its own swap (or TEMP) file on the disk, and these files are stored in the directory pointed to by the TEMP variable in your AUTOEXEC.BAT file. These files begin with the ~ (tilde) character. When you switch back to the non-Windows application, Windows reads the TEMP file back into memory, restoring the non-Windows application to its previous state. Each non-Windows application run in Standard mode creates such a TEMP file, so it's important to have ample room on your hard disk if you intend to run several non-Windows applications simultaneously in Standard mode. If you don't have enough space, you'll get out-of-memory messages from Windows.

With Windows in 386-Enhanced mode, non-Windows applications are run in "virtual machines" that Windows creates using your system's pool of conventional, extended, and virtual memory. In this case, because RAM is more likely to be used in place of swap files for each non-Windows application, switching is faster and hard disk space isn't as important (though it is still used when RAM space is exhausted). The bad news is that each virtual machine Windows creates is an exact copy of the DOS environment existing in conventional memory (from 0 to 640K). So if you have lots of TSRs, memory-resident utilities, and device drivers in your lower 640K, significant amounts of memory get very quickly used up when you run non-Windows applications. Also, RAM-hungry non-Windows applications may have trouble finding space to run in such cramped quarters, resulting in the "Not enough memory to run application" message.

Enter DOS 5, which incorporates intelligent memory management. Designed with Windows 3.1 in mind, DOS 5 (along with HIMEM.SYS) lets you load much of the operating system and the TSRs and device drivers into extended memory, leaving more conventional memory free for applications. So if you are experiencing memory shortages, particularly when running non-Windows applications in 386-Enhanced mode, upgrade to DOS 5.

TIP 206: More About DOS Environment Space

In Chapter 19, I explained what to do when non-Windows applications crash because of low environment space. Here's another take on the subject—this time from within Windows, rather than from the DOS command line.

First, recall that the DOS environment is an important section of memory. In this area, DOS (and Windows, too) conceals internal variables like the DOS search path (the PATH statement), the location of COMMAND.COM, and the structure of the DOS prompt. Occasionally, when running non-Windows applications from within Windows, you may get an "Out of environment space" error.

Here's how to increase the space allocated to non-Windows applications' environment in DOS sessions run from within Windows:

1. Load SYSTEM.INI into a text editor (such as Notepad).
2. Add this line to the [NonWindowsApp] section of SYSTEM.INI:

   ```
   CommandEnvSpace=1024
   ```

3. Reboot Windows, and try again to run your applications.
4. If you still get environment shortage messages with your mix of non-Windows applications, change the number to 1124, and try again.

The CommandEnvSpace= command allocates 1024 (or more) bytes of environment space to all DOS sessions that are run from Windows. The advantage to this approach is that it only affects the environment space for DOS sessions you run within Windows. When you exit Windows, the environment space reverts to whatever is stipulated by your SHELL statement in CONFIG.SYS.

Incidentally, Windows 3.0 doesn't recognize the CommandEnvSpace command, so don't bother trying it with that version. Only the SHELL approach works with 3.0.

TIP 207: Economizing on System Resources

As I've explained earlier, Windows has a discrete amount of the available system resources, and you may encounter out-of-memory messages if your Windows system is low on these resources, even if there is still plenty of RAM available. Windows 3.1 manages system resources better than 3.0 did, but you can still run out, because only 64K of space is allotted in the first place.

In addition to tips such as keeping toolbar use to a minimum (see "About System Resource Shortages" in Chapter 19), you can conserve on System Resources by doing the following:

- Maximize only the program groups that contain your most often needed application icons.
- Put your most frequently used applications into a single program group. Put lesser-used program icons in minimized groups at the bottom of the Program Manager window.

TIP 208: EMM386 Memory Usage

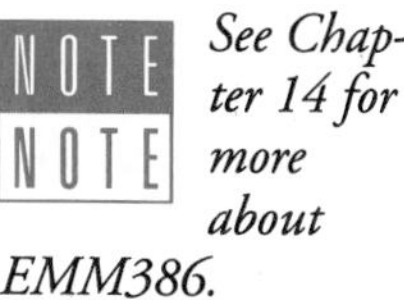
See Chapter 14 for more about EMM386.

The following technical explanation is based on information from Microsoft regarding the use of their expanded memory manager, EMM386. If you're running into memory shortages when using EMM386 or wondering why your memory-usage figures don't jibe, study the next few paragraphs.

EMM386 can report results for memory usage that may not make sense if you don't understand how EMM386 works. EMM386 uses an extra 48K of extended memory in addition to the amount needed for emulating expanded memory. Also, EMM386 always allocates memory in such a way that at least 64K of extended memory remains free. Finally, EMM386 appears to allocate an extra 384K of system memory in addition to the amount that you would expect for extended memory. Here's an explanation of EMM386 memory usage.

Consider the following statement in a CONFIG.SYS file:

```
DEVICE = EMM386.SYS 256
```

For simplification, assume the machine is equipped with only 256K of extended memory. EMM386 will attempt to allocate 256K of extended memory to be used in emulating expanded memory, and the following will be reported when EMM386 installs itself:

```
144K Extended Memory Allocated
384K System Memory Allocated
------
528K Expanded Memory Available
```

This report can be confirmed by using the MEM command from DOS, which displays the following information:

```
262,144 Total Extended Memory
65,536 Available Extended Memory
540,672 Total EMS Memory
147,456 Free EMS Memory
```

Notice that even though EMM386 has requested 256K of extended memory, it only ended up with 144K. This is because 48K is consumed as overhead by EMM386, and 64K is reserved for the XMS driver, HIMEM.SYS. Thus, only 256K – (64K + 48K) = 144K is left for EMS emulation.

EMM386 reports when it loads that 384K of system memory are allocated, and the MEM command reports a total of 528K (384K + 144K) of EMS memory. This is because EMM386, a LIM 4.00 expanded memory manager, has the ability to implement large-frame EMS. In this configuration, part of the conventional memory addressing area can be used by EMM386 for mapping page frames. The LIM 4.00 specification allows up to 384K of conventional addressing area to be used by an EMM. Therefore, the system is reporting that at any given time, EMM386 can use up to 384K of conventional addressing area for large-frame EMS.

TIP 209: Loading TSRs

If you're using the third-party program, QEMM, to load programs into high memory and can't fit everything in, try changing the order of what gets loaded there. Let's say you only have one block of high memory (48K), and you load the following TSRs in this order:

DOSEDIT.COM	6K
PC-CACHE.COM	14K
MOUSE.COM	16K

The K amounts shown above are those reported by MAPMEM.

All these programs should be able to fit in that one 48K section. The problem is that a TSR may initially require more memory than what it eventually uses. For example, MOUSE.COM may initially require 30K to perform various chores before settling down to its 16K requirement. If you load the TSRs in the above order, MOUSE.COM won't fit. By placing MOUSE.COM first, however, there will be enough room to load it and everything else, too.

TIP 210: Out of Memory?

NOTE *Chapter 19 contains lots of other suggestions for freeing up memory.*

One source of the trouble may be low disk space. Windows uses your hard disk to store chunks of memory contents that it doesn't immediately need. Try freeing up some disk space by deleting unnecessary files. To take advantage of the new memory you've just created, you'll have to run the 386-Enhanced option of Control Panel and increase the amount of Virtual Memory allocated to Windows.

TIP 211: Still Out of Memory?

Windows needs as much of the first 640K of RAM (called conventional memory) as it can get. Check your CONFIG.SYS and AUTOEXEC.BAT files for unneccessary programs that may have been loaded into memory when you started your computer. Removing these memory hogs may make available the memory you need.

TIPS FOR NETWORK USERS

TIP 212: Keeping a DOS Window or Session Open After Running a Batch File on a Network

As mentioned in Tip 96, including COMMAND.COM as the last line in a batch file will keep a DOS window open until you type EXIT and press Enter. If you're running on a network, however, COMMAND.COM may not be on your search path, resulting in an error message such as "Bad command or file name" when the .BAT file completes. This is because the DOS command interpreter is typically stored on a file server elsewhere on the network. To ensure that COMMAND.COM is found, use the following line, instead, in your batch file:

```
%COMSPEC%
```

%COMSPEC% is the DOS variable name that always points to the location of the DOS and the command interpreter (COMMAND.COM). With this variable as the last line in your batch file, your DOS window or screen will stay open after running a batch program on a network node.

TIP 213: Use Local Swap Files

One of the most effective networking strategies for increasing your system's throughput is to cut down on data traffic along the network linkage. One operation that consumes significant time across a network—even on a stand-alone computer—is reading and writing to swap files.

One of the things that slows down the initial loading of Windows across a network is the creation of a swap file on the server's hard disk. Then, as you start working with large files or multiple applications, Windows begins using the swap file on the server once the size of your work files exceeds the amount of available RAM in your system. If traffic flow on the network is heavy when Windows attempts a swap, your workstation may have to wait a bit until the network interlink is free before the server can process the swap.

If your workstation has a hard disk, there is a better way. Tell Windows to use your local hard disk for the swap file. Add these lines to the [386Enh] section of your SYSTEM.INI file:

```
PagingDrive=C:
MaxPagingFileSize=1024
```

Of course, if your hard disk has a different logical assignment (drive letter), you'll want to use that designation in the PagingDrive= command. This command tells Windows to use the local drive for swapping. The second command tells Windows what size to make the swap file when you run Windows. One megabyte is ample, and specifying the size speeds up Windows' initial loading. Whatever size you decide to specify for the swap file, make sure you have that much free space on your local hard disk.

TIP 214: Acquire NetWare Tools

A set of the free NetWare tools is a must for any NetWare user. You can get these tools from a number of locations, but a sure source is CompuServe. Get into the NetWare forum, and download a file called TOOLS110.ZIP (this file name may be different for the latest version of TOOLS—perhaps TOOLS115.ZIP or some other number at the time you read this).

What you get is a slick, self-installing group of nine programs that bypass the Control Panel; they accomplish such tasks as making network attachments, messaging with other users, changing passwords, printing, mapping the drive, and displaying information about users on the net.

TIP 215: Keep Your Network Software Up to Date

Network utilities and drivers are constantly being updated as bugs are reported and repaired, and as software developers respond to users' requests. You'll want to occasionally check with your network manufacturer for updated Windows files. If you're using NetWare, the following files are the most likely to have been updated:

IPX.OBJ
IPXODI.COM
NEXTX.COM
TBM12.COM
LSL.COM

TIP 216: Be Careful When You Log In and Out

Caution: In general, Windows isn't happy when you log off a file server to which you were connected when you booted Windows. Logging into additional servers isn't as much of a problem—but beware of logging off the server that is running Windows for you. Since the files Windows needs to run can't be found if you log off that server, Windows will bomb.

TIP 217: Turning Off That Annoying "No Network Running" Message

Do you run Windows both on and off the network? When starting up Windows while you're off the network, you may see an error message warning you that the network isn't running. This annoying message can be turned off if you don't like it, if it confuses other users, or if it always sets you to wondering if something serious is wrong.

While you're on the network, choose the Network icon from the Control Panel and turn off the warning message. If you are not currently on the network, to eliminate the error message you have to edit your WIN.INI file. In the [Windows] section, enter the following line:

```
NetWarn=0
```

TIP 218: Handling Network Printing Hassles

If you're trying to use a printer connected to your network, and you can't print from within Windows, try this:

1. Run Control Panel and double-click on the Printers icon.

2. Make sure that a printer is in the Printers list and is selected as the default printer. If this is not the case, refer to "Selecting the Default Printer" in Chapter 6.
3. Select your printer from the Installed Printers list and click the Connect button.
4. If "Fast Printing Direct to Port" is enabled, disable it.
5. Click on OK and then Close to save the change.

This forces Windows to print through DOS, and it may solve the problem. Of course, printing will be considerably slower—but at least it will work.

TIP 219: NetWare IPX Updates

Attention NetWare LAN administrators: You will probably have to upgrade your client IPX loaders to work with Windows 3.1. Fortunately, Microsoft has created a tool that automates this task. It's available in Microsoft forums in most major on-line services, under the file name NOVELL.EXE. It's also available free of charge in the Windows Drivers Library, available by calling Microsoft.

TIPS FOR LAPTOP USERS

TIP 220: Installing Windows on a Laptop

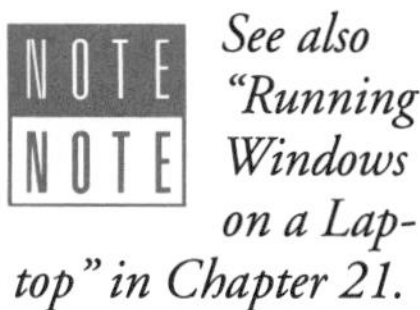

See also "Running Windows on a Laptop" in Chapter 21.

When installing windows on a laptop, you'll probably want to economize on disk space. This is because most laptops have 20 or 40MB drives. You'll also want to choose display and mouse settings that work best with LCD screens.

A complete Windows installation can consume as much as 11MB of hard disk space. By eliminating unnecessary files, however, you can reclaim a good portion of that for use by your programs and data files. Install Windows on your laptop using the Custom Setup instead of the Express Setup. Then, from the screen that lets you deselect files you don't want, turn off the check boxes for the following:

Readme Files

Accessories

Games

Screen Savers

Wallpapers, Misc.

If you intend to use some of the accessories (such as Clock and Calculator), choose those by clicking on the Files button to the right of the Accessories check box in the Windows Setup dialog box. Obviously, if you have a more powerful application that performs the same task as one of the Windows accessories (such as a word processor or communications program) you won't miss the more mild-mannered Windows versions. Finally, install the Help files only for the accessories you don't know how to use, since Help files take up disk space, too.

If you think you might need some of the Windows accessories while on the road, you can install them copied to another directory and zip them up using a program such as PKZIP to save space. Or you can take the Windows master disks with you, and use Windows Setup (in the Main group) to install applications and files you left out of the previous installation (this is a great feature of the new Setup program for Windows 3.1). Just run Setup and choose Options ➤ Add/Remove Windows Components. (See Tip 162 for more details.)

Since virtually all laptops use the VGA screen resolution, install for that resolution. Afterward, you can fine-tune things using the Control Panel's Color settings. I use the normal VGA color settings because my Toshiba T2000SX displays color as shades of gray. I've "reversed" the screen using Toshiba's pop-up utility program (most laptops have something similar), so that Windows displays text and icons as black on white, and DOS sessions are white text on black background. Note that you have to do this before running Windows, since the pop-up won't work when the machine is running in protected mode (that is, when Windows is running). Unfortunately,

I haven't found a way to have a white background for both DOS and Windows. If you like working with black letters on white background while in DOS, then set up your computer to work that way normally (outside Windows), and then choose one of the two Reversed LCD settings in the Color options from the Windows Control Panel. Your icons and a few other elements, such as window buttons and borders, will look a bit "off", but it's workable.

Depending on your screen type, you might want to try several of the other settings. If your laptop has a gas plasma screen, using the Plasma Power Saver option will extend your battery life.

Contrary to popular opinion, none of the screen settings will extend the life of your LCD screen. The parts of the screen that wear out are the back- and side-lighting elements, which aren't affected by what's being displayed. One way you can extend the life of your screen is to shut off the internal lighting whenever possible. On some models, this means closing the lid. On others it means reducing the time-out interval for screen shut-down.

You also can extend battery life by displaying less white on an LCD screen. This is because power is consumed each time a screen pixel is turned on. (Turning on a pixel allows light to be transmitted from the light source to your eyes.) Thus, light-colored pixels use more juice, so if the screen is mostly white, you're consuming more battery power. Even so, I haven't noticed much difference, and enjoy impressive performance from my various laptops running in either normal or reverse video. The hard disk, internal modems, and extra RAM cards consume significantly more power than the LCD pixels, so look to those issues first.

As for mice, a plethora of rodents intended for portables are now available. You be the judge as to whether it's a capitalist plot. I'm happy with my old Logitech three-button. If you have a mouse or other pointing device for which you can't find a specific driver listed in the installation procedure, chances are that it is compatible with the Microsoft-IBM PS/2 mouse driver. Try it.

As mentioned in "Running Windows on a Laptop" in Chapter 21, for pointing devices that are in fact compatible with the Microsoft mouse, the new Microsoft Mouse driver 8.1 gives you some features worth having on a laptop.

Finally, consider what printers you might use on the road. Most printers you'll encounter will emulate either the HP Laserjet II, Epson MX/FX, or Generic/Text printers. Install the drivers for all three of these, and you're pretty sure to have what's necessary if you need to plug into the printer at some gas station or in a friend's office. Just remember to choose the correct driver with the File ➤ Print Setup command from your application prior to printing.

TIP 221: Toshiba Laptops and AutoResume with Windows

If you're using a Toshiba 386SX laptop such as the T2000SX or T2200 SX, there is a trick to getting AutoResume to work properly with Windows. If you don't install a special Toshiba software driver, AutoResume will crash each time you turn off your computer. This is a real bummer, since it amounts to doing a three-key reset from Windows. Open files won't be closed, and TEMP files will be left hanging around on your hard disk. If you haven't saved your work, you'll definitely lose data from your previous session. To solve this problem, get the special driver BIOSXLAT file from Toshiba and modify your SYSTEM.INI file according to directions supplied with the file. Once you have the file installed properly, the Toshiba has something few other computers, desktop or laptop, can offer—the ability to power down and then up again, instantly, without having to quit and restart Windows. Your cursor will be right where you left it, with all programs open and running, waiting for you to continue your work. To get the file and lots of other Toshiba information, call their BBS at (714) 837-4408 with your modem. You'll have to pay long-distance charges, as for a normal voice call, but there's no charge to use the BBS.

TIP 222: Toshiba Laptops and Logitech Mouse/AutoResume Problems

If you are using a Microsoft mouse or one compatible with your Toshiba laptop, and use AutoResume (see Tip 221), your mouse probably works fine when you restart your computer. With Logitech mice, however, problems with wild mouse behavior after a restart have been reported. When you move the mouse, the cursor may jump all over the screen, selecting text, opening menus, and possibly even damaging documents or running programs you didn't want to run. Here's a workable fix I discovered after months of frustration. The problem seems to be that the Logitech mouse isn't reinitialized when you turn the laptop back on. Using the Control Panel to reinitialize the serial port doesn't work, either. What you have to do is start a DOS session and run the Logitech mouse driver as a TSR.

1. Locate the MOUSE.COM file that came with your Logitech mouse. (Make sure it's not a driver for a Microsoft or some other mouse; they often have the name MOUSE.COM, too. Try running the program from the DOS command line to make sure it says Logitech.)
2. Copy the driver to the root directory of drive C (or the appropriate location for your setup).
3. Create a new program icon as shown in the Program Item Properties box shown here:

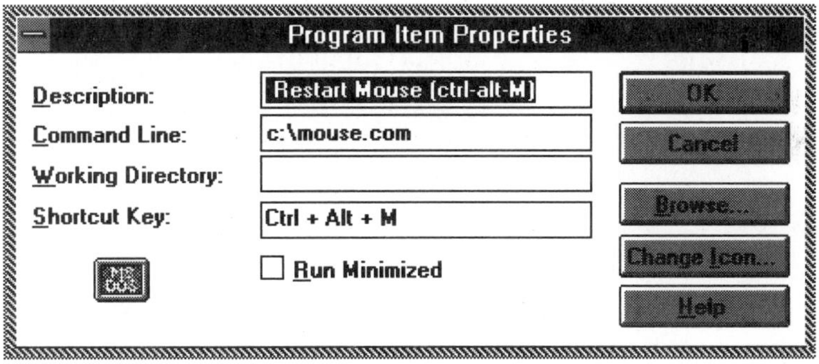

Program Item Properties

Description: Restart Mouse (ctrl-alt-M)
Command Line: c:\mouse.com
Working Directory:
Shortcut Key: Ctrl + Alt + M
Run Minimized

OK
Cancel
Browse...
Change Icon...
Help

You can skip the shortcut key if you want, but having one makes reactivating the mouse easier. (Notice that I've included the shortcut key in the Description box, too, so it will appear as a reminder under the icon. You might want to use this technique with other icons you create.)

4. When you restart your laptop, if the mouse acts freaky, press Alt-Tab a few times to get to Program Manager. Then type Ctrl-Alt-M or double-click on the Restart Mouse icon you've just created.

The screen will clear, a DOS session will run, and you'll see a notice that the Logitech mouse is being loaded, as shown here:

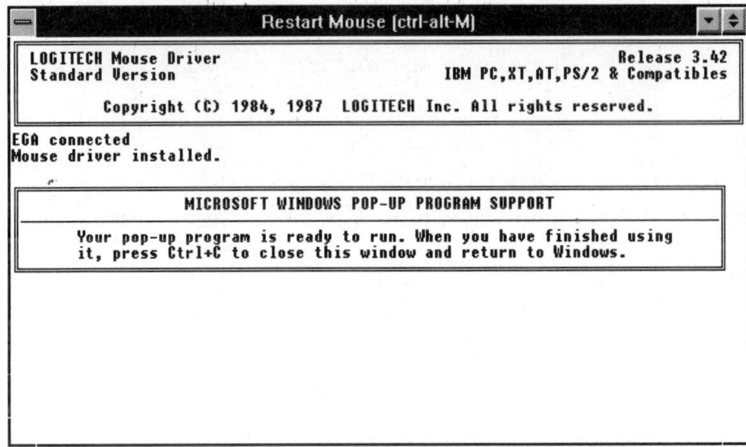

Windows has now loaded the mouse driver as a TSR and reinitialized the mouse.

5. Press Ctrl-C to exit the TSR. This unloads the driver from memory, which is OK because you don't really need the driver. Windows has its own mouse driver, which is still working. You just needed to wake up the mouse.

GAMES TIPS

TIP 223: Two Suggestions for Solitaire

Frustrated with Solitaire? Try these two suggestions:

- Select Outline Dragging from the Game Options dialog box. From now on, if you drag a card over a stack where the card can be played, that stack will change colors!
- Even more sneaky, is fixing it so you can turn over just one card from the deck—even if you're in Draw Three mode. When you click on the card pile, hold down the Ctrl, Alt, and Shift keys simultaneously. You'll get just one card instead of three.

TIP 224: Cheat at Minesweeper!

It's possible to beat Minesweeper with less-than-ethical techniques. After starting Minesweeper, make sure that the upper-left corner of the desktop is not covered by any windows. Type **XYZZY** (it must be all caps) and press Enter. Now, hold down the Ctrl key while you move the cursor over the playing field. Look very closely, and you'll notice that one pixel in the extreme upper-left corner of the desktop keeps changing from black to white to black. When the pixel is black, you're over a mine; when it's white, you're safe!

CHAPTER 21

FEATURING

Product Reviews of Program/ File Manager Replacements and Windows Utilities

Advice for Running Windows on a Laptop Computer

A Catalog of Windows Shareware and Information Sources

Other Products to Use with Windows 3.1

This final chapter covers some of the better programs you might want to run with Windows, including programs that do the job of Program Manager and File Manager and popular utilities. There's some advice for using Windows on a laptop. Finally, I'll point you toward some sources of shareware and freeware, as well as general Windows information.

PROGRAM MANAGER AND FILE MANAGER REPLACEMENTS

Not long after Windows 3.0 came out, a flood of Program Manager and File Manager replacements started to hit the market. These are generically referred to as Windows "shell replacements." Seems like folks felt the supplied Program Manager and File Manager left something to be desired.

The biggest beef was with Windows 3.0's File Manager, which admittedly was pretty lame. Now with 3.1's greatly improved File Manager, there isn't much cause for complaint. Still, some "power users" may find File Manager short on features.

Another complaint about Microsoft's arrangement of the graphical user interface centers on the allegedly unnecessary separation between the Program Manager and File Manager. Why separate them? The Apple Macintosh interface combines these two functions (running programs/manipulating files) into a single program, the Finder. I think of Windows' File Manager as analogous to the Macintosh Finder: you can copy, move, delete, and run programs from it. Being able to create easily accessible collections of your favorite programs and documents with the Program Manager is an extra convenience not found on the Macintosh.

As of this writing, there are several better mouse traps. But the whole idea of Windows and its appeal to both individual and corporate computer users rests on the proposition that what PCs need is a standard user interface. Once a significant number of users have mastered the essentials of Windows through experimentation, study, expensive training, and assimilation of tips and tricks such as those printed here, it's false economy to abandon the industry standard, unless your computing efficiency will skyrocket. Of course, this is just my opinion! But with that said, here's some information about a few of the replacement shells available as of the release of Windows 3.1.

Norton Desktop for Windows

The most popular of the shell replacements is Norton Desktop for Windows (by Symantec/Peter Norton Computing Group), which came out much before Windows 3.1. NDW combines the File Manager and Program Manager into one interface. It also includes a lot of utility programs for checking the integrity of your hard disk, unerasing files you accidentally creamed, backing up your hard disk (manually or automatically), totally erasing files (for security reasons), and so forth. Non-disk-related utilities include niceties such as a better calculator (it has a rewindable tape) and a Viewer program that lets you easily view the contents of many types of files. Its File Manager replacement is very much like the Windows 3.1 File Manager, which suggests that Microsoft got a few ideas from Peter Norton.

When you run NDW, your Desktop doesn't look that abnormal, but there are some notable differences to standard Windows. Figure 21.1 shows my Desktop upon running NDW on a 1024 × 768 Super VGA screen.

FIGURE 21.1:

Norton Desktop for Windows combines aspects of the File Manager and Program Manager and includes a suite of useful utility programs—a file viewer, "disk doctor," backup program, file finder, batch program writer, and more.

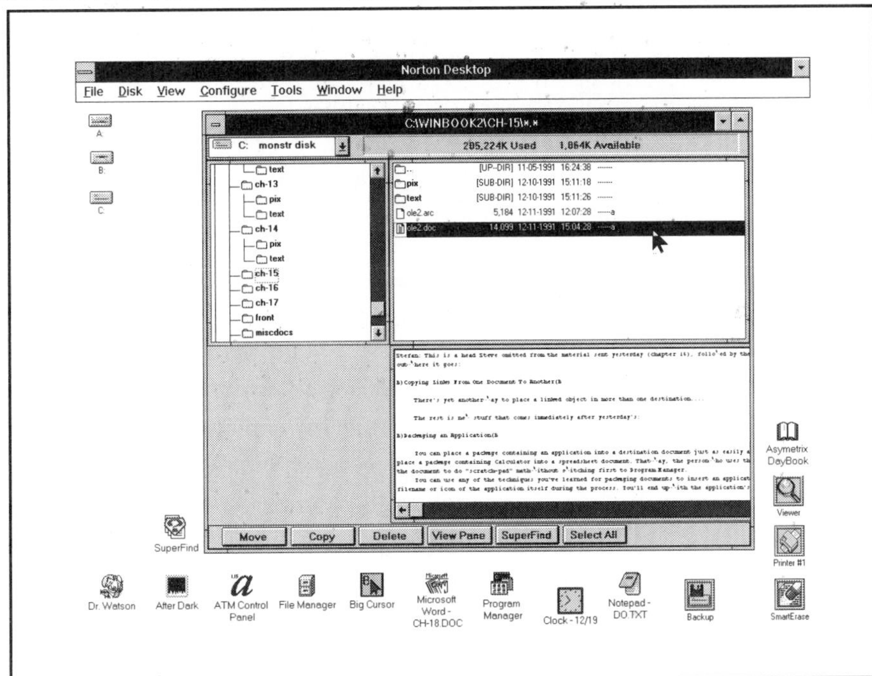

Along the top of the Desktop are menus containing commands that pertain to both file and program management. In the upper-left corner there are disk-drive icons for drives A, B, and C. Clicking on one of these opens the drive into a window like the one shown for drive C. The bottom pane in the drive window shown is the Viewer pane. Simply selecting a file in the listing above displays its contents below, at least well enough to figure out what the file is. Other buttons at the bottom of the file window are quite useful, particularly SuperFind, which speedily locates files. It's faster than File

Manager and has a zillion options, most of which you can get an idea of from its dialog box:

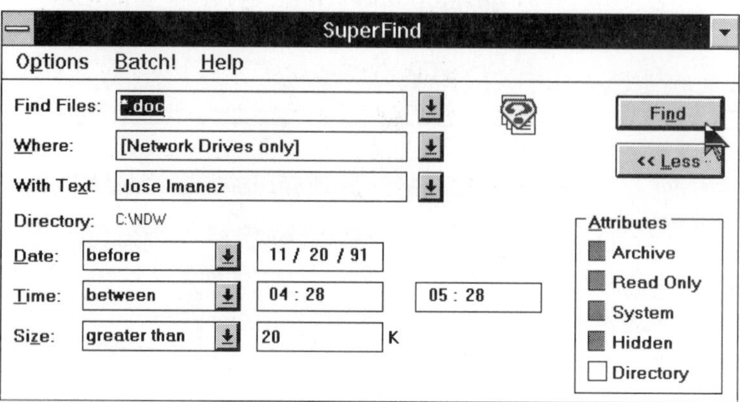

Also note that the normal Program Manager is also running, as indicated by its icon being shown at the bottom of the Desktop. Thus, you can get back to the Program Manager and even File Manager if you want, while still having the benefits of NDW. Things get a little confusing at first, since you have two shells running at once—and being inside of NDW is so much like being on the Windows Desktop, what with the icons at the bottom of the screen and you having to use of all your existing groups. But, after a week or so of use, you can easily become addicted to the added shortcuts and utilities that NDW offers. For more product information, call Symantec/Peter Norton Computing Group at (800) 441-7234. NDW sells for about $130. You may also wish to look at some of the books that SYBEX has recently published on the product: *Understanding Norton Desktop for Windows* by Peter Dyson, *Norton Desktop for Windows Instant Reference* by Sharon Crawford and Charlie Russel, and *Up & Running with Norton Desktop for Windows* by Michael Gross and David J. Clark.

HP NewWave

Whereas Norton Desktop for Windows is a relatively new product, Hewlett-Packard has been working on NewWave almost as long as Microsoft has pounded away at Windows. Like IBM, HP knew a good idea when it saw it (probably on the Macintosh) but early on recognized one inherent problem with Windows—it requires the user to understand and deal with DOS files and directories. HP decided that this runs counter to the philosophy of a true GUI, since users should deal with objects (such as documents) rather than wrestle with DOS files names, directory trees, and so on. This is arguably more parallel to the real world—where you type letters, send them off, put them in folders, and then store them away in a filing cabinet—than DOS is.

After about five or six years of work, NewWave version 4 was released in the spring of 1992, offering a good working alternative to Windows' Program Manager and File Manager, based on this real world metaphor.

Though not a replacement for all of Windows (it requires Windows 3.0 or later), its sheer size is a testament to its comprehensiveness. NewWave came to me on nine 720K floppies and a big box of documentation, and needed about 10MB of free disk space to install it! Installation was simple and straightforward, however.

In contrast to Windows, NewWave combines the File Manager and Program Manager into a single metaphor called the "Office" (see Figure 21.2). From the Office, you can run, print, copy, move, file away, or throw away documents using familiar office tools like folders, a file cabinet, and a trashcan.

FIGURE 21.2:
HP NewWave combines the Windows File Manager and Program Manager into one and insulates the user from the DOS concept of files and directories. Here you see the Office in the background, a session of NewWave Write, and the Save As dialog box, which requires only a descriptive name, not a DOS file name or directory.

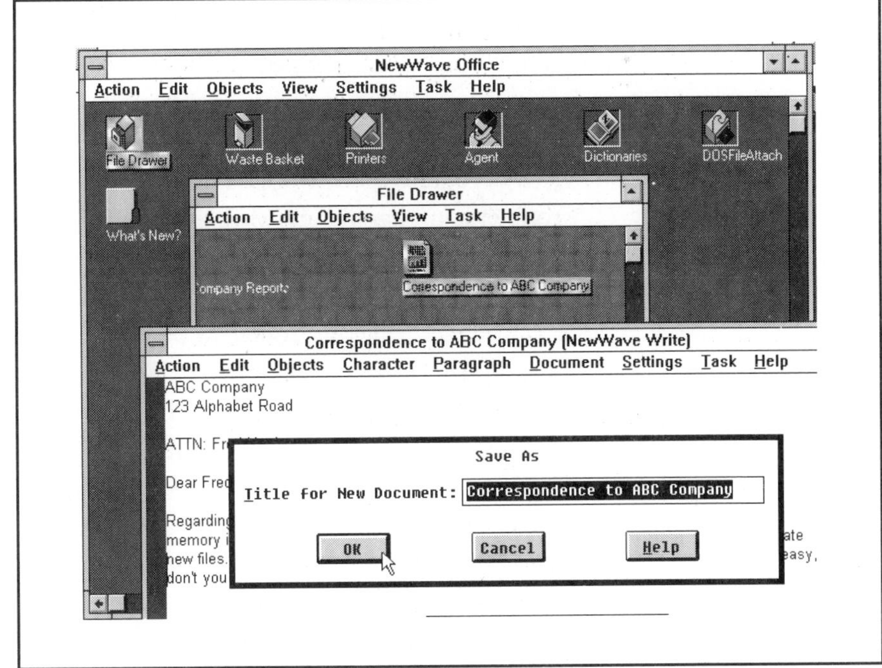

Extensive use of "drag and drop" is implemented. As with the Macintosh interface, you can throw away documents by dragging them into the trash, or print by dragging a document's icon into the Printer icon. You can empty the trash whenever you want. Moreover, Windows' Program Manager and File Manager are still available if you want to use them.

A significant feature is that, unlike with Windows, you are not bound by DOS's eight-character length for file names. Names in NewWave may be as long as 32 characters. NewWave does the work of dealing with DOS file names.

In fact, *files* and *applications* no longer exist as concepts in NewWave's world. Instead, you have slightly different concepts under the monikers *tools* and *objects.* A *tool* is a utility program such as the Waste Basket or printing program that doesn't actually create documents. An object is a document such as a letter, chart, or spreadsheet. The distinction between applications and documents is dispensed with entirely, eliminating a great source of confusion to computer novices. If you want to edit an existing letter, you click on its icon. To create a new document you simply choose Create a New... from the Objects menu, choose the type of document (Lotus 1-2-3, WordPerfect, PageMaker, etc.) from a list, and click on OK. Once saved, the document is automatically given an icon. You can then drag it into a new or existing folder (naming the folder if you want to) and put the folder in the File Drawer. A utility called the Finder Tool can later help find icons that meet certain criteria (such as all charts for ABC Company) once they're stored in folders, just in case you forget where they are.

A program called Bridge Builder connects the DOS and Windows environments to that of NewWave. It automatically sets up pointers to various applications and documents and creates object and tool icons in the NewWave environment, just as Setup does for Windows.

A macro program similar to but more sophisticated than Recorder is also supplied. Dubbed "The Agent," it claims to be more reliable, using a scripting language that doesn't bomb when you move windows or icons around on the screen (since it doesn't use x-y coordinates for mouse movements, but rather sends commands directly to the controlling application). The Agent can watch you perform either a Windows or DOS-based task, record it, and replay it at a predefined time. You can later edit the macro and add logical (conditional) commands to it (such as If...then...).

Network support within NewWave is well thought out. It lets you drag and drop items into a server, earmarking them for network availability. You don't have to know where the server, drive, or subdirectory information is stored, just what icon represents the workgroup. Team members working on the same documents then can check in and out of the files using passwords, with document revisions and revisors stored in a log. Any network supported by Windows is supported by NewWave.

Seven hundred pages of online help with extensive use of keywords are built-in, using the Windows Help system.

Previous versions of NewWave had their own version of OLE to allow mixing of dissimilar data types (such as text and video) within a single document. For applications adhering to HP's standard, this was elegantly implemented, allowing creation of "compound documents" derived from both Windows and DOS application sources—the latter of which is not possible in Windows. As of version 4, however, NewWave is strictly compatible with Microsoft's OLE specification, which means it will support the sharing of data between any OLE-capable Windows programs but with no additional advantages. A spokesman at HP stated that later versions of NewWave will offer additional bells and whistles in the OLE department.

NewWave is quite a different animal from Norton Desktop, which is essentially a file-based set of utilities and a Windows-type interface that requires a working knowledge of DOS files and directories. Still, NDW is likely to be one of the primary competitors to NewWave (along with WinTools, described next). HP NewWave costs about $195 (list price). You can phone Hewlett-Packard Company at (800) 752-0900.

WinTools

WinTools (by Tool Technology Publishing) is as much of a different environment from Windows as NewWave is. In fact, it has some interesting parallels to NewWave, in that it's one of the few truly object-oriented, "drag and drop"-based interfaces. However, it consumes much less disk space (my copy came on only a single 3½" disk) and required only a few minutes to install.

Once installed, it took over my Windows system (though there's an option to leave the old Program Manager in control at boot up), offering me so many new options and working procedures that I found myself wondering how they got them all on one disk. Unfortunately, I also found that my

StartUp group didn't execute automatically, and that returing to normal Program Manager operation to test other shells required editing my SYSTEM.INI file, which shouldn't be necessary.

WinTools, dubbed "Aporia" in a previous incarnation, is a product for the rugged Windows individualist. It even comes shipped in a unique recycled brown-paper carton (no plastic shrink-wrap!)—which gets two points in my book. If you're happy with the concept of Windows in general, but unhappy with how Microsoft has executed that paradigm and want to "roll your own," check out this program. If you're clever, you can recreate Windows in ways you thought impossible. Beware though: WinTools gives you enough rope to hang yourself—and you can't figure out how it works by just fiddling around. You'll have to read the manuals and follow the tutorials. Also, it doesn't offer keyboard alternatives to mouse operations.

As the name implies, WinTools consists of a suite of tools. In addition to taking over the Windows interface and creating new, fancier icons from your existing programs and documents, you're given about ten new icons, called tools, as shown in Figure 21.3.

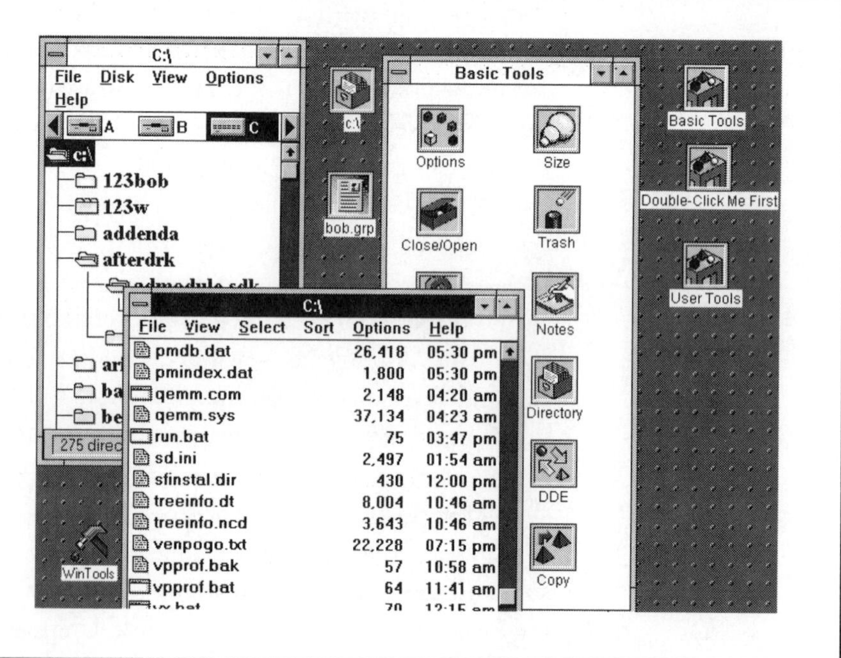

FIGURE 21.3:

WinTools converts your Windows interface into a "drag and drop" environment. For instance, to open a file, you drag the file icon in the file window to the Close/Open icon in the Basic Tools window. To delete a file, you drag it to the Trash icon.

Most of these tools work via dragging and dropping. With few exceptions, double-clicking on them does nothing, requiring that you drag an object into them to achieve an effect. For example, to make a copy of a tool, you drag it into the Copy tool; to change the options of a given tool, you drag it into the Options tool. A dialog box then pops up, wherein you change settings in the normal way.

As an option, an application called Big Sky replaces Windows' Task List. Much like WideAngle (reviewed in the "Windows Utilities" section under "AttiTools"), the task switcher gives you up to a 4 × 4 matrix of virtual screens (thus 16 screens or Desktops), which you can quickly switch between, preventing the confusion caused by overlapping application windows.

Once you've mastered these tools, you can move on to create your own. DOS and Windows applications can become tools, as can DOS batch files. Then you can use your own tools by dragging and dropping, similar to the way you drag a document file into an executable program in the File Manager and have it simultaneously run the program and open the document. The advantage here is that you don't need the File Manager to do it. You can arrange these tools anywhere on your Desktop. An image library of over 100 graphics allows you to easily create custom tool icons.

The File Manager replacement is divided into two tools, one for directories and one for files. Clicking on the lower-right corner of either window opens the dialog box for setting the filter. Directory updating is also very quick, because of WinTools' use of a cache for file information.

As with NewWave's Agent, automatic scheduling can be set up for the execution of tools. However, scripting of the tools is limited, since conditional branching isn't provided.

Probably the best feature of WinTools is that you can create Lotus-style tool bars that will work with any application by passing prerecorded keystrokes to it. For example, suppose you rely on several different word-processing programs, depending on the job at hand. If you're like me you probably mix up their commands, which is a pain. Making an identical tool bar customized for each program can prevent this. If you wanted to change a font or italicize a word, for example, you'd just click on the icon in the tool bar which passes the correct command to the application. As another example, you could create a tool for your electronic mail system. Just dropping a file on it would send it to coworkers.

The authors of WinTools are purported to have been LAN specialists in the past, and seem to have placed network support high on WinTools' list of capabilities. If you're managing a network, options that easily control sharing, locking, password protection, and limited access to tools, directories, and files could be quite beneficial.

The documentation is attractive, well-written, spiral bound, and contains full-color screen images. On-screen help is plentiful. WinTools is available for $149 from Tool Technology Publishing. Phone (415) 459-3700.

SALVATION

Salvation (from Vitesse, Inc.) is a less ambitious approach than Norton Desktop, NewWave, or WinTools. It is more along the lines of PubTech's product described below, being a simpler File Manager and Program Manager replacement with a few niceties. If you'd like a more predictable setup than the stock Windows arrangement, without the hassle of learning one of the more inclusive packages, consider this one.

A combination file and program screen called the Main Screen is shown in Figure 21.4. From here you can set up and launch your most-used programs or documents as well as work with files and directories. Note the status bar at the bottom of the screen that reports the amount of disk, RAM, and resources currently available. The status panel in the upper right displays a clock and the current configuration of options. Program buttons are user-definable and are stored on "pages," allowing the creation of as many buttons as you want. Clicking on a button then runs the application or document without having you open the requisite Program Manager group, remember the applicable shortcut keys, or find the file with File Manager. Over 300 custom icons are supplied, useful when designing your own button icons. A scheduler will automatically run programs in your absence. You can also recover any programs erased during a Windows session prior to quitting Windows.

The Salvation text editor is almost everything I've wanted in an ASCII text editor. It will convert tabs to spaces and vice versa, save or strip control characters, reset or set "high bits," and do a variety of things with carriage-return/line-feed pairs.

Large buttons on the right bring up dialog boxes for disk operations, such as copying, moving, comparing, deleting, formatting, verifying, duplicating, searching, and so forth—handy for some tasks, but not for

FIGURE 21.4:

Salvation is a simple and inexpensive File Manager and Program Manager shell replacement. Customizable buttons, 300+ icons, a good text editor, and scheduled launching round out the package.

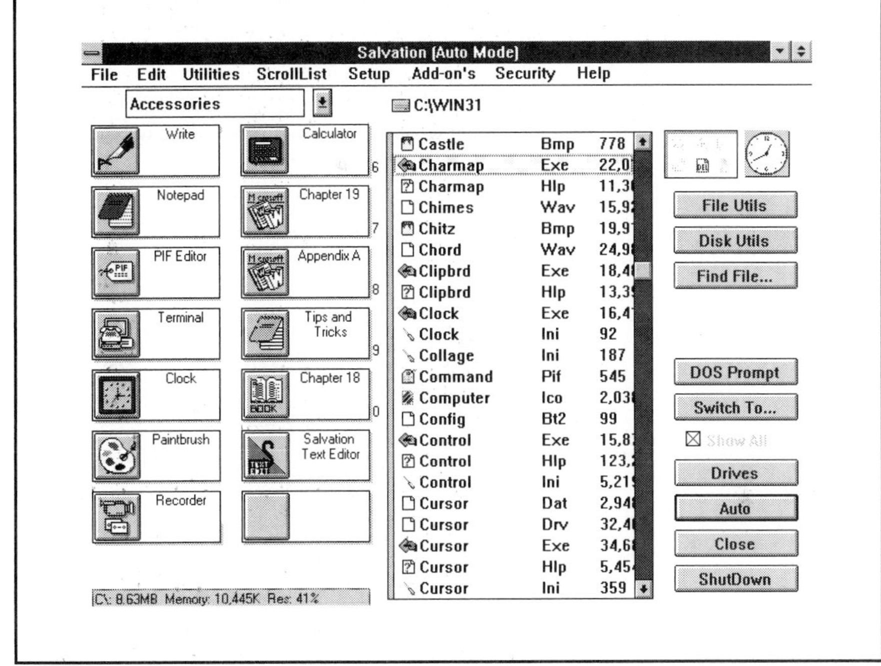

others that are easier in the Windows File Manager (such as copying and moving). A variety of modes makes running programs, creating associations, and viewing graphics files via the Clipboard pretty easy, too. However, it doesn't have a file viewer on the order of Norton Desktop for Windows.

Installation took me about five minutes. But learning some quirks of the shell took about an hour, and the installation program didn't warn me that I was out of disk space, which led to problems after installation. The documentation is not for the novice—and it skipped some obvious points such as a discussion of associations—but it is extensive. The index could be more complete, however.

Overall, I think this is a useful program, particularly as an application launcher. It organizes your applications into one solid window and keeps them put. The good text editor, disk utilities, and security features are icing on an affordable cake. Salvation is available for $69.95 from Vitesse at (818) 813-1270.

PubTech File Organizer

This package received the *PC Magazine* "Editor's Choice" and "Best Buy" by *PC World* for shell replacements. However, that was before Windows 3.1, which now provides some of the same features. As with the other shells covered here, this is a replacement for the File Manager and Program Manager. A host of utilities programs are included in the deal as well. One feature that Windows doesn't have that you get with this program is the ability to create and store multiple Desktop setups, calling them up later. This helps organize and recall programs and documents to the Desktop for specific tasks, while quickly removing irrelevant ones when not needed.

Like NewWave and WinTools, there are object-oriented features to File Organizer with lots of drag and drop functionality. All files, documents, utilities, printers, and drives are represented by icons—similar to the Program Manager icons. You can pull just about any type of object onto the Desktop, be it a trashcan, disk drive, program, or document. You can even use the Desktop as a temporary holding tank for an object until you find its proper destination, such as a file directory. And each icon can have up to 128 characters of text attached to it to remind you or others just what it's about.

Additional utilities provide for the backing up and restoring of files; text searching through files; keyboard remapping; screen dimming; ASCII text editing; a pull-down menu for launching favorite programs; macro recording and editing; and icon editing. There is no file viewer as in Norton Desktop for Windows, however, nor a true undelete function for files, though you can recover erased files from the trashcan until you empty it.

The ASCII text editor is far superior to Windows Notepad, in that you can edit huge files. It also lets you *append* text to the Clipboard rather than wipe out what's on it whenever you copy something to it—a fast way to cull selected tidbits from various text files and join them. It also has case conversion, undo, the ability to print a marked block, and the ability to insert a file on disk into the file you're editing. You can also configure the editor to emulate the commands of popular word processors like Microsoft Word, WordPerfect, and WordStar. This is a terrific feature!

PubTech File Organizer is available for $199.95 from Publishing Technologies, Inc., at (800) 782-8324.

BeckerTools

If you really want to go for the gusto when it comes to hard-disk management accessories, BeckerTools (by Abacus Software) may be your ticket. This one really takes some studying to get it under your belt, but if you need an extensive collection of disk-utility programs all under one roof, and prefer running your applications from a File-Manager-type interface, check it out.

In addition to performing many types of disk activities such as moving, copying, formatting, deleting, printing, compressing and decompressing, and editing files in ASCII and Hex, you can also examine and alter disk sectors, sort directories, print a directory tree, find bad sectors, unerase files, examine File Allocation Tables (FATs), and change file-creation times and dates of files. You can also assign your ten most-used applications to shortcut keys (Ctrl-0 through 10), configure mouse buttons to perform file-related functions, and quickly format floppy disks.

Figure 21.5 shows my drive C open within BeckerTools. Note all the icons on the left. All the menu commands have icons that replicate their use,

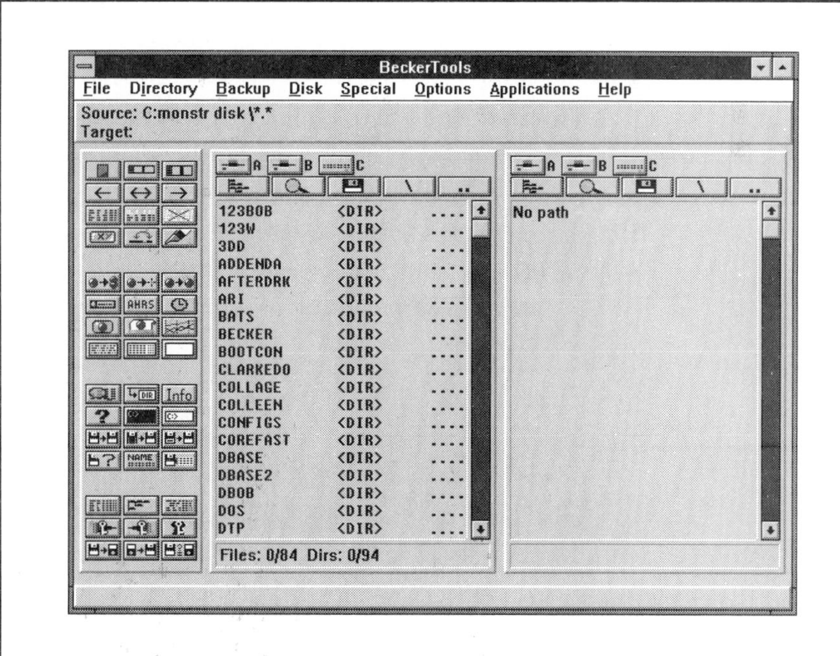

FIGURE 21.5: *BeckerTools offers a veritable plethora of disk utilities in one File-Manager-type shell.*

so once you know what the icons do, you don't have to open menus to choose commands.

For product information, call Abacus at (800) 451-4319. BeckerTools retails for $80.

Freeware/Shareware Shell Replacements

If you're on a tight budget, there are a few cheapie Program Manager replacements that render application launching and switching a bit simpler. You might want to try them out before proceeding with one of the more costly items I have described above:

Alfred

This will start programs from a pop-up menu a bit like StraightLine (described next under "Windows Utilities"). It has user-definable menus. You can find it on CompuServe in the Windows Advanced User Forum by typing **GO WINADV.** The file is named ALFRED.ZIP. Or you can write to the author, John Rotenstein, P.O. Box 165 Double Bay, NSW 2028, Australia. This is freeware.

Desktop Helper

This is a shareware program that makes launching and task switching easy. It's activated by clicking once on the Desktop, bringing up a menu that lets you launch, task-switch, rearrange windows, set preferences, or exit Windows. Write to author Robert E. Alleger, 317 Monrow Ave., Edgewater Park, NJ 08010. CompuServe mailbox: 70240,264. Registration fee is $15.

Usher

This is also a shareware program. As with Desktop Helper, clicking once on the Desktop brings up a launch menu. Programs on the menu can be subdivided by categories you define. Selecting a category opens a submenu with subchoices in that category. This is an efficient menu-driven alternative to the Program Manager. System information and some other niceties are also a click away. Write to author George Browning, 5124 Melbourne Road, Raleigh, NC 27606. Registration fee is $15.

WINDOWS UTILITIES

There are more Windows utilities around these days than you can shake a stick at, and the list seems to be growing exponentially. It would take a whole catalog to cover them in any comprehensive way here. However, I've sorted through the collection of programs I've received for editorial review to tell you about a few of the more popular and readily available ones. For up-to-the-minute information and reviews on the latest programs you can add to your Windows system, see the section on "Windows Information Sources" at the end of this chapter.

hDC Micro Apps

There's a collection of utilities from a company called hDC that is well worth considering as an addition to your Windows setup. It includes FileApps, Power Launcher, FirstApps, and Windows Express. hDC calls their utility programs "micro apps," and supplies a unique means, called the MicroApp Manager, for running and switching to these utilities. When run, MicroApp Manager changes the Control box on every application window to a little red hDC logo. Clicking on it brings up the usual Control menu, but along with it you also get a couple of other cascading menus that list all the hDC micro-apps you have installed, and let you easily run or switch to them and choose any of the utilities functions. (Clicking on any minimized program icon offers the same choices.) Having utilities right at hand for launching programs, copying and moving files, examining system resources, and so forth, is a great convenience. You don't have to open the Program Manager or File Manager anymore.

Though I had a problem installing one of the hDC programs at first, a call to the company solved it and I was pleased with the competency of the technical support person there. hDC is active on CompuServe, in the WINAPA section of the Microsoft forum; you'll find tips, tricks, and hints for their products listed there.

Here's a short rundown of each utility:

FirstApps

This is a set of nine micro apps that customize and enhance Windows. First-Apps lets you do everything from graphically viewing your system memory to turning your Desktop background into a fully interactive calendar. FirstApps includes: Memory Viewer (see Figure 21.6), Art Gallery, Desktop, Work Sets, Auto Save, Character Set, System Enhancer, Alarm Clock, and Font Viewer. Character Set does what the Character Map accessory that comes with Windows does, so that's not really necessary anymore. The Auto Save feature is definitely worthwhile, since you can set it up to make Windows programs automatically save your work at preset intervals or after a certain number of keystrokes. The Work Sets option launches preset groups of applications that you like to use together, or closes them down and launches another set for some other task you're working on. Font Viewer shows you all your currently installed system fonts, but so does the Windows Control Panel, so no big deal. Art Gallery is a nice little repository for bitmap and metafile images: you can add, delete, copy, and paste images from or to library files that it creates. Memory Viewer displays current conventional, expanded, and extended memory usage. System Enhancer offers a number of features, two of which are as follows: you can tell it to close all applications and shut down Windows from anywhere—you don't have to get to the Program Manager; and you can run any application from any other application (no need to go first to Program Manager or File Manager).

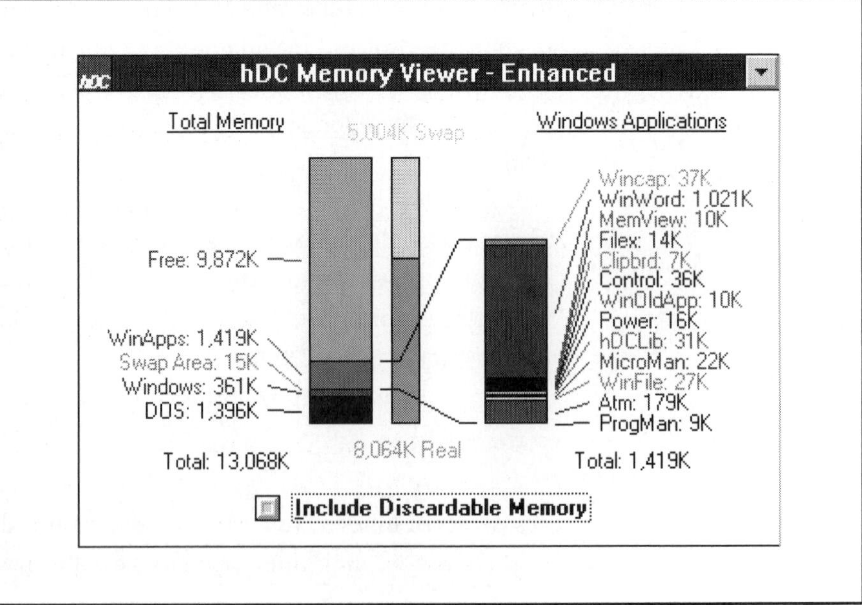

FIGURE 21.6: *hDC FirstApps contains nine utility programs. Here you see the Memory viewer.*

FileApps

As the name implies, this is a suite of file-management utilities. You can run, undelete, search for, and encrypt files, check out disk usage, and transfer files between desktop and laptop computers (this requires a special cable that you order from Travelling Software). A disk viewer gives you a graphical display of disk usage with directories listed in order of size, which lets you easily open or trash files. Of course, you can do most of these things with other programs, like Norton Desktop. But FileApps is small, and easy to learn and use. The File Search utility can search through files for specific text strings, too. Found file names and matching text strings can be dumped on the Clipboard for later reference.

As for its shortcomings, FileApps doesn't have a file viewer—something I need all the time to see what's in all those mysterious files cluttering my hard disk. This drawback is almost compensated for by another feature though: If you double-click on a document that doesn't have an association, a dialog box lets you make it on the spot, rather than just giving you an error message as File Manager does. You can opt to make the association either permanent or temporary, which is great. Then the document opens in its source application. This is almost as good as having a viewer, though not as efficient.

Windows Express

Windows Express is a menuing system much like the menu front ends for DOS that have been in use for years. It lets you set up multilevel menus of work projects for everybody on a network, for example, or for each user of a single system. Each menu choice can include a description of the project, due dates, and so forth. The program seems like a natural for corporations trying to enhance system security and develop a standard front end for Windows workstations, since it provides users with intuitive, easy-to-use folders of applications and documents like that shown in Figure 21.7. Icons can be rendered password-protected and also immobile so users can't accidentally drag them to another folder or group. This way, every user will find programs or documents in the same place every work session. There's also a separate Windows Express editor program you can use to set up your menus. Among other options, it can import your existing Program Manager .GRP files into its own folder format. This simplifies setting up your menus if you've already

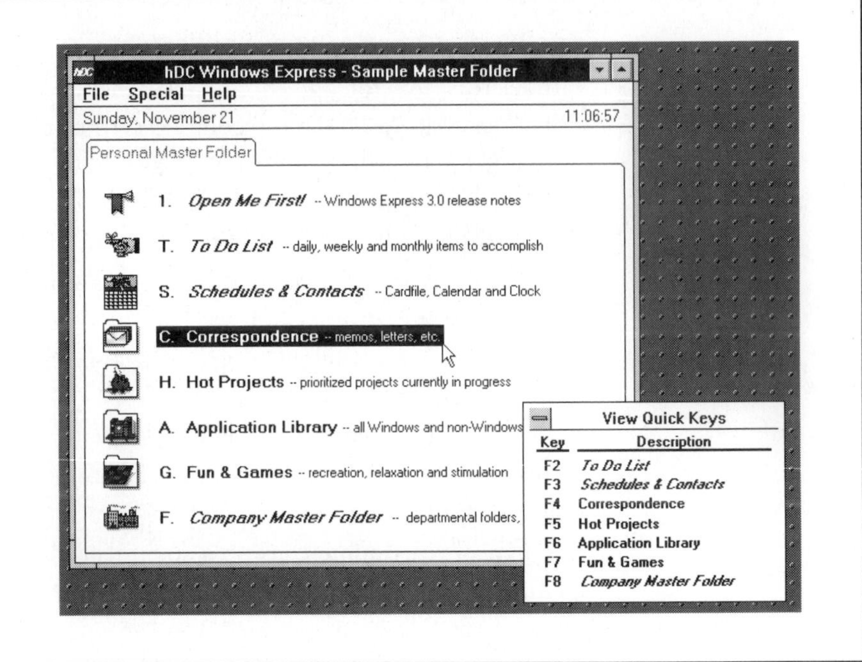

FIGURE 21.7: *Windows Express lets you set up an easy-to-use menuing system for tasks that any user can understand. It also can provide system security with passwords and disabled file functions such as MOVE, DELETE, or COPY.*

arranged applications and documents into some logical arrangement for your office.

Power Launcher

This is the most comprehensive of the hDC products. If you consider yourself a power user and feel constrained by Windows, definitely check out this program. If value can be judged by the sheer number of useful features per dollar, Power Launcher probably wins the bargain contest hands down. This is not a program for the weak at heart, though. It could take weeks to figure it all out. This is partly due to Power Launcher's ability to carry out tasks no other Windows program can—chores you may not have even considered possible.

For example, you can completely automate the launching of applications, predetermining the size and placement of windows and passing command-line parameters such as default document directories to them as they are run. You can execute DDE commands automatically, and call DLLs

(Dynamic Link Libraries). You can create custom toolboxes that launch sets of programs with a click of the mouse. A scheduler lets you preset timed application launches. You can even get around the 128-character DOS PATH limitation using hDC's own path association file.

Three "power utilities" in the package—Power Mouse, Power Keyboard, and Power Toolbox—let you create and assign macros to mouse/keyboard combinations, and create custom icon toolboxes that change when you switch applications. A "virtual Desktop" arrangement like WideAngle's can set up as many as 64 work spaces, with myriad ways to jump among them. (However, you don't see the names of the programs running in each window, so I prefer WideAngle for virtual Desktop management.)

Another utility launches programs into any of the workspaces. Some 50 predefined scripts are supplied, which can perform tasks such as closing down all your open windows, iconizing them all, or ending a Windows session, including closing open DOS sessions and windows (a great feature) in one fell swoop. Another feature can cause a Windows application to automatically bring up the File Open dialog box when run, so you don't have to open the File menu and choose Open.

Power Launcher can work in conjunction with other shells like Norton Desktop, Salvation, and Progam Manager. However, installing it as *the* shell is possible and advantageous. hDC claims that Power Launcher consumes about 50 percent fewer system resources than Program Manager or Norton Desktop do. Combine it with the other hDC utilities and you can dispense with the Program Manager altogether.

hDC has a collection of useful Power Launcher tips written up, too. You might want to contact them once you become a Power Launcher power user. Call hDC Computer Corporation at (206) 885-5550, dept. P. Prices range from $99.95–129.95.

AttiTools

There's another highly visible firm in the Windows utilities aftermarket called Attitash, Inc. Their line of utilities, dubbed "AttiTools," includes Dragnet, Catalyst, and DiskSpace. WideAngle, another utility, is sold separately. These have been well reviewed in a variety of magazines and deserve consideration if you're in the market for utilities. They have recently added a program launcher called SlingShot to the family, though I haven't seen it yet.

WideAngle

This is a virtual Desktop organizer like that supplied with WinTools and Power Launcher from hDC. It sets up nine workspaces, each of which can have multiple Windows applications or a single DOS window running. You can instantly jump between applications by clicking on the correct pane in the icon (if your eyes are that accurate), by clicking on a telephone-like number pad that you can keep on the screen, or by assigning hotkeys. Figure 21.8 shows a sample setup with the WideAngle application maximized. Normally, when you're working with applications, you'd only have the bottom part of the screen (number pad and program list) visible.

Another WideAngle feature, called XRay View, gives you a whole different way to switch between applications. It lets you see the frames of all overlapping windows simultaneously and click on the title bar of the one you

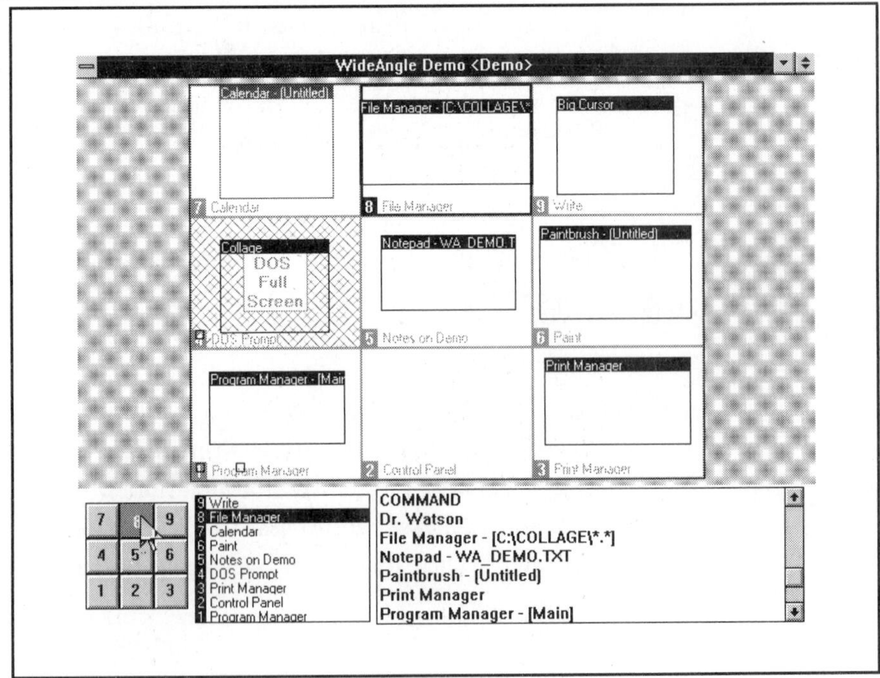

FIGURE 21.8:
WideAngle from Attitash Software lets you create nine virtual application areas so you can run programs without overlapping their windows.

want to switch to (see Figure 21.9). This is great if your Desktop, like mine, gets cluttered with a bunch of overlapping windows and you're not the kind who likes using the virtual Desktop approach of spreading everything out onto different work areas.

Overall, WideAngle is the best of the virtual Desktop utilities I've tried. Icons can be set to be always on top of other windows. On a VGA screen it's particularly easy to select the program you want or to activate XRay View.

Dragnet

This is a text search-and-retrieval utility. Type key words or phrases into a dialog box and the program runs off to look through every file on the target disk for files containing them. You can use wildcards and also combine search criteria using Boolean AND and OR—for example, as Figure 21.10 shows, to find all files with references to New York *or* to Paris (or both).

Dragnet can scan through word-processing, graphics, spreadsheet, and database files, too. Once found, text is displayed in context, in a viewer window, sent to the Clipboard, or sent to a file. Files and/or sections of text can also be

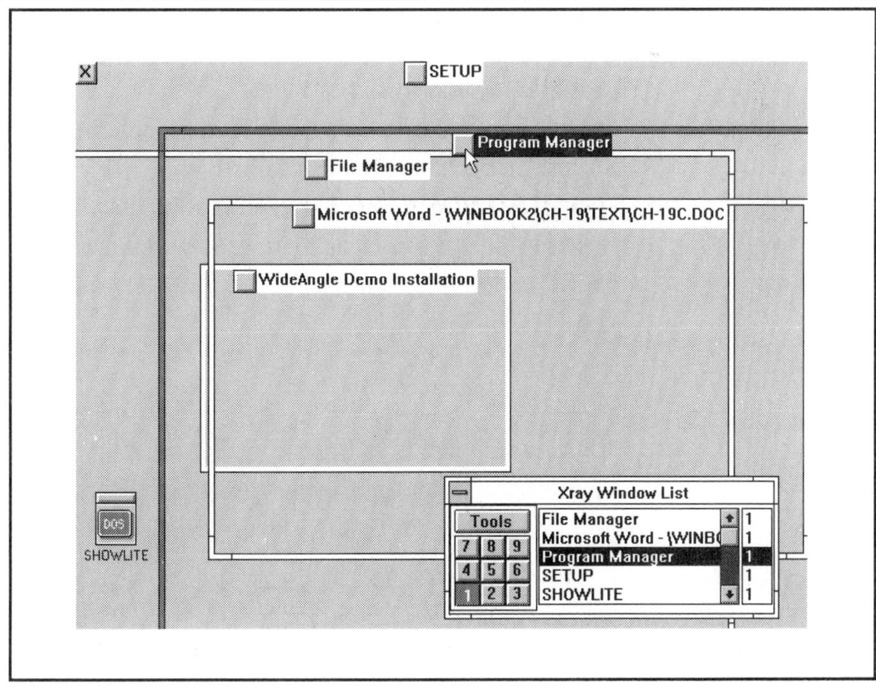

FIGURE 21.9: *WideAngle's XRay View lets you see overlapping windows and choose the one you want to switch to.*

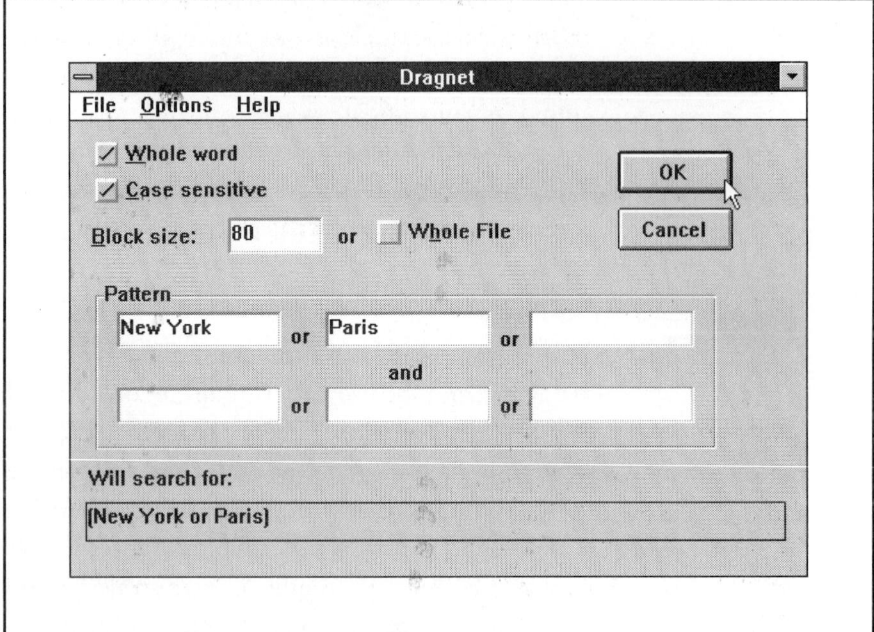

FIGURE 21.10: *With this setting, Dragnet will search all files for references to New York, Paris, or both.*

retrieved and consolidated. For example, several columns of spreadsheet data, some database records, and some text from a letter could be found and easily consolidated into a report. A built-in viewer allows you to see located material without running the source application. A list of files containing found material can be transferred via DDE to Attitash's File-Manager-like program, called *Catalyst,* and it'll show up in what amounts to a Search Results window similar to the File Manager's. With a tool like this, precisely naming files becomes less of an issue, since you'll be able to call them up later, on the basis of their contents.

DiskSpace

This is a bit like hDC's Disk Viewer micro app. It gives you a graphical display of your hard disk, but organized by file type (extension) rather than by directory. You can see how many files of a certain extension you have and what percentage of disk space they occupy. It'll also show you the number of files of different sizes you've got lurking around. For example, I often have some files of zero kilobytes (empty files) taking up directory space for no good reason. Files using obsolete data formats (such as WKS when you're now using WK3 format) or files that you otherwise think should be dealt with can be passed via DDE to Catalyst to be deleted or compressed with its own compression command. This is a pretty easy way to recover lost disk space.

Attitash Software can be reached at (800) 736-4198. The AttiTools package lists for $99. WideAngle, only sold separately, lists for $99 too.

Almanac

This is a shareware calendar program that greatly improves on the one that comes with Windows. For starters, it looks like a regular wall calendar, as you can see in Figure 21.11. It can also display each month's holidays (even for different countries and religions). The Gregorian or Jewish calendar can be stipulated, as can the display of moon phases. Your geographical location's time and azimuth directions for sunrise and sunset are available for each day, too. You can add your own recurring holidays to the calendar as well, using

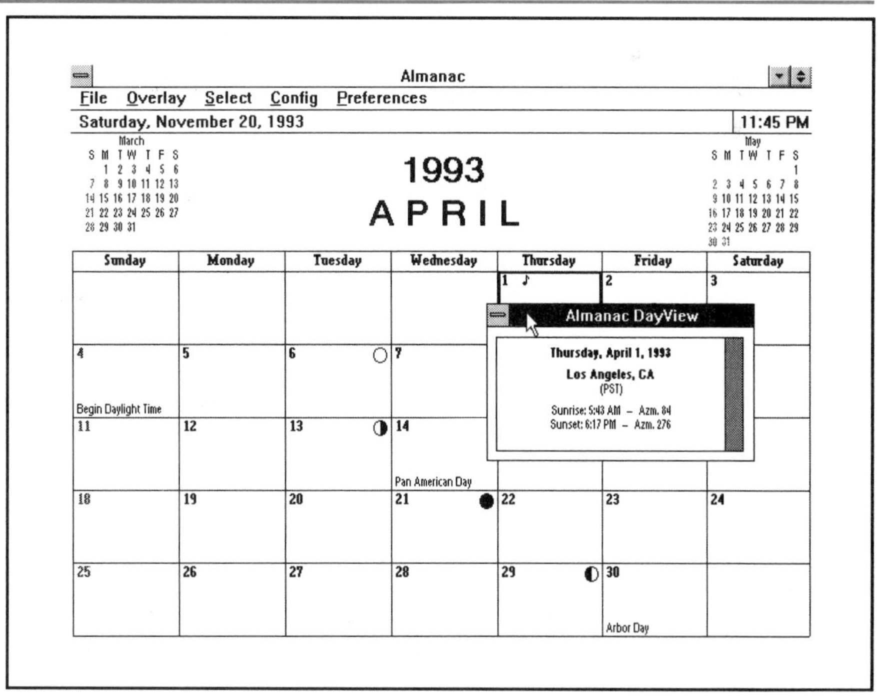

FIGURE 21.11: *Almanac is a shareware calendar program that does calendars and scheduling on the computer the way we're all used to doing them on paper.*

overlay files. To distinguish it, any event on the overlay file can be shaded with a different color, and you can have up to ten overlay files active at one time. You can view and enter notes on the calendar by day, month, and year.

By double-clicking on different areas of the calendar, you can bring up dialog boxes to enter schedule information, alarms, and different calendar views such as a year view. A "Desktop" mode includes a daytimer for appointments and a spiral notepad for general notes about the day, along with the alarm clock. The notepad allows up to 800 characters of information to be attached to any schedule entry. You can print the day's schedule, or the monthly or yearly calendars. Fonts for both screen viewing and printing are selectable.

Almanac is available from Impact Software at (714) 590-8522 for $34.95.

MakeUp

If you want to dress up the typefaces in your documents, consider this program from Bitstream. At about $150 it's not cheap, but it's pretty impressive, and certainly an improvement over Adobe's TypeAlign. To get the kind of features included in this program you'd normally have to buy an expensive, professional package like CorelDRAW or Arts & Letters. MakeUp supports Adobe Type 1, Bitstream Speedo, and TrueType fonts, and allows you to rotate, flip, skew, and stretch text and objects. Drawing tools for common shapes are also supplied. Special effects include a chiseled look, shadowing, and embossing. You can color your text with patterns, washes, and solid colors to match HSV, SYMK, and Pantone color standards. Typographic controls and image support for a variety of graphic file types are also included. Call Bitstream at (800) 522-3668.

WinSleuth Professional

WinSleuth Professional (from Dariana, Inc.) is the only program I know of that performs a thorough investigation of your hardware, DOS, and Windows setups. It does a detailed analysis of your system, reporting possible conflicts with your CONFIG.SYS, AUTOEXEC.BAT, SMARTDrive, TSRs, device drivers, I/O ports, memory allocations, and so forth. It also can test your hardware, including keyboard, ports, mouse, disk drives, and RAM chips. Much of the information generated is designed for programmers or systems integrators, but some is certainly of use for typical end-users as well.

Each of the 48 tests or system reports can be chosen from a normal drop-down menu or from a toolbar of icons, and WinSleuth can tell you more information about your Windows environment than you thought existed.

For example, it knows the tracking speed of your mouse in Mickeys, total number of unlocked memory blocks available, the vertical scroll arrow height, hard-disk partition information, and disk usage for each subdirectory (useful for quickly figuring out which directories are gobbling up your hard-disk space). And this is only a fraction of the available information.

One particularly nice feature, easily worth the price of admission, is called the Installation Assistant. It reports all the available ROM space, IRQ lines, DMA channels, and I/O ports, so that you can properly set up and install new cards into your system without creating hardware conflicts and resultant inexplicable system crashes. No more pulling out all your plug-in cards to determine what's using which ports and interrupts. There's also some friendly online advice about choosing such settings wisely.

Another useful feature analyzes your running Windows setup, producing a written report that suggests improvements to your system. It took about 30 seconds to run on my system and gave me a two-page report of modifications I should make to my SMARTDrive and SYSTEM.INI files. A complete or selective report of your system's health can be printed, just like going for a physical exam at the doctor's office. Figure 21.12 shows the dialog box for printing such reports.

WinSleuth's manual is well-written (and as a writer who makes his living translating computer manuals from technobabble into English—with the help of my editors—I can't say this very often), and includes some mini-articles on interesting topics relating to PC hardware and Windows operations. Call Dariana, Inc., at (714) 562-5777. WinSleuth Professional retails for $169.

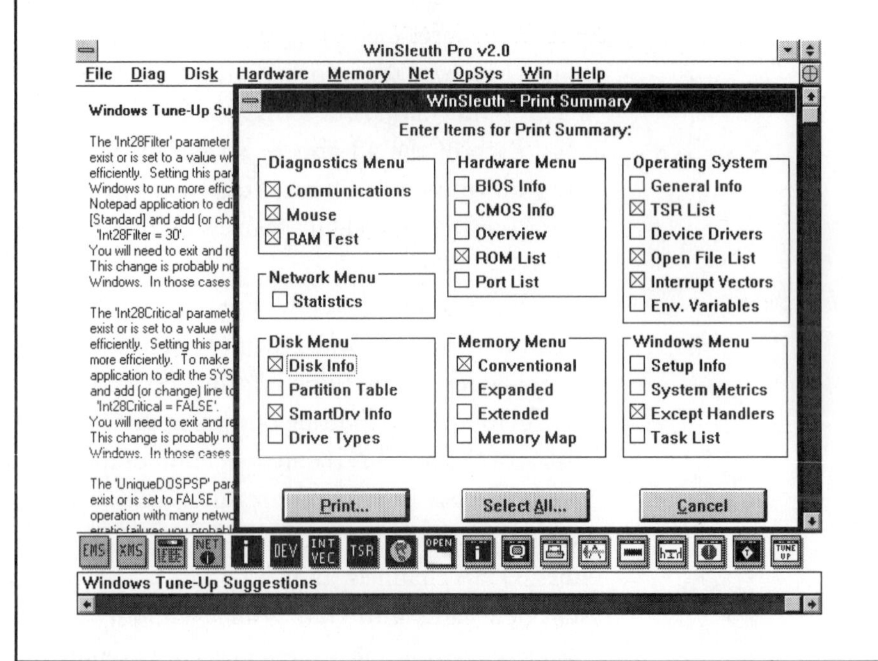

FIGURE 21.12: *WinSleuth Professional diagnoses your hardware and software setup, making suggestions for performance improvements. Findings can be printed, as this dialog box shows. Forty-eight diagnostic tools are accessed from the menus or from the toolbar at the bottom of the window.*

WINSPEED

The screen-refresh rate is a major determinant of your system's overall speed. A software product called WINSPEED, developed by Panacea, Inc., apparently can make a terrific improvement to the screen-refresh rate by modifying the screen drivers used with many monitors. Particularly on 286 and 386 systems, as much as a four-fold increase in screen updating has been noted by some testers. As an added advantage, the program replaces or recreates the appropriate screen fonts for use with the screen and resolution you choose during installation. Since users of Super VGA monitors often forget to install the higher-resolution screen fonts that look so much better on these screens, this is a thoughtful feature.

WINSPEED only works with specific video cards. However, the list of supported video cards is quite long, so I won't print it here. But since many video cards use the same essential components, that doesn't matter. If your card uses any one of the chip sets below, WINSPEED should work with it. Check the manual supplied with your card, look at the large chips on the card, or call Panacea at the number below if you're in doubt about which chip set your card uses:

ATI VGA Wonder (all models)

Paradise chip set

Trident 8800 chip set

Tseng ET-4000 chip set

Video 7-V7 chip set

ZyMOS 51 chip set

You can call Panacea at (800) 729-7420. The program retails for $79.

Click!

This is a great utility. What it does is take a snapshot of your Windows system at the time you shut down. Then when you start up Windows the next time, everything is returned to the exact state it was in when you left. You don't have to drag documents into the StartUp group or arrange them in any particular order just to get the document you were working on last to come up on top. This program also works in DOS.

Click! sells for $80 and is made by Modulo Informatica Ltd. You can write them at the following address:

164 President Wilson Ave.

11th Floor

Andar-Centro

Rio de Janeiro, Brazil

or call them at 55-21-210-3277, ext. 229. (Their fax number is 55-21- 240-8442.)

StraightLine

StraightLine (by First Genesis Software, Inc.) is a simple program that, once you get used to, you may not be able to live without. All it does is offer the straightest line between two points. That is, it lets you jump between applications super easily from a list that pops up right under the pointer when you press the right mouse button (see Figure 21.13). For programs that you haven't assigned to the list yet, you use a one-time Run command to browse for the program you want, or type in its name. If the program is in your system's path, it'll run with just its executable name or PIF, just as with the File or Progam Manager's File ➤ Run command. It also has a great command that will immediately minimize all running applications and windows to clear up your Desktop, or jump between open windows without using the Task List. For product information, call First Genesis Software at (612) 544-4445. StraightLine retails for $99.

Cursor-Altering Programs

Do you spend a lot of time looking around your screen for the pointer? I've found several programs to address the problem. I'll tell you about four of them: BCursor, ChngCrsr, Microsoft Mouse Driver 8.1, and Cursorific!.

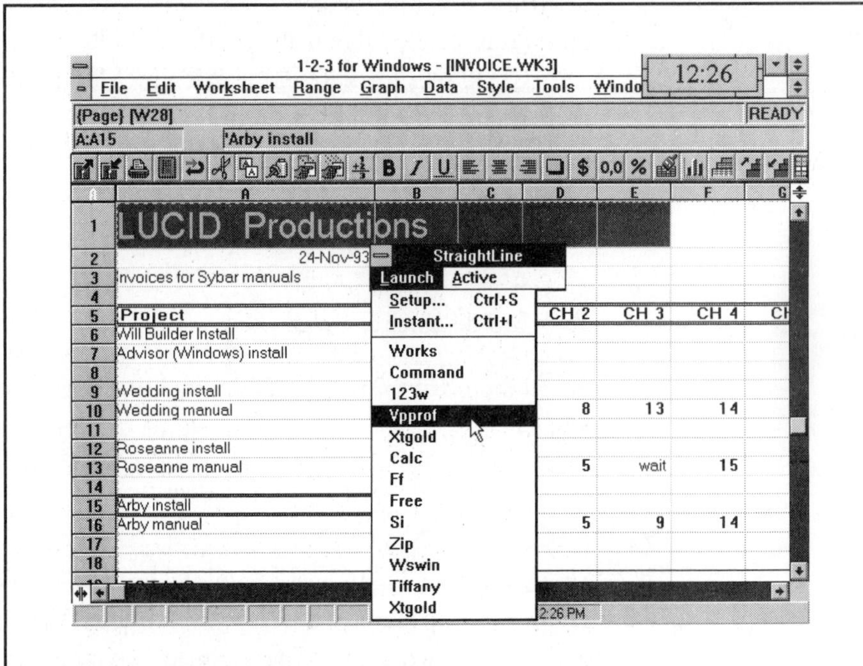

FIGURE 21.13: *StraightLine is a pop-up configurable program launcher activated by clicking the right mouse button.*

BCursor

This doubles the pointer's size and turns it solid rather than hollow. It's particularly useful on laptops, where the pointer often seems to disappear when you move the mouse (this is called *submarining*). BCursor is a public-domain program available on many BBSs.

ChngCrsr

This is a shareware program also available on many BBSs. ChngCrsr modifies the look and/or size of both the hourglass and pointer cursors, and allows editing of them as well. After a 21-day evaluation, you must register and pay a small fee. Adding either one of these programs to your StartUp group will render your pointer always visible.

Microsoft Mouse Driver 8.1

This is Microsoft's newest mouse driver. This version adds new options for your mouse control. With this driver, you can determine the acceleration speed, horizontal and vertical sensitivity control, color, and size of the mouse pointer. You can also set the pointer to increase in size when you move it quickly—a good feature for LCD (laptop screen) users. If you didn't get this version of Microsoft's mouse driver with your copy of DOS or Windows, you can order it by calling Microsoft at (800) 426-9400. For users of version 8.0, the update is free. For new purchasers, the price is $25.

Cursorific!

Unfortunately, none of the above programs or drivers addresses the problem of increasing the size of cursors other than the normal pointer, particularly the text (I-beam) cursor, which is often the hardest to locate—especially on an LCD screen. Cursorific! (I hate those names with exclamation marks after them) tackles the problem, but you won't get it for free. This program lets you modify the look, shape, and size of all the Windows cursors. Over 80 cursor shapes and sizes are supplied. You can even draw your own, such as a company logo. Figure 21.14 shows one of three sets of arrows you can assign to the normal pointer, just to give you an idea. Note that you can flip the pointer's direction horizontally and vertically. Such flipping is a nice feature for left-handed mouse users. Cursorific! is available for $49.95 from AApex Software at (800) 728-7650.

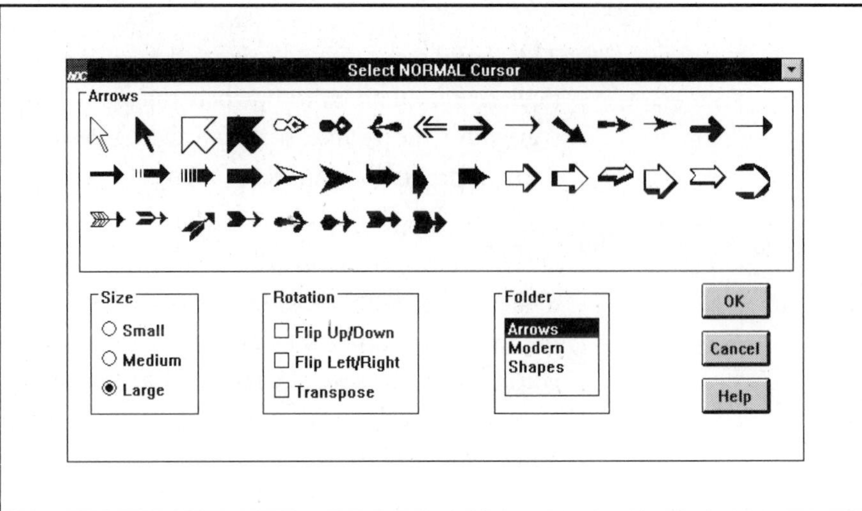

FIGURE 21.14:

Cursorific! lets you change the shape and size of many of the Windows cursors and pointers. Here you see a few of the choices that are available.

RUNNING WINDOWS ON A LAPTOP

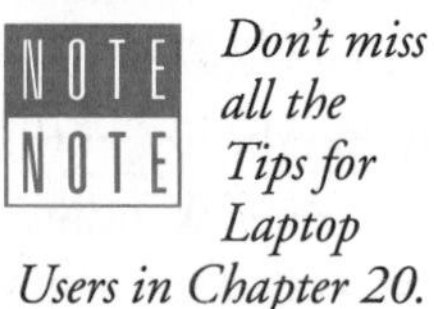

Don't miss all the Tips for Laptop Users in Chapter 20.

Are you shopping for a laptop computer on which to run Windows? Here are some things to consider when comparing models. Though many laptops are available now that will run Windows, they aren't all created equal. You'll want one that has at least a 386SX processor running at 16 MHz and containing a minimum of 4MB of RAM (just as with a desktop machine). For only a small additional outlay you'll be able to acquire a faster 20 MHz 386SX. For a significant speed advantage above an SX, check into a 386DX running at 33 MHz. There's a new rash of these and prices are dropping. A 40MB drive is sufficient, though you could get by with a 20MB drive running a data compression/expansion program such as Stacker to simulate 30–40MB.

Several other laptop-specific issues should be addressed while shopping: weight, maximum RAM, screen size and quality, power-saving features, and standby modes.

You'll have to decide which weight is acceptable. Don't forget to add in the power supply's weight. Try carrying it around for awhile before deciding. Six pounds is heavier than you might think.

As for RAM, most laptops will take up to 5MB, which is acceptable. Check the price of add-in RAM. If you're spoiled by a fast desktop machine and intend to use lots of programs, consider a laptop that will accept more than 5MB. I have 9MB in my Toshiba T-2000SX. This gives me a large (4MB) disk-cache and allows me to run many programs simultaneously with as few disk "hits" as possible. This arrangement increases overall performance, as well as extends the operational time I get from a freshly charged battery, since the hard disk is powered up less frequently (the hard disk powers down if it's not used for awhile). Shop around for third-party RAM upgrades. I got an 8MB upgrade at about one fourth Toshiba's price from tote-a-lap (yes, a lowercased name) in Foster City, CA. These people offer rock-bottom prices in laptops and laptop upgrades. Their phone number is (415) 578-1901.

If you intend to operate your laptop from batteries, power-saving features are a must. How long does the machine really run on batteries? Do they charge quickly? Are they user-replaceable? One great feature that was pioneered by Toshiba is a standby mode, sometimes called Resume, Auto-Resume, or Sleep. Machines with this feature let you turn off the machine and then resume your work where you left off. This is especially great if it works with Windows (check to see that it does!). If it does, you can boot up and run Windows, load all your projects, leave off right in the middle of a document, and put the machine in Sleep mode. Then you can return to work as much as a week later, almost instantly. No waiting while the machine boots DOS and Windows and runs the programs in the StartUp group. This is how computing should be. Ask the salesperson what happens if the battery dies in Sleep mode (some battery power is required to keep the machine semialive), and note whether the mouse comes back to life when switching the unit back on from Sleep mode. As a rule, I've found Zenith and Toshiba to have done more homework on these issues than other manufacturers.

Finally, consider the screen. Though most laptop screens are fine for text work, not all are up to snuff with the detail required by Windows. The screen must be VGA-compatible with eight or more shades of gray. How bright is it? Does it need constant adjustment? Is it backlit (electroluminescent) or edgelit (fluorescent)? The usable life of fluorescent lighting tubes is about ten times that of electroluminescent lighting panels. Does it have an antireflective surface? If you can afford a color LCD screen, more power to you. Active-matrix color LCD screens are far better than passive-matrix color ones. They are "faster," so the pointer doesn't get lost, and there are no "trails" left when moving objects around on the screen. A gas plasma screen is very fast and leaves no trails, but is usually an ugly orange color and consumes lots of battery power. If the computer has an output for a CRT monitor, does it have an option for SVGA (which will give you roughly twice the amount of detail)? Most don't, but some do. This is a nice feature if it will work with your monitor.

Attention Intel 386SL Laptop Users!

Windows 3.1 includes facilites to manage the Advanced Power Management (APM) features included in newer notebook and portable computers. Spend some time familiarizing yourself with the APM options in Control Panel. The APM driver will only be installed (and available in Control Panel) if you have a laptop computer containing the Intel 386SL chip set.

CONVERTING FILES ACROSS PLATFORMS

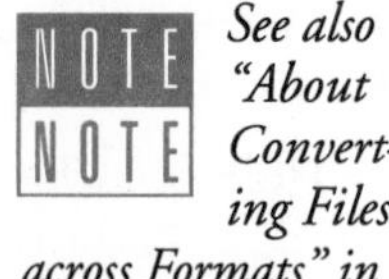

See also "About Converting Files across Formats" in Chapter 20.

Do you ever need to copy information from a Macintosh to your PC? Mac-IN-DOS allows PCs to read and write Macintosh 1.44MB high-density 3½" disks. You can exchange certain text, binary, and graphics files (ASCII, WKS, EPS, PCX, GEM, and TIFF) both from the Macintosh to the PC and from the PC to the Macintosh. Text files can be translated while being copied. No cables or hardware needed. Another program, called Mac to DOS, offers about the same advantages. Note that these programs *only* work if the Macintosh disk is a high-density type. Mac-IN-DOS retails for $99. Call Pacific Microelectronics, Inc., at (800) 628-DISK. Mac to DOS retails for $79. Call Peripheral Land, Inc., at (800) 288-8754.

If you need to read low-density Macintosh disks, consider investing in a Central Point Deluxe Option Board. At this writing it lists for $179. This expansion card connects to your 3½-inch disk drive and lets you read, write, and format low-density (720K) Macintosh disks. Contact Central Point at (503) 690-8090 for more information.

WINDOWS FREEWARE AND SHAREWARE SOURCES

With Windows having become so popular, lots of small-time, do-it-yourselfers are busy tapping away at their cottage industry keyboards, writing Windows utilities and applications. Striking gold in the software business isn't as easy a prospect as it used to be way back before microcomputers were called "PCs." You need deep pockets to finance the engineering and mass marketing of serious applications these days, since the competition consists of multimillion-dollar corporations. Cognizant of this, many smaller software makers now offer Windows products through alternative channels.

Two popular distribution schemes of this ilk make software programs called *freeware* and *shareware* available. Such programs are found in some computer stores, over information networks such as the CompuServe Information Service, and through mail-order catalogs. Either the software carries a miniscule price tag of several dollars or there is none at all until the end of a free trial period. Freeware is absolutely free, but you can't copy it for resale. Shareware uses an honor system that encourages you to send in a registration fee if you decide to continue using it after the trial period. Fees and arrangements vary from product to product. Some are as high as $100, others as low as $5.

See the Mastering Windows Companion Disk order form at the end of this book if you're interested in shareware. It's an effortless way to get your hands on 8MB of the most popular and useful Windows shareware programs (as judged by WUGNET—the Windows User's Group Network).

Contrary to normal antisoftware copying ethics, the authors of shareware progams want you to make copies and give them away to friends in the hope of upping their registration-fee receipts. The good news for we users is that we get to test software before purchasing—and even if you do decide to buy, packages are far less costly than the commercial stuff. Also, lots of offbeat utility programs, games, and other whimsical goodies that no software company CEO would consider marketable are often available for the taking.

The inventory of such items is in constant flux, so covering them here in an up-to-date manner isn't possible. But the following descriptions of a few useful programs may give you the feel of a few of the Windows utilities you can expect to find:

> **Fast-Paste** is a product from the Public Software Library. It allows you to use the right and left mouse buttons for cutting and pasting in a windowed DOS program.

Program Manager Modifier lets you add custom commands to the Program Manager's menu bar for the tasks and applications with which you regularly work.

CCSWAP lets you swap the function of the Ctrl and Caps Lock key under Windows. This is a much-needed program for the great number of folks who use programs that rely heavily on the Ctrl key. Cases in point are SideKick, WordStar, dBASE, PC-Write, NewWord, and many others that utilize the WordStar cursor-movement and editing codes. IBM gave many of us tendonitis when they moved the Ctrl key down below the Shift key with their "enhanced" keyboard. This program fixes this problem.

WinROACH is a cute little ditty that germinates humorous animated roaches that scurry around on your Desktop and hide under the active window. When you close the window, the exposed roaches scurry away to find shelter behind the next active window.

Whiskers lets you reassign your mouse buttons to particular keys, notably the Enter key for quickly OKing dialog boxes without having to aim the pointer precisely.

There are many full-blown programs as well, with topics ranging from tax preparation to multifeatured word processors. With Windows applications development becoming relatively simple to master through object-oriented programming products, such as Borland's C++ and ObjectVision or Microsoft's Visual Basic, you can bet there will be a rash of low-cost Windows applications in the near future—even ones that you can create!

On the downside, you should be advised that few shareware and freeware sources provide quality technical support. However, in my experience, the software is generally of high quality. There is a slightly higher risk that your system will fall prey to a virus through these sources than from mainstream manufacturers, but most distributors carefully check their products for such nuisances before distribution. To be on the safe side, you should use a virus-protection program before loading files from unknown sources onto your hard disk. A good one is Norton AntiVirus (by Symantec/Peter Norton Computing Group) for $129.95.

There are four primary sources for shareware and freeware:

- Local computer stores sometimes have a large cardboard bin of shareware and freeware disks. Prices are very reasonable, often just the cost of the diskette itself. These bins seem to appear at local and national computer shows, too.
- Information networks such as CompuServe contain many programs downloaded by other Windows users. Look for comments left on the service by users who have previously tested the programs you're interested in. They may report unseemly bugs you'd rather avoid. Many bulletin board systems will show you a tally indicating the number of users who have downloaded a program, which is somewhat indicative of its usefulness and quality. CompuServe has several forums for Windows users through which you can access volumes of information about Windows and available programs. Get a modem and join CIS by calling (800) 848-8990. Once connected, log on and type **GO WINDOWS.** Then type **GO WINNEW** to enter the system as a new user and receive information about the Windows forums available to you.
- User's groups are a great source of freeware and shareware, because you have the advantage of talking to others who have used the product or program. Check computer magazines and newspapers for listings of user's group phone numbers and meetings. Many of these will be listed in the Windows forums of CompuServe. One user's group of particular note is called WUGNET, mentioned next under "Windows Information Sources." This is an international group of users, product developers, programmers, and computer journalists.
- Mail-order catalogs are also a good source. Shareware and freeware mail-order services typically charge a per-disk fee to cover their costs and make a small profit. The advantage is that you can peruse a catalog of products to compare their features quickly, rather than pay online per-minute charges on a BBS to read about the programs. It's usually the case that paying a shareware

vendor for a disk doesn't make you a registered user. You'll typically still have to register with the author of the program once you decide to use the program. Five of the more reputable mail-order sources are the following:

Public Software Library, (800) 242-4775

PC-SIG, (800) 245-6717

Public Brand Software, (800) 426-3475

Software Excitement!, (800) 444-5457

The Software Labs, (800) 359-9998

WINDOWS INFORMATION SOURCES

Listed below are some information sources (books, periodicals, and online services) to help keep you up-to-date on the quickly developing world of Windows computing. This is only a portion of the many sources available, but as of this writing, they are the most notable ones.

Windows Resource Kit

A valuable source of technical information about Windows is available from the horse's mouth. This package should be purchased by anyone seriously into Windows. It comes in a sturdy three-ring binder and includes a couple hundred pages of information about installation, configuration, running DOS applications, networking, and troubleshooting. It also contains lists of Windows programs and compatible hardware, as well as a disk full of helpful utilities, system resource viewers, drivers, and accessories. You can order the Windows Resource Kit by calling Microsoft at (800) 642-7676.

Windows Online Information Database Service

Windows Online Information Database Service (WOL) is an online service out of Danville, California, that gives you access to Windows programs and information, by modem. This professionally run BBS, dedicated solely to Windows, claims to have over 2500 Windows files online. The folks who run it promise to have 25 or more new, posted files every day, and say they'll "find every Windows 3.X file that lives and post it for members to download." They have a half-dozen or so staff writers who send in tips, reviews, and product updates. They also have an international e-mail system for exchanging messages with other Windows users. There are 11 phone lines, so busy signals are rare.

Six-month memberships to WOL are $49 and come with 60 minutes per day and up to 300 downloaded files. One-year memberships are $89 and allow 700 files. You can pay online with MasterCard or Visa. The WOL modem number is (510) 736-8343. Their voice/fax number is (510) 736-4376.

WOL also publishes a newsletter called the *WOL Weekly*, an electronic Windows-related magazine that you download and then use your Windows Help engine to read. It's a bit like an interactive magazine, with hot spots to click on that let you jump between topics, view full-screen graphics, look up cross-references, and so on—just like the help files that come with programs. It takes a couple of full-time programmers, as well as WOL's writers, to put the thing together, but it's a great idea in the world of electronic publishing: an interactive magazine that uses a program we all have on our computers—the Windows Help engine.

Windows BBS

Here is a relatively new commerical BBS that specializes in Windows shareware and user-to-user help and information sharing. As of the summer of 1992, this BBS claims to have 600 Windows programs and data files. The board is optimized for file downloading. To cut down on your search time and save long-distance charges, download the file DIR.ZIP—this is a directory of all the downloadable files. Unzip and read it off-line, and then call back and download what you want.

At this writing, six-month subscriptions are $16.20; you get one year for $25. Discounts are available for students and WUGNET members. There is modem support for 1200, 1400, or 9600 bps (V.32). Use settings of 8 data bits, no parity, and 1 stop bit.

The phone number for the Windows BBS is (607) 722-0177. They also sell programs on disk if you don't want to bother downloading. Prices are very reasonable.

CompuServe

Online help is available to solve many of your Windows problems. CompuServe, for example, has several forums to help you. Typing **MSWIN** at the ! prompt gets you in touch with Microsoft personnel, new printer and screen drivers, and other technical advice from the makers of Windows. Other forums are reached by typing **MSAPP**, **WINAPA**, and **WINAPB.**

WUGNET

A group called WUGNET (Windows User's Group Network) has its fingers in all kinds of Windows-related activities, from sponsoring books about Windows to writing and publishing Windows software. WUGNET offers support services for Windows users and developers, publishes a bimonthly journal, and maintains a user's group forum on CompuServe. The Windows Journal is typically a meaty collection of Windows-related information for professionals and serious Windows, OS/2, and NewWave users and developers. It's about 50 pages long and contains a copious amount of useful information. Be prepared for pretty technical stuff, though. Logging on to their CompuServe forum will get you tons of free programs, reviews, and technical information. Once a member, you get disks of programs every two months. To reach them on CompuServe, type GO WUGNET from anywhere on the network. There you will find more information about joining. Ninety-five dollars gets you a one-year subscription (six issues of the journal), six disks, and 24-hour access to WUGNET Online on CompuServe. Call (215) 565-1861. Their fax number is (215) 565-7106.

Windows Magazine

This four-color glossy magazine is published monthly and contains reviews, features, and news about Windows. It's a comprehensive magazine on the topic of Windows, Windows applications, and tips, and costs about $30 a year. If you can find it, check out their *100 Best Windows Products* back-issue, from February 1992. Call them at (800) 284-3534.

Windows Tech Journal

For technical reading and tips on nothing but programming with Windows, check out this magazine. It's a start-up from Eugene, Oregon, but it's a nicely put together glossy job. I recently met the founder, J.D. Hildebrand, at the Windows-OS/2 Conference in San Jose and was impressed with his down-to-earth style. He's landed some good columnists/programmers, and arranged for the code discussed in the magazine to be available on CompuServe and several BBSs around the country. (This magazine appears to be to Windows what *Dr. Dobb's Journal* was to CP/M in the early days of microcomputers.) *Windows Tech Journal* costs about $30 per year. Call the magazine at (800) 234-0386.

The Programmer's Shop

If you're a programmer or are considering getting into programming, a good source for progamming tools is *The Programmer's Shop.* This is a catalog of Windows languages, libraries, and tools. Since it also carries utilities, applications, and hardware, it's a source for nonprogrammers as well. *The Programmer's Shop* is available by calling (800) 421-8006.

The Windows Shopper's Guide

This is a big, thick catalog of Windows products abstracts and services arranged by category and cross-referenced conveniently by category, name, and manufacturer. My current issue is about an inch thick. It's also available on disk for use with Asymetrix's ToolBook if you want to dispense with the paper and look up things more quickly—though that's more expensive ($139.95 a year). I've used the catalog about 30 times in the last few weeks, and I have to say it's pretty handy. It's intended primarily for MIS directors, power users, consultants, distributors, retailers, marketeers, and systems integrators. But if you need easy access to names, prices, products, product descriptions, and addresses of manufacturers who offer Windows programs and services, check this thing out. It comes out twice a year and costs $23.45 for one copy, $43.95 for one year (two issues), or $83.95 for two years (four issues). *Windows Shopper's Guide* is available from WhiteFox Communications, Inc., at (800) 669-5612.

Supercharging Windows

This SYBEX book by Judd Robbins offers advanced users both explanations and demonstrations of Windows' most important, sophisticated, and sometimes difficult-to-understand capabilities. Two 5¼" disks packaged with the book contain 2MB of Windows applications and utilities selected by the author.

Windows Quick & Easy

I've written this SYBEX book for beginners who may prefer a visual approach to learning about computers. Give this book to someone who keeps asking you about how to do this or that in Windows. Scheduled for release later in 1992.

APPENDIX A

FEATURING

Requirements for Installing Windows

Running the Setup Program

Altering Your Setup

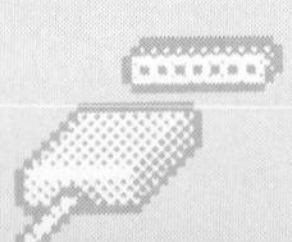

Installing Windows

efore you can use Windows, you have to install it on your computer. Many programs are difficult to install, but fortunately Windows is not one of them. The Setup program supplied with Windows 3.1 automates the installation process fairly successfully on most systems. You cannot install Windows simply by copying files onto your hard disk. The files on your installation disks are compacted so that they can fit onto fewer disks. The Setup program expands the files during installation. That's why you can only install Windows with the Setup program.

Setup installs the Windows system files, the necessary printer and screen drivers for your system, and the appropriate printer and screen fonts. If a network is detected, Setup installs the appropriate network driver. It detects memory-resident programs and drivers, alerting you to any potential conflicts. Finally, it installs the accessory applications ("applets," as Microsoft calls them) supplied with Windows and searches your hard disk for other Windows and non-Windows programs, creating icons that you'll later use to run the programs.

You can use the Setup program in two ways. The Express option takes care of most of the details for you, and speeds up the process as well. All you are asked to supply is what type of printer you have and the port to which it's connected. The Custom setup lets experienced users control details of the installation procedure, including:

- the directory where you want to store Windows files
- your mouse
- your keyboard and keyboard layout
- the type of computer you're using
- your monitor (screen) type
- the language you will work in
- the network you are on, if any
- the printer and printer port you use, if any
- changes to your AUTOEXEC.BAT and CONFIG.SYS files, if necessary
- applications on your hard disk that you want to run with Windows
- which optional Windows components to install
- virtual-memory settings (when running in 386-Enhanced mode)

This appendix describes the Express setup only, since you're more likely to use that option; there's also plenty of on-screen help for the Custom setup procedure. You should allot 15 to 30 minutes for the Express setup procedure.

Once you've performed the initial setup of Windows, it's possible that you'll want to modify some aspect of it later—for example, when you get a new video screen, mouse, or keyboard, or switch to a new type of network. The second half of this appendix explains how you use the Setup program to make such changes.

REQUIREMENTS FOR INSTALLING WINDOWS

Before beginning to install Windows, take a minute to evaluate your system's components to ensure that they meet the requirements of Windows. If you aren't sure what's in your system, you can try running Setup anyway to see what happens. If there is a problem or conflict, you'll be alerted to it.

Operating System MS-DOS or PC-DOS version 3.1 or later (preferably DOS 5).

Computer An IBM-compatible PC-AT, PS/2, 80386, or 80486 computer that is IBM-compatible. You need at least an 80286 machine to run in Standard mode, and an 80386 machine to run in 386-Enhanced mode. Note that 8086 and 8088 machines cannot be used with Windows 3.1; they can only run Windows 3.0. (Modes are described at the beginning of Chapter 2.)

Memory A minimum of one megabyte, and preferably more. The optimal amount you should have depends on the Windows mode you want to work in and the number and size of the applications you intend to use. To work in 386-Enhanced mode, your computer needs at least 640K of base RAM and 1024K of extended RAM. For Standard mode, it needs at least 640K of base RAM and 256K of extended memory. Note that any memory over 640K should be set up as extended memory, not expanded memory. (Chapter 16 explains memory usage in detail.)

Disk Drives The amount of free hard-disk space that Windows 3.1 requires depends on your type of system and whether you already have installed Windows 3.0. Here are the minimum requirements for installation. Note that the minimum figures do not include optional components such as accessory programs, tutorial and help files, network drivers, or a printer driver. The maximum requirements include all components installed, including printer and network drivers.

SETUP TYPE	MINIMUM SPACE (APPROX.)	MAXIMUM SPACE (APPROX.)
New	8.0MB	10.5MB

SETUP TYPE	MINIMUM SPACE (APPROX.)	MAXIMUM SPACE (APPROX.)
Upgrade	5.0MB	5.5MB

If your system is tight on disk space, the Setup program will suggest an installation that omits ancillary files—such as screen savers, readme files, and some accessory programs and their related help files—in an attempt to achieve a functional Windows installation with your remaining disk space.

Your system must also have a floppy disk drive to install the program. As supplied, the Windows disks are in 1.2MB (5¼-inch) or 720K (3½-inch) format. If your floppy drive only reads 360K disks, you'll have to request lower-density disks from Microsoft.

Screens Windows supports many screens. Drivers are included for CGA, MDA, Hercules, EGA, VGA, Super VGA, and 8514/A—and a few permutations of these. To really see and use Windows efficiently, you should have at least an EGA setup and preferably a VGA or Super VGA. For other types of screens, such as high-resolution 1024 × 1280, 1024 × 960, and so forth, you'll have to acquire a software driver from the screen's manufacturer.

Mouse A mouse isn't required, but it's practically a necessity. This book assumes you have a mouse. All the major mouse types are supported.

Printer A printer is optional. Drivers that work with over 190 printers are included with Windows, so it's likely that your printer is among them.

Modem A modem is also optional, but required if you want to use the Terminal program for communications or have the Cardfile program dial phone numbers for you. A Hayes-compatible modem is recommended.

IF YOU ARE UPGRADING FROM WINDOWS 3.0

When you run the Windows 3.1 Setup program, your system is checked for an existing copy of Windows 3.0. If one is found, you'll be asked whether you want to install Windows 3.1 into another directory or replace Windows

3.0 with 3.1. Unless you have a specific reason for keeping both, install 3.1 over 3.0. Less disk space will be used this way and Setup will see to it that incompatible or outdated files, drivers, fonts, and settings are removed or replaced.

Setup recognizes and preserves any existing Windows settings, such as Program Manager groups and Desktop settings you've made. In addition, applications, fonts, and certain drivers are also preserved. Only the Windows system files, device drivers, and accessories are replaced with the new versions.

Specifically, when you choose to upgrade your existing Windows installation, Setup does the following:

- preserves existing Program Manager groups
- preserves existing system-information settings for your computer, monitor, mouse, keyboard and keyboard layout, language, network, and the associated drivers
- preserves settings relating to the use of your system's upper-memory area (HMA)
- uses any existing swapfile (virtual memory) setup from Windows 3.0
- maintains all non-Microsoft installed drivers (i.e., those from other manufacturers)
- updates existing device drivers (such as mouse and printer drivers) that were supplied with Windows 3.0
- preserves the LOADHIGH= line and its order in your current AUTOEXEC.BAT file
- preserves the DEVICEHIGH= line in your CONFIG.SYS file

Even though the installation procedure is relatively nondestructive to your existing setup, reading between the lines in Microsoft's manual suggests to me that things might not be as copacetic as you'd like. For example, they suggest you "...be sure to make backup copies of any data files and programs you have added to your system." So just to be on the safe side, if you've "tweaked" your AUTOEXEC.BAT, CONFIG.SYS, WIN.INI, and SYSTEM.INI files, and/or have added programs and drivers and PIFs to your WINDOWS or SYSTEM directories, you may want to make backup copies of them. I've successfully installed Windows 3.1 several times with no glitches, but I still make a habit of creating a backup directory (\WINBAK) and copying all the .DRV, .GRP, .INI, .PIF, and .SYS files from my Windows directory into it before doing an update. I then add copies of my CONFIG.SYS and AUTOEXEC.BAT files to this directory. This way, if my system acts weird after the update, I can do a little sleuthing by comparing the files.

RUNNING SETUP

Before running Setup, you should terminate any automatic messaging software you might have, such as network E-mail programs that write directly to your screen. Such programs may interrupt Setup and cause it to bomb.

Just follow the steps below to install Windows on your system. (These are instructions for a single-user PC, not for a network. Consult the Microsoft Windows User's Guide for information on network installations.)

1. Put the first disk, labeled Disk 1, into your floppy drive.
2. Log on to your floppy drive by typing **A:** (or **B:** if that's your floppy drive's letter) and pressing Enter.
3. Type **SETUP** at the prompt and press Enter to start the Setup program.
4. The first screen will come up, informing you about Setup and giving you the options of exiting, continuing, or reading some helpful information about the installation process. Press F1 if you want to read more about the Setup program, then look at the bottom of the screen to see which keys to press. If you've already installed the program from these disks, there will be an indication to that effect. You are warned that you're only to make legal copies. Click on Continue to go ahead and perform the installation.
5. During the installation procedure, Setup checks quite carefully to see what memory-resident programs and device drivers you have loaded into your system. It is pretty savvy at identifying them and determining which ones would cause difficulty with the installation process. You may see a message during the beginning phases of installation suggesting that you cancel Setup, remove one or more memory-resident programs from your system, and start the installation again. It's a good idea to do as instructed, since otherwise you could go through all the hassle of setting up Windows

only to find that it doesn't work right. Edit your CONFIG.SYS and/or AUTOEXEC.BAT files accordingly. A text file called SETUP.TXT on Disk 1 of your Windows 3.1 floppy should provide last-minute specific instructions about working with the offending memory-resident program(s). You can view the SETUP.TXT file with Notepad (if you already have an earlier version of Windows on your machine) or with any ASCII or ANSI text editor.

6. Now you see a screen that asks whether you want to use Express Setup or Custom Setup. Choose Express if you don't want to bother with controlling the details of your system that are listed at the beginning of the appendix. If you're upgrading from Windows 3.0, Express Setup will also keep your existing 3.0 printer driver setup, which saves you a little hassle, too. For detailed information about Express and Custom setups, press F1 and read the resulting Help screens. The rest of the installation described in this appendix assumes that you choose Express.
7. Press Enter. Setup will look for any existing version of Windows on your disk. If it finds it, you'll be asked whether you want to keep it and install the new Windows system in another directory or overwrite the old Windows with the new one. Change the path name if you want to keep the old one. Otherwise keep the path name the same. As mentioned above, if you already have an existing Windows installation, don't worry about losing anything as a result of choosing to install the new Windows in your exisiting Windows directory. Setup will not wipe out your old group files (.GRP), .PIF files, and .INI files. If you are using a shell other than the Microsoft one (such as Norton Desktop for Windows), this will be recognized too, so you won't have to reconfigure it.
8. Setup will now start installing files from the floppy disk. A little gauge on the screen will keep you updated on its progress. Prompts will instruct you to change disks from time to time. After a couple of disks, the screen will change to something more colorful, and the mouse will become active. (If it doesn't, skip to the next section, "If Setup Crashes.") Just follow the instructions on the screen. You can use the mouse to click on Continue, or just press Enter after inserting each new disk. (*Clicking* means

positioning the pointer on the item in question and clicking the left mouse button once.) If you decide you want to bail out of the installation process at any time, just click on the Exit Setup button.

9. If you are asked what type of printer you have, just follow the instructions on the screen for choosing the printer and the printer port. If you see a list of available printer types, and yours isn't showing, you'll have to scroll the list up to see additional choices. If you don't know how to do this, here's how: Position the mouse pointer on the little up or down arrows in the box of printer names and press and hold the left button to scroll through the listings until your printer type is displayed. Then release the button. Click on the correct printer name. This highlights the name. Click on Install and you will be prompted to insert a disk with the correct driver for your printer. (Refer to Chapter 6 for more details about installing printers.) Follow the instructions on the screen to complete the installation of the printer.

NOTE *You can run the tutorial later by choosing Windows Tutorial from the Program Manager's Help menu.*

10. Eventually the Program Manager will appear, with several windows popping up. (If you had an existing Windows installation, all your familiar group windows will appear.) Now you'll be asked whether you want to run a short tutorial that will show you how to use a mouse and elucidate the basics of Windows. If you desire edification on either of these two topics, click on Run Tutorial or press **R**. If you aren't familiar with the basics of Windows, I suggest running the tutorial. It'll take you through the steps of moving and aiming the mouse and selecting objects, as well as identifying the basic elements—menus, title bars, scroll bars, and so forth. It only requires about five mintues at the most. Then follow the instructions on the screen. If you're among the initiated, skip the tutorial; you'll be shown a box saying that Windows 3.1 is now set up.
11. Remove the disk from your floppy drive.
12. Click on Reboot or type **R** to restart your system.
13. Wait for the computer to reboot. At the DOS prompt, type **WIN** and press Enter. Windows will now load. You should see the Windows sign-on screen, followed by the Program Manager's window and some program icons.

You can now turn to the front of this book and learn how to work with Windows. However, you might want to skim the remainder of this appendix quickly, since it may come in handy later for altering and maintaining your Windows setup.

If Setup Crashes

About halfway through the installation process, Setup switches over to running within the graphical user interface of Windows. To do this, it uses the screen and mouse settings you specified or, if you didn't change them, its own settings on the basis of the hardware it detected in your system. If your hardware is too offbeat for Setup to recognize, however, or you chose the wrong settings, Setup might bomb, presenting you with a blank screen and not progressing any further. If your screen is blank, your hard or floppy disk isn't being accessed—and if 30 seconds or so go by, then this is probably what has happened.

There are several steps you can now take. The first is to read the file SETUP.TXT that came with your Windows disks. This text file can be read with any text editor that reads ASCII text files. It contains information about software or hardware configurations that require special handling to set up and start Windows successfully.

The second solution is explained in the next section. Try that approach first, making sure that your hardware choices are correct. You might want to try a variation on your actual equipment. For example, if Setup is bombing when you select VGA, try VGA Monochrome; or if your screen can emulate EGA or CGA, try those settings just to see whether Setup will make it through and whether Windows will run—then try to solve the incompatibility problem another way.

As a last resort, you can erase all the files in the directory that Setup created and start Setup again with Disk 1. This is a drag, because of the time the installation takes, but it may be necessary. If you do this, start Setup this time with the command

```
SETUP /I
```

which tells Setup to ignore the system hardware and use its own defaults (which may or may not be correct, of course). Take extra measures to ensure that your hardware settings match your actual system this time. You'll have to set them all manually.

Changing Your System Settings from the DOS Prompt

Use this procedure if Windows didn't boot up the first time or if you need to install a driver supplied with some special hardware such as a screen, printer, or network after Windows is installed and working properly.

If you or Windows were wrong about the actual hardware in your system, it's possible that nothing will happen at the end of the Setup procedure: your screen may go blank, your keyboard may lock up, your mouse may not work, or some other evidence of a system crash may become apparent. If so, all you can do is reboot and then run Setup from your DOS prompt. Luckily, it works from there just as well as from within Windows. Normally, you won't have to do this since Setup can usually guess correctly about your hardware installation, particularly the screen type. But I've met with failure a time or two during installation when the wrong screen or mouse type was accidentally detected and installed (see note below about mice). If most of the installation went OK and the important files were all copied over from the floppy disks correctly, you may be able to change just a few settings and fix Windows without redoing the whole shooting match.

You can also use this technique of running Setup to install a driver not supplied with Windows or to update a driver for your hardware. You should be aware that Microsoft adds drivers to their own collection over time, and that they may have one if you can't get one from the manufacturer of your hardware. Make sure to follow any instructions that come with such a driver before following the steps below, or it may not work optimally (in other words, such things as screen fonts may be wrong).

A note about mice is in order here. If your mouse isn't working correctly after installing Windows, Setup may have inadvertently installed the wrong mouse software driver. You'll want to check the mouse settings to see if this has happened to you. The most common cases of mistaken identity are as follows. Some Microsoft-compatible Logitech mice are detected as "Microsoft or IBM PS/2" by the Windows 3.1 Setup program. If you have a Logitech mouse, be sure to install the Logitech driver by selecting the Logitech line in the mouse section of Windows Setup. If your Mouse

Systems mouse is detected as "Microsoft or IBM PS/2", don't change this setting. Your mouse is truly Microsoft compatible and it works better with this driver than with the Mouse Systems driver. However, if your Mouse Systems mouse *wasn't* detected at all, then install the Mouse Systems driver by selecting the appropriate Mouse Systems entry in the mouse section of Windows Setup.

1. If you're not at the DOS prompt, get there by exiting Windows. (Don't use the DOS prompt icon in Windows.)
2. Switch to your Windows directory (typically C:\WINDOWS) with the CD command, such as **CD C:\WINDOWS**.
3. Type **SETUP**. Setup will start. If you get a "bad command or file name" message, Setup didn't get far enough the first time to install the SETUP program on your hard disk, or a path to the Windows directory has not been set yet. Go directly to Jail, do not pass Go, do not collect $200—i.e., bad news. Try installing from the beginning again, choosing Custom Setup so that you can verify Setup's hardware choices. Sometimes Setup doesn't detect systems correctly. If *that* doesn't work, read SETUP.TXT; it's on Disk 1. Look for information regarding memory-resident programs you might be running, or anything about your particular hardware.
4. A screen will appear, listing the current hardware and software configuration. To change a setting, highlight it with the up and down arrow keys on your keyboard and press Enter.
5. A list of choices for that setting will now appear. Highlight the correct one for your system and press Enter. If you're installing a driver not supplied with Windows, but supplied from the manufacturer of the hardware, choose Other (it's at the bottom of the list).
6. You may be prompted to insert a disk that has the driver on it. You can specify the drive and directory where the driver is located, though the default is drive A. Insert the disk—or specify the path if it's on the hard disk—and press Enter. Occasionally a driver may have more than one disk, in which case you'll also be prompted to insert each one. In any case, the driver files and any associated files, such as screen fonts, will be copied to the hard disk.

7. The updated hardware list will be displayed. Press Enter again and you will be returned to the DOS prompt.
8. Enter **WIN** to start Windows.

ALTERING YOUR SETUP

The Setup program can be run again any time you want to modify the hardware setup or install new programs in your Program Manager groups.

CHANGING YOUR HARDWARE SETUP FROM WINDOWS

Typically, you'll want to run Setup when you add a new type of screen, mouse, or network. You can run Setup two ways. If you've successfully installed Windows and it runs correctly, you can run Setup from Windows:

1. Double-click the Windows Setup icon in the Main group. The Windows Setup window will then appear, listing the current information about your screen, keyboard, mouse, and network.
2. You can make changes to these settings by opening the Options menu and choosing Change System Settings. All the current system settings are displayed in each of four lines of the Change Systems Settings dialog box.
3. Open the drop-down list box(es) for the setting(s) you want to change, select the appropriate choice(s), and click on OK.
4. You may be prompted to insert a disk and indicate which drive it's in. This is because Setup may need a driver file that's on the disk.
5. Open the Options menu and choose Exit.
6. Now a dialog box will give you one or two choices, depending on the changes you made. You'll have the option of restarting Windows or rebooting. If you have the option of rebooting, click on that button. Otherwise choose Restart Windows. Restarting windows or rebooting is necessary to ensure that the changes are applied.

Note that you can also run Setup from the DOS prompt. Just follow the instructions in the previous section, "Changing Your System Settings from the DOS Prompt."

Adding New Applications with Setup

From time to time you may acquire new programs that you want to incorporate into your Windows application groups. Though new programs can be added with a variety of techniques, as described in Chapter 3, you can use the Setup program to automate this task for you. Setup will add the new program's icon to the appropriate Program Manager group so you can run the program easily.

Here are the steps for adding a new program with Setup:

NOTE *You can also add printer drivers to your system from the Control Panel within Windows. Refer to Chapter 6 for information on installing and removing printers.*

1. Install the application on your hard disk according to the manufacturer's instructions. Often such an installation will automatically place the necessary program icons into the Program Manager for you, making any additional steps unnecessary. If it doesn't, continue to the next step.
2. Run Setup by double-clicking on the Windows Setup icon in the Main group.
3. From the Setup window, open the Options menu and choose Set Up Applications. You'll see the following dialog box:

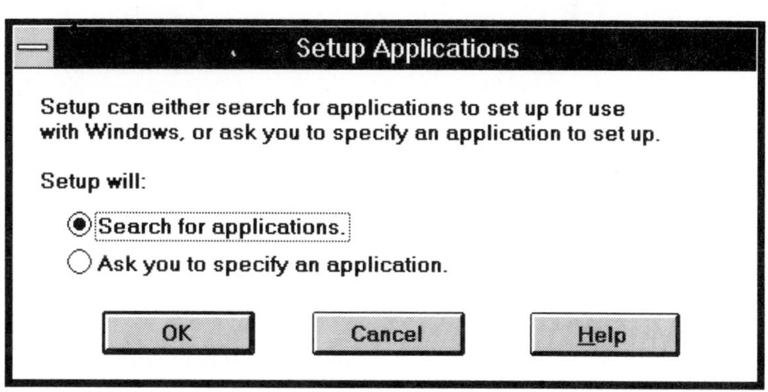

4. If you want to see a list of applications you can choose from, choose the first option and click on OK. If you know the name of the application you want to install, choose the second option and click on OK.

If you choose the first option, you will see a dialog box, from which you choose the application you want to install and the Program Manager group into which you want to install it. If you don't know the actual name and path name of the executable file (such as WP5.EXE, DBASE.EXE, etc.) then use the Browse button to bring up a file dialog box with which you can look around through disk directories to locate the file. Highlight the file and click on OK, or double-click the file name when you find it. You're done. Look in the Applications group in Program Manager for the new icon.

If you choose to have Setup search for programs for you, you'll see the following dialog box:

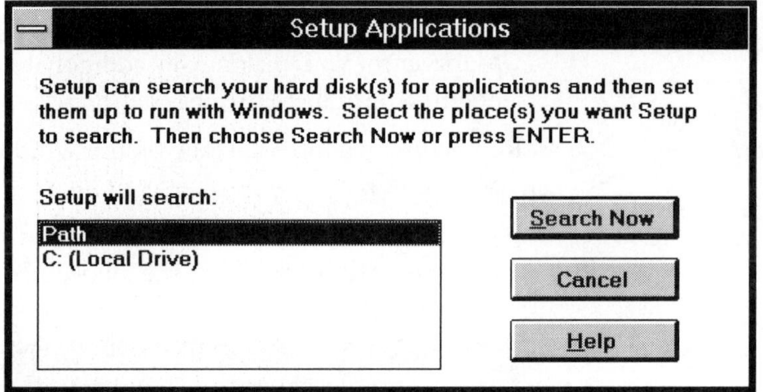

Now do the following:

1. Highlight the drive you want Setup to look on, or leave the default setting of Path if you want it to search only through files in your DOS search path, as set in your system's AUTOEXEC.BAT file. If you want it to search more than one drive, or the drive and path both, click on each one while holding down the Shift key.

2. Press Enter or click on Search Now. Setup will search through the selected drive or path for the application. If Setup comes across a program that's used with more than one popular program (such as Q.EXE, which can be Quattro Pro or Quicken), you may be asked for clarification.
3. After searching the disk or path, Setup then presents you with a list of programs it found. Programs it recognizes are displayed in upper- and lowercase letters. Programs it doesn't recognize are in all uppercase. To add your program, click on the application's name in the left box. Then click on Add. This moves the name to the right box. Don't do this for programs you've added previously (such as during the initial installation) or you will have duplicate program icons in your Program Manager groups.
4. Click on OK. Setup will add the appropriate icon(s) to the Applications group in the Program Manager. Refer to Chapter 3 for details on managing your icons and groups.

APPENDIX B

FEATURING

Using Shortcut Keys for Windows Operations and All Windows Accessories

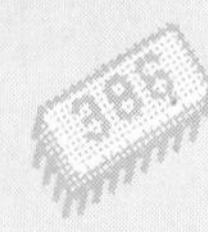

Keyboard Shortcuts

This appendix lists keystrokes you can use in lieu of or in addition to the mouse when you're running Windows and some of the supplied applications. You might want to use this list for reference if you're using a laptop computer on the road without a mouse, or simply to speed up your work by keeping your hands on the keyboard. Touch typists in particular often find keystroke commands preferable to mouse procedures.

Of course, keystrokes for Windows applications that you purchase aren't listed here. With so many available programs, each with its own keyboard commands, this isn't possible. However, lots of applications have similar keyboard commands, especially ones that apply to editing, cutting, copying, pasting, saving and opening files, and exiting.

IF YOU CAN'T REMEMBER A KEY COMMAND

If you're stuck without a mouse and need to execute a command on an application's menu:

1. Press Alt and the underlined letter of the menu you want to open. If it's the wrong menu, press the → or ← key to open the correct one.
2. Look for the shortcut key for the command you want. Commands on a menu often have their keyboard-equivalent commands listed to their right—an easy reminder when you forget. If there is one, mentally note it or jot it down for future reference. Then press Alt to dismiss the menu. Next time, use the shortcut key.
3. If there isn't a shortcut key on the menu, use the ↓ key to highlight the command you want and press Enter—or, to make the process even faster, just press the underlined or highlighted letter in the command's name.

HELP SHORTCUT KEYS

All Windows applications use the same Windows "Help engine." The keys below pertain to any application that has Help available:

Display Help for currently active application; may or may not be context-sensitive Help	F1
Change pointer to question mark so you can click on command or region to get Help on (only in some applications)	Shift-F1
Jump clockwise through hot spots in Help window	Tab
Jump counter-clockwise through hot spots in Help window	Shift-Tab

Jump to help or pop-up explanation on selected hot spot	Enter
Momentarily highlight all the hot spots in Help window	Ctrl-Tab
Copy all or selected portion of Help topic to the Clipboard	Ctrl-Ins
Paste contents of Clipboard into annotation box	Shift-Ins

KEYS THAT APPLY TO MANY WINDOWS APPLICATIONS

The following keys are ones that work throughout Windows. They apply to dialog boxes, application and document switching, and other Windows procedures.

General Keys

These are shortcut keys for general tasks:

Bring up a Help screen if the application has Help available	F1
Switch to Task List	Ctrl-Esc
Switch to the next application, whether it is running in a window or as an icon	Alt-Esc
Switch to the application you last used	Alt-Tab
Switch to next running application in forward order (release Alt when correct name shows)	Alt-Tab
Switch to next running application in reverse order (release Alt when correct name shows)	Alt-Shift-Tab
Cancel the Alt-Tab switching process and stay with current application	Alt-Esc

Place image of the entire screen on the Clipboard (DOS applications must be in text mode)	PrtScr (may require Shift key)
Place an image of the active window on the Clipboard	Alt-PrtScr (may require Shift key)
Open an application window Control box	Alt-Spacebar
Open a document window Control box	Alt-Hyphen
Quit a running application or close a window	Alt-F4
Close the active group window or document window	Ctrl-F4
Switch a non-Windows application between windowed and full-screen mode	Alt-Enter
Move or size a window	Choose Move or Size from Control box, then press ↑, ↓, ←, or →, followed by Enter

Menu Keys

These commands affect the displaying and choosing of commands from menus:

Activate the menu bar	Alt or F10
Choose the menu or command with underlined or highlighted letter	Single letter (upper- or lowercase both work)
Move between menus	← or →
Move between commands	↑ or ↓
Choose the highlighted menu name or command	Enter
Cancel the highlighted menu or deactivate the menu bar	Esc or Alt

Dialog Box Keys

These commands control what you select in a dialog box:

Move between sections and options	Tab
Move in reverse order bewteen options and sections	Shift-Tab
Quickly jump to a section or choose an option	Alt-*underlined letter*
Move the selection cursor between options within a section	↑, ↓, ←, or →
Open a drop-down list box	Alt- ↓
Move the cursor up or down within a list box	↑ or ↓
Move to the last item in a list box	End
Move to the first item in a list box	Home
Quickly scroll up or down in a list, one screen at a time	PgUp or PgDn
Select or cancel an option or item in a list	Spacebar
Select or clear a check box	Spacebar
Select all the items in a list box	Ctrl-/
Cancel all except the current item in a list box	Ctrl-\
Extend or contract the selection in a text box	Shift- → or Shift- ←
Extend or contract the selection to the last letter in a text box	Shift-End
Extend or contract the selection to the first letter in a text box	Shift-Home
Close a dialog box without putting changes into effect	Esc

KEYS FOR MOVING THE CURSOR AROUND

These keys quickly move the text cursor within text boxes or within text-based applications:

Up a line	↑
Down a line	↓
Right one character	→
Left one character	←
Right one word	Ctrl- →
Left one word	Ctrl- ←
Beginning of line	Home
End of line	End
Up one screen	PgUp
Down one screen	PgDn
Beginning of document	Ctrl-Home
End of document	Ctrl-End

TEXT SELECTING KEYS

Here's a list of keys that select text within Windows applications. First place the insertion point (I-beam) at the beginning of the text you want to select. Then use the keys to extend the selection in the direction you desire. If there is already a selection, it may be cancelled or it may be extended further or possibly contracted when you use these keys. What happens depends on where the insertion point is relative to the *anchor point* (the point from which you began the selection process). Experimentation is the best way to learn how selecting, extending, and contracting work:

One character left or right	Shift- ← or →
One line of text up or down	Shift- ↑ or ↓
Previous word	Ctrl-Shift- ←
Next word	Ctrl-Shift- →
Previous full screen of text	Shift-PgUp
Next full screen of text	Shift-PgDn
To beginning of line	Shift-Home
To end of line	Shift-End
Text to beginning of document	Ctrl-Shift-Home
Text to end of document	Ctrl-Shift-End

Text Editing Keys

Use these keys when editing text. Note that not all of these keys will work with all applications. Some applications use other keys, particularly for cut, copy, and paste operations:

Delete a character to the right of the I-beam	Del
Delete a character to the left of the I-beam	Backspace
Delete selected text	Del or Backspace
Cut all selected text and put it on the Clipboard	Shift-Del or Ctrl-X
Copy all selected text on the Clipboard	Ctrl-Ins or Ctrl-C
Paste text on the Clipboard into the active window	Shift-Ins or Ctrl-V
Undo the last editing action	Ctrl-Z or Alt-Backspace

PROGRAM MANAGER SHORTCUT KEYS

Group windows in Program Manager use the following keys:

Move between items within a group window	↑, ↓, ←, or →
Move between group windows or group icons	Ctrl-F6 or Ctrl-Tab
Start the highlighted application	Enter
Tile the open group windows	Shift-F4
Cascade open group windows	Shift-F5
Close the active group window	Ctrl-F4
Quit Windows	Alt-F4

FILE MANAGER SHORTCUT KEYS

Use of the File Manager can be accelerated or accomplished without a mouse using the following keys. Operations are broken down into three categories, corresponding to the three primary task areas of the File Manager: drive selection, directory procedures, and file procedures.

KEYS FOR SELECTING DRIVES

These shortcuts are useful for selecting drives:

Move between the drive, tree, and file areas	Tab
Change to the drive icon that matches the specified letter	Ctrl-(*drive letter*)
Move between drive icons	← or →
Change drives once icon is circled	Spacebar

Add a new directory window for circled drive icon	Enter

Directory Pane Keys

These keys are used in the directory (or tree) pane:

Select the next directory or subdirectory in tree	↑
Select the previous directory or subdirectory in tree	↓
Scroll up one screen	PgUp
Scroll down one screen	PgDn
Jump to the root directory	Home or \
Jump to last directory in list	End
Jump to next directory beginning with a particular letter or number	*letter* or *number*
Expand current directory	+
Collapse current directory	–
Display or hide any subdirectories of the highlighted one	Enter
Display contents of highlighted directory in a new window	Shift-Enter
Select the previous directory at the same tree level (if there is one)	Ctrl- ↑
Select the next directory at the same tree level (if there is one)	Ctrl- ↓

File Pane Keys

These keys are used in the file pane. The word *file* below also applies to directory folders if they are displayed in the file pane:

Scroll up a screen	PgUp

Scroll down a screen	PgDn
Move up or down a file	↑, ↓, ←, or →
Jump to first file in the list	Home
Jump to last file in the list	End
Jump to next file beginning with a particular letter or number	*letter* or *number*
Jump to next directory window	Ctrl-Tab
Jump to previous directory window	Shift-Ctrl-Tab
Back up one directory level	Highlight backup icon (↑ . .) and press Enter
Select multiple consecutive files	Shift-arrow key
Select or deselect nonconsecutive files	Shift-F8, then arrow keys and spacebar for each file
Select all files	Ctrl-/
Deselect all files except current one	Ctrl-\
Open directory, document, or application	Enter
Open directory in a new window rather than in existing pane	Shift-Enter

CLIPBOARD SHORTCUT KEYS

These keys are useful in the Clipboard:

In application, cut selected item to the Clipboard	Ctrl-X or Shift-Del
In application, copy selected item to the Clipboard	Ctrl-C or Ctrl-Ins
In application, paste item from Clipboard to target document	Ctrl-V or Shift-Ins

In Clipboard viewer, delete whatever is on the Clipboard	Del
Copy entire screen image to the Clipboard (this works for non-Windows applications only if they are running in text mode)	Shift-PrtScr
Copy the active window's image to the Clipboard	Alt-PrtScr

CALENDAR SHORTCUT KEYS

The following keys pertain to the Calendar:

Day View

These keys are for Day view in the Calendar:

Previous time	↑
Next time	↓ or Enter
Next day	Ctrl-PgDn
Previous day	Ctrl-PgUp
Jump to specific date	F4
Set alarm	F5
Enter a special mark for the day	F6
Enter a special time	F7
Switch to Month view	F9
Move to the previous screen	PgUp
Move to the next screen	PgDn
Jump to first time on the schedule	Ctrl-Home
Jump to twelve hours after the first time	Ctrl-End

Jump between the appointment area and the scratch pad	Tab
Cut selected text to the Clipboard	Ctrl-X
Copy selected text to the Clipboard	Ctrl-C
Paste Clipboard's contents into the appointment area or scratch pad	Ctrl-V

Month View

These keys are for Month view in the Calendar:

Jump to the previous week	↑
Jump to the next week	↓
Jump to the previous month	PgUp
Jump to the next month	PgDn
Enter a special mark for the day	F6
Jump between calendar and scratch pad	Tab
Switch to Day view	Enter

CARDFILE SHORTCUT KEYS

These shortcuts apply to the Cardfile:

Jump to card whose index line starts with character *n*	Ctrl-*n*
Jump to first card in file	Ctrl-Home
Jump to last card in file	Ctrl-End
Scroll one card/page in Card/List view	PgDn
Scroll back one card/page in Card/List view	PgUp

Find next card meeting previous Find criterion	F3
Go to specific card	F4
Dial first or selected phone number on card	F5
Edit index line of current card	F6
Add a new card	F7
Cut to Clipboard	Ctrl-X
Copy from Clipboard	Ctrl-C
Paste from Clipboard	Ctrl-V
Undo last operation	Ctrl-Z

PAINTBRUSH SHORTCUT KEYS

Though not a program you want to do any extensive mouseless work in, it is possible—hard to believe, but true:

Jump pointer among the Toolbox, Linesize box, Palette, and drawing area counter-clockwise/clockwise	Tab/Shift-Tab
Select a tool, color, or linesize once in correct area	Position with arrows keys and press Ins
Move cursor around in the workspace	↑, ↓, ←, or →
Draw with current tool	Ins- ↑, ↓, ←, or →
Draw text	Position with arrow keys, press Ins, and begin typing
Jump to left side of drawing	Shift-Home (NumLock should be off)
Jump to right side of drawing	Shift-End (NumLock should be off)

Scroll up one screen	PgUp
Scroll down one screen	PgDn
Jump to top of drawing	Home
Jump to bottom of drawing	End
Undo all or portion of objects not pasted down	Press Backspace, then move cursor over area
Undo everything not pasted down	Ctrl-Z
Left-click equivalent	Ins
Left–double-click equivalent	F9-Ins
Right-click equivalent	Del
Right–double-click equivalent	F9-Del

WRITE SHORTCUT KEYS

In addition to some of the text-selection keys described under "Keys That Apply to Many Windows Applications," you can use the following keys in Write. Note that some shortcut keys involve the 5 key. Make sure to use the 5 key on the numeric keypad, not the one above the *T* key on the main portion of your keyboard. If using a laptop that doesn't have a number pad, you'll have to activate your numeric overlay keypad (if your laptop computer has this option) to use this key.

Navigating in Write

These shortcuts are for navigating in Write:

Jump to next sentence	5- →
Jump to previous sentence	5- ←
Jump to next paragraph	5- ↓
Jump to previous paragraph	5- ↑
Jump to next page	5-PgDn

Jump to previous page	5-PgUp

Text Editing

These keys are for editing text in Write:

Cut selection to the Clipboard	Ctrl-X or Shift-Del
Copy selection to the Clipboard	Ctrl-C or Ctrl-Ins
Paste from the Clipboard	Ctrl-V or Shift-Ins
Insert manual page break	Ctrl-Enter
Insert optional hyphen	Ctrl-Shift-Hyphen
Undo last typing or editing	Ctrl-Z or Alt-Backspace
Select picture when cursor is above the upper-left corner of the picture	↓
Move or resize a picture	Edit ➤ Move or Size Picture ➤ ↑, ↓, ←, → ➤ Enter
Jump between document and Find or Replace dialog box	Alt-F6
Jump between document and Page Header or Page Footer dialog box	Alt-F6

MEDIA PLAYER SHORTCUT KEYS

Use these shortcut keys for using Media Player:

Jump between buttons	Tab/Shift-Tab
Choose a button	Spacebar
Jump the playing position forward or back when scroll bar is selected	→/←

Jump the playing position forward or back in large increments when scroll bar is selected	PgDn/PgUp
Jump the playing position to the beginning when scroll bar is selected	Home
Jump the playing position to the end when scroll bar is selected	End

SOUND RECORDER SHORTCUT KEYS

Use these keys for the Sound Recorder:

Move between buttons and scroll bar	Tab/Shift-Tab
Choose a button or scroll bar	Spacebar
Move forward or backward in the scroll bar	Select bar ➤ ← or →
Jump back 1 second with scroll bar selected	PgUp
Jump forward 1 second with scroll bar selected	PgDn
Jump to beginning of sound with scroll bar selected	Home
Jump to end of sound with scroll bar selected	End

APPENDIX C

FEATURING

Networking with Windows for Workgroups

Sharing Resources—Files, Printers, and Directories

Using Mail, Chat, and Schedule+

Maintaining and Monitoring the Workgroup Network

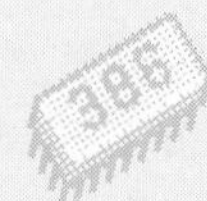

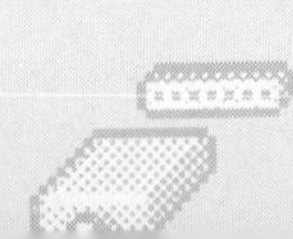

Using Windows for Workgroups

n late 1992, Microsoft released Windows for Workgroups, a new product that performs much the way Windows 3.1 does, but with additional benefits to the business user. Windows for Workgroups is a superset of Windows 3.1, designed for people who want their Windows computers interconnected on a local area network (LAN).

Local Area Networks are nothing new, and those that connect PCs have been around for close to ten years now. For the most part, however, the common nomenclature for PCs that are strung together has been *LAN*. Now with the release of Windows for Workgroups and an increasing number of programs designed with multi-user capabilities, Microsoft is pushing the term "workgroups." When a big software maker like Microsoft throws its weight around, the computer industry at large pays attention. Thus, this new term is winding its way into computer vernacular, and there is some confusion between the terms LAN and Workgroup. Here's the real difference—think of a LAN as any number of PCs hooked together to allow the sharing of information between them or to let workers share costly peripheral equipment such as laser printers, high-speed modems, plotters, and so forth.

Once you have your PCs successfully hooked up on a LAN, though, you may need to organize a bit. If you have lots of workstations, pandemonium can break loose because each user has so many choices—like which of 20 printers to use, or which of 100 workstations' hard disk drives to log on to. The lists in your network dialog boxes become a nightmare.

It makes more sense to divide users into logical groups—groups of workers that have something in common. Those who are in the marketing deparment, for example, will want to run the same programs, share a customer database, and send electronic mail to a small group of coworkers. In another type of organization, the group members might be located in the same area of a building, so connecting them is a logical choice based on proximity.

On a given Windows for Workgroups network, you can have many workgroups. And although dividing a LAN into workgroups is great for organizing things, it doesn't lock you out of the rest of the newtork. Being assigned to one workgroup doesn't prevent you from communicating with people in other workgroups, nor from sharing their shared devices such as directories and printers.

Prior to Windows for Workgroups, the networking of Windows machines necessitated buying a third-party LAN operating system from a manufacturer such as Novell, Microsoft, or Banyan. Now Windows for Workgroups gives you everything Windows does, *and* it incorporates basic networking right in the same package.

Windows for Workgroups is a *peer-to-peer* network operating system that, in short, lets any workstation on a network become a sort of "mini-server." That is to say that any workstation can share its printer and hard disk directories with other users. The only restriction to sharing these items, called *resources*, is that a workstation must be running Windows in 386-Enhanced mode. (Workstations running in Standard mode can still connect to the network using other stations' shared resources, but can't share their own.)

Windows for Workgroups presents an advantage over many other DOS-based networks in that it can utilize Windows' virtual memory management scheme, and thus consume very little system RAM (memory in the lower 640K). The networking software components (server, redirector, and transport) are efficiently shuttled off to the hard disk when they're not needed—just as is the case with any other Windows program. Only about 10-20K of system RAM of each workstation is sacrificed to keep the network "alive," leaving more room for large DOS applications. Also, due to the capabilities inherent in utilizing Virtual Device Driver architecture, Windows for Workgroups offers quite credible performance and "robustness" (resistance to crashing). If your network consists of—or will eventually grow to—no more than 50 workstations, Windows for Workgroups will provide very good performance, often better than competing products. However, its security provisions, when compared to some other more extensive networks such as NetWare, are somewhat lacking.

A LITTLE NETWORK BACKGROUND

Windows for Workgroups is a distributed network. (See Figure C.1.) Unless you use Windows for Workgroups as an adjunct to an existing network that has a server, a Windows for Workgroups network contains no central "server" per se. Instead, every workstation is in effect a server, capable of sharing its

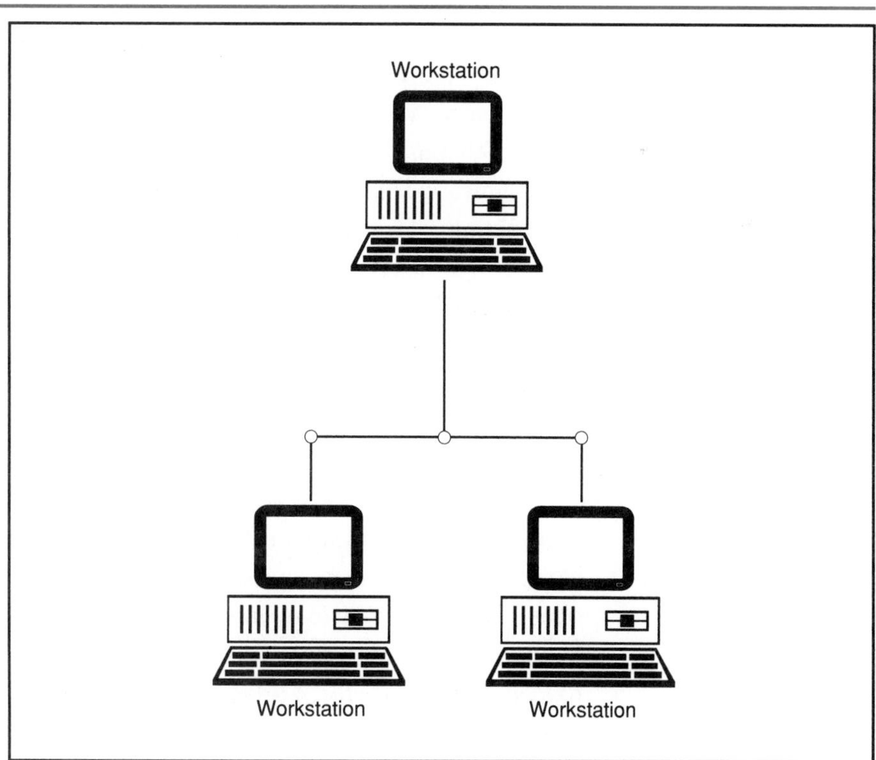

FIGURE C.1:
A typical distributed server workgroup.

resources and using those of others. To prevent invasion by prying eyes, accidental erasure of files, or unauthorized use of printers, access to those resources can be restricted by passwords.

Once the network is set up, users manually choose which items they want to share, issuing commands in new versions of File Manager and Print Manager. A new Clipboard called "Clipbook Viewer" is used to share information between documents. Then workstations on the network can manually log on to the network and choose which resources they want to *connect* to, entering passwords when required.

For example, a typical workgroup might consist of a number of writers who are working on the same documents, such as newsletters, annual reports, or a magazine. Using Windows for Workgroups, one writer can start a document and then close it. Another can open it from a second location and continue working on it. A third writer could then finish it and print it. All this can be done without passing a disk around the office, and without introducing possible confusion through having multiple copies of the document.

Using the Mail program that comes with Windows for Workgroups, the three writers could have been sending efficient paperless memos to each other about the project, while also organizing their work schedules, meetings, and submission due dates using the Schedule+ program.

Finally, Windows for Workgroups incorporates an extended version of DDE (Dynamic Data Exchange) that lets applications that support DDE exchange information between documents and applications that are on other workstations. This way, one user could share, say, a section of a spreadsheet for use by others. This is done through a new utility (similar to the Clipboard) called Clipbook Viewer. Other network users could incorporate this shared object into a variety of documents, trusting that if the original is updated, the changes will be reflected in their documents.

Other Networks Not Excluded

One interesting thing about Windows for Workgroups is that, though it can work alone, it's also designed to augment most existing networking systems—not necessarily to replace them. If you already have one of the popular Windows-compatible networks, such as Novell NetWare or Microsoft LAN Manager, Windows for Workgroups will probably recognize and work with it. (For a complete list of compatible networks, check the Microsoft documentation or read the NETWORKS.WRI file in your Windows directory.)

Once Windows for Workgroups is correctly installed, not only will you be able to share information with other users on the network, you'll have access to any dedicated server machines on the network. Windows for Workgroups will also add new features to the operation of your LAN.

For example, if your network has a dedicated server (such as with Novell NetWare 386), the server will still function normally after Windows for Workgroups is installed, but you'll have the additional capability of direct peer-to-peer communications. Thus, you could use files, directories, and printers in the directories of other users, rather than having access only to files on the server's hard disk. Figure C.2 illustrates a network with a dedicated file server.

FIGURE C.2:
Windows for Workgroups can be added to many existing server-based networks, adding peer-to-peer functionality while retaining the advantages of a high-speed dedicated file server topology.

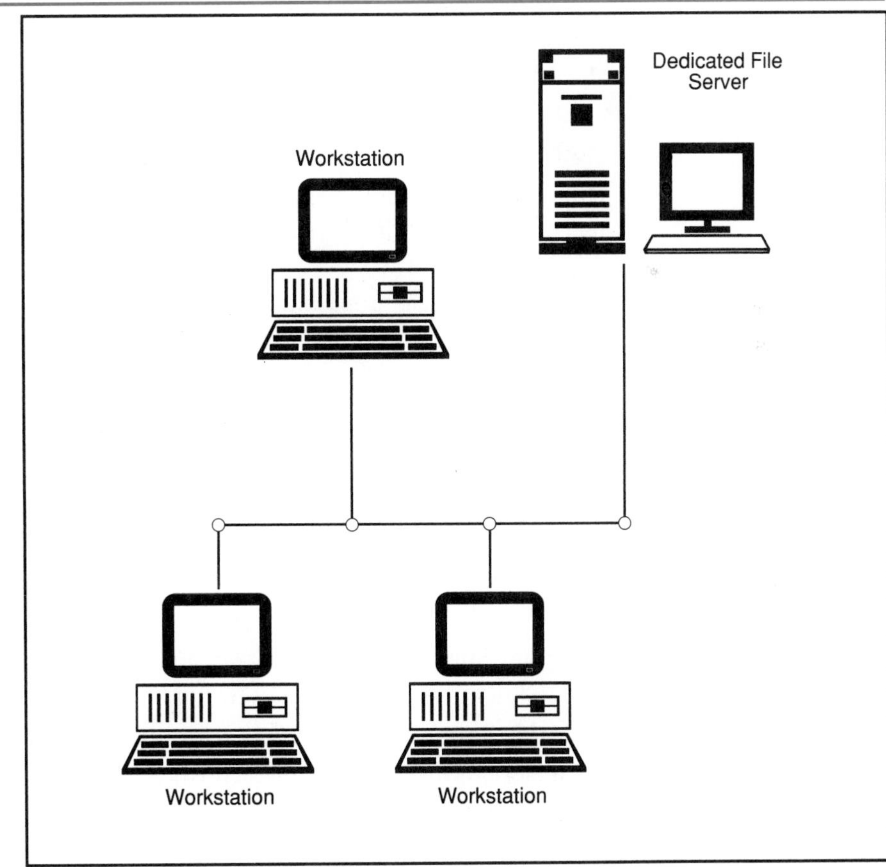

If you don't already have a network, Windows for Workgroups will operate on its own as a rudimentary LAN. All you need are network cards, cabling, and Windows for Workgroups installed on each computer. Windows for Workgroups may meet all your networking requirements, possibly precluding the purchase of higher-priced network software.

Unfortunately, prescribing a particular network software or topology (hardware) isn't a simple matter. Before choosing Windows for Workgroups, you'll want to consider your security needs, your need for data integrity (using a single server prevents multiple copies of data files), for automated backup equipment, and for overall system throughput. Some of these, particularly the last, will be affected by your hardware (mostly by the type of network cards and cabling). For large installations, you should contact a network specialist before embarking on a course of action.

WHAT CAN WINDOWS FOR WORKGROUPS DO?

With Windows for Workgroups you can:

- Share printers among a number of Windows for Workgroups workstations.
- Set up an electronic mail system between users on the network.
- Allow network members to share hard disk space, files, and programs located on any network workstation.
- Set up a groupware appointment scheduling system designed for coordinating groups of workers.
- Set up net DDE "hot-links" to share data between programs that support DDE, even between documents on different workstations.

As Windows for Workgroups becomes more popular (Microsoft's pundits predict almost 30% of Windows buyers in 1993 will be purchasing Windows for Workgroups instead of single-user Windows), a new breed of applications programs tailored to take advantage of workgroup arrangements will develop. We'll probably see tremendous growth in "workgroup programs," such as group video conferencing, group document editing programs, and variations on electronic mail including sound and other multimedia attractions.

In this appendix, I'll cover the basics of installing Windows for Workgroups, describe the additional accessory programs supplied with the package (Schedule+, Mail, Clipbook Viewer, Chat, Net Watcher, and WinMeter), discuss the enhancements to Print Manager, File Manager, and Control Panel, and finally, suggest overall strategies for getting the most from Windows for Workgroups.

INSTALLATION AND REQUIREMENTS

To run Windows for Workgroups, you need Windows for Workgroups software, a network card for each computer, and the cabling that attaches the cards to one another (network cabling). If you already have Windows 3.0 or 3.1, installing Windows for Workgroups simply updates your existing Windows files to add the necessary network drivers and additional accessory programs.

Windows for Workgroups comes on a series of disks, just as does Windows. Before installing the software, consider whether each workstation you intend to add to the network meets several requirements:

- You must be running at least DOS 3.3 or a later version (DOS 5.0 is preferable).
- Workstations with a 386SX or higher processor (386DX, 486SX or DX, etc.) should have at least 3MB of RAM (4MB is recommended). All memory above 640K should be set up as extended memory.
- Workstations with 286 processors (and workstations with 386/486 processors that you want to run in Standard mode) need at least 640K standard memory and 256K extended memory (preferably 1024K). Running in Standard mode doesn't allow you to run the server software, but you can run the client software, which means you can't share printers or directories with other users, but you can run accessory programs, send and receive mail, and perform other network-related activities.

- Each workstation needs at least 10MB of free hard disk space and at least one floppy drive. If you already have single-user Windows 3.1 on the target machine, you'll only need about 3MB of free disk space for the Windows for Workgroups installation.
- Each workstation needs a compatible network card and cables. Check with the manufacturer to ensure that your network cards are compatible with Windows for Workgroups, or check the Microsoft compatibility guide that comes with the package.
- Your printer must be Windows-compatible if you want users to be able to print from the network.
- If you want to take advantage of the sound capabilities built into Windows for Workgroups, you'll need a Windows-compatible sound card, such as the Sound Blaster. (See Chapter 15, "All About Windows Multimedia," for more about sound cards and the PC speaker driver.)

To install the program, follow these steps:

1. Make sure your network boards are installed properly into each workstation, and that the switches on the boards are set for the correct IRQ, port, and base address. Also, ensure that the network wiring is correctly installed. Installation of Windows for Workgroups assumes each computer has a network card in it. To copy its correct driver files into the machine from the floppy disks, Setup will look for the existing card. Consult the manual that comes with the network boards, and read the installation section in the Microsoft manual to set up the switches or software settings for the boards (some boards don't have physical switches). The main thing is to avoid conflicts with any video boards, printer ports, sound boards, and mouse cards in the individual workstations.
2. Quit Windows and get to a DOS prompt.
3. Insert disk 1 of the Windows for Workgroups set into the correct drive.
4. Log on to the correct floppy drive and type:

   SETUP ↵

5. Answer the questions as prompted, inserting and removing disks as requested. (You'll be alerted if you don't have enough disk space, or if there are any problems.) There are two basic types of installation—Express and Custom. You should probably opt for Express, because it is easy, and it allows Setup to ensure that the new installation will work.
6. If, after installation is done, you have trouble getting onto the network, or other maladies have made themselves known, read the Troubleshooting section in the Microsoft Windows for Workgroups *Getting Started* manual.
7. Run Windows for Workgroups again.
8. Read the rest of this appendix to learn how to use the new Windows for Workgroups utility programs, and the modified File Manager, Print Manager, Control Panel, and Clipbook Viewer.

LOGGING ON

After you've successfully installed Windows for Workgroups (and possibly taken a few minutes to wipe your brow now that you've got all those cards in, switches set, cable run, and software transferred), the next step is to run Windows for Workgroups and log on to a workgroup.

1. When you turn on your computer, Windows may come up automatically (if you have added the line WIN to your AUTOEXEC.BAT file.) If it doesn't, type in WIN and press ENTER. The sign-on screen now says Windows for Workgroups instead of just Windows, and you're greeted with a new dialog box, asking you to enter a user name and a password. Enter those now.

If you've already established your user name and password, you'll see a box like this:

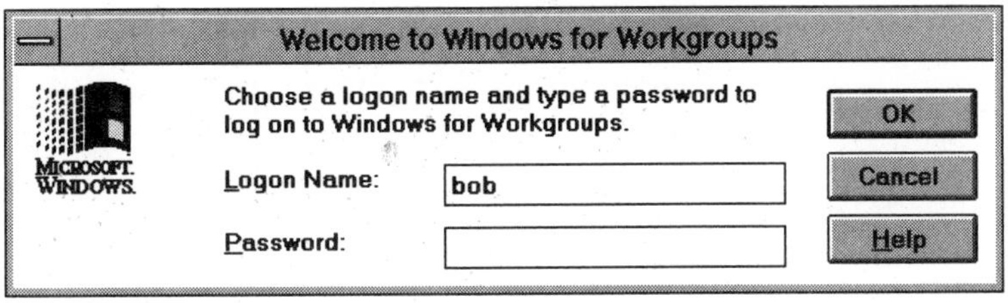

Welcome to Windows for Workgroups

Choose a logon name and type a password to log on to Windows for Workgroups.

Logon Name: bob

Password:

OK Cancel Help

2. Enter the name they want to use in the Logon Name box. Enter the password in the Password box. A second dialog box will appear asking you to verify your password.

Unless this is the first time you've been connected to the network, Windows for Workgroups will attempt to connect you to the last workgroup in which you were active. If some of the workstations in that workgroup aren't turned on, or don't have Windows running, you'll get a message to the effect that you cannot be connected to that computer. Don't worry about it—click on the Continue button, and Windows for Workgroups will continue booting up. You can later tell the operator of the other station to turn on their computer and run Windows, if you need to connect to that station in order to gain access to shared files or printers.

SHARING AND USING A FILE OR DIRECTORY

The two operations of most interest to 99% of Windows for Workgroups users will be sharing files and sharing printers. Let's discuss file sharing first.

Before we get into the procedure for sharing files with other users on a Windows for Workgroups network, let's consider a few things about how networks manage file access and avoid "data collisions"—catastrophes that can cream your files.

PRIMER ON SHARING DATA FILES

As you may know from experimenting within single-user Windows, you can't open a document file in two applications at once. For example, if you try to open a text file in two different sessions of Excel, it'll work the first time, but not the second. When you try to open it in the second session of Excel, you'll be alerted that the file isn't available or is in use by another program.

Now consider a workgroup of two users—Jill and Joe. Suppose Jill is working on an annual report in a program such as Word for Windows. Now Joe gets on his computer to make his changes to the report, and he tries to open the same file. No way! An error message pops up, whether he's on a network or not. If Joe and Jill both opened the file and were allowed to edit simultaneously, only those changes would be saved that were made by the person who saved the file last. Joe's changes would be overwritten if Jill saved the file and closed it last.

One major chore involved in maintaining any network software is to ensure that this data collision problem doesn't happen. The network operating system sees to it that no two people work on the same data file simultaneously, and alerts you to possible trouble.

Some software specifically designed for workgroup use on networks lets multiple users update records within the same file simultaneously. For example, some database programs achieve this by using a technique called *record locking*, which keeps one user from editing the same data *record* as another user, but allows both users to edit records within the same file. Most programs only do *file locking*. That is, if the document *file* is in use by one person, nobody else can use it.

The moral to this discussion is this: you'll see lots of dialog boxes while using Windows for Workgroups, many of which are about document file conflicts. Some will say you can't use the file you want. Others will say you can only use it as "Read Only," which means you can look at the file, but can't modify it. Just get used to seeing these dialog boxes. Read them, click on OK, and try again later, when the other user has closed the file. Understand that Windows for Workgroups is doing its job to prevent loss of data.

About Sharing Program Files

So much for sharing data files. What about sharing programs? Programs (applications) are stored in files too. As you probably know, they usually have the extension .EXE. For example, the WRITE program is called WRITE.EXE.

Sharing application programs is much simpler than sharing data files. Most programs can be used by any number of people simultaneously, because they are simply read into your computer. Just using a program doesn't alter its program file. Occasionally the changes you make to program settings or preferences are written to disk, but they usually go into an initialization (.INI) file stored in the Windows directory, or elsewhere.

As a rule, most non-"network aware" programs can be used on networks by multiple users. Some exceptions at the time of this writing are programs that use support or temp files that can only be opened by one user at a time. If you're having trouble with multiple users running programs simultaneously, contact the manufacturer of the specific program to determine a possible fix. When purchasing new programs for use on your network, look for Windows for Workgroups compatibility statements in the advertising or on the product box, and buy Windows for Workgroups products when possible, or products that give you a discount on upgrades as they become available.

Sharing a Directory

With the basic theory under your belt, let's move on to the actual techniques for sharing data and programs on a Windows for Workgroups network.

Before other workgroup members can use your files, you have to *share* the directory in which they are stored. Then anyone who wants to use your shared directories has to *connect* to that directory. Likewise, before you can use someone else's directory, they have to intentionally share it, and you have to connect to it.

Sharing and Connecting are done from File Manager. Once you set up the directories to share and connect to, Windows for Workgroups will remember the settings and reinstitute them whenever you run Windows—a nice feature and a real timesaver. Shared directories can have passwords, and can have specific privileges—*Read Only* or *Read/Write*. If you have a bunch of files that you want people to be able to see but not to alter, you just put them into a new directory and share it as Read Only. If you want only specific people to be able to alter the files, you share them protected by a password. I'll explain all this a little later.

The Windows for Workgroups File Manager has a new look that includes a configurable tool bar, some new icons, and some new commands. Note that network drives (volumes) in the drive bar look a little different than normal hard disks. Also note the new icon for shared directories—it looks like a folder with a little hand under it. This shows up after you share one of your directories, meaning that other users now have access to it.

To share a directory, do the following:

1. Click on the directory.

2. Choose Disk ➤ Share As. A dialog box like the following one appears:

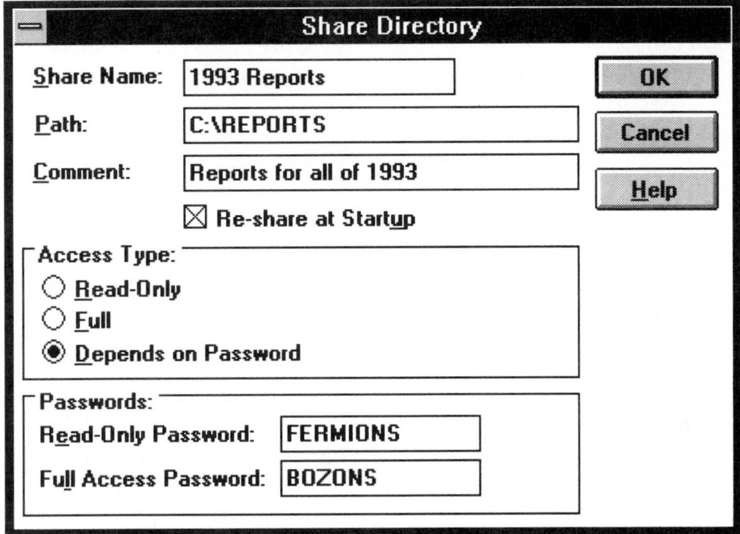

3. Notice that I've filled in some information. I wanted to share the C:\REPORTS directory. Other users will see it listed with the name "1993 Reports" and description "Reports for all of 1993." Fill in these areas according to your needs. The default entry in the Share Name field is the directory name, and that's what will appear to other workstations unless you alter it.
4. Next, choose the access type if you want to restrict the use of the directory.

TYPE	RESULT
Read-Only	Nobody except you can write to files or erase files.
Full	Anyone can access the directory. They can read, write, and erase files.
Depends on Password	If passwords are entered in the Passwords section of the dialog box, only users who enter the correct password will be allowed access to the files.

If you don't enter a password in one of the Password boxes, no password will be required for the stipulated access. Thus, if you want users to have to enter a password for writing but not for reading, leave the Read-Only Password blank, but enter a Full Access Password.

In the figure above, both Read and Write access are password protected with the passwords FERMIONS and BOZONS, respectively. (Case isn't important in password protection.)

CAUTION *Note that a user has the same rights to all subdirectories of a shared parent directory. Be careful not to share directories that have subdirectories unless you want those to become accessible with the same level of restriction.*

5. Click on OK, and the directory becomes available to any other users who are attached to your workgroup. It will appear in the File Manager window with a little hand under it—a little reminder that you're making an offering to the public.

When you want to remove the directory from public offering, follow these steps.

1. Check to see that nobody is using the directory. You can do this by running Net Watcher, an application in your Accessories group. It will tell you who's using what. Or you can ask around. If you don't want to bother doing either of these, take the lazy person's approach and move on to Step 2.
2. Choose Disk ➤ Stop Sharing. You'll see a dialog box displaying a list of all your shared directories.

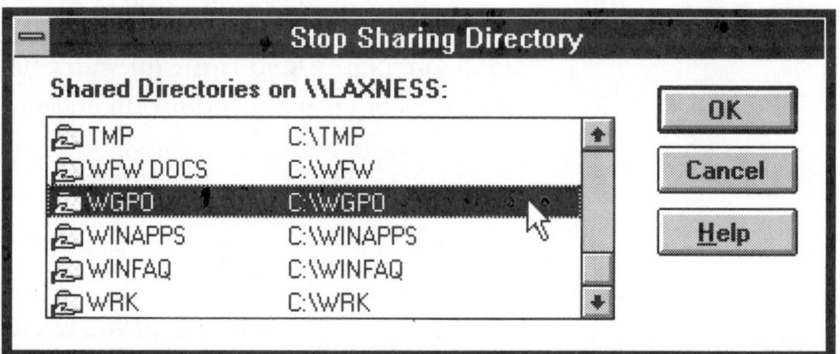

3. Double-click on the directory you want to stop sharing. (You can select more than one by pressing the Ctrl key and clicking on each directory, then clicking OK.) If workgroup users are currently connected to the directory, you'll see a message indicating this and warning you against terminating the share.

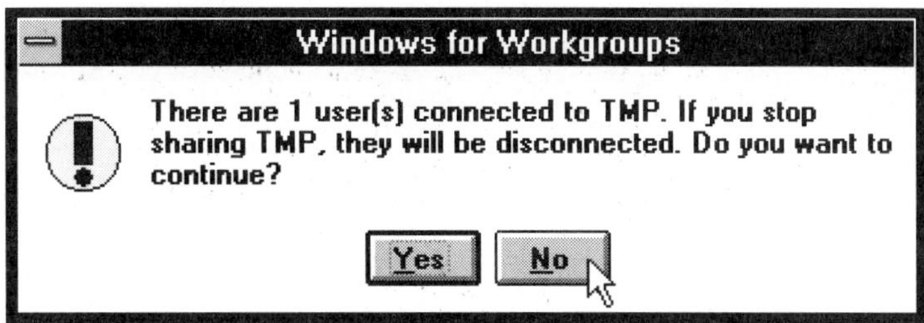

If you really want to terminate, click on Yes, but be aware that other users may lose some data. There may be another warning dialog box, also telling you how many files are open. Closing a shared directory in this way is a great way to lose friends, so normally you'd click on No, get the other user to sign off of your directory, and then try again later. If you want to know what's really going on with a directory (i.e. who's using it and if files are open) do the following:

1. Highlight the shared directory in the directory pane of File Manager. (It should have the "shared" icon—the hand—under it.)
2. Press Alt-Enter or choose File ➤ Properties. Click on the Open By button. (This is a new button in the Properties dialog box that only appears in Windows for Workgroups.) A list will pop up, showing who has connected to the directory, which files are open, and what access privileges apply. The list may help you make a decision about terminating the connection.

Connecting to a Directory

NOTE *The volumes available to you and the exact layout of dialog boxes may look different if you're using Novell NetWare or another network in addition to Windows for Workgroups.*

What about connecting to a directory that someone else has shared? You'll want to do that to run programs on their computer, or access data files stored there. Here's how:

1. From File Manager, choose Disk ➤ Connect Network Drive. A large dialog box appears, as shown in Figure C.3.
2. File Manager will assign the next available drive letter to the new connection. You don't have to change this unless you want to. In the example above, G was the next letter. You can change this from the Drive drop-down list if you desire, but normally you can just leave it alone.

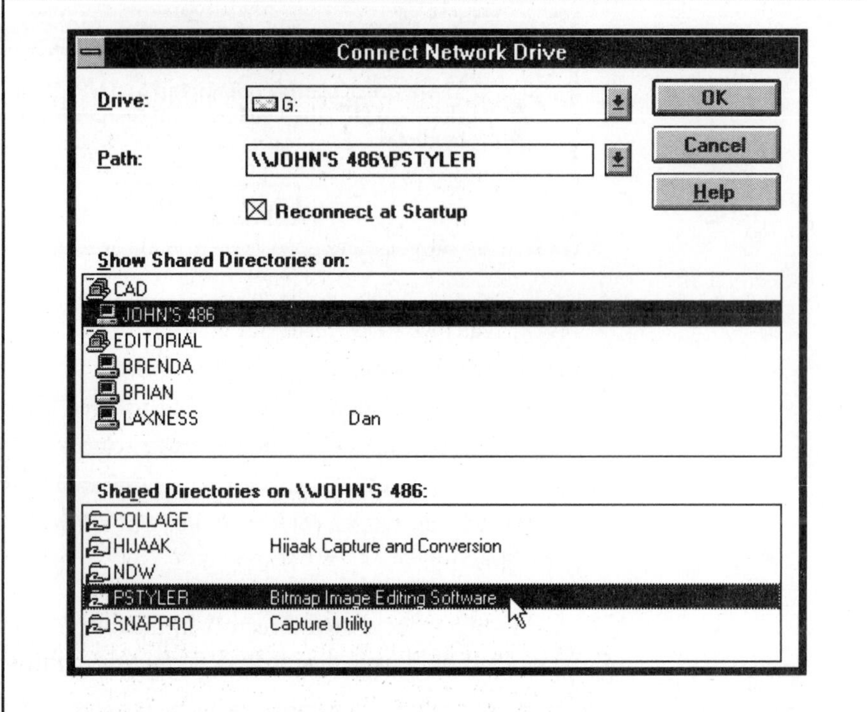

FIGURE C.3: *Connecting to a Network Drive is achieved from the Disk menu. Double-click on the workgroup, then choose the user station. The shared directories appear in the lower pane. Double-click on the directory to which you want to gain access.*

3. All the workstation users in the group will appear under it in a list. You can double-click on any other workgroup name to see a list of workstations in that group. (This is like double-clicking a directory to see a list of its subdirectories.)
4. Click once on the workstation containing the directory you want to use. Its shared directories now appear in the bottom pane, along with their names and descriptions.
5. Double-click on the directory to which you want to connect. If the drive is password protected, you'll be asked to enter the password. If not, you'll just move to the next step—a new drive icon will appear on the Drive bar near the top of your File Manager window. Like any other disk icon, you can select this one to see the files it contains, run programs, and so forth.

To disconnect from a network directory, do the following:

1. Finish any work you're doing, such as editing files and running programs on that drive.

2. Select the drive in File Manager.
3. Choose Disk ➤ Disconnect Network Drive.
4. Choose the drive from the resulting list. It should already be highlighted.
5. Click on OK.

The drive will be eliminated from the Drive bar in File Manager, and your access to that drive will end.

About the Toolbar

As with toolbars in other programs, File Manager's is just a shortcut for common procedures. Click on a button and something happens. At first you won't remember what the buttons do, since the pictures on them are so small. The easiest way to figure it out is to choose Customize Toolbar from the Options menu.

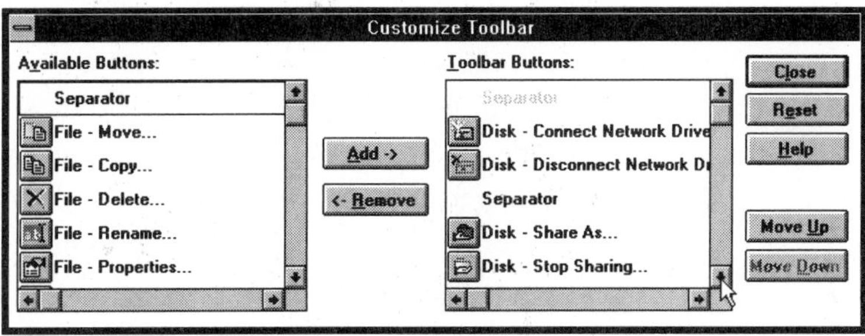

From here you can see the description of each button. You can also add and remove buttons. Whatever buttons you have showing in the right side of the box when you click OK will be on the customized toolbar.

That's it for the salient new features of File Manager. For more information, you may want to browse around the File Manager Help file by pressing F1. Also, see Chapter 4 for a complete discussion of other File Manager commands and procedures. Anything not discussed here (with the exception of Mail) works identically in both Windows 3.1 and Windows for Workgroups. Mail is covered below, under Sending and Receiving Mail.

SHARING PRINTERS ON THE NETWORK

One great advantage of connecting to a workgroup is being able to use printers that are connected to other people's workstations. You can also easily share your own printer so that other users can print on it. Since printers vary widely in their capabilities, printer sharing is a great way to offer workstation users the best tool for the job.

For example, when you have to print out a quick draft, there's no reason to use a color PostScript printer, so you might want to choose the HP Laserjet connected to Joe's computer. When you need to print an architectural diagram, you might want the plotter connected to Jill's workstation. For mailing labels you might want to choose the dot matrix printer that's loaded up with the labels and connected to Brenda's computer. You get the idea.

Sharing and connecting to printers is done from Print Manager, which, like File Manager, has a toolbar and new commands relevant to workgroups.

When you print to shared printers, Print Manager takes care of queuing the print jobs, just as it does when you run single-user Windows. The only difference is that the Print Manager dialog box displays workgroup and workstation names along with the file names for each print job, so you can examine the order of the jobs waiting to print.

Let's first look at sharing your printer. Then we'll discuss the procedure for connecting to another printer when you are ready to print. Be sure to read the chapter on Print Manager earlier in this book for details about pausing, resuming, and canceling print jobs, as well as other details of Print Manager that are not specifically workgroup-related.

SHARING YOUR PRINTER WITH OTHER USERS

NOTE *You can only share your printer if you are running in 386 Enhanced mode.*

To share your printer:

1. Run Print Manager. The new Print Manager window comes up. It will look something like Figure C.4.
2. Select the printer you want to share (by clicking on it).

FIGURE C.4: *The Print Manager window.*

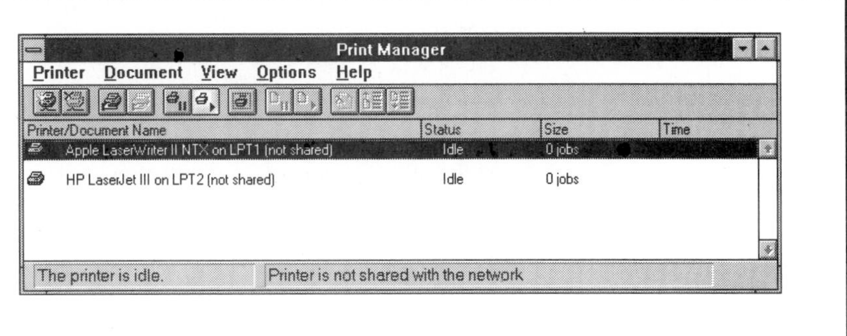

3. Now click on the Share icon, or choose Printer ➤ Share Printer As. The following dialog box comes up:

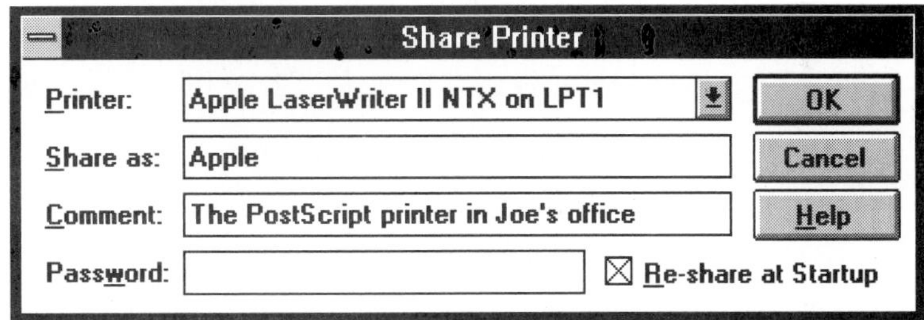

4. Fill in the box accordingly. Note that the Printer name will be filled in already. In the graphic above, a typical shared printer dialog box, I've filled in a description and a name. These will appear to others on the network when they are browsing for a printer to use. If you include a password, other users will be prompted to provide it before printing will be permitted. If you turn on the Re-share at Startup box, the printer will be shared automatically each time you run Windows for Workgroups.

5. Click on OK. The printer is now shared. Its icon will show a little sharing hand and the name of the printer will be bracketed, like this:

   [shared as Apple LaserWriter]

6. You have to keep Print Manager running for other users to connect to your newly shared printer. You can, however, iconize it and leave it on your desktop. If you try to close it, you'll get an error message reminding you that you should leave it running if you intend to continue sharing the printer.

To unshare your printer and reclaim it for your local use only:

1. Select the printer as you did above.
2. Choose Printer ➤ Stop Sharing Printer.
3. Make sure the correct printer is selected in the resulting dialog box. Double-click on the printer name, or select it and click on OK. A dialog box may alert you to the fact that others are using the printer or are connected to it. Answer accordingly.

Connecting to a Network Printer

Connecting to a network printer is similar to connecting to another user's directory. You just use the Print Manager to browse the network for available printers—those that other users have shared. Then you decide which port to connect to (LPT1, LPT2, or LPT3) and issue the Connect command. Here are the exact steps:

1. Run Print Manager.
2. Click on the far left icon in the toolbar or choose Printer ➤ Connect Network Printer. A dialog box similar to that in Figure C.5 will appear.
3. Choose the port to which you want to connect the printer. This may seem like a silly step, since you aren't actually connecting the printer to a plug on the back of your computer. Still, because of the way DOS works, you have to decide to which port you want to assign the printer. Only one printer can be assigned to each port. Typically you'll use LPT1—if you have a local printer hooked up to your computer, it's probably on LPT1. Then you'd assign the network printer to LPT2 or LPT3.
4. If the printer you're seeking is "owned" by someone outside of your workgroup, double-click on his or her workgroup. For example, in Figure C.5, I had to double-click on Editorial to display the names for Brenda and the other workers.
5. It's not immediately obvious who has a printer available. But if you now click on each user (in my case Brenda, Brian, and Dave), available printers show up in the bottom pane.
6. Once you see a printer you want, select it in the bottom pane.

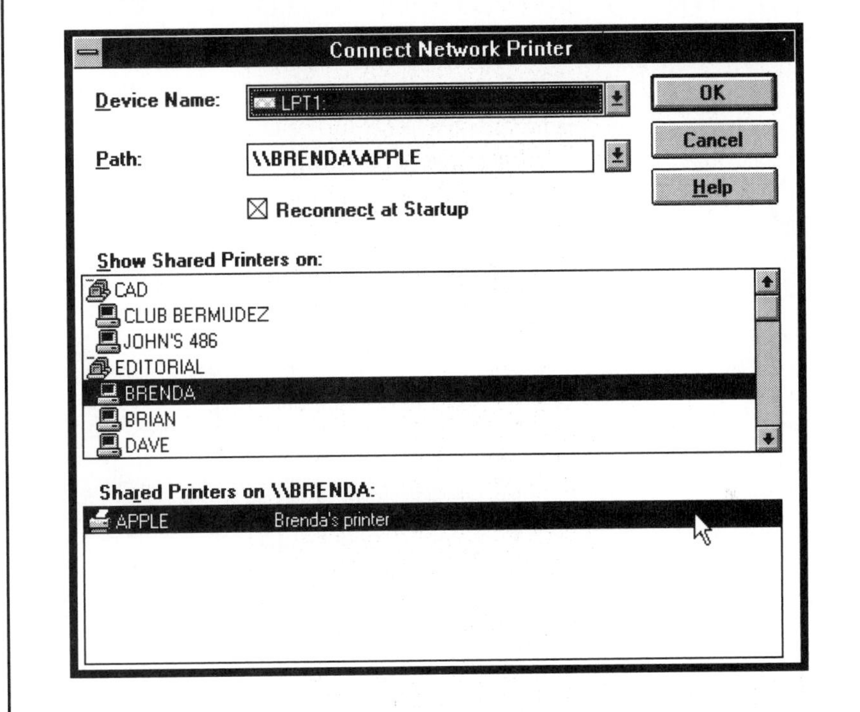

FIGURE C.5:

Use this dialog box to connect to a network printer. Click on each user in the upper box to see who has shared a printer. Then choose the printer from the bottom window. Don't forget to choose the port (Device Name) to which you want to connect.

7. If you want to connect to this printer each time you boot up Windows, check the Connect at Startup box.
8. Click on OK. If the Device Name (port) you select at the top of the box is already in use, you'll be told there's a conflict and given another chance. If the printer is shared with password protection, you'll be asked to enter the password. Otherwise, the printer is now connected. You're done.

To later disconnect from the printer:

1. Get to Print Manager again.
2. Choose Printer ➤ Disconnect Network Printer (or click on the second icon from the left in the toolbar).
3. Choose the printer from the resulting list and click on OK.

ADJUSTING WORKGROUP OPTIONS WITH CONTROL PANEL

The Control Panel in Windows for Workgroups has some additional options that affect workgroup operations. These affect such things as the name and the comments that other users see when browsing computers on the network, configuration of your network adapters and protocols, log on and log off procedures, and so on. These options used to be set from the Windows Setup program, but they've been moved to the Control Panel. Let's look at each option now.

NOTE *See the discussion of Control Panel in Chapter 5 for a discussion of the other Control Panel commands.*

1. Run Control Panel.
2. Double-click on Network. You'll see the following network dialog box:

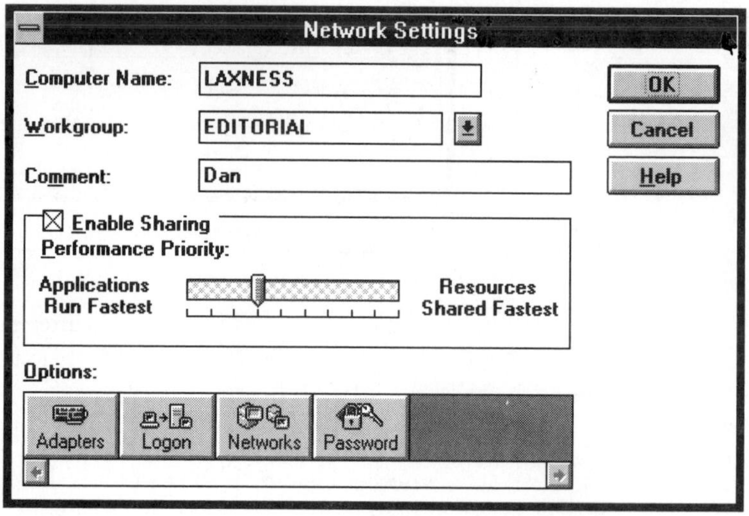

Here's a brief description of what each option in the dialog box does.

NOTE *Depending on your current network status, you may have more or fewer option buttons in the bottom part of the dialog box.*

Computer Name This is the name you gave your computer when you installed Windows for Workgroups. If you want to change it, just type in a new name.

Workgroup This indicates the name of the workgroup to which you belong. To see and choose other workgroups, open the drop-down list.

Comment Other users will see this comment when they open dialog boxes that list all the workstations on the network. Typical comments are things like "Dan's Computer" or "The 386 in Accounting." Just type in the comment you want others to see. You can change it at any time.

Enable Sharing This option determines whether others can use your directories, printers, or Clipbooks. You turned it on to make shared resources available, and now with one simple switch you can lock out everyone on the network from using your system. If your system automatically shares printers and directories upon running Windows, this option makes it easy to prevent use of your system without having to un-share resources one at a time. This is useful when you want to use your computer to do a tape backup or some other task during which you don't want anyone on your system.

When sharing is enabled, the Priority slider becomes active. Sliding it to the left will slow down performance for others using your resources, but will increase your local performance; sliding it to the right does the opposite.

Adapters Click on this button if you want to add, remove, or configure settings that pertain to the network card in your computer. The dialog boxes you get from this button are not for the non-initiated. They control things like interrupts, I/O ports, and base memory addressing, as well as network protocols, buffer sizes, time-outs, and transmission retries. These settings were probably automatically made when you installed Windows for Workgroups and told it (or let it guess) what type of network card you have. If you remove your network card and install a new one, you'd use this button to remove the old software driver and load the driver for the new card.

Logon Settings Use this button to change your personal password (the one you enter when you boot up Windows for Workgroups), or to log on or off the network. If several different people use your computer to work on the network, you'll use this button to log off before the next person can log on. Just click the Logon button and then click the Log Off button in the resulting dialog box.

If you later try to connect to shared resources without logging on, you'll be reminded to log on again. You do that from the same dialog box. Just click on Logon.

Another option in the Logon Settings dialog box is called "Log On At Startup." If you turn this off, you won't be asked to log on when you run Windows for Workgroups. Your workstation will still connect to the network and automatically share any resources that were set for auto-sharing, but you as a user won't be prompted to log on. You'll have to use the Network option in Control Panel to log on before you can use shared resources.

Networks You use this button to add or remove drivers for networks other than Windows for Workgroups. As I explained at the beginning of this Appendix, Windows for Workgroups can work in tandem with some other popular networks, notably LAN Manager and Novell NetWare. This offers certain advantages (such as increased security and performance).

However, successful integration of Windows for Workgroups and another network requires slightly modified versions of the other network's workstation drivers. The Networks button provides an easy way to install those drivers and ensure that they work seamlessly with Windows for Workgroups. When you choose to install drivers for another network, you'll be prompted to insert some of your original Windows for Workgroups disks.

You can also remove network drivers from the workstation's software configuration via the same dialog box.

You have to restart your computer before the changes will take effect.

SENDING AND RECEIVING MAIL WITH MAIL

Windows for Workgroups comes bundled with a program called Mail. This is an electronic mail (e-mail) program that allows users on the network to exchange communiqués—for example, to send memos around your office. E-mail cuts down on paper use and ensures instant transmission of your messages. Electronic tricks are available that allow for easy "Cc-ing" (carbon- or courtesy-copying) to others, broadcasting to predefined groups of associates, and more, with a minimum of effort. In addition to traditional text, your e-mail can include other "objects," such as sound, graphics, and portions of documents (like charts and data). Eventually you will even be able to include live video in e-mail.

Overview

Here's a brief overview of a Mail system. First, a Postoffice is created. This amounts to a file that's located in a special complicated directory tree on one workstation.

Once the Postoffice is set up by the Postoffice administrator, each workgroup user runs the Mail program and registers an account on the system. They choose and enter their Name, Mailbox ID, and Password. Once an account is open for a user, that user can send and receive mail.

When a letter is sent to you, it's stored on the Postoffice machine until you read it. Then you can reply to the mail, keep it for future use, or chuck it.

That's basically how it works. Now for the specifics of getting up and running with Mail.

Establishing the Postoffice

Here's how to get your Mail system up and running. Note that when you install Windows for Workgroups, the Mail program is added to each user's Main group in Program Manager, so everyone on the network already has the program. All you have to do is run it.

Because you can't share mail with people who are registered on another Postoffice, you'll want only one Postoffice per network. Also note that only the user of the machine that hosts the Postoffice can maintain and manage Postoffice accounts, so make sure that person is willing to be the administrator before deciding the location of the postoffice.

1. First, decide (by consensus, volunteer, or decree) who's going to be the Postmaster. The Postmaster has to maintain the Postoffice, deal with people who forget their passwords, and so on. It doesn't take a lot of time, but it does take some attention.
2. The Postmaster then runs Mail. A dialog box will come up saying "Welcome to Mail." You'll have two choices at this point—either to connect to an existing Postoffice or to create a new one. Choose to create a new one.
3. You're now asked to choose the directory for the Postoffice. Choose a directory on your local computer. Mail will create a subdirectory to that directory, and call it WGPO. All mail and associated files will go in WGPO (WorkGroup PostOffice) and in a number of subdirectories that Mail creates below WGPO.
4. You'll be presented with a new user "account form" to fill in as a user of the new Postoffice.

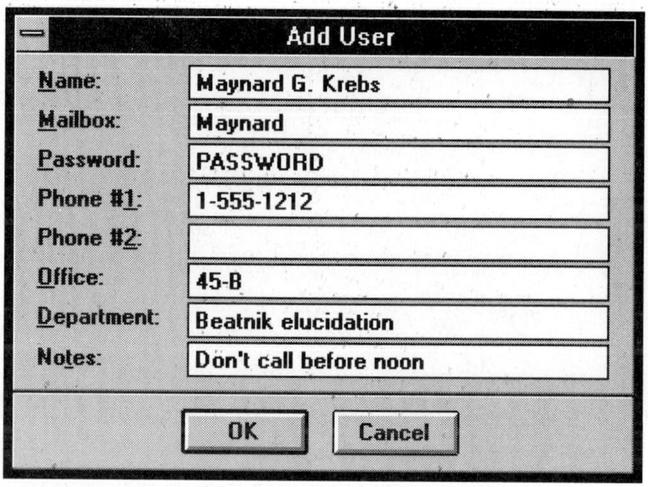

Add User

Name: Maynard G. Krebs
Mailbox: Maynard
Password: PASSWORD
Phone #1: 1-555-1212
Phone #2:
Office: 45-B
Department: Beatnik elucidation
Notes: Don't call before noon

OK Cancel

NOTE *The Postoffice computer has to be on at any time people want to use the mail system. If you have another brand of mail system, you may be able to link it with Mail. Microsoft sells kits to allow this with some popular mail programs.*

You only have to fill in three of the fields in the box—the first three. The others are optional information that users on the network will be able to see (for their convenience). The Mailbox name must be a unique ID—typically it's the user's first name, though it could be a nickname. The Mailbox name can be up to 10 characters long, and can't include spaces, punctuation, or special symbols. The Password has the same restrictions. For security reasons, the Password should not be the same as the Mailbox name.

5. You must share the WGPO directory with Full Access rights to all users. I advise that you do not require password protection for the directory, as it complicates the use of Mail unnecessarily.

Users Now Establish Accounts

Now each user has to establish a Postoffice account. Here are the steps for a typical user.

1. Run Mail from your workstation.
2. When you see the dialog box about creating a new account, choose "Connect to Remote Postoffice."
3. You'll be asked the location of the Postoffice. Use the resulting dialog box to browse the network and find the WGPO directory on the Postoffice workstation. Choose this directory and select OK.

4. You'll see the new account form shown above. Fill in the information about yourself. (Only the first three fields are required.)

You now have an account in the Postoffice. The next time you run Mail, it will connect to the Postoffice automatically, but you'll be prompted to enter your Mailbox and Password before you can send or receive mail. If you want to change your password or mailbox, ask the Postmaster. It has to be done from the Postoffice workstation, using the Mail ➤ Postoffice Manager command.

Checking Your Mail

OK. Let's get down to using the system. When you first log on, you'll see two windows, left and right, as in Figure C.6.

FIGURE C.6:

The Mail screen. Here you see the basic Mail setup with folders of mail on the left. Double-click a folder and you'll see the messages that have been stored there. To see new messages, click the Inbox folder.

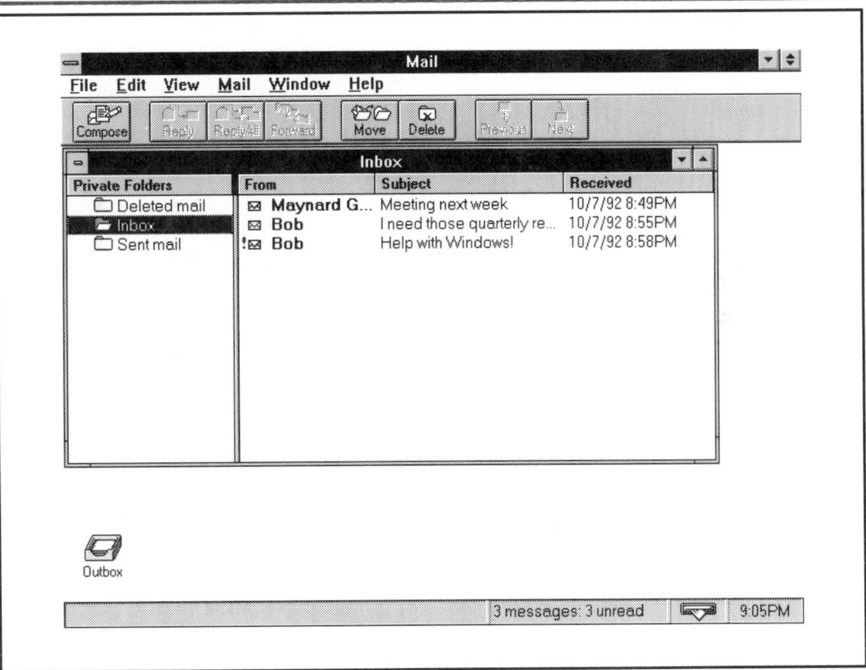

On the left is a list of folders. Folders contain mail that you've already received and filed away. You can create as many folders as you like to keep you mail organized.

On the right are short descriptions of mail you may have received. Note that there are three pieces here, all unopened. You can tell they are unopened because the little envelope icons to the left of the sender are still closed. When you have read a piece of mail, the icon changes to an opened envelope. Note the (!) symbol to the left of one of the messages. This means that the sender tagged this message as high priority.

So much for the lay of the land. How about checking the mail and reading a message?

1. Open the View menu and choose New Messages. This causes your workstation to check for new messages that might have come in after you ran Mail.
2. Now click on the Inbox folder on the left side of the screen, as in Figure C.6. If there is no in box choice, but a little icon at the bottom of the Inbox screen, double-click on that. The in box might be down there if you iconized it at some point.
3. In the right pane, double-click on the message you want to read. It will pop up in a message window like the one you see in Figure C.7.

FIGURE C.7:

Read a message by double-clicking on it. The message will appear in a window where you can read it. You can even edit the message if you like, and send it back by clicking on Reply in the toolbar.

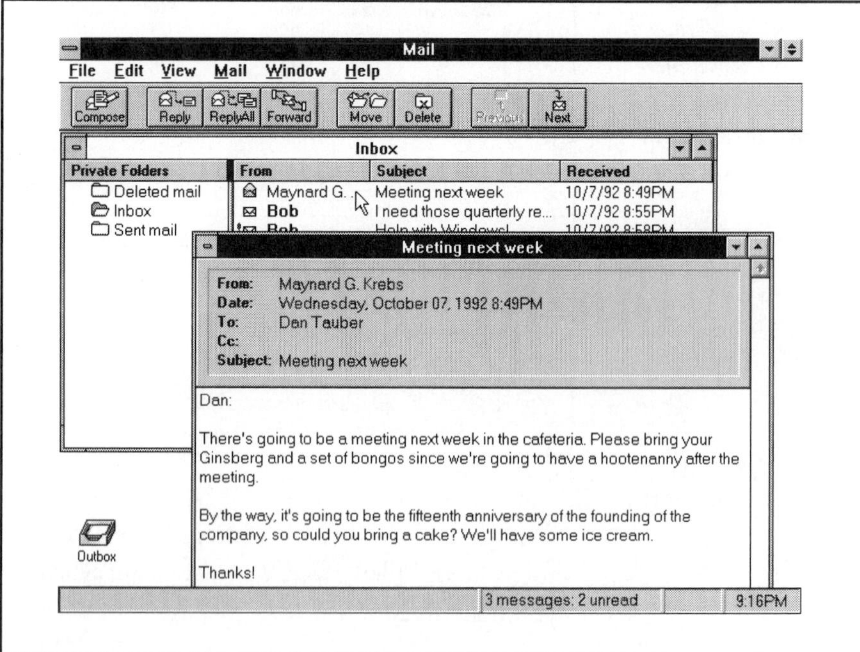

Note that the first message's envelope is open. You can close the window by double-clicking its Control box, or you can iconize it to get it out of the way for a minute. If you close it, it's still listed in the right side of the listings. You can then drag it into another folder, such as Deleted Mail, the same way you drag files into directories in File Manager.

Suppose Dan wanted to respond to this message from Maynard. He just clicks on the Reply button at the top of the Mail window, and up comes a new dialog box with the message in it, waiting to be appended. For Dan's convenience the original message from Maynard is already entered, sort of like attaching a copy of someone's memo to your response. The cursor waits for him to type in his response and click on Send.

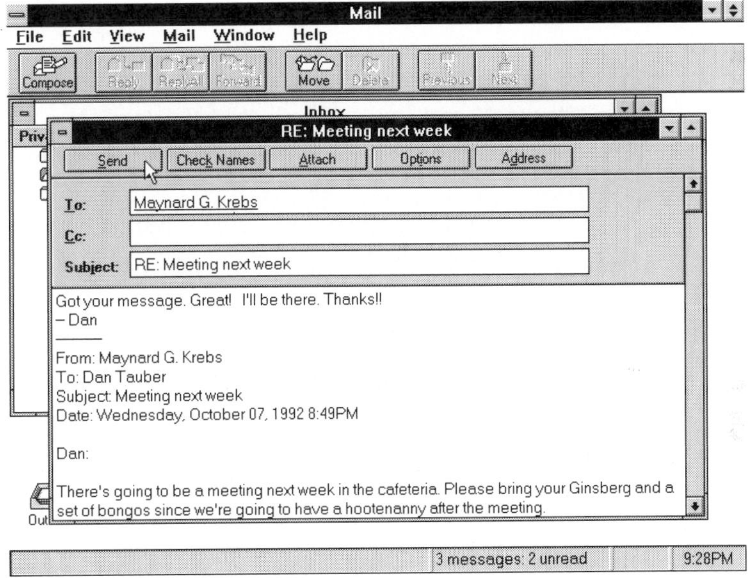

Sending a New Message

Creating a new message and sending it is easy once you know a few basic steps.

1. Click on the Compose button.

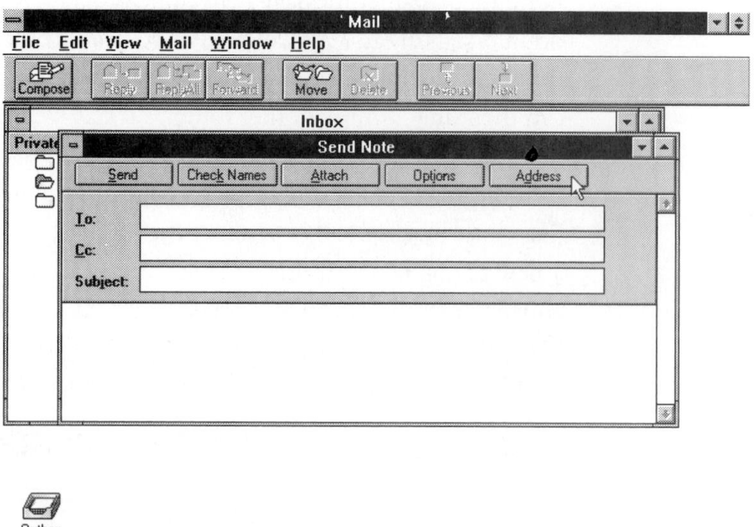

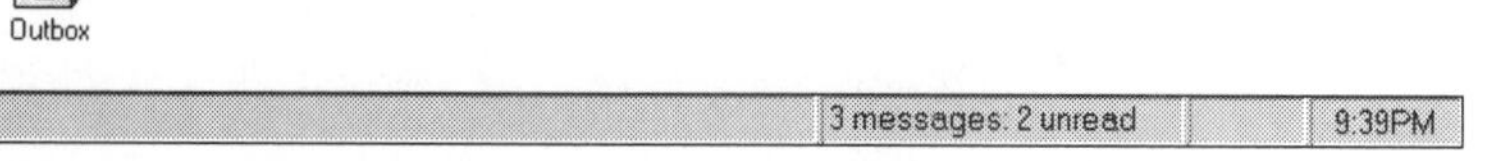

This message is used to create and send a new message. You have to fill out some fields, but they're no big deal since you can select from a list.

2. With the insertion point in the To: field, click on the Address button (see pointer above). A list of names will appear. Just choose the person(s) to whom you want to send this memo. You can choose multiple people by Shift-clicking or Ctrl-clicking, just as when selecting files in File Manager. You can jump to a name by typing the first several letters. You can also use the scroll buttons to scroll the list.
3. Click on Add, and the selected parties (or party) are added to the list in the lower half of the Address list.

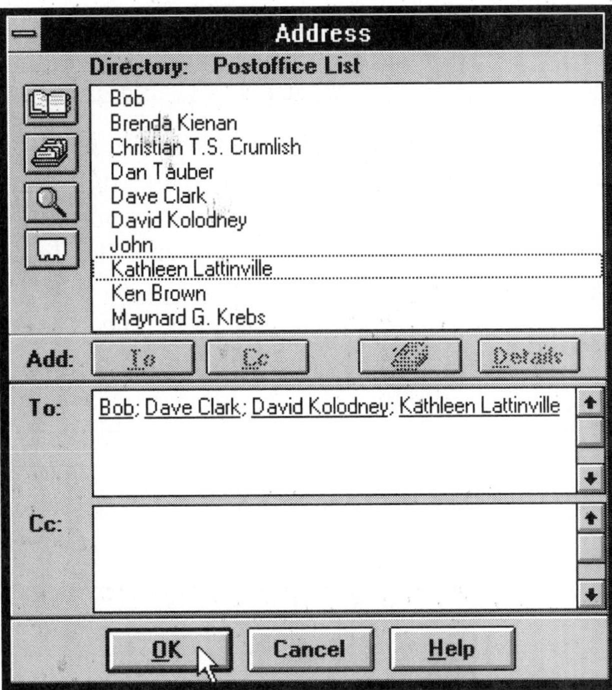

4. Click on OK. The major recipients have now been specified.
   Now fill in the people to whom you want to send copies. You do this the same way you just chose the primary addressee(s). Click in the Cc: area, then on Address. (You can leave this blank if you want, and no one will get copies.)
5. Now type in the subject of the mail. That will show up in the recipient's Inbox listing so they know what your message is about.
6. Write and edit your message in the message window. (Text wraps automatically, and will rewrap to fit the window if you resize it.)

7. Click on Options if you want a return receipt when the recipient reads the message, or if you want to tag the message as high priority or low priority. (A low priority message gets a little down arrow to the left of it on the receiver's screen.) OK that dialog box.
8. You can attach any kind of file, such as a database, spreadsheet, or a graphics file to your message. Of course the receiver must have access to a program that can read the file, otherwise it won't do them any good. To attach a file, click on Attach, then choose the file from the resulting File dialog box, and click on the Attach button in the dialog box. Then Close the Attach dialog box. An icon of the file is placed in the text area of your message. The ability to attach a file allows you to edit text in your own favorite word processor and send it that way rather than compose and edit it with Mail's editor. You can attach other types of OLE objects into a message via the Paste Special command on Mail's Edit menu. (See Chapter 14 for more about the use of OLE.)
9. Finally, click on Send, and the message is sent.

If you want to bail out and not send the message, just double-click on the Control box of the message window.

As you can see by opening a few menus, there are many commands to play with in Mail. The Help system is very good, so you shouldn't have trouble getting on-screen help to explain some of the more advanced features. Don't hesitate to Press F1, use the Help menu, or click on a Help button to learn about additional features.

You might first want to research how to create new folders (everybody gets three at first: Inbox, Deleted, and Sent Mail). You can create as many as you like, via the File ➤ New Folder command. Some can be private and others public. Dragging a message into the public file allows any user with an account in the Postoffice to read the file.

Quitting Mail

When you've finished reading and sending mail, you can just quit as you would with any application. When you re-run it, the Postoffice is checked for mail. If you don't quit mail, that's OK too. If you receive mail while Mail is running, your cursor will change shape, or your machine will beep and the Mail icon (if iconized on your desktop) will change to show a piece of mail coming through the mail slot.

SCHEDULING WORKGROUP ACTIVITIES WITH SCHEDULE+

Managing time in an office environment is a challenge. Scheduling your own meetings and appointments and events is difficult enough. But when you add the hassles of scheduling for a group of colleagues, things can get pretty hairy.

Schedule+, a time-management program that runs on your Windows for Workgroups network utilizing the Mail Postoffice, can help iron out the wrinkles. Schedule+ displays the times when coworkers are available for meetings, so when you suddenly need to call people together you just request the amount of time needed, and the program figures out the rest.

You can also record your personal appointments for a given day, and Schedule+ will graphically display how the appointments dovetail—or conflict. You can set alarms as reminders, and have those reminders alert you and/or the person at another workstation—someone you assign to be your assistant (your secretary, receptionist, social director, valet, or whatever). You can grant other users access to your schedule with the Set Access Privileges dialog box, which you select from the Options menu.

Finally, Schedule+ allows you to create a prioritized Task list of chores you need to tackle. Tasks can be organized by due date, alphabetically, or by their description. Related tasks can also be grouped as *projects*. Schedule+ will even help you assign times to work on the tasks.

If you're logged in to your Postoffice, a Messages window lets you see a list of your meeting requests and responses to your requests.

STARTING SCHEDULE+

To start up Schedule+:

1. Click on its icon in the Main group.
2. You will be prompted for your Mailbox name and password if you aren't logged into the mail system already. The Schedule+ main screen now comes up, as you see in Figure C.8.

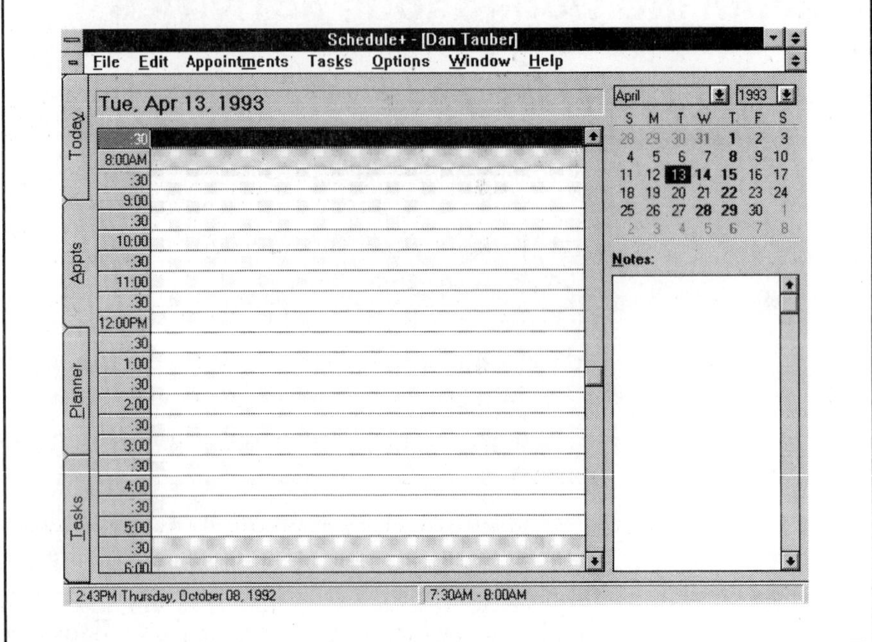

FIGURE C.8: *The Schedule+ workspace. Click on the tabs at the left to change views.*

CREATING NEW APPOINTMENTS

If you're going to use Schedule+, the first thing you should do is set up an appointment list for yourself. This will help you keep track of your schedule, and provide a basis for Schedule+ to arrange meetings with other users.

1. Make sure your schedule is displayed, and that it's not another workgroup user's schedule showing. Choose Window ➤ *your name*. In other words, open the Window menu and choose your name from the list of names. (Other users' names are on the menu, too, if their schedules are open.) Your blank schedule should appear, looking like Figure C.8. If it doesn't, click on the Appts. tab on the left side of the screen.
2. Choose the correct month and year for the appointment from the upper-right area of the window. Then click on the correct date in the little calendar.

3. To set an appointment for a given time, double-click on the start time in the lined area. For example, click on the number 12:00 PM to schedule a lunch appointment. A dialog box comes up:

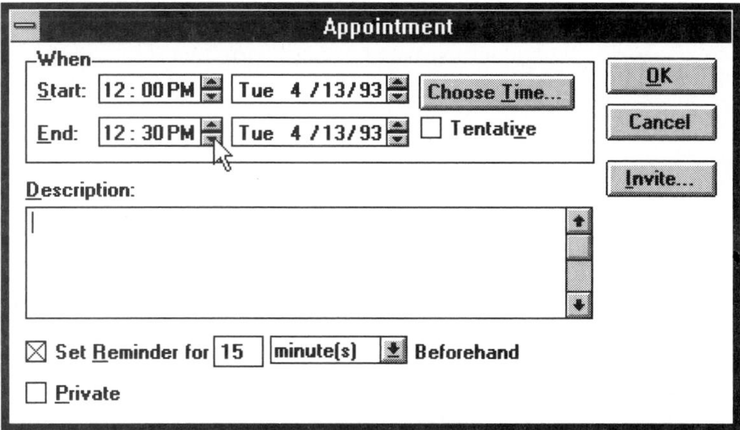

4. Adjust the End time to reflect the duration of the meeting. If you want to choose the time graphically, you can do that, too, by clicking on the Choose Time button.

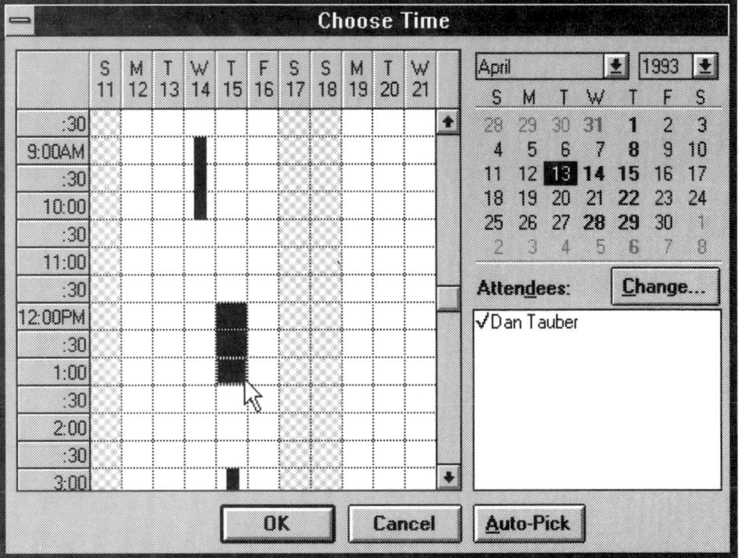

To set the time here, just drag across the appropriate blocks in the grid as you see the pointer doing above. A dark square will already be in the correct start time, just to help you get oriented to the grid. (For now, ignore the other stuff in the box pertaining to attendees—it's there for calling meetings, which we're not covering just yet.) Click on OK when you're happy with the time grid.

NOTE *You can move an appointment to a new time by dragging the upper (dark blue) edge of the appointment in the Appointment list view. Just drag it to the desired start time. You can decrease or increase the length of time of an appointment by dragging the bottom line of the appointment's perimeter (the gray bar) up or down.*

5. Click on the Tentative check box if the appointment isn't confirmed. When you set an appointment as tentative, it still appears in your appointment book, but in a gray color. The appointment won't appear in your Planner, however. (The Planner is the graphical display of appointments marked with vertical colored bars). When other users look at your schedule, tentative appointments won't show, so you'll appear to be available at those times.
6. Type in the description of the appointment in the large text area. You can type information in here if you want, such as directions to a meeting, or what not. If you want the program to alert you in advance of the meeting, turn on Set Reminder and set the amount of advance warning. (This is turned on by default, but can be turned off from the Options ➤ General Options dialog box.) Notice that you can set up advance warning for a time months ahead of the actual appointment by opening the Beforehand drop-down list. My memory isn't that long-lasting, but yours might be.
7. Set the Private box on if you don't want other workgroup users to know what you're doing during an appointment. When another user tries to schedule you in to a meeting, their screen will show that you're busy (not available for meetings), but they won't know if you're actually closing that important deal with Nabisco or if you're down at the racetrack.
8. Click on OK and the appointment is added to the selected day's activities.

Setting Up Recurring Appointments

Many appointments are of the recurring type. You might have a staff meeting every Thursday, for example. Schedule+ can set these automatically for you from now 'til the year 2019. Suppose you have a recurring lunch date every Tuesday.

1. Select the correct day for the first occurrence of the appointment, in the upper-right corner of the window.
2. In the appointment area, click on the correct start time for the appointment.
3. Open the Appointments menu and choose New Recurring Appointment.

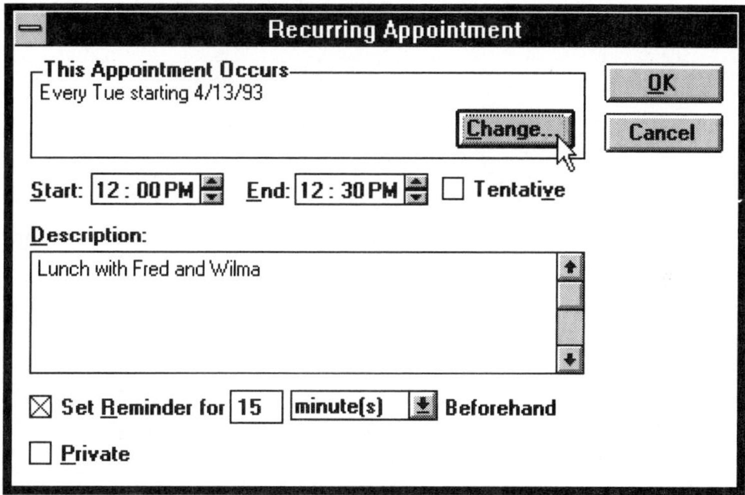

4. Fill in the box as you see fit, particularly the start and end times and the description.
5. Now for the tricky part. You have to declare how the appointment recurs (monthly, weekly, daily, etc.) Click on the Change button.

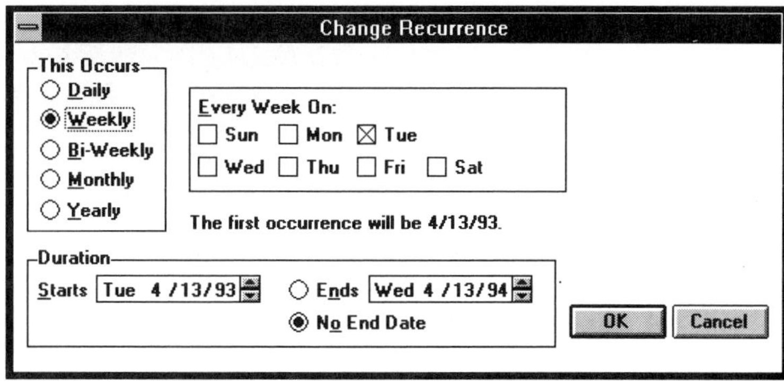

Make settings as you see fit. Note that, as a default, there is no end date to the appointments. In this case, I'll be set for lunch with Fred and Wilma until the year 2019.

6. OK the Change Recurrence box and you're returned to the Recurring Appointment box. OK that one, and you're done. The appointment line now has a new icon in it, indicating that it's a recurring appointment.

Working with the Task List

The next major section of Schedule+, the Task list, helps you track your projects and assign time to get that old "to do" list done. Here's how to add tasks to the list, prioritize them, and mark them as completed once you've done your duty.

1. Get to the Task list by clicking on its tab (on the left side of the window). You'll see a new Task list that looks something like Figure C.9.
2. Type in a task in the New Task box. For example: *Write letter to the Editor.* Click on Add to add it to your Task list.
3. In the Task list below, you'll now see the new addition. Double-click on it to open a new dialog box that lets you declare a few things about the task itself.

Task
Description: Write letter to the Editor
Project: <None>
Due Date: None By Thu 10/ 8 /92
Start Work: 0 day(s) Before Due Set Reminder
Priority: 3 Private
OK Cancel

FIGURE C.9: *The Task list with no tasks yet entered*

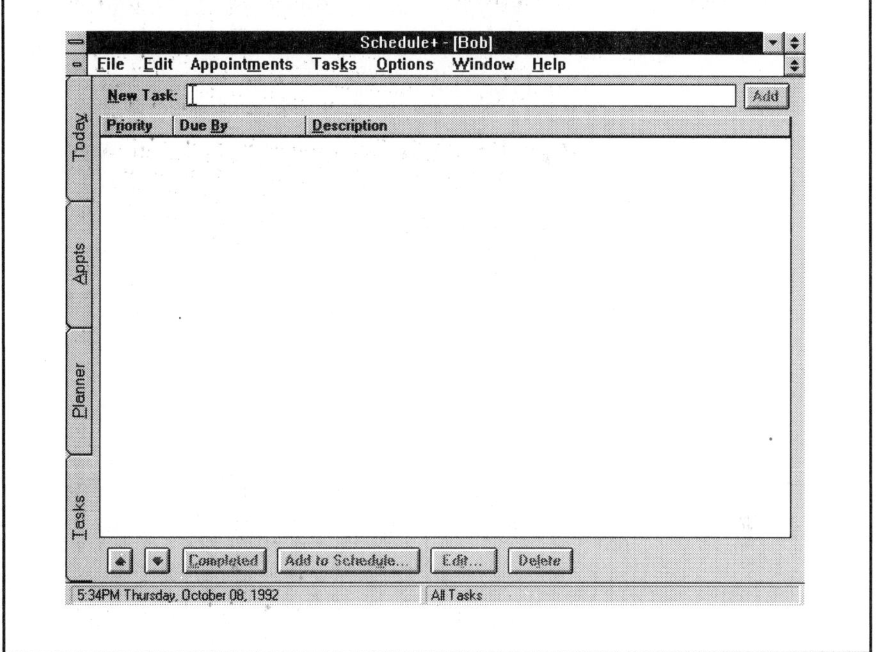

The most important things here are that you can assign the task to a project, and you can set the due date and priority.

4. Once you have some projects set up, they'll appear in the drop-down list. Until then it will read <none>. To create a project, type one in the Project box. For example, I've entered Writing Projects.
5. Setting the Due Date By button on will activate the options that are grayed out. If the task has a due date, turn the button on, then set the due date by typing it in or by using the tiny arrow buttons. The Start Work option allows you to specify an estimated amount of time for completion of the project. If, after you set it, you also set the Reminder check box on, Schedule+ will alert you to get started on the project well in advance—a little nag.
6. Set the priority by typing a number from 1 to 9 or a letter from A to Z. When organized by priority, tasks with numbers will come before those with letters.

7. Click on OK, and the item is added to your Task list.

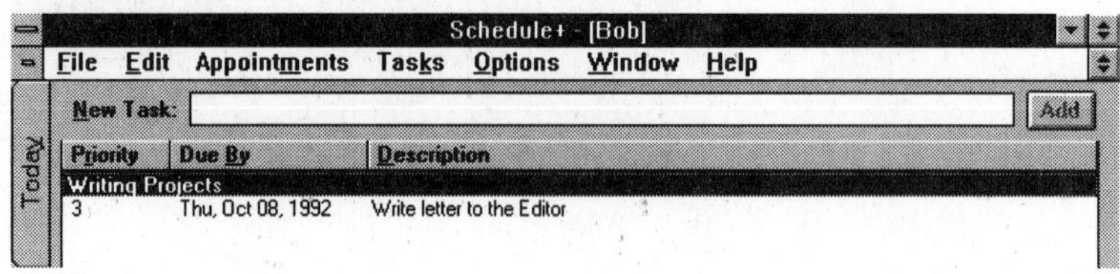

Note that there is now a project category called Writing Projects, under which one task is listed.

You can add new tasks to this project, or create new projects, as you just did. You can also create them from the Tasks menu using the New Tasks and New Projects commands.

Double-clicking on a task brings up the dialog box you just filled in, so you can edit the task description.

When you are finished with a task, highlight it and click on the Completed button at the bottom of the screen. It will be added to the Notes box on your Appointment screen—a little pat on the back for having completed the task, I suppose.

Deleting a Task from the List

You can eliminate a task from the list if you decide not to continue with it—it won't be completed, just canned.

1. Get to the Tasks screen.
2. Click on the task in question.
3. Press Del or choose Edit ➤ Delete Task.

Scheduling Time for a Task

You can have the Task list schedule time in your appointment book to ensure you keep a time slot open for working on the task. Here's how:

1. From the Tasks screen, select the task.
2. Click on the Add to Schedule button.

3. The Choose time box comes up:

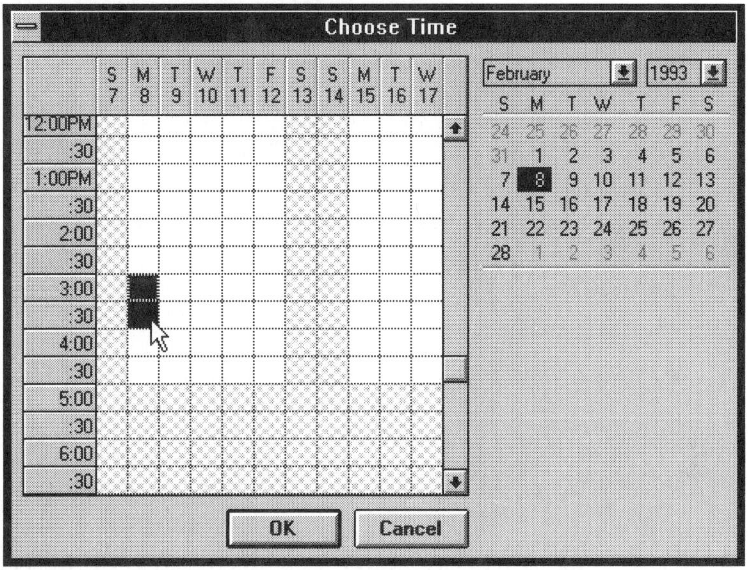

4. Choose the time slot by selecting the date and dragging across the grid. I've chosen 3:00 to 4:00 Monday for the time slot.

5. Click on OK. The task is now on the Task list as well as on your appointment schedule.

Scheduling a Meeting

When you want to schedule a meeting with users in your workgroup, do the following:

1. Make sure you're logged in to the Postoffice. If you aren't, Schedule+ can't send out the requisite meeting announcements to each person you'd like in attendance.

2. Bring up the Planner screen by clicking on its tab.

3. Now look over to the lower-right corner, under Attendees. Your name is already in the list. Since you're calling the meeting, the program assumes you want to be there. Click on Change to add or remove people from the list.

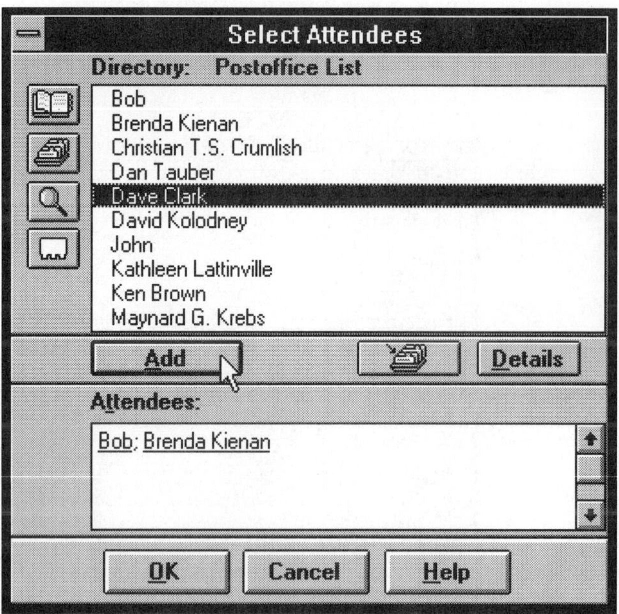

4. Construct your list of desired meeting attendees by clicking on their names in the list, then clicking on Add. You can select several non-adjacent names by Ctrl-clicking. You can select a range of names by Shift-clicking. You can also select one at a time by double-clicking each desired person. When you're happy with the list, click on OK.

5. All the attendees' names appear in the Attendance list on the Planner screen now.

6. Set the meeting time by choosing the correct month, year, and day from the calendar in the upper right. If you have appointments on that date, they will show up on the planner as vertical bars. Also, other attendees' schedules are now collectively overlaid on your planner, with your schedule in one color and everyone else's in another color. (Wherever the other people's schedule overlaps with yours, the colors are combined.) In any case, your job is to look for a free time (an area without a bar) when your meeting could be held. Clicking on an attendee in the list to the right will alternately include them in the display or remove them from the grid so you can see whose schedule might be conflicting with the desired meeting time. (Only if all the check marks to the left of

names are turned on will the Planner be showing everyone's schedule simultaneously.) Choose an acceptable meeting day and time by dragging vertically on the grid.

NOTE *Don't drag horizontally unless you want to schedule a very long meeting, spanning complete days!*

If you want Schedule+ to help pick the time, choose Appointments ➤ Auto Pick, but remember that it only searches forward in time from the current location of the cursor on the Planner grid.

7. Now click on the Request Meeting button to prepare your meeting announcement. Here's an example:

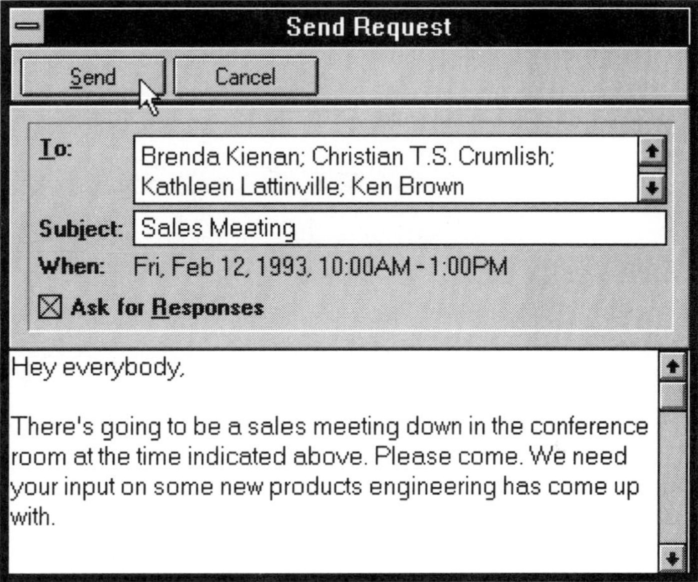

8. Click on Send. Schedule+ sends out announcements with the time of the meeting automatically entered. If there are no conflicts with other people's schedules, Schedule+ informs you that the meeting was successfully booked.

There are many more options with Schedule+, but this should get you started. You might research the use of response requests for meetings. Attendees then have to let you know if they plan to attend a meeting. Printing schedules is another area of possible interest. Privileges can be altered to allow a meeting planner to enter meeting times directly into everyone's schedules without waiting for responses (sort of authoritarian meeting planning). You can also create archives of schedule data for later reference.

CHATTING WITH OTHER PEOPLE ON THE NETWORK

Chat is a little freebie program that comes with Windows for Workgroups. It's actually pretty useful if you need to converse with others and you don't want to use the phone, or when you want to contact another user whose phone is terminally busy. You just call them on the network instead. Here's how:

1. Run Chat. It's in the Accessories group.

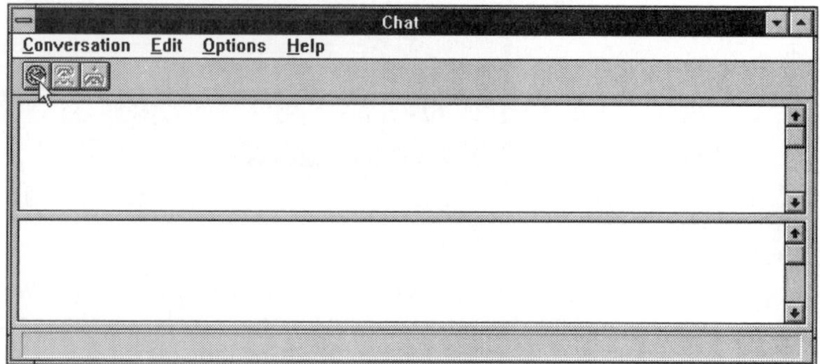

2. Click on the Dial icon or choose Dial from the Conversation menu.
3. From the resulting dialog box, choose the workstation you want to call and click on OK. The user will be called. If either of you has a sound card or PC speaker driver installed on your system, the sound of a phone ringing will be heard. A little phone icon appears on the caller's screen with the receiver bouncing around as if the phone is ringing really loudly. The caller's name appears under the icon.
4. The called party now must click on the pick-up icon or choose Conversation ➤ Answer.

5. Both the caller and the called parties type in the upper halves of their Chat windows, respectively. The responses are seen in the lower half.

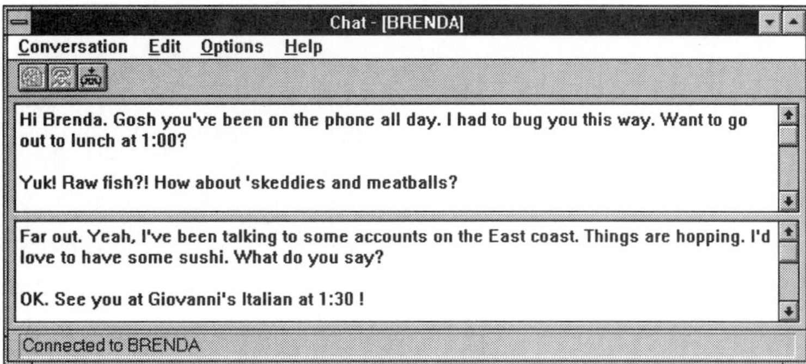

6. When you are finished talking, just click on the hang-up icon, or choose Conversation ➤ Hang Up.
7. Quit Chat when you're through.

WHO'S USING MY SYSTEM? MANAGING YOUR CPU TIME

Finally, let's look quickly at two more small programs that help you monitor workgroup usage of your workstation. One's called WinMeter and the other is called Net Watcher.

WinMeter

WinMeter simply creates a "live" graph that displays how much of your computer's CPU time is spent on your local work versus doing things for other users on the network. If you find that your system is slowing down too much on the network, this might help you figure out what's going on.

1. Run WinMeter. It's in the Accessories group.
2. Adjust the window so you can see it easily. WinMeter works even as an icon, but it's easier to see when enlarged a bit.

3. Unless you've changed your colors, WinMeter displays your local CPU use as purple, and the use by others as aqua. The Settings menu lets you change colors, and the time intervals at which CPU time sharing is calculated.

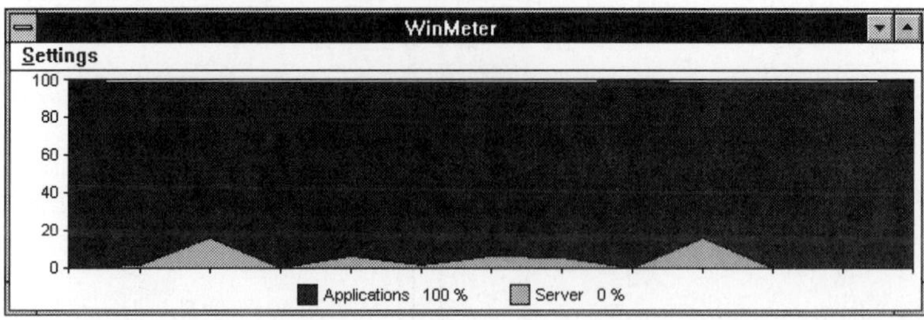

NetWatcher

NetWatcher displays information about who is connected to your computer and what resources (directories, printers) they are using. You can disconnect users from your station using this program, if you decide that's warranted.

1. Run NetWatcher. It's in the Accessories group. The window will look something like that in Figure C.10.

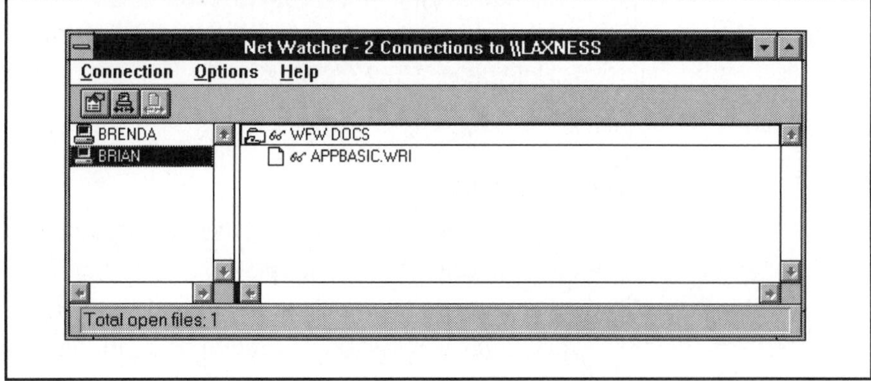

FIGURE C.10:
The NetWatcher screen. Current users of your workstation are listed in the left pane. Click on one to see which of your resources is being used.

2. The left side lists all the users connected to your resources. Click on a user, and the printers, directories, and other resources they are using are displayed in the right pane. Shared files that are currently open are also listed. A pencil icon indicates that the user can

Write to the file or directory. The glasses icon means she or he has Read-Only permission to the file or directory.

3. You can use commands on the menus to determine more about specific users, and to close files that they're using.

QUITTING WINDOWS FOR WORKGROUPS

When you're ready to quit Windows for Workgroups, all you have to do is:

1. Switch to the Program Manager.
2. Open the File menu and choose Exit Windows. (You can also double-click on the Control box.) So far this is just like quitting single-user Windows.
3. Click OK on the familiar "This will end your Windows session" message.
4. If anyone is connected to your computer, you'll see an error message:

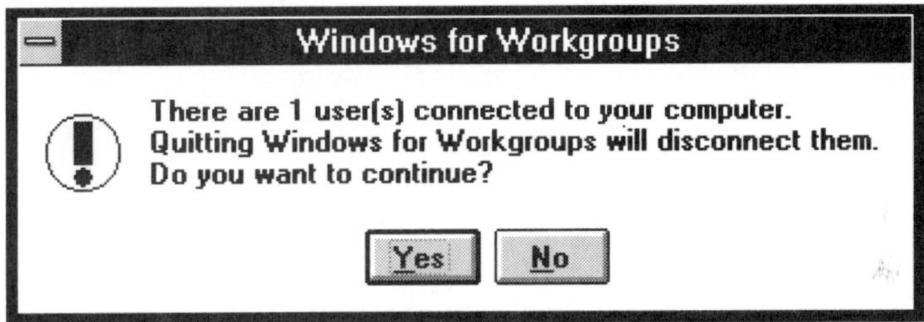

5. Click on Yes if you want to disconnect the user. Click on No if you want to wait until she or he is done using your computer.

You can use NetWatcher before you quit to determine what, if anything, the user has open, or what resource, such as a printer, is being used. Beware that cutting users off without checking can cause loss of data, even if they only have Read privileges on your computer. If a user is running a program from your hard disk and is editing data with that program on her or his own computer, loss of contact with your workstation may kill the application program he or she is using, preventing the user from saving work when she or he is through editing it. Users connected to your machine should be asked to disconnect from your computer, or end any tasks related to your computer, before you quit. If they have files open, you will get a second warning dialog box before the exit is complete.

This has been a quick overview of Windows for Workgroups, but it should be enough to get you started. Don't forget that much of the material in the rest of this book applies to Windows for Workgroups as well as Windows 3.1. There is much more information available on the topic of Windows for Workgroups in the Microsoft manuals and in other books devoted to the subject. For example, you might want to read *Networking with Windows for Workgroups*, by Cheryl Currid & Company (Sybex, 1993).

INDEX

- Page numbers in **boldface** are the primary source of information on a topic.
- Page numbers followed by an *f* refer to figures.
- Page numbers followed by a *t* refer to tables.

C

D

E

F

G

J

K

L

M

N

S

T

U

V

W

X

Z

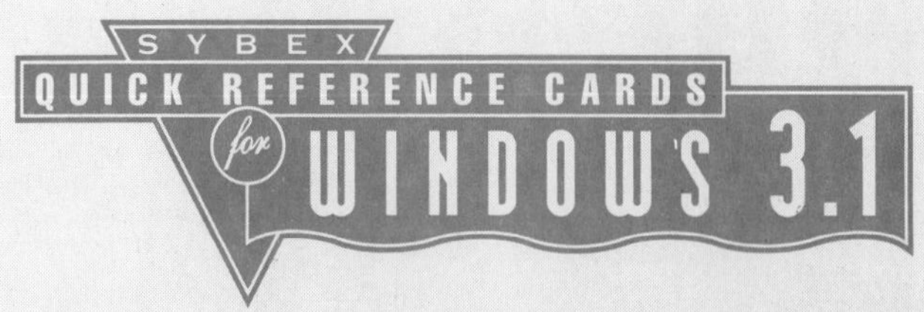

Quick Reference Cards Place Answers at Your Fingertips

Now you can save time and effort by using these unique Quick Reference Cards from SYBEX to answer your questions about Windows 3.1 commands and functions. These cards have been designed to fit in a standard Rolodex® card file and are color coded so you can quickly access the information you're looking for. Look for Quick Reference Cards in other SYBEX *Mastering* titles and build a card library covering all of the software products that you use.

QUICK REFERENCE—ESSENTIAL WINDOWS PROCEDURES

STARTING AND EXITING WINDOWS

Start Windows in a specific mode

To start Windows in Standard mode, Enter **WIN /S**.

To start Windows in 386-Enhanced mode, Enter **WIN /3**.

Exit Windows

Activate the Program Manager window and double-click its Control box.

PROGRAM MANAGER

Add a new group

From Program Manager, choose File ➤ New ➤ Program Group. Fill in at least the description in the dialog box.

Add a new program icon

Drag document or program file from File Manager into the destination group in Program Manager.

Remove a group or program icon

Highlight the window or icon to be deleted. Press Del.